STREET CHILDREN AND THE ASPHALT LIFE

STREET CHILDREN AND THE ASPHALT LIFE

(In 3 Volumes)

Volume 1

(Selection and Enumeration of Street Children)

Editor

P.C. Shukla

ISHA

ISHA BOOKS

Delhi-110033

Street Children and the Asphalt Life
(Selection and Enumeration of Street Children)

Rs. 2500 (Set)
Rs. 835 (Each Volume)

ISBN : 81-8205-212-2 (Set)
ISBN : 81-8205-306-4 (Vol. 1)

Published in 2005 in India by
Isha Books
D-43, Prithviraj Road,
Adarsh Nagar, Delhi - 110033
e-mail : ishabooks@hotmail.com

Laser Typesetting at : Global Printers, New Delhi
Printed at : Chawla Offset Press, Delhi

Contents

Preface

Street children are the casualties of economic growth, war, poverty, loss of traditional values, domestic violence, physical and mental abuse. Every street child has a reason for being on the streets. While some children are lured by the promise of excitement and freedom, the majority are pushed onto the street by desperation and a realisation that they have nowhere else to go. In many countries, street children are named after their main survival activities. What is obvious is that street children are poverty-stricken and their needs and problems are a result of wanting to meet basic needs for survival. They go through the struggle of providing themselves with basic things such as food, shelter, health and clothing. Providing targeted interventions that meet the needs of street children requires an understanding of who they are, what they need, what they do and how they can be identified.

It is estimated that there are between 10 and 100 million street children in the world today. These children live a transitory life style and are vulnerable to inadequate nutrition, physical injuries, substance use, and health problems including sexual and reproductive health problems. Some street children are part of entire families who live on the street. Others are born to older street girls. Some street children are 'on the street', which means that they still see their families regularly and may even return every night to sleep in their family homes. Children 'of the streets', on the other hand, have no home but the streets. Even if they occasionally spend time in institutions for

children or youths, they consider the streets to be their home. Although street children support themselves in many different ways, they need the assistance of caring adults and charitable services provided by governmental or non-governmental organisations. Despite peer solidarity and support through charitable services, street children have extremely high rates of morbidity, disability and mortality.

Improving the quality of life of street children is a difficult and challenging task. Street education is a very effective way to support street children as it occurs at locations where they live. Street education can involve many types of activities, for example, counselling about harmful effects of substances or about prevention of STDs, improving literacy and educating street children on the importance of seeking assistance on health issues or other social problems that could be addressed. It can be of vital importance in meeting the needs of street children in the areas of substance use, sex education, life skills, health education and literacy.

The present work in three volumes provides a comprehensive analysis of the problems of street children. The first volume *Selection and Enumeration of Street Children* narrates the status and burning issues of street children around the world. The second volume *Delinquent Street Children* discusses the crime trends among street children, the reasons that makes them criminals and the measures to reduce the delinquent activities. The third volume *Street Children and the Future Directions* discusses about the precarious future of street children. It explains the effective interventions to be taken to protect them from physical and mental vulnerabilities. This work will prove to be a useful reference material for sociologists, researchers, policy-makers, child welfare agencies and all who working for the empowerment of street children.

Editor

1

Understanding Street Children

Every street child has a reason for being on the streets. While some children are lured by the promise of excitement and freedom, the majority are pushed onto the street by desperation and a realisation that they have nowhere else to go. In many countries, street children are named after their main survival activities. What is obvious is that street children are poverty-stricken and their needs and problems are a result of wanting to meet basic needs for survival. Street children go through the struggle of providing themselves with basic things such as food, shelter, health and clothing.

Providing targeted interventions that meet the needs of street children requires an understanding of who they are, what they need, what they do and how they can be identified. A 'child of the streets', having no home but the streets. The family may have abandoned him or her or may have no family members left alive. Such a child has to struggle for survival and might move from friend to friend, or live in shelters such as abandoned buildings.

Some children live on the sidewalks or city squares with the rest of their families. Families displaced due to poverty, natural disasters, or wars may be forced to live on the streets. They move their possessions from place to place when necessary. Often the children in these 'street families' work on the streets with other members of their families. in institutionalized care, having come from a situation of homelessness and at risk of returning to a homeless existence.

The typical age of a street child varies from place to place. In developing countries children as young as eight live completely on their own. In developed countries, street children are usually over the age of twelve. The proportion of girls among street children is reported to be less than 30% in developing countries and about 50% in many developed countries. There are a number of reasons why there are fewer street girls:

— Fewer girls may be abandoned by their families. Girls are often socialized (taught by their families and culture) to be submissive and caring and therefore they tend to have fewer behavioural problems as compared to boys. Since girls have fewer behavioural problems, they have less conflict with their families and do not need to leave their home. Families might get rid of girls by other means, e.g. 'marrying them off ' when they are as young as 13. The girl would then have another family.

— The authorities or individual members of the community may pick up girls on the street more quickly. For example, girls may be recruited to do domestic work in private households or to work in the commercial sex industry.

— Street girls may be less 'visible' to researchers or educators. Some street girls disguise themselves as boys to protect themselves from harassment by the police, welfare workers, employers and other street children and others may only appear on the streets at night.

Girls on the street have more difficulties and are often overlooked by street educators. Street girls are looked down upon in many societies and are easily exploited. They usually have less economic opportunities than boys and are given less money than boys for similar activities. Educational opportunities are denied to them and street educators usually engage street boys in various activities while paying little attention to girls. It is important to seek and work to improve the situation of street girls because by doing so, you would be:

— Ensuring that young girls and boys have equal opportunities.

— Boosting their low self-esteem. They may then participate in income generating activities and thus break the pattern of vulnerability.

— Ensuring that street girls have improved nutritional status.

— Helping minimize the possibility of early unwanted and high-risk pregnancies by providing them with information about sexual and reproductive health.

— Ensuring the return in investment into future generations, as young women with some education tend to ensure that their own children are educated.

Reasons for Why Street Children on the Street

The reasons why street children live on the street vary. However, there is one explanation that holds true for both developed and developing countries - poverty. Most street children go onto the street to look for a better way of life. The following are some of the common reasons:

— *To earn money for themselves and support their families.* Street children work on the streets to earn money for themselves. Some children need to work to support their families. Some children may have been denied a chance to go to school or have dropped out of school and have nothing to do. They can earn money by begging, carrying or bearing, car washing, drug trafficking, juggling, performing music, running errands, scavenging, sex work, shoe shining or vending.

— *To find shelter.* In overcrowded households, children may decide to leave home to make room for younger siblings and elderly family members. Others are on the streets because they do not have an alternative. They may have become separated from their families during civil unrest or their parents/ caretakers may have died from illnesses such as AIDS or killed during armed conflict. Other children may have nowhere else to go when they are released from institutions such as a jail or a detention centre.

— *To escape from family problems including rejection.* Many children feel that living on the streets is better than coping with problems in their homes. These problems can include conflicts with parents, physical or sexual abuse or neglect (e.g. an abandoned disabled child). Some children are forced to leave home by their families because the family does not approve of a child's behaviour or its consequences, e.g. pregnancy, homosexuality or substance use.

— *To escape from work demands in the home.* In many cultures, children are expected to participate in routine family tasks. At times the demands on children may be more than they can take. This leads to the child feeling that he or she is a slave or a servant. Such children leave home in search of freedom from adult demands.

— *To escape from a children's institution.* Street children may feel that children's homes are 'like prisons'. They cannot adjust to rules after experiencing the freedom of the streets. At times the personnel in these institutions may abuse children.

For example, studies in the Philippines have found that various characteristics of the child, the child's family, the local community and the society explain why some children are on the streets.

Family Causes

— Poor, uneducated and large families.

— Lack of knowledge and skills needed for parenting.

— Lack of responsibility on the part of parents, family conflicts and parental behavioural problems e.g. giving priority to material gains, substance use, gambling.

— Physical abuse of the child.

— Rebellious behaviour and attitudes of the child.

Lack of Opportunities in Local Community

— Inequitable distribution of resources and opportunities in the community, e.g. lack of adequate employment opportunities, problems in working conditions, lack of recreational activities.

— Congestion in slum areas, and inadequate/poor housing facilities.

— Restrictive and inflexible educational system.

— Poor law enforcement and exploitation by law enforcers.

Societal Influence

— Political and economic conditions, e.g. poverty and underdevelopment of resources.

Problems of Street Children

Street children have a greater burden than other poor children who are supervised by adults. Their problems could be grouped into three classes: social, physical, and psychological.

Social Problems

— *Poverty and illiteracy:* They lack basic resources to sustain a healthy living. They usually have no financial means to buy decent clothing (which may be necessary in cold places), and no money to buy food, which is crucial for their development. Because of the costs of services most street children cannot afford to go to school. Even where schools are free, many children cannot afford to buy uniforms, shoes and books. Street children live in places where they are not adequately protected from the environment. They rarely have access to facilities that they need for hygiene and sanitation, such as toilets and clean and safe water supply. They are therefore more vulnerable to health problems resulting from poor sanitation.

— *Discrimination and lack of accessible resources:* When the community makes plans, it does not take into consideration the street childrens' plight. Street children tend to be excluded from participating in most of the activities and facilities of other children. This is one reason why street children often do not have access to medical, educational, recreational and vocational resources. They face problems such as lack of vaccinations; poor health, illiteracy and they cannot acquire skills needed for finding jobs.

— *Violent Environment:* The street is an unprotected environment and street children are exploited frequently. In some places, street children may even face the possibility of physical injuries or death from violence. Common sources of violence are: the police, gangs, drug syndicates, those who operate commercial sex businesses, death squads, other street children, families and sexual partners.

— *Stigmatization:* Society usually perceives street children as difficult children who are out there to cause trouble. In general, the public thinks that street children are uncontrollable and violent, have substance use problems, have no morals, have lost all the ability to feel emotions such as love and that they turn into terrorists and revolutionaries. They tend to be unsympathetic to the street childrens' plight. This negative attitude may be a result of the society's inability to care for its people.

Physical Problems

— *Lack of adequate nutrition:* Even though some street children can usually get enough to eat, they do not have nutritious diets. This leads to malnutrition, anaemia and vitamin deficiencies.

— *Injuries:* Injuries may be caused intentionally (including injuring self while intoxicated or when depressed) and unintentionally, e.g. due to use of tools which have been designed for adults. The rate of injuries is usually higher for male than for female street children.

— *Sexual and reproductive health problems:* Sexual and reproductive health problems affect both girls and boys. However, street girls are more vulnerable to physical and sexual abuse and exploitation. Common sexual and reproductive health problems include sexually transmitted diseases, HIV/AIDS, unwanted pregnancies and unsafe abortions. Pregnant street girls do not receive adequate antenatal care.

— *Common diseases:* Street children experience many common diseases such as tuberculosis, skin diseases, dental problems and parasitic diseases which can be prevented easily if these children have enough resources and their basic needs are met.

Psychological Problems

— *A Stressful Past*: Many situations and events that pushed these children onto the street in the first place (like natural disasters, man-made disasters, exploitation and conflicts) may have a lasting impact on their well being.

For example, the family conflict that pushed the child onto the streets continues to deprive the child of emotional and material support for years afterwards. When the child has his or her own baby, neither the new parent nor the baby will have the benefit of the previous generation's support.

— *A Transitory Lifestyle:* Street children in some large cities move frequently from district to district or between cities. Sometimes they do this by choice, but at other times they are forced to move to hide from the police, welfare authorities, gangs, and drug syndicates. This type of lifestyle leads to problems of social isolation and loneliness and difficulties in developing emotional attachments to special individuals.

— *Mental Health:* The stresses that street children experience make them vulnerable to emotional problems, psychiatric disorders and learning difficulties. They do not receive adequate care for these conditions.

— *Substance use:* Many street children are involved in harmful use of psychoactive substances. This can lead to overdose, increase the chance of accidents, violence, unwanted pregnancy and unprotected sex. Over time, the continued use of substances can lead to complications such as brain and liver damage.

Survival of Street Children

Survival for street children means obtaining food, clothing and shelter, and protecting themselves against violence and other forms of abuse. It depends on personal strengths. The child's resourcefulness (the ability to solve problems quickly and efficiently with available resources), and resilience (the ability to recover from shock, depression, and other difficult circumstances) determine his/ her survival. Resourcefulness and resilience would depend upon the child's creativity, hard work, intelligence and concern for one another.

In Brazil, many street children travelled regularly to the beach in Buenaventura at weekends, some three to four hours away by automobile. To be able to do this, the child would have to negotiate a ride on a freight truck, raise money by shining shoes and begging to feed himself, and successfully negotiate transportation back within a set time frame. This is no small accomplishment for an unsupervised 10-year-old.

Peers are individuals who share common interests and needs. Peer groups tend to be homogeneous in age and gender. The peer group has a strong influence on street children because of the child's need for acceptance, belonging and protection. The group often determines the process of change, socialization and development among street children by providing emotional and material support.

Street children often help in one another's survival. They often join together to form emotional and material support networks. The networks can range from a simple circle of friends to an organized, business network. Experienced street children teach new comers how to survive. Members of the group share food, clothing, shelter, information and psychoactive substances.

Psychoative Substances

The word 'substance' describes any psychoactive material which when consumed affects the way people feel, think, see, taste, smell, hear or behave. A psychoactive substance can be a medicine or an industrial product, such as glue. Some substances are legal such as approved medicines, alcohol and cigarettes, and others are illegal, such as heroin and cannabis. Each country has its own laws about substances. The percentage of substance users among street children varies greatly depending on the region, gender and age. Some studies have found that between 25% and 90% of street children use psychoactive substances of some kind.

To understand substance use a framework called the Modified Social Stress Model is used. The model explains the complex relationship between factors that affect the onset and continuation of substance use. The model suggests that positive and negative aspects of six vulnerability/protective factors affect the risk of substance use. These are stress, normalization of behaviour and situations (acceptance) of substance use in the community, effects of behaviour and situations, attachments, skills and resources. It introduces the Modified Social Stress Model as a useful way of understanding substance use among street children.

Types of Psychoactive Substances Street Children Use

The types of psychoactive substances street children use can be many and varied and it may be difficult to determine what substances they are using. Substances which are sold on the market can be identified by their generic name. This is the standard name used through out the world. However some substances are marketed under various names known as trade names and others have 'street names'. For example, diazepan is the generic name while valium is a trade name.

Alcohol

Alcohol is a depressant which inhibits or decreases some aspects of central nervous system activity (ie., activity of the brain, spinal cord, and some major nerves). Substances containing alcohol include the following: wine, beer, spirits, home-brew, some medicinal tonics and syrups (e.g. cough syrups), some toiletries and industrial products.

Nicotine

Nicotine is a stimulant; that is any substance which activates, enhances or increases central nervous system activity. Nicotine is found in the following substances: cigarettes, cigars, pipe tobacco, chewed tobacco, snuff, nicotine gum, spray, skin patches. Most cigarettes have about 1-2 milligrams of nicotine.

Diacetlymorphine (Brown Sugar)

Diacetlymorphine is a generic name for heroin and 'brown sugar' or 'smack' are some of the names it is called by on the streets. It is important for the street educator to know the general categories of substances and the effects that substances can have on a street child. The following examples of substances in their general categories may not be the ones used in your country, they are merely illustrative.

Opioids

Substances in this group may act as analgesics (they relieve physical pain) and depressants. They may be synthetic or made from opium poppies (opiates). The following substances are examples of opioids:

— *opiates:* codeine (such as in some cough mixtures), heroin, morphine, opium

— *synthetic opioids:* buprenorphine hydrochloride (Temgesic), methadone (Physeptone), pethidine.

Hallucinogenic Substances

Hallucinogenic substances can alter a person's mood, the way the person perceives his or her surroundings and the way the person experiences his or her own body. There are many different types of hallucinogens, some of which are chemically produced and others which are naturally occurring.

— *LSD (Lysergic Acid Diethylamide):* in its pure state LSD is a white, odourless powder. It is usually mixed with a lot of other ingredients. It is often put into capsules, liquids, tablets, and as small spots on absorbent paper.

— *mescaline:* made from the pulp of the peyote cactus.

— *psilocybin mushrooms:* Psilocybin is the hallucinogen found in some mushrooms. It is usually made available as dried mushrooms.

— *PCP (phencyclidine):* this substance was used as an animal tranquilliser.

Cannabis Plant

The cannabis plant grows in many parts of the world. Preparations containing different concentrations of cannabis are consumed. marijuana: the leaves and flowers of the marijuana or hemp plant. hashish (oil and resin): these forms of cannabis are made from the resin of the flowering heads of the plant tablets containing THC (Tetrahydrocannabinol, the main active ingredient in cannabis)

Hypnosedatives

The drugs in this group are made synthetically and do not occur naturally. There are a large number of different drugs in this group. All are slightly different, but all subdue the body's nervous system. This group of substances activate, enhance or increase central nervous system activity.

— *caffeine:* caffeine has been around for thousands of years. It is found in different amounts in coffee, tea, cocoa, and chocolate. It is also in some soft drinks and in some medicines.

— *coca products:* coca leaves, coca paste.

— *cocaine:* cocaine is produced from coca leaves.

— *amphetamines:* amphetamines are found in prescription drugs and included in some diet pills, as well as in various forms on the street. On the streets in the Philippines they are called shabu, a Japanese word for fast/quick, and in Australia speed or goey.

— *MDMA (Ecstasy):* this substance is a type of amphetamine which has both stimulant and hallucinogenic effects. It can be in the form of a tablet, capsule, or oil which is usually mixed with other substances.

— *khat:* the leaves and buds of a plant found in East Africa, which are chewed or brewed as a drink.

Inhalants

Inhalants include a wide range of easily available products including aerosols, volatile solvents and gases. The following substances can all be inhaled: aerosol sprays, butane gas, petrol, glue, paint thinners, solvents, amyl nitrite (poppers)

Some substances do not neatly belong in any of the categories above. kava: a drink made from the roots of a shrub, which is used in the South Pacific for social and ceremonial purposes. betel nut: this substance is the seed of an Asian palm tree. It has been noted through the WHO project on substance use among street children that street children claim that inhaling through a wet carbon paper, inhaling vapour produced by a mixture of fibre matting and boiling toothpaste, inhaling fumes from burning insects, and inhalation of raw sewerage can produce desired effects.

Efforts should be made to learn about the types of substances that are being used by the street children locally. This information could be obtained from specialists in your community, such as pharmacists and medical personnel. The specialists may provide samples of the products so that you are familiar with them.

Methods of Using

Substances can be used in many different ways. They may be:

— Chewed, swallowed or dissolved slowly in the mouth.

— Placed on a mucous membrane (such as inside the anus or vagina, or nose, or under the eyelid).

— Rubbed into the skin.

— Injected under the skin or into a vein or muscle with a needle.

— Smoked or inhaled through the mouth or nose, or inhaled by placing a bag over the head known as bagging.

The way the substance is taken also influences how fast the substance reaches the brain or other organs. Injecting a substance is especially dangerous because of the risks of infection that are carried through the blood (blood borne). In particular, sharing needles or other injecting equipment and the way the substance is prepared can spread HIV (the virus that causes AIDS), hepatitis B and C, and other infections because of contamination with infected blood.

Effects of Substances

Any substance can be harmful to a human body if taken in large enough doses, too frequently or in an impure form. The health effects of substances can occur immediately or in the long-term. The effects are influenced by the dose, the method of administration as well as whether the substance is used with another drug. The long-term effects often take a long time to appear and are usually due to damage of body organs. Be aware that some signs attributed to substance use may be due to other conditions, e.g. poor concentration can be a sign of glue sniffing, but it could also be caused by stress or worry about a life event, about pregnancy, or as a result of head injury. Effects of individual substances are presented below:

Alcohol

The effects of alcohol will vary from person to person. Children, young people and women are usually more affected by alcohol than adult men because they tend to have lower body weights, smaller livers, and a higher proportion of fat to muscle. This leads to faster absorption of alcohol in the body.

— *Immediate effects:* These include drowsiness, uninhibited actions (a person is more likely to do things that normally he or she would stop himself/ herself from doing), loss of physical coordination, unclear vision, slurred speech, making poor decisions or impairment of memory. Excessive drinking over a short period of time can cause headache, nausea, vomiting, coma and death.

— *Long-term effects:* Drinking large amounts of alcohol regularly over a long period of time can cause loss of appetite, vitamin deficiency, skin problems, depression, loss of sexual drive, liver damage, heart ailments, nerve and brain damage or loss of memory.

— *Associated health risks:* These occur when alcohol is taken with other substances or drugs. Taking alcohol with drugs that depress the body's systems, such as hypnosedatives or cannabis, can increase loss of judgement and loss of physical coordination. Combination with hypnosedatives can lead to coma, respiratory depression (person stops breathing) and death.

Although alcohol has calories and provides energy it can also prevent the absorption of necessary vitamins and other nutrients. In general, a person taking substances can easily overlook the importance of good nutrition. Street children use substances to relieve hunger and this can lead to malnutrition. Alcohol may increase feelings of sadness and isolation in young people who are already depressed. A serious state of depression can also be a consequence of long-term excessive alcohol use.

Regular drinking of even small amounts of alcohol during pregnancy can damage the health of both the mother and the foetus. Heavy drinking can lead to miscarriage or foetal alcohol syndrome (slowed growth and mental disabilities in the baby). Alcohol can be passed to the infant through breast milk.

Nicotine

Nicotine, the active substance found in tobacco is addictive in nature. Once a street child starts using tobacco, they are likely to continue using it for a long time.

— *Immediate effects:* A person feels alert immediately after using tobacco, and then feels more relaxed a few minutes later. There is also an increase in pulse rate, a temporary rise in blood pressure, dizziness, nausea and reduced appetite.

— *Long-term effects:* These effects may be due to the nicotine or the form in which it is taken. Heart and lung disease, blockage of arteries (peripheral vascular disease), high blood pressure, breathing difficulty, cancer of the lung (with cigarette smoking) and cancers of the mouth (with pipe smoking and tobacco chewing) may occur.

Smoking during pregnancy can reduce the amount of oxygen available to the unborn and may affect the baby's growth and development before, and after birth. This usually leads to low birth weight in the baby. Similar problems may accompany the use of cannabis during pregnancy.

Opioids

Substances in this group may act as pain killers and/or depressants. Some are used as medicines while others are illegal. Opium, morphine, codeine (constituent of some cough mixtures) and heroin are derived from opium poppies directly or through chemical processing (opiates), while buprenorphine (Temgesic), methadone (Physeptone) and pethidine are made synthetically (opioids).

— *Immediate effects:* Opioids often produce a detached and dreamy feeling, sleepiness, reduction in the size of the pupil of the eye, nausea, vomiting and constipation. Overdose leads to unconsciousness, respiratory depression (failure to breathe) and death.

— *Long-term effects:* The main danger is the development of dependence and the chance of overdose that can cause death. Tolerance and dependence can develop quickly.

— *Associated health risks:* Opioids may be injected into the body. Injecting the substances with a needle that is not sterile or is shared between users can transmit blood borne infections including HIV, hepatitis B and C, and may result in septicemia (infection in blood).

A mother using opioids, hypnosedatives and stimulants exposes the baby to the substance. If the pregnant or lactating (breastfeeding) mother stops using these substances suddenly the baby will experience withdrawal. Amphetamines may lead to miscarriage and cocaine can cause developmental delays.

Hallucinogens

These substances can alter a person's mood, the way the person perceives his or her surroundings and experiences his or her own body. A user may also hallucinate (perceive something that does not exist).

— *Immediate effects:* The immediate effects are those of change in perception and in the awareness of things happening inside and outside one's body. Things may look, smell, sound, taste, or feel different e.g. seeing colours, lights, pictures. 'Bad trips' may also occur. The term refers to unpleasant and disturbing feelings e.g. panic, fear, anxiety, confusion and alteration in the sense of reality. The nature of the experience is partly determined by the setting in which the hallucinogens are taken. Unintentional injuries and suicide may happen under the influence of hallucinogens.

— *Long-term effects:* Many users report getting the experiences first obtained under the influence of substance, days or even months after they have stopped taking the substances. These experiences are called 'flash backs'. Regular use of hallucinogens can decrease a user's memory and concentration and can result in depression and other mental health problems. PCP is particularly likely to cause lasting mental health problems.

Cannabis

Cannabis may make a user euphoric at first, and then relaxed and calm. Large doses can change perceptions in ways similar to that seen with hallucinogens.

— *Immediate effects:* feelings of well being, relaxation, loss of inhibitions, loss of motor coordination and loss of concentration. There may be increased pulse and heart rate, redness of the eyes, and increased appetite. Large quantities can cause panic, hallucinations, restlessness and confusion.

— *Long-term effects:* there is no evidence that using cannabis occasionally in small quantities causes any significant long lasting health problems. Regular use over a long time increases chances of dependency, impairment of memory and concentration and may worsen mental problems such as schizophrenia.

Hypnosedatives

These substances are depressants. They make the nervous system less active. Health workers often prescribe them for treating sleep difficulty and anxiety because of their calming properties. There are a large number of different drugs in this group.

— *Immediate effects:* all substances in this group cause effects similar to alcohol. They slow down a person's thinking and movements and decrease the ability to concentrate. They cause 'hangovers', or problems such as slurred speech, sleepiness and lack of coordination after the intoxication has worn off. Low doses reduce feelings of anxiety while higher doses cause sleep or unconsciousness. Alcohol increases their effect. Repeated doses cause other associated health risks because the substance is not broken down (metabolised) quickly. Unintentional injuries and suicide can occur.

— *Long-term effects:* regular use of these substances can lead to dependence, and continued heavy use can result in problems with memory, ability to learn, and problems with coordination. Convulsions and delirium (an acute confusional state) can occur when the substance is withdrawn.

Hallucinogens may cause mental heath problems such as depression, with suicide being a risk. They may also worsen a pre-existing mental disorder such as schizophrenia.

Stimulants

Stimulants enhance or increase central nervous system activity. They are popular because they make people feel energetic, self-confident and they decrease the feeling of hunger. They are often used to reduce weight and help people stay awake for work. If too much of the stimulant is taken, the person may become anxious, irritable, suspicious, panicky, and/or threatening to others.

— *Immediate effects:* caffeine in coffee and teas spreads quickly through the body and makes a person feel awake. Too much of caffeine can cause an increase in heart beat, anxiety and upset stomach. The effects of cocaine and amphetamines are similar except that the effects of cocaine last for less time. These are excitement, decreased need for sleep and food. High doses can cause anxiety, panic, high blood pressure, convulsions and aggression. With crack (cocaine which is smoked) a person usually experiences a brief intense feeling of intoxication and an exaggerated feeling of confidence. The mood then quickly changes to a low feeling and may prompt the person to repeat the dose. Overdose is commoner with crack than with other forms of cocaine.

— *Long-term effects:* coffee and tea may cause anxiety, depression, stomach upset and difficulty in sleeping. Longterm use of amphetamine and cocaine can cause dependence, inability to sleep, irritability, and mental health problems such as feelings of suspiciousness and hallucinations. Similarly, heavy use of khat can result in dependence and physical and mental problems.

Inhalants

Like alcohol, they make a person uninhibited at first and drowsy later.

— *Immediate effects:* Feelings of happiness, relaxation, sleepiness, poor muscle coordination, slurred speech, irritability and anxiety. Hallucinations and fits can occur with heavy use. The most immediate danger to the user is of 'sudden sniffing death'. Death could also occur as a result of suffocation.

— *Long-term effects:* Regular long-term use may lead to nose bleeds, rashes around the mouth and nose, loss of appetite and lack of motivation. Some of the solvents are toxic to the liver, kidney, heart and brain.

Young people who use substances such as inhalants may like the experience and get relief from their tension. This limits the development of other more constructive coping strategies: For example the use of hypnosedatives can help street children feel less anxious, but they do not change the cause of the street child's anxiety.

Some substances do not belong in any of the above mentioned categories. Examples are:

— *Kava:* is used in the South Pacific for social and ceremonial purposes. It causes mild sedation and feeling of well being. Heavy use can cause dependence and medical problems.

— *Betel nut:* is often chewed in parts of Asia and the Pacific. Regular use can cause dependence and diseases of the mouth, including cancer.

— LSD can increase the chance of a miscarriage and complications during pregnancy. Babies of mothers who use hallucinogens, may be born with physical deformities.

In many areas, street children use more than one substance at the same or different times. In developed countries, this often includes using alcohol, nicotine, opioids, stimulants, hypnosedatives, hallucinogens and inhalants. Combined use of substances makes the assessment of substances that the child is using more difficult. In addition, it complicates the process of detoxification or withdrawal. Combination of substances increase the risk of overdose and thus the chances of accidents, death, violence and suicide.

Patterns of Psychoactive Substance Use

Two important factors that determine patterns of substance use in the community are the price and availability of the substances. Street children almost always choose the least expensive and most readily available ones, e.g. inhalants such as glue or petrol. If they decide to drink alcohol, they tend to pick the cheapest beverage with the highest alcohol content. Patterns of substance use vary greatly among street children and may change over time. Some develop a regular pattern of use while others may be quite haphazard.

A street child may change his or her pattern of use over time. Use of substances does not mean that he or she will automatically progress to using other substances or to use more intensively. Included under patterns of substance use are experimental, functional and harmful use, abuse and dependant use. Functional and experimental use relate to the issues of adolescence and survival on the street as outlined in the previous modules. Explained below are intoxication, harmful and dependent use.

Intoxication : Intoxication is a temporary state that follows the use of one or more substances resulting in a change in the person's alertness, thinking, perceptions, decision making, judgement, emotions, or behaviour. An intoxicated person is more likely to suffer from burns, suffocation, seizure, poisoning, overdose, sudden death etc. They may also be involved in accidents, violence, unsafe sex and rape.

Intoxication is highly dependent on the type and dose of substance and is influenced by an individual's level of tolerance and many other factors. It is not always clear when street children are intoxicated as intoxication with different substances has different signs and symptoms. In general, an intoxicated person will have the following common signs; they may be exceptionally sleepy, have trouble in thinking and speaking and talking to them may be difficult. Their eyes may be dilated, they may giggle or laugh inappropriately (sometimes in response to hallucinations) their mood may switch quickly between highs and lows and they may become aggressive. Even when it appears that a street child is intoxicated, it should be remembered that some of the signs and symptoms may be caused by other physical or psychological states, such as hunger, sickness and emotional difficulties.

Harmful use : Harmful use is a pattern of substance use that results in damage to physical or mental health. Most physical harms experienced by street children following the use of substances occur as a result of intoxication, hence health damage can also occur with experimental and occasional use. Other harms result from the way in which the substance is used. Injecting drugs is particularly dangerous because it can lead to an overdose or it may increase the risk of hepatitis, HIV and other infections from contaminated needles and syringes.

Smoking substances can result in disorders of the respiratory system and burns. Some substances such as leaded petrol, benzene and coca paste are particularly toxic and can cause health damage in even small amounts. As most street children have not been using substances for long enough it is unusual to see them with disorders such as alcoholic liver disease or smoking related lung cancer or heart disease which occur late in life.

Dependent use : This is a pattern of substance use in which the user has a strong desire to take the substance and can not control its use. Thus substance use gains priority over other activities for the user. Long-term use increases tolerance as their body adjusts to the substance so that the same amount of substance no longer produces the effects. They may also experience physical withdrawal reactions if he or she goes too long without the substance. Users who are dependent may continue to use substances despite very serious consequences. They may spend more and more of their day involved with substances.

Withdrawal : When a person stops taking a particular substance that he or she has been using regularly, he/ she may experience adverse effects known as withdrawal symptoms. Unless young people have been using large amounts of the substance for a long time, they rarely need to be weaned off a substance in a medical setting. They can be assessed and managed in other safe places with their cooperation. The most dangerous withdrawals are from alcohol and hypnosedatives, which may trigger convulsions and delirium. In these situations medically assisted detoxification may be advisable. Common withdrawal symptoms of various substances are shown in the table.

Substances	Withdrawal symptoms
Alcohol	Anxiety, tremors, vomiting, sweating, convulsion, delirium (confusion & hallucinations)

Nicotine	Nervousness, sleep difficulty, abdominal pain, poor concentration, muscle spasms, headaches, cough, changes in appetite
Opioids	Anxiety, sweating, muscle cramps, runny nose, vomiting, diarrho ea, sleep difficulty
Hallucinogens	No significant withdrawal symptoms
Cannabis	No or mild withdrawal symptoms
Hypnosedatives	Anxiety, irritability, inability to sleep, muscle cramps, convulsions, delirium
Stimulants	Caffeine: headaches, tiredness, aches and pains, anxiety
	Amphetamines:fatigue, hunger, irritability, depression, suicidal feelings, sleeplessness
	Cocaine: fear, depression, nausea, vomiting, tremors, muscle pain, tiredness
Inhalants	No significant withdrawal symptom

Conflict with Family

Everyone, including street children, occasionally has conflicts with family members, friends, strangers, and lovers. Like other young people they also want the excitement of taking a risk from time to time. Substance use can sometimes make these experiences unpleasant or even dangerous. Here are some consequences for the family and community.

— Important responsibilities may be forgotten, and disagreements can become emotionally or physically destructive.

— Substance users with little income are constantly faced with the problem of finding money to purchase substances. Some of them may steal or use violence to get the money and others might join illegal businesses or the sex industry to earn enough money.

— Activities such as building a fire can become dangerous if the children involved are under the influence of substances because of the lack of safety already present in the situations where they live.

— The demand for illegal substances has produced wealthy and powerful organizations that manufacture and distribute substances in some parts of the world.

Modified Social Stress Model in Substance Use

The Modified Social Stress Model is a framework which has been used by the WHO street children project to understand the vulnerability to risk behaviour and situations associated with substance use. This model could also be applied to sexual behaviour. The model has six major components; stress, normalization of behaviour and situations, effect of behaviour and situations, skills, attachments, and resources. Stress, normalization of behaviour and situations and effect of behaviour and situations (the experience of substance use) are viewed as factors that may increase vulnerability.

Skills, resources and attachments are seen as factors that may reduce vulnerability to risky behaviour and situations. However, each of these factors has aspects which can increase vulnerability (risk factors) or decrease it (protective factors). The model serves as a guide to factors which may contribute to street children engaging in various risk behaviours. The basis of the model is this: if many risk factors are present in a person's life, that person is more likely to begin, intensify, and continue the use of substances, and experience related problems.

Conversely, the more protective factors that are present, the less likely the person is to become involved with substances. Vulnerability can be understood better if both risk and protective factors are considered at the same time. Besides providing a conceptual understanding, the framework is useful for planning interventions to prevent or treat problems such as those related to substance use, sexual and reproductive health including HIV/AIDS/STDs, at both the individual (street child) and the community level.

Stress

Stress is the way a person feels (e.g., anxious, tense, burdened) in response to real or perceived stressors. A stressor may be observable (e.g., violence, poor living conditions, a physical disability), or it may be less visible to others (e.g., emotional abuse, trauma). The more stress a child is under, the more likely he or she is to use substances. Street children often have extremely stressful lives. There are five types of stress:

Major life events : Dramatic events that have a profound effect on the survivors. They include death of parents, abandonment, serious accidents, natural disasters, demolition of home by authorities, war, physical and sexual assaults, and suicide attempts. Street children may use substances after the event to lessen the pain of the event and to help them adjust to their new situation, which is inevitably worse than before.

Enduring life strains : The lives of street children are usually filled with long-term problems that are difficult to solve: poverty, denial of human rights, psychological difficulties, illnesses, and lack of educational and recreational opportunities. Rejection or a sense of rejection by family members, friends, school, health or other services, and society in general can also make the street child feel a se[illegible] similar to that experienced when someone close to one dies. Using substances may provide excitement, or help in imagining a better future and offer relief from physical pain. Substances are sometimes used to decrease guilt feelings and pain related to providing sex for money.

Everyday problems : Most of a street child's time is spent working on survival issues; finding food, clothes and shelter, and avoiding violence and the police. They often have ongoing conflicts with other street children, merchants and community members or authorities. This daily struggle is tiring and leaves little time for other things. Substance use offers a quick and easy escape from day-to-day problems.

Life transitions : Transitions in life, such as moving neighbourhoods or cities, changing peer groups, or beginning a romantic relationship, are always stressful because they require people to behave in new ways. People may use substances during the transition to reduce their anxiety. If a street child's new friends use substances, he or she may imitate their behaviour in order to be more easily accepted. Although stressful, some life transitions may result in a positive situation for street children. A family move may bring the street child who stays with his or her family at night into contact with different people who may have a positive influence.

Adolescent developmental changes : All young people go through physical, psychological, and social changes during their adolescent years. These changes are particularly difficult for street children who are becoming adolescents because they have no one to explain to them about these changes. They may not have had access to adequate adult role models and they may not get the opportunity to gradually assume more adult roles and responsibilities or negotiate such roles with parents and other adults. For example, street children may have to find a new source of income after puberty and may be enticed into commercial sexual activities. It can be confusing and depressing for street adolescents to cope with the immaturity of their bodies, especially while they are dealing with adult responsibilities.

Street children want to be accepted by their peers even more than the typical adolescent. Joining in when their companions use substances or engage in other activities that can harm health are ways to be accepted more easily. Sometimes stressful events and situations may be associated with positive outcomes for street children. The change brought about by the event may ease their situation in some cases, e.g. the marriage of a widowed parent may be stressful, but it may improve the family situation. The rebuilding of a community after a natural disaster may bring new educational resources or work opportunities for street children and their families.

A family move may bring the street child into contact with people who may have a positive influence. Growth and strength that come with adolescence are highly valued by many boys and girls. They may believe that they will not be abused as much, that the smallest members of their community will admire them, and that they may get better jobs. Stressors may lead to a positive outcome in yet another way. If the child negotiates a difficult situation successfully, it may enhance his or her self-esteem.

According to the Modified Social Stress Model, a person is more likely to become involved with substances if using substances is considered normal in the person's environment. Many street children live in places where other street children, the adults in the neighbourhood, and even the entire society accept the use of some substances. This makes it easy for them to use substances as well. Factors that encourage a group or an entire society to accept the use of a particular substance include:

—*Legality and law enforcement* : If a substance is legal, it is much more likely to be accepted or normalized in general society. The use of illegal substances that are tolerated by the authorities could be acceptable to many people, including street children.

Availability : The easier it is to get a substance, the more likely it will be normalized, as with the use of caffeine, alcohol, and tobacco which have become normalized in many countries across the globe. On the other hand, restrictions imposed on the manufacture and sale of psychoactive medicines limit their availability and make it less likely that their use will be normalized. The same principle holds for illegal substances. If they are easy to obtain, they are more likely to be normalized. The use of cannabis, which is widely available in some places, is acceptable to many members of the community even though it is illegal. Coca paste is used by many youths in the Amazon basin where it is produced. Volatile solvents, including petrol and glue, are readily available in almost all areas of the world.

Price : The more affordable a substance is, the more likely it is to become normalized within a group of consumers. Substances that are normalized among some street children are the ones that are the least expensive (and most available). Glue, solvents, and petrol are cheap in most areas. Crack cocaine has become one of the favourite substances of street youth in the United States, partly because of its low price.

Advertising, sponsorship and promotion : When substances are promoted (through advertisement or sponsorship of activities) in a community, residents are presented with the idea that using substances is normal and even desirable. Many promotional campaigns for tobacco and alcohol are designed specifically to encourage their use by young people. These include advertisements and sponsorship to activities at sporting events with celebrity athletes, youth festivals, and at 'rock' concerts. People involved in the drug trade may promote illegal substances in some communities. Street children are easily influenced by advertising, promotion and sponsorships. Without many heroes and successful role models in their own confined world, they often fantasize about the lives of celebrities and look to them for inspiration and direction.

Media presentation : A frequent and positive portrayal of substance use on television, in films, books, comics, and street theatres encourage normalization. Characters are shown smoking cigarettes, drinking alcohol, or taking substances in an atmosphere of excitement, danger, or sex. Equally problematic is the depiction of substance use as a normal, everyday event. Street children, many of whom were raised in stressful or atypical homes, may be easily influenced by what they see in the media because they many not have other sources of ideas and information.

Community acceptance : People tend to accept the use of a substance when the production and sale of the substance is an important source of income for the community. Some street children live in areas where substance production and trade are the major source of income for most of the residents.

Cultural role : Substances that have a place in the traditional culture of a society are usually normalized. The use of at least one substance has a cultural purpose in almost every society in the world. In religious activities, some Christians and Jews drink alcohol and some indigenous communities use hallucinogens. In parts of Asia, opium may be smoked during social gatherings and for relaxation. Cannabis is used for cooking and socializing in parts of Africa and Asia. When deciding whether it is normal to use substances, a person looks at the behaviour of people who are similar to him or her. These people, called a peer group, might find the use of certain substances acceptable in certain situations, even though it would not be acceptable to the general society.

The peer group for a street child is usually other street children of similar age who are involved in the same type of work as he or she is. Each peer group has its own unwritten rules about the use of substances. Working children in Mumbai, for example, accept the use of solvents, but they don't approve of sleeping tablets because the effects last too long and they feel too tired to work.

Experience of Substance Use

Many street children use substances because the substance adds something to their life such as entertainment, or it temporarily solves a problem. Street children use substances because substances lessen hunger, add excitement, decrease physical and emotional pain, induce sleep, may increase energy levels to work, improve alertness, provide a form of recreation, provide a feeling of belonging to the peer group or may even give the courage to commit crimes. If a substance produces a positive or desired experience for a street child, he or she might use it more frequently. The effect that a substance has differs from person to person, and from occasion to occasion.

The exact effect that a particular substance has on a particular individual depends on the user, the substance and the setting. Some street children claim that even if they don't like the effect of a particular substance, they may still continue to use it because the experience they have is better than the boredom of their daily lives and thus it becomes a desirable experience. Hallucinogens are an example of such a situation. Hallucinations have been described as having a 'magical' feeling, even though some of the experiences can be very frightening. Understanding what the street children like about the effects is important in planning interventions. Negative experiences of taking substances such as a bad 'hangover', frightening hallucinations or panic reactions can decrease the likelihood of use.

Attachments are personal connections to people, animals, objects and institutions. Having at least one person with whom someone has a close bond and feeling of acceptance has been found to be vital to developing a sense of positive self-esteem. A desire for close relationships can make a street child vulnerable to close relationships with people who can have a negative influence. A street child is more likely to develop strong attachments to other people if:

— He or she spends a lot of time with them

— He or she performs well in that group in any activity

— He or she is consistently rewarded by the group

Street children are less likely to begin using substances and more likely to stop using them if their strongest attachments are with people and things that are not connected with substance use. Unfortunately, the situation of many street children makes it difficult for them to keep in contact with their families, to succeed at school or work, or to surround themselves with friends who do not use substances. Negative attachments are connections to people or institutions that are associated with substance use, abuse or exploitation such as drug syndicates or peers who use substances. Negative attachments make substance use more likely.

Skills are competencies. Competencies include physical and performance capabilities such as juggling, vending, craft, and self-defence, and psycho-social skills (e.g self-awareness, assertiveness, problem solving etc.) needed to deal effectively with the demands of everyday life. These skills are often called psychosocial life skills. All young people need to develop physical, psychological, social, moral, and vocational competencies as a part of their healthy development.

Coping strategies are the cognitive, behavioural and social abilities that help a person manage stress. Competencies become coping strategies when they are used to manage stressful situations, e.g. seeking support from others or retreating in the face of danger. Competencies also help young people prevent health problems and cope with them if they occur. If street children have more skills it is less likely that they will need substances to meet challenges or to cope with problems. If they do use substances, they will have a greater ability to control the amount of use and avoid problems related to substance use.

Children may be exploited because of their age and general vulnerability during the process of skill development. This may include being paid less or being forced to work longer hours compared to other older workers. Under such circumstances, children may use substances to stay awake or to keep up energy levels and then use different substances to sleep or relax. The skills developed to survive on the streets, such as the ability to steal or lie to people in authority, can have a negative side in increasing illegal activities such as drug trafficking. This can result in increased use of substances in the community and by the individual. Lying prevents the development of trusting relationships.

Resources are used to meet physical and emotional needs. Resources can be inside a person, such as a willingness to work hard, or in the environment, e.g. schools, money, and people who care about the person. Examples of resources are:

- Internal resources.
  - Intelligence.
  - Capacity to work.
  - Educ ation.
  - Vocational skills.
  - Religious faith.
  - Optimism.
  - Sense of humour.
- External resources.
  - Information.
  - Family.
  - Other street children.
  - Street educators.
  - Positive role models.
  - Community organizations.
  - Educational and vocational training services.
  - Health services.
  - Employers.
  - Recreational facilities.

Even though street children usually have many internal resources, they often lack external ones. Without external resources, it is often difficult for street children to learn new skills that would help improve their lives.

2

Street Children and Social Menace

The United Nations Center for Human Rights has estimated that by the year 2000 half of the world's population will be under 25 years of age and located in cities, and that significant numbers will be living in poverty. The United Nations also estimated that by the end of this century there will be almost 250 million more urban children in the 5-to-19 year old age cohort then there were in the mid-1980s; that more than 90% of these youths will be living in developing nations; and that by the year 2020 there will be some 100 million indigent urban minors in Latin America alone. It is likely, furthermore, that many of these children will be living in the streets.

The use of the street as a place to live and/or work is not unknown to most industrial economies, but the presence of vast numbers of unsupervised and unprotected children is a phenomenon that is visible only in developing nations. Numerous scientific studies and media stories have reported the widespread use of inhalants, marijuana and cocaine, and Valium among street children. Also common is the use of coca paste and Rohypnol. Risk of exposure to HIV is rapidly becoming an area of concern because of the large number of street youths engaging in unprotected sexual acts, both renumerated and non-renumerated.

Some 55 million people, 33% of Brazil's total population, are under age 16 and 35 million children are living in families earning well under the minimum wage. Almost half of all

Brazilian families live below the poverty line (88% of the minimum wage), and almost a third are below the indigency line (53% of the minimum wage). More than 18% of Brazil's population is illiterate, and 35% of children between ages 7 and 15 are not enrolled in school. In addition, with the exception of Haiti and Guatemala, malnutrition is more prevalent in Brazil than in any other Latin American or Caribbean nation. According to official government statistics, 1,000 children die from hunger and malnutrition each day in Brazil.

Moreover, Brazil's infant mortality rate in 1993 was 52 per 1,000 live births, one of the highest in Latin America and exceeded only by Peru (88) and Bolivia (98). In the poorest regions of the country and in impoverished areas near industrial centers, 10% of the children are expected to die before they reach 5 years of age. These discouraging numbers documenting the destitution of millions of Brazilians become even more bewildering when one considers that Brazil has a higher per capita GNP — $2,770 — than any other Latin American country (except Uruguay).

Brazil is a relatively wealthy country and possesses the tenth largest economy in the world, but the distribution of resources within its population is highly skewed. In fact, in 1996 the World Bank reported that for the second year in a row Brazil had the most lopsided income distribution in the world. For example, the wealthiest 20% of the population earned 65% of the country's total income, leaving only 12% for the poorest half. When Brazil is compared with other countries, the problem of inequity becomes even more obvious.

The wealthiest 10% of the population earned 30 times more than the average income of the most impoverished 40% — a proportion that is ten-to-one in Argentina, nine-to-one in the United States, and only five-to-one in most European countries. Moreover, there is a staggering amount of land concentration in Brazil, with 43% of the total land area owned by 1% of the population. The striking economic disparity that exists between different segments of Brazilian society has its roots in regional inequalities and racial discrimination. During Brazil's "Economic Miracle" of the 1970s, government funds and foreign loans flowed into the industries of the south, resulting in improved standards of living and employment opportunities in that area of the country.

In the agricultural northern regions, however, the poverty rate increased 9% over this same time period. Further, the aim of the Brazilian government to achieve "economic growth at all costs" led to a decrease in spending for health care, social programs, and educational initiatives. As a result, the proportion of malnourished children under age 5 increased from 13.7% in the late 1970s to 30.7% by the end of the 1980s.

With respect to economic disparity and racial inequality, Brazil is thought to have the largest black population of any country outside of Africa, with about 70 million people, or 46% of the total population being Afro-Brazilians. Blacks in Brazil are typically overrepresented in the lowest income levels and represent the majority of the under-employed. Several studies have documented that incomes of white Brazilians are, on average, twice that of black Brazilians. In addition, a World Bank study found that almost 30% of Afro-Brazilian children live in households with incomes at the lowest wage levels.

An important consequence of regional and racial economic inequalities in Brazil has been a massive influx of migrants from rural to urban areas. Over the past 20 years, cities throughout Brazil have absorbed over 29 million migrants seeking employment and a better life for themselves and their families. Others were evicted from their land by mining projects or cattle raising. This influx of migrants created a seemingly inexhaustible pool of unskilled laborers in Brazil's large cities. Moreover, the infrastructure of these urban areas has increasingly been unable to expand to meet the demands for health care, education, and employment.

As a result, slum dwellings, unemployment, hunger, and violence have risen dramatically. Currently, 75% of all Brazilians live in cities, and among them are 52 million boys and girls under age 19. The Southeastern region of Brazil, where São Paulo and Rio de Janeiro are situated, is the most heavily populated section of the country. It is estimated that in metropolitan Rio de Janeiro and São Paulo alone there are several million children living in extreme poverty. And it is this destitution which drives children to the streets in an attempt to survive.

New Face of Child Labor

Throughout Latin America, meninos de rua (in Brazilian Portuguese) or niños de la calle (in Spanish) represent the new face of child labor □ youths working in the urban informal sector. Their occupations range from shining shoes, selling cigarettes, flowers, newspapers or chewing gum, to hauling garbage, drug trafficking, petty theft, street robberies, and prostitution. The existence of street children in the large metropolitan areas of Brazil is not particularly new. The international media began to document the condition of large numbers of Brazilian street children as early as the 1970s.

Despite the significant media attention over the past 15 to 20 years, however, much remains unknown about their daily lives and activities. In fact, even approximating the actual size of the population of street children has proven difficult. Estimates of their numbers in Brazil have ranged from 7 to 17 million, but more informed assessments suggest that between 7 and 8 million children, ages 5 to 18, live and/or work on the streets of urban Brazil. While the vast majority of street children are boys, Brazilian government estimates put the number of street girls at approximately 800,000, with almost two-thirds of them working as prostitutes in various parts of the country.

Part of the problem in estimating the number of street children lies in the distinction between what are known as "children on the street" and "children of the street". Children on the street work in informal sector occupations in order to supplement the family income, but return home at night to sleep. These children typically reside in households headed by impoverished, single women and spend most of the day and night in the street selling candy or gum, guarding cars, shining shoes, or carrying groceries.

By contrast, children of the street have oftentimes completely severed ties with their families. They seemingly choose to leave homes where hunger, neglect, and exploitation are commonplace, making life on the street preferable. A very small number of children actually live full-time in the streets, often engaging in illegal activities in order to survive. In fact, children of the street are more typically associated with theft, drug sales, petty theft, prostitution, and gang activity.

Younger children often begin their careers on the street by begging, but rely increasingly on crime to support themselves as they age and become less successful at panhandling. Young street girls commonly use prostitution as a way of supporting themselves. As indicated in Table 1, the United Nations Children's Fund estimates that the number of "working children" (children on the street) and "street children" (children of the street) throughout Latin America total as many as 40 million.

Table 1. "Working Children" and "Street Children" in Selected Latin American and Caribbean Nations

Country	Working Children	Street Children
Argentina	2.35 million	20,000*
Bolivia	72,000	200
Brazil	7.4 million	8 million**
Costa Rica	53,000	5,300
Ecuador	1 million	4,000
El Salvador	231,000	10,000
Guatemala	1.62 million	1,000***
Haiti	120,000	10,000

Honduras	275,000	800
Mexico	10 million	250,000

*Includes Buenos Aires only.

**May include children working, but not living, on the street.

***Includes Guatemala City only.

As the number of street children and their related criminal activity continue to grow, so does public opposition to their presence. Over the past twenty or so years, public opinion has shifted dramatically. Youngsters who were once looked upon as deserving of compassion and sympathy are now viewed at best as a nuisance, and at worst as a danger to public safety — future criminals who ought to be locked up. Although popular views characterize these children as delinquents and thieves, perhaps Nancy Scheper-Hughes most accurately described street youths in modern Brazil as simply "poor children in the wrong place".

Perhaps it was this sentiment that enabled the Brazilian National Congress was to pass the Child and Adolescent Act in 1990. This statute was designed to reform the legal status of children in Brazil and to create councils that would act as children's rights advocates, with an eye toward integrating impoverished children into the larger society. However, negative attitudes toward street children by the Brazilian people prevail and public resistance to such reforms continues to frustrate attempts to implement the statute.

Children of the Favelas

Important to understanding the presence of large numbers of street children in Latin America in general, and in Brazil in particular, is a comprehension of the nature of primate cities and what life is like in the thousands of primate city shantytowns. Most developing countries contain one or more "primate cities," urban areas that grow in population and influence far beyond the other cities in the region or nation.

In many Latin American countries, and in other developing nations as well, the largest cities may have several times the combined populations of the next two or three urban areas and may also have a significant share of the national population.

Mexico City's population of 16 million, for example, accounts for 20% of the nation's population, while other cities are considerably smaller: Guadalajara (1.6 million), Monterrey (1.1 million), and Puebla de Zaragoza (1.1 million). Similarly, the populations of Brazil's two largest cities — São Paulo and Rio de Janeiro — combine to account for some 16% of the national population.

Primate cities typically are located on the coast or in other areas close to transportation routes, since many were political and economic centers when under colonial rule. The orientation of such cities had been toward supplying the developed nations with raw materials and other goods, rather than toward the urban areas and hinterlands of their own country. Among the greatest difficulties experienced by these cities in Latin America are those of stimulating industrialization and providing employment. People who move into these urban locales do so, not because of the employment opportunities the cities provide, but because the living conditions in rural areas seem so much worse.

Rural-urban migrants believe that the cities offer a better life and at least the hope for employment. Some do find work in small enterprises, but the lack of sophisticated technology and industrial production methods does not provide for the large pool of unskilled labor that characterized the Western industrial revolution. As a result, the unemployment rates in the cities of many developing nations exceed 25% of the labor force.

Common features of the primate city landscape are the sections comprised of shanties, shacks, and makeshift huts inhabited by those who have no other shelter. Known as barriadas in Peru, ranchos in Venezuela, villas miserias in Argentina, or favelas in Brazil, these squatter settlements have been estimated to house as much as one-third of the urban population. Mexico City has some 4 million squatters, Calcutta has 2 million, and Rio de Janeiro has over 1 million.

Favelas have been a feature of urban Brazil for generations. Favela in Brazilian Portuguese means "slum." Yet it is a particular type of slum that takes its name from Morro da Favela, a hill near Rio de Janeiro where the first one appeared in the late 1880s. In 1963, the noted journalist and biographer John Dos Passos commented:

> In Rio — this was in 1948 — there were said to be three hundred thousand people living in favelas. Today there are nearer a million. You come on favelas in the most unexpected places. In Copacabana a few minutes walk from the hotels and the splendid white apartment houses and the wellkept magnificent beaches you find a whole hillside of favelas overlooking the lake and the Jockey Club. In the center of Rio a few steps from the Avenida Rio Branco on the hill back of one of the most fashionable churches you come suddenly into a tropical jungletown.

Similarly, in 1966 travel writer John Gunther described Rio's favelas as "vertical" in character — since they were situated on hillsides:

> This came about partly because much of the land in Rio is too steep for normal building purposes and, when urbanization began on a serious scale, speculators let the hills alone. So the squatters swarmed to the cliffs, scraped off plots from jungle shrubbery, and built their miserable huts out of tin cans, hunks of stone, and cardboard, on the sharpest slopes. The irony is that they now have the best views in the city. But there are no amenities whatever, not even water or a postal service. Filth and flies are everywhere. Dogs howl, and children drip with slime.

The favelas situated on the hillsides of Rio de Janeiro are the best known and most notorious. They began to appear at the end of the nineteenth century, and spread rapidly after 1930 as shelters for newly-arriving migrants. Fleeing regions hard-hit by drought and unemployment, rural Brazilians thronged to cidade maravilhosa, the "marvelous city" of Rio de Janeiro, lured by its illusionary riches. There has been a steady stream even since, and at the close of the 1980s it was estimated that some 1,500 "favelados" were arriving each day.

Little has changed since Dos Passos and Gunther made their observations three decades ago. In the great majority of the favelas, migrants from all over Brazil have recreated a semi-rural way of life, in neighborhoods with names which often reflect a bittersweet Brazilian humor — Morro da Esperança (Hill of Hope), Chácara do Céu (Sky Gardens), and Nova Brasília (New Brasília). In Rio de Janeiro, the favelas have been estimated by Brazil's Municipal Planning Institute to number 545 and house more than 1 million persons — some 14% of the city's population. Clustered on the hill and mountainsides that overlook Rio's fashionable beaches and elegant shopping and high-rise centers, the favelas are slums in which only a small portion of households have electricity, running water, or sewage facilities.

Juramento, for example, like most other favelas, is a self-contained realm of the very poor, with 30,000 residences and a dozen or so entry points. There is no glass in the windows of the shacks, no electricity or water other than what can be tapped from city lines, and when it rains the gutters run with mud and refuse. The hill is riddled with alleys and passageways, but there are no official street names, and no mail service or telephone lines. In the absence of public medical facilities and unemployment benefits for the more than 50% of out-of-work favelados, disease and social problems multiply. There is prostitution and drug use, and a key feature of most favelas is cocaine trafficking.

Within such a setting, it is no wonder that so many children retreat from the favelas to the streets — in Rio de Janeiro, São Paulo, Belo Horizonte, Porto Alegre, Santos, Fortaleza, Recife, and other Brazilian cities. And in Rio, a city where street children have received considerable media attention, they withdraw from the favelas to Copacabana,

Ipanema, Lapa, Botafogo, Tijuca, and other sections of the "asphalt city." The total number of street youths in Rio de Janeiro has been the topic of considerable media conjecture and exaggeration, with some estimates as high 1 million. Local public health officials put the number of "children of the street" at 2,000 - 3,000, which still is a major social problem.

Drug Use

Anecdotal accounts of drug abuse among street youths in Brazil are commonplace. Numerous media stories have reported the widespread use of inhalants (such as glue, gasoline, lighter fluid, bim — a mixture of ethyl alcohol, sugar and benzene), marijuana and cocaine, and Valium among street children in Rio de Janeiro. Also common is the use of coca paste and Rohypnol. Common not only in the drug-using communities of Brazil, but also in those of Colombia, Bolivia, Venezuela, Ecuador, and Peru, is the use of coca paste, known to most South Americans as basuco, susuko, pasta basica de cocaina, pasta de coca, or just simply pasta.

Perhaps best known as "basuco," coca paste is one of the intermediate products in the processing of the coca leaf into cocaine. It is typically smoked straight, or in cigarettes mixed with either tobacco or marijuana. The smoking of coca paste became popular in South America beginning in the early 1970s. It was readily available, inexpensive, had a high cocaine content, and was absorbed quickly. As the phenomenon was studied, however, it was quickly realized that paste smoking was far more serious than any other form of cocaine use. In addition to cocaine, paste contains traces of all the chemicals used to initially process the coca leaves—kerosene, sulfuric acid, methanol, benzoic acid, and the oxidized products of these solvents, plus any number of other alkaloids that are present in the coca leaf.

When the smoking of paste was first noted in South America it seemed to be restricted to the coca processing regions of Bolivia, Colombia, Ecuador, and Peru, appealing primarily to street children and low-income groups due to its cheap price when compared with that of refined cocaine. By the early 1980s, however, it had spread to other South American nations, including Brazil, to numerous segments of the social strata, and throughout the decade paste smoking further expanded to become a major drug problem for much of South America. Among the Rio's street youth of the 1990s, the smoking of pasta de coca remains an enduring problem.

By contrast, Rohypnol is a legal drug in Brazil, readily available in pharmacies in many parts of the world. Also known by its generic name flunitrazepam, Rohypnol is a benzodiazepine drug having anticonvulsant and sedative effects, slowing psychomotor performance, and inducing muscle relaxation and sleep. It is used for the short-term treatment of insomnia. However, its use can lead to the development of physical and psychic dependence, with the risk of addiction increasing with dose and duration of use.

Rohypnol is similar to Valium, but ten times as potent. It was first introduced in the 1970s, and is legally available throughout Europe and Latin America. Since the 1980s it has been used to counter some the negative side effects of cocaine abuse. In addition, combining Rohypnol with alcohol, cocaine, or marijuana reportedly produces a fast hit followed by a mellow state which lasts for several hours. Many street youths in Rio de Janeiro see their use of inhalants, coca paste, marijuana, Rohypnol and other drugs as an escape — a way to dull their hunger and facilitate acts of prostitution and other crimes. And as one young female prostitute observed:

> When I was prostituting at the boarding house, my father would go there and want to pay me to have sex with him. I would never do it and every time he would leave, I would smoke a lot of marijuana to try and forget the things that he would say.

Indeed, it has been observed that drug use by street children is a nearly universal phenomenon because these youths are confronted with the harsh realities of street life on a daily basis. Given that drug abuse among youths has emerged as a concomitant of life on the streets, the paucity of scientific studies which have examined this and other related topics among street children in Brazil is troubling. Although previous research on drug use among street children is limited, existing studies have found rates of use to be high. A survey among 119 street children in São Paulo, for example, classified 45% as heavy drug users, indicating the use of up to three drugs a day.

In a study of street youths in Belo Horizonte, a city of 2 million people some 452 km northeast of Rio de Janeiro, 84% of the children living full-time in the street had histories of illegal drug use, 10.6% reported injection drug use, and 83.5% were sexually active. Additionally, in an earlier study involving this same sample, 82.6% reported having had sex while under the influence of drugs and/or alcohol. In comparison, of the working but "home-based" children interviewed, only 25% had histories of illegal drug use and none reported the use of injection drugs. A similar study supported these findings by reporting higher rates of drug use among "street-based" youth than "home-based" youth, 76.9% vs. 29.1%, and earlier onset of drug use — 9.8 years versus 11.2 years.

Moreover, a 1992 study of 98 street children in Rio de Janeiro found that 90.8% believed drug abuse to be a problem in the community and 38.8% stated that drug use was a personal problem for them. The most commonly used drugs among these children were glue (13.3%), marijuana (13.3%), alcohol/tobacco (12.2%), and cocaine (11.2%). Nearly 70% of this sample refused to respond to questions about injection drug use. The most in depth study of drug use among street youths was conducted in 1992 by the Guidance Center on Drugs and the Treatment of Drug Addicts of the University of Brasília. The research sampled 150 males ages 10 to 17 in Ceilândia, one of Brasília's satellite towns, and examined three groups of street children — youths with no school or family ties, youths receiving assistance from social welfare institutions (typically delinquents), and youths enrolled in local schools.

The data indicated that a full 100% of the street youths interviewed used drugs. Solvents and inhalants, typically cobbler's glue, were the most commonly used. "Frequent use," defined as daily or several times a week, was found among 88% of the entire sample, and among 72% of those in social welfare institutions. In addition, 32% of the youths reported the use of marijuana and/or cocaine. The latter drugs are purchased from local dealers, while the inhalants can be obtained legally in in a variety of places.

The fact that solvents and inhalants are the drugs most frequently used by street youths was not an unanticipated finding of the Brasília study, because prior studies have found these drugs to be common among other youth populations as well. In a study of 1,836 São Paulo students (ages 9 to 18 years) from low socioeconomic backgrounds, 24% reported lifetime use of inhalants and 4.9% reported use in the last 30 days. Moreover, in a 10-city survey of 16,300 Brazilian public school students 26.2% reported lifetime use of psychotropic drugs — typically solvents and inhalants.

Risky Sexual Behaviours

Regardless of whether they reported any use of illegal drugs, street children have frequently related engaging in risky sexual behaviors. Street studies in Rio de Janeiro have concluded that a "second shift" of children are visible on the streets at night. Unlike their daytime counterparts, these "second shift" children tend to be older and are more likely to be female. Among them, prostitution is frequent by both boys and girls. A 1992 study of 62 children found that 48.4% had engaged in sex, 60% with adult men, 16.6% reported sex for money, but only 33.3% reported any use of condoms. In addition to solicitation for prostitution, many street children have reported incidents of rape. Scheper-Hughes and Hoffman observed that street girls and boys are frequently raped by police and others.

Surprisingly, however, the perpetrators are not always male. Vasconcelos noted that older street girls will sometimes force younger girls to have sex with them, thereby continuing the cycle of violence of which they too have been victims. A survey of 52 HIV seropositive street youths under age 16 in Rio de Janeiro found that 28% had had anal intercourse, presumably forced. Of those ages 7 to 12, 63% had had anal intercourse and 57% had been forced to have anal intercourse by older street children. Although this type of sexual violence appears to be common, it is not always necessary. Many street children use sex as a way to gain affection and attention. For this reason, younger girls at times voluntarily seek sexual contact with older girls. Sexual activity among boys is also relatively common.

Some 21% of street boys interviewed in a 1991 study reported same-sex anal intercourse. Heterosexual anal intercourse was reported by 43% of these same respondents. Despite high rates of sexual activity among street children, attitudes regarding condom use are for the most part negative and usage rates are low. Various studies have reported the proportion of sexually active street children having ever used condoms to be in the range of 8.2% to 33.3%.

Risk of exposure to HIV is rapidly becoming an area of concern because of the large number of street youths engaging in unprotected sexual acts, both renumerated and non-renumerated. On the whole, the World Health Organization reckons that there are between 50,000 and 100,000 HIV positive children and adolescents in Brazil. Going further, it has also been estimated that between 1% and 2% of Brazil's population of 7-8 million street children, or between 70,000 and 110,000 individuals, are HIV positive. A study in 1987-1988 at the FUNBEM Hospital in Rio de Janeiro found that among 3,389 street children, 50 (1.5%) were HIV positive. However, a more recent study conducted between May 1991 and January 1994 found that of 126 street children interviewed and tested, 94% reported HIV risk behaviors, and 6% were HIV seropositive.

Violence Against Street Children

Street children throughout Latin America are viewed by many police groups, merchants, and other citizens as undesirable, pariah populations. In Brazil, they are targets of fear, and are seen by the upper classes and the political right-wing as being:

> . . . a blemish on the urban landscape and a reminder that all is not well in the country. Unwanted and considered human waste, these ubiquitous tattered, mainly black children and adolescents evoke strong and contradictory emotions of fear, aversion, pity and anger in those who view their neighborhood streets, boulevards and squares as 'private places" under siege.

Because of their drug use, predatory crimes, and general unacceptability on urban thoroughfares, street children have frequently been the targets of local vigilante groups, drug gangs, and police "death squads." Perhaps most notorious have been the death squads, which initially appeared in Brazil in 1968, and principally in Rio de Janeiro, at first to avenge the terrorist murder of a well-known police officer. The death squads proliferated during the years of Brazil's military rule, which ended in 1985. As the killings spread, political and community leaders were often targeted, and the victims were easily recognized. Their hands were always tied behind their backs, their tongues cut out, and a crudely drawn skull and cross-bones were left on the corpse with the initials "E.M."—"Esquadrão de Morte"—appended.

News reports have suggested that there are many such police assassination squads in Latin America. Guatemala had its La Mano Blanco (The White Hand), Argentina its Anti-Communist Alliance, the Dominican Republic its La Banda gang, and in Brazil, Paraguay, Honduras, and El Salvador simply Esquadrão de Morte or Esquadron de Muerte—"Death

Squad." All were organized, but unofficial, police vigilante organizations established with the aim not only of preserving their respective political regimes through selective political murders, but also of eliminating those viewed by the police as "undesirables"—trade unionists, drug dealers, thieves and other criminals, and not surprisingly, street children.

Many of the death squads still exist, particularly in Brazil, and street children are common victims. Because they survive, in part, through prostitution and crime, they have become the targets of retributive violence by police death squads and merchants' vigilante groups. Considered to be bad for business, store owners hire off-duty police officers or professional killers to eliminate the "disposable children." Their elimination is also seen as a mechanism of "social cleansing." There is considerable public support for the death squads as the result of perceptions that street children are dangerous criminals. Residents of the poorest communities are often the strongest supporters of violent solutions to local crime, perhaps because their neighborhoods are the least secure.

The most notorious of the death squad killings of street children occurred in 1993 in Rio de Janeiro. At 1 A.M. on July 25th, as 50 homeless youths were sleeping on the grounds of the Candelaria Cathedral in the downtown section of the city, a group of gunmen drove up and began shooting.

Four of the youths died instantly, a fifth was shot and killed as he ran, two more were abducted, beaten, shot and dumped in the gardens of the nearby Museum of Modern Art, and an eighth died several days later, never waking from a coma. Eight others were also shot, but survived their wounds. Three members of the Military Police were arrested for the crimes, and the shootings were reportedly provoked by an occurrence earlier in the day in which some of the children had allegedly thrown stones at a military police vehicle after one youth had been detained for drug use. The incident captured headlines worldwide. A commission was established to investigate the "Candelaria massacre," but its progress was slowed when two of its members were slain in Rio de Janeiro by unidentified gunmen.

Nevertheless, on April 30, 1996, one of the police officers — Marcos Vinicius Borges Emmanuel, who had admitted to one of the killings — was convicted on six counts of murder, five counts of attempted murder, and several counts of grievous bodily harm, and received a sentence of 309 years. Street children are also the targets of drug gangs. Because Brazil's Protective Child Statute holds that children under 18 years of age may not be arrested unless caught in the act of committing a crime, to the drug gangs the youths' impunity makes them ideal couriers. But they are often killed because they know too much, steal too much, or get caught in the crossfire.

The hierarchy of the favela drug trade is a vertical one, and children are recruited into the lowest level, serving primarily as lookouts. They progress to running errands for the hillside dealers, and if they are successful, they begin delivering drugs to customers. Survivors from these operations may become armed "controllers" (security guards who protect the operation and proceeds of drug transactions). Finally, there are the corporate levels of the local drug business, but few children ever last that long. Most die while they are still at the lower end of the hierarchy. When a hillside dealer is dissatisfied with a child's work, or decides that the youth is dangerous as a witness, he or she is simply killed. And altogether, it is estimated that as many as four to five street children are murdered each day throughout Brazil, and two each day in Rio de Janeiro alone.

Proposals and Programmes for Street Children

Although there have been many proposals and programs for addressing the problems of Brazilian street youth, it would appear that only minimal headway has been achieved. At the most general level, programs appear to be of four types: a) the correctional approach; b) the rehabilitative perspective; c) outreach strategies; and, d) the preventive outlook. The correctional approach views street children as a matter for juvenile justice organizations. This correctional vision seems to dominate the thinking of much of the public and criminal justice authorities. The result is that thousands of street children are housed in institutions.

In Brazil, the National Foundation for Child Welfare (FUNABEM) operates twenty treatment centers and "reform" schools for abandoned and delinquent youth. Conditions in these facilities have been described as both crowded and abusive. However, some changes appear to be underway, involving the substitution of correctional initiatives with community-based treatment alternatives. The rehabilitative approach has been gaining momentum throughout Latin America. This perspective holds that street children are not delinquents as much as they are victims of poverty, child abuse and neglect, and untenable living conditions. Because street children are seen as having been harmed by their environments, hundreds of church and voluntary programs have been organized in their behalf. These typically provide housing, drug detoxification, education, and/or work programs. But there is a difficulty. The programs benefit only a limited number of youths, and are unable to address the needs of the millions of boys and girls who continue to call the streets their home.

Because the institutional capacities and resources of virtually all programs are limited and unable to accommodate the overwhelming majority street children, services are also provided through a variety of outreach strategies. In São Paulo, for example, the Catholic Church supports young lay workers who provide educational, counseling, and advocacy services to children in a street setting. In addition to teaching basic hygiene, literacy, and business skills, the general program approach is to instill self-reliance and empowerment so that children will find solutions to their problems. However, it would appear that this street educator model is overly ideological, and fails to deal with the immediate physical and safety needs of street children.

Most recently, outreach strategies have been focusing on HIV prevention and risk reduction. The effectiveness of these initiatives, however, is unclear. The preventive approach attempts to address the fundamental and underlying problem of childhood poverty. In this regard, UNICEF is conducting educational campaigns to alert policy makers to the causes of children moving to the streets. In addition to policy advocacy, UNICEF provides technical assistance and support for promising local efforts. Those receiving UNICEF's focused attention are of two types:

1) programs which provide daytime activities, schooling, jobs, and other alternatives to street work for high risk children; and

2) efforts focusing on the prevention of family disintegration—cooperative day care centers, family planning clinics, small business services, and community kitchens.

The most comprehensive effort on behalf of Brazilian street youth is the National Movement for Street Children (Movimento Nacional de Meninos e Meninas de Rua/ MNMMR), a nationwide coalition of street children and adult educators founded in 1985. MNMMR initiatives focus on shifting the management of street children away from the criminal justice system, codifying the rights of children into law, and structuring innovative approaches for providing education and training for youths directly on the streets where they live. MNMMR projects are targeting an estimated 80,000 youths, the great majority of whom work on the streets and live in nearby favelas, with the remaining actually living on the streets.

Street children in Brazilian cities are legion. Their actual numbers are difficult to estimate, however, and have often been exaggerated. As one observer put it: They seem to be everywhere: begging in front of restaurants, peddling cigarettes in sidewalk cafes, shining shoes outside the train station, washing clothes in public fountains. Take a morning stroll on the elegant, black-and-white mosaic sidewalk that curves along Rio's Copacabana Beach and you'll smell them; dozens sleep under the palms there, and the beach serves as a toilet. For those who work the streets during the day, returning to their favela homes at night, life is harsh and unkind.

For the rest who live in the streets day and night, life is mean and unusually short. And for the great majority of Brazil's street children, it would appear that few changes are likely. Prostitution, drug use, infections, and illiteracy are common, yet there are few programs available to address the many needs of youths. After his election in 1991, Brazilian President Collor de Mello announced a dramatic plan to build 5,000 model schools called CIACs (Centros Integrados de Apoio à Criança/Integrated support Centers for Children) for indigent children and youth over a four-year period. They were conceived to offer indigent youths comprehensive classroom instruction and after school care, three meals a day, medical and psychological attention, shower facilities, sports and cultural activities, and a library.

3

Health Issues

Children of the street have oftentimes completely severed ties with their families. They seemingly choose to leave homes where hunger, neglect, and exploitation are commonplace, making life on the street preferable. A very small number of children actually live full-time in the streets, often engaging in illegal activities in order to survive. In fact, children of the street are more typically associated with theft, drug sales, petty theft, prostitution, and gang activity. Younger children often begin their careers on the street by begging, but rely increasingly on crime to support themselves as they age and become less successful at panhandling. Young street girls commonly use prostitution as a way of supporting themselves.

Children on the street work in informal sector occupations in order to supplement the family income, but return home at night to sleep. These children typically reside in households headed by impoverished, single women and spend most of the day and night in the street selling candy or gum, guarding cars, shining shoes, or carrying groceries. Numerous scientific studies and media stories have reported the widespread use of inhalants, marijuana and cocaine, and Valium among street children. Also common is the use of coca paste and Rohypnol. Risk of exposure to HIV is rapidly becoming an area of concern because of the large number of street youths engaging in unprotected sexual acts, both renumerated and non-renumerated

The presence of vast numbers of unsupervised and unprotected children is a phenomenon that is common throughout Latin America, and in few places are the street children more visible, and reviled, than in Brazil. Estimates of their numbers in Brazil have ranged from 7 to 17 million, but more informed assessments suggest that between 7 and 8 million children, ages 5 to 18, live and/or work on the streets of urban Brazil. Accounts of drug abuse among street youths in Brazil are common place.

Brazil's street children are targets of fear. Because of their drug use, predatory crimes, and general unacceptability on urban thoroughfares, they are frequently the targets of local vigilante groups, drug gangs, and police "death squads." Although there have been many proposals and programs for addressing the problems of Brazilian street youth, it would appear that only minimal headway has been achieved. The United Nations Center for Human Rights has estimated that by the year 2000 half of the world's population will be under 25 years of age and located in cities, and that significant numbers will be living in poverty.

The United Nations also estimated that by the end of this century there will be almost 250 million more urban children in the 5-to-19 year old age cohort then there were in the mid-1980s; that more than 90% of these youths will be living in developing nations; and that by the year 2020 there will be some 100 million indigent urban minors in Latin America alone. The use of the street as a place to live and/or work is not unknown to most industrial economies, but the presence of vast numbers of unsupervised and unprotected children is a phenomenon that is visible only in developing nations, and particularly in Latin America.

Brazil is often referred to as the land of perpetual promise. It is also a land of great diversity. It is the rain forests of Amazonia and the factories of São Paulo; it is the turquoise beaches of Bahia and the swamps of the Pantanal; and it is Carnaval in Rio de Janeiro and the gauchos of Rio Grande do

Sul. And Brazil is Copacabana and Corcovado, the samba and capoeira, and soccer, feijoada, Pelé, cachaça, and world beat. But at the same time, Brazil ranks near the bottom of the hemisphere in its standard of living, health status, and social indicators. Some 55 million people, 33% of Brazil's total population, are under age 16 and 35 million children are living in families earning well under the minimum wage.

Almost half of all Brazilian families live below the poverty line, and almost a third are below the indigency line. (1) More than 18% of Brazil's population is illiterate, and 35% of children between ages 7 and 15 are not enrolled in school. In addition, with the exception of Haiti and Guatemala, malnutrition is more prevalent in Brazil than in any other Latin American or Caribbean nation . According to official government statistics, 1,000 children die from hunger and malnutrition each day in Brazil. Moreover, Brazil's infant mortality rate in 1993 was 52 per 1,000 live births, one of the highest in Latin America and exceeded only by Peru and Bolivia. In the poorest regions of the country and in impoverished areas near industrial centers, 10% of the children are expected to die before they reach 5 years of age.

These discouraging numbers documenting the destitution of millions of Brazilians become even more bewildering when one considers that Brazil has a higher per capita than any other Latin American country. Brazil is a relatively wealthy country and possesses the tenth largest economy in the world, but the distribution of resources within its population is highly skewed. In fact, in 1996 the World Bank reported that for the second year in a row Brazil had the most lopsided income distribution in the world.

During Brazil's "Economic Miracle" of the 1970s, government funds and foreign loans flowed into the industries of the south, resulting in improved standards of living and employment opportunities in that area of the country. In the agricultural northern regions, however, the poverty rate increased 9% over this same time period. Further, the aim of the Brazilian government to achieve "economic growth at all costs" led to a decrease in spending for health care, social programs, and educational initiatives. As a result, the proportion of malnourished children under age 5 increased from 13.7% in the late 1970s to 30.7% by the end of the 1980s.

With respect to economic disparity and racial inequality, Brazil is thought to have the largest black population of any country outside of Africa, with about 70 million people, or 46% of the total population being Afro-Brazilians . Blacks in Brazil are typically overrepresented in the lowest income levels and represent the majority of the under-employed. Several studies have documented that incomes of white Brazilians are, on average, twice that of black Brazilians.

An important consequence of regional and racial economic inequalities in Brazil has been a massive influx of migrants from rural to urban areas. Over the past 20 years, cities throughout Brazil have absorbed over 29 million migrants seeking employment and a better life for themselves and their families. Others were evicted from their land by mining projects or cattle raising. This influx of migrants created a seemingly inexhaustible pool of unskilled laborers in Brazil's large cities. Moreover, the infrastructure of these urban areas has increasingly been unable to expand to meet the demands for health care, education, and employment. As a result, slum dwellings, unemployment, hunger, and violence have risen dramatically. Currently, 75% of all Brazilians live in cities, and among them are 52 million boys and girls under age 19.

The Southeastern region of Brazil, where São Paulo and Rio de Janeiro are situated, is the most heavily populated section of the country. It is estimated that in metropolitan Rio de Janeiro and São Paulo alone there are several million children living in extreme poverty. And it is this destitution which drives children to the streets in an attempt to survive.

Child Labour

Throughout Latin America, meninos de rua or niños de la calle represent the new face of child labor — youths working in the urban informal sector. Their occupations range from shining shoes, selling cigarettes, flowers, newspapers or chewing gum, to hauling garbage, drug trafficking, petty theft, street robberies, and prostitution. The existence of street children in the large metropolitan areas of Brazil is not particularly new. The international media began to document the condition of large numbers of Brazilian street children as early as the 1970s.

Despite the significant media attention over the past 15 to 20 years, however, much remains unknown about their daily lives and activities. In fact, even approximating the actual size of the population of street children has proven difficult. Estimates of their numbers in Brazil have ranged from 7 to 17 million, but more informed assessments suggest that between 7 and 8 million children, ages 5 to 18, live and/or work on the streets of urban Brazil. While the vast majority of street children are boys, Brazilian government estimates put the number of street girls at approximately 800,000, with almost two-thirds of them working as prostitutes in various parts of the country.

Favelas Children

Most developing countries contain one or more "primate cities," urban areas that grow in population and influence far beyond the other cities in the region or nation. In many Latin American countries, and in other developing nations as well, the largest cities may have several times the combined populations of the next two or three urban areas and may also have a significant share of the national population. Primate cities typically are located on the coast or in other areas close to transportation routes, since many were political and economic centers when under colonial rule. The orientation of such cities had been toward supplying the developed nations with raw materials and other goods, rather than toward the urban areas and hinterlands of their own country.

Among the greatest difficulties experienced by these cities in Latin America are those of stimulating industrialization and providing employment. People who move into these urban locales do so, not because of the employment opportunities the cities provide, but because the living conditions in rural areas seem so much worse. Previous research has suggested that rural populations have been "forced" to relocate because of increasing agricultural density and the inability of the land to support its people. Rural-urban migrants believe that the cities offer a better life and at least the hope for employment. Some do find work in small enterprises, but the lack of sophisticated technology and industrial production methods does not provide for the large pool of unskilled labor that characterized the Western industrial revolution. As a result, the unemployment rates in the cities of many developing nations exceed 25% of the labor force.

Common features of the primate city landscape are the sections comprised of shanties, shacks, and makeshift huts inhabited by those who have no other shelter. Known as barriadas in Peru, ranchos in Venezuela, villas miserias in Argentina, or favelas in Brazil, these squatter settlements have been estimated to house as much as one-third of the urban population. Mexico City has some 4 million squatters, Calcutta has 2 million, and Rio de Janeiro has over 1 million.

In 1963, the noted journalist and biographer John Dos Passos commented: In Rio — this was in 1948 — there were said to be three hundred thousand people living in favelas. Today there are nearer a million. In Copacabana a few minutes walk from the hotels and the splendid white apartment houses and the wellkept magnificent beaches you find a whole hillside of favelas overlooking the lake and the Jockey Club. In the center of Rio a few steps from the Avenida Rio Branco on the hill back of one of the most fashionable churches you come suddenly into a tropical jungletown.

The favelas situated on the hillsides of Rio de Janeiro are the best known and most notorious. They began to appear at the end of the nineteenth century, and spread rapidly after 1930 as shelters for newly-arriving migrants. Fleeing regions hard-hit by drought and unemployment, rural Brazilians thronged to cidade maravilhosa, the "marvelous city" of Rio de Janeiro, lured by its illusionary riches. There has been a steady stream even since, and at the close of the 1980s it was estimated that some 1,500 "favelados" were arriving each day.

In the great majority of the favelas, migrants from all over Brazil have recreated a semi-rural way of life, in neighborhoods with names which often reflect a bittersweet Brazilian humor — Morro da Esperança, Chácara do Céu, and Nova Brasília. In Rio de Janeiro, the favelas have been estimated by Brazil's Municipal Planning Institute to number 545 and house more than 1 million persons — some 14% of the city's population. Clustered on the hill and mountainsides that overlook Rio's fashionable beaches and elegant shopping and high-rise centers, the favelas are slums in which only a small portion of households have electricity, running water, or sewage facilities. Juramento, for example, like most other favelas, is a self-contained realm of the very poor, with 30,000 residences and a dozen or so entry points. There is no glass in the windows of the shacks, no electricity or water other than what can be tapped from city lines, and when it rains the gutters run with mud and refuse. The hill is riddled with alleys and passageways, but there are no official street names, and no mail service or telephone lines.

In the absence of public medical facilities and unemployment benefits for the more than 50% of out-of-work favelados, disease and social problems multiply. There is prostitution and drug use, and a key feature of most favelas is cocaine trafficking. Within such a setting, it is no wonder that so many children retreat from the favelas to the streets — in Rio de Janeiro, São Paulo, Belo Horizonte, Porto Alegre, Santos, Fortaleza, Recife, and other Brazilian cities. And in Rio, a city where street children have received considerable media attention, they withdraw from the favelas to Copacabana, Ipanema, Lapa, Botafogo, Tijuca, and other sections of the "asphalt city." The total number of street youths in Rio de Janeiro has been the topic of considerable media conjecture and exaggeration, with some estimates as high 1 million. Local public health officials put the number of "children of the street" at 2,000 - 3,000 , which still is a major social problem.

Use of Drug

Street children most often use inhalants, including industrial glue, paint thinner and other solvents, as well as marijuana and coca leaf byproducts, because they are inexpensive and easily obtainable. One of the most pressing health problems facing street children is drug abuse, which offers an escape from the harsh daily realities of family break-up, poverty, hunger, violence and homelessness. For most street children, drug use is associated with hunger, homelessness and despair. Street children in Kenya say they sniff glue to help them eat the rotten food they forage through for survival. Street children in Central America say that the chief attraction of sniffing glue is its price: Two days' worth costs about 50 cents in Columbia, and a week's supply costs about 75 cents in Honduras, far less than the cost of maintaining a regular diet.

Anecdotal accounts of drug abuse among street youths in Brazil are commonplace. Numerous media stories have reported the widespread use of inhalants, marijuana and cocaine, and Valium among street children in Rio de Janeiro. Also common is the use of coca paste and Rohypnol. Common not only in the drug-using communities of Brazil, but also in those of Colombia, Bolivia, Venezuela, Ecuador, and Peru, is the use of coca paste, known to most South Americans as basuco, susuko, pasta basica de cocaina, pasta de coca, or just simply pasta. Perhaps best known as "basuco," coca paste is one of the intermediate products in the processing of the coca leaf into cocaine. It is typically smoked straight, or in cigarettes mixed with either tobacco or marijuana.

The smoking of coca paste became popular in South America beginning in the early 1970s. It was readily available, inexpensive, had a high cocaine content, and was absorbed quickly. As the phenomenon was studied, however, it was quickly realized that paste smoking was far more serious than any other form of cocaine use. In addition to cocaine, paste contains traces of all the chemicals used to initially process the coca leaves—kerosene, sulfuric acid, methanol, benzoic acid, and the oxidized products of these solvents, plus any number of other alkaloids that are present in the coca leaf.

When the smoking of paste was first noted in South America it seemed to be restricted to the coca processing regions of Bolivia, Colombia, Ecuador, and Peru, appealing primarily to street children and low-income groups due to its cheap price when compared with that of refined cocaine. By the early 1980s, however, it had spread to other South American nations, including Brazil, to numerous segments of the social strata, and throughout the decade paste smoking further expanded to become a major drug problem for much of South America. Among the Rio's street youth of the 1990s, the smoking of pasta de coca remains an enduring problem.

Rohypnol is a legal drug in Brazil, readily available in pharmacies in many parts of the world. Also known by its generic name flunitrazepam, Rohypnol is a benzodiazepine drug having anticonvulsant and sedative effects, slowing psychomotor performance, and inducing muscle relaxation and sleep. It is used for the short-term treatment of insomnia. However, its use can lead to the development of physical and psychic dependence, with the risk of addiction increasing with dose and duration of use. Drug use by street children is a nearly universal phenomenon because these youths are confronted with the harsh realities of street life on a daily basis. Given that drug abuse among youths has emerged as a concomitant of life on the streets, the paucity of scientific studies which have examined this and other related topics among street children in Brazil is troubling.

A survey among 119 street children in São Paulo, for example, classified 45% as heavy drug users, indicating the use of up to three drugs a day. In a study of street youths in Belo Horizonte, a city of 2 million people some 452 km northeast of Rio de Janeiro, 84% of the children living full-time in the street had histories of illegal drug use, 10.6% reported injection drug use, and 83.5% were sexually active. Additionally, in an earlier study involving this same sample, 82.6% reported having had sex while under the influence of drugs and/or alcohol. In comparison, of the working but "home-based" children interviewed, only 25% had histories of illegal drug use and none reported the use of injection drugs (Campos et al., 1992).

A similar study supported the findings by reporting higher rates of drug use among "street-based" youth than "home-based" youth, 76.9% vs. 29.1%, and earlier onset of drug use — 9.8 years versus 11.2 years. Moreover, a 1992 study of 98 street children in Rio de Janeiro found that 90.8% believed drug abuse to be a problem in the community and 38.8% stated that drug use was a personal problem for them. The most commonly used drugs among these children were glue, marijuana, alcohol/tobacco,and cocaine. Nearly 70% of this sample refused to respond to questions about injection drug use.

The most in depth study of drug use among street youths was conducted in 1992 by the Guidance Center on Drugs and the Treatment of Drug Addicts of the University of Brasília. The research sampled 150 males ages 10 to 17 in Ceilândia, one of Brasília's satellite towns, and examined three groups of street children — youths with no school or family ties, youths receiving assistance from social welfare institutions, and youths enrolled in local schools. The data indicated that a full 100% of the street youths interviewed used drugs. Solvents and inhalants, typically cobbler's glue, were the most commonly used. "Frequent use," defined as daily or several times a week, was found among 88% of the entire sample, and among 72% of those in social welfare institutions.

The fact that solvents and inhalants are the drugs most frequently used by street youths was not an unanticipated finding of the Brasília study, because prior studies have found these drugs to be common among other youth populations as well. In a study of 1,836 São Paulo students from low socioeconomic backgrounds, 24% reported lifetime use of inhalants and 4.9% reported use in the last 30 days.

HIV/AIDS

Street children are being further marginalized by the rapid spread of AIDS. Their lifestyles and struggle to survive land them in the highest-risk categories for contracting the disease, with their sexual exploitation and drug use putting them at particular risk.

In Brazil, which has one of the highest numbers of AIDS cases, public health officials describe AIDS as a "time bomb" among street children. They are particularly worried because unprotected sex with multiple partners is a way to make a living for many of Brazil's abandoned street children. A significant number of street girls work in brothels or on the streets as prostitutes, placing them at even higher risk of acquiring sexually transmitted diseases, including H.I.V./ AIDS.

In addition to solicitation for prostitution, many street children have reported incidents of rape. Scheper-Hughes and Hoffman observed that street girls and boys are frequently raped by police and others. Surprisingly, however, the perpetrators are not always male. Vasconcelos noted that older street girls will sometimes force younger girls to have sex with them, thereby continuing the cycle of violence of which they too have been victims. Of the 98 street children interviewed by Eisenstein and de Aquino, 53.1% were sexually active and 44.9% reported being forced to have sex. Similarly, a survey of 52 HIV seropositive street youths under age 16 in Rio de Janeiro found that 28% had had anal intercourse, presumably forced. Of those ages 7 to 12, 63% had had anal intercourse and 57% had been forced to have anal intercourse by older street children.

Although this type of sexual violence appears to be common, it is not always necessary. Many street children use sex as a way to gain affection and attention. For this reason, younger girls at times voluntarily seek sexual contact with older girls. Sexual activity among boys is also relatively common. Some 21% of street boys interviewed in a 1991 study reported same-sex anal intercourse. Heterosexual anal intercourse was reported by 43% of these same respondents. Despite high rates of sexual activity among street children, attitudes regarding condom use are for the most part negative and usage rates are low. Various studies have reported the proportion of sexually active street children having ever used condoms to be in the range of 8.2% to 33.3%.

Risk of exposure to HIV is rapidly becoming an area of concern because of the large number of street youths engaging in unprotected sexual acts, both renumerated and non-renumerated. On the whole, the World Health Organization reckons that there are between 50,000 and 100,000 HIV positive children and adolescents in Brazil. Going further, it has also been estimated that between 1% and 2% of Brazil's population of 7-8 million street children, or between 70,000 and 110,000 individuals, are HIV positive. A study in 1987-1988 at the FUNBEM Hospital in Rio de Janeiro found that among 3,389 street children, 50 (1.5%) were HIV positive. However, a more recent study conducted between May 1991 and January 1994 found that of 126 street children interviewed and tested, 94% reported HIV risk behaviors, and 6% were HIV seropositive.

Unwanted and considered human waste, these ubiquitous tattered, mainly black children and adolescents evoke strong and contradictory emotions of fear, aversion, pity and anger in those who view their neighborhood streets, boulevards and squares as 'private places" under siege. Because of their drug use, predatory crimes, and general unacceptability on urban thoroughfares, street children have frequently been the targets of local vigilante groups, drug gangs, and police "death squads."

Perhaps most notorious have been the death squads, which initially appeared in Brazil in 1968, and principally in Rio de Janeiro, at first to avenge the terrorist murder of a well-known police officer. The death squads proliferated during the years of Brazil's military rule, which ended in 1985. As the killings spread, political and community leaders were often targeted, and the victims were easily recognized. Their hands were always tied behind their backs, their tongues cut out, and a crudely drawn skull and cross-bones were left on the corpse with the initials "E.M."—"Esquadrão de Morte"—appended.

Many of the death squads still exist, particularly in Brazil, and street children are common victims. Because they survive, in part, through prostitution and crime, they have become the targets of retributive violence by police death squads and merchants' vigilante groups. Considered to be bad for business, store owners hire off-duty police officers or professional killers to eliminate the "disposable children." Their elimination is also seen as a mechanism of "social cleansing." There is considerable public support for the death squads as the result of perceptions that street children are dangerous criminals. Residents of the poorest communities are often the strongest supporters of violent solutions to local crime, perhaps because their neighborhoods are the least secure.

Street children are also the targets of drug gangs. Because Brazil's Protective Child Statute holds that children under 18 years of age may not be arrested unless caught in the act of committing a crime, to the drug gangs the youths' impunity makes them ideal couriers. But they are often killed because they know too much, steal too much, or get caught in the crossfire.

The hierarchy of the favela drug trade is a vertical one, and children are recruited into the lowest level, serving primarily as lookouts. They progress to running errands for the hillside dealers, and if they are successful, they begin delivering drugs to customers. Survivors from these operations may become armed "controllers". Finally, there are the corporate levels of the local drug business, but few children ever last that long. Most die while they are still at the lower end of the hierarchy. When a hillside dealer is dissatisfied with a child's work, or decides that the youth is dangerous as a witness, he or she is simply killed. And altogether, it is estimated that as many as four to five street children are murdered each day throughout Brazil, and two each day in Rio de Janeiro alone.

Intervention Strategies

At the most general level, programs appear to be of four types:

a) the correctional approach;

b) the rehabilitative perspective;

c) outreach strategies; and,

d) the preventive outlook.

The correctional approach views street children as a matter for juvenile justice organizations. This correctional vision seems to dominate the thinking of much of the public and criminal justice authorities. The result is that thousands of street children are housed in institutions. In Brazil, the National Foundation for Child Welfare operates twenty treatment centers and "reform" schools for abandoned and delinquent youth. Conditions in these facilities have been described as both crowded and abusive. However, some changes appear to be underway, involving the substitution of correctional initiatives with community-based treatment alternatives.

The rehabilitative approach has been gaining momentum throughout Latin America. This perspective holds that street children are not delinquents as much as they are victims of poverty, child abuse and neglect, and untenable living conditions. Because street children are seen as having been harmed by their environments, hundreds of church and voluntary programs have been organized in their behalf. These typically provide housing, drug detoxification, education, and/or work programs. But there is a difficulty. The programs benefit only a limited number of youths, and are unable to address the needs of the millions of boys and girls who continue to call the streets their home.

Because the institutional capacities and resources of virtually all programs are limited and unable to accommodate the overwhelming majority street children, services are also provided through a variety of outreach strategies. In São Paulo, for example, the Catholic Church supports young lay workers who provide educational, counseling, and advocacy services to children in a street setting. In addition to teaching basic hygiene, literacy, and business skills, the general program approach is to instill self-reliance and empowerment so that children will find solutions to their problems. However, it would appear that this street educator model is overly ideological, and fails to deal with the immediate physical and safety needs of street children. Most recently, outreach strategies have been focusing on HIV prevention and risk reduction. The effectiveness of these initiatives, however, is unclear.

The preventive approach attempts to address the fundamental and underlying problem of childhood poverty. In this regard, UNICEF is conducting educational campaigns to alert policy makers to the causes of children moving to the streets. In addition to policy advocacy, UNICEF provides technical assistance and support for promising local efforts. Those receiving UNICEF's focused attention are of two types:

— Programs which provide daytime activities, schooling, jobs, and other alternatives to street work for high risk children; and

— Efforts focusing on the prevention of family disintegration—cooperative day care centers, family planning clinics, small business services, and community kitchens.

The most comprehensive effort on behalf of Brazilian street youth is the National Movement for Street Children, a nationwide coalition of street children and adult educators founded in 1985. MNMMR initiatives focus on shifting the management of street children away from the criminal justice system, codifying the rights of children into law, and structuring innovative approaches for providing education and training for youths directly on the streets where they live. MNMMR projects are targeting an estimated 80,000 youths, the great majority of whom work on the streets and live in nearby favelas, with the remaining actually living on the streets.

Street children in Brazilian cities are legion. Their actual numbers are difficult to estimate, however, and have often been exaggerated. As one observer put it: They seem to be everywhere: begging in front of restaurants, peddling cigarettes in sidewalk cafes, shining shoes outside the train station, washing clothes in public fountains. Take a morning stroll on the elegant, black-and-white mosaic sidewalk that curves along Rio's Copacabana Beach and you'll smell them; dozens sleep under the palms there, and the beach serves as a toilet.

For those who work the streets during the day, returning to their favela homes at night, life is harsh and unkind. For the rest who live in the streets day and night, life is mean and unusually short. And for the great majority of Brazil's street children, it would appear that few changes are likely. Prostitution, drug use, infections, and illiteracy are common, yet there are few programs available to address the many needs of youths.

The existence of "street kids" who are Aboriginal is obviously more marked in metropolitan and semi-urban areas than elsewhere. While there are at times "marginal" children without permanent carers or home camps in remote Aboriginal communities, it is in the cities that such youths are more noticeable.

In many ways young Aboriginal people are no different from any other youthful segment of the general population. They quickly become obsessed with the ideas, activities and preoccupations of their peers, learn quickly from the mass media, and are in the process of establishing their identities as adults. Their health is low on their list of priorities, and risk-taking is normal behaviour. They are the healthiest of the age groups among the Aboriginal population, having survived the high infections and mortality of early childhood, and having (for the most part) not yet developed the symptoms of chronic illness which cause premature death in middle-aged Aboriginal people. But they are vulnerable to violence, accidents and poisonings, the leading causes of morbidity and mortality among them.

None developed serious learning or behaviour problems in childhood or adolescence". These were what the researchers termed "resilient children", and the research endeavoured to understand this resilience, despite considerable physical, social and environmental odds. The "protective" factors were found within the children themselves, in the families, and in their wider social networks. Some of the sources of resilience seemed to be constitutional, within the individuals, and associated with temperament; they included high activity levels, a low degree of excitability and stress, and a high degree of sociability. These were not particularly gifted children, but they were able to use whatever talents they had effectively; usually they had a special hobby they could share with a friend.

The family environment also seemed to contribute to the children's ability to deal with stress. They tended to come from families with four or fewer children, and "in spite of poverty, family discord or parental mental illness, they had the opportunity to establish a close bond with at least one caretaker" who gave them positive attention in their early years. If a biological parent was not available, the resilient children seemed to be adept at attaching themselves successfully to surrogate adults. Girls appeared to be positively influenced if their mothers were employed, and if they were responsible for younger siblings; resilient boys had "some male in the family who could serve as a role model".

> When we interviewed them at 18, many resilient youths mentioned a favourite teacher who had become a role model, friend and confidant and was particularly supportive at times when their own family was beset by discord or threatened with dissolution...With the help of these support networks, the resilient children developed a sense of meaning in their lives and a belief that they could control their fate. Their experience in effectively coping with and mastering stressful life events built an attitude of hopefulness that contrasted starkly with the feelings of helplessness and futility that were expressed by their troubled peers.

By the age of 30 these men and women "seemed to be handling the demands of adulthood well", although they reported more health problems than their low-risk peers. Despite problems in their adolescent years (such as teenage motherhood, delinquency and mental health problems), many individuals were able to bounce back in their twenties and thirties. Significantly, one of the most critical of influences was the reliance on informal rather than formal sources of support, "kith and kin rather than mental-health professionals and social-service agencies". In conclusion, Werner and his colleagues state that "risk factors and stressful environments do not inevitably lead to poor adaptation". They suggest that it might be possible to shift the balance from vulnerability to resilience through intervention, and point out that individual differences among children living in adverse conditions mean that there is a need for greater assistance to some than to others.

For Aboriginal children in Australia, the process of identifying particularly vulnerable children who lack the "protective" factors that will assist them to withstand stress, is poorly focused. Even if such children were identified at an early age, the provision of appropriate support services is made extremely difficult as a result of inconsistent funding arrangements, federal-state squabbling, "mainstreaming" arguments, and insufficient sensitivity to Aboriginal ways of doing things.

Distance and isolation compound the difficulties. As usual, it seems, we must fall back on the requirement that the "Aboriginal community" marshal its own resources and networks to overcome the disadvantages that childhood ill-health, parental unemployment and discord, and societal disdain load onto young Aborigines. This, of course, is a circular argument: there may be no "community" at all, or the community may itself be embattled and unable to operate as a supportive environment in and of itself.

In Australia, in the Adelaide metropolitan area (as one example) some Aboriginal youths are now living in squats, but in general Aboriginal youths are living with relatives. Even those from bush communities (such as Yalata) usually have a relative with whom to stay.

However, the homes for many of these urban Aboriginal youth are not stable, and young people are often in transit from one to another, with no consistent caregivers. This constitutes an important difference between Aboriginal and non-Aboriginal youth: Aboriginal youths may not be literally "homeless" but may suffer from the disadvantages of an uncertain and changing caregiving environment. Urban

Aboriginal and other youths in Adelaide have a diversion scheme in operation called the Youth Support Scheme; it is based in Banks Street, in close proximity to Hindley Street, which has perhaps the liveliest nightlife scene in the city. The scheme started in January 1989; it was initially a one-year project but was later extended, and is funded under state social justice funding.

The scheme is a crisis intervention program: the police ring the service if they pick up young people and the staff try to increase the level of cautionings in order to prevent incarceration and the taking of formal proceedings against kids. The service is also involved in co-counselling and liaison with the police, and even undertakes to do training days with the police. Workers also compile social background reports and participate in case conferences for the children's court. Teams of street workers (in pairs) cover the Hindley Street area on Thursday, Friday and Saturday nights from 7 p.m. to 1.30 a.m. There are approximately 500 individuals, Aboriginal and non-Aboriginal, on their files, but "the majority" of their case load is Aboriginal youth.

The main presenting problems seen by the Youth Support Scheme workers are: threatened and attempted suicide; offending; street behaviour (potential offending); drug overdoses or reactions; and alcohol problems . Also aimed at street kids in the centre of Adelaide, is The Second Storey, a drop-in and health centre, which is used primarily by 14 to 17-year-old teenagers. The centre has a half-time doctor and full-time nurse and its clinics are booked out for three to four weeks ahead. There are also youth workers, one of whom focuses on drug and alcohol issues, and family planning clinics are conducted.

The place has a relaxed atmosphere, with coffee available and table tennis. However, very few Aboriginal youths now make use of The Second Storey, although this was not the case when the centre first opened. For this reason, the Aboriginal drop-in centre in Hindley Street now has a part-time community health nurse. In Perth, the Aboriginal Child Care Agency is providing services to street kids, and estimates that over half of the street kids in Perth are Aboriginal, some as young as eight or nine years old. Choo reported:

> the community needs rehabilitation programs, recreation facilities, a drop-in centre for young Aboriginal street kids, and education for their families, in order to change their lifestyles to exclude drug and alcohol abuse and chronic gambling.

In Darwin, facilities for street kids and other Aboriginal children in need were under some pressure. Casey House, a refuge, provides short-term crisis accommodation for up to three months, housing up to ten at a time. There is also another refuge for young pregnant women. The clientele of Casey House always includes some young Aboriginal people. Between July 1989 and June 1990, for example, Aboriginal residents comprised 14% (n=18) of the total (n=132); and in the four months July to October 1990, Aboriginal residents comprised 26% of the total. Some youngsters ask for help from Casey House without becoming residents (it was said that some dislike going to bed by 10 p.m.).

Staff at Casey House help their residents with contraceptive advice, taking them to the Family Planning Association, and act as advocates on their behalf with social security, schooling and legal issues. They stressed, however, that unless their clients actively want to stop using alcohol or drugs, there is little they can do. There are no outreach health workers or legal workers for young people in Darwin - the available assistance is all crisis-oriented. As in other locations, the absence of Aboriginal workers was said to hinder effective contact with the Aboriginal population.

Sport and Recreation Facilities

Sport and recreation facilities are often seen as a panacea for a variety of social ills among young people. They are mooted as part of the "solution" to drug and alcohol use and juvenile crime in particular. A critique of earlier policies which proposed youth movements (of various kinds) as a means of producing happy and non-threatening youths is provided by Cahill and Ewen. They observe that the notion of one small population group "rescuing" another much larger group has produced timidity in addressing new issues affecting young people such as homelessness, unemployment, and sexuality. Further, they point out that youth inevitably implies orientation to the future, and yet the history of youth policy is full of "responses to today's problems with yesterday's solutions".

In a review of the impact of sport and recreation on juvenile crime, Gail Mason and Paul Wilson comment:

> it cannot be concluded...that sports, recreation and wilderness programs are the new answer to high rates of Aboriginal and non-Aboriginal delinquent behaviour. However, we are now in possession of sufficient facts upon which to base the conclusion that sport and recreation do have the ability to play a role in the reduction of offending behaviour.

The impact of sports and recreation on the health of young Aboriginal people has not been measured; indeed it would be difficult to do so. But the indirect influence of participation in social or sporting activities is undoubtedly positive, and "keeping up the side" is a useful persuasive lever to use in educational programs about the ill-effects of petrol sniffing, and drinking among young Aborigines. Several remote communities with keen basketball and football teams use these arguments in attempts to reinforce the view that sniffing petrol (for example) makes the muscles weak and the brain slow and thus adversely affects an individual's sporting activities.

Access to recreation facilities is also used in some communities as a "reward" for not using drugs. Sport and recreation are also classic diversions from the obsessions of group sniffing or drinking. In Arnhem Land a Christian revival which incorporated mass choreographed movement to modern spiritual rock music attracted large numbers of young people, diverting many from their previous participation in sniffing groups. Once again, it seems that remote-urban factors can be influential. While there are better equipped and functioning sports and recreation facilities available in urban areas, they are not specific to Aboriginal youth, and this may serve as a deterrent, particularly if instances of racist abuse or discrimination have occurred.

In remote communities on the other hand, while hardware and supervising staff may be limited, the discreteness of the community may reinforce the popularity of a particular activity. Obtaining funds to purchase and maintain equipment, and to hire supervisory staff, is difficult for many remote communities. The YMCA no longer has a formal role in the provision of workers to Aboriginal communities, as these functions have been taken over by state or territory departments. Communities have to think ahead, apply for funds by the appropriate dates, and often must take responsibility for the employment of recreation officers. Often too they must raise the money themselves for specific items.

In the Northern Territory, for example, there are 16 communities with Aboriginal recreation officers funded by the relevant territory department; all but one are male. Training is non-existent or sporadic, though, and supervision difficult. There are two field staff who offer support to these communities, and one is based in Alice Springs. In Central Australia, however, several quite large communities have no youth worker or recreation officer, and the responsibility to run and supervise out-of-school activities often falls on the community adviser, or the teachers.

Already stretched by their other responsibilities, these people often baulk at the extra work involved. In some remote communities (particularly in Western Australia, and in Arnhem Land) the adults dominated the distribution of funds and resources and the control of access to some buildings within settlements. Their priorities took precedence over those of young people - despite the fact that in many communities over half the population is under 19 years old. In some communities heavily influenced by fundamentalist Christian beliefs, for example, adult Christians refused to allow the use of public or church-owned buildings for events such as roller-skating, play, or band practice. In these cases, some pointed consciousness-raising is required to enable the youth of the communities to lobby for resources and facilities.

Rural towns are often flash-points for Aboriginal white confrontation, and local town councils often take alarming decisions which have poor outcomes in terms of race relations. In Port Augusta, South Australia, for example, an uproar among the Aboriginal community followed a proposal to impose a 10 p.m. to 6 a.m. curfew for city residents aged 16 and under. Aboriginal people perceived the curfew to be discriminatory and believed that Aboriginal, not white, children would be victimised by it. The town is not atypical, in that a local survey found that only four out of 123 17-year-old Aboriginal youths interviewed were employed. Of the 99 individuals interviewed in the 17 to 21 age group, only 11 had jobs.

The town has no games centres, bowling alleys or amusement arcades; Aboriginal youths amuse themselves by swimming off the jetty, going to Friday night movies and playing football. Broome in Western Australia is probably not a typical example of a rural town, with many visitors from bush communities. It has an active Police Youth and Citizens Club, well equipped with indoor sports, an oval, gym shed, roller skating rink, a canteen, BBQ, pool, and ablution blocks. A committee of 15, of whom four are Aboriginal, run the PYCC. A "healthy" proportion of users of the club are young Aborigines, but there is a membership and use charge for the facilities.

Also in Broome is a drop-in centre used by Aboriginal children and teenagers. This is housed in a tin house, and operates in a low-key way as a place for youngsters to listen to rock music, play pool, and table tennis, and watch videos. Because the building is basic and homely, and the coordinator well known to the kids, the centre performs a valuable function for town dwellers, and has some visiting children from communities such as Lagrange and Derby as well. The place runs on a minimal budget of $40,000 per year; the building was donated by Lord MacAlpine, the pool table is second-hand, and the truck used to take kids out on weekend camping trips is borrowed from a local college. The girls are raising the $6000 needed to visit Perth for basketball by having raffles.

Teenage Aboriginal boys in Broome said that they would like discos for their age group and more frequent trips out camping. Broome has five Aboriginal bands and numerous other solo and duo performing musicians - a keen interest in Aboriginal rock music is supported by the Broome Musicians Aboriginal Corporation. Thirteen recordings have emanated from Broome musicians, although the band Scrap Metal is the only one with top sales. The corporation holds concerts and organises voice and music recording workshops; there are alcohol free family concerts as well. There are Aboriginal rock bands in communities throughout the Kimberleys, and four members of the cast of "Bran Nue Dae" (the rock musical from Broome) are under 18.

The World Summit for Children, organised by the UN in New York, brought together 159 state delegations and encouraged governments everywhere to take a new look at their measures to help and protect children. The Declaration on the Survival, Protection and Development of Children agreed at the summit committed all those present to improve child health and security, to enhance the role of the family, to develop appropriate education, to mount an attack on poverty, and to protect the environment. The follow-up United Kingdom Implementation Report acknowledges that work with NGOs in the areas of education, health care, water supply and sanitation needs to be a central component of the international development strategy to help children.

The importance of the relationship between housing and poverty, and its particular relevance to the situation of children, is not however always acknowledged in international development policy. Secure, good quality housing and its associated infrastructure (water, sanitation, drainage, electricity and waste disposal) is vital to people's wellbeing, but many poor people find that they do not have sufficient access to them. Similarly, relocation, forced eviction and the impact of natural disasters (all acute problems to poor families living in rudimentary facilities) particularly threaten children's welfare and development.

For example, poor quality, insecure housing imposes enormous health and safety costs on its inhabitants. Children's educational opportunities are also severely restricted by a family's need to concentrate time and money on maintaining shelter and related infrastructure, often requiring children to take on basic domestic responsibilities and / or income-generating tasks from an early age. Addressing the housing and shelter needs that lie at the root of child poverty in urban areas is therefore vital to development.

Homeless International supports community-driven housing and infrastructure programmes that have distinct benefits in terms of local social and economic development, cost savings and improved income opportunities, which consequently provide the foundation for children and young people to address the effects of poverty. The outcomes of many of these initiatives demonstrate why housing and shelter issues should be placed in the centre of development thinking generally, and policies for the alleviation of child poverty in particular.

Inadequate Housing

Inadequate housing and infrastructure facilities pose direct threats to children's physical safety. Poor people often live in temporary homes constructed with whatever impermanent, basic materials are available. They frequently have little option but to live on marginal land (flood plains or steep slopes for example), with the consequence that they are the first to suffer the effects of earthquakes, landslides, cyclones and floods. In addition, a combination of overcrowding, the use of open fires or kerosene stoves and flammable buildings leads to danger from burns, scalding and accidental fires. Inevitably in these conditions, children are especially vulnerable.

Community-managed upgrading programmes can greatly reduce the safety risks faced by poor families and children. For instance, Homeless International has established a Loan Guarantee Fund to operate in Andhra Pradesh (India), funded by the UK Department for International Development (DfID), the European Commission and a number of UK-based housing associations. It is intended to help families unable to access conventional housing finance, to obtain credits from local finance institutions for the creation of self-managed housing solutions. The Guarantee Fund is used by Homeless International to secure a loan made to a local NGO, the Youth Charitable Organisation (YCO), which in turn extends loans to families and recovers them through community-based women's organisations (the Mahila Mandals).

Families use the loans to improve their housing and basic infrastructure with technical support from YCO and the Mahila Mandals. Between the early 1990s and August 2000 the Loan Guarantee Fund helped poor people in the area secure finance for 850 homes, with a further 550 in the pipeline, which have demonstrably improved the security of families and children. An independent report by Richard Platt of the University of Bradford found that from a sample of 100 households, all agreed that their newly constructed concrete and clay houses had increased security from theft, cyclones and monsoon rains. The risk of fire was also felt to have diminished. Following the success of this initiative, Homeless International has supported the creation of Guarantee Funds in Bolivia and Mumbai (India) which are based upon a similar model.

In addition to the direct safety risks of living in inadequate housing, children's safety can also be threatened by the need to take on informal work, often on the streets or in other dangerous areas such as garbage dumps. Street children, often without even basic shelter facilities, exemplify the risks to children working in the informal sector. Those in Mumbai run the risk of being picked up by police, branded as criminals and put in grim remand centres from which approximately two-thirds of them try to run away. However the issue of street-children working in the informal sector remains complicated, as many of them rely on, and benefit from, the moneyup-front generated by such activities.

Homeless International supports ongoing work which aims to help reduce the vulnerability of street children in India, without taking away the independence provided by cash from their informal work activities. SPARC (an NGO who assist poor communities to initiate development activities) and Sadak Chaap (meaning "stamp of the street", the children's own organisation), carry out a range of activities to ensure the operation of night shelters to which street children can come and go as they wish. All of the shelters were built by local street children with help and advice from SPARC staff and the women of Mahila Milan (MM).

Both of these groups provide wider support for training and opportunities for employment within the shelters, while it seems to be the case that community members are viewed as role models by some of the children. The most important result with regards to children's safety is that many street children now have a safe refuge at night, which can often be the springboard for further activities aimed at reducing vulnerability and increasing their opportunities to develop.

A case study of Sandip has now made the decision to start formal education after staying in the Churchgate shelter and is going to move to the shelter at Mulund together with another boy from Bengal. Sandip is originally from Pune so he is more comfortable with the language of Marathi than

Hindi, but will learn both. Sandip is from a broken family, who could not support him emotionally. When he first came to Mumbai he stayed in a shelter run by another NGO for two months before running away.

Fayyaz is from Hyderabad. His mother and father were labourers, so he worked with them breaking rocks while his younger brother made incense sticks. He doesn't want to go home and has also been staying in the Churchgate shelter since he came to Mumbai with another boy. He has probably been in the city for a year, during which time he was involved in a train accident that left him scarred. Sunil is from Mumbai where he was living with his sister and her husband. They used to send him out to work and his brother-in-law would beat him. He is now staying at the night shelter, which has given him the base to become involved in catering work. As a result of his new skills he is able to earn 10 Rupees per day.

Insecure Tenure and the Threat of Eviction

The continuing uncertainty caused by the threat of eviction or living in impermanent accommodation is detrimental to children's wellbeing. Firstly, children can often suffer from the effects of feeling 'rootless' and / or 'roofless' implying an unsettled situation hardly conducive to social development or formal education. Secondly, insecurity of tenure does not encourage families to invest in housing and infrastructure improvements, leading to the health, safety and other problems. Lastly eviction itself can be emotionally damaging, not to mention dangerous, especially in the all too frequent cases where inadequate provision has been made for relocation. The Global Campaign for Secure Tenure has been organised by UNCHS , the lead agency within the UN system for co-ordinating activities in the field of human settlements.

The Campaign aims to highlight the relationship between poverty and social exclusion, and recognises that the most severe impacts are on women and children. Slum/Shack Dwellers International (SDI), an informal international network of poor communities and federations who share ideas and experiences about land, infrastructure and housing, have agreed with UNCHS to take the lead in promoting the campaign. The initial global launch took place in Mumbai, India at an event organised by NSDF, the Indian branch of SDI. Subsequent regional launches have been organised by SDI members, such as the Asian Coalition for Housing Rights (ACHR) in Manila (the Philippines) and by the South African Homeless People's Federation in Durban.

Homeless International supports many of the NGOs that work with federations involved in promoting the Campaign under the SDI umbrella, and addressing practical tenure issues has been important in many of the initiatives carried out by our partner organisations. Land tenure issues in the Philippines are particularly illustrative. There are many dangers facing informal settlement dwellers in Payatas, such as the 'garbage avalanche' which killed hundreds of waste-pickers and made many more families homeless in July 2000. However, community-led initiatives in Payatas have resulted in a range of savings and credit schemes, training, and development programmes. Many of these were demonstrated in the run-up to the Launch, to expose the barriers facing families without secure tenure, whilst illustrating communities' abilities to organise development activities.

The President of the Philippines has now committed to supporting the Secure Tenure Campaign. Homeless International supports the 'Dialogue on Land and Shelter for the Homeless in Zimbabwe' (Dialogue Zimbabwe), an NGO which aims to strengthen the Zimbabwe Homeless People's Federation. Communities within the Federation carry out a range of activities to secure land tenure such as negotiating with municipalities, surveying their own settlements (records are vital in proving occupation), demonstrating community-designed houses and developing communities' capacities through community exchanges, savings groups and information dissemination.

In India, SPARC has been instrumental in halting illegal evictions and demolition of homes belonging to families in the Railway Slum Dwellers Federation (RSDF). SPARC has enabled the Federation to build a partnership with the State authorities to ensure relocation to safe and secure homes. The results of these and other initiatives which promote and establish security of tenure undoubtedly benefit family life and hence children's wellbeing.

Poor Quality of Housing and Sanitation

Ill health is often caused by poor quality housing and sanitation, imposing economic costs on top of direct physical and emotional suffering. Researchers in the field of urban development issuespoint to the prevalence of diarrhoeal diseases, typhoid, respiratory difficulties and the increased effects of many other infectious diseases in the overcrowded, insanitary living conditions frequently faced by poor families and children. The foundation of safe, secure housing can however dramatically reduce child mortality and morbidity rates as well as reducing the problems of ill health more generally. For example the survey by Richard Platt recorded 100% agreement between households that family health had improved as a result of new and improved housing with better ventilation and sanitation.

Homeless International supports communityled infrastructure initiatives that provide, rehabilitate and maintain toilets and sanitation facilities in poor communities and informal settlements. Of particular interest is the infrastructure program in Mumbai, which is partly funded by DfID, the European Commission and a UK Trust. The Alliance of SPARC, Mahila Milan (MM) and the National Slum Dwellers Federation (NSDF) have worked with communities to construct 70 toilet blocks, establish nearly 2000 household water connections and manage solid waste and legal electricity connections benefiting a total of more than 14,000 households in the first two years.

The toilet block constructed at Chikhalwadi, which includes a separate toilet area for children, has been recognised by the World Bank as a suitable pilot project to establish norms and conditions for community toilets. This is significant because the planning and design was a community-led process, ensuring that the facilities have had specific benefits for children. For example, children often get elbowed out of the queue for 'adult' toilets and end up soiling the ground outside, which is one of the biggest contributing factors to deteriorating common facilities. Secondly, the design of the children's toilets is specific to their needs, because it is safe (the handrails allow children to squat without danger of falling into the trench, a genuine danger in other rudimentary facilities) and open (children dislike dark cubical designs). They are also efficiently hygienic as trenches can be sluiced with minimal water.

Finally the use of facilities is also free to children, which is important because poor families are ordinarily reluctant to pay for children to use toilets. The open design is also socially beneficial because the toilets are separated into areas for girls and areas for boys, each forming a communal area where children can chat whilst using the facilities. This last point is genuinely important, as the social nature of defecating is very much a part of children's culture in India.

For example, a DfID grant has enabled Homeless International to fund an education and credit programme in Bolivia which helps poor families to upgrade their adobe housing in order to prevent infestation by Vinchuca beetles. These beetles live in rough adobe walls and are vectors for the debilitating Chagas disease, which is incurable and eventually leads to death. Simple housing improvements, such as plastering walls and replacing thatch with tiled roofs, eradicate the beetles' habitat and community control of Chagas disease becomes possible. In addition, educating and training school-children and young people has been central to construction and also encouraging good household habits in cleaning, tidying and keeping animals away from living space. Young people are very much seen as a driving force for change.

Finally in the area of children's health, improving the general living environment is important. Dealing with garbage and sewerage as well as general slum rehabilitation is a key concern of many of Homeless International's partners. Often this involves developing constructive relationships with municipal authorities in order to create solutions that work at the community level. Of course this benefits communities in general, but children are again the group most vulnerable to ill health and hence benefit greatly from initiatives which improve their living environment.

Education and Training

Impoverished living conditions affect children's educational opportunities and achievement in two ways. Firstly, as mentioned earlier, the increased likelihood of young children working domestically or in the informal sector to boost household income diminishes the opportunity for children to participate in educational activities. This is especially true of girls, who tend to shoulder significant household responsibilities. Secondly, insecure, temporary housing in overcrowded areas, or rough living on the streets, is clearly not conducive to formal study or learning. For example, many poor families without legal electricity supplies must either access supplies illegally, expensively and dangerously or "must burn meagre fuel rations in kerosene lamps, so their children can study after dark."

Homeless International has supported community-led infrastructure initiatives with the Alliance and with YCO, which have resulted in better study conditions as well as providing a basis for families to send children to school in Indian communities. Skills training in relation to housing and infrastructure improvements can also provide spin-off benefits in addition to the actual benefits of better living conditions.

In Tanzania for example, Homeless International has supported PEHOLE, a local NGO, in combined youth training and construction work, which has improved both skills and housing in the area.

In conjunction with the Alliance and Sadak Chaap, street children in Mumbai have learned skills in driving, catering, masonry, surveying, recycling, composting and household electrification, often as part of construction projects and related activities. In the case of' catering, skills were learnt through planning and cooking meals for other children in the night shelters. Their success in taking on major catering assignments can be measured by the fact that, in combination with the RSDF, Sadak Chaap caterers fed all 7000 visitors attending the slum dwellers' Housing Exhibition organised by Mahila Milan in 1997. Skill development (within various housing improvement activities) and informal education play important roles in providing a base for poor children to develop and grow.

Health Conditions in Slums Areas

India has the fastest-growing segment of urban poor on earth, with urban population believed to be doubling or even tripling from a mid-1990s figure of 250 million, thus possibly propelling the urban population to 660 million by 2025. Ahmedabad is India's seventh-largest city, with an estimated 1997/98 population of 3.6 million. Its population has grown at a rate of 37.6% per decade for most of the past century. The city has 2,432 slum pockets, with a population of over 1.2 million. These slums are characterized by crowding and poor environmental health conditions, which cause waterborne diseases, malnutrition, respiratory illnesses, and skin conditions and which produced a gastroenteritis epidemic in 1988 and a jaundice epidemic in 1993.

In 1996, the World Health Organization (WHO) Regional Office for South East Asia found the most frequent causes of death of three million Indian children under five to be the same ones found throughout the developing world: acute respiratory infection (ARI) (20%), diarrheal disease (28%), and measles (11%). The 2000 NFHS maternal mortality ratio (MMR) for all India was 540 per 100,000 live births, in contrast to 276 per 100,000 live births for all urban women. The government of Gujarat estimates the MMR for the city of Ahmedabad to be 319 per 100,000 live births. MMRs specific to slums in India have not been located.

NFHS morbidity data for children under 35 months in the two weeks preceding the survey show that diarrheal disease affected 20% of urban children and 19% of those in rural areas. ARI affected 16% of urban children and 20% of rural children. In the Counterpart International survey, 22% of mothers in Ahmedabad slums reported that their children had ARI symptoms in the preceding two weeks, and 37% of children had diarrhea in the same period.

The NFHS found 47% of all Indian children under three to be underweight, using weight-for-age measurements. Fifty percent of rural children under three and 38% of urban children under three showed signs of malnutrition, meaning that even without disaggregating the data by slum and nonslum, one-third of all urban children in India were malnourished. The Counterpart International survey found that rates for moderate and severe wasting in slum children in Ahmedabad of 21% were notably higher than the NFHS Gujarat State rate of 16%.

Disaggregated data from the 1996 UNICEF Gujarat statewide MICS showed malnutrition in children under five in urban slums to be a serious problem, especially for the 12-to-23-month age range. Two-thirds of these children were malnourished, and over half of children in the other age ranges above 6 months were also. In contrast, 28% and 41% of children in the lowest two socioeconomic quintiles of rural Gujarat State were malnourished.

Specific micronutrient deficiency rates for slum populations were not found, but the Opportunities for Micronutrient Interventions Project (OMNI) reports that xerophthalmia resulting from vitamin A deficiency affects between 5% and 7% of preschool children (seven million to nine million!) and causes an estimated 60,000 children to go blind in India each year.

Iodine deficiency is a serious problem nationwide. The OMNI Fact Sheet on India notes that iodine deficiency disorder causes an estimated 90,000 stillbirths and neonatal deaths each year. According to latest NFHS figures, anemia among children age 6 to 35 months is uniformly high: 74% for all India, 74.5% for Gujarat State, 71% among urban children, and 75% among rural children. Slum children will undoubtedly have high anemia rates.

Iron deficiency anemia among pregnant women is estimated by OMNI at 70%, and as high as 90% among preschool children when hookworm infection is present. Data specific to slum dwellers were not found, but it is safe to assume that young children in slums where sanitation is a serious problem are likely to have high intestinal parasite infection rates.

Health Determinants

Forty-one percent of slum children are exclusively breast-fed for the first three to five months. This is lower than the national DHS average of 55% and the rate of 65% for Gujarat State. Twenty-three percent of slum children age 6 to 23 months had received no solid food the previous day. Grains rather than a variety of foods were the predominant complementary food. ??Vitamin A supplementation: Eleven percent of mothers of children 12 to 23 months of age reported that their child had received a vitamin A supplement. The figure for vitamin A supplementation coverage for all India is between 25% (UNICEF) and 30% (DHS).

Fifteen percent of all children age 12 to 23 months in the slum study were found to have proof of full immunization, whereas the DHS Gujarat State data showed 53% of children fully immunized. Thirty-seven percent of slum children received measles immunization-a percentage lower than the DHS rates for rural children (45%) and urban children (69%) of same ages. Twenty-one percent had received polio immunization-a percentage higher than the DHS rate for rural children (10%) but close to the DHS rate for urban children (23%).

Only 18% of children with diarrhea in the slum study were given oral rehydration therapy (ORT)-a much lower figure than DHS rates for Gujarat State (42%) and for children in rural areas (35%) and urban areas (33%). However, care-seeking from health providers was relatively good for episodes of diarrhea: 61% from a qualified provider. This is close to the DHS rate for rural diarrheal disease care-seeking (60%). The DHS urban rate is 75%. Care-seeking for symptoms of ARI was equally high in the slum study population: 86% of mothers. The DHS rates of mothers seeking care for ARI were 75% for urban areas, and 61% for rural areas.

Two percent of children in the slum study had slept under an insecticide-treated bednet the previous night, whereas 23% of mothers claimed to have a bednet in the house. No comparison data were found. Only 9% of mothers stated that they washed their hands before food preparation, before eating, before feeding children, and after defecation. Thirty-four percent of mothers in the slum study claimed to have received two doses of tetanus toxoid vaccine, and 46% claimed to have received more than two doses. These rates were lower by about half than the DHS rates for two or more tetanus toxoid doses: urban women, 82%, rural women, 62.5%.

Coverage for child immunization and micronutrient supplementation services was uniformly higher in rural areas than in urban slums. The proportion of rural children receiving all immunizations (59%) was nearly double the urban slum rate (30.7%).

Environmental Health Indicators

According to a "quick slum survey" carried out in two slum neighborhoods prior to work undertaken in the Ahmedabad Parivartan Slum Improvement Program, water was supplied at public standpipes, two for each slum.One neighborhood comprised 42 households; the other, 105 households. In the larger slum each standpipe served between 262 and 420 persons.

A more detailed profile of the water and sanitation situation emerges from a U.K. Department for International Development (DFID) environmental case study of cities that includes Ahmedabad:In 1991, 26% of urban households were in areas deemed slums. Of these slum households, only 23% had piped water connections, and only 26% had individual household sanitation. Most slum households obtained water from shared standpipes and suffered erratic water supply. Sixteen percent had no water source at all.

In contrast, 87% of nonslum urban households had individual water connections, and 73% had individual toilets. The case study mentions a 1998 survey of 7,512 slum households that found 80% without a water connection and 93% without toilet facilities of their own. Shared toilets were also rare, and an estimated 500,000 people out of a population of 3.6 million defecated in the open. The Gujarat State MICS found that in urban slums, 52% of the population defecated in the open, whereas in rural areas the rate was 70%. In this case, lower rates do not mean better rates. Densely populated urban slums mean high numbers of people exposed to a contaminated environment and at risk for fecal-oral communicable diseases. Small children are especially vulnerable. Drainage presents a problem, because few slums are hooked up to the city sewer system, and in the peripheral areas, there are no drains. Hygienic disposal of sewage and wastewater is impossible, and storm water causes flooding in the rainy season.

Ahmedabad is considered India's most polluted city. The concentration of total suspended particulates is nearly twice the recommended maximum levels, and other common air pollutants are well above WHO standards.In addition to everincreasing numbers of vehicles, a main cause for this unacceptable level of air pollution is the presence of industries within the city limits and the city's weak Pollution Control Board.

Indoor air pollution is a serious problem in Ahmedabad, contributing to respiratory disease. A 1995 study found that 41% of the city's households use wood, cow dung, charcoal, or kerosene for cooking, often with no ventilation.These households were among the poorest, and already-malnourished women and children suffered severe respiratory problems as a consequence of indoor air pollution. Surveys of slum households found women, as well as girls who sit with their mothers while cooking, to be afflicted with coughs and lung problems.

An environmental risk assessment carried out in Ahmedabad in 1995 gave indoor air pollution, pollution from vehicles, and suspended particulate matter the highest risk rating of all risk factors studied. Of the total population, 90% was at risk for ill health from ambient air pollution, and 41% of poor households using biomass cooking fuels were at risk for health consequences, especially respiratory infections, from indoor air pollution.

Health services are the responsibility of the Ahmedabad Municipal Corporation, which runs family welfare centers, municipal health treatment centers (where slum dwellers prefer to go), and referral hospitals, as well as Anganwadi Centers for maternal and child health services.All services are accessible to slum dwellers, and some services (e.g., Integrated Child Development Scheme) are concentrated in slum areas. A number of private practitioners also work in the slum areas of Ahmedabad. Fifty-two private practitioners were identified in the program area of one child health project covering six urban slums with a population of 183,000.

A study of the health care preferences and expenditures of 100 Ahmedabad slum dwellers found that although nearly all respondents had gone to municipal health services at least once, 77% preferred to see a private practitioner for common diseases (colds, cough). The reason given was nearby location and shorter waiting time. Public providers were used for immunization, maternal and child health services, and treatment of major illnesses. Public health facility fees are low, and this is attractive to many, but credit is sometimes available from private practitioners.

The Philippines is one of the fastest urbanizing countries in the world. Its 1999 urban population was estimated at 38.6 million and is expected to increase by 61% by 2010. This growth is mainly occurring in informal squatter areas. In 2000, the population of Metro Manila, a megacity comprising 17 cities and municipalities, was 10.5 million. An estimated 35% of the urban population lives in slums lacking basic services. The World Bank states that conditions in Manila's urban slums are worse than in the poorest rural areas of the country. The urban poor are mainly squatters who live in cramped, flimsy, one-room shelters in unhealthy environments.

In Metro Manila, 11% of informal settlers live along waterways or other dangerous areas, such as railroad tracks and dump sites.There are a fair number of anecdotal descriptions of the living conditions of urban squatters in Manila, but recent studies of the urban poor are hard to come by. No studies containing data on family practices that are determinants of child health were found.

The DHS IMR for all the Philippines is 36/1,000; for Metro Manila the rate is 24/1,000. A Philippines Department of Health study from 1993 found the IMR to be three times higher in the slums of Manila than in the rest of the city (thus, about 72/1,000). The DHS mortality rate for children under five is 55/1,000 nationally, with an urban rate of 46/1,000 and a rural rate of 62.5/1,000. No slum comparison rates were found.

The MMR for the country is 172 per 100,000 live births. No data on MMR for urban or urban slum areas were found. Causes of illness in children under three nationwide during the two weeks preceding the 1998 DHS survey were diarrhea (7%) and ARI (13%). No comparison slum data were found. The Mega-Cities Project states that rates of TB are nine times higher in the slums of Manila than in nonslum areas, without specifying an age group.Incidence of diarrhea (in adults and children) in these same slums is twice as high as in wealthier sections.

A recent news item reports that the highest number of dengue cases comes from the most depressed areas of Quezon City (Metro Manila), including 138 children between January and July 2001. The city government's health department head attributes this to the lack of sanitation among slum dwellers. No data on vaccine-preventable illnesses, HIV/AIDS, accidents, and malaria for slum children under five were found.

UNICEF figures show that 28% of all children nationwide are underweight. The Mega-Cities Project states that three times as many children suffer from malnutrition in slums as in nonslums. A study of Smoky Mountain (a Manila garbage dump) scavenger children aged 8 months to 15 years found that 80% had at least two species of intestinal parasite; 20% had Giardia, and 32% had Escherichia coli. Vitamin A deficiency has declined nationally, but subclinical levels persist in 35% of preschool children. It is endemic in disadvantaged areas of urban Manila, where xerophthalmia affects 1.5% to 3% of children.

Anemia is reported in 43% to 49% of older infants and pregnant women. A 1987 food and nutrition survey found that 50% of small children in Metro Manila's squatter areas were anemic. The national goiter rate is 15%, with large regional variations. Data on urban slums were not found. Only anecdotal evidence of malnutrition in urban slum children was found.

A 1986 UNICEF studyfound that only 16% of lowincome households have water connections. Others rely on artesian, open wells and public taps. The urban poor have no public toilets and resort to open pits, which pose a serious threat of fecal contamination in overcrowded squatter settlements. A compilation of studies on the urban poor of Metro Manila for a pro-poor advocacy Web sitestates that water services are generally not available for the urban poor. People either buy water or obtain it from privately owned faucets.

In addition, 66% of Metro Manila's urban poor have no toilets and resort to the river, open pits, or the "wrap and throw" method of human waste disposal. The Mega-Cities Project claims that 50% of the metropolitan area is directly served by piped water and that the 35% living outside the distribution area must buy water from vendors or rely on groundwater.Compounding the water supply problem, the El Niño phenomenon has created a water shortage crisis. As an example of discrepancies in urban data that are not disaggregated by slum and nonslum or by other economic indices, UNICEF country statistics show 92% of total urban population covered by potable water supply and the same percentage with adequate sanitation.

In an overview of Manila, the Mega-Cities Projectstates that air pollution is a major environmental problem. Emissions from the city's 800,000 cars account for 60% of total air pollution, oil-fired power plants account for another 30%, and industrial plants account for 10%. An Asian Development Bank on-line report on the health and nutritional status of children in the region states that prior to a mandated ban on leaded gas in Metro Manila, the average child was at risk of developing with nearly five intelligence quotient points less than children raised in a lead-free environment.

A 1999 survey of 106 families from urban poor communities in Metro Manila found that all the respondents had access to schools, health centers, and markets. incidence of TB, diarrheal disease, parasitic infections, dengue, and severe malnutrition affecting slum children. The crowded and dangerous conditions of the slums, the serious water supply problem and lack of proper sanitation, severe air pollution, and effects of the Asian economic crisis would all begin to explain the poor health status of small children. However, empirical evidence from studies of determinants of child health in urban slums, especially family practices, was not found. Like the residents of Ahmedabad's slums, Manila slum dwellers have access to health facilities and other institutions, which can be viewed as a positive among many negatives but is a situation requiring further investigation.

Egypt, like the Philippines and India, has experienced rapid urbanization in recent decades, due in large part to rural-urban migration until the 1973 war, and thereafter mostly due to natural increase of the urban population.Urban poverty has increased faster than rural poverty. The Greater Cairo region and Alexandria have 3.3 million poor people and over 1 million ultrapoor who are excluded from a range of social and municipal services. The poor are concentrated in overcrowded and underserved squatter settlements.According to the 1986 population census data, around 50% of the total population of Cairo lived in eight poor neighborhoods.

Many of the shantytowns or "random housing areas" (informal squatter or slum settlements with a mix of tenured and nontenured residents) within and around Cairo were created in the last decade. The inhabitants are among the poorest of the poor in Greater Cairo.The results of sociological and other urban studies are extremely hard to access, because data are frequently not made public and funding for such studies is very limited.The 1997 UNICEF MICS sampled random housing areas in addition to disaggregating data by "urban" and "rural."

The proximity of the random housing areas to municipal services and the presence of well-off (legal) residents produced results that were, for the most part, similar to all-urban figures but that nonetheless provide a glimpse into urban poor-urban nonpoor disparities.A decadal study of an unauthorized urban settlement in the heart of Cairo called Manshiet Nasseris a rare source of child health information. By the late 1990s, over 500,000 people resided there. Data in this study are from the late 1980s and mid-1990s.

The DHS IMR for all Egypt is 55/1,000, broken down into an urban rate of 43/1,000 and a rural rate of 62/1,000. The DHS mortality rate for children under five is 69/1,000, with an urban rate of 53/1,000 and a rural rate of 79/1,000. The 1997/98 UNDP Human Development Report gives an under-five mortality rate of 31/1,000 for all Cairo; it is unclear why this figure differs so much from the DHS urban figure.

The national Maternal Mortality (MMR) is 174 per 100,000 live births, whereas the rate for Cairo is 200. Data on maternal mortality for urban slums were not found. DHS morbidity data show that 9.5% of all children suffered from ARI (8% of urban children and 11% of rural children), and 7% suffered from diarrheal disease (6.1% of urban children and 7.8% of rural children) in the two weeks preceding the survey. The Manshiet Nasser survey of the mid-1990s found that 69% of children had had some form of infectious disease, 49% had had a respiratory illness, 42% had had diarrhea, and 22% had had both in the preceding two weeks. These rates are extremely high compared with national DHS data from 2000 noted above.

UNICEF data showed that 12% of all children were moderately to severely underweight, and DHS data showed that 4% were malnourished (3% of urban children and 5% of rural children), using weight-for-age measurements. Mild anemia affects 18.5 % of all children six months to five years old; 15% of urban children, and 21% of rural children are affected (DHS). One study found anemia in 31% of preschoolers and in 34% of schoolchildren. Prevalence of Ascaris and other parasites was high (25% to 30%), but place of residence was not clear.

In the squatter settlement of Manshiet Nasser, the poor nutritional status of children is illustrated by the finding that children at nine months of age were at the 25th percentile of the healthy population and remained undernourished for the second and third years of life. The 2000 Egypt DHS found that 8% to 9% of children in Cairo as a whole were undernourished, whereas 18% in a same-age group were undernourished in the squatter settlement.

The prevalence of malnutrition in children in squatter settlements was lower in boys than in girls. Over twice as many girls (15%) as boys (6.4%) were underweight.o Nearly ubiquitous intestinal parasitic infection (90%) was found in two-year-olds in the Cairo squatter settlement, and 21% of these infected children were hosts to three or more species. This is a strong indication of poor environmental conditions and hygiene behaviors.

The bulk of information related to selected health determinant indicators comes from the study of Manshiet Nasser.This unauthorized settlement in Cairo, created in the 1960s, housed 64,000 residents in 1984, with a growing population density of 40,000 per square kilometer-dense, but not as dense as the teeming urban slums of South Asia. By the late 1990s, over 500,000 people resided in the settlement. The anthropological and epidemiological study conducted there in the mid-1990s yields some information on determinants of child health:

In the two weeks preceding the survey, 55% of mothers had sought professional help for diarrhea, and 65% had sought help when more clinical signs were present. These rates are as good or better than the DHS rate of 52% for all urban areas. In the two weeks preceding the survey, 53% of mothers took their ill children for professional treatment for signs of ARI-a lower rate than the 77% the DHS found for all urban dwellers.

Attack rates for diarrheal disease during the first year of life were lowest for wholly breast-fed children (42%), higher when they were given other foods besides breastmilk (54%), and higher yet when receiving no breast milk (69%). Where breast-feeding was never initiated, the diarrhea attack rate was highest, at 73%. Successful breast-feeding is associated with giving birth with the help of a daya (a traditional birth attendant) rather than in a hospital or maternity clinic.

Children living in homes or buildings with both water and sewer connections experienced diarrheal attack rates 22% lower than children in households without facilities. The DHS found that 38% of urban children were given ORS or home fluids for diarrhea. In Manshiet Nasser, many mothers were aware of the recommendations for ORT for diarrheal disease, but regarded it as one of several options, and a labor-intensive one at that. The mean duration of breast-feeding was between 16 and 17 months. The average age for receiving supplemental foods was 10 months. At 6 months, 52% were still receiving only milk.

Regarding infants no longer being breast-fed, households with adequate home sanitation were able to achieve 26% better standardized weight for them than households without facilities. Households with and without facilities achieved the same nutrition results while infants were being breast-fed. Only 12% of households had soap near the toilet. Households with both water and sewer connections were 3.4 times as likely to have soap available in or near the toilet. This finding shows that infrastructure promotes health by facilitating good hygiene practices.

Sixty-three percent of births were attended by dayas, and 80% of births occurred at home. Medical monitoring of pregnancy and birth was nearly nonexistent and was not considered necessary by most women. In comparison, 2000 DHS data show that for all Egypt, 52% of deliveries are at home. In all urban areas, 30% are at home, and in rural areas, 65% are at home, making the urban settlements' proportions much higher. DHS data also show that in all urban areas of Egypt, 17% of births are attended by a daya, whereas in rural areas the proportion is 47%. Again, proportions for Manshiet

Nasser are much higher, although the data are separated by a decade.

The UNICEF MICS found tetanus toxoid vaccine coverage very low in Cairo (36% of pregnant women) compared with the rate for urban areas in general (44%). Interestingly, the coverage rate for random housing areas was slightly higher (49%). The 1997 UNICEF MICS found that only 83% of households in unauthorized settlements have access to piped water in their homes, whereas access was nearly universal in Cairo as a whole. Access to some means of sanitary disposal of excreta is available to 99% of the Greater Cairo population, with access falling to 95% for unauthorized settlements.

The percentage of households with access to a public sewage network within 100 meters of the residence is 92% for Greater Cairo, but only 68% for unauthorized settlements. According to the Mega-Cities Project, sewer connections are available to 70.9% of the population of Cairo.In the settlement of Manshiet Nasser, obtaining water for household consumption is a time-consuming occupation of women and girls. In the 1980s, water was collected from standpipes or private taps and sometimes delivered to homes by entrepreneurs using donkey carts.

Sanitation was in the form of pits dug into rock beside dwellings and sludge emptied occasionally by laborers. Urban upgrading projects in the 1990s have brought a coordinated water and sewer system, but actual coverage is unclear. Air pollution: The Mega-Cities Project calls Cairo's air pollution among the worst in the world: 2.1% of all deaths can be attributed to it. Its air lead levels are among the highest in the world, and studies have shown that children growing up in Cairo are in danger of losing an average 4.25 intelligence quotient points as a result of lead pollution.

According to UNDP, there were 4.9 health units per 100,000 persons in Cairo in 1998.Access to the health care system is limited for the poor. Public expenditure on health was low, at 1.5% of total public expenditures, in 1996, whereas private spending on health was substantial, with private voluntary organizations and Islamic health centers expanding in urban areas to respond to gaps in public coverage. Poor illiterate women are the group the most affected by the low coverage in public health facilities. Nonetheless, the public sector is the largest provider of health care to urban poor.

4

Homelessness

Chamberlain and MacKenzie delineate there are three broad approaches to defining homelessness, referred to as conventional, radical and literal. The term "personcentered" is preferred to the term "radical". The conventional approach is to define homelessness in terms of the character of a person's housing situation. A person's housing situation renders them homeless, not merely on the basis of whether there is "shelter", but when it fails to meet the "minimal housing conditions that a particular community believes people have a right to expect". These are the culturally relative and socially constructed conditions of a "home".

A person would be homeless if they felt that where they were living was not in the affective sense a "home", such as feeling emotionally unsupported or physically unsafe. The National Youth Coalition for Housing definition is located within this approach when it cites as the central criterion "the absence of secure, adequate and satisfactory shelter as perceived by the young person". The third approach identifies someone as homeless when they are without shelter in the literal sense.

In the United Kingdom this approach has been used by local authorities where "rooflessness" has been employed as the criterion for determining who are homeless young people. This is the most narrow approach as it does not include those people whose "homelessness is characterised by continual insecurity and frequent moves". The conventional approach appears to be gaining increasing acceptance in Australia. In a relatively unspecified form it was used in the HREOC Inquiry where homelessness was described as being more than a total lack of shelter, where "for many children and young people it signifies a detachment from family and vulnerability to dangers".

Young people are homeless if they are living without any family assistance in the following circumstances:

— no accommodation

— temporary accommodation : with friends, relatives or moving around between various forms of temporary shelter.

— emergency accommodation : refuge or crisis accommodation etc.

— other longer term supported accommodation for homeless people . e.g. hostels, youth housing pro - grams, transitional accommodation.

Generally consistent with the "conventional" approach, Neil and Fopp state that a definition of homelessness should be: one which gives weight to the most basic requirements of a home, that is, that state in which people have no access to safe and secure shelter of a standard that does not damage their health, threaten their personal safety, or further marginalise them through failing to provide either cooking facilities, or facilities that permit adequate personal hygiene.

The inclusion of normative notions of home, vulnerability and safety, in some conventional definitions begs continued debate as to what constitutes a minimum community standard in relation to these, and who determines this. In turn such questions lead to various percept ions about the minimum community standards regarding the housing, income support and social resources which should be made available to young people of various ages. There are two other important dimensions to homelessness:

— First, there is a time dimension. Homelessness may be chronic, it may consist of a single acute crisis in a person's life, or it may be an enforced state entered and exited intermittently.

— Second, for homeless people, homelessness is not an event, but a process - one that involves constant adaptation. The way people react once homelessness has occurred, and the mechanisms they adopt to cope with the stresses it generates, in turn add to, or detract from, their subsequent chances of exiting permanently from homelessness.

Mackenzie and Chamberlain maintain young people go through various stages before developing an identity as a homeless person, and assert that the first key transition is the permanent break from family and home. The second break is the shift to chronicity, which refers to the young person accepting homelessness as a way of life. This stage of chronicity may be accompanied by crime, prostitution, drug abuse, and young people who have entered this stage are often reluctant to change their lifestyle.

MacKenzie and Chamberlain also maintain that the first stage can occur as quickly as two to three weeks after leaving home, if the young person leaves school and home at the same time. They suggest that this permanent break can be delayed if school attendance is maintained, thus maintaining relationships with teachers, friends and significant others. Such an approach acknowledges what Chamberlain and MacKenzie elsewhere referred to as a "temporal dimension" of young people's homelessness. The temporal concepts they describe apply from the point of a young person leaving home, that is, in relation to young people "being" homeless.

Defining and investigating prevention and early intervention requires in addition to this, the application of a temporal dimension to the experience of young people in the period before they experience homelessness as defined in the conventional sense. It is from this perspective that it is critical to accommodate and respond to the felt homelessness of young people, which is characterised by feelings of insecurity, a lack of safety or of not belonging, and is central to a person-centered definition of homelessness.

Causes of Homelessness

Frequently in the research, factors associated with becoming homeless are confused with outcomes of homelessness. Common examples of this concern mental illness and crime, both of which are at times "linked" to homelessness without any clear understanding of whether this occurs prior to first becoming homeless, whether it accompanies the situation of homelessness or whether it is an outcome of homelessness. There is also the tendency to view personal characteristics as causes of homelessness. From this perspective homelessness is viewed as a personal behaviour rather than as a feature of a particular society.

"popular view" of the causes of homelessness as where:

— personal characteristics of homeless people are regarded as deficiencies;

— personal characteristics are confused with and become causes or explanations for homelessness;

— the direction of causation, from personal characteristic/ deficiency to homelessness, is presumed;

— symptoms are confused with and become causes

Structural factors including:

— the creation of adolescence as a period of dependence on families,

— a changing social structure which offers little support to families,

— a general breakdown in notions of community,

— an economic system which seriously disadvantages many people and contributes to rising unemployment, and

— a society which creates expectations for a standard of living which is unachievable for many young people and families.

Some study shows that, Particular social, institutional and economic structures create conditions for the emergence of the category "homeless youth"... such social structures, rather than individual characteristics, create barriers that prevent homeless youth from effectively making transitions into adulthood, especially though the education system. External factors are those which deny a viable self determination and include policies and practices of government, corporate and non-profit agencies which create barriers to young people establishing an independent household. Inadequate levels of income support to avoid poverty, the lack of access to public housing, discrimination by landlords and other constraints experienced by young people because of their juvenile status can be seen as external factors. Additional external factors which particularly impact on young people can include the actions, inaction, and orientations of statutory welfare authorities, juvenile justice authorities, the police, schools and non-profit human services.

The institutional context of young people's lives cannot be viewed as outside and somehow separate from the process of young people becoming homeless. Situational factors are those which arise from an individual's immediate relations and in the case of young people, most significantly their family relations. These factors include high levels of family conflict or stress, sexual, physical or emotional abuse, domestic violence, alcohol or substance abuse. Different types of factors can overlap in such a way as to make it impossible to determine priority of causation; for example, poverty and other income related issues can underlie factors such as family stress and conflict in many cases.

Emergence of Adolescence

With the emergence of adolescence as a recognised stage of life, came the view that this period was one of "storm and stress", of crisis and upheaval for young people. These theories, which continue to have popular appeal, were essentially theories of abnormality. Though there is virtually no empirical support for this approach to young people the images of young people as problematic, as dangerous threats to social order, as deviant and troublesome or as naive victims, have heavily influenced relations between social institutions and young people.

The Australian media have been found to portray young people in a highly stereotypical, generally negative way, with a substantial focus on crime. Bessant theorises that the public fascination with the youth "problem" reflects the tendency to use young people as "repositories for our collective fears and anxieties" and argues that the treatment of youth as some "exotic species" helps create typologies of deviance which justify intervention by the expert into the lives of young people and their families, in an endless quest to "normalise" young people to the satisfaction of the older community. The concepts of adultcentrism and ageism are useful for naming some of these age-related social dynamics.

Adultcentrism has emerged in the family therapy literature to describe the tendency by adults to view the world from an adult perspective and in so doing not understand or appreciate how children and young people are viewing things. At the same time age relations as a determinant of young people's experience can be overstated and infer that young people constitute a homogenous group. While age relations are significant considerations' socio-economic status, gender, ethnicity and race are more significant contextual factors. These interact with age relations producing quite different dynamics for differently located young people.

Young people's attitudes and perceptions do not support the notion that they constitute a group at odds with the values of mainstream society. Rather, studies show that young people value their relationships with parents and family members, and have respect for parents. Even where young people have been forced to leave home because of difficult circumstances they usually want to re-establish or maintain contact and have some level of relationship with their parents or other family members.

Model of Social Management

Australia is described homelessness as a mixture of "corporatist" and "economic rationalist" models where economic decision making is largely market driven, with rationalist assumptions underpinning taxation policy and government spending, and where instead of universally directed services there is an emphasis on targeted welfare delivery. Burke makes the point that homelessness is much more a problem in dominantly economic rationalist societies such as the United States and Britain, and contends there is evidence that Australia is moving more towards the economic rationalist model.

Unemployment and Poverty

Employment is an important avenue for escaping homelessness. Unemployment plays a key role in becoming homeless. In the past two decades full-time employment opportunities for young people have been substantially eroded with every recessionary period seeing an over-representation in jobs lost to young people which are never recovered in following periods of relative employment growth. In 1966, 59% of 15- to 19-year-olds in Australia were in full-time employment; in 1992 this was 20%. Similar downward trends have occurred in the United Kingdom, USA and Europe. So serious is the issue that the National Council for the International Year of the Family notes: "Youth unemployment was described as a 'black hole', a direct and insidious form of abuse against the young person by economic and labour market circumstances".

The viability of independence is largely predicated on young people having access to a viable income, and this is not within reach for most independent young people. Related to this is the factor of family income and employment. The data from Australian Bureau of Statistics reveals that 17% of Australian families had no parent in paid employment, while among sole parent families, 43% were not in the labour force. Any analysis of homelessness must consider the financial stresses on families and young people within families resulting from low income and unemployment.

Young cites Australian statistics indicating that the occupation of the father has an influence on the children's homeleaving, with blue collar workers' children leaving home at an earlier age than those from white collar jobs. Where the father was unemployed or not working, a high proportion of their children left home to live with a partner or because of conflict, especially so with daughters. In the United Kingdom patterns of home leaving in terms of reasons, the timing, reversability of the process, and type of accommodation moved to, have been found to vary between classes, and are closely related to differences in access to educational opportunity.

The National Youth Coalition for Housing point out that if the allowance was an incentive to leave home, more young people leaving home would have sought SAAP assistance because of the long waiting time for YHA. In a survey of agencies conducted across the United Kingdom, withdrawal of benefits to 16- and 17-yearolds was seen as a major factor in increasing youth homelessness.

Low Incomes and High Housing Costs

The combination of low incomes and high housing costs mean that young people seeking to form independent households face great difficulties. As the Maas report for the National Youth Housing Strategy points out, 80% of young people on low incomes are in private rental accommodation. A range of factors is well canvassed, factors which result in a lack of access to affordable housing for young people on home leaving. These include access to and adequacy of wages or income support for young people, discrimination against young people in gaining rental accommodation, and continuing low levels of access to generally unsuitable public housing stock.

Statutory Welfare Intervention

Being removed from home because of protective concerns may reduce the risk of physical or sexual abuse but it may have the unintended consequence of propelling a child or young person into homelessness. The pattern of transience and multiple care givers that many young children experience as a result of state welfare authority intervention meets the definitional requirements of homelessness in some important respects. That the intervention by the state authority is warranted in cases of abuse or neglect is not at issue; what is highlighted is the phenomenon whereby statutory intervention which removes a child from the family home, rather than removing the abusive or neglectful perpetrator, may well render the child vulnerable to the conditions that constitute homelessness. The experience of young people leaving care has been characterised as one of particular vulnerability given that little support is available from the State to assist these young people to establish a stable independent living situation.

Schools

The connection between early school leaving and young people becoming vulnerable to homelessness. The earlier young people left school, the longer they were likely to remain homeless. Few homeless young people continue their schooling even if they have not re ached the minimum age for leaving and there is evidence that between two-thirds and three-quarters of homeless students do not complete the school year in which they become homeless.

Inflexible structures in schools, especially secondary schools; the notion that curricula areas are largely irrelevant for students not aiming for tertiary study; the poor quality of teacher-student relationships; the practice of rejecting or neglecting underachievers; and the policies of suspension or expulsion of difficult students. Interviews with young people reveal that developing rapport with an understanding teacher was a crucial element in making their school experience positive. Patterns of truancy and school failure recur throughout the narratives of young people who become homeless. Despite this, there is little evidence that schools are assuming systematic measures to address the needs of the broadest cross-section of students.

Child Abuse and Family Violence

Abuse often takes a multidimensional form, illustrated by a recent Australian study which found that when the primary abuse was physical, emotional abuse also occurred in 45% of cases, with neglect occurring in 44%. Most difficult to define is emotional abuse, where definitions range from emotional deprivation from a carer to a broader ecological definition of the child inhabiting a situation or ecology characterised by patterns of interpersonal and intersystem relation - ships which have an influential and detrimental effect on the child's emotional development.

Factors which may contribute to an abusive ecology in families include marital conflict, family separations, stress resulting from life crisis such as unemployment or the death of a parent, restructured or blended families, the presence or absence of a family network for support, gender stereotypes maintained within the society, and learned patterns of aggression and dominance. A substantial number of

Australian studies indicate escape from physical, emotional and sexual abuse as common reasons for early homeleaving.

The statistics on sexual abuse as an antecedent to early home leaving are quite variable. The difficulty in building a clear picture of the level of incidence is due in part to the pattern of "late" disclosure among homeless young women, who generally refrain from revealing details of sexual abuse until such time as considerable trust has been established between themselves and human service workers, and the reluctance by young men generally to disclose experiences of sexual violence.

Family Conflict

Family conflict is the most commonly cited reason by young people as to why home leaving resulting in homelessness occurred. Some interviews with 100 young homeless people in Australia revealed that "family conflict is a unifying theme in all of the accounts". There is also a substantial body indicating that marital conflict is correlated with a significant number of emotional problems in children. One effect of high levels of marital conflict is to increase levels of children's anger and aggression, particularly in male children.

As children get older it is inevitable that some shift in roles and expectations within families occurs. The need for parents and adolescents to change roles and assumptions as the young people move towards independence was one finding of the study of 92 families by Wolcott and Weston. A family's communication patterns, problem-solving abilities, belief systems, and structure of relationships will influence whether adolescence is a time of normal challenge and adjustment or becomes a crisis of conflict.

In one Australian study the most common "sources" of conflict prior to leaving home, identified by young people listed in descending order were: father, mother, need for independence, personality clash, view of life conflict between the parents, social life/peers, alcohol misuse, conflict over young person's partner and clash with stepfather. It appears conflict triggered home leaving, together with those attributes which render a family and young person more vulnerable to stress correlate with a higher incidence of homelessness.

Correlations between restrictions placed on children by parents, and their homeleaving is had distinct gender dimensions: restrictions on the independence and freedom of sons will force them to leave home sooner and more likely for the reason, independence. Restrictions on daughters are relatively more likely to result in their leaving home because of conflict. Among daughters, also, there is some indication that marriage may be used as a means of achieving independence from a restrictive family situation.

The sex of both the adolescent and the custodial parent may also be factors in the contexts for conflict within families. Some study concludes that as female adolescents get older, they develop closer affective relationships with their mothers, while male adolescents do the reverse; both male and female adolescents revealed a pattern of using their fathers less for support as they age. It suggesting mothers are the preferred parent to turn to in times of distress and in particular, that female adolescents differentiate between parents and refer significantly more to mothers than fathers.

In a Canadian study of early home leaving indicates the factors associated with early home-leaving include the sex of the young person, racial/ethnic background, education level, employment and income. The results, based on the views of 2,033 young people aged 15 to 24 were that:

— young people from stepfamilies were two and a half times more likely to leave home due to "conflict" than young people from biological families;

— young women were significantly more prone to early home leaving than young men;

— young people with greater access to material wealth were less likely to leave home early.

Some studies shows that in cases of family breakdown or separation, the structure of the family after the event is more critical to the long-term adjustment of the child than the event of separation itself. Edgar, in commenting on all the findings on divorce produced by the Australian Institute of Family Studies, indicated that the research confirms: "that it is the degree of conflict, not divorce per se, that traumatises children". High levels of conflict within a family regardless of the family structure is seen to be associated with poor adolescent adjustment. There is a temptation, encouraged in the popular media, to overstate the significance of the single parent or blended family as social "problems" in themselves. This is particularly so of single parent families, given historical data which indicates single parent families are not a new phenomenon.

In 1891 the percentage of families comprising single parents with children was 17%, a figure which matches contemporary statistics. In the 19th century it was mortality rather than divorce, that accounted for this figure, yet as McDonald points out: "despite the currently high divorce rates, marriages today are more likely to be still intact after 30 years than were marriages 100 years ago".

Peer Group Influence

High levels of family acceptance and support correlated with peer groups being seen as sources of support, while: antisocial conformity was found to relate to a family atmosphere that was high in conflict and which emphasised achievement and independence combined with a lack of support for intellectual development. Joining particular peer groups may then compensate for the young person feeling less accepted by parents. There is a body of research indicating the importance of peer group friendships for adolescents as a source of support, but at the same time, a strong theme emerged that peers do not replace family and parental bonds during adolescence.

Mental Illness

The HREOC report into human rights and mental illness, estimated that 15% of Australian adolescents suffer from a recognisable psychiatric disorder with more recent research citing a figure of 20%. There is evidence that serious depressive illness has increased dramatically among adolescents and young adults and the dramatic increase in suicide particularly among young males is well documented. The correlation between homelessness and mental health problems is well supported though it is also recognised that this correlation does not distinguish mental health issues as antecedents or products of homelessness.

Further there is the caution that young people are at times pathologised as "ill", when in reality there may be social and contextual reasons underpinning the "symptoms". "homeless young people have a high risk of depression and suicide" and there is a clear pattern of suicidal attempts and/or ideation appearing as warning signals: for example, these are reported by 25% of young people who are at risk of becoming homeless. In the Western Australian Child Health Survey 16% of adolescents reported having had suicidal thoughts. In the same study, the adult caregivers/teachers reported that only 3% of the adolescents had spoken of suicide. This discrepancy supports the conclusion that the caregivers' perception of children/young people often differs from the self-perception of children/young people.

Long-term Process and Event Based Antecedents

Long-term processes, such as abuse, may culminate in events which have the effect of removing important protective factors, or which may lead to processes becoming entrenched and so result in home leaving. Recent study suggest, about 20% of respondents gave drug and alcohol mismanagement as a reason for their homelessness, but connected this with physical and/or sexual abuse experienced within the family, and 25% of this same group had come from families where one or both parents had died These life experience factors, such as separation from or death of a parent, are significantly over-represented among samples of young people who become homeless.

The same broad pattern was found in a study for Hanover Welfare Services of 33 families where there were two major patterns in becoming homeless. One pattern involved family hardship and disruption from early childhood. For these young people the underlying causes were seen as: poverty, violent and often drunken fathers, sexual abuse, the difficulties of single mothers, the loss of a parent, parents separating and repartnering, conflicts in relation - ships, and the trauma of children being made Wards of State or put in foster care.

The second pattern arose from a sudden event such as job loss or the death of a parent. Plass and Hotaling extend the notion of a "lifelong" process to the point of concluding that there is evidence for intergenerational transmission of "running away" from home. In a study focusing on 108 parent-child cases involving running away, and a control group of 224 cases of children aged over 10 years, it was concluded that: ... parents of runaways were significantly ... more likely to have run away themselves than were parents of non - runaways: 24% of the parents of runways said they were runaways themselves, compared to 11% of the parents of non-runaways.

Other issues for Homelessness

There are a number of additional issues relating to the cultural and personal contexts of young people which also need to be understood in any discussion of home leaving leading to homelessness. A range of factors has been mentioned already having particular impact on young women. Issues for other groups of young people include: For Aboriginal and Torres Strait Islander young people:

— a general lack of adequate accommodation;

— high mobility among families;

— an education system which is poorly oriented to their needs, and a tendency to leave school at an early age; and

— over-representation in the juvenile justice system.

For young people from non-English-speaking backgrounds:

— the particular impact of family structure;

— conflict between parents and offspring over morality and personal freedom, especially for young women in some cultural groups;

— conflict arising from parents' struggle to maintain cultural identity;

— more severe restrictions on the freedom of young people, and stricter discipline, than that imposed on their peers; and

— a reliance on community elders or clergy to resolve family conflict.

For young people with an intellectual disability:

— a greater risk of chronic homelessness than other young people;

— high levels of pressure on families and frustration by parents;

— negative school experiences and lack of ongoing educational opportunities; and

— a pattern of highly unstable or inappropriate accommodation.

For gay and lesbian young people:

— conflict with the parent/guardian arising from parental attitudes regarding the sexual orientation of the young person.

Prevention and Early Intervention

There are four levels of intervention:

— activities which assist an individual on the point of homelessness;

— activities which focus upon the development of living skills in those people whose lack of such skills threatens them with homelessness or a re turn to Chomelessness;

— community development activities which focus on overcoming barriers at a local level to a SAAP user's reintegration into the community;

— advocacy at a broader policy level to overcome structural barriers to secure housing.

This approach to early intervention illustrates a mixture of structural, external and situational strategies, implying that almost all action can be understood within the parameters of early intervention. At the literal level prevention is stopping something from happening. Implicit is the element of prediction where an event will occur unless some action is taken to hinder or stop it. Prevention frameworks have increasingly been applied in social policy contexts such as health, crime and labour market contexts. It has also been argued that something cannot be prevented unless "unambiguous causal links can be demonstrated between the intervention strategies and the problem which they are intended to eradicate".

Commonly, a layering approach has been adopted with a number of types of prevention being defined: a primary focus aimed at strategies which would prevent the emergence of a problem, a secondary focus which would address problems identified in their early stages, and a tertiary focus which would address mitigation of their most damaging effects. The approach taken by MacKenzie and Chamberlain uses the point of leaving home as a demarcation between early intervention, which occurs as soon as the young person becomes homeless, and generally in the first few weeks following leaving home, prior to becoming chronically homeless, and prevention which occurs when a young person is at risk but is not actually homeless.

The definitions of early intervention and prevention proposed by MacKenzie and Chamberlain match to some extent the secondary and tertiary prevention levels. In the definition used in the present research, prevention incorporates primary prevention level and that aspect of secondary prevention which builds up the protective factors around young people. Indeed prevention can be enhanced by building up protective factors not only around young people but around their families and communities. This definition is influenced by understandings of the causal factors of homelessness as being to some extent situational, though predominantly external and/or structural. Prevention can address each of these levels. For example, prevention that is both situational and protective may take the form of a parenting skills program incorporated in the school curriculum.

Prevention aimed at external factors may be targeted at programs or policies that improve the pool of suitable public housing stock for young people. Prevention aimed at structural factors may include change to age based systems of youth wages and income support. Early intervention in our definition incorporates the tertiary prevention level , together with intervention in relation to specific young people and their families seen as vulnerable to homelessness. Early intervention is distinct from prevention in that it is aimed at addressing situational factors that may contribute to a particular young person becoming chronically homeless. Early intervention can occur prior to homelessness in response to a difficulty or crisis perceived by a young person, family member or carer to be a possible antecedent to early home leaving or homelessness.

Social scientists have become more adept at defining the risk factors than the factors which protect against youth homelessness. We can conceive of protective factors as the other side of the coin to the risk factors. Resources and relationships are the elements which provide protection against youth homelessness. Prevention needs to aim at maintaining or rebuilding young people's attachments by increasing the level of protective factors, thereby decreasing the risk factors.

The Western Australian Child Health Survey provides an example of a protective factors approach in relation to healthy child development. These have some relevance to homelessness prevention and early intervention. The report highlights the three areas of family, school and the social environment and goes on to list particular avenues for prevention. These include improved preparation for parenting, high quality day care and preschool education, building parental competence, improved support for families with adolescents ; life skills education, healthier school environments, in particular, addressing the problematic transition from primary to secondary school, using schools as a venue for parent education; and supporting locally initiated action, and countering harmful socio-cultural influences particularly in the mass media.

A range of other protective factors, particularly structural and external factors can be extracted on the antecedents to homelessness among young people. There is a lack of consensus, and large variability in the use of "at risk" terminology as it applies to young people. The term is generally used "to denote a set of presumed cause and effect dynamics that place the child or adolescent in danger of negative future events". Commonly cited in discussions about particular future problematic events are references to signals of being at risk such as school exclusion, drug and alcohol use, low self-esteem and various forms of abuse.

At risk terminology is almost always explored at the level of the individual, family or population sub-group implying that the antecedents of the particular negative event are located in people themselves or in their interaction with their immediate environment. The assumption is that the young people themselves are in some way lacking rather than seeing the economic, social and institutional contexts of their lives as lacking.

For example, in a review of the Australian literature between 1980 and 1994 on students at risk, The term at risk is used to describe or identify young people who, beset by particular difficulties and disadvantages, are thought likely to fail to achieve the development in their adolescent years that would provide a sound basis for a satisfying and fulfilling adult life. Of critical importance is the nature of the "risk" phenomenon. Homelessness, drug misuse, suicide, and early school leaving are quite different phenomena. Yet the language of at risk is used relatively indiscriminately to refer to all of these with little if any clarification regarding meaning and the underlying assumptions that accompany a particular pairing.

In recent Commonwealth and State Government social policy, the use of at risk terminology has at times been located within a social justice framework, or used as a synonym for disadvantage. From this perspective the identification of at risk young people and groups of young people is seen to allow speci fic targeting of limited government resources to tackle social problems such as crime, AIDS, and homelessness, and thus enhance access and equity for disadvantaged groups. Such an application has merit although it is likely that in accomplishing such strategies the individuation of social problems often occurs.

Increasingly the term has been a focus for critique. Most common in these analyses is the view that "at risk" can be or is a vehicle for managing young people in a way which locates the source of social difficulty within young people themselves, thereby diminishing the significance of structural and institutional factors which underlie social problems, such as homelessness. Second, depending on the focus of attention, there is generally very poor predictive power in the application of at risk factors to individuals. The term at risk can also have the effect of labelling and further marginalising those it is applied to.

Finally, it seems that the problems people face at any one time could result in a wide range of preventive goals depending on the institutional location of the service, the naming of the "problem", the practice framework of the worker or service, and the views of the people themselves. For multiple reasons the terminology of at risk is not promoted in this research, though it is used descriptively when programs or agencies self-identify in this way.

Home Leaving

The term "home leaving" is preferred on the basis that it places more emphasis on the phenomenon than on an individual's agency. Most people leave their family of origin and establish another household at some point in their lives. There are financial dimensions to this process, most significantly a secure income sufficient to afford private rental housing, the main form of tenure accessed, often with significant difficulty, by young people.

In light of substantial barriers to accessing other housing, it is not this act of leaving home which of itself causes homelessness. There is however a tendency for this to be inferred. For example, early intervention, in the context of youth homelessness, is a process which is based on the principle that if appro - priate action and support is provided at an early stage of a young person leaving home, the spiral towards chronic homelessness can be avoided. Implicit is the view that a young person is of an age where formation of an independent household is not appropriate.

If this is in fact so, then the view that home leaving causes homelessness is still problematic, given that the overwhelming majority of young people for whom independent living is not appropriate, do not commonly leave home without substantial issues existing in the home, and are unlikely to remain at home on returning unless these circumstances change in some positive way. This is not to say that providing support to young people and families prior to or shortly after home leaving occurs is not well placed. It is simply to be clear that home leaving itself does not cause homelessness even when the young person is of an age where they do not have access to sufficient resources to avoid homelessness.

For many young people it is the time gap between home leaving and the availability of adequate material, social and protective resources to form another household which causes homelessness. The availability of these resources is the subject of social policy and is largely outside of the capacity of families and youth services to provide. There is an age under which living independently is not socially or politically sanctioned, generally agreed to be 15 or 16. This is linked to the age at which schooling is no longer compulsory, the benchmark where young people symbolically begin to be seen as economically productive members of the community. This is also the age below which the state has child protection concerns as evidenced by the Commonwealth-State Protocol arrangements for the payment of income security benefits to under 16s.

The National Youth Housing Strategy report cites 15 years as the age when young people, because of lost family connections, having been a ward of the state, or because of moving out of home due to violence or abuse, may need the means and the opportunity to make independent choices.

There is beyond this an age range where home leaving is partially sanctioned, but littered with disincentives. The discrimination young people experience in accessing private rental and public housing, even though they are technically eligible, are examples. The age grading of income support arrangements for unemployed young people and students also typify this partial acceptance. Finally, there is the age where home leaving is acknowledged implicitly in social policy as appropriate and legitimated as such, that is, where individuals gain a full adult rate of material support and access to social resources.

There is clearly a reasonable basis for seeing home leaving of young people under 15 or 16 as an issue for exploration, where the goal of remaining at home in the context of safety and well-being is pursued. This is a matter of considerable public consensus and is reflected in Commonwealth/State divisions of responsibility regarding income support, and the continuing concern within SAAP for under 16s. It is to this age range which the present research has been most directed and to this age range that the term "early home leaving" can be applied with confidence.

The issue of home leaving for those between 16 and the age where employment and genuine adult incomes becomes accessible cannot be addressed without examining and debating the economic, social and political place of young people in Australian society, and the implications this has for responses to home leaving. There are numbers of groups in society for whom home leaving has been considerably more difficult or conditional, such as those with disabilities or those suffering from mental illness.

When the age of availability of full-time work was articulated to the age of sanctioned home leaving, there was little need for social policy to attend to the nexus between home leaving and homelessness, other than that which attended to child protection. As the employment opportunities for young people have been delayed and not replaced by income subsidy arrangements sufficient to sustain an independent household a difficulty has emerged.

Patterns of Home Leaving

Prior to the 1970s it was the pattern for young people to leave home for marriage once they had become financially independent. Leaving home in many ways signified independence. The trend for young people to leave home later has been acknowledged and reflected in ABS data since the late 1980s. Females tend to leave home at a slightly earlier age than males. There is evidence, however, that while the average age of homeleaving is increasing, there may be an increased diversity of ages at which young women leave, with some leaving earlier and some later. Whereas young people, especially females, routinely left home for marriage prior to the 1970s the average age of marriage more recently has increased to the point where it is usual for there to be a period of "independent living" following home leaving.

The underlying reasons for later home leaving can be summarised as the collapse of the full-time youth labour market and increased levels of participation in education and vocational training. Other factors such the interaction of housing costs and availability with levels of income support for young people unemployed or studying, have contributed to the situation where increased numbers of young people are remaining at home. These structural issues have been cited as giving rise to increasing levels of conflict between young people and their parents.

The research suggests that where young adults had once been seen as individuals who had achieved independence, autonomy and responsibility, the evidence shows an amplification of dependence and irresponsibility which goes along with the absence of freedom for an increasing number of young people.

Some reports supports the view that young people are not only leaving home later but that parents are playing a significant role in supporting them financially both while they are at home and subsequently when they leave. The implication is that home leaving is not a clear move to independent living but usually requires, in the current Australian context, a level of continued economic relationship between parents and young people. Where such connection does not exist, or where families have limited income, the implication is that young people are at additional risk of becoming homeless. It is unfair, Ellis argues, that young people should remain at home when otherwise they would have to leave for education/ employment or when parents cannot provide support at the levels required. Hartley summarises the positions of families in this way:

> Some parents were very supportive of their teenage children; others contributed little or nothing to their upkeep. In the latter cases, this was sometimes due to the break - down of relationships between parents and their children. Many, however, particularly widowed parents or those on supporting Parents Benefit with a number of children in their care, simply did not have the financial resources to provide for their older teenage children.

At one level this financial dependency can be seen to create tension against moves to social independence by young people. Hartley and Wolcott point out that harmonious family life for young people in late adolescence now requires interdependence, within a mutually supportive relationship of "equals", yet this equality is highly problematic in a context where young people's financial dependence is so prolonged. Young identified the main reasons cited by young people for leaving home as marriage, independence, work, study, conflict in the family, and travel. She points out that there is a significant difference between home leaving for a clear goal (such as study or taking up a job offer), and home leaving due to conflict.

Further, young people frequently leave home and return a number of times. Fifty per cent of young men and 40% of young women who left returned later to the parental home. It is significant that: "a high proportion of second departures of those who first left because of conflict are also because of conflict". It would appear that there are "positive" connotations attached to the first kind of home leaving, but not attached to the second kind. The sources of conflict, the unresolved nature of that conflict (evident in the fact that the young person leaves yet again) and the availability of sufficient resources to avoid homelessness if staying at home is not possible, are the issues at stake, rather than the home leaving itself. Under ideal circumstances, leaving home is viewed positively by both the young person and the parent/s.

In the case of young people who leave home at a very early age, who are 'kicked out' by parents, and/or who leave in situations of emotional distress, the pattern of leaving is often very complex. Wolcott and Weston's Australian study of 92 families reported that one-third of the young people in their sample stayed away from home for fewer than six days, one-third for a period of one to four weeks, and one-third for a period that ranged from five weeks to more than a year. Young people in these situations may leave one family home to go to another, or where there has been separation or divorce they may move from the mother's home to the father's. It is difficult to establish which home leaving is the critical precursor to homelessness.

In the Wolcott and Weston study, 42% of the young people stayed with a family member or noncustodial parent after leaving home, and 40% with a friend. This difficulty is compounded by a general failure to acknowledge that for many young people, there is not a single identifiable "home" but rather multiple homes. In a study of 104 young people, Smith found that on their first night away from home, the largest percentage (36%) went to a friend's place, and this arrangement could extend for weeks or even longer; 18% spent the first night with a relative or other member of the extended family; 14% spent one or more nights on the street after leaving home; and 22% went directly into a government or non-government service.

Plass and Hotaling in a comparable American study found that 60% of the young people who ran away from home went to a friend's house. This latter study also found that in 40% of the cases, police were a first point of referral by parents of runaways. Tasker found that most young people who had left home a number of times initially sought shelter with friends or another family member.

It is very difficult to estimate the number of young people in Australia who fall into the early intervention parameters used in this research. Any available statistics are inevitably going to include only a small proportion of young people and families experiencing distress that could lead to early home leaving and subsequent homelessness.

Kids Help Line

Kids Help Line, a national free call telephone help service for children, maintains a comprehensive data base and supplied the following data. During 1995 Kids Help Line received 4,000 calls relating to homelessness and/or home leaving, accounting for 6% of all problem-related calls. The number of callers in this category was greatest for females aged 15 and males aged 16, gradually decreasing either side of this peak age of inquiry. The number of calls from males and females is similar. Such findings are consistent with data which indicates the average age of home leaving for females is slightly younger than for males. Calls made to Kids Help Line in the calender year 1995 relating to homelessness and home leaving were rated according to severity (Table 1).

Table 1. Homelessness related calls according to severity – Kids Help Line

Severity	%
Left home – severely distressed	7.52

Left home – distressed	21.65
Left home – okay	32.93
Contemplating leaving	14.94
Inquiry	22.97

Of relevance to the area of early intervention is that 38% of callers, were making inquiries about or contemplating leaving home. Kids Help Line indicated that many of those classified as "left home - distressed" and most of those "left home - severely distressed" are experiencing stress within the first month of home leaving and fall within the parameters of early intervention defined here. A number of other categories are of factors acknowledged as contributing to early home leaving leading to homelessness and include those of family relationship, child abuse, and violence.

5

Refugee Children

Children are especially vulnerable in times of war and conflict because of their dependency on others and their inability to fully understand many of the situations they are forced to confront. Refugee children are frequently exposed to war and violence. Many would have experienced dislocation or lived in exile, and may have witnessed family members and others being physically or sexually assaulted, or even killed. In war torn countries, many children are regularly exposed to bombings. Children as young as seven may have been forced into being child soldiers.

In most refugee situations, children face an increased risk of sexual abuse and violence. Forced displacement and relocation present risks to the safety and security of children, as does the situation in many refugee camps. They are also faced with interruption to family life, schooling, routines and rituals, the loss of their home, and for some the death of parents, family and friends.

Health of Refugee Children

Mass population movements, the destruction of health services, water systems and sanitation, malnutrition, and overcrowding in refugee camps encourage the spread of disease. In countries where children are already vulnerable to diseases, the onset of armed conflict may dramatically increase death rates, with those under 5 years at particular risk.

Oral Health

Refugee children can present with severe caries and gum disease due to substandard dental care and hygiene, and poor nutrition. Refugee families may lack information about the relationship between diet and dental caries. Advice about healthy eating, on the advantages of breastfeeding over bottle feeding, and about oral hygiene is important.

Micronutrient Diseases

The effects of under-nutrition and vitamin deficiencies can be seen in some children following settlement here. Those from Africa and the Middle East are at risk of vitamin D deficiency, with some children suffering from the bone deforming disease rickets. Risk factors include exclusive breast feeding, lack of oral supplementation, dark skin and reduced sun exposure. Other nutritional deficiencies, including thiamine, iodine, vitamin C and vitamin A, may occur in refugees spending long periods in camps. Iron deficiency is the most common cause of anaemia in refugee children and women. In the children this can be due to iron deficiency in the mother, exclusive breast feeding, low iron intake, impaired absorption due to chronic diarrhoea, and parasitic infections.

Delays in physical growth and development may occur due to inadequate nutrition, illness such as chronic infections, the emotional environment and other factors. Where developmental delay is suspected, undiagnosed congenital or birth disorders would need to be considered, as well as more unusual causes such as tuberculosis or parasitic infections. Exotic cerebral infections should also be considered in a child with convulsions. Developmental delay without any underlying abnormality may of course be seen in a child who has had recurrent illnesses and endured traumatic life experiences.

Pre-schoolers and school-aged refugee children will have missed out on formal hearing and vision screening. Assessment of these faculties should be arranged through community nurses or other health professionals. The profile of refugees arriving in Australia has changed in the last three years, with an increasing number coming from African countries such as Sudan, Somalia, Ethiopia, Eritrea, Liberia, and Sierra Leone. Children from these countries are at risk from infectious diseases due to their refugee experience and to the high incidence of communicable diseases in these regions. The types of organism would vary with the geographic origin of refugee.

A recent study in Victoria found the most common intestinal pathogens among African refugees to be Giardia lamblia, Trichuris trichiura (whipworm) and Entamoeba histolytica. Since refugees in NSW do not undergo routine postarrival health assessment, the existence of infectious and parasitic diseases may go undetected among children. Many refugee children may have incomplete immunisation. In particular, arrivals under five years will not have had HIB vaccination. Children who came from conflict-ridden situations may have sustained war-related injuries (e.g. injuries from beatings, landmines, shrapnel, etc) that require assessment or further management.

Traumatised refugee children may show a range of behaviours including poor school performance, behavioural problems, withdrawal from parents and other children, lack of confidence and trust, anxiety, depression, post traumatic stress disorder (PTSD), sleeping and eating disorders, bed wetting, sleep walking, speech problems and psychosomatic symptoms. A child's psychological health is closely linked to the health and security of his/her parents or primary caregiver. Parents who are traumatised and are not coping well may have a diminished ability to support their children physically and emotionally.

Protection Issues

Child protection issues need to be addressed sensitively. Issues that may give cause for concern include the degree of physical discipline, apparent neglect, domestic violence, and female genital mutilation (FGM). FGM is practised in more than 40 countries in Africa, Middle East, Asia, Europe and South America. There are girls and women affected by FGM currently now living in Australia. In those communities where it is common practice, girls born here who have not undergone FGM may be considered unmarriageable. However the practice of FGM is banned by law in NSW. It is also illegal to take a girl out of the country to seek FGM.

Refugee children are, like their parents, survivors. Although some will have health issues as highlighted above, the majority are healthy and keen to start a new life. Previous generations of refugee children and young people have shown how much they have to offer to their new country. Today more than 5,000 children will be displaced by conflict. In all, an estimated 25 million children are living as refugees or are displaced in their home country. These young individuals experience much disruption and loss in their lives - loss of familiar people and surroundings; loss of a sense of order and predictability. They also face difficulties specific to their experience as returnees.

A child attendee at the recent UN Special Session on Children said, "You [session attendees] have spoken about many solutions to help us [children affected by conflict]. What are you waiting for to do something?" The goal here is to highlight some of the vulnerabilities child and adolescent returnees face as documented by field advocates of Refugees International (RI)and by the broader humanitarian community and to recommend practical steps that can be taken on behalf of young people affected by conflict and displacement.

Sometimes international agencies reduce or cease assistance before returnee communities are self-sustaining.

Sometimes, even if international agencies are present, there is a gap between the relief and development operations. Sometimes there is a large degree of difference in the level of services available from camp to return settlements or from urban areas to rural ones. Together, these factors can threaten the well being of children and adolescents. Survival itself is at risk when there is inadequate healthcare, food, or water, and when there is military recruitment of underage youth or the hazard of unexploded antipersonnel landmines.

The deterioration of public health infrastructure during conflict reduces access to emergency care, preventive healthcare, reproductive health services, such as family planning, treatment for sexually transmitted diseases and gynecological complications, and pre- and post-natal care. Complications in pregnancy and delivery are especially likely for children who have children. Without sensitive, timely and adequate medical care, many of these victims die or some will commit suicide because of the humiliation and embarrassment they suffer from their situation. In situations where refugees have changed health behavior, for example in the case of adolescent male condom use in West Africa, young men told RI staff that they want access to the same level of reproductive health services on return, it often is simply not available to them.

Lack of access to food and clean water can threaten the lives of returnees. Children die as a direct result of diminished food intake or by diseases contracted due to malnutrition. In places like the agricultural districts of Kono and Kailahun in Sierra Leone, earlier this year refugees were returning to find 90 percent of the infrastructure destroyed. Farmland has not been worked for 11 years. With returns out of season, promised rations insufficient, and agricultural inputs scarce, food security is a major concern.

It can also take a long time for returnees to return to normal eating habits. In Mozambique, for example, some young couples returning to the country from refugee camps did not know how to prepare any foods other than the maize, beans and oil that had been distributed to them as rations during their time as refugees. They were not familiar with traditional foods or eating practices. They did not know which local foods to use during weaning, and there was no one available to teach them.

Lack of access to clean water can also contribute to high levels of child mortality. Once again the difference in the level of services from refugee camp to returnee site can be difficult. RI staff witnessed the situation of long-term refugees such as those returning from Thailand to Cambodia, children become ill from poor water. To compound the problem, these children may not have access to care in returnee settlements that have poor or absent medical facilities. Returnee children are at high risk of under-age military recruitment-leading to active service and possible injury or death.

In the Congo, UNHCR and nongovernmental organizations located a sizeable number of refugee children living with local Congolese families because they are reluctant to return to Rwanda, afraid to being targeted as militants. Children who have been child soldiers and who have had especially traumatic experiences are at risk for psychosocial distress and marginalization. Girls and adolescents who have been forced to be wives of other soldiers may face life-long impact of being ineligible for marriage, yet having to raise children alone.

Landmines are also a serious threat when refugees and internally displaced families return home and risk crossing mined areas as represented by the situations in Sri Lanka and Angola now. Problems of identity and discrimination are very real for many returnees, particularly children born in a country of asylum. Children are not always given proper documentation or access to registration processes. On return to Burma, Rohingya refugees from Bangladesh were given a card that identified them as returnees, but they did not receive promised identity cards.

Without being considered citizens, Rohingyas continue to have their rights violated. They cannot travel, attend high schools and universities, or own property. Also, there can be tensions between returnees and residents. This can occur when displaced children become minorities on return or when they repatriate to a new location and become victims of discrimination. If a young person is part of a minority group, it may impact on every aspect of their lives - access to education, what language they speak, treatment by schools, police and other institutions, employment, what their aspirations are. According to RI staff who traveled to Afghanistan, gender discrimination against girls also occurs, particularly in rural areas, where they may be unable to access education or health care because they are not allowed to walk outside their homes or villages.

Social Reintegration and Development

During conflict, sudden changes in family structures, caused by death, incarceration or detention, parental participation in active conflict, differences in the timing of return, and disability or disappearance of parents, can leave youth without guidance, role models and sustenance. Long-term effects of exile- strained marriages, family violence, confusion, depression and apathy, displacement and deprivation-can affect family functioning. Changes in family structure and roles can place children and adolescents under obligation to provide for the family and to rebuild the homestead.

Children get separated from families temporarily, or unaccompanied minors who travel in groups or independently, may find themselves in situations of greater responsibility for themselves and others. These are often several siblings, children of extended family members, or even unrelated children, headed by a minor, usually an adolescent girl. Child-headed households are particularly vulnerable to exploitative labor and prostitution. After mass return of

Rwandan refugees from the Congo and the United Republic of Tanzania ended in 1997, it was estimated that approximately 75 percent of returnee households were headed by girls.

One problem observed was that female heads of households may, on their return, lost property rights and custody of children in their care. Access to education is critical for returnees. Education provides an important base for the social and psychological well being of children and adolescents and can promote reintegration. For refugee returnee children, it is important that their home countries recognize the schooling they have undertaken in the country of asylum, and students should be provided with appropriate course documentation.

Returning to non-violent daily activities, like attending school, can start the process of healing. Early education and recreational activities for children and adolescent brings the additional benefits of helping identify youth who are most severely traumatized, or having other problems, such as being exploited or abused by household members or employers. It is also a valuable protection tool for providing alternatives to military recruitment and other forms of exploitation. Child soldiers, who have been leaders themselves, may need access to alternative forms of education.

Financial difficulties, however, may prevent children from attending school. One problem for Roma children returning to Bosnia and Herzegovina was low level of participation in education. Most non-Roma school age children were in school, while only nine percent of the Roma children were in school for lack of resources. To strengthen the availability of formal or informal education in Afghanistan, UNHCR's program included the provision of textbooks and other school material for children, rehabilitation of schools and training of teachers. Individuals involved in running education programs before displacement, and in camps, should be consulted in the task of recreating educational systems.

The physical and psychological well being of children is almost inevitably jeopardized by the material deprivation and stress arising from displacement. It is said that three times as many children are seriously injured or permanently disabled by armed conflict than the millions killed by it. In Afghanistan alone, some 100,000 children have war-related disabilities, many of them caused by landmines. The lack of basic services and the destruction of health facilities during armed conflict mean that children living with disabilities at the time of their return get little support. They may not attend school because their families think that they do not need an education, or because educators think that their presence in the school will be detrimental to the education of "normal" children.

Discriminatory attitudes and practices exclude disabled children from social support and interaction as well, from leisure activities to training. Some children face violence in the family when frustration and rage over a long period of conflict is not abetted by the slow and often faltering process of reconstruction and development. Such sentiments are sometimes taken out on children. Furthermore, studies indicate that exposure to violence puts children at greater risk of future involvement in violence. Many of the daily, household chores assigned to young children, such as fetching water and wood can be very hazardous to children's healthy development since children carry out these jobs in physically damaged and risky environments. On return home, displaced children often take more responsibility for these tasks, putting them at greater risk for physical injury.

Healthcare services in returnee settings rarely address the special reproductive health needs of girls and boys, including family planning, pregnancy as a result of rape, sexual mutilation, having a child at an early age, or sexually transmitted infections, including HIV/AIDS. In addition, little is known about the psychosocial long-term effects of war and displacement. Children often return to the place where they were traumatized. They may face cultural differences as in the case of young women returning to Afghanistan faced with the question of covering themselves with a burka. The ways in which children respond to the stress of armed conflict will depend on individual factors such as age, sex, personality type, personal and family history and cultural background.

The nature of the traumatic events, including their frequency and the length of the exposure, also affect responses. Children affected by conflict display a wide range of symptoms, including increased separation anxiety and developmental delays, sleep disturbances and nightmares, lack of appetite, withdrawn behavior, lack of interest in play, and learning difficulties. In older children and adolescents, responses to stress can include anxious or aggressive behavior and depression, in the most severe cases committing suicide. With supportive caregivers and secure communities, most children achieve a sense of healing and prove remarkably resilient. Nonetheless, the loss of parents and other close family members and other experiences leave a life-long impression and can dramatically alter life pathways.

Guidelines for Protection and Care

Refugee Children and the Rights of the Child

International Treaties

International treaties are important to refugee children because they set standards. When a State ratifies a treaty, the Government of the State promises to the international community that it will conduct itself according to the standards in the treaty. The 1951 Refugee Convention and the 1967 Protocol set standards that apply to children in the same way as to adults:

(1) a child who has a "well-founded fear of being persecuted" for one of the stated reasons is a "refugee",

(2) a child who holds refugee status cannot be forced to return to the country of origin (the principle of non-refoulement), and

(3) no distinction is made between children and adults in social welfare and legal rights.

One article in the Convention sets standards which are of special importance to children: refugees must receive the "same treatment" as nationals in primary education, and treatment at least as favorable as that given to non-refugee aliens in secondary education (art. 22).

The 1969 Organization of African Unity Convention (Governing the Specific Aspects of Refugee Problems in Africa) broadened the definition of "refugee" to include persons in Africa who flee from war and other events that seriously disrupt public order. The OAU Convention makes no distinction between children and adults. The 1984 Cartagena Declaration also expanded the concept of refugee, and although the standard is not legally binding, States in Latin America do apply it. The treaty which sets the most standards concerning children is the 1989 Convention on the Rights of the Child (CRC). While the CRC is not a refugee treaty, refugee children are covered because all CRC rights are to be granted to all persons under 18 years of age (art. 1) without discrimination of any kind (art. 2).

The Convention on the Rights of the Child is important to refugee children because it sets comprehensive standards. Virtually every aspect of a child's life is covered, from health and education to social and political rights. Some of the standards are specific, for example the articles on juvenile justice (arts. 37 and 40), adoption (art. 21) and family rights (arts. 5, 9 and 14.2). Some social welfare rights are expressly qualified by the State's financial capability Rights to health (art. 24), education (art. 28), and to an adequate standard of living (art. 27) are called "progressive rights" because they increase along with the State's economic development.

However, these social welfare rights are not just principles or abstract goals. Because they are "rights," the prohibition against discrimination (art. 2) means that whatever benefits a State gives to the children who are its citizens, it must give to all children, including those who are refugees on its territory The Convention on the Rights of the Child has gained importance to refugee children because of the near-universal ratification of the treaty. The CRC standards have been agreed to by countries in every region of the world, countries of every population and geographical size and stage of economic development, and representing every type of political system and religious tradition.

Because the standards are universal, the CRC can be used as a powerful tool for advocacy: a country cannot claim its uniqueness as an excuse for not living up to universal standards. The widespread ratification of the CRC is important for other reasons as well. When a State is a party to the CRC but not to any refugee treaty, then the CRC may be used as the primary basis for protecting refugee children. Even when a State has not ratified the CRC, UNHCR still advocates its observance because its standards are universal.

UNHCR also applies the CRC to its own work by using the rights as guiding principles. The UNHCR Policy on Refugee Children states, "as a United Nations convention, (the CRC) constitutes a normative frame of reference for UNHCR's action" (para. 17). One of the guiding principles in the Policy states, "In all actions taken concerning refugee children, the human rights of the child, in particular his or her best interests, are to be given primary consideration".

For the well-being of refugee children, UNHCR advocates the observance of CRC standards by all States, international agencies and non-governmental organizations. In 1990, the World Summit for Children adopted a Declaration and Plan of Action. The goals of the World Summit set important standards to work towards in health and education. As follow up, States are encouraged to develop national plans of action, which should include refugee children under the category of "children in especially difficult circumstances." Although the Declaration and Plan are not treaty standards, their widespread acceptance has been a major step forward.

The CRC's major innovation is that it gives rights to children. We are used to thinking of children as having needs that should be met, rather than as having legal rights. Because of the CRC, children now have internationally recognized human rights. Although the rights in the CRC cover almost every aspect of a child's life, there are three rights that are so fundamental that they can be thought of as underlying the entire CRC: the "best interests" rule, non-discrimination, and the right to participate. These three rights are so important and so interrelated that it is helpful to think of them as a "triangle of rights". The three rights of the triangle reinforce each other to reach the objective: "the survival and development" of children (art. 6).

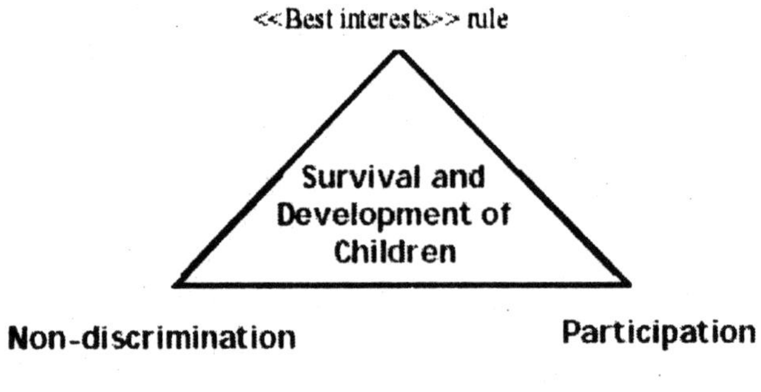

The Triangle of Rights

The Best Interests Rule

The "best interests" rule has two main applications: government policymaking and decisions made about children on an individual basis. Policy decisions Art. 3 requires that, "In all actions concerning children" the State shall make "the best interests of the child a primary consideration." This article requires States to analyze how each course of action may affect children. Because the interests of children are not always identical to adults' interests, and can at times even conflict, the State must carefully separate out the various interests at stake. The government does not have to take the course of action that is best for children, but if any conflicts are identified, the State must make the "best interests" of children "a primary consideration." This rule applies in budget allocations, in the making of laws, and in the administration of the government.

When a decision is being made about an individual child, then the child's best interests must be, at a minimum, "a primary consideration." There are some situations where the child's welfare gets higher consideration. For example, in a case of abuse or neglect, a child can be separated from parents if it "is necessary for the best interests of the child" (art. 7). In an adoption case, the "best interests of the child shall be the paramount consideration" (art. 21). In these cases, how a course of action might affect the child must be looked at closely, which is a requirement similar to that in policy decisions.

A child might be an orphan living in a refugee camp, with grandparents in the country of origin, an uncle in a second country of asylum, and with an unrelated family in another country that would like to adopt the child. In deciding what is best for the child many factors would have to be considered, including "the desirability of continuity" of culture and language (art. 20), the preservation of family and nationality (art. 8), and the child's own desires, which must be considered according to the child's "age and maturity" (art. 12).

The objective is to allow the child to "grow up in a family environment, in an atmosphere of happiness, love and understanding" (Preamble). The decision about a child's best interests can often be difficult; no single answer may be obviously and indisputably correct. (In the example, not enough "facts" were given to make a decision.

The non-discrimination article, art. 2, requires States to "respect and ensure the rights set forth in the present Convention to each child within their jurisdiction without discrimination of any kind, irrespective of the child's ... national, ethnic or social origin ... or other status". In other words, every child within a State's jurisdiction holds all CRC rights without regard to citizenship, immigration status or any other status. Refugee children, asylum seekers, and rejected asylum seekers are entitled to all the rights of the CRC.

Participations is a theme that runs throughout the CRC. Art. 12 provides that:

> "States Parties shall assure to the child who is capable of forming his or her views the right to express those views freely in all matters affecting the child, the views of the child being given due weight in accordance with the age and maturity of the child." In one way or another, nearly every article concerns some aspect of children's participation in society There are many forms of participation For example, there is social participation in family (arts. 7.1, 10) and community life (arts. 15, 17), and participation of those with special needs, such as disabled children (art. 23).

The participation of children in decision-making helps adults make better choices because they are better informed of the thoughts, feelings and needs of the children. But participation also meets a developmental need. It is through participation that children learn decision-making skills and gain the confidence to use those skills wisely.

As children age and mature they have greater participation in decision-making. Three forms of participation in decision making are:

Information input :When primary school children draw pictures, the activity can be just recreation and self-expression. But it can also be participation, provided that adults use the pictures as a source of information about the children's thoughts and feelings in their decision-making.

Dialogue : Children have opinions and can discuss them with adults. When adults give the opinions "due weight", according to the child's age and maturity, then the children are participating in the decision-making process, according to the CRC.

Decision-making : At an older age, young people can make some of their own decisions. For example, under national law adolescents may have the right to get married or to join the army. Even though these choices are usually subject to the approval of parents, the right of adolescents to decide what is in their own best interests shows that participation is a continuum: with an increase in age and maturity comes an increase in control over one's life.

Although the Convention on the Rights of the Child gives individual rights to children, the CRC also emphasizes relationships. The well-being of children and the enjoyment of their rights are dependent upon their families and their community. The CRC recognizes that the family is "the fundamental group of society" and places children's rights in the context of parental rights and duties (arts. 5, 14, 18, etc.). The importance of the community is constantly recognized (arts. 5, 13, 14, 15, 20, 29, 30). Throughout these Guidelines, we stress that one of the best ways to help refugee children is to help their families, and one of the best ways to help families is to help the community. UNHCR's Policy on Refugee Children conveys the same message.

The CRC defines "child" as anyone "below the age of eighteen years unless, under the law applicable to the child, majority is attained earlier" (art. 1). The CRC definition may cause some confusion because it equates child with "minor". The dictionary definition of "child", on the other hand, is a person who has not yet reached puberty, or sexual maturity A person who is no longer a child but not yet an adult is an adolescent, or a young man or young woman.

In advocating "children's rights" in societies where adolescents are performing adult roles of marriage, child-rearing, work or combat, for example, you should be prepared to explain why all persons under 18 should receive the special treatment given them under the CRC. One reason why 18 is the dividing line is because that is the widely accepted age of legal majority, that is, the age a person assumes the legal rights of adults. But there is a more practical reason why adolescents are included under the CRC. Although adolescents may have adult bodies and perform many adult roles, generally speaking they have not fully developed the emotional maturity and judgment, nor achieved the social status, of adults that come with life experience.

In refugee situations, adolescents do need the "special care and assistance" given them by the CRC: they are still developing their identities and learning essential skills. When the refugee situation takes away the structure they need, it can be more difficult for them to adjust than for adults. Their physical maturity but lack of full adult capabilities and status also make them possible targets of exploitation, such as in sexual abuse and military recruitment. In advocating for adolescents it may at times be more useful to focus on their needs in a given situation, rather than the CRC's legal language of "rights of the child," which might be misunderstood unless carefully explained.

All UNHCR staff are encouraged to use the Convention on the Rights of the Child in all aspects of their work, to use the language of children's "rights," and to stress the "triangle of rights" - the "best interests" rule, non- discrimination, and participation. It is good practice to be familiar with the CRC, to know whether the country you are working in has ratified the Convention and whether it has made any reservations, to know whether it has been translated into the languages of that country, and to have ready access to a copy of the Convention.

It is important that you not base your advocacy for CRC standards only on the fact that they are legal rights. Each right has been placed in the Convention on the Rights of the Child because it helps answer a developmental need of children. Successful advocacy reaches out to people's better nature - their natural desire to protect children and their sense of justice - and offers practical solutions to problems. The CRC is not just a legal treaty, it is a moral statement and a practical guide to the welfare of children.

Conservation of Culture and the Right

The conservation of culture and the right to take part in a cultural life are recognized as human rights. Culture provides children with identity and continuity. By learning the values and traditions of their culture, children learn how to fit into their family, community and the larger society. Each society has a unique body of accumulated knowledge, which is reflected in its social and religious beliefs, and ways of interpreting and explaining the world around them.

Culture determines the values held by a social group as well as the rules and controls which ensure that such values are upheld. This includes a society's approach to the raising of its children. Each social group has its particular rules concerning who takes care of children, what they are taught at which age, what is expected of children, how they should be disciplined, and what should be done when things go wrong, such as when children are abused or neglected or their parents are unable to take care of them.

Culture is not static, but is constantly developing and adapting to change. To remain healthy, however, a society must incorporate change gradually to ensure that the various aspects of its culture evolve in a coherent and consistent manner. A refugee movement can disrupt nearly every aspect of a culture. The social upheaval caused by the involuntary movement of individuals, families and communities, can dramatically affect the coherence of their culture. Normal social rules, values and controls begin to break down when the social group which provides the framework for their application disintegrates.

The consequences of this disruption for children, in particular, can be extremely serious. When a society's guiding and regulating mechanisms are lost, individuals find themselves deprived of their normal social, economic and cultural environment. As a consequence, human relationships often suffer. Parental distress and anxiety can seriously disrupt the normal emotional development of their children. Moreover, children often lose their role models in a refugee situation. Under normal circumstances, parents provide the primary role model for their children, contributing significantly to the development of their identities and to their acquisition of skills and values.

Separation from one or other parent, very often the father in circumstances of flight, can deprive children of an important role model. Even when both refugee parents are present, their potential for continuing to provide role models for their children is likely to be hampered by the loss of their normal livelihood and pattern of living. Children's roles also change in refugee situations. If one parent is missing, a child may have to take on adult responsibilities. When a mother has to take over a missing father's productive tasks outside the home, for example, an older daughter may have to substitute for the mother in caring for younger children. As a result, the daughter's developmental needs might be neglected because of overwork, or lack of opportunities for play or to attend school.

The continuity of experience required for normal development may be further undermined for refugee children when they come into contact with different cultures. In many refugee situations, the language, religion and customs of the local population in the country of asylum, as well as that of officials and aid workers may be quite different from those of the refugee community. In such cross-cultural situations, in particular in the context of resettlement, children frequently "lose" their culture much more quickly than adults.

There is a natural tendency for children to try to adapt and conform to a new environment. The mother-tongue is often the first thing to be lost, and with it a vital part of the children's identity. The longer-term impact of such changes will, of course, depend on whether the child and family are temporarily in a country of asylum pending repatriation or are permanently resettled. In either situation, however, a serious consequence is likely to be a growing alienation between child and parent, particularly if the parent is finding difficulty in adjusting to the changed condition and is economically inactive.

Cultural Normalcy

The social and mental well-being of all refugees, but particularly of refugee children, can be most effectively assured by the quick re-establishment of normal community life. Voluntary return to the country of origin is likely to be the easiest way to achieve this. In many refugee situations, however, children and adults alike are obliged to stay for long periods of time in temporary asylum while for others the only solution is resettlement in a third country. Resettlement is dealt with elsewhere in the guidelines, so this section focuses on the important issue of restoring the cultural normalcy of a refugee population remaining for extended periods of time in a country of asylum.

The extent to which cultural normalcy can be restored will depend principally on the degree of fragmentation of the refugee population and on the willingness of the host government to permit refugees to determine their own activities. The following are ways in which the aid worker can assist refugees in re-building a healthy cultural life. Identifying these factors in their particular context is essential for determining programme priorities and anticipating how these factors can affect the outcome of your plans.

Community Development

Community development is an extremely important mechanism for regenerating normal social organization.

Traditional leadership

A refugee population may already include part, if not all, of its traditional leadership. The aid worker can help to strengthen and reinforce traditional leaders by consulting and working through them. Preservation of the refugees' traditional form of social organization enhances not only their well-being but also the effectiveness of assistance efforts.

New leaders

Where a fragmented refugee population lacks traditional leaders, it may be necessary to assist the community in identifying new ones. In this situation it is of critical importance to ensure that the non-traditional leaders given support and credibility by the aid worker have the best interests of their community at heart rather than their own self interest.

Living together

Community re-building or development can be achieved most easily if refugees are able to live in groupings which approximate those in the country of origin. This process can be helped considerably by promoting living arrangements whereby extended families and members of the same village of origin are able to settle close together. Serious problems have arisen in the past by filling up camps or settlement sites on a "first come, first served" basis. On the one hand this is likely to impede the reforming of coherent social groups, and on the other hand it can result in the inappropriate mixing of distinct tribal groups or clans, sometimes with devastating consequences.

People-Oriented Planning

To restore cultural normalcy, the aid worker will have to know the background of the refugees. "The Framework for People-Oriented Planning in Refugee Situations, Taking Account of Women, Men and Children" provides a framework for analyzing who the refugees are and determining factors shaping the context within which refugees conduct their daily lives. These broad interrelated factors may include, inter alia: community norms, social hierarchy, family and community power structures including mechanisms for protection especially for women refugees and for child refugees; economic activity including division of labour according to gender; religious beliefs and practices; demographic considerations; national attitudes towards refugees in both the country of origin and the receiving country; and attitudes of refugees to development/ assistance workers.

Refugee Participation

Refugee participation - or permitting refugees to take back control of their own lives - is fundamental to developing, or re-building, a healthy community. Through participation, refugees can regain influence and control over their lives which, in turn, will have a positive impact on the raising of self-esteem. Consulting refugees on matters such as house construction and layout, food preferences, or requirements to regenerate religious activities, can make a critical difference in the restoration of cultural normalcy. There are many ways in which UNHCR and its implementing partners can seek and encourage refugee participation: through formal representation by traditional or elected leaders; through refugee committees; through informal contacts between refugees and staff, or through the employment of refugees, especially in decision-making positions. In many traditional communities where the leadership tends to be exclusively male, special efforts will be needed to encourage the participation of refugee women, to ensure that all aspects of community life are appropriately addressed.

Language

Maintenance of the mother tongue is a critical factor in retaining identity. Refugee children should be encouraged to use and preserve their own language. If refugee children attend national schools in the country of asylum, and if the language of instruction is different from the mother tongue, special provision may be necessary to enable them to retain, and become literate in, their mother tongue.

Religion and Ritual

A crucial element in regaining cultural normalcy is the renewed practice of religious and ritual activities. The disruption of such practices, so common during a refugee movement, can seriously interfere with the opportunities of refugee children to learn about the physical manifestations of their culture. Religious festivals and rites of passage such as birth, transition into adulthood, marriage and death are extremely important in unifying a community and in conferring identity on its individual members. The importance of such activities to community mental health should not be underestimated. For example, the provision of extra food for communal meals, or other material assistance for funerals (burial cloths, coffins, firewood, etc.) can give vital emotional support and sustain culture through a crisis.

Arts and Recreation

Traditional music, dance and other arts are important representations of culture and permit the communication of its values from one generation to the next. In a refugee situation, it is important to encourage the continued practice and training in such traditional skills as well as the celebration of traditional events and festivals. Such activities play an important role in restoring and maintaining social cohesion. Sports, games and other recreational activities also have an important part to play in building up community spirit as well as providing entertainment and relieving stress.

Avoiding Coercive Practices

The instability and uncertainty which characterizes many refugee populations makes them extremely vulnerable to coercion by agencies and individuals wishing to impose alien religious beliefs. It is extremely important, in choosing operational partners, to make every effort to ascertain how an agency intends to support the culture and religion of the refugee community.

6

Violence Against Children

In Russia, a two-year investigation from 1997 to 1999 found that police violence against children appeared to be widespread, in particular against boys accused of having committed small- scale theft or other petty crimes. According to the Moscow-based Committee for Civil Rights, the frequency of police violence against children increased significantly between 1994 and 1998. The group estimated that about one-third of all children facing criminal proceedings are subjected to violence during the detention and investigation process, and that every fourth child has been subjected to police violence on the street, unrelated to the criminal investigation process, before the age of fifteen.

Fifteen- year-old Oleg F. was taken from his school by police officers to a police station, where he was accused of stealing a jacket from another schoolboy. When he refused to confess, police tortured him. According to his account, police first beat him, kicked him, and dragged him around on the floor. Then they handcuffed him, tied him to a chair, and put a gas mask over his head. They cut the oxygen supply several times for about a minute. Oleg F. said he twice almost lost consciousness.

The Indian police regularly torture children to obtain evidence and confessions. One boy, Shantanu G., was accused of committing a robbery at a wedding. He was arrested eight days later and taken to the station. There, his hands were beaten with a baton for an hour until the complainant came and identified Shantanu G. as the robber. Once identified, Shantanu G. was taken back to the enquiry room, hung from the ceiling, and beaten for about forty- five minutes with police batons on the shoulders, back, and thighs. Following this, he was forced to lie on a block of ice while his legs were held in place by police. The police hit him whenever he tried to move. Then he was taken outside and made to lie in the sun for two hours while police asked him where the stolen property was kept.

Two days later, Shantanu G's. parents were brought in and threatened with beating if he did not confess. He confessed, the property was recovered, and his parents were released. He was held for another ten days, and was tortured so badly that two officers had to hold him up in court when he appeared. He was sent to an adult prison, and then to an observation home when the prison inspector-general discovered his age. Immediately after his release, Shantanu G. spent twenty days in the hospital as a result of the torture he received in police custody and in the observation home.

Violence in Detention

Once placed in police lock-ups or detention facilities, children are frequently subjected to severe corporal punishment, torture, isolation, restraints, sexual assaults, harassment, and humiliation. Negligent practices can also facilitate physical and sexual abuse by other children. Prohibitions against ill-treatment frequently are not enforced, in part because it is the officers of enforcement themselves who perpetrate such violence. Fellow officers rarely report such abuse, and supervisors often fail to investigate reports of ill-treatment. Grievance procedures frequently are ineffective, and children's reports of abuse often are not taken seriously or considered credible.

In the United States, Human Rights Watch found that children in juvenile detention facilities in Georgia were bound to a bed at the wrists and ankles for several hours, often face down, as a form of discipline. A subsequent investigation by the U.S. Department of Justice found that staff persistently used excessive physical force against detainees, hitting or slamming youth onto the ground and into walls. Suicidal detainees were forcibly stripped, shackled to beds or even toilets, and sprayed with chemical pepper spray. In Georgia's "boot camp" programs, where children are sent as an alternative to detention, staff routinely punished children by placing them on the ground and twisting their arms behind their backs, up to the neck, for up to a half hour or more.

In the U.S. state of Colorado, a 1996 Human Rights Watch investigation found that in some juvenile detention facilities, attacks and sexual assaults among residents were described as routine events. None of the children interviewed in one centre said that they felt safe; they described staff members as physically abusive and said that assaults by other residents were unreported or ignored by staff.

In the Baltimore City Detention Centre in the U.S. state of Maryland, guards sometimes allowed youths to fight with each other in what is called the "square dance." The two boys who were going to fight were allowed into a little area about eight feet by eight feet, and everyone else was locked in their cells. Jackson F. described a square dance: There's a lot of yelling from everybody, but if it gets too loud the officers will tell you need to be quiet or they'll break up the dance. It ends up with busted heads, slashes over your eyes, broken fingers, cut lips, maybe a broken nose. But you don't go to the hospital for the cuts. If you did, there'd have to be a report, and the guards would have to explain why two guys were out in the square while everybody else was locked in.

Violence in schools may deprive children of their right to an education on equal terms with their peers. In correctional schools in Kenya, children consistently complained about the use of corporal punishment. They told that they were caned for offenses as minor as having buttons missing from a uniform, not doing homework, making noise, accidentally breaking a window pane, fighting with other children, and "going to the gate of the school." In a borstal facility, one boy said, "everyone who comes on duty canes you when you're in there."

Boys also described public beatings: The boy was stripped naked, and made to bend over a stand, shackled at the hands and ankles. They put a wet salted cloth on his back side, and give him strokes of a young supple bamboo cane. The other boys were assembled around to watch. This punishment was used for things like homosexual acts, or trying to escape, or smoking cigarettes or smoking bhang.

Punishments in the schools routinely included beatings, denial of home vacations, confinement in an "isolator," heavy labor, and reductions in diet. Further, there was no recourse to complaint procedures-one eighteen-year-old girl said "[c]omplaining here is like a voice in the desert"-and children at some schools were severely punished for attempting to speak out about what went on at the school to outsiders. One young boy, who was beaten by teachers so severely that he had to be sent to the hospital for treatment of head injuries, was warned by school staff not to talk to doctors about the reason for his injuries or else he would never be able to leave the Labor Education School. Boys and girls alike may be subject to sexual abuse.

In April 1999, children in the juvenile ward of a Pakistani prison rioted after members of the prison staff beat a thirteen-year-old boy for complaining of sexual abuse by the head warden. A legal aid centre reported that such cases were far from isolated, and that they received many reports of sexual abuse of juveniles by both prison staff and adult inmates.

Julia, a fifteen-year-old Jamaican girl who ran away from home, was picked up by police as a child "in need of care and protection" and taken to the local police station. During her second night in the lockup, she said, a police officer came to her and asked her age. When she told him, he asked if she had ever had sex. She said no and said that he tied her down with a belt, and raped and beat her. In clear violation of the Convention on the Rights of the Child, children who have been taken into police custody are frequently detained with adult offenders. In some cases, children who are charged as adults are automatically detained in adult facilities, in other cases children are held in adult facilities because there is simply not enough room for them in juvenile facilities. In either case, little effort may be made to maintain separation between children and adults, as mandated by international law. As a result, children are exposed to physical and sexual abuse and psychological and developmental harm. In the United States, at least forty states adopted legislation in the 1990s making it easier for children to be tried as adults. One of the immediate results in that increasing numbers of children are detained in adult jails while they await trial and sentenced to adult prisons.

In 1995, sixteen-year-old Rodney Hulin, Jr. was sentenced to eight years for arson, and sent to an adult prison in the U.S. state of Texas. Older inmates immediately started to threaten and harass him; within a week he was raped. Hulin requested protective custody, but was denied. His father testified in 1997: For the next several months, my son was repeatedly beaten by the older inmates, forced to perform oral sex, robbed and beaten again. Each time, his requests for protection were denied by the warden. The abuses, meanwhile, continued. On the night of January 26, 1996-seventy- five days after my son entered Clemens-Rodney attempted suicide by hanging himself in his cell. He could no longer stand to live in continual terror. It was too much for him to handle. He laid in a coma for the next four months until he died.

One seventeen-year-old in a Maryland jail reported that the adult inmates in his section continually harassed him by throwing urine and excrement into his cell. When the guards refused to move him, he told them he was suicidal and was removed to the mental health unit. When he returned to his section, he asked to be housed in an isolation cell because it had a steel door and nothing could be thrown into his cell. In the cell, he said, there "[a]in't nothing in it, just a toilet and a bed. I'm the only person in there. I stay there twenty- four hours a day, only come out Tuesday and Friday for a five-minute shower, then get locked back in." Many children in Guatemala are also incarcerated with adults.

Three boys interview ed by Human Rights Watch had been sent to an adult prison where minors and adults were not separated. One boy said that the "adult prisoners make you take your clothes off, they make you 'trade' your clothes. Otherwise they'll beat you up." According to another boy, "in the adult prisons, you have to pay money to get a place to sleep. Otherwise you sleep on the floor, in the garbage. ... Boys who are put in with the adults are often raped. This is very common. ... The guards don't pay any attention."

Capital Punishment

In the last five years, eleven individuals are known to have been executed for crimes committed when they were under the age of eighteen. Eight of these death sentences were carried out in the United States, the only country in the world that continues to claim the legal authority to execute juvenile offenders. The Democratic Republic of Congo, Iran, and Nigeria each carried out one such execution; each has now expressly renounced the practice, which violates the Convention on the Rights of the Child and the International Covenant on Civil and Political Rights. The U.S. state of Texas has executed four juvenile offenders since 1995. Joseph Cannon and Robert Carter were put to death in 1998; Glen McGinnis and Shaka Sankofa were executed in 2000.

All were seventeen at the time of the crimes for which they received the death penalty. The state of Virginia executed Dwayne Allen Wright in 1998 and Douglas Christopher

Thomas and Stephen Roach in 2000, each seventeen years of age at the time of his crime. The state of Oklahoma carried out the death sentence against Sean Sellers in 1999, the first person in forty years to have been executed in the United States for an offense committed at the age of sixteen. Several other juvenile offenders received last- minute stays of execution after their attorneys presented new evidence or raised constitutional issues on appeal.

On August 15, 2001, Napoleon Beazley, convicted in Texas for a murder he committed at age seventeen, came within hours of execution when the Texas Court of Criminal Appeals issued a stay to enable it to consider whether his first appellate attorney provided ineffective assistance. Missouri death row inmate Antonio Richardson received a stay from the U.S. Supreme Court in March 2001. Sixteen at the time of his crime, Richardson may be mentally retarded; his case is on hold while the Supreme Court resolves another case that questions the constitutionality of imposing the death sentence on persons with mental retardation.

In the Democratic Republic of Congo, a fourteen-year-old child soldier was executed in January 2000 shortly after being sentenced to death by the country's Court of Military Order. Established in 1997 by a presidential decree that was itself of questionable legality, the military court does not safeguard the due process rights of those brought before it. In particular, those convicted by the court have no right to appeal; the second president of the military court told Human Rights Watch in late 1998 that those who are condemned to death may legally be executed immediately following judgment.

In a positive step that followed a meeting with Human Rights Watch in May 2001, the Democratic Republic of Congo agreed to spare the lives of four child soldiers who were arrested and sentenced to death by the Court of Military Order when they were between fourteen and sixteen years of age. Elsewhere in the world, Iran executed a seventeen-year-old in October 1999; Nigeria carried out a death sentence against a seventeen-year-old in July 1997 for a crime committed at the age of fifteen. Pakistan's July 2000 juvenile justice ordinance raised the minimum age at the time of the offense to eighteen for capital punishment to be imposed, three years after its last reported execution of an adolescent offender. China and Yemen banned the execution of juvenile offenders in 1997 and 1994, respectively.

Street children risk violence at the hands of the authorities much more frequently than other children. Children on the street are beaten, tortured, sexually assaulted, and sometimes killed. Several factors contribute to this phenomenon: police perceptions of street children as vagrants and criminals, widespread corruption and a culture of police violence, the inadequacy and nonimplementation of legal safeguards, and the level of impunity that officials enjoy. Street children are easy targets because they are young, often small, poor, ignorant of their rights, and frequently do not have responsible adults to look out for them.

Police also have financial incentives to resort to violence against children. They beat children for their money or demand payment for protection, to avoid false charges, or for release from (often illegal) custody. In Bulgaria, police have harassed and beaten street children, chased them away from areas of safety and shelter, jabbed them with electric shock batons, smeared the glue that the children sniff on their faces and clothing, and sprayed them with gas. Police robbed street children of their money, and sought out girls on the street for sexual harassment. Several adolescent girls in 1996 said that police often requested or demanded oral sex from them; they said some of the girls comply but most run away or scream for attention when they are approached.

The Roma ethnic identity of the majority of street children contributed to their discriminatory treatment by the police and was reflected in one police officer's response to being asked why street children ran away when he approached. He answered, "first, most of those kids are not Bulgarians, they're

Roma." Thousands of children living in Guatemala's streets have faced routine beatings, thefts and sexual assaults at the hands of the National Police and private security guards. During a 1996 Human Rights Watch investigation, nearly every child spoke with of habitual assaults and thefts by the police. These assaults occurred on busy city streets in broad daylight, on quiet streets in the middle of the night, in alleys and deserted areas, and in police stations. Often, they were witnessed by passersby or other police officers.

A youth who spent nine years on the street told that The police bother us every single day. They hit us and steal our money, our shoes, our jackets. If you don't give them what they want, they'll beat you up or arrest you . . . .We can't say anything, or they'll hit us harder.

Girls on the street are additionally vulnerable to sexual attacks. Susana F., a sixteen- year old, reported that she was raped by two police officers while a third kept watch. The officers threatened to put her in prison for having marijuana if she made any noise. "I'm sure this has happened to many other girls. But usually they won't say anything about it. . . .Ugly things happen on the street." Guatemalan street children have also been killed in extrajudicial executions. In September 1996, sixteen- year-old Ronald Raúl Ramos was shot and killed by a drunken Treasury Police officer. More than ten other street children in Guatemala were murdered that year under suspicious circumstances, yet by April of the following year, all of the perpetrators were still at large.

In India, where more than 18 million children live and work on the streets, street children have been routinely detained illegally, beaten, and tortured and sometimes killed by police. In 1995 and 1996, Human Rights Watch interviewed one hundred street children; all reported a fear of the police, and sixty reported police abuse in the form of detentions, beatings, extortion, or verbal abuse. Fifteen- year-old Rakesh P., a porter in India, told of being awoken by police on a railway platform and taken with three other boys to the police station. At the station, Rakesh P. was made to lie on his back with his arms outstretched. A policeman stood on each of his hands, then his legs were tied and placed in the air. He said that this happened to all four boys.

Another policeman started to beat their legs and feet with lathis while the police called them thieves and sons of prostitutes. Rakesh P. said he was beaten for a long time and so badly that his legs and feet bled. The next morning the police sent the other children to observation homes, but they did not send Rakesh P. because they had injured him so badly they did not want a magistrate to see him. Instead he was carried to the street by two strangers. He was not charged with any offense. Rakesh P. had to walk with a cane for eight weeks because of the injuries he sustained.

The scale of violence against street children in India sometimes included custodial deaths of children. Between 1986 and 1995, fourteen children are known to have died in custody in Andhra Pradesh province, but no police officers were prosecuted in that period. Street children in Kenya experience similar abuse at the hands of police. Children told Human Rights Watch in 1996 that they were frequently kicked, slapped, or hit with a rifle butt for no reason other than the fact that they were street children. Street children were often subject to extortion, and street girls were asked for sex in addition to money to avoid arrest or to be released from police custody.

In 1996, eighteen months after the acquittal of one Kenyan police reservist for killing a street boy, another street boy was killed by a police reservist. Children present at the shooting could identify the police officers who came toward them with a whip and guns. Two boys had hidden in a ditch. One of them escaped through a tunnel, but the policeman pointed into the ditch and shot the other. The boy who escaped told Human Rights Watch that his friend was shot at point blank range, that he had his arms raised in surrender when he was shot, and that the reservist spat on his body before he walked away.

Violence in the Schools

Many children around the world experience violence as a regular part of their school experience. Instead of facilitating the healthy development of children, schools are too often the source of violence and abuse that undermine children's opportunities to learn, cause children to drop out of school altogether, or cause psychological trauma, physical injury, disability, and even death. In the past two years, Human Rights Watch has conducted three investigations into violence against children in schools, examining the use of corporal punishment in Kenya, harassment and violence against gay, lesbian, bisexual, and transgender students in the United States, and sexual violence against schoolgirls in South Africa.

In the United States, children were often victimized because of their sexual orientation or gender identity. Lesbian, gay, bisexual, and transgender youth who attend public schools were relentlessly harassed and sometimes physically attacked. They were beaten, kicked, spit on, cut with knives, strangled, thrown against lockers, and dragged down flights of stairs. Girls are also at particular risk. In South African schools, the reports showing that rape, assault, and sexual harassment of girls was widespread and committed by both teachers and male students. Girls were raped in school toilets, in empty classrooms and hallways, and in hostels and dormitories. They were frequently fondled, subjected to aggressive sexual advances, and verbally degraded.

In some countries, including South Africa, schoolgirls may also be subjected to virginity examinations. Such examinations were recently reinstituted for girls studying in government medical high schools in Turkey. A July 2001 decree allowed tests on girls "known to be having sex or engaging in prostitution." Those girls who fail the virginity examinations are to be expelled from school. The examinations, banned since 1999, involve intimidation and pain and violate girls' right to bodily integrity. In the past, girls have attempted suicide rather than submit to this abusive examination.

In addition to the specific acts of violence that they endure, children are also victimized by the routine failure of teachers and school authorities to act effectively to prevent violence and abuse or to respond adequately when it occurs. Rather than punish perpetrators, school authorities frequently choose inaction or compound the problem by encouraging the victim to move to another school. The results of school violence can be devastating. Children may become depressed and anxious and have difficulty concentrating on their studies. They may use alcohol or other drugs or engage in risky sexual behaviours as a way of dealing with stress. Many skip classes while others change schools or drop out altogether. Some commit suicide.

Corporal Punishment

In school one girl was slapped so hard that two of her teeth came out. The teacher was very angry because some of the girls failed a test, and so the teacher gave these girls a choice: three slaps from his hand or ten strokes with his cane. This girl chose the three slaps and so he hit her on her face three times, very hard, and her mouth was bloody and her two teeth came out. In at least sixty- five countries, corporal punishment is permitted as a method of school discipline. Children may be spanked, slapped, caned, strapped, or beaten by teachers as a result of misbehaviour, poor academic performance, or sometimes for no reason at all. In 1999 Human Rights Watch investigated the use of corporal punishment in Kenyan schools, visiting twenty different schools and interviewing more than 200 children.

Kenyan children were commonly hit with a wooden cane, though they were also subject to flogging with whips made of rubber, slapping, kicking, or pinching. Boys were commonly hit on the buttocks, while girls were hit on the palms of their hands. Children were also beaten on the back, the arms, the legs, the soles of the feet, and even the face and head. Children received anywhere from two to twenty or more cane strokes at one time. At some schools, caning happened only once or twice a week, while in others, children reported that they and others were caned on and off throughout the day, nearly every day, routinely receiving five or more strokes each time.

Corporal punishment was widely used to punish unsatisfactory academic performance. In Kenyan classes, for example, it was not uncommon for teachers to strike children for giving the wrong answer to a problem. If a school did not perform well on national exams, an entire class might be caned regardless of the individual performance of each student. Children were also caned for not being able to afford school fees.

One child who dropped out of school because he could not afford schools fees said: If you couldn't pay fees, you would be caned six times, and sent home to bring the money from your parents. You would go home, and there is no money, and then you would go back to school because you still want to learn, and you would be caned again. Bruises, swelling, and cuts have been regular by-products of school punishment in Kenya. More serious injuries, including broken bones, temporary or permanent hearing loss, knockedout teeth, or internal injuries were not infrequent.

In the most extreme cases, children have died as a result of corporal punishment; several such deaths were reported in the Kenyan press over the past several years. In the few cases that led to prosecutions, the teachers were acquitted because they had not known that the child suffered from a preexisting medical condition which made the child particularly vulnerable to injury. Post- mortem results for one child, who died in 1996 after being caned by three teachers, showed that the child had a heart condition. This condition-rather than the beating-was found to be the cause of death and the case against the teachers involved was dismissed.

Many severe beatings have never been reported to authorities, as children and parents fear retaliation from teachers and headteachers. Human Rights Watch received numerous reports of serious retaliation against people who challenged severe corporal punishment. According to many interviewees, complaints from parents about excessive punishment could lead to more severe punishments in the future for the child, or punishment of the child's siblings or cousins.

In April 2001, Kenya's Minister of Education formally banned corporal punishment in the schools as a matter of policy and proposed to Parliament the elimination of the sections of the Education Act of 1968 that provided for corporal punishment and its implementation. Human Rights Watch welcomes this positive development but remains concerned that the official notice did not provide penalties for teachers who continue to carry out corporal punishment and that there has been no plan to provide teachers with training in alternative methods of discipline. Many teachers continue to express strong disagreement with the ban, illustrating the need for widespread in-service training and education for teachers on the harmful effects of corporal punishment and effective alternative methods for maintaining classroom discipline.

Girls constitute nearly two-thirds of the 130 million children out of school in the developing world, according to estimates by the United Nations Children's Fund in 1998. While much attention has been directed towards this gender gap and barriers girls face in getting to school, the obstacles girls encounter at school also merit serious consideration-gender-based violence chief among them. It is no surprise that girls, much more frequently than boys, are raped, sexually assaulted, abused, and sexually harassed by their classmates and even by their teachers.

In 2000, Human Rights Watch investigated the phenomenon of gender-based violence in the schools of South

Africa. Based on interviews with dozens of students, teachers, and government officials, Human Rights Watch found that on a daily basis, South African schoolgirls of every race and economic group encounter sexual violence and harassment. Girls were raped in school toilets, in empty classrooms and hallways, and in hostels and dormitories. Girls were also fondled, subjected to aggressive sexual advances, and verbally degraded at school.

A thirteen- year-old girl in Johannesburg did leave school, not because she wanted to abandon her education but because she was gang raped by male classmates and felt unsafe at school while the boys remained there. "I left school because I was raped," she said, "My mom asked me if I wanted to go back to school. I said no." A medical research study found that among those South African rape victims who specified their relationship to the perpetrator, 37.7 percent said their schoolteacher or principal had raped them. Girls interviewed by Human Rights Watch reported routine sexual harassment by teachers, as well as psychological coercion to engage in "dating relationships."

In some cases, girls acquiesced to sexual demands from teachers because of fears that they would be physically punished if they refused. In other cases, teachers abuse their position of authority by promising better grades or money in exchange for sex. In the worst cases, teachers operated within a climate of seeming entitlement to sexual favours from students. One fifteen- year-old girl spent weeks away from school because she was scared of the teacher who had sexually assaulted her. She said, "I didn't go back to school for one month after... everything reminds me of what happened. I have dreams. He is in my dreams. He is in the classroom laughing at me. I can hear him laughing at me in my dreams."

The trauma associated with the assault that caused the girl to miss so much school has cost her academically: "My grades are horrible," she told Human Rights Watch. Many girls interrupted their schooling or left school altogether because they felt unsafe in such a violent environment. Most girls, however, remained at school and suffered in silence, having learned a lesson that sexual violence at school was inevitable and inescapable. Interviews with girls subjected to sexual attacks, their parents, teachers, and social workers showed that these girls were not performing up to full potential, were losing interest in outside activities, and were failing their higher education matriculation exams.

Too often, school authorities concealed sexual violence and delayed disciplinary action against perpetrators of violence. Schools responded with hostility and indifference to girls who complained about sexual violence and harassment. Girls described a persistent response pattern whereby schools discounted or failed to take seriously their reports of sexual violence and harassment. Sometimes school officials appear to have failed to respond adequately because they simply did not know what to do; other times they ignored the problem; still other times they appeared to have been afraid to assist. In many instances, schools actively discouraged victims of school-based sexual violence from alerting anyone outside the school or accessing the justice system.

At several South African schools, school administrators not only failed to prosecute perpetrators, they even refused to cooperate with official investigators. A prosecutor told Human Rights Watch that in her experience schools could not be relied upon to assist with investigations, particularly where a school employee was the accused perpetrator. While the South African government has pub licly recognized the problems of its criminal justice system in prosecuting violence against women and girls, Human Rights Watch found that coordination between the education and justice systems on investigating cases of sexual violence was often ineffective, ill-conceived, or nonexistent. Human Rights Watch found a great deal of confusion over responsibility for resolving problems and repeatedly encountered breaks in the chain of communication between school officials, police, and prosecutors, with all actors shifting responsibility and sexually abused girls getting lost in the shuffle.

Acts of sexual violence and violence against girls at school that remain unchallenged by school officials exact a terrible cost to educational quality and equality in South Africa in addition to violating girls' rights to bodily integrity. A school environment where sexual violence and harassment is tolerated compromises the right of girls to enjoy education on equal terms with boys-a lesson that is damaging to all children.

Harassment and Discrimination

A 2001 Human Rights Watch report found that lesbian, gay, bisexual, and transgender youth in many U.S. schools are subjected to unrelenting harassment from their peers. Despite the pervasiveness of the abuse, few school officials intervene to stop the harassment or to hold the abusive students accountable. Over time, verbal harassment may escalate into sexual harassment and other forms of physical violence. These violations are compounded by the failure of federal, state, and local governments to enact laws that would provide students with express protection from discrimination based on their actual or perceived sexual orientation or gender identity. Such abuses are not limited to the United States.

Researchers studying lesbian, gay, bisexual, and transgender youth in Australia, Canada, France, New Zealand, and the United Kingdom, among other countries, have reached similar conclusions about the pervasiveness of antigay violence in schools. The Europe Region of the International Lesbian and Gay Association concludes that teachers and other adults are "more likely to reject than support" gay and lesbian youth. Amnesty International reports that gay youth elsewhere in the world suffer torture and ill- treatment because of their sexual orientation or gender identity. Harassment and violence against lesbian, gay, bisexual, and transgender youth takes many forms, including taunts, obscene notes or graffiti, the destruction of personal property, unwelcome sexual advances, mock rapes, and brutal physical attacks.

Lesbian, gay, and bisexual youth were nearly three times as likely as their peers to have been involved in at least one physical fight at school, three times as likely to have been threatened or injured with a weapon at school, and nearly four times as likely to skip school because they felt unsafe, according to a 1999 survey of youth risk behaviours administered to Massachusetts students. Discrimination, harassment, and violence hamper students' ability to get an education and take a tremendous toll on their emotional well-being. Perhaps because so many lesbian, gay, bisexual, and transgender youth experience abuses on a daily basis, these youth are more likely than their heterosexual peers to use alcohol or other drugs, engage in risky sexual behaviours, or run away from home.

A disproportionate number of lesbian, gay, bisexual, and transgender youth attempt or consider suicide-youth who report attractions to or relationships with persons of the same sex were more than twice as likely as their heterosexual counterparts to attempt suicide, a 1998 study found. The abuse of lesbian, gay, bisexual, and transgender youth is frequently predicated on the belief that girls and boys must adhere strictly to rigid rules of conduct, dress, and appearances based on their sex. That is, homophobia is linked to stereotypical gender roles. Boys are expected to be athletic, strong, stoic, and dominant relative to girls. Girls are expected to be attentive to boys and to accept a subordinate status to them. Regardless of their sexual orientation or gender identity, youth who violate these rules run the risk of punishment at the hands of their peers and at times by adults. Transgender youth are the most vulnerable to violence by peers and harassment by adults.

Discussions of antigay violence in schools often focus on the youthful perpetrators of these acts and fail to consider the responsibility of teachers and other school officials to maintain a safe learning environment for all youth. Even more disturbing were the accounts heard of teachers and administrators who actually took part in acts of harassment. "It's one thing to talk about being gay in a negative sense," a Massachusetts girl stated. "It's another thing to see an adult, a person you respect, talking negatively. Once you see a role model degrading you, it tears you apart." Even teachers who were themselves lesbian, gay, bisexual, or transgender admitted to us that they did not always stand up for students who were being harassed.

Nevertheless, the help of teachers and other adults is critical in ensuring that students are safe in their schools and able to enjoy their right to an education. In virtually every case where lesbian, gay, bisexual, and transgender youth reported to Human Rights Watch that their school experience was positive, they attributed that fact to the presence of supportive teachers. Schools also play an important role in securing the rights of youth to free association and expression, particularly the freedom to seek, receive, and impart information. This right includes the right to have access to information about sexual orientation and gender identity. Many lesbian, gay, bisexual, transgender, and heterosexual students in the United States have formed school clubs, often known as "gay-straight alliances," to provide each other with peer support, seek information about issues related to sexual orientation and gender identity, and ensure that schools respect their rights.

Despite the benefits of such student groups, many of the youth interviewed had to overcome opposition from school administrators, their local school boards, and their communities before they could start gay-straight alliances at their schools. Failing to protect gay youth ultimately harms all youth. When adults fail to teach respect for all youth, and indeed for all human beings, they send a message that it is acceptable to demean, attack, and discriminate against others because they are different or are perceived to be different. This is a message that can only hurt its recipients.

Violence in the Workplace

Violence of any type may have serious mental health consequences and infringe on the right of children to the enjoyment of the highest attainable standard of health and development. The obligation to protect requires more than having laws on the books. When children are subjected to abuse and other forms of violence, the Convention on the Rights of the Child requires the state to "promote [their] physical and psychological recovery" in a setting that "fosters [their] health, peer-respect, and dignity."

The International Labor Organization estimates that 250 million children between the ages of five and fourteen work in developing countries- at least 120 million full time. Children are often expected to work long hours that keep them out of school, and subjected to gruelling conditions and health and other hazards. In addition, many children are also subjected to beatings or other forms of violence by their employers or supervisors.

In the cotton fields of Egypt, where over a million children work each year to remove pests that damage the crops, physical abuse by foremen is routine. Children typically gauged the leniency of a foreman by the severity and frequency of the beatings that he administered. One ten-year-old boy worked under two foremen. "One of them I hate; the other one I like," he told Human Rights Watch in late 1999. "The one I hate used to beat and kick me whenever I missed a leaf. The other one beats and kicks me lightly."

Severe maltreatment caused some children to quit work entirely or seek employment under the supervision of a different foreman. A nine- year-old Egyptian girl described a steady process of attrition from her work group. "The last group I was in started with twenty-two [children]," she said, "but you know, children don't like to be hit, so they turn up in another foreman's group. Our group ended up with twelve."

In India, an estimated 15 million children are bonded labourers, working in conditions of servitude in order to pay off debts incurred by their family. Most work in the agricultural sector, while others work in domestic servitude, prostitution, or the production of silk, beedi, handwoven carpets, jewelry, leather and other products. During an investigation in late 1995 and early 1996, Human Rights Watch found that bonded child labourers were frequently punished for arriving late, working slowly, making a mistake in the work, talking to other workers, or even missing work because of illness.

With very few exceptions, the beedi rollers interviewed all complained of being beaten. A ten-year-old bonded beedi roller told us: The agent would beat me with a stick if I was not there on time, he beat me if I could not roll 1,500 beedies a day, and he beat me if I was tired. I had to roll eight beedies a minute. If I failed he would beat me. If I looked around, he beat me. He made me put a matchbox under my chin; if it fell, he beat me.

Girls were subjected to sexual abuse, and those working inside Indian factories were frequently targeted for sexual assault by the factory owners. The practice was so prevalent that it was difficult for these girls later to get married. Because of the high rate of abuse, everyone assumed that the factory girls had been "touched," that is, molested or raped by their employers. As a consequence, they were shunned as potential brides.

In Kenya, a study of girls working as housemaids found that of twenty- five girls aged nine to sixteen years who were interviewed in depth, eighteen were HIV-positive. Of those eighteen, most had worked in several homes and reported being sexually abused in all or most of them. Fifteen of the girls said their first sexual experiences were coerced and were with their employer or someone in his family or circle of friends. Kenya is estimated to have about 1 million children who have lost parents to AIDS and many more whose parents are ill with the disease.

In Kenya and many other African countries, these AIDS-affected children are likely to have to leave school and seek work, and they may wind up on the streets or in jobs that put them at risk of violence. In Sri Lanka, Human Rights Watch spoke to about seventy children during a 1998 investigation of the treatment of child domestic workers. Almost all of the children reported being punished by their employer for being "naughty," for being careless, or for not completing assigned tasks. The punishment ranged from deprivation of privileges, to smacking, and beatings with a cane or stick.

Several children had been deliberately burnt. Some of the children had been badly injured during these "punishment" sessions and many had scars caused by beatings. Several of the Sri Lankan girls interviewed also experienced sexual abuse at the hands of their employer, their employer's children, or their employer's friends. Such abuse is frequently known to agents who arrange for the children's employment. One agent told of how he had recruited over a thousand children for domestic service when he knew that the primary purpose of the recruitment was sexual.

In Ecuador, where Human Rights Watch interviewed forty- five children who had worked on banana plantations in early 2001, that girls working in banana packing plants routinely experience sexual harassment in the workplace. "He goes around touching girls' bottoms. . . . I was taking off banana plastic coverings, and he touched my bottom. He keeps bothering me," one twelve-year-old girl said, speaking of one of her supervisors. "He gave my cousin the nickname 'whore.'" Another twelve- year-old girl told us, the boss of the packing plants makes lewd remarks "when we bend down to pick up plastic bags."

In Burma, the government has forced millions of people, including many children as young as twelve years old, to work without pay on the construction of roads, railways, and bridges. Many of these forced labourers have died from beatings, exhaustion and lack of medical care. In 1996, Human

Rights Watch witnessed a group of schoolchildren being forced to clear streets of small rocks. One of the children, a young boy about twelve years of age, was kicked in the face by a soldier when he temporarily stopped working.

Orphanages

In some countries, children are abandoned at alarming rates, due to poverty, restrictive population control policies, and cultural traditions that value boys more than girls. Prejudice or policies against children with disabilities may lead parents to institutionalize children who are disabled or perceived to have disabilities. Once institutionalized, orphans and abandoned children may experience such extreme neglect or abuse that their lives may be endangered. They may be denied interaction, stimulation, medical care, and education and frequently learn to live in fear of the people who are their only providers of care.

In Russia in the 1990's, children were abandoned to the state at a rate of more than 100,000 per year. Many were placed in orphanages, where they were exposed to appalling levels of cruelty and neglect. They were often beaten, locked in freezing rooms for days at a time, or sexually abused, and were often subjected to degrading treatment by staff. Found in a 1998 investigation that Russian babies who were classified as disabled were segregated into separate rooms where they were changed and fed, but were bereft of stimulation and lacking in medical care. Confined to cribs, they stared at the ceiling and were not encouraged to walk or talk. At age four, these and other children who are labelled retarded or "oligophrenic" were sent to locked and isolated "psycho- neurological internats."

One child welfare advocate estimated that the death rate in internaty was twice the rate in the general population. Similar findings were made in other parts of the former Soviet Union. A 1996 national statistic from Ukraine indicated that "approximately thirty percent of all severely disabled children in special homes - a staggering figure - die before they reach eighteen." Children deemed "educable" and who passed a test at age four were sent to a dyetskii dom, or children's home. While conditions in these standard orphanages were better than in the internats, children were also subject to abuse, neglect, and gratuitous cruelty. In some cases, adult staff members, with the informal consent of the orphanage director, struck and humiliated children. In other instances, the adults engaged other orphans with them to punish a child "collectively."

One student recalled that one teacher would grab a student, strip off his or her clothes, and force the student to crawl on all fours in front of everyone. "Then the rest of us children had to kick the child and sit on him like a horse - to humiliate him. The kids push and kick and pull hair and ride him like an animal. The teacher was an active sadist." This pattern was particularly insidious because the favoured children developed a repertoire of vicious and injurious punishments which the older, stronger orphans inflicted upon the younger or weaker ones. Some of the punishments included forcing a smaller child into a small wooden clothes chest and throwing him out the window; "in the wind," where smaller children were held upside down outside a window; and "velociped".

A 1996 report by Human Rights Watch on China's state orphanages found a horrifying pattern of cruelty, abuse and malign neglect. The most recent nationwide figures available at the time showed that the majority of abandoned children admitted to China's orphanages were dying in institutional care, with mortality rates in some institutions exceeding 75 percent. In China's best-known and most prestigious orphanage, the Shanghai Children's Welfare Institute, the majority of infants brought to the Institute before 1993 died within a few months of arrival. Between 1986 and 1992 alone, the brutal treatment of orphans in Shanghai, which included deliberate starvation, torture, and sexual assault, led to the unnatural deaths of well over 1,000 children.

Medical records and testimony obtained by Human Rights Watch from official inquiries that had been suppressed showed that deaths at the Shanghai orphanage were in many cases deliberate and cruel. Child-care workers reportedly selected unwanted infants and children for death by intentional deprivation of food and water-a process known among the workers as the "summary resolution" of children's alleged medical problems. When an orphan chosen in this manner was visibly on the point of death from starvation or medical neglect, orphanage doctors were then asked to perform medical "consultations" which served as a ritual marking the child for subsequent termination of care, nutrition, and other life-saving intervention.

Deaths from acute malnutrition were then, in many cases, falsely recorded as having resulted from other causes, often entirely spurious or irrelevant conditions such as "mental deficiency" and "cleft palate." At the Shanghai orphanage older children in particular were subject to many forms of cruel and degrading treatment, including beatings and torture at the hands of orphanage employees. A number of girls also reported that they had been raped or sexually assaulted by various men on the orphanage staff, including the orphanage director. One six- year-old girl suffered brutal abuse by a senior staff member over a period of over twenty-four hours. After stealing several pieces of candy, the girl was beaten by the staff member with a plastic shoe and wooden mop handle.

The staff member tied the girl's wrists to the metal frame of a high window, forcing her to stand on tiptoe, and then began pummelling the girl with her fists. The girl was left hanging from the window for the remainder of the day. Once she was finally taken down, she was not allowed to sleep, but was kept tied in a standing position throughout the night. The following morning, she was beaten again. In another instance, a fifteen-year-old boy was knocked to the ground and beaten for some ninety minutes by the orphanage director, and then locked inside a shed for four days with little food.

Although the beating was witnessed by a number of other orphans as well as staff, the director later forced staff members to deny that the incident had taken place. One who refused to do so was demoted as a result. Brutal punishments were often inflicted for relatively minor disciplinary infractions, or simply on the whim of child-care workers. These included:

— forcing children to assume the "airplane" and "motorcycle" positions for long periods of time . In some cases, children were also forced to balance bowls of hot water on their wrists, heads, or knees or to squat over bowls of boiling water, so that scalding occurred when the child fell;

— forcing children to kneel on ridged washboards for long periods of time;

— hanging children upside down with their heads submerged in water, until nosebleeds and near-suffocation ensued. This technique, known as qiang shui, was reportedly the one most feared by children.

Children in Armed Conflict

In conflict situations, children are the frequent targets of brutal, indiscriminate acts of violence. In an oft-repeated statistic, UNICEF estimates that during a recent ten-year period, two million children died as a direct result of armed conflict, and an additional six million were injured or disabled. In Sierra Leone, children have been murdered, mutilated, tortured, beaten, raped, and enslaved for sexual purposes. Some of the atrocities committed by the rebel Revolutionary United Front (RUF) were unthinkable. Infants and children were thrown into burning houses, the hands of toddlers as young as two were severed with machetes, and girls as young as eight were sexually abused.

Medical records from one hospital showed that out of 265 war wounded admitted during a three-month period in 1998, approximately one-quarter were children. During a nine-day period in February of that year, 111 children died during rebel attacks in the Bo area, according to reports from humanitarian agencies. Rape and sexual assault of girls are common in armed conflicts. A newspaper reporter in Sierra Leone told Human Rights Watch. "There was rampant raping. I saw a fifteen-year-old girl raped right before me. They left her, but they captured others, and among them was a sevenyear-old girl." Pro-government militias in Sierra Leone, like the Kamajors have also committed atrocities against civilians. Over twenty civilians were killed by militias, including nine children, in four attacks documented by Human Rights Watch in June and July 2001. Some nineteen more civilians, including eleven children, were wounded.

Child Soldiers

Human Rights Watch has documented the recruitment of children as soldiers in armed conflicts in Burma, Colombia, the Democratic Republic of Congo, Lebanon, Sierra Leone, and Uganda. The use of children as soldiers places their lives and well-being at great risk. They may use high-caliber weapons at the front lines of combat, lay explosives and serve as human mine detectors, participate in suicide missions and commit atrocities. They may risk attack while carrying supplies or collecting intelligence. Apart from the inherent risks of combat, child soldiers are also frequently subjected to sexual abuse and other forms of brutal treatment by fellow soldiers or their commanders.

In Uganda, the rebel Lord's Resistance Army (LRA) has abducted thousands of children to fight against the government of Uganda and the Sudan People's Liberation Army. The rebels prefer children of fourteen to sixteen, but have also taken children as young as eight or nine. They tie the children to one another, and force them to carry heavy loads of looted goods as they march them off into the bush. Children who protect or resist are killed. Children who cannot keep up or become tired or ill are killed. Children who attempt to escape are killed. Their deaths are not quick- a child killed by a single rebel bullet is rare. If a child attempts to escape, the rebels force the other abducted children to kill the would-be escapee, usually with clubs or machetes. Any child who refuses to participate in the killing may also be beaten or killed.

In 1997, Human Rights Watch interviewed dozens of children who had escaped from the LRA. Fourteen-year-old Thomas C. told us: I saw quite a number of children killed. Most of them were killed with clubs. They would take five or six of the newly abducted children and make them kill those who had fallen or tried to escape. It was so painful to watch. Twice I had to help. And to do it, it was so bad, it was very bad to have to do.

In the Democratic Republic of Congo, thousands of children have been recruited by government forces, pro-government militias, and rebel forces. A 2001 Human Rights Watch report on the recruitment of children by the Rwandan-backed Congolese Rally for Democracy-Goma (RCD-Goma) found that children were beaten, ill-treated, and used as cannon- fodder.

A former recruiter for the RCD-Goma told that they were trained on how to use arms and how to shoot, and that was the end of it. Some of the kids were even sent to battle without arms. . . . They were ordered to make a lot of noise, using sticks on tree trunks and the like. When they succeeded in diverting the attention of government troops, that is to say when they drew government fire on their unarmed elements, these units, known as the Kadogo Commando, would be literally allowed to fall like flies under government fire. The experienced troops would then attack the government troops when their attention was diverted to the Kadogo Commando.

Thousands of children have also been recruited by the Rally for Democracy-Liberation Movement (Rassemblement

Congolais pour la Démocratie-Mouvement de Libération (RCDML) with the assistance of the Uganda army. In 2000, Human Rights Watch found that recruiters for the RCD-ML would routinely tour villages on recruitment missions lasting several days to a week. Teams typically returned from these missions with a truckload of 100 to 200 children and youth, aged 13 to 18. Ugandan army instructors would then provide three to six months of infantry and weapons training at Nyaluke camp. According to one news agency, conditions at Nyaluke were deplorable: "living conditions are terrible, and many children die before completing the training, due to abuse and lack of health assistance."

In Burma, unknown thousands of children have been forcibly recruited by the Burmese Army. These children are used as porters, guards, and combatants. A 1996 Human Rights Watch report found that some porters were extrajudicially executed or accidentally killed, and all were subjected to cruel, inhuman, and degrading treatment. Interviewed one fifteen-year-old boy who was beaten when he could not carry his load. His father said he was lucky to be alive. Children used as guards are also beaten if they fell asleep during duty, or left their posts even briefly.

One former Burmese soldier told Human Rights Watch he was recruited at age fifteen. At the military training school where he was sent there were five hundred other recruits, none older than himself. He described the brutal and brutalizing treatment he and all the recruits experienced in this training camp, which included beatings, sleep deprivation, and starvation. Several boys who joined the army at age thirteen toldof being sent to front- line action after just one year of training - when they were still only fourteen years old. In Colombia, thousands of children have been recruited into guerrilla forces and progovernment, military backed paramilitaries.

In late 2000, independent observers reported to Human Rights Watch that dozens of children were among the guerrillas registered as killed or captured after an encounter between government troops and the FARC-EP. The Colombian Army announced that thirty-two of those captured were aged seventeen or under, including several younger than fourteen, and a third were females. Of those killed, twenty were said by the army to be children. Thousands of children have been killed during the Colombian conflict. Children who escape the guerrillas are considered deserters and can be subjected to on-the-spot execution. If guerrillas believe a child has given information to the Colombian security forces, the punishment is death.

Even children who have been captured by the authorities, convicted, and placed in juvenile detention centers are at risk of being killed. Between 1994 and 1996, the Public Advocate's Office found, 13 percent of the children convicted of belonging to guerrilla groups and imprisoned were killed while in custody, apparently by other child guerrillas in the same facilities.

Impunity

Human Rights Watch has found that acts of violence against children are ignored or covered up. Incidents are rarely investigated and perpetrators even less often punished. Many perpetrators enjoy impunity for their actions and go on to abuse other children. The result is that many children are victimized not only by the initial abuse, but also by the failure of authorities to take effective action against the perpetrator or by acts of retaliation in response to their attempts to seek justice. For street children who suffer police violence, reporting is seriously hampered by the fact that children must complain directly to the police about police abuse.

The threat of repercussions by police is a serious deterrent to any child coming forward to make complaints or testify. Thus, the majority of cases of police abuse of street children go undetected and unreported. The cases that are reported are often only superficially investigated. One Kenyan boy, who witnessed a police reservist shoot and kill another street child in 1996, told Human Rights Watch that police investigating the incident never interviewed any of the other street children present. Although an inquest file was opened, the reservist was never charged. One child said, "The afande is still around. He still comes after us and tries to beat us."

Two years earlier, another Kenyan reservist shot and killed a fifteen-year-old street boy at close range less than two months after having shot and killed five other street boys. The reservist admitted to the shootings but claimed he had acted in self-defence. A judge found insufficient evidence that the most recent victim was armed, but acquitted the defendant, saying that the boy "was killed in the course of arrest after having committed a crime." Street children interviewed after the ruling said that it signaled to police that they could shoot street children at any time and claim that children were stealing as justification for their conduct. In Guatemala, the rape of sixteen- year-old Susana F. by police officers, also illustrates the failure of police to investigate properly attacks against children.

Children in institutions also face formidable challenges to reporting violence. Children are frequently not told of mechanisms for reporting abuse, if they exist. Reprisals are a frequent concern. One boy in a detention facility said that boys could complain to the prison inspector, but that boys were afraid to do so because "once the inspector's gone, they'll beat you again, so you don't bother to complain."

Children who were caught attempting to send letters of complaint to outsiders were confined in the "isolator" for ten days, according to one Bulgarian NGO. One boy who was beaten by teachers so severely that he had to be sent to the hospital for treatment of head injuries was warned by staff not to discuss the reason for his injuries with doctors or else he would never be able to leave the school. In South Africa, schoolgirls who reported sexual abuse by their male classmates or teachers were treated by school officials with indifference, disbelief, and hostility. Repeatedly, parents in South Africa told Human Rights Watch that schools asked them not to get the police involved or draw publicity to problems of sexual violence at school.

In one instance, a school principal persuaded a parent to drop rape charges against a teacher, promising "to take care of the matter." Nothing was done, and the teacher continued to teach at the school. In another instance, it was found that a teacher accused of raping a student had been reported at other schools for similar offenses. None of the schools reported him to the police, leaving him free to continue his pattern of abuse in new schools and against additional children. In Kenyan schools, teachers who have injured children through caning or whipping are rarely disciplined, let alone dismissed or prosecuted. In some cases, parents press charges against abusers.

However, in almost every case known to Human Rights Watch, teachers have either been acquitted, the cases have been dismissed, or teachers have been convicted but handed extremely light penalties-generally just a small fine. Most continued to have children in their care, teaching in the same schools in which they previously abused children. Many Kenyan children have been reluctant to report corporal punishment for fear of reprisals. A twelve- year-old girl told us, "Even if you have been beaten unfairly and your parents are angry at the teacher, it is better for them not to complain, because if they complain, the teacher may then form a grudge against you and then you will suffer more." Another child said that if a child "reported badly to the parent, sometimes the teachers will be angry and cane more strokes."

In the United States, numerous accounts of teachers and administrators who refused to act to protect lesbian, gay, bisexual and transgender students from harassment out of the belief that they get what they deserve. The director of a Houston group for lesbian, gay, bisexual, and transgender youth described a case involving a boy who openly identified as gay at school. "The harassment began to get physical," she told us. " The assistant principal told him that if he didn't walk around telling people he's gay, there wouldn't be any problems." In orphanages, Human Rights Watch found that authorities have generally reacted to critiques of their facilities by blocking access to the institutions; punishing or threatening to fire workers if they speak about abuses; and in some instances, promoting those who are responsible for wrongdoing.

An Russian advocate reported: The problem with all the institutions is that the director hires all the personnel. That means that the doctors and nurses are required to write papers according to what the director wants. So if something is done by the director, they can't report it because they will be fired. When workers in Shanghai's orphanage tried to expose abuses, they were demoted and harassed. The orphanage director, accused of abusing and raping children in the orphanage, used his control over bonuses, staff assignments and housing allocations to harass his opponents and reward supporters. A speech therapist was suspended from her duties and transferred to a position cleaning bathrooms and windows. An orphanage driver was attacked and badly beaten by a group of employees loyal to the director. Eventually, all of the critical staff were forced from their jobs.

Legal Standared

The protection of children from violence is a key component of the Convention on the Rights of the Child. The convention is the most comprehensive treaty on the human rights of children and has been ratified by every country in the world except Somalia and the United States. Reflecting almost universal consensus on children's human rights, the convention recognizes that children are entitled to special care and assistance and that the best interests of the child must be a primary consideration in all actions concerning children. Under article 19 of the convention, youth have the right to protection from "all forms of physical or mental violence, injury or abuse, neglect or negligent treatment, maltreatment or exploitation including sexual abuse, while in the care of parent(s), legal guardian(s), or any other person who has the care of the child."

Article 19 of the convention protects youth from private acts of violence and harassment as well as from acts committed by state agents. By its terms, the state's obligation to protect extends to "all forms" of violence or neglect committed against a child while that child is in the care of another person. In fact, the Committee on the Rights of the Child's concluding observations on country reports have addressed problems of violence or threats of violence by youth against other youth in schools and other institutions. The right of children to protection from violence is also found in the International Covenant on Civil and Political Rights (ICCPR) and the Convention against Torture and Other Cruel, Inhuman or Degrading Treatment or Punishment. Under article 24 of the ICCPR, children enjoy the right "to such measures of protection as are required by [their] status" as minors.

In addition, both the ICCPR and the Convention against Torture prohibit cruel, inhuman, or degrading treatment. Human Rights Watch views the obleigation to protect youth from violence, as delineated in article 19 of the Convention on the Rights of the Child, as one aspect of the "measures of protection . . . required by [one's] status as a minor" to which youth are entitled under article 24 of the ICCPR. This view is consistent with the Human Rights Committee's general comment on the scope of article 24, which notes that "every possible economic and social measure should be taken . . . to prevent [children] from being subjected to acts of violence and cruel and inhuman treatment." Protection from violence is also an essential component in securing other human rights.

7

Prevention of Street Migration

Children are now found on the streets of cities in both the developing and developed world, programmes for street children have a longer evolutionary history in developing countries, and in particular Latin America. Through systematic research and attention to the voices of street children and their families, policy makers and practitioners are moving from understanding the more observable risks posed to children in the street environment, to the conditions that push children there in the first place. Intervention initiatives for homeless street children are now well established in many countries throughout the world.

Intervention Initiatives

Intervention initiatives for street children are now well established in many countries throughout the world. Awareness of the risks to physical and psychological health that children face in the environment of the street has led to the establishment of a myriad of programmes which seek to protect the child from the high risk aspects of street life. Seeking to address the immediate needs of children in the streets, many organisations have established shelter and/or feeding programmes, basic health services, street education and income generation support. In general, such intervention strategies may be regarded as maintenance strategies; they aim to support and protect the child while in the street environment, aiding physical and psychological development while reducing exposure to high risk behaviours and situations. Such street based contact is usually the first step in the long process of reintegrating the child in his or her family or community.

The diversity of creative and effective strategies for working with children and reintegrating them in the community continus to grow. However without a complementary prevention agenda, reception centres, drop in centres, street education programmes, all indicate a fundamental acceptance of the inevitability of street life involvement for children. Moving attention from the street to the factors which bring children to the street has been a logical step in the evolutionary development of many street child projects.

Preventive Approach

It is important to try and define 'prevention'. Ager defines a preventative approach as one "marked by an attempt to anticipate risk and put in place actions considered likely to reduce the likelihood of the onset of difficulties, rather than respond to needs only when such difficulties have clearly arisen". In child centred programmes in general, and street child programmes in particular, the advantages of focusing on prevention to protect children from engagement in environments that are potentially damaging to their development are obvious. Once children are initiated to street life, it is much more difficult to reintegrate them in their community of origin as they have become assimilated by the community of the street.

However, the real challenge to developing a prevention agenda is in 'anticipating risk'. Given the myriad of causal factors pushing children to the street, from macro-level factors such as war, displacement and chronic poverty to micro-level events at the familial level such as family breakdown, where should the focus of prevention work aim to fall? The first step must be an understanding of the predisposing factors to street life. The next step is to understand the immediate family and situational factors which push children to the street. Preventative action can then be targeted at those vulnerable points when children are at high risk of precipitation to the street.

Levels of Prevention Responses

Tolfree argues it is useful to distinguish between two levels of prevention responses: developmental prevention and responsive prevention. Tolfree identifies prevention as actions which enhance the capacity of communities, families and children to cope with the conditions which give rise to a particular problem. However, similar processes are often at play in the creation of street children. He defines the main aim of developmental prevention as likely to be "to provide a range of facilities or services which support families, enhance the quality of life for children, families and communities, and serve to create the social conditions in which the likelihood of family stress and breakdown is diminished".

When applied to street children, the main objective of developmental prevention may not be to prevent a very specific outcome, such as the movement of children to street life, but to support the material or psychological resources of the community or family so that their ability to provide for the best welfare of their children in enhanced.

Responsive prevention refers to more focused strategies which aim to influence the circumstances of specific families identified as at risk. From the perspective of prevention of street migration, it is suggested that prevention strategies can be assigned to one of the following categories.

— Developmental prevention strategies are strategies which seek to address the familial, situational, economic and psycho-social factors which predispose children to street life involvement (such as the Child to Child programme and the case study from "El Tuerto")

— Responsive preventative strategies, in particular, may seek to identify families and children who are at particularly high risk - that is, whose children are most likely to opt for street life.

The aim may be to equip families which are under severe pressure, such as in times of serious family disharmony or acute economic stress, to cope more effectively with their problems (the case with CEDRO and JUCONI).

— The term may also refer to family or community based strategies which address the needs of children that have been reintegrated in their community of origin. Programmes such as JUCONI and Link Romania runs a follow on programme, during which educators visit former street children who are with their families, in order to strengthen reintegration and address the conflicts which may precipitate children back into street life.

As a programme objective, the 'prevention of street migration' is a difficult one to present to planning meetings and donors. While chronic poverty, both rural and urban, is indisputably the context of enormous hardship manifest in a variety of ways. In different countries (and even in different regions within the same country), the push factors may differ enormously and at a local level, will influence the profile of the street child population in any city or country. The proportion of girls to boys on the streets varies according to local conditions.

For example, in Muslim countries, girls are very rarely found on the street as the presence of unaccompanied girls in that environment is socially unacceptable. The proportion of family based street children compared to homeless street children is also influenced by social and political factors. For example, three quarters of street children in Addis Ababa, Ethiopia are family based and cited poverty as responsible for their initiation to the street. By comparison, in Rwanda, half of Rwandan street children are homeless, and a third orphaned as a result of the genocide and social upheaval . Other factors which influence the numbers of children on the street are factors such as levels of access to primary and secondary education, or the existence of alternative sources of demand for child labour in the informal or uncontrolled economic sector.

As the case studies of JUCONI and CEDRO, and the analysis from Angola and Ethiopia show, it is important to look carefully at the social causes of street migration. One of the more interesting and useful findings to emerge from the observations of project partners and researchers in the developing world is that most children who live on the streets do not flee only poverty, but also violence and family stresses exacerbated by poverty. Research from a number of sources is uncovering some of the mechanisms by which macro-level forces such as poverty, war, social turbulence and family breakdown impinge directly on parents and children, creating conditions which precipitate children to the street.

There is evidence that the quality of family relationships is a fundamental issue. In Brazil, for example, Rizzini et al. found that homeless children reported higher incidents of corporal punishment at home, 63% compared to 23% of working street children. In Ethiopia, homeless children reported significantly higher levels of abuse at home in the form of violence, shouting between family members and beatings than family based street children. In Peru a national programme was initiated to prevent the migration of children to the streets.

Even in this very short analysis, it can be seen that the 'prevention of street migration' is a highly complex task as the social causes of street migration are very diverse across different settings and difficult to target. Addressing the phenomenon of street migration at its source means addressing large social problems; at a programme level, the challenge is how to intervene in a meaningful way in such a complex environment.

Developmental Prevention

Inevitably, the focus of prevention programmes for street children is fundamentally related to assumptions about causal factors. Programmes which identify poverty as a root cause attempt to raise the socio-economic standard of families in strong push communities for street children. One such example is 'Prevention Programme for Street Children' run by Save the Children USA and Forum for Street Children, Ethiopia. This is a targeted income generation and tutorial support programme for families judged at high risk of their children becoming involved in street life. The programme is based on two core assumptions:

1 Low economic status and the inability of families to provide for their children pushes children to the streets.

2 Participation of children in income generation activities is an economic survival strategy for many families; if children have to work on the streets, 'prevention' means supporting children's continued links with school, family and community to prevent them moving further into street life.

The programme objectives are twofold: raise the economic level of high risk families, and prevent children falling behind and dropping out of school. An evaluation of the programme was carried out after eighteen months. Using visually based drawings and rating scales to represent different programme activities with parents and children, qualitative and quantitative information were gathered about beneficiaries' perception of the programme. With regard to the first objective, 60% of parents said the income generation activities had somewhat eased the difficult economic condition of the family, a quarter reported no difference, and some even said their standard of living had degenerated due to repayment demands and a rising cost of living.

For most beneficiaries the main difference experienced was in their ability to provide an extra meal a day, or provide enjira (a local staple food) instead of bread. The profit made would certainly be insufficient to cover the costs of school fees, books and materials and health care after the programme withdrew its funding for these things. The basic premise, that the credit and savings component should raise the income level of families so children would not be obliged to work had not been realised. A fundamental problem was that given the marginal income levels of families and potential risk of defaulters, loan sizes were small to ensure the minimum risk. However on very small loans, it was difficult for beneficiaries to undertake initiatives that could make any substantial difference to the household income.

The rise in income level was not significant enough to ensure that parent(s) were no longer dependent on the income of their children from street work. Of the evaluation sample (50 children), 72% of children were engaged in income generation activities such as selling the outputs of the mothers income generation project, enjira, local beer, or vegetables, cigarettes or chewing gum, or other street based activities. In fact, in a few cases, the income generation activities of mothers stimulated the need for child street labour. The programme objective was not to prevent street work, but to prevent children breaking ties from family and community and becoming street living. A major component of this was the education and tutorial support programme which aimed to keep children from dropping out of school, thus retaining strong links within the community.

With respect to the education and tutorial support programme, of 300 child beneficiaries, only 2.3% had dropped out of school, and children reported very positive feelings about it. Children from the programme and a matched control group were compared on indicators of school performance at the end of the school year. 59% of child beneficiaries had increased their rank in the class (compared to 39% of the control group), 47% improved their year average (40%) and 25% ranked in the top 10 of their class (12%). The evaluation examined children's daily routine, to see if all these various demands of work and after-school tutorials were in fact creating extra pressure, possibly adding to their work load, rather than reducing it. Using a 'sun scale' depicting morning, mid-day and evening, children estimated the time engaged in different activities in a typical day.

Street working children reported that they commonly worked for an average of 2-3 hours a day on the streets, typically for an hour before school and for another hour in the evenings. 8% worked on the streets only at the weekends. However, children said that their involvement in the tutorial programme after school reduced the amount of time they are available for work. Parents also appreciated this. One mother commented "Most children spend their time after school either playing or working on the street but now most of their time is spent studying". Another said "If the children are at the tutorial programme, there is less chance of them being out in the streets, where they may be involved in a car accident, or get in trouble with the police for selling things". This was echoed by another mother; "If it were not for the programme, my child would be playing on the street, the programme keeps my child out of danger".

Perhaps sadly, children themselves rated the 'play and recreation' element of the tutorial programme, involving sport, handicraft and music, as their least favourite element while the study element was liked best. The reasons children gave as to why they rated the recreation programme their least favourite component included a lack of interest in these activities, ill health, being too hungry to engage in sport, and because it "wasted their time" that otherwise could be spent studying. In terms of prevention objective, the evaluation paints a complex picture. The conceptual base of the programme, of improving the income levels of families in order to make them less reliant on children's street labour is undermined as an objective, because of the dynamics of the labour needs of the household in the face of income generation activities.

However, in tandem with the education and tutorial support programme, children may be prevented from drifting full time to the street as they perceive other future options. If the street literature demonstrates anything, it is that street work and life is a product of children's and families choices in an environment that, because of poverty and stressful family environments, presents few other alternatives for children. Through the tutorial programme, children could see other options to falling out of school and onto the streets. Many reported their aim of completing secondary school, and a few expressed a desire to go to University.

An example of a prevention programme that could be argued to span both developmental and responsive prevention is a parenting programme implemented by Save the Children U.K., in conjunction with local partners in the Caribbean. Noting that a breakdown in family relationships was one of the most significant causal factors of homeless street children, the programme aimed to equip parents with the social skills necessary to communicate with their children, promote self discipline and self esteem, handle anger and conflict in the family and recognise their own needs as parents.

Local research revealed a growing incidence of child abuse by parents; large numbers of teenage pregnancies; a rising crime rate among young people, with particular concern about violent crime and drugs; widespread difficulties among parents coping with adolescent behaviour and a growing number of children living on the streets.... The (parenting) programme evolved out of work with young people who had already experienced a breakdown in family relationships. By tracing back the history of the problems faced by children living on the streets it was possible to identify deficiencies in parenting skills as one amongst a number of significant factors".

A potentially difficult issue to handle in the implementation of parenting programmes is the selection of beneficiaries. At a community level, inviting a parent to participate in a programme on good parenting skills may be likely to cause insult as the insinuation may be that the person is a poor parent. On the other hand, if a programme relies on parents that self select to participate in such training, then the likelihood is that these are individuals already committed and motivated to the ideals of good parenting.

In the SCF U.K. experience, some focused targeting of high risk families was done through probation officers. These officers worked with children in conflict with the law and were among those trained as 'parent group' facilitators. They were able to implement the course with parents of young offenders. The programme was promoted as a national programme and it was felt this contributed to reducing the likelihood that individual parents felt 'singled out' by their participation.

While the majority of homeless children world wide are over 10 years of age, the average age of initiation to the street is 8-10 years of age, although it differs country by country. Childhope Guatemala, with the specific objective of preventing the migration of children to the street, developed nursery education for toddlers and young children in a marginal community in Guatemala city in a strong push community for street children. Childhope Guatemala was concerned to work out a plan of action with the community that would cater for the needs of children and youth in the area. Children will take to the street as a consequence of the breakdown of social bonds, the objective of this programme was to strengthen the social fabric between community and families, and families and children.

Responsive Prevention

Responsive prevention aims to support children and/or

families at critical moments when children are at high risk of being precipitated to the street. Examples of such projects are more difficult to find, as most street child projects have either a community development focus (developmental prevention) or a street focus (intervention). However in addition to CEDRO and JUCONU, some other programme models exist. One example of a project that can be classified as "responsive prevention" is a project being implemented by International Childcare Trust, in Liyavo Settlement Project in Kenya. The objective of the programme is to provide temporary refuge to children in situations of family crisis in order "to avoid children going to the city to wander the streets begging".

As part of an integrated community development programme, they provide an emergency refuge for children who have lost a parent, or who experience family crisis. The causal factors bringing children to their centre will be familiar to those working with street children. Children perceive their options for safety or support as limited. For many rural and urban children in crisis, the street becomes perceived as their best option. Responsive prevention strategies are those which broaden the choices available to children in crisis, giving short term or long term respite from overwhelming circumstances.

The need to respond to the fact that many street children have rural roots is particularly important in many African countries. Yet typically, projects for street children are to be found in the major cities and towns, where arguably, they serve to attract yet more children to the town, fuelled by stories of children claiming that food and riches are to be had for the asking. The Liyavo children's refuge has developed in a particular context, to respond to local problems, in a rural community marked by increasing poverty in a subsistence economy, tribal fighting and ethnic sensitivities in placing children in alternative family care.

JUCONI's Prevention Programme

Few people would take issue with the old saying that

'prevention is better than cure', as "prevention" avoids pain and is a cost-effective use of resources: "cures" are generally far more expensive. Sadly "prevention" has not been the priority nor the success one might expect in the field of development. Clean water and vaccines are known prevention strategies, yet every year hundreds of thousands of children die from avoidable diseases because these are not available to them. Since the nineteenth century, formal education has been taken seriously as a prevention strategy and is more widely available now than at any other time but while it has undoubtedly achieved very positive results, it has not proved a panacea for preventing society's ills.

These two examples, one of prevention strategies that are not fully implemented and the other of a much used strategy which has not yielded all the results expected of it, hint at some of the difficulties inherent in prevention work.

JUCONI (Junto Con Los Niños, Together with the Children), a joint Mexican-British initiative, was founded in 1989 in the central Mexican city of Puebla, with the aim of "seeking and offering alternative lifestyles to children living and/or working on the streets and to youngsters at risk of taking to street life." The personalised educational methodology which JUCONI has developed over the years is designed to ensure that "each girl and boy confront and overcome the problems they face in the street, in their families and within themselves." We do this through an educational methodology which develops children's cognitive, emotional, and social communications skills and their physical health.

JUCONI now has three separate programmes providing reintegration and prevention services for:

(1) street-living children and their families,

(2) street-working children and their families and

(3) street-market working children and their families respectively. Each programme comprises a contact/ outreach service, (3 to 6 months), an intensive change

service (12 to 18 months), and follow-on/sustainability service, (up to 3 years).

Community Outreach

By 1991, JUCONI's reintegration programmes were showing strong enough signs of success for individual children. A survey carried out amongst the girls and boys participating in the programmes as well as others working on the streets of the "industrial corridor" between Puebla's Central Bus Station and in the city's largest market area, showed that the majority came from outlying areas, particularly from small villages swallowed up by the city years ago and from the informal, newer suburbs. JUCONI referred to these areas as "expulsion zones" and chose one of each type of area, San Pablo and San Felipe, which were home to a number of street-working children we were already attending, to begin creating and providing prevention services.

In 1991, JUCONI had introduced week-long Evaluation, Training and Programming Workshops for each programme. Although at that time JUCONI's evaluation instruments were somewhat rudimentary, they nevertheless focused evaluation at the level of each individual participant. Careful analysis of the tangible results achieved for each child, (a practice which continues to this day), helped highlight several important issues which have remained central to the endeavour to provide effective and efficient services.

Reaching the Target Population

The problems of low self-esteem, poor communication skills, inertia etc. that prevent the most vulnerable and excluded from accessing educational and employment opportunities in the community, keeping them on the margins of society, will also prevent them from successfully integrating into a group - even if the group plans to tackle those very same problems. Systematic, intensive and personalised attention is needed to empower them to build the emotional strength and the cognitive and communication skills necessary first to be able to identify new opportunities for themselves and go on to take these up successfully

Capacity for Prevention Work

Integrating prevention work has been a gradual process. In some ways reintegration or "cure strategies" can be easier as they respond to more specific needs, whereas prevention widens the scope: it is harder to diagnose needs in relation to what might happen to someone. It has proved essential to have clear, measurable objectives and to make a careful selection of the action fields/areas to work in.

In each Programme educators divide their work in four fields of human development: Health, Cognitive Development, Emotional Development and Social Development. JUCONI uses an integral assessment tool which systematises detailed information on a child's situation in the four human development fields from the start of her or his participation in JUCONI. This tool is reapplied at set intervals to assess the child´s progress in each service and beyond. Follow-on is the final test as to whether a child or family have been able to sustain progress and whether, 3 to 4 years after contact, these youngsters have not turned to the street as an answer to their problems.

Street-Working Child Programme

Very early on - during the 'contact stage' of the street-working child programme. Prevention work in the street-working child programme also begins in the intensive phase of the programme. This service is home-based: each family is attended by a team of three educators, one specialising in reintegration work with the street-working children, one in prevention work with the younger high risk siblings and one straddling both, focusing on parental guidance.

Generally around 18 months of intensive attention is required before a family meets the criteria to graduate to Follow-On. In Follow-On, families- the former street-working children, high risk siblings and parents - continue to receive visits from educators for up to 2 years to ensure they continue to progress and find solutions to their setbacks.

At first glance, this programme may look like a community project and seem to contradict some of the statements made earlier with reference to the capacity of community work to reach those in danger of becoming street children. The intensive change service for this programme is a Day Centre, a service commonly associated with community work.

A Community-Based Approach

Children had left their family, school and, in one-third of cases, their previous work activities and had inserted themselves into street life and gangs of peer age. Living 'in the wild', they slept in open spaces, made a living by group assaults on bystanders, became sexually active and violent and started using drugs (mainly inhalants: compulsive glue-sniffing) and crack cocaine. There were no reports of drug use previous to the children's entrance into street life. Street children, who named themselves as 'piranhas' due to their habit of clustering in order to assault, tended to concentrate in four of the city's Districts, which were conceived in practice as groups' 'territories'.

Once in the street, each new arrival involved himself with a particular group as a means of survival and got acquainted with the 'subculture of the streets', i.e. other juvenile and adult delinquents, and the 'rules' which govern street life. The latter include seeing stealing (laburo) as 'work' (labour), resolving interpersonal conflicts through violence and dominance, and condoning drug and solvent use. Although street children were not usually 'monitored' by adult delinquents and the offences of both groups were not related, the former tended to take the latter as role models and imitated them.

As a result of their asocial behaviour, street children ran into problems with the local police and the Juvenile Justice system. Thus, most of them had been placed in a reformatory belonging to the government's 'closed system', from which most of them had also escaped back into the streets. There are several facts which contradicted the common beliefs of the time and which were to be taken into account in order to develop a better understanding and a more adequate answer to this social problem, i.e.:

- That the phenomenon was not related to poverty, the risk of previous, frequent exposure to street life or child 'abandonment', but to family structure problems and family violence;
- that the problem was related to the context of becoming adolescent in a conflictive family environment;
- that its scope was limited: there were less than 500 individuals of this kind in the streets in a city of 7 million inhabitants;
- that for cultural reasons, it was gender biased: a 10:1 to 15:1 ratio (depending on the period measured) between males and females;
- that family and/or social reinsertion of these individuals was possible in a high number of cases on the basis of intensive work with the individual, his family and the community.

The research also uncovered that:

- Most (90%) of the children come from rebuilt (with step-father or step-mother) or monoparental families, or from rural families that had 'given' their child to other people (relatives or not) to be raised by the latter in the city. Thus, in almost one-third of cases the children had not escaped from their family of origin but from other family groups.

— That more than half of the children had abandoned schooling several months before leaving home (thus schooling may be considered to be a partial protective factor for this specific kind of behaviour), or they had problems with the police or justice. Thus, it was reasonable to think that, although the adolescent 'running away from home' phenomenon in Lima was considerable, those children who ended up living in the streets were those who lacked an 'immediate social network' due to the immigrant condition of the parents or the 'delinquent social status' (the place and way of living) of the family.

This description also corresponds to the geographical distribution of the population/districts of the city from which the children came.

— That most children had experienced not only a conflictive and violent family context, but mainly a loss of their 'place' and status in the family, having previously experienced serious affective losses (mainly of parents) and having become the hostages of the power struggles which resulted as the family redefined itself..

— In most cases, the child had been the only child who had abandoned home as the price of the new family union. Violence against the child had been the final precipitator of the child's escape from home, but not its main root.

In the aftermath of this process, the role of drug use by street children is a complex one and, it may be summarised as follows:

— Street children are introduced into the use of drugs (primarily inhalants) by their age peers, who organise themselves into small, relatively unstructured 'gangs'. Drug use, then, is a collective phenomenon, not only because almost everybody (97%) does it, but also because it is part of a collective ritual, performed once or twice a day. So, drug use among street children is also a sign of belonging to a group and of conforming to its rules. Therefore, it is an adaptive behaviour.

— It is also adaptive, in individual terms, to the vital context of the children, as a means to evade some important issues they are unable to cope with, such as:

— depression, due to successive and massive personal losses (of one's own status in the family, of loved ones, of one's own family life, of school peers and friends, etc.) and the fact of their present living conditions of street misery and marginalisation;

— low self-esteem, due to the negative attitudes, violence and mistreatment received at home, plus the aggression and marginalisation experienced from the 'normal' adult world and the police during street life;

— fear, due to one's own position in the streets, facing the adult world; thus the stimulating effects of inhalants provide the individuals with feelings of 'powerfulness' and 'mightiness' that allow them to get involved in aggressive and delinquent behaviour;

— lack of acceptable and satisfactory ways to obtain pleasure under the above mentioned vital conditions;

— the hallucinatory effects of inhalants are used to compensate this difficulty. The anaesthetic effect of high doses of inhalants also helps to hide the feelings of cold and hunger experienced during street life.

— Thus, for street children, drug use is the principal means by which to evade one's own depression, fear, low self-esteem and conflicting family memories.

It helps sustain the 'carapace' or 'false (social) self' that these adolescents quickly develop after their entrance to the streets, and that masks one's own access to oneself and to one's own feelings. Thus street children start behaving in a severely disrupted manner and taking collective 'revenge' on the world of adults (collective assault), not for the purpose of 'survival' or food (most of their gains are spent on drugs and solvents), but for pleasure.

Street children lacked the ability and opportunity to adapt themselves psychologically to all these breakdowns of context, and their answer to this process was, at the same time, partial, self-protective, ineffective and harmful (i.e. leaving home, thus diminishing the number of their socialisation contexts, entering into gang life, developing a false-self, becoming frequent drug users).

The programme, named "From Piranha to Dolphin", was conceived as 'open' in several ways:

— It started and permanently continued its work in the streets, trying to build strong interpersonal links between 'street educators' and old and new (in-coming) street children, and to rebuild their trust in the adult world in order to encourage them voluntarily to leave the streets and go into one of the programme's units/houses.

— The resident children and adolescents had the choice of staying or leaving the programme/house where they lived at any time at all.

— Children did not lose their contact with the exterior society; after an average of three months they were actively encouraged and expected to go back to public schooling, learn a trade (at one of 10 programme workshops) or get a job outside the programme while living on one of its premises. Thus, social reinsertion was actively promoted from the moment a child took part in the programme.

The programme remained 'open' to the inputs of a wide range of community sectors: local municipalities donated land for the programme's premises or partially contributed to its costs; volunteers from different groups were engaged in the programme's activities, or were encouraged to develop their own activities in the programme, in order to enrichen the range of social interaction of the children and the programme's range of opportunities; school teachers and possible employers were actively lobbied in order to facilitate the children's integration into these domains; in-kind donations from private individuals and enterprises were actively sought.

The programme remained open as a 'safety network' for adolescents who intended to run away into the streets or who, after having gone back to their family, decided to leave it again, thus avoiding their re-entrance into street life. The programme conceived its goals as a three-step process:

— The child leaving the streets as a pre-condition to:

— the child abandoning drug use (which was sustained by street peer-pressure), before:

— finding an acceptable way of family and/or social reinsertion for each child.

Apart from providing shelter, nutrition, clothing, medical and psychological attention, the programme emphasised - in the context of community life - shared responsibilities, counter peer-pressure (of houses' residents) and a new set of (group) 'rules of life' (i.e. no drugs, no stealing, no violence and no sex - the latter, in the house premises) as an important means to enact a 'therapeutic breakdown of context'. Strong emphasis was placed on helping individuals to restructure their use of space and time, building a 'project of life' (to be monitored and supported by the programme) and in strengthening the self-esteem and sense of achievement of house residents.

From Piranha to Dolphin Programme

Follow-up research carried out on this programme during the past 5 years has provided the following information:

— The "From Piranha to Dolphin" programme has proven effective on 56% of the population it initially reaches in the streets; the remainder is composed of 24% of street children who are attended to by parallel systems, and 20% of children who will not leave the street or who will go back to them. Negative prognostic factors are: greater age and/or extent of street life of individuals, greater extent of time involved in drug use and use of coca paste. Thus, the system is mostly effective with those who have only been users of inhalants and solvents.

— Reincidence in drug use remains very low for the houses' residents: less than 8%.

— Drop-outs remain at a low level: 10% per month, who are mainly new-comers unable to adapt to the system.

— An 18 month follow-up study developed in 1992 gave evidence of rates of reintegration to the educational system of 85% and of labour reinsertion of 65%.

— A 21 month follow-up study developed in 1994 gave evidence of rates of reintegration to the family of 70%, and rates of 'independent emancipation' of individuals of 20%. The same study showed that reintegration to the family processes failed in 15% of cases, and that 'independent emancipation' of individuals failed in two-thirds of cases.

In other words, it was most difficult to help adolescents over the age of 16 to settle into an independent living and working pattern.

Community-Based Programme for the Prevention and Early Social Intervention

Given that police action against drug dealers was demonstrably ineffective, by the end of 1991 it was clear that the only effective way to stop the flow of children onto the streets, and impede their becoming addicted to drugs and solvents was to prevent the entry of new children and adolescents into independent street life.

A study carried out in 1991 showed that around 50% of a random sample of 100 street children came from 6 micro-zones of the city of Lima, between the limits of 8 districts of the city, most of them belonging to the outskirts - impoverished areas which were occupied mostly by immigrants to the city. Discounting 23% of the individuals of the sample who had come to Lima from other provinces of Peru, it appeared that these 6 zones of the city were at the origins of 63% of the cases.

On the basis of this information and of further correlating studies, the author designed a community-based programme for the prevention and early social intervention of child mistreatment and abuse cases at 22 specific small, urban-marginal communities, including the 6 core zones. Initial studies on the attitudes and beliefs of the adult population of these communities revealed the very high incidence of physical punishment (mainly flagellation and child-battering with objects), part of a complex cultural pattern of child raising .

A further epidemiological study on child mistreatment in the city of Lima supported by the author revealed that up to 61% of Lima's poor school age population had been physically mistreated at home, and that child mistreatment was positively correlated with the lower class status and male gender of the victim.

Voluntary Separation

In 1989, the Angolan Ministry of Social Welfare (MINARS) and Save the Children UK began a programme to assist children who had become separated from their family or usual carers as a result of the long running civil war. The programme emphasised family tracing and reunification as a priority though it also included the development of non-institutional care alternatives for children whose families could not be traced. During the mid to late 90s, more and more children began to be registered within the programme who were not separated accidentally because of the war, but had been brought into children's homes by family members, or had left home and were living on the streets, particularly in the capital Luanda. Before this, "street children" had been almost unknown in Angola.

The term "voluntary separation", meaning separation as a result of a decision by children or adult carers, was used to distinguish this from the earlier process of "involuntary" or "accidental" separation caused by the war. Organisations and individuals responded to this by establishing residential homes, aimed, in particular, at street living children. The staff at these projects argued that separation was caused by poverty and family breakdown, and that family reunification was not possible or in the best interests of street living children.

In 1997, MINARS organised a piece of research to test this hypothesis. Its objective was to identify forms of intervention which could assist children who were already "voluntarily separated" and to examine how to prevent more children becoming separated in the future. In all, 173 'voluntarily separated' children and their families were interviewed in the capital, Luanda, and two provincial cities.

Very few of the children are orphans in the full sense of having lost both parents, over 88% of them have at least one parent living - this was especially true for children who ran away. Only a small percentage (18.5%), however, were actually living with both of their parents before separation. A high percentage of children in both groups were living with single carers (60% brought into care, 45% ran away) For those running away the majority of these were single women (41% women, 4% men) but amongst children being brought into care this also included a high percentage of single men (31% women, 29% men). Statistics in wider studies tend to hide figures for single male headed households but two recent studies put the figure for female headed households in urban areas as under 29%.

Factors Contrinuting to Separation

In most cases a variety of factors were mentioned either by

the child or the adult as contributing to separation. Those most commonly mentioned are listed in the following table.

Table 1

Total Sample	%	Brought into care	%	Ran away	%
Economic	53	Economic	67	Economic	46
Supervision	42	Death of a tutor	60	Behaviour of the child	45
Death of a tutor	34	Lack of supervision	35	Lack of supervision	45
Behaviour of the child	33	Incapacity of tutor	35	Violence/fear of punishment	40
Violence/fear of punishment	28	Separation of parents	19	Liberty/Independence	33
Liberty/independence	24	War	19	Relationship conflict	27
Relationship (with non family member of household)	23				

At first glance, economic factors emerge as the most significant reason why children were on the street. However qualitative information shows that this is not always a simple cause and effect. Responses to the changing economic and social situation are demanding new roles of individual members of the household, altering the dynamic of relationships both within and outside it and putting new strains on all its members.

Effect of the Economic Situation

The principle strategy of households in response to the economic crisis appears to have been:

— diversification of income activities into the informal sector.

— the mobilisation of additional labour resources within the household.

Over 72% of families including those who had a relatively better standard of living complained of occasional or frequent moments when they did not have enough food in the house because income from the informal sector fluctuates, and because salaries don't last the month and are not paid on time. Households which appeared to be more economically stable often had at least one member still employed in the formal sector.

Assistance from other family members is the single most important strategy for covering both short and long-term financial difficulties (48%). However, traditional kinship networks are under pressure as everyone faces the same economic difficulties and the war has also cut off vital support to urban households from family who have remained in the provinces. Many households talk of help from friends and neighbours in the form of short term loans or food to cover difficult periods. Support from other congregation members in churches was also mentioned relatively frequently (23%).

Despite these networks, many households are quite simply not managing to survive. Over 24% of the people interviewed in Luanda, 35% in Benguela and 31% in Huambo talk of being forced to sell assets, of reducing the number of meals they eat and of going hungry. Small margins of survival mean that many households are unable to cope with additional shocks and in time lines drawn by families and children, the child's separation frequently followed on from such a period of crisis.

Causes of Crisis

1. Death of a guardian or separation were the most

important factors provoking economic crisis. (57% in the total sample, rising to 77% for children being brought into care). This reinforces the picture that half of children within the sample were living with single carers before their separation.

2. Over 40% of children within the sample have parents who are separated. There is no information from other studies to compare this with directly to see if this is a much higher proportion than the population as a whole.

   Several comments point to the fact that relationships, whether they are formal or informal, are not only a social desire but an economic necessity. This may be one of the pressures that, apart from tradition and the disruption caused by war, is pushing a high rate of serial partners amongst men and women. Individuals who become separated or divorced tend to move rapidly into another relationship and the arrival of a new partner can mean a dramatic change in the household's economic situation. This is true for both sexes, but evidence suggests that women face added cultural disadvantages. Traditional rules governing the practise of polygamy have been weakened by the greater freedom of individuals from community sanction and control in the urban context and there is less social pressure on men and they have less capacity to provide for "their wives". In the event of death, women in informal unions, or who are one of multiple partners, may have little or no entitlement to their resources. Particular types of female headed households, then remain amongst the most vulnerable.

3. Sickness, infirmity or disability of a carer are also some of the cases which display the worst economic situations of the whole sample. Again this is particularly true if they are single and there are no other adults within the house as it effectively means little or no income.

4. Alcoholism is both a cause of economic difficulties and quite often a response to them. Time lines drawn by the children often showed either the start of alcoholism or it getting worse after the onset of an economic crisis.

5. Loss of a job will have varying effects depending on the other sources of income for the household. However, the continuing importance of formal employment has already been noted above.

6. Loss of housing was also a factor provoking crisis. Problems included poor quality which could lead to houses falling down not once but several times in the rains and the high cost of rent which forced families to move frequently or to sell assets to pay.

7. Not displaced: It is interesting to note that there are very few recently displaced amongst the sample and this does not appear to be a major cause of economic crisis for this group. Many in the capital were originally from other provinces but under 15% of respondents in all areas had been settled in the city for less than five years.

Effect of Crisis on Children

In children's qualitative responses, it was evident that a combination of economic and psycho-social factors in the household contributed directly or indirectly to children's decision to separate from the family. This information may provide important indicators of risk in the targeting of prevention work.

1. Children going out to work: One of the first responses to economic problems within the household is for the children who are old enough to be sent out to work or to voluntarily go to look for it. Over half the children within the sample (53%) were engaged in some form of income generating activity. Many of them were contributing to household expenditure or were bringing

back food that they had been able to get during the day for younger brothers and sisters.

2. Lack of adult supervision and growing burden of domestic work and child care: Adults are spending longer and longer periods out of the house in order to be able to make enough to survive. Within the sample in 64% of cases there were no adults in the house during the day. Older children are increasingly taking up the responsibility for child care and domestic chores to fill this gap. In total, 43% of children were the oldest child in the house, rising to 52% of children running away. Within the total sample, on average, children appeared to be spending 50% or more of their time on household chores or looking after younger siblings.

   Added to their work outside the home, the burden of these responsibilities is proving too much for some children, who cannot cope, and may be at high risk of running away. Often work activities themselves involve children with life in the street and may lead to a gradual drift out of the home. These factors have an important impact on relationships, which is explored more fully under 'A Crisis in Authority' (below). The problem of child care is also an important factor amongst cases of children being brought into care, as single carers, in particular men after the death of their wives, are unable to find adequate care and supervision for younger children.

3. Loss of wider opportunities - the problem of education: Many children talk of the inability of their parents to put them in school as a reason for leaving home. However, a certain amount of caution needs to be exercised before taking this at face value. First, many children feel this is an "acceptable" response that interviewers will sympathise with. There are equally a number of family members who say that their children left home precisely because they didn't like to go to school or stopped going

and that this was one of the causes of conflict between them and the child. It is as much the search for wider opportunities in general that can not be found at home, as a desire for formal education that can be a significant factor. That said, the crisis in education in general within the wider community and the desire to ensure that at least one of their children receives some formal education can be an important element in the decision of families to bring children into institutions or on finding them in one the decision to leave them there.

4. Relationships: Another major cause of separation is the relationship between children and someone in the house who is not a family member e.g. stepmothers and fathers as well as wives or husbands of brothers, sisters, aunts and uncles. Children complain of being treated differently in the house to other children. This can include being shouted at and beaten more often, being asked to do a larger share of the work, not being given food or other goods or being made to feel an intruder. In 60% of these cases the child was the only sibling of that father and mother living in the house.

   In some cases there is a direct link between who is the principal income earner in the family and this problem i.e. if the child is not directly related to the principal income earner their entitlement is weaker within the household. However, in only 38% of the cases where a relationship problem was present were economic difficulties also mentioned. In many of these cases the household had a reasonable and in some, very good, standard of living. This does not appear, then, to be a problem that arises directly in relation to competition within the household for scarce resources.

   It may not be a response to a real shortage of resources, but comments that were made in the interviews suggest that it is perhaps linked to a perceived pressure on resources. It may be that the current precariousness of the general economic situation induces a feeling of vulnerability and leads to resentment against any extra element within the household. This can be particularly true if the person who is directly related to the child is absent for long periods or is out of the house during most of the day leaving the main burden or responsibility for care of the child to fall on their partner. Many children within these cases complain of being treated differently when their relation is in the house and when they are absent. Equally, if there is a conflict between the relation and their partner this can be taken out on the child.

5. However, resentment works both ways. Over 60% of the children in these cases were the eldest child and often were being asked to look after younger children or to contribute to the household in other ways. The types of crises of authority that are described below under "The Process of Leaving Home" may also be exacerbated if the person who is most directly delegating tasks to the child is not a relative. The child themselves may refuse to accept their authority or the right to tell them what to do thereby provoking conflicts. Children complain that in these conflicts they are rarely heard as relatives will tend to side with their partners in order not to create problems within the home. This often induces a feeling of rejection and anger in the child who then runs away.

The greater fluidity of sexual relations and weakening of traditional rules and sanctions as to how they are conducted is creating extremely complex family situations. In the current climate parents do not have the economic power to support all the children that result from these unions nor the time to give them all the emotional attention they need. Some children are falling through these gaps.

Leaving Home

Many children are spending increasing amounts of time on the street. This can be a response to economic necessity or a reaction to the burden of responsibilities in the home, but equally may be a simple search for companionship and entertainment. Even children who are studying do so for only a few hours and for the rest of the time may go looking for their own forms of stimulation.

These growing numbers have created a vibrant youthful "street culture" and "street life". As they spend time on the street they meet other children who teach them the ways and the norms of the life, particularly about how best to make money. At the same time children find friendship and moral support and a world completely free from adult demands or strictures - an absence of supervision which can be liberating and is certainly exciting. Many children, certainly initially, participate in this only on a part time basis, returning home at night.

As adults are out of the house for so much time they do not know how their children are spending their day. Some did not know, for example that the child was working. Others talk of thinking the child was going to school and only later realising that he/she had dropped out and was spending their time on the street. Many on realising what is happening respond by telling the child off or trying to punish them, often violently.

There are some cases of extreme abuse, of children being beaten with catanas (machetes) or benches and chairs. Often the most serious cases are also linked to alcoholism. In general, however, punishment for what is seen as "disobedience" or "bad behaviour" tends to be violent to a lesser or greater degree and raise questions about what is or is not considered acceptable punishment. Many children complain of being shouted at or hit and talk of the fear of punishment, even if it is for a single misdemeanour, as a reason for leaving home.

The reaction of adults, whether extreme or not, far from resolving the problem provokes the child to leave even further. Often in response to a first conflict the child will run away and will spend several days sleeping out of the house nearby and then return either of their own volition or brought back by his/ her carers . This often provokes further and often more severe punishment causing the child to run away again. This cycle can continue for several months and is often accompanied by the child as he/ she starts sleeping on the street, becoming more involved with other children who are actually living on it. It may also be accompanied by new larger "offences". Some parents talk of children's behaviour becoming gradually worse, of them starting to steal both at home and in the neighbourhood or beginning to take drugs or in general becoming more "disrespectful."

Finally, the child decides to run away and does not come back. In Luanda this is usually because a friend has invited them to go into the centre of town. From there separation becomes more established. They become further involved emotionally with other children sleeping on the street, they can make better money so the incentive is to stay, but also distance no longer permits them to return home easily even if they want to visit. As children's economic power grows it undermines traditional lines of authority between them and adults within the house. Many adults do not know how to deal with this.

Trying to support the household, to look after other siblings and then faced with a child who no longer appears to listen to them, who they feel is falling into "bad company" and who quite often gets them into serious problems with their neighbours, some adults feel unable to cope. Sometimes after repeated attempts to find their children, they just give up. Others try to pre-empt the situation by bringing their children into care as an attempt to remove them from the influences they feel are pulling them onto the street and where they feel others will be able to help them and, one suspects, "give them discipline" in a way they no longer feel able to.

The research tends to lend weight to the assertion of other writers that many children even among those living on the street maintain some contact with their families and may even return home for periods of time. Some children do not visit home regularly because of the physical distance from home, or anxiety about how their family will receive them. In other cases, children said they would return home if the original cause of the separation was removed. Even when their home situation is bad and they do not want to return, family may remain an important source of identity for children. Children may believe their family will be there if and when they want to return. One child, within the research, when he tried to show the interviewers where his family lived, discovered they had left the area, and no one knew where they were. This produced panic in the child who believed he was "on his own in the world". This can have serious` emotional consequences for the child.

In Angola the growth in numbers of street children has been accompanied by a proliferation of organisations and individuals providing different levels of welfare. These may include initiatives such as the provision of food, clothes, blankets or medical assistance on the street but focus on moving children off the street into permanent homes or institutions. Without wishing to minimise the dedication of staff within these programmes, this response suffers from a number of weaknesses.

The negative psychological effects of long-term institutionalisation particularly on younger children are well documented. Furthermore, the cost of maintaining a child in an institution is prohibitively expensive. In Angola, many homes do not have the resources to support the number of children in their care or the staff with sufficient training to supervise and assist them. Families who believe that their child will have the chance of a better future in an institution may have an unrealistic picture of what opportunities they are receiving in reality.

Another shortcoming is that institutionalised responses often have a tendency to view children "out of context". As a result, they provide for children in isolation from their families and with insufficient attention to their individual histories, or to the very different family contexts from which they may have come. This ignores the fact that strong affective bonds can still exist between children and their families even after separation. Some children continue to visit their families periodically and to use them as one element in a complex network of emotional and material support.

In addition, this 'decontexualised' approach overlooks findings in the research that many of the children were the oldest in their family. Behind them they left younger brothers and sisters who are currently living and suffering exactly the same conditions that led to their separation. By concentrating attention and resources on the one who is "visible", programmes are ignoring the much greater number who are not. In Angola, there are still very few street based programmes such as those established in Latin America and elsewhere. These have attempted to move away from institutionalised responses and have used a variety of methods, such as street outreach and education, halfway houses, and vocational training, to develop an alternative and more flexible response to delivering services to children on the street.

Alongside these programmes and in part informed by them, there has also been a growing emphasis on campaigns for the recognition of the rights of street children both within the law and amongst institutions such as the police as well as the wider public. Most of these types of programme have been motivated by an agenda of counteracting negative images of "street children" and of challenging perceived assumptions about the nature and reality of their lives. This has led to strong emphasis on the positive capacities of street children.

Evidence from Angola suggests that there are different groups of children on the street, some who have found relatively successful and stable strategies for surviving or protecting themselves, others who have not. Nearly all of them are vulnerable to a greater or lesser degree to sickness and violence. Some writers suggest that living on the street is just a passing phase and that children do successfully reintegrate themselves into society but this is by no means conclusive as few longitudinal studies have been undertaken. Children themselves may perceive it as a passing phase but the reality maybe one of reinforcing marginalisation and social exclusion.

In Angola, there is a rising tension between the growing numbers of children on the street and public attitudes towards them. As more children come onto the street the more they create a "street culture" which in turn pulls other children onto the street as it seems a viable and sometimes attractive alternative to the problems they are encountering at home. As numbers of children grow on the street the more they are seen as a "problem" or a "menace" by the rest of society. As the problem appears bigger and more insoluble this provokes a growing indifference and hostility on the part of individuals to their situation. This has clearly happened in Angola, where five years ago there were no street children. When they started to appear there was a greater willingness on the part of individuals to assist them as they were seen as victims of the war whereas now they are seen as "thieves" or "delinquent" and full of "vices".

As society becomes more aggressive towards them so the children themselves risk becoming more alienated and aggressive in response, in turn provoking more violent reactions against them. Angola has not yet seen many incidents of children being shot on the streets, as has happened in Brazil, but the warning is there. There is a need for new approaches which include not only reactive responses to children after they have become separated, but also greater emphasis on supporting reintegration and doing preventative work. These should see "home" and "street" as not separate but linked and should seek to support strategies in each realm which enhance security for children and reduce their vulnerability both in the short and long-term. Putting the issue of security and vulnerability at the centre of interventions, leaves room for recognition of the existing strategies of families and children as a starting point but also suggests the need for public action to support these.

Organisations need to move the focus of their work back along the time line of children becoming separated and to begin to identify children at the point they begin to be separated rather than after a definitive break has occurred. In many instances, this requires a geographical shift of focus from the centre of town to communities in periurban areas and even in some countries, rural ones. There are three possible approaches:

a) *Community development programmes:* Long-term strategies for improving urban services or environments are clearly important in reducing separation but are too broad to probably have a noticeable affect in the short-term. Efforts should be made, as has been attempted with gender, to include an awareness of the particular needs and roles of children of different ages in the planning of programmes and in discussions about the development and use of urban services and spaces.

b) *Community based programmes for children:* These would look at providing specific services and interventions targeted at the needs of children generally or particularly for those groups considered most vulnerable of separation, e.g. children between the ages of 9-12, particularly boys, or children working in markets and streets of peri urban areas. Interventions need to take into account the multiple responsibilities that many children have both within and outside the home. Some possible areas are outlined below:

   — Income generation: Children will and in many cases wish to continue working. The issue then is not necessarily how to stop them working but how to make this less of a burden in terms of their time, to try to prevent the drift into the centre of town and to look at how this can be used to help provide them with skills that will be useful in later life.

— Educational assistance: In the short term it is most effective to think in terms of informal educational activities and life skills training which are useful and appropriate to children's needs. Other possible interventions could include assistance in preparing children for more formal schooling and assistance to families in arranging places for them and registering them. This latter, however, should take into account the position of other siblings at home.

— Entertainment activities: It is somewhat debatable if children will find organised activities as stimulating as their own but some success seems to have been had with street children with activities such as football leagues. In Angola greater use might be made of the great attraction that "video houses" have for children both as entertainment but also as social focal points. Activities could be useful as a means of beginning to work with children, as a way of providing contact with adults outside the home, and as a means of identifying particularly vulnerable children.

— Childcare for younger children: This is clearly a problem directly for younger children but also for older children, due to the responsibilities they are being asked to assume. In Angola, the few experiences of trying to organise additional support systems at a bairro level have not been very successful. One other option would be to organise these in or close to markets and to use the networks which already exist between market women and which are sometimes stronger than those in the bairro to help run them.

c) *Targeting children at risk:* This would seek to identify and target families whose children are at risk of separation. This might be most effectively done through a broader community based programme and some form of community monitoring scheme. Though the profile of children at risk may vary in different contexts what is remarkable about studies is not the differences but the constant repetition of similar factors.

Clearly, the factors contributing to separation in particular street migration in any one family are complex and particular, but it is not impossible to envisage that better profiles could be developed by talking to different groups within communities about who they identify at risk as well as trying to understand the factors which allow certain households who one would assume to be at risk to stay together.

8

Teaching, Training and Skills Development

Street educators educating street children involves helping them acquire knowledge, skills and attitudes in specific areas of need. In order to be effective, the teaching of street children should be planned. You will have to understand the needs of street children and the local situation before you embark on any teaching. It is a waste of resources and efforts to train street children on issues that are not useful or relevant to their lives.

Educational Concepts of Street Education

To teach effectively, you need to understand some concepts that are important for planning, developing and implementing teaching sessions. In terms of street education, they can be defined as follows:

— Learning is a process by which a child's behaviour is changed as a result of experience, usually on a long-term basis. Learning entails acquiring appropriate knowledge, skills and attitudes.

— Learning objectives are statements which describe what the street child should know, be able to do, and how he should feel about issues at the end of a course or session.

— Education refers to learning experiences which are intended to broaden the street child's knowledge and give him/her a stronger base for future learning.

— Training is a procedure which is intended to foster and enhance learning and build upon the knowledge, skills, attitudes and competencies that the street child obtains though education.

Street education is aimed at helping street children acquire appropriate knowledge, skills and attitudes.

— Knowledge. When information is shared with street children, they gain knowledge on the subject, e.g. substance use and sexual and reproductive health. Knowledge helps in bringing about changes in behaviour and can become the foundation for taking appropriate measures for protecting oneself.

— Skills can be learnt through demonstrations and practice. The idea is to teach skills by providing information and practice together. This allows the street children to get the facts and practice at the same time.

— Attitudes are the tendency to behave or think in a certain way. This involves street children's values and beliefs. If street children are supported, they can acquire healthy attitudes and a sense of self-worth. However, attitudes are learnt gradually and you must have patience. Appropriate attitudes provide the foundation for learning and adopting useful skills.

Methods for Street Education

There are some practical methods that can be used to educate and train street children. These methods should be adapted to the needs of street children and to the resources that are available in the community. The common and effective teaching methods that you can use are: group discussions, demonstrations, field visits, games, role play, and brainstorming.

— *Group discussion:* during group discussions, the street children do more talking than the educator. The method provides an opportunity for everybody to participate during the teaching session.

— *Demonstration:* a demonstration is a practical skill presented by the educator. Demonstrations are successful if they are followed by practice sessions for the street children.

— *Field visit* : this method enables the street children to experience real situations. To be effective, the choice of the place to be visited should be relevant to the subject you are teaching or what the street children want to learn.

— *Games* : many educational games are available which could be used to teach street children. The critical part of an educational game is the 'learning questions' that come after the active part of the game. These questions are intended to help the street children in analysing what they have done and in drawing important conclusions. It is important that the games used are culturally appropriate and acceptable in your community. They should also be appropriate to the age of the child.

— *Role play/drama:* this is a method in which problems are outlined, acted out and discussed. During role play, the street children act out roles of certain people in real life. The method is useful in teaching attitudes.

— *Brainstorming:* brainstorming is a fast moving activity during which you gather as many ideas as possible from the participants or street children. It stimulates street children to generate ideas. The method is most useful at the beginning of a teaching session.

Learning Aids

Learning aids are all those things that help a child learn. They could be visual (things that can be seen) or auditory (what the learners can hear). A number of learning aids can be used for teaching street children, e.g. pictures, posters, objects, stories, songs, recording of conversation, overhead projectors etc. Trips and excursions can also aid in learning. Learning aids help in stimulating discussion about the children's experiences and reality.

How to Use

To be effective learning tools, learning aids must meet the needs of street children. The street children should be familiar with them and understand their use. When planning a teaching session, think about the materials that you may need, how they will be used and where they will be used. When teaching, bring them in at the right time and in the right way to help the street children understand. There are a number of reasons why learning aids can be used during teaching.

— To secure interest of the child.

— To transmit information that is difficult to convey with words.

— To reinforce information that other teaching methods have given.

Enhancing Learning

Learning aids and teaching methods alone will not ensure that learning takes place. Here are some principles that you can apply to enhance learning:

— *Ice breaker (starter):* can serve as a short 'warm-up' before beginning a teaching session. It helps in creating a relaxed atmosphere, and provides a good point from which a learning activity can be introduced. This activity in itself also helps children in developing creative expression and observation skills.

— *Participatory learning:* involves giving the street children something to do when teaching. Ask them questions, seek their responses and give them feedback about how well they are doing, what was not done well and how they could have done better.

— *Clarity:* to enhance learning, make sure that those you are teaching can hear and understand you. Speak with a reasonable rhythm, clearly and loud enough for those sitting far from you to hear. Use simple expressions. If you have to write, write neatly. Use appropriate learning aids.

— *Ensure understanding:* clarify any concerns and misunderstandings that the street children may have immediately. If you are teaching skills, check that all learners can demonstrate the skills.

— *Individualize:* it is important to realize that street children, as individuals, are different in many ways. They learn at different speeds, in different ways, and have different interests, experiences and abilities. If a street child is facing difficulties in learning, allocate time for discussions with him/ her, determine the problems together and take measures to assist the child.

— *Motivation:* at all times, strive to keep the street children motivated by making the teaching process interesting. Show them that you recognize and appreciate their personal progress.

Planning to Teach

Before developing a plan for street education, it is important to determine what the street children need to learn. Training should only be given on the knowledge and skills that they lack. Learning needs can be identified through interviews, observation and needs assessment. Needs assessment is a comprehensive investigation which includes interviews, discussions, observations and information about the environment where the street children live.

Lesson Developing

In order to develop an appropriate lesson for street children, you should be aware of various features about street children in your area. Also, before developing the teaching plan ask yourself the following questions:

— How relevant is the lesson to the children's lives and experiences?

— Will the children relate to the content?

— Can they immediately use what they learn?

— How will the street children react to the timing of the activity and style of presentation?

— Does the proposed lesson logically follow the previous one?

— Will they understand the content?

— Will it interfere with their activities?

— Will they play an active part in the lesson or will it be boring or tedious for them?

— What could be potential problems that could hinder learning, e.g. hearing or visual impairment, lack of psychological maturity, ability to follow instructions or low self-esteem?

Lesson Plan

A lesson plan is a framework that outlines the steps of a teaching session. The lesson plan should include learning objectives, duration of the teaching session, content of the material to be covered, teaching methods, assessment and if you are not well conversant with the subject, possible answers. Remember that a lesson plan is only a 'skeleton'.

— *Learning objectives:* these are statements of what you expect the street children to have learnt and what they should be able to do after completing the lesson.

— *Duration of the teaching session:* this will depend on the objectives, the teaching methods and whether you plan to have exercises and field visits. Some teaching methods such as demonstrations, group discussions and field visits require a lot of time. Pay attention to the time allocated to each component of the session in relation to the content and teaching method.

— *Content:* this is the list of the issues you plan to cover during the teaching session.

— *Teaching methods:* these should reflect the objectives: For example, if you plan to impart knowledge, use talks or group discussions; for skills, use practical exercises; and for changing attitudes, use role plays.

— *Assessment:* always plan to assess the street children in order to find out if you have achieved the set objectives. Remember your assessment can be formal or informal.

The use of lesson plans can help in maintaining consistency in what you teach. Even when you are not present, another street educator can continue from where you left off by referring to the lesson plan you had developed. Lessons should be designed to promote the street child's sense of self-esteem and confidence that their actions can help to improve their lives.

Teaching Session

The following details have to be taken care of, to ensure that the teaching sessions are effective:

— Time: schedule the sessions in agreement with the street children. Avoid long sessions. Allocate time for breaks.

— Learning aids: ensure that they are appropriate for the group and are in working order.

— Size of the group: teach a manageable group.

— Place: select a convenient and comfortable place, which is free from noise and interruptions.

— The actual lesson: break up the lesson into manageable portions. Ensure they are presented in a logical manner.

Skills and Knowledge Assessment

Assessment focuses on knowledge, skills and attitudes. It is aimed at determining the street children's performance and progress. This provides feedback to the trainer and the street child about the progress made. Corrective measures can be taken if things are not going well. Most of your assessments will be informal and take place during the teaching session. Formal assessment could be of an oral, written or practical nature. Assessment can be conducted at the following times:

— Before the training begins (pre-test).

— During the teaching process (continuous assessment).

— At the end of the course (final assessment).

Self-assessment : To make improvements on the teaching approach, make an assessment on how you presented a particular session. This could help you in planning your next teaching course better. There are several ways in which the teaching material could be evaluated. You could ask the street children to evaluate you or you could record the session on a cassette and assess your own performance. The information gathered should tell you whether the learning objectives have been achieved, what went well and what went wrong. Ask the street children to talk about what they have learnt and what benefits they have attained.

Programme Evaluation

Evaluation can provide important information for future educational activities with street children. Ask yourself and/ or street children the following questions:

— To what extent did the street children think the training programme was enjoyable, informative, worthwhile and stimulating? Do they have any suggestions for improving the teaching and learning process?

— Have the aims of the teaching been achieved? What kind of change occurred as a result of training? Did they learn facts, principles and skills? Did the programme change their attitudes?

— Did the programme affect their life in a positive way? What did they learn about themselves? Do they do things differently after having gone through the programme?

— Are there any areas in which street children need more teaching/educating?

Educating Street Children on Substance Use, and Sexual and Reproductive Health

Education is a part of efforts directed at health promotion and preventive activities. It is aimed at minimizing or avoiding the consequences of substance use and problems related to reproductive health among street children. Information that forms the basis for such educational activities : Understanding substance use among street children, Understanding reproductive health including HIV/AIDS and STDs among street children, and Responding to the needs and problems of street children: general issues.

Topics on Substance use

The street children can be taught about many issues in relation to substance use. For example:

— Substances that are used locally.

— The effects of substances.

— The consequences of using these substances.

— Relationship between substance use and STDs/HIV/AIDS.

— The dangers of injectable drug use and safer injection practices (e.g. cleaning injection equipment).

— Available services for treatment of substance use.

Another important topic is reducing the risk from overdose among street children. You can educate street children regarding:

— The danger of using multiple substances and of using substances when alone. If an overdose occurs when a child is alone, there is no one around to revive him/ her or to call for medical help.

— The fact that one cannot be sure of the strength or composition of substances that are bought illegally.

— Any myths that they may have about management of an overdose.

Topics on Reproductive Health

The street children can be educated about some important issues on STDs and HIV:

— Common reproductive health problems among street children.

— Reducing the risk of acquiring and spreading STDs, e.g. through safer sexual activity.

— Information on where they can receive treatment and how to use condoms .

— Messages on safe sex among street children.

Street children should be educated about safer sexual practices, which reduce the risk of passing STDs and HIV infection from one street child to another. Specific messages that should be included are:

— Using condoms for all types of sexual intercourse.

— Practicing non penetrative sex such as hugging and kissing, (where this does not conflict with cultural values and beliefs).

— Reducing the number of sexual partners.

— Avoiding sex when a street child has open sores or any sexually transmitted disease.

— Seeking care when they have a STDs.

Although the situation of street children makes it difficult for them to negotiate for safer sex, providing them with a variety of choices gives them an opportunity to adopt an appropriate strategy.

Topics on Pregnancy and Contraceptives

Educating street children about the importance of seeking help at health facilities reduces the chances of complications from pregnancy, abortion and childbirth. However, you can also educate the street children about:

— The importance of developing and maintaining healthy relationships.

— The importance of contraceptives and the varieties that exist (if this is permitted in your culture) and advise them to use them.

— The need to discuss sexual issues.

— The menstrual cycle and how pregnancy comes about.

— Life skills (to be discussed in next lesson).

— The dangers of abortions, pregnancy and childbirth.

— Existing resources related to pregnancy and contraception.

Substance use, violence and involvement in risky sexual behaviour are some of the ways in which street children cope with the harsh reality of their lives. Street children need to develop healthier, more constructive coping strategies that help them to deal with their difficult circumstances. Positive coping strategies stem from the acquisition and practice of psychosocial skills or life skills, practical skills and performance, vocational and livelihood skills.

Life Skills

Life skills or psychosocial skills include decision making and problem solving, creative thinking and critical thinking, communication and interpersonal skills, self-awareness and empathy, and coping with emotion and stress. Demonstration, feedback and practice, group discussion, role-play, and games are key activities that help in developing basic psychosocial skills. Another way to learn a skill is to analyse important aspects of the skill.

Group facilitation

A starting point for training the street educator as a life skills educator will be the training required to become a group facilitator. The street educator should be able to listen to what the street children have to say about their experiences and their needs, and be able to facilitate open and constructive communication in the group. These include: paying attention to the street child who is speaking in the group, asking open-ended questions, repeating key words to prompt further communication where any uncertainty exists, checking with individuals as to what they really want to say, providing feedback, and noticing disparities between verbal and non-verbal messages. Some techniques are fairly specific to group work. To facilitate group work, you should:

— Encourage street children to lay down the rules for behaving in a group, such as the need to take turns while speaking or the need to listen carefully when one member is speaking.

— Summarize what has been communicated. This provides an opportunity for you to check that you have heard accurately what has been said. It also enables the individual speaking to build a better picture of the total situation.

— Before finishing a discussion on a topic take time to check that everyone who wants to contribute has had the opportunity to do so.

— Discern situations when the discussion doesn't move towards the tasks that the group is trying to achieve. If you notice this happening you may have to explore what is going on. A good way to do this is to reflect back to the group the process you have observed and find out whether others in the group share your perceptions. If they do, you can try to discover what is stopping the group from 'working' or achieving its aims.

There are no easy ways for developing these skills. Some people find it useful to concentrate on one strategy at a time and practice it in groups of which they are members, or with friends and colleagues. Like all other skills, the more practice you have of group facilitation, the better you become, and the easier it is to be an effective and sensitive group leader.

To avoid when facilitating life skills with a group of street children

A number of behaviours can be unhelpful or counterproductive in group work. These include:

— Displaying boredom, impatience or hostility.

— Distracting body gestures like fiddling with a pen.

— Being patronizing.

— Devaluing, by minimizing, disbelieving or laughing inappropriately.

— Insisting that your perceptions and beliefs are the only correct view.

— Passing judgement.

— Favouring one person.

— Joining in with the group to scapegoat or bully a particular member.

— Talking too much.

— Filling in a silence too quickly.

— Interrupting.

— Asking too many questions when a child is trying to think something through.

— Drawing conclusions prematurely.

Practicing

After a skill has been acquired, it should be practiced in the safe environment of the group. Role play, where the children act out short scenes from their daily lives, is a very useful method for this. It gives each child the opportunity to try out a skill in situations that are likely to arise in their daily lives. The street children should be asked to:

— Take up different roles, e.g. a street child, a policeman, or a drug dealer.

— Role play a typical scenario and its consequences.

— Go through the same scenario a second time to see how a life skill, e.g. communication skills, can help improve a situation.

How to enhance the application of life skills

Street children will need to be given the chance to experience the positive effects and consequences of positive, pro-social behaviour.

— Give street children positive feedback (positive reinforcement) about their use of life skills .

— Help children develop confidence in their ability to use life skills and in their positive consequences.

— Help them in applying and practicing the life skills in normal everyday situations.

Physical Skills

Street children could be taught:

— Method of using a condom.

— Games and sports.

Vocational Skills

Street children can use and learn a variety of skills that help them survive on the streets. Vocational skills help them earn some money. Vocational education may include:

— Crafts such as jewellery, toys or woodcarvings.

— Performance skills such as music or dancing.

— Domestic work skills.

— Skills on how to search for jobs.

Vocational training should be individualized to fit into the street child's life, interests and goals. A child who begs in buses may be taught how to sing; if a street child works as a vendor in a tourist spot, he may be taught words of a foreign language to enhance his chances of earning money.

Other Topics for Education

Health promotion and disease prevention

Health promotion and disease prevention involves educating street children on what they should do to be healthy. Street children can be educated regarding:

— Promotion of health and prevention of common diseases, e.g. diarrhoea, problems related to cuts and wounds etc.

— Personal hygiene and how to keep food and water clean.

— Importance of seeking help at health facilities.

Rights and laws

Street children's lives are not regulated by formal rules. The only contact they may have with the rules and authority of mainstream society may be negative. For example, the police may detain them for invalid reasons. Consequently, street children may not understand why laws are necessary in a society and how laws can be the basis for their personal rights. Street children need to be made aware of the following:

— Definition of a law, who are the law makers , and who are the law enforcers.

— The rights of individuals who live on the streets and their rights when in custody.

— How to access legal counsel and advice.

— Facilities that cater for abused/ homeless children.

— Laws regarding minimum age for employment, working hours, type of work and minimum pay.

These topics could be taught to the street children through games and field visits, e.g. to police stations, courts and to a legislative assembly.

9

Street Children and Needs-based Approach

This chapter describes various levels of interventions and outlines important areas that need to be considered when responding to the needs of street children. For the most part, as a street educator the interventions you will be implementing will focus on changing or influencing the life of the street child.

Street children need various resources to meet their physical and emotional needs. Resources can be internal (inside a person), e.g. intelligence, capacity to work etc., or they can be external (outside the person i.e. in the environment), e.g. schools, health services, community organizations and people who care. Even though street children usually have many internal resources, they usually lack external ones.

Without these external resources, they may have a hard time learning new skills that would help improve their lives. It may be more difficult for them to develop healthy ideas and practices about substance use if they do not have the benefit of resources such as street education and informational campaigns. If they have fewer ways of coping with stress, they may fall back on substances to relieve it. Your task involves identifying these resources and making them available or accessible to street children.

Levels of Responding

The question of prevention or treatment of substance use and sexual and reproductive health problems and providing support to street children can be approached at three levels:

1) Individual level (street children).
2) Local community level.
3) Beyond the community.

The way an individual street educator responds to the needs and problems of street children depends on the circumstances of the street children, availability of resources and the cultural norms and expectations. The response to these problems must be complimentary and comprehensive, taking into consideration other individuals and organizations in the community who might be needed to implement the selected intervention. There is a need to be clear about your own role in the implementation of selected interventions.

Individual Level

Responding to the needs and problems at the individual level requires targeting street children who are currently using substances, at risk of using them in the near future or at risk of sexual and reproductive health problems. You can target street children either as individuals or groups. The strategies that can be applied at the individual level are building basic skills, counselling and improving access to health services. Each of these are described in the next lesson.

Community Level

Local communities sometimes undertake programmes to help their residents. These programmes may emphasize prevention of health problems, health promotion, community development and referral of substance users for further assistance to health or other services. Interventions for street children should compliment other activities in your community. The strategies that can be employed at this level include community action, providing services and ensuring that resources are available. These are described in the next lesson.

Beyond the Community Level

It is possible for street educators to influence what happens far beyond their area of work, especially in creating safe and supportive environments. They can do this primarily through advocacy, which influences policy development, and may lead to improved health services. Such activities can be regional, national, or even international, with the results directly or indirectly influencing the local area.

Maintaining Support

Whether it is a prevention or treatment intervention, the impact of the interventions needs to be maintained. This can be done by emphasizing the importance of the intervention throughout its application, and by assisting the street child in participating in various activities, e.g. reminding him/her to attend a specific service, assisting with transport, and offering advice and support for not missing the next appointment. Ensure that a particular street child has access to a supportive person when problems arise. You might be that person or you might be able to link the street child with someone else in the community who can provide that support.

Varity of Responses

There are no simple solutions to the problems of street children. A number of individual and social factors contribute to the problems, and therefore a variety of responses are needed to deal with them. Five major categories of responses promote healthy development of street children and help in preventing and responding to their health problems. These are: creating a safe and supportive environment, providing information, building skills, counselling, and improving services. It is generally recommended that these interventions are combined.

A Safe and Supportive Environment

The term environment is used to refer to what a child encounters outside of himself or herself in daily life. It refers to the political, legislative, legal, economic, social and cultural context of the child's life, including opportunities to get an education and gain livelihood skills as well as the opportunity to experience positive relationships with other people. This broader environment influences behavioural choices. The aim of creating a safe and supportive environment is to promote positive behaviour among street children.

Interventions

Environmental factors that may affect street children include: attachments, such as a caring family, friends, and other adults; social norms, such as attitudes towards street children, attitudes towards sexual activity among young people; resources, such as opportunities for street children to go to school, to have a place to play, and to develop livelihood skills and get paid work; and policies, such as laws on child labour and access to health services. Some examples of interventions that can be aimed towards each of these factors are given below:

Attachments

- — Linking children with families or creating family-like groups to help meet the needs of children.
- — Increase communication skills in families and build parenting skills so that parents develop a more positive interaction with their children.

— Youth support groups.

For example, Mpho had been on the streets of Johannesburg for as long as he could remember. After a year at the Centre, at the age of 14 years, he began asking the staff to take him home. On assessment of reasons for his leaving home, it was found that his mother had abandoned him. He claimed that he had a vague idea of where his relatives lived. On three occasions, the staff took him to the township where he said he came from, and drove around while he tried to orient himself to the surroundings, but he could not find the house which he was looking for.

A month later, all the children on the street were invited to attend a major function. One of the members of a band playing at the function began talking to Mpho. It turned out that this was his uncle, the one that he had been looking for. During the same week, a home visit was made, and the street educator gathered information about the child's biological parents. The family had never known his father, and his mother had not been seen in many years. His uncle and aunt agreed to take the child to live with them. The street worker did an assessment of these relatives, and found them to be caring, capable of supporting the child financially, and willing to participate in counselling.

They soon moved to a rural area because they were concerned that Mpho would be tempted to return to the streets. Follow-up was done regularly and recently a letter and a school report were received. Mpho had passed his fifth grade at school. He had also started to settle down and had made a few friends in his new environment.

Another example, during the past few years, a whole generation of street children has been growing up on the streets of Guatemala City. These are babies born to young girls - 13 years old and up - mostly as a result of prostitution. The Casa Alianza Mums and Babies Programme is a residential programme. The environment allows for a bonding to take place between the young mother and her baby. Both mother and child receive full medical support. During the morning hours the mothers either attend school or participate in a job-skills training programme. During this time Casa Alianza staff care for their babies. In the afternoons, the mothers participate in the ongoing activities of the home, which include learning better skills in how to take care of the baby and keep it healthy.

Social norms

— Offering participatory group activities to share and discuss basic facts regarding prevention of HIV/ AIDS and STDs, using peer- and adult-led approaches.

— Using the media to increase the acceptability of talking openly about sexuality.

— Anti-drug, anti-tobacco and anti-alcohol lobbying groups.

Resources

Providing services:

— Developing links to services which provide screening and treatment for substance use, sexual and reproductive health including STDs/ HIV.

— Establishing community youth centres and 'drop-in centres' where street children can go for support, advice, and counselling.

— Making selected commodities available; e.g. condoms and other contraceptives.

Ensuring resources are available :

— Encouraging accessible and sensitive health services.

— Forming youth and special interest advocacy groups.

— Working with local school systems to facilitate re-entry or partial day school participation for street children.

For example, a foundation for street children in Ermita, Manila, established several group homes where street children can live and receive many different services. The staff quickly realized that the group homes were not suitable for all street children. Some children ran away from the homes and returned to street life. The staff organized an outreach programme. It sends street educators out to the places where street children gather during the day or at night. The street educators gradually form relationships with many of the children they meet. They find out the needs of the children, offer advice to them, help them obtain educational and health services, and encourage them to join the programmes at the group's homes.

Policies

Advocacy

Developing a comprehensive street children policy (education, health, welfare, housing and employment policies that do not discriminate against street children). Promoting government policies that reflect the relative risks and the social, economic, and health costs of different substances (less control of relatively harmless substances; strict control of the most harmful substances). Insisting that news and entertainment media provide responsible coverage of sexual behaviour and advocating for the restriction of advertisements which promote substance use and high risk sexual behaviour.

Law enforcement

— Ensuring that guidelines for prescription practices are followed.

— Bringing legal action against individuals who commit violence against street children.

— Ensuring that health, welfare, housing, employment and educational services are fully accessible to street children, the poor, youth, and minority groups.

Enabling environment

— Development of strategies that assure human rights.

— Changing laws which limit access to education and services for girls who are pregnant.

— Forming links with groups of lawyers and others who are interested in protecting the rights of citizens, including street children.

For example, the role of adolescents, particularly working and street youth, in advocating for the passage of a law against child and youth exploitation has been realized in the Philippines. The adolescents on the streets were assisted to hold Regional and National Congresses in which legislators were invited to listen to them. The adolescents also met with them in the Senate and House of Representatives. NGO Coalitions with support from the Department of Social Welfare conducted advocacy sessions and meetings with members of the legislature. The law was passed and its implementation is now to be monitored by an Inter-Department (Ministry) Committee recently established by the President with the support of an NGO Advisory Group.

Another example, A street educator from Bombay reported: "once when I sat with the boys at the railway station platform they were rating the girls arriving from the local trains in order of attractiveness, giving them marks for their looks. I took this opportunity to give them a message. I told them, "Be careful. Do you have a condom? Don't forget to use it." I know this intervention may or may not work. Probably I will not even know whether it worked, but at least the message is given.

Information Lays

When street children and the community are enlightened about issues that affect them, it is easier for them to react positively to these situations. Information lays the basis for interventions that follow, such as the building of skills and counselling. Information on the effects of substance and risky sexual behaviours and resources address two of the components of the Modified Social Stress Model. Street children should be provided with information on growth and development, sexual and reproductive health, substance use, prevention of disease (e.g. dental care), promotion of good health (e.g. physical exercise, nutrition) and other issues such as rights and laws. They should also be told about resources available in the community.

When working with street children it may not be possible to find an appropriate place or time to provide information to them. Take advantage of as many situations as possible whenever you are in contact with street children. It is also possible that the information provided can have a negative influence on street children. Information should therefore be formulated properly and given using the appropriate and accepted channels. Some of the issues you need to avoid are providing information that:

Blame street children for their substance use and sexual activities. Such messages could be misinterpreted resulting in street children not paying attention to the information. Are exaggerated and frightening. Scare messages have been found not to have the desired impact on recipients of the messages. Describe how to prepare and obtain substances can give street children ideas on how else they could prepare and where to obtain the substances they need.

It is necessary to have a thorough understanding of the topic to be communicated and the provider of information should be credible. If street children are being used in the delivery of information, they should also have a full understanding of the messages. Use appropriate media that is acceptable within the local context.

Building skills

The daily life of street children is likely to be full of dangers, pressures and stressors. Children frequently turn to substance use and other risky behaviours to cope with these circumstances and to fit into the street culture. Street children need to develop healthier, more constructive coping strategies. As identified in the Modified Social Stress Model, use of psychosocial skills influence the likelihood of substance use or other risky behaviours.

Building skills is the process of facilitating learning through a set of structured activities. It is intended to equip a street child with new or improved strategies for dealing with the daily life on the street and with specific situations that they are likely to experience. Many types of skills can help a street child to plan and carry out responsible and healthy choices. These include; life skills, practical skills, performance skills, vocational and livelihood skills.

Life skills

Life skills are defined by WHO as 'abilities for adaptive and positive behaviour that enable individuals to deal with the demands and challenges of everyday life'. Some of these skills are mentioned below:

— Decision making and problem solving.

— Creative thinking and critical thinking.

— Communication and interpersonal skills.

— Self-awareness and empathy.

— Coping with emotions and stress.

— Life skills could enable the street children to:

— *Be assertive*: e.g. the ability to state one's dislike for sex or substance use clearly. This skill helps street children to communicate their needs and to resist social pressures.

— *Negotiate*: the ability to discuss and get others to agree to what one wants. A street child could negotiate to use a contraceptive method such as condoms during sexual intercourse.

— *Think critically*: street children can learn to assess potential risks in various situations ahead of time, and think about why they engage in risk behaviour. A street child who knows the problems that may arise from substance use and realises that he or she uses substances as a way of making friends or coping with stress may try to find other ways of addressing those needs and avoid getting involved in using substances.

— *Develop self-awareness and self-esteem*: increasing understanding of personal strengths, interests, personal priorities and goals. This can decrease the attitude of 'just letting it happen'.

— *Make and build friendships*: having real friends can be a source of support and protection and may help street children resist pressure from adults who try to exploit them, for example, for sexual favours.

Life skills can also help street children in taking the opportunity to get off the street. Helping street children think about strategies for getting off the streets will need to include creative ways of getting them to think beyond their current situation.

For example, in South Africa, 'An important part of the work that workers at 'STREETS' engage in is getting the children and youth to think about the future. This is usually facilitated during activities such as art, dance, drama and other creative type workshops. The children and youth are asked to reflect on what they would like to be or do in the future. They are then asked to reflect on what steps they need to take in order to reach their desired goals. On a number of occasions the younger children tend to see going back to school as a step they should take. This is the starting point of getting them to think about going back home and back to school'

Counselling

Counselling is a process of interpersonal communication where the person with a need or problem is helped to understand his or her situation in order to make decisions on how to respond. Before providing any counselling, you must receive training or identify resource persons or facilities where you can refer street children when they need counselling. Counselling is important among street children especially in times of crisis, such as sexual abuse or other forms of violence. It addresses the stress component of the Modified Social Stress Model. Peer counselling has been used for the prevention of pregnancy and STDs, and in the reduction of use of alcohol, cigarettes, and other substances.

The goals of counselling are to:

— Build a trusting relationship that fosters communication.

— Encourage the street child to be active and take responsibility for recommended interventions.

— Reduce the street child's fear and distrust of services that might be necessary for their betterment.

— Provide emotional support.

The main skill that needs to be practiced when counselling is called empathy. This involves listening to the street child, understanding him or her, and communicating this understanding back to the street child. Empathy requires you to respect the street child and show that you believe in the street child's ability to find his/her own solutions. Avoid giving advice, providing solutions, moralising, arguing, sympathising, interpreting or withdrawing. This enables the young person to speak freely in an atmosphere of trust. Your approach to the child must be positive, honest, individualized, and culturally sensitive.

For example, the Aunts Project in Uganda involves selecting and training women to be counsellors in addition to working as prevention educators in villages. Young women can go to the counsellors to talk about a broad range of issues related to relationships, personal goals or other worries and concerns. The programme is aimed at the prevention of HIV. It is based on the premise that HIV prevention will be enhanced by helping girls to explore HIV related issues in the context of their own situation. The girls may be referred by adults or come to the 'Auntie' counsellor on their own for help about issues such as whether to begin sexual activity, how to seek a marriage partner, worries about pregnancy and STDs. The women are known in the villages as counsellors, not AIDS counsellors specifically to make it more likely that young girls will want to talk with them and because this reflects their role of helping clients in various ways. This approach can be explored and linked with both substance use and sexual and reproductive health!

Improving Health Facilities

Health facilities provide general health care, emergency care, disease prevention and health promotion services. These services can play a major role in preventing health problems by promoting and supporting healthy behaviour and identifying and safe-guarding those at increased risk of developing problems. Health services also help in the detection, treatment and rehabilitation of street children with illnesses and injuries when they arise.

The health problems of street children are similar to those of other children. However, their problems are more profound because they often do not have access to services that are available in the community. The common reasons why street children may not seek health services are:

Fear

— Children may not want to appear feeble or different from their peers.

— They may not trust health and welfare services because they believe that these services are a cover for police or child protection agents who want to capture them .

— Because of threats from adults who exploit them (these adults may fear that the children will tell law enforcement authorities about their activities).

Inaccessibility of Services

— Appropiate health facilities may not exist in their neighbourhood.

— Services may be too costly and the process of obtaining care may be too time-consuming.

— The agencies may not assist a child without the presence of a guardian or a legal document.

Attitudes of Health Workers

— Health workers may reject street children because of the stigma attached to them.

— Workers may not feel capable of caring for substance users and may therefore refer them on.

Attitudes of Street Children.

— *Low self-esteem*: they may feel that they will not be attended to at health centres. Resignation: they may feel that the future holds nothing for them, so the idea of making efforts at healthy living may not have much appeal for them.

— *Self-care*: they may be sensitive to their health needs but may feel that they can manage the problems by themselves or with advice from their friends (often the advice is wrong).

For example, A youth from South Africa said: "the clinic staff aren't always friendly to young people. The clinics are overloaded and have long queues. The staff are so busy they don't have time to counsel people properly......"

Another example, during a mission to Guatemala, a WHO officer from the substance abuse department reported the following:

> "While talking to a group of street children, it was found that one of the street children had been stabbed. His friends took him to the hospital but he was not admitted until the officer from the WHO street children project convinced the doctor to clean and sew the wound. When the boy recovered from anaesthesia at the hospital, he was discharged. His friends took him to the park where they stayed. He remained under a tree for several days. Other children would bring food and water for him. They would also encourage him to inhale glue to relieve the pain".

For examples, an NGO called CINI-ASHA in Calcutta has a sick bay unit for children brought in by street educators from various contact centres. This ensures early diagnosis and appropriate health care in the presence of street educators, making the street children feel comfortable. Children are also encouraged to learn the basics of health care. After recovering the child is given the option of joining a vocational training course or non-formal education classes at contact centres of the NGO.

Importance of Involving

Street children can be a great potential resource if given the support and opportunity. Involving street children can result in their commitment to take measures to reduce substance use and reproductive health problems that affect them. They must be given a greater degree of control over the services provided to them. However, they cannot do all that is needed alone and they need the partnership of street educators and others who care about their welfare to ensure that what they are doing is correct and appropriate.

How to Involve

There are many activities in which street children can be involved. These include peer education, advocacy and forming street children's organizations. Peer educators can teach and persuade other street children to adopt new behaviours and skills. For example, peers who are seen as role models can play an important part in making the use of condoms for prevention of STDs and pregnancy acceptable. Similarly they can demonstrate to street children using substances that it is possible to live without using substances.

For example, in Manila, the Junior Educators Programme aims to provide street children with the basic knowledge and skills needed to function meaningfully in society. Street children aged 11-17 years have been trained to provide basic education skills to other children. The programme also serves as a training ground for future staff of a local centre for alternative education. The Junior Educators receive training in communication skills, typing, planning, facilitating meetings and group discussions, poster making, outdoor photography, art, music, and self defence. They are also helped to realize that they are worthy human beings, and that they are capable of understanding the realities of their own lives and doing something about it.

The educators work in the street, in communities where children live and work with their families, and in a local centre where they offer more structured learning activities. The Junior Educators have also been trained in methods of sharing information about HIV/AIDS/STDs, and basic counselling techniques to help peers with problems related to substance use and reproductive and sexual health. Adult support and weekly meetings where they talk about their experiences and learn new skills have been important elements in keeping the programme going.

After a year on the streets of Manila, Edwin and his brother came across Bahay Tuluyan (welcome house), a drop-in centre offering accommodation and legal advice to street children. Regular attenders are trained as counsellors so that they can work with other vulnerable children. Theatre, art and play are used to encourage children to open up.

Impact of Modified Social Stress Model

The Modified Social Stress Model highlights the risk factors and protective factors which influence decisions regarding risky behaviours. This makes it easier to decide on which strategies would help the street child the most.

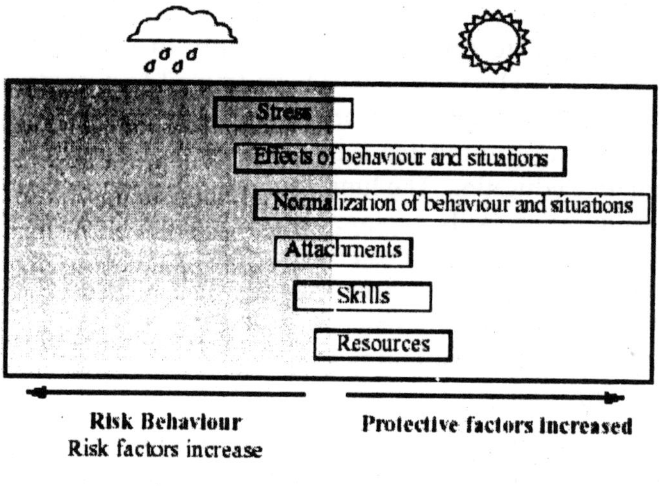

All six components of the model (stress, normalization of behaviour and situations, effect of behaviour and situations, attachments, skills, resources) influence the probability of indulging in risk behaviours. Therefore, intervening in any one of the six areas could help the street child in leading a healthier life. Intervening in more than one area increases the chances of benefit. Intervention should be aimed at various components of the model and arranged according to the level of intervention.

10

Assessing Street Children

Assessments help in formulating workable strategies for responding to the needs and problems of street children. Assessments also help in monitoring whether services are producing the desired effect and whether there is a need for a change in strategies. Results from the assessments should be used to create awareness about the causes of street children's problems and their relationship with other issues. Two questions define the goals of an assessment. These are:

— What specific problems should the assessment address?

— What is the purpose of collecting the information?

There is a danger of collecting information that is of no use to street children if these fundamental questions are not clarified before the assessment begins. The purpose of the initial assessment may be the determination of problems and needs, while the purpose of ongoing assessment may be to provide feedback on the success of the programme. The information gathered should be closely linked to the specific issues to be addressed.

Sources of Information

Assessment helps in understanding the needs and problems of street children. It also provides an idea about their environment. Adequate assessment is essential before any intervention is attempted. Similarly, assessments may be carried out later to monitor the progress and success of the programme. Modification in intervention may be made on the basis of information obtained from the assessment. Information can be obtained from primary and secondary sources. Street children and their families, health care and other service providers are primary sources of information. The common secondary sources of information are:

— Official documents such as surveys, policy statements, professional guidelines, registers and court proceedings on street children.

— Unofficial materials from government or medical institutions and private individuals, e. g. television and radio programmes, evaluation reports on street children, books, newspapers and magazine reports and copies of presentations at professional and community forums can add to the resource materials.

Secondary sources provide the background for designing assessment procedures. Usually they do not provide sufficient information for a complete understanding of the situation of street children. Information should be gathered from primary sources to supplement secondary information. Primary information also gives you qualitative data. Service providers can be an important source because they can provide information on:

— the economic, social and political conditions of the community.

— community attitudes towards street children, substance use, sexual and reproductive health.

— services available in the area, particularly those accessible to street children, potential barriers to their use by street children, and how to overcome such barriers.

— what interventions have worked, or failed

After deciding on the goals of the assessment, the following steps should be followed:

— Make a plan regarding the method for obtaining information.

— Collect the information.

— Organize the information.

— Analyze the information.

— Make conclusions.

— Use the information.

Important considerations during collection of information. The following issues should be kept in mind during the assessment of substance use and sexual and reproductive health problems among street children.

Informed consent :- The street child should agree to participate. To get valid consent, inform the child about the goals and method of the assessment, what they would gain or lose if they participate and also that they are free to refuse to participate.

Confidentiality :- All assessment information should be kept confidential, unless you have the street child's consent to give information to others. Talk to the street child away from peers, family and others. Their presence may compromise confidentiality. Similarly, the confidentiality of the informants is extremely important. In some countries, children and other informants have been murdered for providing information.

Rapport :- The process of assessment is not just the collection of information as it can be an opportunity to engage the street child in a respectful and trusting relationship. The assessment could provide an opportunity for street children to ask questions and get information if they choose to do so.

Burden :- Street children might have been assessed many times by health, welfare, educational, legal and other agencies.

Try not to duplicate assessments that have already been done. Street children tend to have a short attention span, so avoid asking too many questions (it may be useful spread the assessment over more than one session to make the process less demanding).

Priorities :- During the assessment, you may come across conditions and/or situations which require urgent attention, such as injuries or threat of violence. Attend to these priority issues before dealing with substance use or sexual and reproductive health.

Suggested areas for assessment and use of the Modified Social Stress Model for collecting information. The Modified Social Stress Model can help to decide on the questions that can be asked regarding the problems and the potential of street children. Information should be obtained in the following areas:

— Background: age, gender, religion, cultural background.

— Substance use.

— Sexual and reproductive health.

— Physical health and injuries.

— Mental health and psychological trauma.

— Family and social.

— School and vocation.

— Unlawful behaviour.

— Recreational and cultural activities.

Methods for Collecting Information

To obtain quality information about street children, methods suitable for small groups of people should be used. The choice of the method will depend on the type of information needed. These methods are:

- Focus group discussions.
- Case studies.
- Observation.
- Key Informant interviews. (in the street context, the term "informant" often means "police
- Therefore replace the term informant with a more acceptable term when introducing the concept during assessment).
- Narrative research method.
- Surveys.
- Projective methods.

Importance of Questions

Many street children will not speak spontaneously about their lives, especially to a stranger. They have learned to be careful about who they give information to and are suspicious of adults who ask too many questions. Think carefully about what questions you need to ask and how to ask them. Ask questions in a way that will encourage them to speak freely. Approach the child in a manner that will make him/ her feel comfortable. Here are some simple phrases and questions that you can use to start a conversation with the child:

Getting to know each other:- Say who you are and ask the child to tell you his/her name. Address the child by name as it makes the child feel that you respect him or her. If the child does not respond, tell the child where you work and when he or she can come to speak to you. Don't ask questions that might make the child feel threatened or suspicious. Keep the questions simple and general. Show that you are genuinely interested in the child.

Asking questions about a painful subject :- When questioning a street child about something that may be painful for them to think about, spend some time with the child, starting with general questions, and then ask questions that are gradually more specific. Do not assume that you know how the child feels about any event. Emotional reactions occur in specific situations of a person's life. Two people may have completely different emotional reactions to the same event, e. g. death of a father can lead to deep sorrow, but the death of an abusive, violent father can also lead to a feeling of relief. The same person might also feel a mixture of conflicting emotions about a single event, as in the above situation, the death of an abusive father can lead to a feeling of relief, but the child might also feel guilty about feeling relieved at his father's death.

Types of Questions

There are two types of questions: closed and open-ended.

— *Yes and No questions (closed questions)*: These types of questions are formulated to give a simple yes or no answer.

— *Open ended questions*: Open-ended questions encourage further conversation and more information can be gathered about the street child. The process of asking such questions should be guided by the topic being explored.

The WHO Street Children Project on substance use has developed a long list of questions designed to provide information about the six components included in the Modified Social Stress Model. A key question has been written about each of the six components of the model. In addition, many follow up questions or 'probes' have been included to obtain more detail about specific issues. These questions have been written to give ideas as to the type of questions that may be asked and the issues that may be raised in the inquiry. You can select specific questions that are relevant for your needs. Add questions if needed. Consider the age and cultural background of the children before choosing any questions. When choosing questions for adults, consider their professional, cultural, and religious background.

Question Menu A: Street children

Demographic information

These questions provide information on the background of street children:

— Gender of the participants.

— How old are you? Or what year were you born?

— Where were you born?

— Can you read and write? How much schooling did you do?

— Where do you live?

— With whom do you live?

— Where are your parents? Who raised you?

— Where did your parents come from?

— Do you practice any religion? How important is it to you?

— Do you work? What type of work do you do?

Stresses

a) *Major Life Events.* Key Question: Has anything happened to you in your life that has been very difficult? Probes, if needed:

— Have you ever been so sick or injured that you needed to go to the hospital?

- Has any one close to you died?
- Have you ever been in a situation where you feared losing your life or being severely harmed?
- Have you ever experienced a natural disaster, such as an earthquake, flood or fire?
- Are you a refugee?

b) *Everyday stresses*:- Key question: What don't you like about living on the streets? What don't you like about living with your family? Probes, if needed -

- What do you like about living on the streets? What do you like about living with your family?
- What do you try to avoid each day? (Problems, street children, activities)
- Where do you usually sleep? Where do you sleep at other times?
- Where do you usually get your food? What do you usually eat? Do you ever go hungry? If youcannot get food, what do you do?
- Where do you get your clothes? Are they warm/ comfortable enough? What about when it rains heavily? Do you ever get cold? Where and how do you clean your clothes?
- Where do you go to wash or clean yourself? How often?
- Where do you get your money? Do you ever provide sex in exchange for affection, food,clothing, shelter, drugs or money?
- Do you often get hassled? Who hassles you? Why do they hassle you? What do they do?

c) *Enduring life strains*:- Key question: What are the most important problems that you have in your life at the moment, other than finding food, shelter and clothing? Probes, if needed:

— Do you feel good about yourself?

— Are you as physically strong as everyone else?

— What are the most important things that you need right now to get by?

— What are your plans for the future?

— Do you need more education? What kind of education?

— Will you be able to find a job? What kind of job could you get? What type of training would assist in getting the type of job you would like to have? What kind of job would you like?

— Where would you like to live?

— Do you often feel sad, lonely or unhappy?

— Have you ever tried to harm or kill yourself?

d) Life transitions:-Key questions: Have you had to move often? Do you need to move around a lot when living on the streets? Why? Does your family move around a lot? Why? Probes if needed:

— Did you grow up in a different place? What made you move here?

— If you have moved, did you lose contact with close friends or family?

— Is it difficult to make new friends when you move into a new area?

— What makes it easier to fit in with a new group of street children ?

— Have you had different groups of friends? If so, why did you change your friends?

e) Developmental changes of adolescence:- Key Question:What things are good and what things are difficult about growing up and being an adolescent? Probes, if needed:

— What is it like to be an adolescent? Are you like other adolescents? What is different about you?

— Do you worry about growing up? Do you worry about your size or appearance?

Normalization of substance use

Key question: What problems concerning substance use are there in your community ? Probes, if necessary:

— What do street children in your community think of substance use?

— Which substances are all right and which substances are bad to use? Which is the most harmful substance and which is the safest?

— Where do street children get their substances from?

— How easy is it for street children around here to get substances? Is it easier to obtain substances here than elsewhere?

— Do street children prefer using certain substances or do they use different substances depending on their availability?

— In what way has there been a change in the availability of different substances around here over time?

— How much does the cost of substances influence the type and amount of substances that street children use? Has there been a change in the cost of the substances that they use?

— Do street children use more substances when they live on the streets or when they live elsewhere?

— Do most street children use the same substances as their friends? Do friends encourage others around here to use substances? If so, why?

— Do street children get hassled by the police or others because of their substance use?

— Do you think that advertising, sponsorship or marketing of substances influences street children?

Effects of substance use

Key questions: What are the main reasons street children use substances? What effects do they get from using substances such as cannabis, alcohol, tobacco, glue, etc. ? Probes, if needed:

—What substances do you/street children use? Which is the favourite substance? Which is the least favourite substance? You may prompt from the following list:

— Alcohol

— Tobacco

— Cannabis (e. g. marijuana leaf, hashish, resin/oil)

— Natural opioids (e. g. heroin, opium, morphine, codeine)

— Synthetic opioids (e. g. methadone, pethidine, omnopon)

— Cocaine (e. g. coca paste, cocaine salt, crack)

— Amphetamine-like stimulants (e. g. methylphenidate, methamphetamine, MDA, ice)

— Stimulant/Hallucinogens (e. g. MDMA, bromo-DMA)

— Other stimulants (e. g. ephedrine, caffeine)

— Hallucinogens (e. g. LSD, psilocybin, peyote, mescaline, PCP)

— Hypnosedatives (e. g. barbiturates, benzodiazepines, methaqualone)

— Volatile substances and aerosols (e. g. petrol, glue, benzene)

— Others (e. g. khat, kava, pitchuri, nutmeg, betel nut)

— Prescription drugs

— How often do you/street children use these substances?

— How much of the substance do you/street children use each time? Do you/street children get intoxicated?

— How do you/street children take these substances?

— When did you/street children first start using these substances?

— Why do you/street children take them? How do the substances affect you/street children? Do you/street children enjoy them?

— Where do you/street children prefer to go to use substances?

— Who do you/street children use these substances with? Do you/street children use substances when alone? Do you/street children share substances with others?

— What do you/street children find is good/bad about taking substances?

— What effect does taking substances have on your health or the health of street children ?

— How do you feel about your taking substances?.

— What does your family feel about your substance use? Or How does substance use affect family life around here?

— How does your substance use affect your friendships? Or How does substance use affect friendships?

— How does your substance use affect your study or work?

— Have you/street children been in trouble with the police because of (your) substance use?

— Have you/street children had to leave a place you/they were living in because of your/ their substance use?

— Do you/street children go without things such as food or clothes so that you/they can buy substances?

— Does substance use affect your/someone's sex life? Do you/street children usually have sex when you/they take substances?

— Have you/street children ever been in an accident after using substances?

— Have you/street children ever been in fights during or after using substances?

— Do you/street children feel guilty about using substances?

— Do you/street children need help because of (your) substance use? Would you/ street children like help to do something about (your) substance use?

— Has anyone told you/street children that you should do something about your/their substance use? Do any of your friends have a substance use problem?

— Have you/street children ever been treated for a substance problem? Can a person with a substance problem be helped or cured?

— How do you feel about street children who sell substances?

Attachments

Key Question: Who or what is most important to you? Probes, if needed:

— What is/ was your family like? Are you still in contact with them?

— What do you like about your family? What don't you like about your family?

— (If away) What do you miss about your family? Would you like to visit your family or go back and live with them? Would your family welcome you back?

— Who is most important to you in the family?

— What are your thoughts about school? (same for non-formal education) What is/was the most useful thing about school?

— How well did/do you do at school? (same for non-formal education) How did/can you keep up with the schoolwork?

— How did/do you get along with your teachers? (same for non-formal education)

— Would you consider going back to school? (same for non-formal education)

— Do you have a few close friends, many not very close friends, or no real friends? Who is your closest friend?

— Whom do you trust? Whom don't you trust? Who do you turn to when you need help?

— Whom do you admire? Who is your hero?

— Whom do you most agree with -your parents/carers, your friends, your teachers/employer, or your sexual partner?

— Whom do you feel most comfortable with?

— Who admires you? Who says good things about you?

— Who are you most like?

— Do your parents/carers approve of your lifestyle? Do your parents/carers approve of your friends?

— Do your friends approve of your parents/carers?

— Do/did your parents/carers have a substance use problem? Did you leave home because of your parents'/

careers' substance use? Did you leave home because of sexual, physical or emotional abuse?

— Is religion important in your life?

— Do you like your work?

— What is your employer like?

— Do you have a pet? How do you feel about your pet?

— Do you own anything that is very special to you?

Skills, competencies and coping strategies

Key questions: What things do you think you are best at? How have you managed to survive the difficulties in our life? Probes, if needed:

— What are the most difficult problems that you have to deal with?

— How do you usually deal with these problems?

— What could you learn that would help you cope better?

— What do you do when you feel anxious or stressed? What do you do when you feel sad or depressed?

— What do you do when you feel angry? How do you try to control your anger or violence?

— Do you have any problems sleeping? What helps you to sleep?

— What do you do to make you feel better about yourself?

— How do you try to stop street children from forcing you to do something you don't want to do?

— What do you do to try to control your substance use?

— What special skills do you need to work or to earn money?

Resources

- Where do you get your information from? Who do you speak to and listen to? What information do you trust? Who wouldn't you listen to or take notice of?
- Where do you go for medical treatment? Do you feel comfortable there? Are you treated well there? How could the service be improved? Who do you listen to about medical and health information?
- Who do you see to help you find shelter or a place to live?
- Who helps you get food?
- Where do you go to find clothing?
- Where do you go for recreation? What do you do for fun? What would you like to do forrecreation? Do you play any sports? Would you like to play sports?
- Where do you spend most of your time? Where would you like to spend time?
- Are you involved in any educational activity? If so, what are you learning?
- Have you had any training for a job? If so, where? What kind of training would you like? How would it be helpful?
- If you can read, what do you read and what would you like to read?
- Do you watch television, video, movies, or listen to the radio? Which do you trust, and which provides you with the best information?
- Do you read information pamphlets and posters? Do you believe them?
- What kind of information would you take notice of, e. g. colourful, humorous, frightening, serious?

— Where do you find out about information on substances?

— Where would you go to get help for a substance problem?

— Who could give you advice about your diet?

General health issues

— How has your general health been in the past?

— What problems have you had with your health? Have you had any accidents? Do you suffer from any allergies? Have you any problems with your teeth? Have you ever had a sexually transmitted disease?

— Do you suffer from any long term disability?

— Have you ever required medical treatment, e. g. for malaria, tuberculosis, parasite infection? Have you ever been admitted to a hospital? If so, why? Have you had any, operations?

— Have you ever been treated by a psychiatrist or psychologist? Why did you need such treatment?

— Are you receiving any treatment now? Are you satisfied with your medical treatment? How can it be improved?

— Has your substance use caused any problem with your health?

— What immunizations have you received?

— What do you normally eat? Do you think that this is a good diet? How could it be improved?

Risk behaviours

Key Question:Example of asking question directly: Do you take any risks with your life or safety? If so what type of risks? Example of asking question indirectly: Do you think street children take risks with their lives or safety? If so, what type of risks? Probes if needed:

— Do you/street children around here do somewhat risky or daring things? How do you/street children around here show off to your friends? How do you/street children around here prove yourself?

— What do you/street children around here need to do to be accepted by the other street children?

— Do you/street children around here get involved in fights? Do you/street children here carry/use a knife, gun, or other weapons? Do you/street children around here break the law for fun, to be accepted by others, or to survive in the streets?

— Do you/street children around here do risky things to earn money or to get food, clothes, shelter, etc?

— Are you/street children around here sexually active? Have you ever been forced to have sex? Do you provide sex to survive? Have you ever had sex with a person of the same sex? How many sexual partners have you had/ have now?

— Have you any children or have you been pregnant? Have you ever had an abortion? If so, where?

— What are sexually transmissible diseases? What is HIV? AIDS? Have you ever had a sexually transmissible disease? Are you/street children around here at risk of becoming infected with HIV or with other sexually transmissible diseases ?

— Do you use any form of contraception? What type? How often?

— What is 'safer sex'?

— Do you/street children around here experiment with different combinations of substances? What combinations do you/street children around here use? Do you/street children around here ever take substances which you don't know about?

— Do you/street children around here do risky things after using substances, such as committing a crime, climbing buildings or trees, swimming, having sex with strangers, or walking across a busy street?

— Do you use substances alone or with other street children? Where do you use these substances?

— Have you ever injected a substance? How did you inject it? If so, did you share the needle, syringe, water, or any other utensils with someone else?

— Where do you get your clean needles and syringes from? Do you re-use them? How do you clean them and with what?

— Who would you ask to find out more about the substances you use, and how could you protect yourself from any harm?

Menu B: Service Provider

The second menu (Service Provider Question Menu) is for collecting data from adults who are involved with street children. Questions to be asked of adults can also be asked in a focus group, an interview, or a survey.

— *What is the sex ratio of street children?*

— What is the age range and average age?

— Where do they come from? Where do their parents come from?

— What are the literacy and educational levels like?

— Where do street children live, sleep, spend most of the day?

— Where are their parents? Who and where were they raised? Do they come from institutions?

— What is their religious involvement?

— Do they work?

The term, 'street children' is used throughout the sample Menu Questions for Service Providers. Remember the definition of street children used by the WHO Street Children Project on substance use is broadly defined. You will need to adapt the term to fit your local needs. For example, instead of street children, you may want to say "homeless children"or "children living in slums". An organization in Canada, found that the terms "street kids" and "street youth" were preferred.

Stress

a) Major life events.

— What kind of tragedies have street children been exposed to?

— What disasters or major changes has the local community been exposed to?

— How was the community affected? How did the community respond?

— How have these tragedies and disasters affected the children? What help have they received to cope with the trauma of these tragedies and changes?

— What major risks do street children have to contend with on the streets?

— Are street children scared of being harmed? How or by whom?

— Have street children been affected by any major illness?

b) Everyday stresses.

— How do street children spend each day?

— What do they have to do to survive on the streets each day? What are their priorities?

— What are the problems that they have to deal with? How do they cope?

— Where do they sleep?

— How do they find shelter, food and clothing?

— How do they keep clean?

— How do they pay for their basic needs, recreation and substances?

— Are street children involved in survival sex?

c) Enduring life strains.

— What are the social, cultural, health, political, environmental, industrial and economicproblems of the local community?

— How do these affect the street children? What are the future prospects like for street children?

— What are the main social factors which contribute to their homelessness?

— How do street children feel? Do they suffer from depression? What is their self-image and selfesteem like? How do they express their feelings?

— Do street children harm themselves or commit suicide?

d) Life transitions.

— How mobile are street children? What are their movements and why do they move?

— How stable are their contacts with their family, peers and health and welfare services?

— What kind of changes do street children experience? How do they adjust to these changes?

e) Developmental changes of adolescence.

— What problems of adolescence do these street children experience?

— Are these problems similar to other adolescents?

— Are street children concerned about their size or appearance?

— Do they understand the normal developmental changes of adolescence?

Normalization of substance use

— What substance problems exist within the community?

— What substances are used in the community?

— What is the attitude of the community towards different substances, substance use and substance users? What substance use is condoned and what substance use is not accepted by the community?

— Do street children use substances?

— How does the community influence substance use?

— How easy is it to obtain both licit and illicit substances in the community?

— Are substances more readily available for street children?

— Do peers and families influence the substance use by street children?

— How important is advertising, sponsorship and 'pushing' in influencing substance use by street children?

— How are street children who take substances treated by the police or other law enforcement officers?

— What strategies (e. g. health education campaigns) are used in the community to prevent substance related problems?

Substance use and its effects

What substances do street children use? What are the preferred substances? What combinations are used?

- Why do street children use substances?
- How are these substances used or what is the route of administration?
- How often do street children use these substances? How many children are dependent on substances?
- Where are these substances obtained from?
- How do they pay for them?
- Where do they use these substances? Who do they use them with?
- Do they sell substances?
- What are the main problems that they experience through their substance use?
- What are the greatest risks to street children through their substance use?
- What are the greatest concerns that the community and your organization have about the use of substances by street children? Do street children cause problems for the community?

Attachments

- What kind of families do street children have or come from?
- Are street children still in contact with their families? Do they miss their families?
- Could they return home to live with their families?
- What are the reasons for street children leaving home?
- How common is physical, emotional and sexual abuse in these families?
- How do their families feel about their children living on the streets?

— What problems do their parents have? Is it common for their parents to have a substance problem?

— Who are their friends? How strong are these friendships?

— Whom do they trust? Who don't they trust?

— Whom do they admire? Who acts as role models for them?

— Who admires them? Who gives them complements and positive messages? What are street children good at?

— How are they valued in the community?

— What has their schooling experience been like? Why have they left school?

Skills

Competencies and coping strategies What coping skills do street children use to survive on the streets?

— Are there positive learning experiences associated with living on the streets?

— What are the most difficult problems that they have to deal with?

— How do they cope with depression, anxiety, anger and fear?

— Compared with other children, what living and coping skills do they lack?

— How do street children learn new skills?

Resources

— Where do street children get their information from? What information do they trust? Who do they trust as information providers? In what form is the information more likely to be accepted?What information resources are available to them? Have any resources been specifically developed for street children?

— Where do street children go for medical treatment or advice? What medical services are available? How accessible are these services to street children? Is training offered to service providers to improve delivery of services to street children? Has the training been evaluated?

— Are reproductive health services available for street children? Are condoms and other contraceptives easily available to street children? Is testing for HIV and other Sexually Transmissible Diseases (STDs) offered for street children? Is pre- and post-test counselling available? Is treatment for STDs available? Is care and support available for street children who are infected with HIV and those who have AIDS?

— Where do street children go for advice or treatment related to substance use? What substance treatment and advisory services are available to street children? What strategies are used? How accessible are these services for street children?

— Are there any services specifically for adolescents? How are street children treated by these various agencies?

— Do any agencies provide a range of services in one location? What agencies provide an outreach service? How are outreach services provided? Who utilizes the outreach services?

— Where do those children go to find shelter? What kind of accommodation and accommodation services is available? How accessible are these services to street children?

— Where do street children go to find food? What services are available to feed street children? How accessible are these services to street children?

— Where do street children get dressed? What services are available to provide clothes for street children? How accessible are these services to street children? Where and how do they clean their clothes?

— Where do street children go to wash? What services provide facilities for street children to wash? How accessible are these services to street children?

— What do street children do for recreation? Where do they go for recreation? What recreation services are available for street children? How accessible are these services to street children?

— Where do street children go to find formal and non-formal educational opportunities? What educational services are available to street children? How accessible are they for children? What percentage of children are able to read, write, and do basic mathematics?

— Where do street children go to find employment? What vocational training and employment services are available to street children? How accessible are these services to street children?

— Where do street children go for counselling or emotional support? What counselling services are available for street children? How accessible are these services for street children?

— Where do street children go for religious or spiritual guidance? What religious support is available to street children? How accessible is this support to them?

— Where do street children go for legal advice or support? What legal advice and rights are available for street children? How accessible are these services to street children? What human rights abuses do they suffer? Who abuses them?

— Where do street children go for physical protection when they are threatened? What protective services are available to street children? How accessible are these services to street children?

— Are there networks of community agencies which deal with street children? How do these networks operate?

— Has any research been conducted or data collected on the problem of street children in the community?

— Where do agencies dealing with street children go for advice or support?

— What exposure do street children have to the mass media, such as television and radio? What mass media health education programmes are available to street children?

— Where do street children working with street children get their training from?

General health issues

What are the main health problems of these street children? What type of long term disabilities do street children suffer from?

— What is the prevalence of sexually transmissible diseases and other infections among street children?

— How common are accidents and other trauma among street children?

— How common are psychiatric illnesses among street children?

— Do street children suffer from nutritional disorders?

— Do street children experience dental problems?

— What are the common health problems in the general community? How do these problems differ from the problems experienced by homeless children? What factors contribute to these differences?

Risk behaviours

— What kind of risk behaviours do street children indulge in? Which of these behaviours pose the greatest risk to the children and to the community?

— How common is injectable substance use in this group of children? How common is needle sharing? What knowledge do street children have of safer substance using practices? What are the greatest risks to street children through their substance use?

— How common are unplanned pregnancies among street girls? How are these pregnancies managed?

— What contraception is used by street children? What is their understanding of safer sex, and how widely is it practiced?

— How common is survival sex/prostitution in this group of street children?

Methods for Collecting Information

A number of methods that have been used by the WHO Street Children Project.

Focus Group Discussions

A Focus Group Discussion (FGD) is an organized discussion among 6 to 12 individuals on a single topic for a specified duration. It helps in the collection of qualitative information. The process of group interaction stimulates active participation and encourages ordinary dialogue among members of the group. The assessment is better if the dialogue resembles a normal, serious discussion. The focus group technique is especially useful for an in-depth exploration of street children's and service providers' views on the given topic.

Preparing for Focus Group Discussions.

Steps that need to be kept in mind during the preparation for a focus group discussion include:

a) *Decide what you want to know*:- It is not possible to discuss every issue related to street children and substance use or sexual and reproductive health in a single focus group. Decide what information you need to know the most. Make a checklist of the general questions and probes. General or key questions allow group members to reveal their general perceptions and attitudes and specific questions or probes help to develop deeper discussions of these perceptions and in understanding the decision making process of group members. The list will remind the facilitators during the discussion of all the issues that need to be discussed. Ideally, at least one current or former street child could be a part of the planning group for the FGD.

b) *Identify the participants*:- The children themselves can answer many questions but, to get a complete picture, organize a group discussion with service providers, community leaders, ordinary residents, or law enforcers. Participants for these groups can be selected on the basis of the questions that need to be answered.

c) *Characteristics of members of the street children focus group*:- Determine whether you want street children with similar or different backgrounds in the same group eg. vendors, sex workers, those using substances or at risk of sexual and reproductive health problems. Girls should be separated from boys because they often do not speak much in the presence of boys, especially if there are more boys than girls in the group. It is important to get information about street girls because their lives are different from those of street boys in several important ways. They may have more needs and may face more dangers than street boys.

d) *Characteristics of members of service providers focus group:-* Invite members of the community who are in close contact with street children (such as community nurses, doctors, social workers, community development officers, volunteers, vendors who employ street children, parents, teachers, law enforcement officers etc.). It is often helpful to invite service providers from a range of different organizations. Mixing participants from different organizations in the same FGD can promote an interesting exchange of ideas and information and increase motivation to attend.

Plan the Focus Group Discussion

a) *Date and Time*: Ensure that the timing of the discussion is convenient to all participants. The time that suits street girls may be different from the time that suits street boys. Choosing an appropriate time may be particularly important for service-provider groups.

b) *Confirm attendance*: Keep in contact with the participants in person or in writing.

c) *Venue*: Arrange the meeting point. The place should be safe, comfortable and easily accessible. It should offer privacy.

d) *Presentation material/aids and seating arrangement*: Prepare visual aids. Make seating arrangements and place teaching aids in a manner that promotes participation and communication, e. g. sitting in a circle provides better eye contact and improves communication.

e) *Plan the focus group discussion*: Identify the facilitator, observer and recorder, and fix the duration.

Roles of Participants

All participants of the FGD, have an important role in ensuring the quality and progress of the discussion. The roles of various participants are given below:

a) *Facilitator*: the facilitator should preferably be of the same sex as the FGD members, should speak the same language and be familiar with the topic for discussion. Ideally, he or she should have had the experience of working directly with street children. The members of the group must feel that the facilitator cares about them and their problems. It is best to ask street children and service providers who they think would be a good facilitator for their respective groups. The facilitator should:

— introduce the themes being discussed and create a conducive environment for discussions. - establish confidence and trust among participants and ensure that each group member is participating. - control the group, keep discussion focused and help participants present their ideas and feelings to the group. - protect members of the group from personal attacks, putdowns and criticism. With a group of more than six street children or service providers it is better to have two facilitators. A single facilitator might not be able to guide the discussion and pay attention to the emotional needs of the participants at the same time.

b) *Recorder*: this should be someone who can prevent his or her own opinions from influencing the information he or she records. The person must also have writing skills, observation skills, and familiarity with the dialect or slang of the group. The recorder should:

— note the date and time of the meeting, number of group members, and their name and age. - note the proceedings in the words of the group members so that other readers can actually get the 'feel' of the discussion. - from time to time help the facilitator by making suggestions on how to make the discussion more meaningful.

— check the notes immediately after the discussion for completeness and accuracy.

Recording is a critical task because hearing the 'voice of street children' is the very purpose of focus group discussions. Documenting only what is actually stated is a skill that can be developed. One way to practice this skill is to simultaneously record the discussion on paper and on an audio (or video) tape, and then compare the two.

c) *Observer* : The person must have observation skills and should observe:

— the process of the discussion, the flow of dialogue, the emotional atmosphere and problems that hinder communication.

— nonverbal cues e. g. silence, restlessness and posture.

Bibliography

Campos, R., Antunes, C., Jeronymo, M., Raffaelli, M., Payne-Merritt, A., Halsey, N., And Greco, D., "Comparison of behavioral risks for HIV infection among sub-groups of brazilian street youth". *Presented at 8th International Conference on AIDS*, Amsterdam, The Netherlands, 1992.

_____________, Greco, M., Ude, W., Machado, A., Raffaelli, M., Campos, M., and Greco, D., "Female street youths: Social factors associated to behavioral risks for HIV infection". *Presented at 10th International Conference on AIDS*, Yokohama, Japan, 1994.

_____________, Raffaelli, M., Ude, W., Greco, M., Ruff, A., Rolf, J., Antunes, C., Halsey, N., and Greco, D. "Social networks and daily activities of street youth in Belo Horizonte, Brazil". *Child Development* 65:319-330, 1994.

Carlini, E.A., and Carlini-Cotrim, B., Illicit use of psychotropic drugs among brasilian students: 1987 and 1989 surveys. In Brasil - United States Binational Research, eds. M.G. Monteiro and J.A. Inciardi, 151-163. Sao Paulo, Brasil:CEBRID, 1993.

Carlini-Cotrim, B., and Carlini, E. A., "The use of solvents and other drugs among children and adolescents from a low socio economic background: A study in Sao Paulo, Brazil". *International Journal of the Addictions* 23:1145-1156, 1988.

De Paula, I., "Drugs used by 100 percent of street children. Brasilia Correio Braziliense". 10(May):2, 1992.

Dewees, A. and Klees, S.J., "Social movements and the transformation of national policy: Street and working children in Brazil". *Comparative Education Review* 39(1):76-100, 1995.

Eisenstein, e. "Street youth: Social imbalance and health risks". *Journal of Paediatrics and Child Health*, supp. 1, 29:S46-S49, 1993.

WHO, Life skills education in schools: *Geneva, World Health Organization*, 1994.

WHO, UNESCO. School health education to prevent AIDS and HIV: a resource package for curriculum planners: Teachers' guide. *Geneva, World Health Organization and United nations Educational, Scientific and Cultural Organization, 1994.*

Index

STREET CHILDREN AND THE ASPHALT LIFE

STREET CHILDREN AND THE ASPHALT LIFE

(In 3 Volumes)

Volume 2

(Delinquent Street Children)

Editor

P.C. Shukla

ISHA

ISHA BOOKS

Delhi-110033

Street Children and the Asphalt Life
(Delinquent Street Children)

Rs. 2500 (Set)
Rs. 835 (Each Volume)

ISBN : 81-8205-212-2 (Set)
ISBN : 81-8205-307-2 (Vol. 2)

Published in 2005 in India by
Isha Books
D-43, Prithviraj Road,
Adarsh Nagar, Delhi - 110033
e-mail : ishabooks@hotmail.com

Laser Typesetting at : Global Printers, New Delhi
Printed at : Chawla Offset Press, Delhi

Contents

Preface

Street children are the casualties of economic growth, war, poverty, loss of traditional values, domestic violence, physical and mental abuse. Every street child has a reason for being on the streets. While some children are lured by the promise of excitement and freedom, the majority are pushed onto the street by desperation and a realisation that they have nowhere else to go. In many countries, street children are named after their main survival activities. What is obvious is that street children are poverty-stricken and their needs and problems are a result of wanting to meet basic needs for survival. They go through the struggle of providing themselves with basic things such as food, shelter, health and clothing. Providing targeted interventions that meet the needs of street children requires an understanding of who they are, what they need, what they do and how they can be identified.

It is estimated that there are between 10 and 100 million street children in the world today. These children live a transitory life style and are vulnerable to inadequate nutrition, physical injuries, substance use, and health problems including sexual and reproductive health problems. Some street children are part of entire families who live on the street. Others are born to older street girls. Some street children are 'on the street', which means that they still see their families regularly and may even return every night to sleep in their family homes. Children 'of the streets', on the other hand, have no home but the streets. Even if they occasionally spend time in institutions for

children or youths, they consider the streets to be their home. Although street children support themselves in many different ways, they need the assistance of caring adults and charitable services provided by governmental or non-governmental organisations. Despite peer solidarity and support through charitable services, street children have extremely high rates of morbidity, disability and mortality.

Improving the quality of life of street children is a difficult and challenging task. Street education is a very effective way to support street children as it occurs at locations where they live. Street education can involve many types of activities, for example, counselling about harmful effects of substances or about prevention of STDs, improving literacy and educating street children on the importance of seeking assistance on health issues or other social problems that could be addressed. It can be of vital importance in meeting the needs of street children in the areas of substance use, sex education, life skills, health education and literacy.

The present work in three volumes provides a comprehensive analysis of the problems of street children. The first volume *Selection and Enumeration of Street Children* narrates the status and burning issues of street children around the world. The second volume *Delinquent Street Children* discusses the crime trends among street children, the reasons that makes them criminals and the measures to reduce the delinquent activities. The third volume *Street Children and the Future Directions* discusses about the precarious future of street children. It explains the effective interventions to be taken to protect them from physical and mental vulnerabilities. This work will prove to be a useful reference material for sociologists, researchers, policy-makers, child welfare agencies and all who working for the empowerment of street children.

Editor

1 Introduction

Youth homelessness and street children are phenomena, not only of developing countries, but experienced worldwide. Definitions of "street children", "homelessness" and "youth" vary across countries and cultures, as do the causes of homelessness and the associated problems. There are major difficulties in trying to estimate the number of street children and the magnitude of difficulties they experience as these populations are not adequately covered by national census, educational and health data.

Depending on the definition used, estimates of the numbers of street children range from 10 to 100 million, the majority being located in major urban areas of developing countries. By regions, estimates have included about 40 million in Latin America, 25-30 million in Asia, and over 10 million in Africa. Boys predominate (71-97%), but girls often have more difficulties.

Some of these children are "on the street", that is they maintain quite good family contact, often returning home each night. They may be on the streets to work, have fun, to pass time, or due to overcrowding in their homes which may provide little more than a place to sleep. In some countries, these are the majority of street children. Others are "of the street", where the street is their home. Some search for their identity on the streets.

The existence of street children is not something new. Historically, the streets of large urban areas have been both theatre and battleground for the children of the poor. Their lives have tended to be romanticized by some, but in most instances they have been referred to in derogatory terms: "gamin" (urchin) and "chinches" (bed bugs) in Colombia, "marginais" (criminals/marginals) in Rio, "pajaro frutero" (fruit birds) in Peru, "polillas" (moths) in Bolivia, "resistoleros" (little rebels) in Honduras, "scugnizzi" (spinning tops) in Naples, "Bui Doi" (dust children) in Vietnam, "saligoman" (nasty kids) in Rwanda, or "poussins" (chicks), "moustiques" (mosquitos) in Cameroon and "balados" (wanderers) in Zaire and Congo. While their lives have been of genuine concern to some, it is more likely that they have been exploited and marginalized; used as cheap and expendable labour, for sex and for criminal acts.

Most accounts focus on particular groups at a particular time and tend to ignore the historical continuity which exists: most are male, their peer relationships, group life and survival strategies have been much the same whatever the time or place, and they are usually younger in developing than in developed countries. However, more recent economic situations (e.g. recession), political changes, civil unrest, increasing family disintegration, and natural disasters have led to larger numbers of children heading from rural areas and smaller towns to larger cities and their streets.

Some are born on the streets to older street children, some come from families which can no longer support them due to overcrowding or poverty, some are members of whole families who live on the streets (street families) and others come to streets after being orphaned by armed conflicts, natural disasters, or parental death through diseases such as AIDS: one estimate suggests that there will be 16 million children orphaned by AIDS in Africa by the year 2015. The increased availability of a wide range of drugs adds to other potential health risks.

For the purposes of the Street Children Project, a number of distinct groups of young people have been subsumed under the definition of "Street Children":

a) Children living on the streets, whose immediate concerns are survival and shelter.

b) Children who are detached from their families and living in temporary shelters, such as abandoned houses and other buildings, hostels/refuges/shelters, or moving about between friends.

c) Children who remain in contact with their family, but because of poverty, overcrowding, or sexual or physical abuse within the family will spend some nights,or most days on the streets.

d) Children who are in institutional care, who have come from a situation of homelessness and are at risk of returning to a homeless existence.

Lifestyle and Health

While youth is generally a time of relatively good health, the nature of continuous exposure to the streets and the associated lifestyles makes street children vulnerable to a range of health and other problems which are not typically experienced by other young people. Factors which might contribute to vulnerability include:

a) Factors associated with the aetiology of their homelessness or street existence:

— family breakdown

— armed conflict

— poverty

— natural and man-made disasters

— famine

— physical and sexual abuse

— exploitation by adults

— dislocation through migration

— urbanization and overcrowding

— acculturation

b) Factors associated with the physical conditions of homelessness and street life:

— poor hygiene and sanitation

— poor diet

— lack of shelter from the environment

— violence

— transiency of situation and its effects on planning

— possible lack of positive attachments, with resultant emotional and social deprivation

— sensory deprivation

c) Factors associated with survival behaviours on the street and coping with stress:

— criminal behaviour

— begging, including acts of self-mutilation and self-humiliation

— violence

— exploitation by adults

— prostitution/survival sex

— drug use

— involvement in the production, distribution and marketing of drugs

d) Factors associated with inaccessibility to services and resources:

- — inadequate primary health care, including vaccinations
- — lack of access to recreational, educational and vocational opportunities
- — lack of positive role models

The particular health problems which have been identified among street children include:

- — Malnutrition and other disorders of diet. Specific nutritional deficiencies resulting in such disorders as anaemia and endemic goitre.
- — Infectious diseases, including:
  - — skin
  - — respiratory tract
  - — sexually transmitted diseases
  - — viral, including HIV and Hepatitis A, B and C
  - — parasitic
  - — opportunistic
  - — specific infections, such as cholera, tuberculosis, leprosy, rheumatic fever
- — Oral health problems, such as dental caries and gingivitis.
- — Hazardous, harmful, and dysfunctional drug use, including drug dependency.
- — Unplanned pregnancies, often at a young age and with minimal, if any, ante-natal care; risks associated with practices for terminating pregnancies.
- — Skeletal and soft tissue injuries from accidents and violence.

- Industrial and environmental poisoning.
- Non-specific symptoms such as headache, abdominal pains, lethargy and nausea.
- Psychiatric disorders:
  - mood disorders, depression
  - suicide and para-suicide
  - anxiety and phobias
  - post-traumatic stress disorder
  - conduct and anti/dis-social personality disorders
  - psychoactive substance use disorders, including psychoses and organic disorders
  - sleep disorders
  - eating disorders
- Cognitive disorders and learning difficulties.

While other children may have any or many of the above health problems, street life may increase prevalence, morbidity and mortality.

Use of Drugs

The use of drugs by street children, although functional in most circumstances, tends to add to their health and other difficulties. While drugs may be used by street children to keep awake for work, or alert to possible violence, to get to sleep, to anaesthetize physical or emotional pain, or to replace the need for food, they increase health risks and may lead to high levels of exploitation and violence.

The drugs used by street children are usually those which are most readily available and cheap. For example, glue in areas where shoemaking is common, solvents in industrial areas, coca paste and cocaine in coca producing regions, opium and heroin in opium producing regions, and almost universally various forms of inhalants, alcohol, nicotine, cannabis and pharmaceutical products. In developing countries, street children who use drugs do not usually fit the stereotype of the "addict" or "junkie" in more developed nations: anti-social and criminal, poly-using and injecting substances such as heroin and amphetamines. In contrast to more developed countries, street children who use drugs in developing countries often present as much more cheerful in spite of their difficulties, generous, resourceful, helpful to each other, friendly, and younger. Despite this, they tend not to inspire much compassion from the ruling and monied classes, but are usually further marginalized and discriminated against.

Some children voluntarily or under duress become involved with the manufacture, traffic, distribution and sale of drugs. For others, drug use may provide status within the street community. As mentioned above, the greater part of life in some areas revolves around the manufacture, distribution and use of drugs, with access to services and protection linked to compliance with drug traffickers.

Involvement in crime and drug trafficking bring rewards unavailable via compliance with mainstream societal values. For example, in Brazil a child joining the criminal/drug "profession" does so as one would learn most trades; in a highly organized and structured manner. First he, as they are usually males, would be used as an "olheiro" whose job it is to tell others that the police or rival groups are in the area (often by flying kites). The next stage is that of "aviazinho", a transporter of drugs, and thereafter to "indolador", who packs them, an "misturador", who mixes the drugs with other substances to increase the quantity, and finally to the rank of "solado", a "soldier" who sells the drugs.

Due to current Brazilian law, those under 18 years are treated fairly tolerantly. Thus they will be exploited by drug traffickers until age 18, when they risk being killed by members of the trafficking group ("queima de arquivo" - the burning of the archives or knowledge of the trade). In some slum communities (e.g. favelas) a child involved in this process will be respected, and even feared, thereby achieving a status that merely being a poor, street or market vendor does not. He brings in a reasonable wage, and his family may depend on this for survival, and even the provision of "luxuries" such as television sets and stereos. He may also bring protection. By such employment, he can maintain a link with his culture, which may be severed if he enters the "welfare" or "helping" system provided by the state (if available), in which he is labeled "an abandoned child" or a "transgressor" or "delinquent" and is placed away from home.

In addition, drug "bosses" may play a crucial role in providing a purpose, economy and welfare system to marginalized communities. Street children constitute a marginalized group in most societies, where accessibility to health care and other services is severely restricted. For those street children who use drugs, discrimination and marginalization remain major obstacles to effective interventions. The WHO Programme on Substance Abuse (PSA) initiated a pilot project in 1991, with funding support from the international Drug Control Programme (UNDCP), to investigate and respond to the problem of substance use among street children. The project has aimed to address this problem utilizing rapid assessment methodologies and community development approaches. Placing the issue of substance use in the wider context of risk behaviours, a desired outcome of the project is an increase in the utilization of, and access to, health care services by street children.

In 1991, the Programme on Substance Abuse (PSA) made a commitment to develop a project to focus on the issue of substance use with regard to so called "street children". Funding was received from the United Nations International Drug Control Programme for the development and implementation of the project. Street children constitute a marginalized population in most urban centres of the world.

Street children who use drugs are even more marginalized and are neglected in relation to the provision of services. The initiation of the project was seen as an opportunity to raise national and international awareness of the needs of this group, the current tragedy of many of their lives, and to advocate for urgent and planned strategies to be implemented both for preventing and reducing harm associated with drug use by this population.

Particularly in developing countries, where street children are often much younger, they can provide a powerful image of how drugs can affect a whole community. With some street children, most of life revolves around the manufacture, distribution and use of drugs, with their basic means of survival, access to services and protection linked to compliance with and the support of those members of their communities who are involved in the drug industry. Concern for this population has arisen also due to the global spread of HIV/AIDS.

Street children are vulnerable through sexual exploitation and now drug use. Street children who are injecting drug users and/or who practice unsafe sex are also seen as one potential bridge for the spread of infection to the broader community. This could occur via the adults who share injection equipment with them or use them for sex. After some initial research and the development of a model to inform situation assessment and interventions, PSA selected seven countries, representing diverse cultural settings, to pilot the project. These countries were: Brazil, Egypt, Honduras, India, Mexico, the Philippines and Zambia. The selection of the countries reflected the belief that the prevalence and needs of street children are greater in developing countries. The selection does not intend to deny or ignore the plight of street children in more developed countries.

A meeting was held in Geneva (3 to 7 February, 1992) of representatives of key organizations involved in working with street children from the seven countries selected, to obtain a briefing on each participating country's situation with regard to their street children and their drug use, to discuss the project, to consider the role of PSA in addressing the problem, to review the instruments and methodology developed in late 1991, to set objectives and to prepare a plan for implementation of the project. The project was enthusiastically received, and the participating representatives were appreciative that the voices of street children and those working with them were being taken seriously and receiving global attention. They felt that the PSA initiative reinforced, by attention to street children who use drugs, the increasing concern of other United Nations' organizations, such as International Labour Organization (ILO), UNICEF and UNDCP.

It is generally accepted that the best predictor of experimentation with licit and illicit substances by young people is being young. Adolescence is a time of experimentation, exploration, curiosity and identity search and part of such a quest involves some risk taking. However, in some countries, by the time many young people reach adolescence they have been out of home for some time; working, begging, abandoned or sick. By adolescence they have also been exposed to many drugs, especially those easily available or associated with work—glue, petrol, cannabis, tobacco and alcohol.

Within a milieu of social and peer influence and expectations, together with easy drug availability, drug use becomes one aspect of the developmental process, and even a part of life. Most individuals who initiate drug use do not develop significant problems, with experimentation and a variable pattern of use and cessation being quite common. Much use of drugs is not mindless or pathological, but functional. When surveyed, young people in developed or developing countries often indicate that boredom, curiosity and wanting to feel good are perceived as the main reasons for drug use. Other functions served by drug use are to relieve hunger, to adopt a rebellious stance, to keep awake or get to sleep, and to dream.

However, the aetiologies of initiation into drug use and regular, harmful or dependent use may be quite different. It is generally believed that those young people who maintain and escalate their use of drugs are more vulnerable due to the presence of more problematic backgrounds. They usually also lack accessible internal and external resources. Earlier onset of use and continued use are strongly associated with other behaviours, such as precocious sexual activity, crime and educational failure. They are also associated with such environmental variables as: family disintegration, poverty, lack of accessible and useful recreational activities, lack of suitable alternative accommodation if the child cannot stay at home, relocation, oppression and discrimination, the availability of drugs and, in some cases, the pressure of dealers.

Studies shows that drug use by young people is more likely to occur where families: have low quality and inconsistent support of their children; model drug use; approve of use (explicitly or implicitly); lack closeness and involvement in the children's activities; have low educational aspirations; exert weak control and discipline; and emotionally, physically or sexually abuse their children. It is obvious that weak or negative bonds to the family would occur for children growing up in such environments.

Likewise, bonds to society can also be weakened by bad experiences at school. Failure, prejudice, a rejecting school environment (teachers, authorities and/or other students), not being able to stay awake or maintain attention because of needing to work at night to support the family, or being kept awake at night by domestic violence will all impact on educational achievement. In addition, poverty takes its toll: not being able to buy education, educational equipment, or transport to school, or not being able to pay to go on excursions. Families may be embarrassed that they are not able to provide adequately for their children, such as school clothing and books and may choose not to send their children to school to protect them from potentially embarrassing experiences. Bonds may also be weakened where young people work in environments where there is exploitation and adverse working conditions.

It is little wonder then that children from unhappy homes and schools would want to find comfort and support with others with whom they could identify. The streets and their occupants provide such peers, a sense of belonging to a new and often more caring replacement 'family', and a degree of freedom which may not have been possible previously. However, the price paid for this may be a near total absence of privacy, supervision, education, nurturance and security, and the likelihood of hunger, violence, marginal employment and exploitation.

It must also be remembered that not all young people who have experienced such familial and societal abuse end up in trouble or use drugs at dysfunctional or harmful levels. Many survive and do well. The aetiology of problematic drug use by young people, then, is clearly multi-determined and that the individual, the environment and the drugs themselves cannot be considered in isolation.

One way of conceptualizing the use of drugs is the Modified Social Stress Model which was developed by PSA from the work of Rhodes and Jason, and which emphasizes competence and coping. The modified model differs from that of Rhodes and Jason by incorporating environmental, social and cultural variables which may influence drug use, and also by acknowledging the role of the physical properties of the drugs used and their interactions with the user. It posits increased risk for problematic use of drugs as a function of the level of perceived personal (distress)stress, the image that drugs have in the particular community or subculture and the perceived effects on the individual of particular drugs, being offset by positive attachments, the possession of adequate coping strategies and skills, and access to necessary resources.

For example, risk may be greater when stress levels are high, drug use is promoted and condoned in the community, the drug effects experienced by the user are perceived as positive, positive attachments to family do not exist, coping skills are poor and access to resources blocked. The model appears to lend itself to attributing numeric values to each of the variables, which may have positive or negative valance and/or weighting, to assess risk. However, this form of analysis is difficult, time consuming and open to many interpretations. Consequently, the model is suggested as a conceptual framework which can organize information and assist in the formation of plans and interventions.

Normalisation

The variable "normalization" refers to a number of environmental, social and cultural factors which have been shown to, or are considered likely to contribute to or influence drug use. In particular, it refers to the extent to which particular drug use or drug-using behaviour may be considered "normal" in a society or sub-culture (in that it is widespread, visible, fairly resilient to law enforcement interventions and supply reduction strategies) and how that society reinforces this belief. These factors include:

Price : The price of a drug will significantly impact on the extent to which that drug is used. This is particularly so for young people and other populations where finances are severely restricted. When the price of a drug increases, the user with limited financial resources may use one or more of at least five options. First, the user can choose to stop using the drug. Unless something else is offered in its place, it is unlikely that this option would be acceptable to the user. Second, the user may reduce his or her level of drug use while maintaining the same expenditure on drugs. This appears to be a common approach particularly for non-dependent drug users. Third, the user could choose to change to a less expensive alternative drug. This is more likely to occur if the drug user has no preferred drug of use, or if he or she is not entrenched in a certain pattern of drug use. Younger drug users often fall into this group. Fourth, the drug user could use the drug more efficiently. As the drug becomes more expensive, or its purity decreases, the user may change from ingesting or inhaling the drug to injecting it, thereby increasing its bio-availability. This has significant implications as the health risks for injecting drugs are far greater than those for using other routes of administration. Finally, the user can make available more money or services, so that he or she can maintain the same level of drug use. To do this, the user may divert money from other living expenses (e.g. food, rent, clothing) to pay for drugs, or he or she may increase his or her earning power, such as working longer hours, committing more crime, selling more drugs, or using sex to earn money or pay for drugs.

Where incomes are low, the cheapest drugs tend to be consumed. Inhalants, such as glue, solvents and petrol, are cheap and widely used, particularly in developing countries, as may be alcohol in communities where in local brewing occurs, and cannabis and cocaine in producer and trans-shipment countries. Often combinations of drugs are used to achieve the greatest level of intoxication for the cheapest price.

Availability : The availability of drugs to a large extent is culturally determined. The community determines whether a drug is accepted or not and its legal status. Of those drugs which are licit, the community determines which drugs should be controlled and how they should be controlled. There are also those drugs for which there are no formal controls on their availability in different communities, such as caffeine and traditional drugs, including kava, betel nut and pitchuri.

For those drugs which are illicit, availability is determined by the supply of the drug and the vigilance of the drug enforcement agencies. The guaranteed attractive profit margins for supplying certain drugs ensures a continuing supply of those drugs. The trade is so vast, that any increase in the vigilance of law enforcement agencies to increase the probability for detection and punishment for illicit drug production, importation, trafficking, dealing or using is likely to result in only a small impact. The level of vigilance adopted by the authorities varies over time, across communities, and is very sensitive to both the local and international political mood.

Such vigilance, and the very fact of the illicit nature of certain drugs, contributes to the problems which are experienced by the drug user. The illicit nature of these drugs makes the user a criminal, marginalizes him or her within the society, and requires the user to use more drastic means to acquire the drug. It also increases the possibility of corruption on the part of those charged with vigilance.

Advertising and sponsorship : While contentious, certain studies indicate that young people are particularly susceptible to advertising messages; that alcohol and tobacco advertising may reinforce their use of these drugs; and that youth are often targeted in alcohol and tobacco advertising. Young people with little bonding to society are particularly vulnerable, when lacking hero figures and attractive models in their own communities, and having to rely on sporting and entertainment celebrities who may actively promote products such as alcohol and tobacco.

The portrayal of drug use on television and in movies, especially from developed nations, often highlight attractive elements such as danger and excitement, or place drug use in such a context that it is seen to be a normal, everyday event. Rarely are the harmful and unappealing consequences of drug use demonstrated, and when they are it is usually in a stereotyped portrayal. Many young people, having come from a severely disturbed home life, often rely on such media as a window into what may be considered a normal life.

Societal attitudes and reference group norms : Drug use has always been an integral part of most, if not all, societies. Each society has its own attitudes, beliefs and rules in relation to drug use. For any one drug, it may have a different role and pattern of use in different societies. Drug use may be encouraged, such as alcohol for celebrations in Western cultures, coca leaf chewing to ward off hunger and altitude sickness in the Andes, and opium smoking for relaxation in areas of Asia. Societal rules exist, where deviation from accepted drug using practice is negatively viewed within that community. It is important to consider the reference group that different populations relate to.

Many sub-cultures appear to condone drug use which in the wider community would be considered deviant. Examples include the ghetto cultures of certain USA cities, and some favelas in Brazil, where drug dealers often maintain a respected and hero profile in the community due to their material success as compared to the other ghetto/favela dwellers. In such communities it is not surprising to see young people aspire to follow in the same footsteps as these successful "businessmen", and further to this, such goals are achievable for them.

Drugs vary in their physiological actions; a certain drug is more likely to be used if the subjective experience of using that drug (an interplay of the drug's pharmacology on the individual in a certain environment with certain expectations) is an experience which was desired. Characteristics of the drug user significantly influence drug effects, the potential for dependence and the risk of drug-related harm. These characteristics include the individual's physical condition, other substances being used at the same time, his or her expectations and his or her past drug-related experiences. The drug experience does not necessarily have to be positive for the person to continue such drug use. It is not uncommon for street children to report negative experiences through their drug use, however it is claimed that any altered mood or state of conscious provides a welcome escape from the boredom or misery of reality.

Rhodes and Jason describe how bonding tends to occur within three distinct groups: the family, the school/work, and the peer group. Within these three groups, three variables determine the level of attachment and the behaviour expressed: a) the youth's exposure to opportunities and influences within the group, b) the youth's skillfulness of performance within the group, and c) the rewards which the youth receives from the group. Strong attachments to a group are likely to occur if a young person has high exposure to that group, is seen to perform well in that group through learning the necessary skills (such as skate-boarding, busking or pick-pocketing), and is consistently rewarded by that group. Young people who have established strong, positive attachments to their family and/or school/work are therefore less likely to develop attachments to drug using peer groups who use drugs in a harmful and/or dysfunctional manner, and who expect and reward these and other socially unaccepted behaviours.

Negative relationships also exist, sometimes called negative attachments. They lack the positive qualities of a relationship which is fulfilling, affirming and pro-social. They describe situations where, say, a young person is dependent on someone whom he or she despises, feels trapped in a relationship or has attached to anti-or asocial influences. It would appear that those young people who are detached from their families are at greatest risk. They may have minimal or no opportunities for developing attachments within a family, school or work environment, their exposure often being limited to peers who are in a similar position to themselves. This lack of exposure to such positive environments further compromises their capacity to learn how to behave in such situations. They may feel more comfortable with their peers who behave in a similar way and who hold similar attitudes and interests to them.

Even for those young people who do maintain contact with their families, they may find that the rewards that they receive from their peers are more attractive and consistent than those received from their families. If, in these circumstances, their peers are using drugs, or hold positive attitudes towards drug use, these youths are more likely to take up similar drug-using behaviours.

Childhood and adolescence are important times for the acquisition of coping and social skills. This process is in itself dependent on having positive attachments, the opportunity and resources to learn the skills and an absence of overwhelming stressors. To cope effectively, individuals require a wide repertoire of coping and social skills to deal with the wide range of stressors which are likely to be encountered. A young person skilled in one area may not have the necessary skills to cope with problems that may appear in another part of his/her life. If a young person has the capacity to access and utilize effective coping skills at a time of stress it is less likely that he or she will choose to use drugs as a coping strategy.

These skills become cognitive or behavioural. Cognitive skills include self-assurance, cognitive restructuring, cognitive distraction and self-control. Behavioural skills include problem solving, direct action through negotiation or compromise, withdrawal through leaving or avoiding the situation, communication skills, assertiveness, social networking, engaging in alternative activities, and relaxation. Apart from coping and social skills, well developed physical and performance skills are critical for life on the streets. The capacity to fight, to run, to react quickly and to weather physical harm will determine whether they may survive in such an environment. Practical performance skills such as juggling, singing, bartering, making crafts and vending provide the means for an income.

For some youth who are out of home, learning survival skills which the broader community may even consider aberrant or anti-social may be very important. These skills are usually learned from others who have been longer in the same situation. The availability of, and access to resources significantly affects a young person's ability to learn new skills and effectively implement them. Information and education also have the potential to change attitudes and perceptions. Access to health, welfare, educational, vocational and recreational services have the potential to ameliorate some of the stresses that an individual may be experiencing. The lack of resources is a common problem for poor, marginalized and minority communities, those communities where stress levels tend to be highest.

Not all resources may have a positive influence on a person. Research has demonstrated that some prevention and intervention programmes have actually had a negative impact on the audience targeted, resulting in an increase in drug use, curiosity and drug related harm. Just providing interventions or resources does not mean that they are going to produce the desired effect. Therefore it is essential that resources are carefully evaluated to determine their validity, utility, appropriateness, cultural sensitivity, and impact within a community. Educational materials developed for the general population or adolescents may be inappropriate for street children. Consideration of literacy levels is essential. Street children may not be able to relate to images, language and story lines which have been designed for a general audience.

Access to Health Services

Traditionally, young people under-utilize existing health services. A number of factors contribute to this. Of significant importance is that the majority of health services have been developed by adults for adults. Many such services rarely recognize the unique issues of young people, particularly those of street children, and rarely try to accommodate for their often age-appropriate behaviours. Therefore, many young people view health services as unfriendly, threatening, mystifying, unhelpful and inappropriate.

Further to this, young people rarely identify that health is a major concern for them. This is more so when day to day survival is the paramount concern for many on the streets. In addition, young people often regard themselves as invulnerable, focus on the here and now, and do not concern themselves with the longer term consequences of their behaviour. If they are marginalized and believe that no one cares about them, the present is all they have. The presence of death squads and similar, in some cities, merely reinforces such beliefs.

For those who are unwell or concerned about their health, there may be a reluctance to seek help as it might make them different from their peers, or cause employers to look for someone in better health. There may also be no services available, or those that do exist may not provide appropriate services or are too expensive. For those using drugs and involved in activities regarded by society as aberrant (for example, "survival sex"/prostitution), the situation is worse. This is despite the fact that adults are the main clients of street children engaged in sex work, and are usually in charge of drug manufacture, distribution and sale.

Street children involved in such activities are often poorly understood by mainstream services. Agencies which do provide services for this population are themselves also often marginalized, regarded with suspicion, attacked, or barely tolerated by government, the population at large, or those involved in crime; whether the services are drug-related or not. When "drug use" becomes a part of the presentation at a health service, there may be a tendency to refer the young person on to a specialist agency, if one exists. Where they do exist, specialist drug services tend to poorly understand issues pertinent to young people.

Young people tend to be treated as mini-adults, and their particular needs get ignored. All of this helps to reinforce the mythical and "special" image held of drug use, and discourages health workers from developing skills to deal with the presenting problems. Denial becomes a major factor: denial by the adolescent that he or she has possible health problems, denial of a capacity by workers to respond, and denial by society at large of its role creating an environment which accentuates the difficulties of drug-using street children, and the part it can play in developing useful responses.

Given scarce resources, in developed as well as developing countries, street children, especially those who use drugs, do not usually receive high priority. Alternatively, the existence of street children may be viewed as a problem to be dealt with by the police and military, and street children are then "criminalized", placed in prison-like institutions or even killed. At other times, programmes which are regarded as effective in developed countries are replicated in developing ones. The results are usually less than useful, and can demonstrate cultural insensitivity.

It also must be recognized that, where street children are particularly marginalized and/or fear for their lives, they may not trust any services which exist. They may believe that the services are merely "fronts" for the police or welfare agencies, and that they will be captured. In fact, surveillance of services is not uncommon in some places. Alternatively, more senior drug or crime "bosses" may fear that children will tell the authorities about them, and so put overt or covert pressure on the children not to use services. The families of street children may hold the same views. The high level of mobility of many street children also makes it difficult to engage and maintain them in services, including treatment, welfare and other programmes.

Many health and welfare agencies, particularly governmental agencies, have fixed rules and admission criteria which exclude unaccompanied minors from receiving services. Some agencies will not see any unaccompanied youths under a certain age or anyone who does not have the necessary documentation for identification. For those agencies which are prepared to see such youths, it is common for specific treatments to be refused without parental or guardian consent.

Many street children are below the "age of consent", do not have parents or guardians, do not know a trusted adult who could accompany them for treatment, and do not have the necessary documentation. Although these obstacles relate particularly to the accessing of health services, similar problems exist for street children in trying to access housing, welfare benefits, educational opportunities and employment. After being turned away from different services on a number of occasions, and not having any adults to advocate on their behalf, these youths consider it pointless to try again, even when they are in great need.

Reports from a number of countries have revealed cases where street children have actually died on the streets after having been refused emergency treatment at local hospitals. Some NGOs working with street children provide a specific service in which they provide adults to escort children to services and assist them through the registration and processing phases. Some organizations have provided identification cards to street children in order to improve their access to services.

It has been recognized that many organizations, predominantly NGOs, work at the "coal face", developing nd implementing programmes for street children in developed and developing countries. Particularly in developing countries, these organizations have been working in very impoverished communities for many years, they have developed good networks among the street children and, in some cases won the respect, trust and support of their local communities. They have a good understanding of their communities, cultures and customs. However, they often lack an effective structure within which they can plan and deliver their services, particularly to street children who use drugs, and may lack a capacity to advocate for their street children at higher governmental levels.

Determining Reliability of Informaton

It has been described that a major problem working with street children is that of determining the reliability of the information that they provide. Lack of trust towards this population and disbelief in the "stories" that they tell significantly influence the accessibility to and quality of services provided. Service providers may feel uncomfortable with this lack of trust and, where possible, will try to avoid contact with street children. They may be cautious in treating these children, suspicious that they are exaggerating or lying about their ailments or other problems. They may feel resentful about being misled by some of the tales told, or they may dismiss what may be valid complaints as an attempt by the children to manipulate them.

Fabio Dallape states in his book about *working with street children in Nairobi, Experience with Street Children*: "children don't care to answer questions correctly. In fact, they rarely give correct answers to your questions whether you are a foreigner or a local. Whether you belong to their same tribe or not, they tell you what they think you want to know from them. They enjoy elaborating on the hardship of their life and how they must survive. They want to impress you, in fact they act like actors in the theatre".

Similarly, it is well recognized that there may be problems in obtaining reliable histories from substance users, particularly those who use illicit drugs. While many are critical of the validity of self-reports by adolescents, there is some evidence to suggest that self-reports may be more reliable and valid than believed. Those health and welfare workers or researchers gathering information need to be sensitive to the individual or group being interviewed. Although data collection methodologies require inbuilt validity checks, special consideration needs to be given to the interpretation of messages being given.

The "reality" for street children (and for drug users) is very different to that of investigators, service providers and the immediate community. Their conceptualization of issues is determined by very different thought processes based on very different life experiences. For example, as part of this project, when one street boy in Rio de Janeiro was questioned about his understanding of religion, he replied that it was a place he could go to sleep and shelter from the rain. This demonstrates the importance of not rejecting their responses as being unreliable, but the need to explore further what they are trying to say. In relating the stories of their lives, they may be communicating in a way which is open to misunderstanding.

Issues in Geneder Difference

In general, males and females are not equally represented in populations of street children. In most, if not all, communities males overwhelmingly outnumber females. Although it is not clear as to why this is the case, there are a number of factors which may contribute to this phenomenon.

For many cultures and specific communities, the phenomenon of street children is new and is perceived to be a consequence of a rapidly developing economy and urbanization. Not only is it new, but it is often considered to be an embarrassment to and viewed as a failure of their respective societies. It appears that in these communities the least tolerated aspect of this problem is having to witness young girls on the street. Where communities feel a need to protect their children, often it is traditionally girls who are afforded the greatest protection, or who are placed in roles which keep them at a distance from the outside world. This community intolerance, which differs for street children according to gender, is a critical factor in determining how a community responds to the problem of street children. For example, many Islamic cultures do not tolerate girls living or working on the streets.

For children who work, including those who have families, it appears that boys are more likely to be involved in activities which put them on the streets, for example, street vending, running messages, providing street entertainment, washing cars, collecting scrap, pick-pocketing, shoeshining, riding trishaws, and involved in drug dealing. Whereas girls, often are employed or earn an income off the streets, for example working in factories, making crafts, employed in domestic services, involved in commercial sex and vending.

It is also reported that often girls who work on the streets are under the supervision of an adult. For example, while her mother stays in the background, a young girl may sit on the roadside selling farm produce or small goods or may approach passing cars or pedestrians begging for money. These apparent differences may reflect cultural beliefs that males are stronger, more independent and are able to fend for themselves on the streets. Some cultures consider that it is the responsibility of the male child to be the provider for the family, thus forcing him out to earn an income.

For those children who have left their families, the gender differences are still evident. Physical, sexual and emotional abuse are common reason for children leaving home. As survival on the streets is less threatening for boys, it may be an easier decision for a boy to leave an abusive family setting than for a girl. And, if a girl does leave home, it may be more likely that she finds alternative accommodation with other family members or friends. Often girls who end up on the streets are recruited into the commercial sex industry or are taken into institutional care. It appears that this is less likely to happen for boys in similar circumstances.

The reasons why there is such a large gender difference with regard to the numbers of street children are obviously complex and multifaceted. The preceding discussion only alludes to some possible factors which require further investigation. In particular, any such inquiry needs to address specific cultural issues which determine the differences observed. The differences between street boys and girls are not solely those of numbers and activities. Street girls are at a greater risk of experiencing certain health problems than boys.

Girls are more vulnerable to sexual exploitation and both physical and sexual abuse. Girls also experience specific problems related to adolescent female development and reproductive health. On the streets, risks are considerable with unplanned pregnancies often complicated by minimal or no ante-natal care, poor nutrition and hygiene, violence, sexually transmitted diseases, no shelter, and the possible use of drugs. Some girls risk unsafe abortions outside of the health care system. Often girls who complete a pregnancy will have no support in their attempts to mother their babies. Apart from these specific, well-known reproductive health problems, attention needs to be given to other gender specific health issues as they relate to street children, including the use of psychoactive substances.

Development and Implementation of the Street Children Project

For development and implementation of the Street Children Project, seven developing countries were selected to represent a range of cultures and regions: Brazil, Egypt, Honduras, India, Mexico, the Philippines, and Zambia. All WHO regions, apart from the WHO European Region (EURO), are represented. Each of these countries had a representative, selected on the basis of prior contact with PSA, at a meeting at WHO in Geneva during 3 to 7 February 1992. Canada joined the project at a later time.

The criteria used to then select the participating organizations/individuals in those countries were:

Essential:

a) to be an organization (nongovernmental or government) which provides a direct service to street children, including those who use drugs; to be flexible and to recognize that it would benefit from receiving support in dealing with street children who use drugs

b) to have extensive and current practical experience working with street children

c) to have a capacity to conduct basic research

d) to have a capacity to train other people working with street children

e) to be recognized and respected by the local community within which it works

f) to agree in principle with the project aims and objectives

g) to be receptive to the trialing of a new model for the assessment of the local situation and planning for an appropriate response.

Desirable:

a) to have clearly identified a gap in services for street children who use drugs

b) to have no strategic plan or formal intervention developed for the management of street children who use drugs

c) to be a relatively young organization with limited support, but credibility and respect in the community.

Aims

The meeting in Geneva during February 1992, agreed to the following aims:

— To improve the health, welfare and quality of life of street children in the selected sites. It recognizes that many NGOs have well researched and developed strategies in existence and aims to build onto and further develop these where they exist.

— To facilitate the work being done by existing agencies which currently provide services for street children, with a particular focus on improving strategies for the prevention, assessment and management of drug problems in this population.

— To assist local organizations in identifying the needs of street children.

— To assist local organizations in planning a coordinated and holistic response to the identified needs and thereby develop appropriate prevention and treatment strategies.

— To facilitate local organizations to develop and/or strengthen structures which will involve the local community, and particularly street children, in the development and implementation of local projects.

— To facilitate the work of local organizations in improving the accessibility of primary health care and welfare services for utilization by street children who use drugs. To identify those obstacles which impede access to these services for youths, and to ensure that this population is not discriminated against.

— To facilitate, through training, an improvement in the skills of health care workers and other community members in dealing with the health problems of street children, particularly the problems related to drug use.

— To improve the community's attitude towards and understanding of the problems of street children through the activities of the local organization, and therefore reduce the likelihood of discrimination of this population, particularly for those who use drugs.

— To promote the utilization of operational research, as feasible, in order to facilitate information gathering and project management.

— To promote the use of empowerment methodologies by local organizations as an important mechanism for dealing with the drug problem among street children.

Objectives

In working towards the aims of the project, the following objectives were agreed upon.

a) The identification of and collaboration with appropriate agencies, which work with street children in the communities being targeted, for the implementation of the pilot project.

b) The establishment of a community advisory committee at each site with representation from services which work with or are in contact with street children, local welfare and other agencies involved in emergency relief, housing, education and vocational training; local medical and other health care services; the criminal and/or juvenile justice system; the local community including the business sector; and street children themselves.

c) The development of a mechanism for establishing representative focus groups of street children and a structure within which these groups may be conducted.

d) The development of a strategic plan for the coordination of activities (including prevention, treatment and rehabilitation) directed at improving the health (in its broadest sense) and welfare of the local population of street children.

e) The formal or informal engagement of an appropriate local medical service, by the local organization, to provide primary medical care to the population of street children.

f) The development of an advocacy role for the community advisory committee with the purpose of:

- improving community attitudes towards and understanding of the problem
- recognizing and tapping into sources of funding and other resources
- reducing discrimination against street children
- influencing government policy and practice at all levels

— and identifying obstacles to change

g) The development and utilization of operational research methods, as far as possible, to test the alternative methodologies of intervention.

h) The development and utilization of empowerment methodologies by local organizations where appropriate.

Expected Outcomes

Process outcomes:

a) The establishment of an effective model which may be used to assess the needs of street children in relation to drug use and to structure an effective response.

b) The establishment of a strong and influential network of individuals and agencies who work with or come into contact with street children.

c) Improved advocacy for the population of street children who use drugs.

d) The development of local strategic plans to address the problems of street children, particularly in relation to drug issues.

e) The establishment of a mechanism for consultation with street children.

f) The identification of innovative and appropriate mechanisms for the assessment of street children and for delivering outreach health services to them.

Impact outcomes:

a) An increase in the number of contacts and quality of contacts between street children and health and welfare services, particularly for those street children who use drugs.

b) An improvement in the health of street children, including a reduction in problems associated with drug use.

c) An improvement in the community's perceptions of the problems of street children, particularly those related to drugs.

d) An increase in the confidence and competence of health and welfare workers in the management of drug problems of street children and therefore, a reduction in the perceived need by these workers to refer this group of street children onto specialist services.

Methodology—Process and Procedures

The following guide was developed to assist in the site implementation of the methodology.

The site representative who attended the Geneva meeting was to convene a meeting with local staff to discuss the Geneva workshop and the strategy for implementation. Where possible all site staff were to have access to the documentation prepared by PSA and the meeting participants.

A separate meeting, a training workshop, was to be held for staff directly implementing the project, to cover the Geneva material in more detail and to provide additional training as necessary, for example in group work techniques and referral procedures. It was recommended that, given limited resources, staff already working with street children and who have some level of rapport and trust developed with them would be the likely ones to implement the project.

Rapid Assessmenmt

Focus groups are a form of Rapid Assessment, and are regarded as very useful in obtaining information quickly from specific populations. They are particularly useful in assessing a situation, determining the needs and attitudes of the population under focus, and for planning appropriate interventions and responses. They are usually easy to organize, flexible, and through open-ended questioning allow for issues raised by the group to be elaborated and followed. They often elicit information which could not otherwise be disclosed through the use of other methods, such as questionnaires. However, they also raise issues of trust in the group and, without effective leadership, can be open to manipulation by high-status group members.

Often, a number of focus groups need to be conducted with the same group of participants to increase trust, to obtain useful information on a broad range of issues, and to take into account fatigue, and the short attention span and concentration difficulties of some participants. Parallel focus groups with different participants can be conducted to increase the sample size, to cross-check for reliability and validity of information, or to highlight differences within a group, or sub-group, that may have important implications for the development of interventions and responses.

On-going focus groups can be used to monitor a situation and to assist in the evaluation of a project, especially by highlighting changes which need to be made to strategies. These changes may be needed to take account of broader social, cultural or political changes which impact on the strategy, or smaller, local ones which may have gone unnoticed. This process forms part of action or operational research, ensures that the project maintains relevance, is focused and monitored. It is also empowering, as participants see that their views are valued and become a part of the ongoing development of the interventions.

The success of any focus group will depend on the skill of the facilitator. It was recommended that they be carefully chosen, have contact with street children, be trusted by them, and have group work skills, for example, be able to lead a discussion, keep it focused, deal with emotional issues that may arise, be supportive and nonjudgemental, and be able to record the discussion in the least obtrusive and threatening manner. The facilitator should also have a good knowledge of the project, the participating organization, referral resources, the local community and its culture and customs. The facilitator must ensure that what is recorded and observed truly reflects the discussions of the group, and the consensus and differences that emerged. To enable this, the facilitator should feedback to the group their observations for verification by the group. This is also part of the empowering process.

It was recommended that the above issues be taken into account when setting up focus groups.

Initial Focus Groups

It was recommended that an initial focus groups be conducted with groups of street youth known to the participating organization. They should involve a range of street children, particularly those who use drugs. The purpose of these groups was to determine the types of services utilized by this population, the people and organizations they regularly come into contact with, the services they would be prepared to utilize, and their perceptions and attitudes toward various individuals and organizations in the community. The information from these groups would assist in selecting people who could be approached to become members of the Community Advisory Committee and of the Service Providers Focus Groups.

Later, the formation of focus groups with less attached street youth would be necessary to obtain a broader information base. Some form of encouragement to participate may be necessary, such as an outing or the provision of food. The setting for the group also requires special attention, and preferably would be a familiar and safe venue. Six to ten participants per group was considered to be the optimal size of such a group.

Community Advisory Committee

Utilizing the information obtained from the initial focus groups, the participating organization would be able to determine the most appropriate individuals and organizations who could be invited to become members of the Community Advisory Committee. It was recommended that the Community Advisory Committee membership should reflect those services the street children use or see a need for. Membership should also extend to those services that have a key role in dealing with or making policies relating to street children, such as police, juvenile justice system, local and state officials, and community leaders.

The purposes for establishing a Community Advisory Committee are: to share information, skills and ideas; to increase cooperation and enhance referrals; to provide support for the project; to influence community attitudes; to form a larger and more powerful body to advocate for the needs of street children, and to give a sense of "ownership" of the project to the community.

The Community Advisory Committee would determine its own terms of reference, relevant to the local situation. Part of their role should include attempts to safeguard the rights of street children, as outlined in the United Nations Convention on the Rights of the Child, including the rights to receive adequate food, shelter, health care, educational and vocational opportunities, criminal justice, love and respect.

Initial Service Providers Focus Groups

It was also recommended that a focus group be conducted with professional and non-professional workers who provide services and employment to street children (including health, housing, educational and recreational services) and with people who are in daily contact with street children (e.g. vendors and community members). The Community Advisory Committee may be an appropriate and convenient group of service providers for this task. However, if there are too many administrators as members of the Community Advisory Committee who are not currently, or who have never been, service providers, another group or a series of groups may be more appropriate.

Strategic Plans

It was recommended that by utilizing the information from the various focus groups and the framework of the preliminary strategic plan, a Strategic Plan would be developed. This plan should cover both prevention and management strategies, and be able to fit into any overall strategic plan of the participating organization. The plan should contain specific objectives and expected outcomes to enable easy monitoring and evaluation, and strategies for addressing service gaps and needs identified.

The plan should also identify those who are responsible for each intervention strategy. For example, street educators, primary health care providers, administrators, local leaders, government authorities or departments. It was recommended that any Strategic Plan should be a living document, which is constantly reviewed, improved and fine-tuned. The on-going focus groups can provide useful information to assist in this monitoring process, as can reconvened service provider or Community Advisory Committee focus groups.

It was also recommended that the engagement of an existing primary medical service, if not already part of the participating organization's network, should be a central part of the Strategic Plan. If not already providing an outreach service targeting street children, this primary medical service could be encouraged to do so as one of the objectives of the plan. Organizations that serve the needs and interests of street children were strongly encouraged to develop clearly stated policies addressing the type and quality of services that should (or should not be) provided to street children by the organization. The written policies might address such issues as:

— Organizations to which referrals will (or will not) be made and for what purposes.

- The nature and scope of educational interventions and services that will be provided to help street children reduce risks associated with drug use, sexual behaviour or other important behaviours or conditions.
- The protection of street children's rights to privacy and confidentiality, especially in relation to drug use and/or HIV infection, including who needs to know and why; and under what conditions would information about a youth be given to others.
- The nature and scope of street children's participation in the organization's efforts to reduce use and/or HIV infection.
- Providing education and services to meet the needs and concerns of street children who divulge that they are infected with HIV.
- Persons who the organization will use as street workers/educators/counsellors; the extent to which they will be trained, and the determination of their competency.
- Strategies to avoid discrimination and moral bias.

Without well documented policies to address such issues, staff will not be able to act with confidence in matters that are inherently controversial or that may conflict with community standards. Additionally, without written policies, staff may unknowingly act in ways that are not considered appropriate by the organization decision-makers.

Modifies Social Stress Model

All participating organizations reported that the conceptual framework as presented in the Modified Social Stress Model was very useful, simple to understand and had wide application. It was considered that the integrated and holistic nature of the model provided a good structure for undertaking rapid situation assessments and planning appropriate responses. It was considered that the model could be used to address other risk behaviours, not only that of substance use. One way of examining the usefulness of the Modified Social Stress Model is by reviewing what information in relation to the six variables was elicited from the street children, service provider, and community advisory committee focus groups and/or interviews.

Many of the street children were involved in work such as: shoeshining, carrying goods in markets, running errands, traffic light or street corner vending (some carrying trays with them, others set up tables outside taverns at night, or business houses during the day), clowning, playing music, piece work, cleaning cars, garland selling, helping their mothers sell rural produce. Others were involved in commercial or survival sex.

Much of the work involves risks and stress. For example: young girls selling eggs outside taverns where intoxicated adults leave and sexually exploit the girls; children standing in heavy traffic inhaling exhaust and other fumes and at risk of injury from vehicles; expectations of, or forced unsafe sexual practices by adults; having earnings taken by bigger or stronger persons and threats from criminal groups (including the illicit drug industry).

Many have dreams of a future. For example, to become pilots, teachers, police officers, doctors, nurses, lawyers, businessmen, farmers and tradespersons. It is interesting to note that most of these are caring, service areas of work, or law enforcement. Most wanted education and fairly traditional futures. When reality tested, dreams change. For many the thought of leaving the streets behind induced fear: a move from something known, albeit difficult, to something poorly understood and which they felt they had little confidence in their ability to deal with.

Mechanism for Consultation with Street Children

Selection and training of street educators

Most street educators and facilitators were selected from within existing organizations due to their: proven ability to engage street children and engender trust; skill in group work and dealing with sensitive issues which may arise; knowledge of local culture, communities and resources; and previous work with street children. Most were psychologists, social workers, teachers, and in some cases students of these professions or persons who had undertaken other training courses offered by the participating organization(s). In one case, volunteer youth participated, providing programmes in juvenile/criminal justice institutions, with few difficulties. The difficulties encountered, in this case, related to the use of a female volunteer with Muslim youth, and due to lack of trust and high levels of suspicion by some staff of the institutions. In Bombay, ex-street children were utilized to help identify and engage street children.

The overall difficulties encountered will be reviewed below "under street children focus groups". Reports indicated that the street educators and facilitators went about their tasks with dedication and enthusiasm, enjoyed the process, learned a great deal of new information, and learned how to utilize a conceptual model to aid this. Where regarded as necessary, training sessions for street educators and facilitators were run. The content of these sessions varied from centre to centre. The range of topics chosen included: drugs and their use, epidemiology and aetiology of drug use, drug dependency, detoxification, adolescent development, psychology of street children, HIV/AIDS, behavioural patterns, sexual problems, health, emotional problems, interview and group work skills, and a briefing on the street children project.

Sessions contained information input and skills acquisition. In many cases the training was regarded as a continuous process, and plans were made to provide for this.

This was seen to be particularly important in relation to the emergence of new information, or where emotional issues arose and street educators felt unskilled in dealing with these. It is again unclear from most responses as to whether ex-street children were involved as facilitators or interviewers, or merely used to locate children due to their work as outreach workers or street educators. This issue also needs to be addressed in Phase II of the project.

Street Children Focus Groups

Each participating organization conducted a number of street children focus groups. The populations of the various groups reflected what was easily available, the normal group-work and activities of some organizations, and moving out and/or snowballing to new populations not previously engaged with services. In some cases camps were held, in others children were interviewed in groups in parks or on the streets. At other times, children were interviewed individually where a group was seen as too threatening or dangerous to safety, or likely to reveal unusable and unreliable information. Food and/or a recreational or enjoyable activity were often provided to engage the children for the lengthy process of the focus groups.

Various questions were deleted from the lists in the Menu in some cases, as certain topics were viewed as inappropriate or culturally insensitive to ask in those cases. One centre (Brazil) developed a useful mechanism for recording information from a number of children in a group setting. This format set out each question on a new page, with boxes in a semi-circle to represent individual group participants. As children spoke, their data were recorded in the box allocated to them for that particular question/issue. In Egypt some of the topics were turned into multiple choice questions.

In Rio 14 groups were conducted, with a total of 106 young people (reduced to 98 for analyses), aged 18, of whom 49% lived on the streets, 43% lived at home, and 8% in institutions. Interviews were conducted in the streets (Saes

Pena Square), at various agencies and institutions, and in the Favela do Lixao. In Toronto there were two groups: a group of young people in regular contact with a service dealing mainly with out of home gay and lesbian youth, and youth from the "Ambassadors Program", a peer education and counselling programme for "street kids". In Montreal one group was conducted with a cross section of young people out of home.

In Cairo and Alexandria 194 street children were interviewed - 138 in Cairo and 50 in Alexandria from one open juvenile detention centre in Alexandria, three open/semi open juvenile detention centres (Giza, Ein Shams and Misr ElKadima) and one closed centre (Marg-Cairo) in Cairo. There were 6 children from St. George Orphanage in Alexandria who were interviewed. Ages ranged from 9 to 23 years, with a mean of 14 years. About 30% still lived with their families and 65% were working regularly. Group processes and individual interviews were used as appropriate. There were 23 groups conducted in Cairo and 7 in Alexandria, which met about 5 times each.

In Tegucigalpa there were five groups: 1) abandoned male children living in the streets and using substances (aged 12-22) which met 11 times, with an average of 6 participants; 2) abandoned male children living in the streets and not using drugs (aged 8-15) which met 11 times, with an average of 9 participants; 3) institutionalized male children who had a history of problematic drug use (Casa Alianza Honduras - closed centre) (aged 12-17) which met 14 times, with an average of 8 participants; 4) market vending male and female children who are in school and not using drugs (aged 8-11) which met 28 times, with an average of 8-11 participants; 5) market vending male children who are not in school and not using drugs (aged 8-9) which met 12 times, with an average of 8-11 participants.

In Bombay 65 children were interviewed: 23 boys living in the streets and mainly working as shoeshine boys and coolies along the Western Railway network, particularly Borivalli, Kurla, Chembur, Govandi and Mankurd Railway Stations, and 38 boys and 4 girls living in slum areas near the railway lines, such as Indira Nagar, Adarsh Nagar and Shivaji Nagar, mainly involved in rag and scrap trades. Individual interviews were conducted, as it was felt that this would be the most reliable means of obtaining information. Three on-going focus groups are being held.

In Mexico City 11,172 street children had been identified from previous research falling into 5 groups: Children who were selling goods, children who were providing services, children who were marginal service providers, children who were street performers and artists, and children involved in crime. 886 children had been interviewed in groups and 739 gave usable data; 72% were male (54% between 14-17 years), and 28% female (34% between 13 and 14 years), 1,020 lived in the streets and 10,152 worked in the streets.

In Manila groups were conducted by the participating NGOs: Maryville: 2 groups, each of which met 3 times: 10 males aged 9-11, and 8 males and 2 females aged 13-15. All except one member were at school and living with their families. At least 50% of waking time was spent on the streets. FCED: 2 groups, each of which met twice: 3 males and 2 females aged 8-12 all living with their families, but working on the streets, and 16 males aged 11-16 most of whom lived on the streets. The first group had 10 participants, but the second group had 16 as the original 10 brought peers. Masigla: 2 groups, each of which met twice: 2 males and 3 females, aged 12-15 most of whom lived on the streets, and 5 females and 6 males, aged 13-19 who were residents of a group home for street children.

In Lusaka Red Cross/SKI selected out specific children from their regular groups in Garden and Mtendere Compounds: one for 10 street boys from the SKI Drop-In-Centre in Garden Compound, aged 8 to 12, and one for 12 school boys and girls aged 7 to 14 from the Chitulmko Primary

School Anti-Drug Youth Club in Mtendere Compound. CYP Africa Centre interviewed 31 children, all male except one; 16 from Matero Compound and 15 from Mtendere Compound, aged 16-24.

In all, over 550 street children participated in focus groups or were interviewed using the PSA format in the 10 cities. In addition, Mexico City contributed information from an extensive research project conducted earlier. Most participating organizations found that to use the whole menu and list of questions was far too long for both the attention/ concentration span of the street children. It was necessary to conduct a number of groups to cover all issues. It appeared that in some cases the sessions were conducted with fairly strict adherence to the question lists.

Having greater familiarity with the process and question areas, it may be possible to have a more open, less structured and directive discussion where all topics are covered, but not in any rigid order. There was some difficulty in getting some children to return, and others needed to leave part way through to go to work. Only a few behavioural problems were evident, and these were mainly from the children who were drug users. Some children were actually inhaling solvents during some sessions.

Many of the reports commented on how much useful information came from the street children focus groups. In some cases, workers were confronted with new information that became very useful in developing strategies and interventions. For example, in Manila, the groups told the facilitators: that it was common for boys and girls to have sex after inhaling glue; that sex was used to obtain cannabis; that in non-tourist venues some had sex with adults in cinemas where pornographic movies were shown; that one form of substance use was to put wet carbon paper on their faces for 3 minutes and then inhale; that they mixed a local mint candy ("Stork") with "7-Up" and gained a cannabis like effect; and that they boiled toothpaste with cut up fibre matting and inhaled the fumes.

All reports indicated how involved the children became in the process, and how moved the facilitators were at times by the open disclosures of very painful and distressing information. At times, this required individual follow-up after the group. Many reports of focus groups noted how the behaviour of the participants changed over time. For example, hygiene, appearance and in group behaviour improved and more respect towards all participants was shown. Some street children even brought others in to become group members. This demonstrated a wide degree of acceptance by the children of the process; notwithstanding that the groups were long and sensitive material was being brought up and discussed.

There was fear of disclosure expressed in some settings, particularly in areas where children were known to have been killed and in some state institutions where it was alleged that drugs were available, and that staff were involved in their distribution and in physical and sexual assaults on inmates. In other cases high-status street children dominated discussions until facilitators were able to redress this. High-status children refer to those street children who are positioned high in the hierarchical structure of any particular group of street children, those who wield power and influence either through fear or respect. However, from the reports the information from the children was regarded as reliable and valid, but issues of staff and child safety require constant attention.

In some cases there was evidence of certain moral, cultural or religious values and positions entering the process of the focus groups. It is not clear from the reports whether these were attempts to provoke discussion, or to "educate". This issue requires attention. Although some girls were involved in focus groups in different centres, they were in general under-represented in the process. For those groups where girls were present, boys often dominated the discussions. It appears that little attention was paid to gender issues in the discussions. In some centres it was extremely difficult to access any street girls.

It appears that, overall, the use of the focus group methodology was highly successful. It was a practical mechanism for consultation, provided much new and highly relevant information, and allowed street children to have a voice and be seen to be taken seriously. However, the lists of prompt questions need to be reduced.

Innovative Mechanisms for the Assessing of Street Chidren

In a number of settings, primary health care was provided as part of the participating organizations range of services. In others, links had already been formed with health facilities, and in some, new connections were formed. The mere existence of services or links to them does not imply, however, that they are accessible to street children who use drugs or that they have the expertise and/or willingness to provide such services.

Recognizing the brief history of the project, it is not clear from the reports that there was a development of "innovative and appropriate mechanisms" or an enhanced capacity of existing services and facilities to provide for the needs of street children who use drugs. It is not so much that they "need" specific techniques, as the health consequences of drug use are widely recognized and, in most cases treatable.

It is more a willingness to receive these children as clients, treat them with nonjudgemental respect and without discrimination, and develop better mechanisms of access via community health nurses and physicians, mobile and extended hours services, locating health services in non-health venues, and the use of appropriate, safe and user-friendly buildings and facilities.

Most centres were still in the process of preparing strategic plans and considering appropriate responses. Some centres used street children themselves and other youths for the assessment process. Specific centres where street children congregate were targeted, for example, train stations, market places and juvenile detention centres. In targeting these locations, the local community and authorities were consulted and encouraged to participate in the process. As a result of the project specific new activities and strategies were implemented.

For example, railway station children in Bombay built a shed where they could attend informal lessons and they established a support group; in Egypt, Caritas was considering establishing a specific street children programme; a brick-making enterprise was established in Lusaka; training materials for street educators were prepared in Tegucigalpa; and a young people's street theatre group has incorporated the theme of drug use and AIDS in their drama in Manila.

Obstacles for Developments

In addition to the above, other obstacles to better meeting the needs of street children who use drugs emerged.

These included:

— corruption

— entrenched drug cultures supporting communities, where some thought they would be worse off if the drugs industry were removed

— how to keep the community involved and contributing, informed without boring and overwhelming them, and ensuring that they have a useful role

— the expectation of some potential community advisory committee members that they be paid or offered some other incentive

— the isolation and marginalization of services and workers, even within their own organizations

— staff working part-time on the project who already have full time work commitments

— finding "real" and acceptable alternatives to drugs and the streets

— the absence of fathers in many cases

— media influence promoting drug use

— burn out of staff

— the mobility of much of the target population

— the existence of services which require ongoing attendance by street children who can be rather unreliable

— the mix of different "tribes" and languages in some cities with little preparedness to integrate at any level

— the understandable tendency of some of the population to be preoccupied with getting enough for themselves, rather than seeing cooperation as desirable

— promises by the powerful not followed through

— being unable to establish outreach services where their existence contravenes the law

— the infiltration or surveillance of some agencies by the "authorities"

— suspicion of research and outreach work by organization staff, who may wonder if there is a "hidden agenda"

— competition for funding and other resources between agencies

— suspicion and fear regarding staff and client safety, when "outsiders" become interested or involved

— a lack of confidence and fear in having to deal with drug issues; and

— misinformation about drugs and also street children.

There may not be much that can be done about many of these obstacles, but clearly recognizing them may assist in developing realistic intervention strategies.

Street Girls

The phenomenon of "street families" is spreading throughout the world. Children are being born on the street to adolescent street girls, creating second and even third generation street children. In the Mabini district of Manila, a 16 year old girl with her three month old baby and 18 year old boyfriend were found sleeping out in a park. Not far away, an adolescent mother stood in the distance while her four year old son sat outside a nightclub begging from pedestrians while nursing his baby sister. The mother was dependent on her children to earn an income and feared that a welfare agency would remove them from her custody.

In Mexico City, a family camped on the median strip of one of the major roads. While the young father juggled and danced at the traffic lights, the young mother, with baby in her arms approached motorists asking for money. Elsewhere, in the city, a middle-aged mother sat in the shade of a square, sending her two young daughters out to pull on the shirts and trousers of passing tourists asking for money. It was considered that the younger and dirtier the girls were, the more successful they would be in their begging endeavour.

In a "group home" for street children in Rio de Janeiro, a 14 year old girl had just given birth to a baby a month before. She was planning to remain in the home and raise the baby herself. Her pregnancy was a main factor influencing her decision to seek permanent shelter off the streets. In the same home street children ranged from the age of 4 to 18 years, both boys and girls. It was acknowledged that the residents were sexually active and information on safer sex, including condom use, was provided.

At the Second International Conference on Street Youth in Rio de Janeiro in September 1992, a panel of six street girls described how they had been severely beaten and their lives threatened by the police. They further described how they had regularly been sexually abused. One of the beaten girls was pregnant. A NGO residential institution for street girls was visited in Manila. Many of the residents were under the age of 10 years. Most had been involved in the commercial sex industry. Some described how that having sex was the only time they felt wanted and loved.

In Bombay, informal education classes were held for "slum" children. Whereas most of the boys were extroverted and actively participated, a small group of girls sat quietly at the back appearing withdrawn and depressed.

In Rio de Janeiro and Manila street boys reported that they often had sex with street girls after inhaling solvents. In Sydney, within a period of five months, four adolescent girls died from overdose of a combination of heroin and benzodiazepines. They had been living on the streets. These brief vignettes provide some content within which the broad spectrum of gender issues may be considered. Although they are only examples, they may help to orientate further discussions on how the specific issues of street girls may be addressed.

2

Trafficking and Sexual Abuse among Street Children

According to recent UN data, there are nearly 150 million street children in the world today, and the number is rising daily. That means nearly one of every 60 people living on the planet is a child living on the streets. Half of them die within first four years of their street life. In other words, a child who ends up in the street at age 8 has a 50% chance of dying before the age of 12.There are many unfortunate incidents which cause children as young as 3 years old to end up on the streets.

The vast majority of these children have been abused and abandoned by their own families. In Guatemala, for instance, 64% of street girls interviewed by Human Rights Watch turned out to be victims of incest. Other reasons include extreme poverty of a family, death of parents, unstable socioeconomic situation in the country, and armed conflicts that cause many people to flee their homes, therefore instigating many families to fall apart. Once on the street, children must resort to begging, robbery, and even prostitution in order to survive. Many join gangs where they are introduced to crime, violence, and drugs. They become addicted to inhaling glue, paint thinner, and/or other toxic substances destroying brain cells and organ tissues.

Street educators in Guatemala, Mexico, Honduras, Russia, and other countries regularly find numerous grossly intoxicated kids as young as 6 years old trying to escape the pain, hunger, and desolation of street life in the poisonous fumes. Neglected by society and government, street children are deprived of education, proper nutrition, and medical care. They suffer and die from various, often easily treatable, diseases such as head lice, skin parasites, pneumonia, tuberculosis and a host of sexually transmitted diseases, including, yet not limited to, gonorrhea, syphilis and AIDS. Because of the grave lack of outreach and shelter programs, street children often have no place to go and no one from whom they can seek help and protection.

Protection is what these street children desperately need because they are prime targets of disturbed, exploitive adults. Child murderers, angry shopkeepers, and pedophiles are a daily threat to the safety and lives of desperate street children. Sexual exploitation of street children by locals and foreigners alike is widespread. For example, a Swiss couple, William and Lily Marti, was arrested in Bombay in 2003 for taking pictures of 8 and 9 year old children in exchange for money. The couple was also accused of kidnapping, molesting, and sexually abusing street children throughout India.

Similarly, in 2004, Stephan Irving, a 56 year-old pediatrician from New York was prosecuted for traveling to Mexico to visit places like Castillo Vista del Mar hotel, which provides shelter and food to street children as young as 6, in exchange for sexual activities.However, it is important to note that exploitation is rarely reported. Many believe the most serious threat to street children comes from the very people responsible for their safety and protection - local governmental and law enforcement officials.

Unfortunately, police brutality and corruption is common worldwide, and is especially widespread in developing countries with large populations of street children. Unspeakable police brutality reflects the governments' perception of street children as parasites to be exterminated, rather than as children needing homes and nurturing. A growing number of politicians inaccurately blame increasing levels of violent crime on children and teens, instead of looking at the actual numbers of street children who are victimized or murdered on a regular basis by official security forces.

Police overwhelmingly view and treat these street children as sub-human; unworthy of basic human rights. While it is true that street children are sometimes involved in petty theft, drug-trafficking, and other criminal activities, the police often assume that violence and brutality are the only means of dealing with this problem. They unjustifiably see a hardened criminal in every street child.

For the police and other security forces, street children represent easy and silent targets. They are young, small, poor, ignorant of their rights, and often have no family or advocates who will come to their defense. It does not require much time or effort to detain and torture a child to coerce a confession, and street children are unlikely to register formal complaints.

Latin American countries are especially notorious for their vicious and sadistic practices against street children. Death squads and armed police forces regularly comb the city streets to perform savage "social cleansings". In Honduras, brutal murders of street kids by government forces reached such high levels that it led to an international scandal in 2001. The UN appointed a Special Rapporteur to investigate hundreds of extrajudicial executions of street children throughout the country.

Numerous witnesses saw armed men in civilian clothes that drove around in unmarked vehicles and had, on several occasions, forcibly abducted street children. Often their dead bodies were found in deserted areas outside the city limits. The children appear to have been tortured before being shot in the head, execution-style. Police, meanwhile, demonstrated an alarming lack of concern with the situation, and, at times actively covered up the crimes, including failing to record and investigate the murders, and quietly disposing of evidence.

Police actions are informally sanctioned by high ranking governmental officials. For example, the Minister for Public Security of Honduras denied any police involvement in the killing of any street child. The children, according to him, were "out of their minds" and not to be trusted. His point of view was fully supported by the country's Human Rights Commissioner, whose son incidentally, was arrested in November 2000 for attacking a 10 year old street boy and poking a lit cigarette in his eye.

Arbitrary detention of street children is also a common practice, even though it grossly violates international and domestic laws.Law enforcement and government authorities often try to justify roundups or prolonged detention of street children as means of identifying them and re-uniting them with their families. Neither the manner of the arrests or the lack of actual re-unification attempts reflects this law enforcement "justification". In fact, many street children often have no family to claim them. Meanwhile, they are held in deplorable conditions. In some instances, the police beat detained street children claiming that it is a method of crime prevention.

In Bulgaria, for example, children who have been held in lock-ups reported that they were beaten by police with electric shock batons, clubs, chains, rubber hosing, boxing gloves, and a metal rod with a ball at the end.In Paraguay, police practiced interrogation of street children by placing plastic bags over their heads while they proceeded to kick and hit their bodies, especially the testicles and the back.

Police are known to place pins under the children's fingernails and give them electric shocks. The hypocrisy of the authorities is most evident if one considers that the police are especially active in "cleaning up" the streets at times of major events that attract close national and international attention. The children are arrested on vague or false charges, sometimes just for being homeless or for begging.

Brute force and obscene language are used in abundance by police during roundups that frequently happen at night, in order to avoid public witnesses and political condemnation. Many street children have described being grabbed, kicked, hit, whipped, caned, and/or clubbed while being held in police custody.Security forces have also been known to abuse and exploit street children for personal gain. One commonly reported practice is for the police to extort money or services from the children by threatening to imprison them if they refuse to pay.

Girls living on the streets are especially vulnerable to sexual abuse from security forces that sometimes coerce street girls into sexual acts in exchange for their freedom. In extreme cases, police will blatantly rape girls and threaten to kill or maim them if they report the abuse. From police custody, the children may be sent before a juvenile court which often places them in special institutions called "remands", or juvenile homes. The remands are mostly degenerated into jail-like custodial centers. Many children sent to such homes in India and Latin America have died as a result of severe beatings and torture performed either by the staff or by older children.Few advocates, lawyers, or prosecutors speak up for these abused children who rarely have the financial resources to pay legal fees.

Family members willing to intervene usually have financial constraints of their own. The street children's stories remain untold, and their lives are often neglected and forgotten. Widespread impunity allows violence against street children to continue. Casa Alianza in Latin America files hundreds of criminal complaints on behalf of street children each year, but only a handful result in prosecution.

Almost always when an investigation is ordered, it is done by the police themselves, and in some cases, by members of the same department, station, or remand house staff in which the alleged abuse occurred. Adding to the police brutality is the cruelty and indifference of society as a whole, which has turned its eyes and hearts away from the children of the street. In Bulgaria street children of Roma (gypsy) ancestry are often attacked and viciously beaten by skinhead gangs armed with bats, chains, knives, steel capped boots, and gas guns.

In Guatemala, street children are often murdered when they fall asleep in public places. Casa Alianza's reports that a homeless boy was killed by three unidentified civilians who covered the boy's head with a cloth as he slept then crushed his skull with a concrete block. The shocking ruthlessness of the murders and abuse, and the fact that there has been so little public outcry, seems to illustrate the general disregard for street children by the public.

Street children desperately need programs and services. Unfortunately, there are relatively few shelters or outreach programs anywhere in the world. And the one's that do exist, like at Casa Alianza, struggle daily for justice and the recognition of the human rights of street children. Governments need stronger enforcement measures and international penalties for non-compliance. Police must be made accountable for their crimes against homeless and poor children. There is much to be done.

These are only a few of the ideas that are needed to make a difference; there are countless others. One of the most important things that can be done is to become aware and educated on the issue, then to inform those around you. You may be surprised at just how few people will know anything about street children, and equally surprised at how many people may be willing to help you in your efforts to educate people about one of the largest groups of vulnerable children in the world.

Trafficing and Sexual Abuse of Street Children in Nepal

Street children are highly vulnerable to sexual abuse and

exploitation. Their vulnerable conditions in the street, increase in the cases of pedophilia, and the expanding sex market appear to be some of the major causes of sexual abuse and exploitation of street children. Child Workers in Nepal (CWIN) indicates that foreign pedophiles abuse about 5 per cent of the street boys in Nepal. There is no available information on Nepali pedophiles so much so that presently all pedophile activity is considered synonymous with foreigners only. The situation of pedophilia is further compounded by the lack of national legislation on the issue and as a result it is speculated that Nepal may increasingly become a hotspot for pedophiles and sex tourists.

From a child labour perspective, the problem of street children is among the worst forms of child labour-jeopardizing the physical, mental and emotional development of the child. It is against the fundamental principles of child rights and an expression of social injustice. Although there is a growing concern about elimination of all forms of abuse and exploitation of children, the problem of trafficking and sexual abuse/exploitation of street children has yet to be studied in Nepal.

Among the areas that need further scrutinization are the different forms of sexual abuse, an identification of the abusers and how they operate and the circumstances that lead to children ending up in abusive conditions, including whether they were trafficked. Children's own views about the situation is seldom taken into consideration and this study looks carefully at how children define their situation and how they can change it to the better.

Street children, the homeless population of both sexes below 18 years of age who work full time in the street and in other public places. This means that two categories of street children are included in this study:- 'off the street children' and 'on the street children'. The former refers to the children living full time in the street, the later refers to children who work in the street but live with their parents in Kathmandu. Nepal is also a signatory to the Convention on the Rights of the Child, 1989 and has recently (September 2001) ratified the ILO Convention 182 on the Worst Form of Child Labour.

Trafficking

Trafficking means the recruitment, transportation, transfer, harbouring or receipt of persons by means of threat or use of force, or other forms of coercion, abduction, fraud, deception, abuse of power or of a position of vulnerability or of giving and receiving payment or benefits to achieve the consent of a person having control over another person for the purpose of exploitation

- Exploitation - prostitution of others or other forms of sexual exploitation
- forced labour or services
- slavery or practices similar to slavery
- servitude
- removal of organs

The recruitment, transportation, transfer, harboring or receipt of a child for the purpose of exploitation shall be considered as trafficking in children

- A child is anyone under the age of 18 years
- consent of victim is irrelevant

The majority of the street children in the valley come from the periphery districts of Kathmandu. Most of them come from Nuwakot (n=13), Kathmandu (n=12), Sindhupalchok (n=8), Dolakha (n=7), Chitawan (n=5) and Kabhrepalanchok (n=5). Note that those children reporting origin as Kathmandu are those children who have either migrated to Kathmandu with their parents when they were very young or they were born in Kathmandu from migrant parents. Such children are mostly involved in manual work such as rikshaw-pulling, rag picking, factory workers, taxi-driving, vending, stone-quarrying, retail shops or begging.

The migration pattern of street children interviewed indicates that both boys and girls tend to migrate to the Kathmandu valley. Out of the eight girls interviewed six originated from outside the valley and two from Kathmandu valley itself. The birth districts reported for girls interviewed were Nuwakot (n=1), Kathmandu (n=2), Dolakha (n=1), Illam (n=1), Sunsari (n=1), Rupandehi (n=1) and Bara (n=1). As expected, an overwhelmingly majority of the street children were born in rural areas (65%) with 32 percent reporting their birth place as urban areas.

Table 1 shows the single year age distribution of the respondents. The median age of respondents is 13 years indicating that half of the respondents are under 13 years of age and half are above it. This indicates that street life begins from early childhood.

Table 1. Distribution of Respondents by Age, Kathmandu, 2001

Age	Boys	Girls	Total
7	2	0	2
8	5	0	5
9	1	0	1
7-9	8	0	8 (8.0)
10	8	1	9
11	3	0	3
12	20	1	21
13	14	0	14
14	16	0	16
10-14	61	2	63 (63.0)
15	11	1	12
16	7	2	9
17	5	3	8
15-17	23	6	29 (29.0)
Total	92	8	100
Median age			13 years

Note: figures in parentheses indicate percentage.

According to the age groups, the majority were from 10-14 years of age (63%), followed by children in the age range of 15-17 years (29%). Of the total children interviewed, eight were girls. The age distribution of girls range from 10 to 17 years of age. Of them, one girl was 10 years old, one was 12 years, one was 15 years, two girls were 16 years and 3 were 17 years old.

Caste/ethnic Groups

The phenomenon of street children affects most caste/ethnic groups of Nepal. Unlike the traditional beliefs- that street children come mainly from most backward caste/ethnic groups such as Tamang and Dalit, street children also come from the so called higher caste groups such as Chhetri and Brahman. Yet the highest number of street children are from Tamang, one of the indigenous groups of Nepal, that reside in the periphery districts of the Kathmandu valley such as Nuwakot, Sindhupalchok, Kavre, Dahding, Rasuwa and Makawarpur.

In terms of the broader categories of caste/ ethnicity, 52 percent comprises the hill ethnic groups, followed by Brahmin/Chhetri (21%), Dalit (13%) and Tarai origin groups such as Tharu, Paudar and Teli (Table 2). The girls are also from different caste/ethnic groups such as Magar (n=1), Newar (n=1), Chhetri (n=1), Sahu/Teli (n=1), Damai (n=1), Tamang (n=1) and Sherpa (n=1).

Table 2. Distribution of respondents by caste/ethnicity

Caste/ ethnicity	Boys	Girls	%	Caste/ ethnicity	Boys	Girls	%
Hill ethnic groups	47	5	52.0	Brahman/ Chhetri	20	1	21.0
1. Tamang	23 2	25.0	8.	Chhetri	14	1	15.0
2. Newar	9	1	10.0	9. Brahman		4	4.0
3. Magar	6	1	7.0	10. Giri/Puri		2	2.0
4. Gurung	5		5.0	**Dalit**	**12**	**1**	**13.0**

5. Sherpa	2	1	3.0	11.	Kami	5		5.0
6. Limbu		1	1.0	12.	Damai	7	1	8.0
7. Rai		1		1.0	**Tarai groups**	11	1	12.0
13.					Shaha/Teli	3	1	4.0
14.					Paudar	2		2.0
15.					Tharu	5		5.0
16.					Indian	2		2.0
Total						92	8	100.0

Literacy Status

Most street children are deprived of basic education. Three fifth of the total respondents could not read and write. Similarly, only 49 reported that they have ever attended school. Of the children who have been in school, the mean grade completed was 3, with a minimum of 1 grade and a maximum of 10 grade. Table 3 shows the distribution of respondents by illiteracy according to various characteristics of the respondents. None of the girls reported that they could read or write. The age pattern among the illiterate street children indicates that as the age of street children increases, the likelihood of being literate also increases implying that street children, to some extent are exposed to education with increase in age.

Table 3. Illiteracy by sex, age and caste/ethnic groups, Kathmandu, 2001

Characteristics	Illiterate	N
Sex		
Boys	52 (56.5)	92
Girls	8 (100.0)	8
Age group		
7-9	7 (87.5)	8
10-14	38 (60.3)	63
15-17	15 (51.7)	29
Caste/Ethnicity		
Hill ethnic groups	30 (57.7)	52

Brahman/Chhetri	9 (42.9)	21
Dalit	10 (76.9)	13
Tarai groups	9 (81.8)	11
Indian	1	2
Don't know	1	1

Note: Figures inside brackets indicate percentage.

There is a distinct pattern of literacy status according to caste/ethnicity of street children, the most deprived are the Dalit, Tarai origin, and hill ethnic groups. An overwhelmingly majority of the children from Tarai origin (9 out of 11) and Dalit origin (10 in 13) are reported to be illiterate. The literacy status is relatively better among Brahman/Chhetri (9 in 21). A question was asked to those respondents who did not attend school about their perceived reasons for not attending school. Of the total street children who had never been to school (n=51), the majority reported that they were not sent to school by their parents (29 in 51), followed by poor economic condition at their home (18 in 51) and only 4 out of 51 reported that school was far from their house.

Family Situation

The average family size of the respondents was 6.4 as compared to the national average of 5.2 in 2001. A larger family size may have implications on availability of sufficient food, care and support and financial coping. The distribution pattern of respondents by their family size suggests that a large family size may be one of the reasons why children leave home. 55 per cent of the total respondents reported that they have 5-7 family members and more than three-fourth street children originate from a family size with more than four. Yet it is difficult to conclude that larger family size is exclusively associated with the phenomenon of street children as 23 per cent of respondents were from the family size with 1-4. A large number of respondents reported that they their own mothers are not their home caretakers. One-third of the respondents have had stepmothers at home. Absence of own parents, particularly the mother is directly associated with the deprivation of children from education, nutrition, health and love.

Family poverty in association with death and/ or absence of own mother of a child is also an important reason for children coming in the street. More than two-thirds of the respondents complained that they had faced ill treatment at home by their family members, particularly by their stepmother, step-father and sometimes by their own alcoholic parents. The majority of the respondents reported that they face physical abuse. Other forms of abuse reported included mental abuse (23%), no food (7%), lack of schooling (2%) and thrown out from the house (2%). One girl told us that her close relatives sexually abused her.

Illiteracy among Parents

Illiteracy among parents may be another contributing factor behind why children leave their home. The literacy level among the mothers of the respondents is extremely low as only 4 in 100 street children's mothers were literate, this literacy is far lower than that of the national average of female literacy of 40%. Literacy among parents may have a positive multiplier effect on children's life. Educated parents may earn more and there is a higher possibility that they will send their children to school as they themselves are aware and value the importance of education. In the Nepalese context, it is common for children to follow their parents traditional work such as tailors, musicians, goldsmiths etc (considered Dalits) and education is less prioritized as these children undergo apprenticeship at an early age with their parents. If Dalits constitute a major part of the street child population, traditional beliefs, customs and practices may be among the root causes. Therefore parents' literacy and education are among the key intervention areas for combating the phenomenon of street children.

Child Migration and Working Conditions

An overwhelmingly majority of street children in Kathmandu valley were from outside the Kathmandu valley. Only four out of 100 street children interviewed reported that they were from Kathmandu valley. Among these four street children, two girls reported that their origin is Kathmandu while for other two boys their parents were migrants but they were born in Kathmandu. A question was asked to the migrant respondents about their age at first leaving home. The median age for street children who left home is nine years indicating that half of them left their home before the age of nine. It appears that children start leaving home from early childhood, in some cases already from the age of six years old. At the other end of the scale, two cases did not leave their home until they were 15 years of age.

Among the migrant street children, about 23 per cent came with their parents. Similarly, three fourth of the street children came with either their peer groups, or were brought by their relatives or by employers. It is striking to note that about one-fifth of the total interviewed street children reported that they came alone. These are mostly 'run away children' (Table 4). The mean age of such run away children was 10 years. There is not a common reason for children to leave home. Every street child reported their individual history. However, in general, children leave their home due to poor household economic conditions, adverse familial environment and the desire for modern consumer items, which is a growing phenomenon in urban Nepal.

Table 4. Company at the period of first movement

Company	N	%
With parents	22	22.9
With friends	40	41.7
With employers	3	3.1
With relatives	12	12.5

Alone	19	19.8
Total	96	100.0

A non-supportive family environment stands out to be among the leading reasons for child migration. About 38 per cent of the total migrant street children reported that they left their home because of dysfunctional family conditions such as domestic violence (either against children or fighting between the mother and the father), scolding and physical abuse by alcoholic fathers and step-mothers including neglect in the family and lack of care and support. Desire for consumer items in the city life is the second most important reason for child migration.

In Kathmandu there are two types of street children: "off" the street children and "on" the street children. The former are children that spend the day and night in the street and latter are children who come to the street for work during the day and they stay at home at night with their relatives and/or with parents. About two-third of street children are of the category 'off the street children' and the rest are 'on the street children', who live in their own rooms (n=12), own huts (n=7), hostel/ transit homes (n=4)1 and working places (n=3). Most respondents reported that the latter types of children are the children of those parents who are labourers, rickshaw-pullers, rag pickers, vendors, hookers, beggars and small tea stall venders.

In order to identify the living circumstances, a question was asked to those street children who are currently in the street. The majority of street children live with their peer groups and about 15 per cent live with their own parents and/ or relatives. However, from the key informant interviews and case histories of the respondents, many street children live with foreigners such as tourists and so called 'social workers'.

The median duration of stay in the street among the respondents is estimated to be 4 years indicating the fact that half of the respondents have already spent 4 years in the street and half have not. Street-children are found to be involved in a variety of economic activities. Rag picking, however, is among the major sources of income. A substantial number of them also depend on begging. Other sources of income among street children include portering, sex work, stealing and pick pocketing. There is no fixed amount of earning among street children. Their earnings range from Rs. 40 to 150 per day. It was also found that street children have been economically exploited by both the police and the leaders of street children including junkyard owners. Street children also run the risk of losing their money to junkies and leaders of street children. It is reported that sometimes they lose all the money earned to local thugs or lose it as they do not have a place for safekeeping. Sometimes they have to pay 25-75 percent of their total earnings to their leader/police/ junkyard owner as commission. None of the off the street children were sending money back to their family home. They spend all their earnings on food. A large portion of their income is spent on drugs (boot polish), alcohol and tobacco. A few of the street children support their family.

We can see the gangs of street children occupy specific geographical areas in the city of Kathmandu. These are gangs of 5-12 street children. Most street children stay with their own gang in a particular locality for years. They have their own 'territory'within which they work. For example, we have been informed by the respondents that there is a street children's gang in Basantapur whose area is Basantapur, Bisal Bazar and New Road. Similarly, street children in Thamel occupy areas in Thamel and Chhetrapati. The street children gang around Bir Hospital works in the periphery of Bir Hospital, and sells newspaper in the Bus Park areas. There were about seven street children who were involved in selling daily Nepali newspapers such as the 'Kamandar' and 'Sandhayakalin' These children range from 10-15 years. These children are assisted by the Women Cell of the Valley Traffic Police, Kathmandu. Sometimes they earn about Rs. 50 per day by selling these newspapers.

Of the three rupees that the paper sells for - rupee one is paid to the publisher, rupee one is kept by the child hawker and rupee one is deposited in the name of the hawker in the women cell. On the one hand it seems to be providing a safe working environment for the children, but they still live in the dangerous environment of the street without any access to education. What the deposited money earned by the children by selling newspaper is spent for, is not clear.

The leader of the Bir Hospital gang collects money from the earnings of the other members on a daily basis. He spends it in buying rice, kerosene, vegetables and other essentials for the group as a whole. This pooling of money and equal distribution of food among its members reinforces the sense of group belonging and creates solidarity between group members. There is a tendency that most of these children do not go to work unless they finish their previous earnings. They live from hand to mouth through the pooling and redistribution system within the group.

Child trafficking include: heard about child trafficking, definition and perceptions of trafficking, sources of knowledge, whether they know about cases of child trafficking either from their place of origin or from working places and type of work trafficked children would be expected to perform. A large majority of the respondents had heard about child trafficking (59%) (Table 5). However, It differs according to age, sex, literacy status, caste/ethnicity and father literacy status of the respondents.

Table 5. Heard about child trafficking

Characteristics	Heard of child trafficking		
Age	n	%	N
7-9	2	25.0	8
10-14	33	52.4	63
15-19	24	82.8	29
Sex			
Boys	52	56.5	92

Girls	7	87.5	8
Literacy status			
Illiterate	26	43.3	60
Literate	33	82.5	40
Caste/ethnicity			
Hill ethnic groups	31	59.6	52
Brahman/Chhetri	14	66.7	21
Dalit	7	53.8	13
Tarai origin groups	4	36.4	11
Indian	2	100.0	2
DK	1	100.0	1
Father literacy status			
Literate	18	69.2	26
Illiterate	41	55.4	74
Total	59	59.0	100

The level of education seems to be linked to the awareness of child trafficking among street children. For example, more than fourth-fifth (82.5%) of the literate respondents were aware of child trafficking as against only 43 percent for the illiterate ones. The pattern of awareness also differs with the caste/ethnicity of respondents, Brahmin/Chhetri (67%) being most aware and the Tarai origin groups (36%) and the Dalits (54%) being least aware.

Father's literacy also accounts for the awareness among children as evident in Table 5. It is essential to note the there is no exact term for the word trafficking in Nepali and when translated it loosely stands for "sale and purchase of children" therefore it was necessary to ask further related questions. How do respondents perceive child trafficking? The majority perceive child trafficking to be employment of children with force or with coercion in work, followed by 'giving false promising for good employment' (10/59) and child selling (10/59). Similarly, respondents also understands child trafficking as child exploitation and prostitution.

Some children also regard child trafficking as children working in hotel/restaurant. How did the respondents hear about child trafficking? The responses are summarized in Table 6. The highest number of respondents heard it from their friends (21/ 59), followed by teachers (9/59), parents (8/59) and social workers (8/59). Other sources of awareness about child trafficking as stated by the respondents were relatives, radio/TV including police. Among those respondents who reported that they have heard about trafficking, 34 knew that there has been child trafficking either from their origin or from their working places.

Table 6. Sources of trafficking

Sources	N	%
Friends	21	35.6
Teachers	9	15.3
Parents	8	13.6
Social workers	8	13.6
Relatives	5	8.5
Radio/TV	4	6.8
Police	1	1.7
DK	3	5.1
Total	59	100

Are the respondents aware of the nature of work a traffick trafficked ed child would have to do? A little less than half of the total respondents feel they are aware of the nature of work a trafficked child is doing. The majority of respondents reported that it is domestic child labour, followed by sex worker and work in hotel/restaurant.

In order to identify whether the respondents were trafficked either from their origin or from the previous place of residence, a question was asked to all the respondents (migrant and non-migrant) whether they perceive that they were forced/tricked to leave their home/ previous place of residence against their will. This is the basic criterion of identifying whether the respondents were in the trap of recruiters, traffickers, employers or brokers employed in this study.

There are only a few studies indicating the magnitude of internal child trafficking in Nepal, related to street children. Table 7 summarizes the processes of internal child trafficking as found in the case of street children in Kathmandu valley i.e. places from where children are trafficked, types of traffickers/recruiters, means of abduction and means of transport used for bringing children to the destination. From rom where are children traffick trafficked? ed? Children are either directly trafficked from their place of origin or from the working places in urban areas. The phenomenon of internal child trafficking is found in most districts of Nepal. Children trafficked originate from ten districts of Nepal. They include Sindhupalchok (n=3), Chitawan (n=2), Nuwakot (n=2), Kavre (n=1), Kathmandu (n=1), Kaski (n=1), Lamjung (n=1), Gorkha (n=1), Mahottari (n=1) and Rautahat (n=1).

Table 7. Process of child trafficking

Place from where children were got	N
Birth place	8
Street in Kathmandu	2
Gangabu bus park	4
Persons involved in bringing children	
Local broker	2
Relatives	4
Peer groups (grown up street children)	5
Recruiters	3
Ways of recruiting/trafficking	
Promising good employment	8
Promising escape from poverty	2
Promising escape from domestic violence	4
Means of transport used	
Public bus	10
Trucks	3
On foot	1

Leaders of street children (ex street children, who spent their life in the street during childhood), relatives and local brokers including recruiters are the main persons involved in child trafficking. When street children grow up and are no longer able to stay as beggars in the street they go to their home and bring children from their villages. It is reported that they bring younger children for three purposes:

a) for becoming a leader of street children with large number of street children under them

b) for recruiting children in hotels/restaurants for commission and

c) for employing them as drug traffickers as it is easier for younger children to traffic drugs.

Some children were brought by their close relatives for domestic child labour. How do recr recruiters/uiters/traffick traffickers ers force/trick children to leave home or previous place of residence ? A majority of children are trafficked by false promises of good employment in Kathmandu. Children's household poverty and domestic violence are identified by recruiters/traffickers when they look for potential children. However, none of the respondents reported that they were provided any drugs during travel to the destination. It appears that the trafficker has the full confidence of the child who is absolutely unaware of what awaits him at the end of the journey. None of the children were aware that they were being trafficked.

The trafficked children sooner or later leave the masters or employers working place as they are not treated well and not paid. Among the 14 respondents reporting that they were first trafficked, 13 ran away from their employers or masters houses and only one respondent told us that he was rescued by NGO personnel i.e. by Human Welfare Centre. After having left their employers half of the children came directly to the street, four went to work as hotel boys, and only one was taken to a rehabilitation center. However, in the case of health during the work of masters/ employers houses or working places, the majority of the respondents did not feel that their health was in danger though many seemed to be psychologically depressed affected.

Some street children who were trafficked for domestic child labour also ran away from the master's house and came to the street. From the case histories of children who are now living in the hostels of Human Welfare Center it is known that most children do not know whether they were trafficked because most of them came to Kathmandu at a very young age. Yet it is evident that children are trafficked by relatives, leaders of street children, recruiters directly either from the origin or from the working places. Mostly, such trafficked children are put in the worst forms of child labour such as carpet weaving, domestic child labour and hotels. There are also few cases in which younger children are directly brought to street by the leaders of street children.

Sexual Abuse and Exploitation

Various forms of negative media, cheap cinema, availability of alcohol and drugs in the market, pornographic activities including sex tourism can have adverse impact on street children's life. Street children are vulnerable of being sexually abused or exploited as they are exposed to these activities. The fact that children are left to the gang protection only inscribes in them a distinct coping strategy and survival techniques.

Abuse of alcohol and drugs can have far reaching consequences for any child. The use of alcohol has become common among street children. This process has been fortified by several reasons. Firstly, the expansion of urban culture where modern media plays an important role. Secondly, easy access to alcohol market with no legislation regarding drinking age. Several types of alcohol with different brands are available in the market. Among them, four types of alcohol were commonly taken by the respondents: Jand or Chhang (rice or corn beer), home made alcohol (raksi), local alcohol and beer.

Jand or Chhang stands out to be the most popular among the sample population probably because of easy availability and the cheap price. An overwhelmingly majority of street children have consumed alcohol at some stage of their lives and more than one-thirds arę regular users (Table 8).

Table 8. Alcohol and drug use by the respondents

Alcohol/drug use	Both sex		Girls
	(n)	(%)	(n)
Ever taken alcohol			
Never taken	16	16.0	1
Yes, regular	36	36.0	
Yes, sometimes	44	44.0	5
Yes, rarely	4	4.0	2
Ever taken drugs			
Never taken	35	35.0	4
Yes, regularly	45	45.0	
Yes, sometimes	17	17.0	4
Yes, rarely	3	3.0	
Total	100	100.0	8

In case of drug abuse, two third of the respondents stated that they have experimented with drugs at some stage. A substantial percentage of respondents were regular drug abusers. 'Boot polish' is the most common drug among street children. Other drugs such as cannabis, iodex, kerosene and petrol is also reported to be used by the respondents. Expensive drugs such as heroin, opium and tranquilizers are less prevalent among street children.

Table 9 shows the number of respondents reporting sexual abuse/exploitation faced by their peer groups according to the respondents' age and sex. Of the total street children interviewed, 63 per cent stated that they have heard about sexual abuse/ exploitation experienced by their friends while 27 percent reported that they did not know about it.

Reporting of sexual abuse/exploitation varies with the respondents' age and sex. Older children in comparison to younger boys and girls over boys reported such events among their friends.

Table 9. Respondents reporting sexual abuse status among their peer groups (in number)

	Sexual abuse of their friends			
Age	Yes	No	Don't know	N
7-9	1	2	5	8
10-14	37	6	20	63
15-17	25	2	2	29
Sex				
Boys	58	10	24	92
Girls	5		3	8
Total	63	10	27	100

There are several forms of sexual abuse/exploitation a victim can face (several forms of sexual abuse/exploitation even in one act). Therefore, multiple forms of sexual abuse/exploitation were reported to be faced by the respondents' friends. The most reported forms of sexual abuse stand out to be masturbation, oral and anal sex. Other forms of sexual abuse such as kissing, commercial sex, teasing and rape (two girls reported that they were raped) are also common especially among girls.

Involvement in Pornography

Street children were involved in pornographic activities i.e. whether they have ever watched any x rated films and whether their naked photographs have ever been taken. It is evident that pedophilias who have access to the market for such products are the main abusers and these Pedophilias can easily attract children by giving money, medicine food or merely sympathy. A little less than two-thirds of the respondents have watched x rated films. Five respondents reported that they watch such films regularly and 37 per cent of the total respondents watch it sometimes (Table 10).

Table 10. Respondents reporting having watched x rated films

Categories	N
Ever watched	
Not at all	34
Yes, regular	5
Yes, sometimes	37
Yes, only one time	12
Not stated	12
Total	100
Persons showing x rated film	
Leader of street children	34
Foreigner	9
Local people	8
Others	8
Place of show	
Lodge	25
Friends place	11
Transit home	8
Paying money	1
Not stated	7

Street children get access to x rated films mostly through the leaders of street children, foreigners and also local people. Mostly such films were shown in lodges, followed by friends' places. The child rights issues also reported that street children are shown educational films in transit homes intending to teach street children the reproductive systems including the negative consequences of sexual exposure with multiple partners and the involvement in pedophilic activities. However, with little follow up and guidance this exposure may have an unintended negative impact on street children.

Eleven in 100 street children reported that their nude photographs were taken. (Table 11). Both foreigners and local people were reported to be the photographers. Hotels/ lodges including some of the public but lonely places such as temples, riverbanks were places where nude photos of street children were reported to be taken. To be able to get children to pose in the nude, photographers can only get access to and permission from the street children if they become close to such children and are able to win their confidence or on the other hand create dependency of some kind.

Table 11. Status of taking nude photography

Categories	N
Whether photographed nude	
Yes	11
No	89
Persons who took photographs	
Foreigners/Tourists	4
Local people	3
Not stated	4
Place of Photography	
Hotel/lodge	5
During bathe time	4
Other public places	2

Causes of Sexual Abuse

This section deals with sexual abuse/ exploitation faced by the respondents: prevalence and differentials of sexual abuse/ exploitation by selected characteristics, such as forms and frequency of sexual exploitation, persons involved in sexual exploitation, while also attempting to look at the context and root causes of sexual exploitation among street children.

The proportion reporting sexual abuse/exploitation, however, varies with age, sex, caste/ethnicity and duration of stay in the street of the street respondents. It can be rightly summarized that the number is probably much higher as many would prefer to keep their secrets to themselves due to feelings of guilt, shame and fear.

Two thirds of the oldest street children have been sexually abused/exploited. There is also substantial proportion of youngest children who have been sexually abuse/exploited. With regard to the sex of the respondents, six out of eight girls interviewed reported that they were sexually abused/ exploited while the comparable figure for boys is 34 percent. In terms of caste/ethnicity, Brahman/Chhetri children were exposed more to sexual abuse as against other groups considered. The duration of stay in the street also matters for the risk of sexual exploitation. The longer the period in the street, the higher the possibility of sexual abuse.

Several forms of sexual abuse/exploitations were reported in the survey among street children. The most common forms reported include giving and receiving masturbation, oral and anal sex. Out of 37 street children who faced sexual abuse/exploitation, at least 30 experienced one of the listed abuses. Girls also face the same forms of sexual abuse including commercial sex as indicated in the total cases. These girls are often found around the public toilet areas of Kathmandu. It is not quite clear why such girls stay around the public toilets, are the places where low-paid men often come searching for sex. Some street boys also work as brokers.

It appears that these girls have now come to a stage of complete desensitization, beyond stage of guilt, shame or fear. The implication of such practices would have long term adverse impact on the individual girl's physical and psychological life as most of the time their clients refuse condom use during intercourse. In the case of sexual exploitation among boys, it is mostly by pedophiles who attract children by providing 'good' food, clothes, lodging and money.

Most respondents, who reported that they were sexually abuse/exploited or involved in sex work willingly, a large majority of them were paid by the abusers/clients. Those not being paid may be sexually bused/exploited/raped by street junkies and/or leader of street children.

It is important to understand how children were initially sexually abused/exploited in order to combat the phenomenon of sexual abuse/exploitation among street children. A majority of the street children were first sexually abused/exploited by promise of good money. Thirty in 100 street children reported that they were involved in sex because of some form of coercion. Some street children first got into sexual activities with the promise of good food, good clothes and peer pressure. The average age at which street children are initially sexually abused/exploited is 11 years - 2 or 3 years before the age of puberty in the case of girls.

Hotels/lodges are the places where street children were first sexually abused or exploited. Other places of sexual exploitation include the street itself, client houses/rooms, temples and river banks. One girl in Bir Hospital area told us that she was first sexually abused by a gang of three junkies inside the Khullamanch (open stadium) in Ratna Park. This suggests that it is essential to sensitize the lodge and hotel owners on the issue of pedophilia including travel agencies and public place authorities.

Every child in the street is vulnerable to sexual abuse be it from foreign pedophiles, sex tourists, locals, their own peer or leaders. Life in the street is harsh and difficult and children have to adopt different survival strategies and in some cases it is to numb themselves to the abuse they have to adhere to. As they have but little public sympathy and no support from the government, they have little access to justice or a platform for complaints thus they tend to create their own sense of belonging, justice and survival mechanisms.

3

HIV/AIDS and STDs among Street Children

Sexually transmitted diseases and HIV infection are among the commonest health problems in the area of sexual and reproductive health in the world today. These conditions are a major cause of morbidity and mortality among the young. It is estimated that one in every 20 adolescents worldwide contract sexually transmitted diseases each year. 34.3 million people are now living with HIV the virus that causes AIDS.

Already, 18.8 million people around the world have died of AIDS. 3.8 million of them children. Half of the people who acquire HIV become infected before they turn 25 and die from AIDS before their 35th birthday. By the end of 1999 the epidemic had left an accumulative total of 11.2 million AIDS orphans. Orphans are defined as those having lost their mother before reaching the age of 15. Street children are particularly vulnerable to HIV/AIDS/STDs because of their circumstances.

STDs are diseases that are passed from one person to another mainly through sexual intercourse. The most common STDs are: chlamydia, syphilis, trichomonas, genital warts, chancroid, genital herpes, hepatitis B and HIV infection. Some STDs, such as syphilis and HIV can also be transmitted through exposure to contaminated blood and from a pregnant woman to the unborn child. During your work with street children, you may encounter children needing help or treatment for STDs.

Awareness of some of the common complaints will help you recognize or suspect the presence of these conditions. You could then refer the child for expert care. A street child complaining of any of the following may have a sexually transmitted disease:

— Abnormal discharge from the penis, anus or vagina.

— Burning or pain on passing urine.

— Pain in the abdominal or groin area with fever.

— Pain during sex.

— Blisters, rash or sores on the genital organs.

HIV destroys certain white blood cells that form an important component of the immune system. As the power or ability to resist infections depends on the immune system, such individuals become vulnerable to many types of infections, even those that heal quickly in people with normal immunity. The destruction of the protective white blood cells takes place gradually and therefore a person may be infected with the virus for many years without feeling unwell.

As the virus is present in the body, the potential for spreading the disease exists even during this period. After this initial dormant period, the person develops swelling of lymph glands, fever, loose motions, loss of appetite, loss of weight, and fatigue. After a period varying from six months to as long as 10 years, the illness becomes more active and serious infections and related conditions occur. This stage of the illness is known as AIDS (Acquired Immunodeficiency Syndrome).

Almost all HIV-infected people will ultimately develop HIV-related disease and AIDS. Remember that the complaints attributed to HIV/AIDS (fever, loose motions, loss of appetite, loss of weight, fatigue, skin lesions etc.) are common and are also seen in many other diseases. There is no way that anyone (including doctors, street children or you) could diagnose that the street child has HIV or AIDS by simply looking at him/her. The presence of HIV infection can only be confirmed by a blood test.

Although the typical age of a street child varies from place to place, the age range includes children in the adolescent period. Sexual behaviour begins before adolescence; during adolescence, major physical and psychological changes occur. These include rapid physical growth and development, social and psychological maturity which bring about enormous social and psychological pressure. Young people, especially boys are exposed to continued pressure from peer groups as sexual experiences may be viewed as achieving or demonstrating competence.

Street children are exposed to situations that make them vulnerable to sexual and reproductive health problems on a day to day basis. Their vulnerability to these situations is increased by their lack of understanding of the changes associated with adolescence, the lack of knowledge and skills which could help them to make healthy choices and their inability to access the appropriate services.

In broad terms, sexual health is a personal sense of sexual well being as well as the absence of disease, infections or illness associated with sexual behaviour. As such, it includes issues of self-esteem, selfexpression, caring for others and cultural values. Sexual health can be described as the positive integration of physical, emotional, intellectual and social aspects of sexuality. Sexuality influences thoughts, feelings, interactions and actions among human beings, and motivates people to find love, contact, warmth and intimacy. It can be expressed in many different ways and is closely linked to the environment one finds oneself in. The environment can hinder or enhance sexual expressions.

The WHO defines reproductive health as a state of complete physical, mental and social wellbeing and not merely the absence of disease or infirmity in all matters relating to the reproductive system and to its functions and processes. This definition suggests that people with adequate reproductive health have a satisfying and safe sexual life, can have children, and can make a choice as to whether they would like to have children and if so, when and how to have them.

Adolescence is the transitional period between childhood and adulthood. It begins with the biological changes associated with puberty and proceeds through a process of psychosocial changes. Each aspect of maturation does not develop at the same rate. Development in adolescence can be uneven and deviations from the norm can cause alarm in the adolescents and those around them. The general information below will give you an understanding of the importance of sexual reproductive health among street children, most of whom are in this phase of development.

Puberty refers to the sequence of physical events by which a child is transformed into a young adult. The characteristic physical changes include those in the reproductive organs and the external genitalia in both sexes, breast development and hip enlargement in the female, facial hair growth and change in voice-pitch in the male. Puberty leads to menarche (onset of menstrual flow) in females and to the onset of ejaculation (of seminal fluid) in males.

Adolescents select characteristics from many people,- peers, parents, teachers, relatives, religious leaders and famous people. They blend certain of these people's features with their own characteristics to become a unique new person. The new person or identity is not one's final self, but it forms the basis of what one will become. If adolescents manage to work through the contradictions of this process they will develop positive and healthy feelings towards themselves.

The advent of sexuality and the need to manage it in some way are major features of the adolescent experience. Uncertainty, conflict and a struggle often accompany the awakening of sexual feelings over appropriate avenues of expression. Cultural factors also play an important role in the psychosocial aspects of adolescent development and in the sexual conduct and meaning adolescents generate concerning sex. Adolescence serves as the intermediate stage between the shaping experiences of the gender in childhood and the development of the full-blown male or female adult identity.

Sexual activity may signify different things to different people. Such meanings are derived from collective, individual and interpersonal experiences and expectations. Street children have a great need to fill the void of normal relations because many have left their families or do not have a family. Street boys sometimes describe sex as "play between friends". Comfort sex is often exploitative in nature, even though such a relationship provides the child with shelter, basic needs and protection.

Sometimes, street children use sex as a way of expressing physical power. The younger street children comply for fear of being beaten. Some street boys have said that they have sex with prostitutes because it is a symbol of strength and being a 'real man', and to show friends that they are in control. Sex is used to control other street children and make them obey demands and respect 'hierarchies' on the street. A street child in Mwanza, United Republic of Tanzania said, "he rapes me because he wants me to know who is in power".

Initiation sex occurs to initiate newcomers to the group. It is thought to be a way of making the new street children feel they 'belong'. It is a passage to identity formation. Usually the victims are threatened with violence if they do not agree. Most street children see this type of sexual experience as something inevitable. When a street child is found not to be 'going along' with the group (norms), they may be punished for not abiding by the 'rules'. Sexual assault is used as a way of punishing a street child.

A risky sexual behaviour is one that increases the likelihood of adverse sexual and reproductive health consequences. These health consequences may include unwanted pregnancy, unsafe abortion, HIV/AIDS and STDs. Examples of such behaviours are: sexual activity under the influence of substances, sexual intercourse with drug users, unprotected sexual intercourse, commercial sex/survival sex/ prostitution, and unprotected sex with a same sex (particularly between males) partner.

Substance use may influence sexual behaviour in ways that increase the risk of acquisition of HIV and other STDs. The street child's decision on sexual behaviours such as whether to use a condom during sexual activity, whether to negotiate for sex or to use force (rape) depend on the level of intoxication. In general alcohol and other substance use often accompany the early sexual experiences, especially among boys.

In Australia and Canada, many street children engage in commercial sex while intoxicated as they say it helps them not to think about what they are doing. Having unprotected sex with substance users can lead to sexual and reproductive health problems because such persons are more to likely engage in risky sexual behaviour. The risk of acquiring HIV infection through unprotected sex from a sex partner who injects substances is particularly high.

Sexual Intercourse

Unprotected sex is common among street children. This could result in a variety of sexual and reproductive health problems. Street children spend a lot of time in settings where casual sexual encounters occur (taverns or 'crack houses'). Their risk of acquiring blood borne diseases and STDs such as HIV, syphilis and hepatitis is increased by the fact that they often have sex with persons at high risk for these diseases (people with multiple sexual partners or those sharing injection equipment for substances).

Sometimes street children engage in this type of sexual activity due to the immediate need to secure food and shelter, or as a means to obtain substances or to support their families. Street children sometimes have sex with other street children of the same sex. This is much more common among boys. In addition, street boys are often sexually exploited by older men. Engaging in unprotected sexual intercourse can lead to acquisition of STDs.

Sexual violence including rape is very common on the streets. Both street girls and boys are at risk. The perpetrators may be strangers or people known to them. Sexual abuse may also occur within the family e.g. forced sex with a stepfather. Because of the unprotected nature of the sexual intercourse, there is a high risk of STDs and other reproductive health problems.

Street girls may become pregnant because of unprotected sex. Because the reproductive system is not fully developed, they are prone to complications related to childbirth such as premature delivery and obstructed labour. These can cause injuries or death to the baby and the mother. The baby born to such mothers may have a low birth weight and may be prone to infections and illness. Coping with the needs of the child may be difficult for a street girl.

Pregnant street girls may feel pressured into terminating their pregnancy. They often have no one to turn to for support and advice and they may not have access to reproductive health services for safe termination of pregnancy. They may seek the services of unqualified persons or induce the termination themselves. Unsafe abortions could lead to infections, bleeding, or even death. Damage to the reproductive organs can cause infertility (inability to have children). The stress of the experience could also lead to psychological problems such as depression.

STDs and HIV infection are consequences of unprotected sexual intercourse with an infected individual. The risk of STDs increases if a person has more than one sexual partner, or a partner (including prostitutes) who has other sexual partners.

HIV Transmission

Since the discovery of the virus in 1983 by scientists in France, the routes of transmission were confirmed. HIV infection can pass from one person to the other through the following ways:

— Through unprotected sexual intercourse: a person infected with the HIV virus can pass it on to another when his or her body fluids (e.g. semen, vaginal fluids or blood) enters the other person's blood stream through unprotected sexual (vaginal, anal and oral) intercourse. The virus can enter the bloodstream through cuts, abrasions etc. on the body surface or mucosa. A street child's (street girl) immature vaginal mucosa can easily be broken during sexual intercourse, facilitating the entry of the virus into the body. Sexually transmitted diseases increase the risk of transmission of HIV because some of them cause genital ulcerations or sores which can facilitate the entry or transfer of the HIV infection.

— Through contaminated blood or blood products: such as receiving infected blood, using contaminated needles and syringes when injecting drugs, or through skin-piercing equipment contaminated with HIV. The pattern of substance use among street children can have an influence on HIV transmission in two ways:

— Due to practices connected with the administration of the substance e.g. sharing needles and syringes or mixing the substances in the syringes contaminated with blood.

— Substance can affect perception, judgement and behaviour, making it more likely that they would engage in unprotected sexual intercourse especially with other substance users using injectable substances.

— From an HIV infected mother to the child: this could occur during pregnancy, childbirth and in infancy through breast-milk.

Even with the current level of knowledge, HIV/AIDS generates fear and misunderstanding in many people. HIV/AIDS is surrounded by many myths among people in many countries. It is important to understand how HIV/AIDS is perceived in the local community in order to develop appropriate educational messages. Illustrated below are some examples of common misunderstandings about HIV/AIDS.

Boys and girls talk about the stress of unwanted sex. Street girls report being sexually assaulted by older street youth, army men and other adults. Street girls also talk about the stress of feeling they are defenceless in the face of sexual advances/assaults. A number of stressors can have a profound influence on the reproductive and sexual behaviour of the street child. These include lack of companionship and acceptance, sexual abuse and unwanted sex, economic pressure from family and adolescent development.

Street children often get their information about sexual and reproductive health issues from the media. Sex and substance use are often presented in the following way in the media: Sexual themes are used to sell many products in the media in ways that make sex seem very exciting and desirable or as something very normal. Such images influence sexual behaviour among street children.

Sex is rarely presented as having any negative consequences. Sexual relationships presented rarely incorporate ideas and images that promote or support responsible sexual behaviour (e.g., delaying sex until older, using condoms and other contraceptives to prevent sexually transmissible infections and unwanted pregnancy). Such presentations increase the possibility that the street child will indulge in risky sexual behaviours. Advertising shows stereotyped images of men and women, showing men in dominant, unfeeling roles and women as submissive. This encourages the role of force in sexual encounters.

Pornography exists in a variety of forms (videos and films, magazines, photos, sculpture and drawings) within all cultures. Pornography is presented in a much more attractive manner than many of the materials used to promote responsible sexual behaviour and consequently significantly influences the norms that shape sexual behaviour and attitudes towards relationships.

Attitudes towards sex and sexuality are a basic part of every culture. Such attitudes are influenced by religious, social and economic factors. The expectations and norms (accepted practices) of the society greatly influence how the street child perceives sexual practice and activities. Such practices affect the sexual and reproductive health of an individual. For example, if sex may be accepted only within marriage in a culture where early marriage is the norm, it would protect against infections, but it would be associated with problems related to early pregnancy and childbirth.

The attitude towards the role of men and women is interrelated within each culture to sexual behaviours and practices. The low status or value placed on girls or women increases the likelihood of sexual reproductive health problems in them, e.g. men may demand sex as their right and may refuse to accept the responsibility for contraception.

Girls and women often have little control over men's sexual access to their bodies, and the conditions under which sexual encounters take place. Street girls appear to have internalized their role as sexual beings, and see sex as a way to meet their needs. Just as boys understand 'being a man' as behaving in a dominant fashion, girls understand 'being a woman' as pleasing men sexually. In both childhood and street experiences, girls have learned that selfesteem, acceptance, and love are usually available only through sex.

If the street child's earlier sexual experiences were positive, he or she is more likely to seek these experiences. If sexual activity brings feelings of power or control to someone who otherwise feels powerless, such feelings may be sought through aggressive sexual demands or violence against others. Street children may enter a sexual relationship to avoid the feeling of loneliness or rejection or to feel desired and accepted. Sex is often used like substances, to help street children forget worries and anxiety or for relaxation, pleasure or comfort. Negative sexual experiences decrease the chance that a child will indulge in sexual activity. Early and unwanted sex may also lead to distorted perceptions of sexuality.

The people who are supposed to be protecting them may sexually assault street girls and boys in some situations. One of the lasting effects of child sexual assault can be a difficulty in forming and maintaining intimate, trusting relationships. Some of these children keep forming relationships with potential abusers and others become frightened of developing closeness with anyone.

Street children are more likely to have positive sexual and reproductive health if their strongest attachments are with people who support and practice responsible sexual behaviours (e.g. the use of condoms/contraceptives). Attachments to people who take advantage of them, or allow or encourage risky behaviours increase the vulnerability of street children. Trading sex for friendship and protection is common.

4

Street Children and Violence

Street children are particularly vulnerable to violence within juvenile justice systems. They are more likely to come into contact with the juvenile justice system in the first place, and they are simultaneously less able to defend themselves against violations of their rights within that system. Grassroots development and human rights organisations have identified the situation of street children in detention and juvenile justice as necessitating immediate, sustained and coordinated action.

Physical Violence

Violence by state officials (police and military) against children on the streets is perhaps the most obvious, and the most 'traditional' form of violence associated with street children. However, it is important from the beginning to make clear the links between wider social, economic and cultural factors and different forms of violence. The connection is obvious: street children invariably come from the poorest sectors of society, and it is this initial socio-economic disadvantage, and the resulting lack of protection, that renders them so vulnerable to violence. This is often compounded by racial discrimination because street children - for reasons linked yet again to poverty - are more likely to come from ethnic, racial and indigenous minorities. Violence against children on the streets must therefore be seen in its wider context as the visible end of a spectrum of structural violence against which these children struggle to survive on a daily basis.

Violence against children on the streets, including extra-judicial execution, therefore springs from their socio-economic and cultural situation and their racial and ethnic identity, all of which contribute to the process of dehumanising these children. Not only are street children (especially those who actually live on the streets) an embarrassing, visible reminder of a society's failure to provide for and protect its most vulnerable children, but they are also considered a threat to that very society by the way in which they live. It is therefore easy and more comfortable to either not see them at all, or to fear them and see them as more animal than human. This results in them being transposed from 'children' to 'street children' to 'undesirables' to 'discardables', the most extreme manifestation of which are the death squads and vigilantes made famous in Latin America.

In Brazil, a military policeman is quoted as saying "99.9% of policemen think that the street child is an unsolvable problem. He cannot be helped, and so he must die. It is a way of resolving the problem....". Dehumanisation is the most dangerous threat posed to vulnerable children in that it absolves people, especially the authorities, of the obligation to accord them their human rights. It is this lack of political will - sustained by negative public pressure - resulting in woefully inadequate national protection for street children, that brings us repeatedly to international human rights fora to explore the possibilities of expanding protection mechanisms for children who fall through national safety nets.

Since international attention was drawn to the responsibility of governments for such killings - made famous by the outcry over the 1993 Candelaria massacre in Rio de Janeiro - the problem has not gone away. Nor has the investigation and prosecution of the perpetrators improved. Casa Alianza released a report in April 2001 regarding the murder of more than 650 children and youth in Honduras over the past 3 years. Some 60% of the cases have not been investigated sufficiently to determine who the killers were. In the 40% of the remaining cases where the killer has been identified, one half of them were police or Honduran authorities .

There have, however, been developments in the way in which these killings are carried out. For example, in Brazil, international pressure has driven killings away from tourist centres to the outskirts of cities, and statistics for extra-judicial killings are deliberately blurred to conceal an accurate picture of the true level of violence against street children . Likewise, there has also been a move away from uniformed assassins in groups, easily identifiable as military and police state agents (death squads), to individuals dressed in civilian clothing.

The NGO Jubilee Campaign states: "The increasing trend over recent years which has made almost indistinguishable the difference between policeman and security guard, death squad and security firm, has only served to augment the numbers of children assassinated in Greater Rio de Janeiro" . This blurring of the identity of the perpetrators of violence against street children serves to deliberately confuse allocation of state responsibility for these crimes at local and national level, once again revealing a gap in the protection offered to at-risk children which needs urgently to be filled at the international level.

One final link between economic circumstances and violence is that of exploitative child labour to which street children are particularly vulnerable. An explicit example of this is a six-year-old girl on an Indian railway platform being forced by an adult to whip herself in order to gain sympathy and an increase in the money gathered from begging. Further harmful (worst forms of) child labour to which street children are prone, and which are at high risk of incurring violence, are commercial sexual exploitation and drug-trafficking.

Psychological Violence

In addition to suffering extreme forms of physical violence, street children are also particularly vulnerable to psychological violence, which can play on and exacerbate existing insecurities and lack of self-esteem (based once again on their wider socio-economic and cultural circumstances). The overall stigmatisation of street children and the aforementioned dehumanization process form a continual backdrop of degradation of street children. For example, verbal abuse against street children (such as derogatory remarks made about a child's mother and family situation) are common, often carrying the implication that 'you are such a bad / worthless child that even your parents don't want you, you have no value...'. Furthermore, racial discrimination can also be a significant component of verbal abuse.

Domestic Violence

Referring once again to the spectrum of violence and disadvantage that street children experience, let us step back momentarily from the issue of violence against street children in the public arena, to examine violence in the private arena - a notoriously difficult area for human rights protection. The psychological abuse suffered on the street, as mentioned above, is very often the continuation of abuse suffered at home, prior to migrating to the street.

The vast majority of street-living children are victims of domestic violence, and/or sexual and psychological abuse to such an extent that life on the streets, with all the obvious dangers it entails, is still considered preferable. Street children therefore have to be seen as double victims of violence: both before and after moving to street life. Violent socialisation patterns and poor communication skills experienced in the home, including gender socialisation (patterns of violence against women) can be absorbed by children and perpetuated after their migration to the streets. Furthermore, these cycles of violence can also be exacerbated by the development of 'survival' violence on the streets as a form of self-defence and protection.

It goes without saying that the pressure of extreme poverty on families (which may also be linked to alcohol and drug abuse) impacts on levels of violence in families, once again reinforcing the links between wider socio-economic circumstances and violence, to which street children are subject not only on the streets but within the home as well.

Sexual Violence

Amongst street-living children, girls are in a minority (estimates range between 3 and 30%, depending on the country in question). However, these girls are amongst the most vulnerable children in the world. Domestic violence, sexual abuse, neglect and rejection are just some of the factors pushing girls to sever their family relationships and fend for themselves in situations of violence and extreme vulnerability.

In addition, due to cultural constraints, research has shown that the move to the street for girls is more traumatic and the rupture more permanent than for boys. Programmes in Kenya, Senegal, Bolivia, Brazil and Guatemala report that girls on the street display more psychological damage than boys - a combination of both sexual abuse and rupture in the family. This internalization by girls of the effects of domestic violence, sexual abuse and family break-up has been described as "psychological death"- which finds expression in violent behaviour, depression, withdrawal and self-mutilation .

After transition to the street, girls are particularly vulnerable to sexual violence. Because of their 'non-normative' sexual activity (possibly involving multiple partners, 'survival' sex in exchange for food, shelter and protection, and the difficulty in drawing boundaries between this and sexual abuse and commercial sexual exploitation), they suffer a perceived loss of rights over their bodies - which is yet another manifestation of 'otherness' or dehumanisation. This is compounded by gender stereotypes in male-dominated cultures which define these girls as not 'nice girls'.

Combined with a general taboo of sexually active children, especially girls, and even a fear of them, this results in exceptionally high levels of sexual violence against street girls. Recent information from Nairobi, Kenya, reveals that street girls are shaving their heads, flattening their chests and wearing up to four pairs of trousers in order to disguise themselves as boys and give themselves more time to escape gang rape on the streets at night . These high levels of violence are, of course, further exacerbated by their lack of protection at local and national level, with state agents often directly implicated in the abuse.

Particularly worrying is the added vulnerability of street girls who are already mothers themselves. Finally, let us not forget the specific impact of HIV/AIDS on street children, which is an inherent risk involved in the sexual violence which they experience. Evidence shows that men are looking for increasingly younger girls (and boys) for sex, and - added to the vastly increased risks of HIV transmission from adult to child - street children are once again at the brunt of a society that treats them as disposable, worthless, 'inhuman' commodities.

General Background of Violence

In many countries, a general background of conflict can both contribute to the increase in numbers of street children (through displacement and the creation of orphans), and in the increased levels of violence against street children. For example, the number of street children in Guatemala swelled during the 1980s. This was due to both the influx of unaccompanied children fleeing violence in neighbouring countries such as El Salvador and Nicaragua, and as a result of the 36-year civil war in Guatemala itself, the effects of which continue to impact on the country today.

The exceptionally high levels of widespread violence at that time led to a prevailing culture of violence and systematic torture with a strong political and ethnic/racial dimension. An example of how this endemic violence manifested itself against street children can be seen in the case of the 1990 brutal murder of five street children, four of whom had been horrifically tortured with their eyes gouged out and their ears, noses and tongues cut off by off-duty police acting with impunity in a typical 'signature' crime along the lines of 'see no evil, hear no evil, speak no evil against our authority' .

In another example, South Africa is currently suffering exceptionally high levels of societal violence, especially rape - across all sectors of the community. From January to June 1998 alone, 23,374 rapes were reported to the police nationally. Of these reported rapes, 19,836 cases were children under the age of 18. It is also widely accepted that reported rapes account for only a small percentage of actual rapes - estimated between 1 in 20 and 1 in 30 . Although these figures do not specify numbers of street children (who are even less likely to report rape), it may be assumed that street children are particularly vulnerable to these particularly disturbing trends in the prevalence of rape and sexual assault.

Once again - it would be reasonable to assume that high levels of general societal violence are linked to socio-economic circumstances, frustration at high levels of poverty, political instability and ethnic or racial tension. All of these factors impact negatively on street children as they are particularly vulnerable to this aggression being vented on them: they can even be seen as the causes of these wider societal problems, being scape-goated for crime levels due to their visibility in street crime.

Likewise, unprotected refugee, immigrant and/or minority children can become easy targets for nationalist aggression and suspicion. This perception that they are to blame for other problems can therefore compound the levels of violence against street children. Futhermore, where countries are experiencing widespread conflict and high levels of violence, street children inevitably sink even lower down a government's list of political priorities, thus further exacerbating the lack of protection and recourse to justice to which street children already have very limited access.

Violent socialisation patterns experienced in the home prior to children migrating to street life can manifest themselves in violence which is both necessary for self-protection on the streets, and which - in the absence of non-violent communication skills - is considered a normal recourse to resolving disputes. Violence is also prevalent in gang culture. It can be used to maintain discipline and assert authority within the hierarchy of the gang as well as taking the form of inter-gang violence.

Violence can also be related to substance abuse . First, certain types of drugs can induce violent behaviour per se or can lead to violent behaviour as a consequence of the need to obtain further drugs in order to satisfy addiction (i.e. crack has particularly violent associations due to its high addictiveness).

Secondly, involvement in the drug trade (often linked to gangs) carries a high risk of violence, both against children and by children. Younger street children are involved as couriers and then become increasingly involved in the business as they get older. The average life expectancy of gang members in Rio is about 29 . One report from Brazil lists the following reasons why children involved in the drug trade are killed:

— inter-gang drug wars;

— those who make mistakes or who try to cheat their employer are killed to set an example to others;

— younger children with outstanding debts are disposable;

— even children who become a threat to the gang leaders - as they get older and have amassed experience of the trade - can be eliminated.

These 'genuine' drug-related deaths are in addition to those that are disguised as such to conceal killings of street children by police and local extermination groups . This type of gang violence mainly affects boys, but girls are also subject to violence - both physical and sexual - within gangs. The socio-economic and cultural links to drug and gang related violence are clear: street children abuse substances to quell pangs of hunger, for escapism, for 'Dutch courage' in a dangerous and hostile environment, to bond with their peers, and simply to get through the day. For similar reasons, street children join gangs in response to social exclusion, loneliness and the need for protection, in a society that has failed to provide them with their basic physical and emotional needs.

International Protection Mechanisms

It goes without saying that the different types of violence discussed above are not adequately dealt with at a national level: street children are not a political priority because they have no voice with which to express their concerns. Street children represent high government expenditure with little short-term (election term) returns on state investment (although the longer-term costs to society of failing to provide for these most marginalized children are very great indeed). In addition, there is usually no public pressure on governments to deal with street children issues, including violence against street children - violence which is often condoned or even perpetrated by 'concerned citizens' or 'vigilantes' from amongst local communities themselves: "One person pulls the trigger, but many others support the pulling of that trigger. Many want it pulled. They even pay for it to be pulled. They think it's right" .

Reports show that vigilantes in these crimes are not necessarily motivated by economics so much as by a response to the failure of the State to combat crime and the public perception that street children are a threat to 'decent', 'normal' society, failing to recognize that street children are the product of the failings of that very same 'decent', 'normal' society. This lack of political will and absence of public pressure naturally creates a culture of impunity whereby violators of street children's rights act secure in the knowledge that they will go unpunished. Implicit in this culture of impunity is the involvement of the local police and judiciary which can make it nearly impossible for NGOs and human rights defenders to obtain justice for street children who are victims of violence.

It is only after expensive and exhausting legal battles lasting for up to 10 years that Casa Alianza and CEJIL (Centre for Justice and International Law) have managed to win compensation for the families of murdered street children in Guatemala. Although the Inter-American Commission and Court of Human Rights finally found the State of Guatemala guilty of violating numerous provisions of the American Convention on Human Rights in a landmark decision, the costs and length of time involved in this process are extremely prohibitive. Furthermore, outside of Europe and the Americas, the majority of the world's children do not have access to any reliable regional human rights systems.

If violence against street children is therefore not being adequately dealt with at the national - or even regional - level, then there is an obvious need for it to be dealt with at the international level. Unfortunately, however, protection mechanisms currently available at this level are also inadequate. Although some of the existing UN Special Rapporteurs (such as those on Torture and on Violence Against Women) examine cases involving children on an incidental basis , there is no mechanism specifically to address violence against children, although the need - as has already been demonstrated here today - is great.

In the words of Bruce Harris, Regional Director of Casa Alianza in Latin America: "What actions [can] the UN Commission on Human Rights take in instances such as these [in Honduras] where the governmental authorities do not respond; where impunity reigns in the judicial system and where no individual complaints are accepted by the Committee on the Rights of the Child. What concrete actions can the Committee take, or do we just have to continue to report on more and more killings each year?"

Even whilst recognising the advances being made regionally in Central America in terms of legal compensation for street children's families (and the potential impact this may have in terms of longer-term prevention of violence against street children) Bruce Harris admits: "We cannot speak of justice because our kids are dead" .

Surely true 'justice' will come only when children are prevented from being placed in situations at risk of violence in the first place. Therefore, whatever international protection mechanism is under discussion, be it a Special Rapporteur on Violence Against Children or an Optional Protocol to the CRC, the Consortium for Street Children is concerned that the scope of its mandate should go beyond the limitations of an 'urgent action' procedure - as necessary as this obviously is - to examine the causes of violence against children as well, in order to make the links between socio-economic and cultural and civil and political rights violations explicit.

The majority of forms of violence against street children are linked to their low socio-economic position, and ethnic and racial origins, which impact on their lack of access to national and regional protection mechanisms - access being an issue that will also have to be taken into account in any potential international mechanism on children and violence. Without addressing these background causal factors, any mechanism will have limited effect.

5

Child Prostitution

Street and slum children throughout the world are seen to be particularly at risk of HIV/AIDS/STD infection because of the special circumstances of their situations. These include the need to perform "survival prostitution", greater freedom to experiment with sex, lack of adequate protection and socialization and the inherent dangers of street life. They represent an especially vulnerable group both in terms of the reasons for their coming to and being on the streets, and what could happen to them when on the streets and slums.

In Uganda, children constitute a fifth of the population and are presently a rapidly growing segment. Unfortunately, over 20,000 children in Kampala are estimated to be living on the streets and in slum areas where they are exposed to a number of problems ranging from drug and substance abuse, violence, unemployment, prostitution to lack of access to appropriate services. 4000 children were living on the street in 1996. The number has now increased due to HIV/AIDS, poverty and wars, which have raged for over 18 years. In 2001, Uganda Youth Development Link, in a conference paper on psychosocial problems of children under rehabilitation from commercial sex, noted that child prostitution is on the increase.

Major targets of exploitation are street and slum children, housegirls, students living independently in hostels and those in day schools. Due to constant lack of food, clothing and other basic needs, these children engage in sex with multiple partners for survival. Girls say that life on the streets is hard and so those who have stayed longer on streets introduce new girls to all sorts of behavior and a culture of illicit survival. Sex is the most readily available means of survival. Almost every girl living on the street acknowledges the exchange of sex for food, clothing, drinks, shelter and money.

Coupled with the above factors, the main slum areas in and around Kampala city like Kisenyi, Katanga, Katwe and Bwaise have poor housing where children often become victims of sexual abuse and drug abuse at a tender age. Findings from a study done by Save the Children UK in the year 2003 in one slum of Kampala city revealed that "82% of residents in slum areas live in single room houses with over 6 children and thus children were likely to experiment sex so early while trying to initiate into practice they hear and see from adults".

Further more, some children in the slums, especially girls engaged in survival sex, live independently where they rent small rooms as individuals or groups. This is one of the reasons attributed to the ever-increasing age of first sexual encounter where children start sex at an early age of 14 years and give birth as early as 15 years. Generally, there is scarcity of information on the situation of drug and substance abuse in the country, mostly due to the fact that no major study has been conducted in Uganda.

Drug abuse is illegal, though it has been update since 1964 Act, save the national authority drug statute of 1993 which vaguely touches on the issue of drug misuse. It is difficult to obtain accurate data on the extent and nature of this latent problem. Available data from Police, NGOs and Health centers however, suggests an increase in use and abuse of drugs in Uganda. There is higher reported use of drugs and substances in urban areas compared to rural areas. According to reports 30% of the cases admitted in Butabika mental hospitals are drug and alcohol related. However, the problem of drug and substance abuse is gradually and steadily spreading to the rural areas concentrating mainly in small rural trading centers and towns.

The street and slum children culture is also highly synonymous with use of alcohol and drugs. Drug abuse culture plays a functional role among them to escape and reduce stress, daily problems as well as serving as a cure for their health maladies. It plays a recreation role and consolation for lack of access or absence of services. Drug abusing culture is also highly promoted in films, makeshift video halls and disco places. On the demand side, peer pressure, especially among the youths, appears to be promoting the scourge.

Article 33 in the Convention on the Rights of the Child prohibits use of narcotic and psychotropic drugs among children. According to the Convention on the Rights of the Child in article 1, anybody below 18 years is a child and therefore drug dealings involving children are against the rights of the child. Subsequent studies by Rogers Kasirye in 1995, 1998 and 2000 among the street children in Kampala city found out that 8 out of 10 children interviewed were using one or more substances of abuse; paintthinner, commonly referred to as 'tina', heroin and cannabis use taking foremost position.

Today, drugs like alcohol, cannabis, aviation fuel and opium are also widely used among street children because they are cheap and easy to get. Drug use is a mode of survival for children living on the street because it helps them face the dangers and challenges of being on the street comfortably. Drug and substance abuse is also becoming a common phenomenon among school going children. UYDEL, in a study done on drug and substance abuse in schools of Kampala and Wakiso found that 71% of the students were using drugs with alcohol and cannabis taking the biggest percentages. Nakamyuka another study among senior secondary students indicated that 68% of the students using alcohol were between 14-17 years. This may be due to the fact that it is cheap and to make matters worse Uganda has no clear policy on alcohol thus making its consumption a widely accepted social activity in society.

The commercial sale of traditionally produced spirits is regulated by the Liquor-Licensing Act of 1964. Such a law is out dated, inadequate and worse still not enforced. There is no law to regulate alcohol producers advertising in the media. It is estimated that alcohol causes suffering to at least 70% of the population either directly or indirectly. Again, 50% of the hazardous acts such as sexual activity are blamed on alcohol consumption. 5-10% of the population who regularly use alcohol experience alcohol related problems like ill health, mental disturbance and loss of employment.

Most drug users in the slums especially the young people say they use drugs to feel good, escape personal identity or to rebel against authority. However, recreational drug users are more likely to report being motivated to use drugs to relieve personal distress or cope with emotions like anger and loneliness. Efforts in preventing and reducing drug abuse are to an extent hampered by lack of precise knowledge of drug abuse patterns and trends and more broadly by the lack of information on the effectiveness of prevention and treatment activities undertaken in Uganda.

Child prostitution is the most dominant form of Commercial Sexual Exploitation of Children. Country studies conducted by ECPAT in East Africa point out with regard to Uganda's case that girls are often hired in pubs as cleaners or domestic workers but later encouraged or promoted to become prostitutes. Several documents show that prostitution is prevalent in all major regions of the world. ILO estimates that over 1.8 million children around the world are involved in prostitution.

As in many countries around the world (India, Jamaica and Russia), it is noted that the demand for children in the sex industry is growing not only for tourists but also inhabitants and that more and more children are being forced into the trade. Child prostitution is considered by the International

Labour Organisation to be the worst form of child Labour (Legislation Convention 182). Article 34 of The Convention on Rights of Children, ratified by the Government of Uganda in 1990, further protects children from sexual abuse and exploitation including prostitution.

The majority of the victims are girls who are the victims of HIV/AIDS, poverty and wars. There are two categories of child prostitution; one is survival sex aimed at securing basic needs and the other is commercial sex for financial gain. The major targets of commercial sex are in slums, street and hostels where sex is offered in exchange for money or handouts. Survival sex is identified with seasonality and irregularity.

Seasonality relates to periods when a child can engage in prostitution to lack of basic needs like shelter, school fees, culture events such as funeral rights and circumcision, food, transport, peer pressure; characterized with high entry and exist in this business therefore, an irregularity in practice. They view sex trade as a profitable business. Under this category, there are no seasonal child sex workers but rather those who are permanent in practice.

Many children in this group live independently. They rent small rooms as individuals or in groups. Many left school early and the majority are young and have not had children. These are preferred because they are considered inexperienced and vulnerable to exploitation especially men and women. Interestingly, there are adult pimps who go in the villages and recruit children in disguise by promising them employment, later to be lured into prostitution.

There are known places in the slums where these children congregate in small rooms sleeping in small groups. The most conspicuous form of identity among Commercial Sex Workers is that of group identity. This implies that children identify themselves with "solidarity groups" referred to as "ebiduula" within their areas of work. They have principles to which every member must conform. Some of the principles relate to amount of money charged for services based on "short" duration and overnight and more.

According to the recent study on Commercial Sexual Exploitation of Children in Uganda (Ministry of Labour Gender and Social Development, 2004) sexual encounters can take place in the workplace, homes of colleagues, rented rooms or lodges. Other contact points are roadsides or streets, wells or springs. This population is very nomadic and characterized with high entry and exists in their sexual business. There are grave consequences of child prostitution including contracting HIV/AIDS and other STDs, early pregnancy and criminal abortions.

These some sometimes lead to death and early school dropout, yet there is no explicit government policy on child prostitution in Uganda save the government being a signatory to the CRC in 1991 and ILO Conventions 132 and 189 in the year 2002. Children involved in prostitution have sought ways of dealing with problems they experience in work. In cases of pregnancy the option considered mainly is illegal abortion; marriage is the least considered. Indeed UYDEL's clinic receives many cases of post abortion care: by August 2004, 40 cases had been received.

Some opt to temporarily leave the practice until they give birth and later come back. Positive responses appear to be lacking among them due to inadequate knowledge and access to services. Children involved in sex work are stigmatized in the slum communities where they live; thus the whole business is done in secrecy. Many are considered wild cat - 'Malaya'. Some despise it because of religious considerations conceiving it to be adulterous and to contravene the law of God as well as the state.

The negative attitude towards children involved in Commercial Sex is translated into harassment by supposedly secure groups such as the police and Local Defense Units. Prostitution is one of the worst forms of sexual exploitation of children and is highly linked to and fuelled by the use of drugs. Street and slum children use inhalants such as sniff fuel, glue, paint thinner and others use cannabis and heroin to be able to take on several customers and absorb the pain that go with it. Others use alcohol, cannabis, smoke "bhangi" or chew "khat" to gain courage and confidence.

The use of drugs has been compounded by the spread of HIV. There are beliefs among some groups that the use of drugs such as cannabis provides a self-cure and lowers the risks of spread of HIV in the body. Experience and work with slum youth has also shown that significant proportions of young people abusing drugs are at a high risk of engaging in commercial sex involving multiple partners. Young adults who use alcohol are 7 times more likely than non-drinkers to have sex. This is due to the fact that there is always need for drugs that require large sums of money to meet the constant demand.

The buying, selling and use of drugs is one of the major factors behind the growing demand for services of sex workers because one facilitates the other. The use of drugs appears to increase the sex appetite of the users. Hence the more drug users increase in number, so likely will be the demand for sex services increases.

Uganda AIDS Commission noted that "as we fight HIV/AIDS, it is important we also fight those factors that increase risk of acquiring the disease. Drug abuse and prostitution are very big factors in this. People who are drunk easily catch HIV/AIDS because of irresponsible behavior like having unprotected sex. Modes of administration of drugs in the body like intravenous drugs such as injecting heroine and cocaine exposes the drug abusers to the risk of HIV infection. Drugs lead to domestic violence which leads to street children who can be sexually exploited and hence catch HIV/AIDS".

Working with drug abusers and child prostitutes requires advocacy in areas of treatment and rehabilitation. Many don't have money to help themselves get access to treatment. It also requires bringing the governments' attention to the urgent need to review the laws of drug supply and demand and to put into action the international conventions on drug abuse and other treaties.

In Uganda, government is yet to appreciate and recognise the problem and threats that production, sale and consumption of alcohol, tobacco and drugs pose to its citizens. UYDEL, based on their field experience, adopted a drug abuse Peer-to Peer prevention approach to reach out to fellow slum/ street youths in Kampala slums. These peers play an educative role about drug abuse and encourage safer sex among their peers. It has however been duly observed that the Peer to Peer prevention approach alone may be inadequate in enhancing effective behavioral change and flow of information among the youth. This approach should occasionally be reinforced by public film and drama shows.

Florence (19 years) lives in Kasubi, one of the suburbs in Kampala District, Uganda. She went to school but stopped in senior four when her sister who was supporting her died of AIDS. She had no one to turn to for assistance to continue with her education since her mother had died and the father is unemployed and not living with her. It is during this time that she met the father of her child who was a street boy with no job. The child is now staying with the grandparents (paternal) as she is trying to look for work.

In Kasubi, where she is currently staying, is a suburb characterized by many street and slum youth who engage in anti-social activities like drug and substance abuse, commercial sex and theft among others which put them at risk of contracting HIV/AIDS. Florence says that many of the young girls in this area are involved in commercial sex (prostitution) and that in order to accommodate and attract clients they smoke pipes (okufuwa emiddi). The contents of these pipes are tobacco and Marijuana (Njaga), which are highly addictive drugs. She says that "Some smoke these pipes every minute and others can smoke them 10 -15 times in a day."

Florence is a Peer drug educator. After the training she tried to talk to some of her peers in Kasubi where she lives who are using these pipes about the dangers of the contents in the pipe. But she says it is not easy to convince them to stop or change the habit since change is a gradual process and a lot of patience is needed if one is to change completely. owever she has managed to convince six peers to alter their habits. Currently 3 have completely stopped using the pipes and the other three are still using it but less frequent than they used to (they used to blow it 8 - 10 time a day and now they have taken to blowing only 2- 3 times a day).

To effectively address the problem of child prostitution requires first classifying the children involved as a vulnerable group that needs special protection against risks and vulnerabilities that drive them to and sustain them in the practice. As seen earlier, most of the risk factors that force or attract children into prostitution are rooted in poverty. Interventions therefore undertaken at any level need to priotitise reduction or elimination of poverty.

In addition, the elimination of child prostitution cannot be the responsibility of only one actor in the name of government or Third Sector Participants (NGO community), but rather the responsibility of a number of actors. This therefore points to the need for public-private partnerships in addressing the problem. Further still, it could be appropriate to employ a pluralist approach that underlines the need to devise complementary measures in extending social protection to embrace areas or categories of people that are not covered by schemes in place. It is important to underline the complementary role of informal safety nets based on family and community systems in promoting protection of children against sexual and other different forms of exploitation. It is necessary to work closely with these arrangements.

An effective safety net needs to be developed as a response to the problem of child prostitution and drug abuse among slum and street children. Discontinuity of both practices requires at point of entry an Information, Education and Communication (IEC) Programme accompanied with provision of psychosocial counseling services. UYDEL with support from Pathfinder, International Labour Organisation and World Food Programme runs a shelter programme to integrate the street and slum youths in their communities. So far 560 youths above 16 years who graduated from the streets and slums have already benefited from a vocational skills training programme with local artisans and have been assisted to get employment at building sites, in saloons, workshops and tailoring.

Working with children involved in drugs and prostitution therefore requires provision of viable alternatives. This may include vocational skills, skills training and sports. Sensitization alone is not an adequate method of preventing use of drugs and prostitution because basing on experience and practice with these children, they are drawn into drugs and prostitution because they have nothing to do.

In short, protecting children from drug abuse and prostitution is not a responsibility of Government alone. It is everybody's responsibility to embrace prevention, withdrawal, rehabilitation, advocacy, awareness and observation and respect the rights of children if a lasting solution is to be arrived at lest we continue hearing cases of abuse and violation of rights of the child.

Commercial Sexual Exploitation

"Commercial" refers to the exchange of money; "sexual" to the sexual acts that are purchased or viewed; "exploitation" to the fact that a person is used unjustly for the advantage of another. There are three primary aspects of commercial sexual exploitation of children: stripping, pornography, and prostitution. There are different types of exploitation, the many facets of each type, and the various effects on individuals, families, and communities.

Strip clubs regularly promote dancers through their association with the porn industry; porn stars often earn more money by stripping than by performing in hard-core videos. Strip clubs are doubly articulated to the porn industry- both through the overlap in performers and the conventions of their routines and through zoning regulations that set them apart as a clearly male form of entertainment.

Child Pornography

The legal definition of the term 'child pornography' varies from state to state and under Federal law. Under most definitions, child pornography involves a visual depiction of a child that is sexually explicit. Child pornography can be behaviorally defined as the sexually explicit reproduction of a child's image. In essence, it is the permanent record of the sexual abuse or exploitation of an actual child.

Child pornography can be divided into two subcategories that focus on actual use. First, commercial child pornography is that which is produced and intended for commercial sale. The second is homemade child pornography. Homemade simply means it was not originally produced primarily for commercial sale. Generally homemade pornography is used solely by the individual that exploits the child. The question of what constitutes child pornography is extremely complex because the standards applied are highly subjective and contingent upon a host of cultural, sexual, moral and religious beliefs that do not readily translate into law.

Significant effects of pornography are feelings of aggression and abuse. Exposure to particular kinds of erotic imagery can result in an increase in aggressive sexual fantasies, aggressive behavior, acceptance of anti-female attitudes, and specifically, in male aggression against females. Case histories of victims and perpetrators of pornography demonstrate that pornography serves as a catalyst for sexual and other physical abuse of human beings. Some researchers believe that if the perpetrators had not been exposed to or involved in creating pornography, many of the victims would not have been killed, raped, or otherwise abducted. Oftentimes the violence portrayed in pornography becomes real as the offender 'plays out' the pornography on the people, and most often prostitutes, that they encounter.

The feelings of aggression identified above do not solely affect adults, but also children. There are many cases where children, imitating pornographic scenarios, sexually or otherwise physically abuse other children. A woman who testified at the Minneapolis anti-pornography hearings in 1983 said that her daughter was gang raped by four tenth grade boys who used pornographic magazines to threaten and terrify her. In addition, pornography seriously affects the children involved in its production. Pornography is psychologically damaging to the child, it ruin's a child's self image, it is exploitative, it makes children vulnerable to adults in unnatural ways, it spreads incorrect information about sex, it forever invades a child's privacy, and it complicates a child's moral development.

Pornography poses an even greater threat to the child victim than does sexual abuse or prostitution. Because the child's actions are reduced to a recording, the pornography may haunt him in future years, long after the original misdeed took place. A child who has posed for the camera must go through life knowing that the recording is circulating within the mass distribution system for child pornography. In addition, pornography can be used for blackmail, profit, instructional aids to indoctrinate other victims, self gratification, conditioning to lower a victim's inhibitions, advertising, collections, sexual record, access to other offenders and markets.

Because production, distribution and sale of child pornography are secretive businesses, the determination of the extent of the problem is extremely difficult. There are neither national reporting systems nor statewide data-processing procedures to establish accurate statistics on child pornography. Even in areas where there are reporting systems in place, children are unlikely to come forward. This is because children are afraid to tell anyone about the incident out of fear of punishment or blame.

Also, there is a lack of standardization in data gathering, since definitions of sexual offenses vary by state and community. There are no national statistics on sexual-assault victims by age or sex. As a result, postal inspectors confirm that it is almost impossible to determine the extent of child pornography that flows through the mails.

Pornography businesses cite estimates from $4 billion to $7 billion a year in US sales. Both production and sales of pornography are at an all time high, and the industry is moving into newer technologies such as the Internet. The number of erotic books published between 1991 and 1996 increased by 324% while the overall number of books published increased by only 83%. New estimates of adult videos show that the number of hard-core video rentals rose from 75 million in 1985 to 490 million in 1992, then to 665 million in 1996.

Child pornography represents a part of the booming sex industry. Child pornography remains a major problem in the United States. By one estimate, the sex industry in the United States grossed $5 billion in 1980. Others estimate that $8 to $10 million dollars a day is spent on pornography. The best estimate of the approximate number of US consumers who 'read' at least one porn magazine in 1996 totaled just over 5.5 million. An estimated 43% of American males were exposed to at least one of the seven porn magazines in 1995. This is likely to be an underestimate since there are actually hundreds more than the seven porn magazines that were the focus of this analysis.

The volume of material produced by child pornographers and pedophiles on a routine basis within the United States is enormous. The evidence confiscated from sex rings and convicted pedophiles indicate that many offenders produce child pornography for their own consumption in sufficient quantities to warrant elaborate classification and index schemes. One reason that the presence of pornography is so extensive is that pornography is much in demand and expensive, yet can be produced in the United States at a minimal cost and risk to the photographer. In addition, no federal enforcement agency has sought to comprehensively monitor or identify the volume and distribution of child pornography manufacturers within the United States.

The amount of income generated from the sale of child pornography is a matter of widespread speculation because of the absence of reliable data. Studies shows that $1 billion is generated by child pornography. The profitability of child pornography has never been in doubt because of the high ratio of income to expense. The photographer who has a large clientele or a steady buyer at the wholesale level is assured of enough profit to offset the risk of detection, arrest, and confiscation of his goods. In addition, the rapid growth of communications technology is making it easier and safer for pornographers to operate outside the limits of the law.

Children are being exploited by pornographers throughout the United States. Authorities on the sexual exploitation of children estimate that 7% of the pornography market in the US involves activity between children and other children and adults. Statistics based on information from three states, estimate that between 40,000 and 120,000 children were involved each year in pornography and/or prostitution. Estimates of the number of children involved across America range from the thousands to the hundreds of thousands. One thing is clear, a significant number of children are being sexually exploited through the medium of child pornography.

Pedophile

A pedophile is a person who derives gratification from engaging in sexual activities with minors. Child pornographers may be teachers, lawyers, doctors, law enforcement officers, members of the clergy, laborers: In sum, child pornographers are from all walks of life. Although it is usually assumed that most pedophiles or child molesters are males, we have observed an increase in the number of recorded incidents involving female pedophiles. Beyond the collecting of child pornography, traits of pedophiles are difficult to isolate.

The single most distinctive characteristic of a habitual child molester is a compelling interest in collecting adult and child pornography. Law enforcement investigations have verified that pedophiles almost always collect child pornography or child erotica. Child pornography and child erotica are used by pedophiles in the following ways:

— Sexual arousal and gratification.

— Lower children's inhibitions for further sexual abuse.

— Blackmail the child to keep the secret of sexual abuse.

— Medium of exchange with other pedophiles.

Pedophiles believe that if they do not do physical damage, they have not harmed the child. Pedophiles believe that society is wrong for condemning them for expressing their true sexuality. If there is no evidence to prove molestation, pedophiles will deny ever having sex with a child. The pedophile will often state that the child enlisted the sexual services of the adult. Pedophiles maintain an inventory of all the child pornography they own. Most pedophiles want to recount their thoughts and experiences to someone else. Some male pedophiles are impotent with adults.

The standard strategies of a pedophile are alternating affection and abuse to leave the child confused, and telling the child that the sex is special but must be kept a secret from others. There are several organizations in this country and around the world that openly voice support adult sex with children. Organizations and publications that advocate adult-child sex are scattered throughout the world. They perform an assortment of functions and exist for the following purposes:

— To recruit and expedite the exchange of information and correspondence among pedophiles.

— To act as a medium for advertisers and distributors of soft-core child pornography.

— To promote political activism and organization.

— To alert members and subscribers to recent court decisions and active criminal investigations.

— To provide a bulletin board news services as to the whereabouts of sexually available minors.

— To raise funds for legal representation of accused pedophiles.

— To offer sexual stimulation in the form of erotic fiction or suggestive photographs of minors.

The information superhighway has given a technological boost to pedophiles. As yet on-line services are only self-regulated and acquisition of ideas and materials are easily sent across public bulletin boards. Pedophiles can easily contact each other and can contact children without postal service restrictions applying and without leaving the privacy of their own homes. An example of the ease in which the sexual exploitation of children occurs over the Internet is the Orchid Club. The Orchid Club was once a lurid corner on the information superhighway, an Internet conference room or 'chat' room were members thousands of miles apart could meet in cyberspace and trade homemade child pornography, both in words and pictures.

As home access to the Internet grows rapidly, so too does the threat that this on-line medium will expand opportunities for sexual exploitation of children. About 10 million people use on-line services and tens of millions more use the Internet worldwide.. There is only a click of a mouse between a normal kid's chat room and a pedophile chat room. Given the anonymity that is possible on the Internet, an increasing number of pedophiles are feigning youth in their electronic personae as they troll through various forums looking for children to abuse. Pretending to be a child, the pedophile may converse with a real child in an open chat forum. This is only a short step away from a 'private' one on one chat room.

The computer offers multiple opportunities for identity bending, as users are free to adopt the gender, age, sexuality, race, physical appearance, and other characteristics they so choose. And on the Internet, the line between producers and consumers of pornography breaks down as users download pornographic images and texts from adult bulletin boards and post them to newsgroups, themselves becoming disseminators if not exactly the 'original' producers of pornographic images.

Child pornographers have little difficulty recruiting willing participants. The pool of susceptible child victims includes runaways, throwaways, teen prostitutes, children from broken homes, homeless youth, drug addicted children, and relatives or neighborhood youths looking for quick money, excitement, or adventure. Most children in prepubescent child pornography were not abducted into sexual slavery. Rather they were seduced into posing for these pictures or videos by a pedophile they probably knew.

Children in general have certain characteristics that make them ideal victims from the offender's point of view. Some of these characteristics include: natural curiosity, they are easily led by adults, they need attention and affection, they also need to defy parents at some level, and finally, children are often not believed when they report instances of sexual abuse. The following characteristics as typical of a sexually exploited boy: between the ages of 8 and 17, an underachiever at school or home, usually without previous homosexual experience, comes from a home where the parents are absent in some manner, has no strong moral or religious obligations, usually has no record of previous delinquency, and suffers from poor sociological development.

Pornographic activity is a commonplace aspect of life for those involved in prostitution. Based on the number of studies examining the connection between prostitution and pornography, it seems impossible to deny the existence of a significant link between the exploitation of minors in prostitution and in pornography.

A recent study refers to the interrelationship between pornography and juvenile prostitution, but there is no empirical research demonstrating such a relationship. Weisberg found that there appears to be no involvement between pornography and prostitution for males. However, some studies have shown a direct link between female prostitutes and pornography. Female prostitution and the sex exploitation industry have also been shown to correlate with other criminal activity, such as organized crime and drug dealing, as well as with sexually transmitted diseases, promiscuity and child sexual abuse.

Juvenile Prostitution

Juvenile prostitution is one of the pivotal crimes of sexual trafficking. From it other forms of exploitation develop, such as involvement in pornography, apprenticeships, and recruitment.

Juvenile Male Prostitutes

It is unknown just how many male prostitutes there are in the United States. However, it is believed that approximately 35-40% of juvenile prostitutes are male. Some researchers believe the number to be at least equal to the number of female prostitutes. Some studies estimates that there are approximately 100,000 to 200,000 full-time juvenile hustlers of both sexes.

Historically boys have been involved in organized prostitution to a greater degree than girls. Callboy networks exists throughout the country. In addition, boy prostitution is often more hidden than female prostitution, frequently taking place in city parks, street corners in certain neighborhoods, bars, bathhouses, and motels. Research differs as to whether boys who prostitute themselves are gay or bisexual. Some believe that one of the most distinctive attitudes of juvenile prostitutes is that many do not consider sex with an adult male a homosexual activity. However, more recent research has found that most adolescent male prostitutes identify themselves as gay.

Popular juvenile male hustlers have several traits in common: youthful appearance, including smooth feminine features and a lack of muscle tone, exceptional sexual sophistication or skills, easy rapport with customers, and a façade of naiveté tempered with street sense. The world of adolescent male prostitutes is distinctive for their freelance status, passive roles in sex, lower earnings, bisexual behavior, and methods of customer-hustler communication. Boys tend to age out of prostitution earlier than girls, in their mid-teens and early twenties.

Another feature is also important; violence is endemic to this lifestyle. The opportunities for bodily harm, either to them or their customers, are rampant. An indicator of this is that runaway boys have been victimized and murdered in large-scale serial murder cases more often than girls. The mortality rate for young men is high due to drug overdose, AIDS, and violence. Juvenile male prostitutes come from many racial groups, but researchers overwhelmingly concur that the majority are Caucasian. Adolescent prostitutes first become involved in prostitution at an early age. Most researchers agree that the vast majority of juvenile prostitutes are under age 16 when they first engage in prostitution and the average age for the first prostitution act is 14.

There are several categories of male prostitutes:

1. Situational prostitutes- young men who engage in prostitution only under certain circumstances or occasions.

2. Habitual prostitutes - young men involved in inner-city street life for which prostitution is an intregal aspect of a street lifestyle.

3. Vocational prostitutes - young men who view prostitution as a career and regard themselves a s professionals.

4. Avocational prostitutes - vocational prostitutes who regard their work as part time employment.

There are several explanations for how juvenile males become involved in prostitution. The foremost influence is peer pressure, the subtle actions of friends can prod a novice to experiment with prostitution. A second explanation is prior sexual abuse, either within the family or by a stranger. A third indicator involves prior homosexual experience or preference that encourages an adolescent male to experiment with prostitution. One final explanation involves environmental factors such as lack of adequate parental supervision, illiteracy, the absence of a structured set of values, and the depreciation through abuse of the value of the human body.

Most studies concur that fathers of male prostitutes, more often than mothers, are either absent or ineffective. While girls also mention glamour and excitement as their reason for entering prostitution, boys involved in hustling nearly always cite their reasons as financial. .

The average age of entering prostitution varies depending on the study. Some studies found that girl prostitutes are as young as 5 or 6 when they begin to prostitute. However, most find that the vast majority of female teens selling their bodies falls between the ages of 15 and 17. Another study found that the age of initiation ranges from nine to twelve. In a separate study the children used as prostitutes in some area ranged from 4 to 12 or 13 years. In a study examining 620 homeless youth it was reported that 76% of the involved youth had sexual intercourse before age 15 years, and 26% had sex before their 10th birthday.

A girl who begins prostitution at fourteen will have submitted to the sexual demands of four thousand men before she is old enough to drive a car, eight thousand men before she is old enough to vote, and twelve thousand men before she is deemed mature enough to buy a single beer in most states.

The demand for underage females, may, in fact, rival that for adult prostitutes. Profit expectations are linked to several factors: the hustler's age and appearance (the younger, the more expensive), the type of sexual act, the location, the opportunity for blackmail, and the customer's willingness to pay exorbitant fees.

One of the precursors to entering prostitution was prior sexual mistreatment at the hands of their father, stepfather, uncle, or mother's boyfriend. Most studies have found the home life of the juvenile who becomes involved in prostitution characterized by violence, lack of parental love and affection, and alcohol abuse. Parental abuse or neglect is widely considered a typical childhood experience of girls who become prostitutes.

Another common factor for many females that become involved in prostitution is a high drop out rate. This may be caused by change, which seems to be an important factor is increasing psychological disorientation and disruptions at home or school and which may lead to prostitution. A related indicator is that many adolescents that enter prostitution have minimal financial employment possibilities.

A general list of factors that lead to an underage female engaging in prostitution include: recruitment, peer pressure, conditioning, a destructive self-image, a need to survive, and a subcultural drift away from the mainstream. Others include: money, social excitement, imitation, anger toward men, lack of parental attention, early sexual experience, drug addiction, and being a runaway.

A recent study divides motivators for prostitution into three needs. 1) Economic needs of obtaining money for basic items such as food, housing, and shelter. 2) Status needs: the desire to acquire esteem and prestige and to accumulate those material items (cars, clothes, jewelry) that confer social status upon an individual. 3) Psychological need: the adolescent's desire for adventure, to meet new people, and/or to escape a problematic family or other living situation.

A primary method of procuring a juvenile for prostitution is through the use of feigned friendship and love. The initial phase of procurement is essentially an information-gathering mission in which the pimp attempts to identify the youth's vulnerabilities. The pimp then uses the information that the victim naively provides him to tailor his recruitment strategy to meet what he perceives her needs to be. He will then offer to meets any unmet needs. He will then fawn over her. Pimps then use a combination of flattery and charm, the promises of money, protection, companionship, and intimacy to con a young woman into prostitution.

Another description of this process focuses on the mental process of the child. The deviant drift begins with the first phase, where a child adapts to a negative self-image. The negative self-image is followed by acculturation. The third stage is assimilation of the lifestyle and the acceptance of the identity of a prostitute.

The Enabler's study showed that the process of prostitution was subtle: first a weakening of ties with outside individuals, a need to develop ways to survive, and an unrealistic view of prostitution all led to their involvement in this life.

Female juvenile prostitutes come from all socioeconomic levels, nearly all experienced disruption of family relationships, frequently at an early age. Many grew up in families in which one parent was absent, all had left home at least once by the time that they were 14 years old, and nearly half had lived in out of home placements prior to becoming involved in prostitution.

The average age at which they started prostitution was 14. Most, at the time of engaging in prostitution, were not school nor attending regularly. Nearly all stated that they were using drugs at the time they started prostituting. In addition, they were not working.. At the time they turned out most had low self-esteem and a poor self-image. Other common factors are physical, sexual and psychological abuse in the families of origin.. Violence of all forms appears to be an expected aspect of prostitution. In order to survive the violent life of prostitution, juveniles develop an illusion of control over aspects of the prostitution process.

Both range in age from 12 to 18. Both come from all socioeconomic backgrounds, but recent studies note the presence of a substantial number of youth from middle class backgrounds. Studies of both male and female juvenile prostitution reveal that an overwhelming number come from homes broken by separation or divorce. Both physical and sexual abuse characterize the childhood histories of both. Both begin prostitution at an early age. One difference between male and female juvenile prostitutes is that male prostitutes are rarely introduced to prostitution by pimps and rarely work for pimps.

Much of the physical abuse of female prostitution come from the pimp, thus eliminating a major source of violence for the males. However assaultive behavior from the customers comes to both males and females. The use of drugs and alcohol appears to characterize young prostitute's lives.

There are no consistent patterns or profiles that explain why minors are drawn into prostitution. However, the most frequent of all experiences is the dysfunctional family. Absent in these homes are nurturing relationships, positive child rearing practices, and concern for the well being or happiness of the children; physical and sexual mistreatment is often prevalent. Incest or other intra-familial sexual abuse is common in the dysfunctional family. Evidence indicates that families of juvenile prostitutes are more sexually deviant and more sexually abusive than those found in general populations.

Adolescent homosexuality may put a male at a higher risk of running away and getting involved in juvenile prostitution. The majority of girls who become child prostitutes appear to have suffered childhood traumas associated with early sexual experiences. This demonstrates that the violation of fragile child sexuality, if it is combined with other family tensions or emotional deficiencies - whether in the child or in the family - makes the probability of catastrophe in puberty extremely high.

In US, from 1970 to 1983 the number of reported arrests of underage prostitutes climbed by over 150%, although the number of juveniles aged 14 to 17 actually declined by nearly 10%.

Teenage Prostitution

Teenage prostitution is an elusive and complex phenomenon. Teenage prostitutes remain an unknown population for a variety of reasons. They have limited involvement in family or school settings and they are not likely to admit their sexual activities. In attempting to describe juvenile prostitution in contemporary society, it is critical to accept at the beginning how hopelessly incomplete the evidence is or can ever be. The nature of prostitution, its existence outside the law, outside legitimate business, and outside mainstream society, makes it wholly unsuitable for 'scientific' study. The number of children involved in prostitution is hopelessly elusive. In fact, no reliable estimate exists or is even possible, given the absence of census data on the subject, the inherent limitations of police information, and the weaknesses of unsupported estimates by social service providers and popular journalists who reach only a tiny fraction of juvenile prostitutes in highly specific settings.

Studies on child prostitution are too few and difficult to compare. Few researchers have specifically dealt with the area of prostitution among adolescent girls. Since the only visible part of adolescent prostitution is on the street, it is difficult to determine the total number of adolescents involved. Foremost is the use of false identification papers for the 'older-looking' kiddie pro that can easily pass a casual street examination by police officers. A second reason is the arrest priorities of police organizations, which do not focus on the easily released prostitutes. Third is the realization that neither the juvenile hustler nor customer is likely to file a complaint in the event either person is victimized. The 'see no evil, hear no evil syndrome' represents a fourth reason. A fifth reason that underage hustlers escape detection is the absence of effective curfew, truancy, and loitering laws or ordinances.

When faced with complaints about prostitution, exploiters merely shift the trade to new locations. The cumulative effect of all of these circumstances is that many juvenile prostitutes, even those in plain view, become 'invisible.'. Unless a concerted effort is made to identify and intercept minors engaged in prostitution, they are often overlooked.

Worldwide the number of juvenile prostitutes is estimated to be in the tens of millions, perhaps as high as 100 million. UNICEF put out a background paper estimating the number of street children who are partially or fully abandoned worldwide to be about 80 million. In Brazil the numbers range between 700,000 and a million Brazilian child prostitutes between the ages of 9 and 17 years. In the Philippines it is estimated that 20,000 children are involved in prostitution. It is estimated by Thai sources that there are over a million prostitutes in Thailand.

Other studies support findings of juvenile prostitutes totaling 400,000 in India, and 80,000 in the Philippines. In Tokyo, Japan 8% of the schoolgirls are estimated to be prostitutes. The chamber of commerce recently reported that the number of child prostitutes under age 14 in Bogota, Columbia has quintupled in seven years. In Moscow, over

1,000 youths are estimated to be in the sex-for-sale business. In most cases the actual number of child prostitutes tends to far exceed the estimates. UNICEF estimated that in Asia alone there are over one million minors enslaved as prostitutes.

Prevalence of Juvenile Prostitution

In US, every city and county across the country, juveniles can be found selling their bodies for money, drugs, or a place to stay. It is estimated that there are anywhere from 300,000 to 2.4 million juveniles in the United States on the streets selling themselves. Other, nonofficial but more accurate, sources estimate that as many as half a million children under the age of 16 are involved in prostitution, with that number doubling or tripling when including 16 and 17 year old prostitutes. Among street prostitutes in the United States, half or more are under age 21. Indeed some 40 percent may even be younger than 18 years old.

Not only does prostitution exist across the United States, but its presence is increasing. A recent survey of child prostitution in all 50 states concluded that it had increased in 37% of the cities. FBI statistics further support: there has been a 183% increase in the number of females arrested for juvenile prostitution, and a 245% increase for males. Two trends of adolescent prostitution are evident: the number of adolescents involved in prostitution has increased in recent years and the entry age into prostitution has decreased.

Money is a central aspect to the commercial sexual exploitation of children. By one estimate, $40 million a day, $14 billion a year, is spent on prostitution in the United States. The initial premise used by pimps and customers to entice juveniles into this lifestyle is that prostitution brings wealth. The average income of adolescent prostitutes is difficult to determine. Subject to the weather and a client's generosity, a day's earnings can range from $50.00 to several hundred dollars. Most earn less than $300.00 per week. That rate translates into several thousand dollars a month and tens of thousands of untaxed dollars earned annually by a single juvenile hustler. However, if there is a fortune to be made working on the streets, it has eluded these particular juveniles; nowhere will you find a wealthy male or female prostitute.

Instead of prosperity, anyone involved in prostitution can expect to contract some type of venereal disease, from gonorrhea to AIDS, in addition to range of psychosomatic illnesses derived from the stressful nature of their activities.

Sexual Trafficking

The broadest definition of sexual trafficking is the sexual exploitation of a person under the age of eighteen for pleasure or financial gain. This can include a multitude of crimes: child pornography, prostitution, sex rings, molestation sex tourism industry, white slavery, bogus adoption schemes, nude dancing or modeling, apprenticeship or recruitment for prostitution, procuring, and indenturing. Campagna uses a broad definition because each offense represents a specific market that shares several characteristics with the other markets, including an underage victim, one or more adult offenders, and a mixture of sexual pleasure and financial motivation. When the commercial element is present, the victim is compelled to exchange the use of his or her body for money, food, shelter alcohol, or drugs.

A narrower view of sexual trafficking is simply the moving of individuals in large numbers across national borders, sometimes known as the "white slave trade." There are two types of traffic, one in which the participant is aware of the circumstances and one in which they are not. The first involves hiring an individual to engage in prostitution in any country, state or territory other than that in which they live. The second form is known as 'disguised traffic' and involves hiring women or girls to work away from their homes in an industry in which they will likely come into contact with pimps and prostitutes.

Victims are coerced into prostitution by being forced to repay debts to the employment agency that paid for their ticket to another country and found them employment. It should be noted that it is not only women that are trafficked, many males and children are also victims of sexual trafficking. One kind of traffic specializes in young children. There is little empirical evidence for making a specific link between sex tourism and child prostitution, but it is evident that it exists.

One of the greatest obstacles to the study if sexual trafficking in minors is the popular misconception that a wealth of information about these offenses has already been accumulated. The unfortunate fact is that such a foundation of knowledge does not exist. Theories and stereotypes abound, but hard facts are woefully absent.. There remains an enormous volume of illegal behavior connected with sexual trafficking that is, at best, only partially reflected in official statistics. In short, more is known about the volume and nature of shoplifting in the United States than about any specific offense relating to the sexual exploitation of children.

Estimates of the number of victims of trafficking vary considerably due to the variations on the definition of trafficking. Thousands or even millions of individuals are supposed to be trafficked worldwide, depending on the source. Advocates say that more than 1 million children are affected by the child sex trade each year. This number is growing, according to human rights groups and child advocates.

Sexual trafficking occurs not only in Europe, but worldwide, not only from north to south, but from Latin America to southern Europe and the Middle East, from southeast Asia to the Middle East and central and northern Europe, from South America to North America and Europe, and from eastern Europe to western Europe. According to a United Nations official, trafficking in women is more profitable than arms or drug smuggling.

Constant Demand Supports

The various market entrepreneurs operate on the premise that demand, though it may be periodically restrained by law enforcement, will never disappear. Trafficking is supported by various human desires, including sexual gratification, the pursuit of profit, and a depraved sort of personal fulfillment.

Sex Tourism

Sex tourism is traveling to another country for the purpose of sexual exploitation. Package holidays are arranged for tourists through travel agents in the developed world.. Sexual experience is an explicit part of the package, indeed it may be the only object of the journey. The inclusion of sexual pleasure in the relationship between foreign travel and enjoyment is not a recent phenomenon. The assumption of the eighteenth century, as for many twentieth century travelers, was that unregulated sexuality is typical of non-Western societies.

During the Vietnam War, US servicemen generated a thriving sex trade that generated the third largest source of Thailand's foreign earnings. After the US withdrawal, the economy faltered, but Thailand rebounded with tourism. The past 40 years have seen a clear trend toward the commercialization of sex within the tourist industry. In recent years there have been many reports of sex tourism in the South East Asian countries of Thailand, South Korea and the Philippines. Tourists who take advantage of sex package holidays travel from all over Western Europe, the United States, Australia and Japan.

In the 1970s and 1980s the Spartacus Gay Guides, published in the Netherlands, provided male homosexual tourists with up-to-date advice about the availability of sexual contacts in most countries. Development expert Tim Bond estimated that there are about 2,000 boys between the ages of 7 and 17 that make their living prostituting themselves in the tourist areas of Sri Lanka. A factor in the rise of sex tourism is in part the erroneous belief that countries like Thailand were at low risk for HIV.

In US, there are clear differences in sexual preference which affect the extent to which minors are involved in sex tourism. Whatever the case, sex tourism tends to emphasize the ready availability of young sexual partners in tourist resorts. In 1973 a guide entitled Where the Young Ones Are gave male tourist information about the availability of child prostitutes in the US. However, once again we are faced with a lack of empirical evidence identifying the extent of sex tourism.

Tourism has emerged out of an exploitative system in which national images are manipulated by profit seeking companies for sale to pleasure seeking customers. Rather than an aberration, sexual tourism is a part of normal international relations – economic, political and ideological. Many if the host nations exploit this as a vital component of national growth. Tourism has become too important to national economies for governments to take ready action against prostitution.

For example, in Thailand tourism is the third largest component of the GNP, in the Philippines it is the fourth. The main stimulus for sex tourism comes from customer demand. Tourists to such places expect to enjoy a relaxation of the moral restrictions of their own culture, they expect 'complete erotic freedom.'

Sex Rings

In the context of exploitation of children, a sex ring can be defined as a situation in which one or more adults conspire and organize for the purpose of promoting illicit sexual acts with and among minors. These acts include the production of pornography, prostitution, adult molestation of children, the sale and transportation of minors for sexual purposes, the use of juveniles to recruit other youths into the ring, and the use of blackmail, deception, threats, peer pressure, or force to coerce or intimidate children into sexual activity.

A child sex ring need not, and usually does not, involve any moneymaking element. When something of monetary value if exchanged, it is usually given by the offender to the victim, as part of the seduction or 'grooming' process. A child sex ring can involve a daycare center, a school, a scout troop, a Little League team, and neighborhood or runaway children. It can also involve interfamilial molestation of children, including the use of marriage or a live-in relationship as a methods of access to children and the use of family children to attract other victims.

The following elements seem common to all rings: a high level of planning and cooperation among offenders, multiplicity of victims, longevity of the group, victimization of minors by other children, extensive range and sophistication of sexual activities, and the potential to spill over into the public domain of exploitation, as in the sale of child pornography..

There are three types of sex rings. In solo rings, the adult operates alone with a small group of children. In transition rings, the adult has begun to exchange or sell pornographic photographs of children and tries to pressure the child in the next ring level. In the syndicated ring there is a well-structured organization formed for recruiting children, producing pornography, delivering sexual services, and establishing an extensive network of customers.

The risk of catching AIDS or other sexually transmitted diseases is not a significant deterrent for these youth (or for clients). Adolescent prostitutes tend to view disease as a risk that is part of the job. Safe sex is practiced generally, although adolescents new to the street and others desperate for cash will forego the use of a condom if a client pays or offers a premium. However when forced to weigh the risks against the rewards, many felt, at least for a short time, that the risks were worth it. For the youth on the street who is living hour by hour, struggling to meet the daily needs of shelter, food, and clothing, information about a disease that may kill them in ten years is irrelevant.

According to an AIDS specialist a large runaway shelter, an estimated 40% of the runaway, homeless teens may carry the AIDS virus. In Los Angeles, information gathered by youth services indicates that 80% of street youth have been involved in prostitution, 40% have used injection drugs, and depending on their ages, between 15 and 25% are HIV infected. In San Francisco it is estimated that one in four street kids is HIV infected. And there is no reason to believe that the infection rate among street kids will not continue to escalate. About 20% of new cases of AIDS are among young adults in their 20s. Given the virus's' latency period, that means that most were infected in their teens.

There are multiple health problems that are a direct result of engaging in prostitution, and as a result, many adolescent street prostitutes are in relatively poor health. For some it is the result of a poor diet and stress while for others it is directly related to a sexually transmitted disease. Sexually transmitted disease constitutes the most notorious risk to youth prostitutes because almost 30% of those involved take no precautions against venereal disease. In addition, child prostitutes face other health risks including infections, sterility, permanent injuries from abuse, damage from drug abuse, and HIV/AIDS infection.

Also, trauma from beatings and rape, complications from persistent bladder infections and repeated exposure to venereal disease often results in chronic pelvic inflammatory disease (P.I.D.) and infertility. Other, more serious risks, include: robbery, arrest, violence, rape, murder, psychological injury. These risks are well known to the average prostitute and are identified as something that they dislike.

Although STDS and HIV have created a public health crises, there is also the psychological distress resulting from the violence that must also be considered. A study of prostitutes resulted in a diagnosis of posttraumatic stress disorder (PTSD) for many individuals. PTSD can result when people have experienced "extreme traumatic stressors involving direct personal experience of an event that involves actual or threatened death or serious injury; or other threat to one's personal integrity; or witnessing an event that involves death, injury, or a threat to the physical integrity of another person; or learning about unexpected or violent death, serious harm, or threat of death or injury experienced by a family member or other close associate.

Some women have fears about the physical aspects of sexual intimacy. Others report that after years of sexual abuse and training themselves to dissociate their minds from their bodies during the sex act, it becomes difficult to reintegrate. Others engage in sexual avoidance, and still other women remain celibate for a period to heal from the abuse. Long term effects include flashbacks and nightmares. Public hospitals report that 15% of all suicides are prostitutes.

In a study of 620 homeless youth, those involved in prostitution were diagnosed as having multiple health problems, with an average of 4.1 diagnoses per youth. A diagnosis of pelvic inflammatory disease was more than 14 times as likely for those involved in prostitution. A diagnosis of rape was nearly 3 times as likely to be given to a youth involved in prostitution.

More than 74% of those involve din prostitution were also diagnosed as abusing drugs or alcohol. Compared to other homeless youth, those involved in prostitution were twice as likely to have a serious mental health problems. Also, they were twice as likely to be actively suicidal or to have previously attempted suicide. The high level of multiple drug use, including intravenous drug use, and the greater likelihood of a gay or bisexual male involvement, combined with an large number of different sex partners, place the young people involved in prostitution at high risk for contracting and transmitting HIV.

Role of Media

The media plays a powerful role in the commercial sexual exploitation of children. The American culture rewards youthful appearance, seductive behavior, and sexual attractiveness. As a result, the images in media usually portray the joys and rewards of sex, rarely the problems and responsibilities. In doing this, the media acts as an advertising agency for prostitution. In light of the predominance of such images, it is not unreasonable to conclude that impressionable and naive adolescents would accept them at face value and wish to imitate the behaviors and lifestyles portrayed. It is clear that there is a general lack of awareness on the part of the public, the police, and many social service providers of the depth and complexity of the phenomenon of adolescent prostitution. Because of this lack of understanding, mainstream media sexualizes stereotypes of hypersexuality and unconditional sexual availability.

Juveniles that are runaways have an increased chance of becoming involved in prostitution. Between 11 and 66 percent of runaways become involved in prostitution; the rate is somewhat higher for females than males. An urgent need exists for a large-scale study of male and female runaways to determine how many become sexually exploited, in what ways, who is at the highest risk of exploitation, and what are the short and long-term effects on personality and social functioning.

It is estimated that anywhere from several hundred thousand to over 2 million children run away from or are thrown out of their homes each year in the United States. Many youths do not run far to get into prostitution, many end up in the same state. In studying the reasons for running away from home, rural children face more difficult circumstances than urban children in most areas. Children are running away due to physical abuse, violence due to alcoholism in the home, or other bad family situations.

The overwhelming majority of juvenile prostitutes admit to using drugs as part of their lifestyle, and an alarming number admit to heavy use or even addiction. Numerous studies find that male prostitutes are significantly involved in drug use. The most tangible consequences of involvement in juvenile prostitution is the extremely high probability of suffering violent assault. The vast majority of young female prostitutes will be beaten by their pimps and abused by their customers, often repeatedly. Young male hustlers are less vulnerable, but it still remains a substantial risk. The risk of violence for both sexes is part of the game.

Women are tied-up, gagged, whipped, and paddled, engaged in acts involving urination and defecation, are penetrated by objects and animals, gang raped, and forced to participate in humiliating circus-like sex shows for the voyeuristic pleasure of one or more men. Prostituted women have revealed a pattern of responses that is shockingly similar to those expressed by women who have been sexually abused or raped by their husbands. Most women reported feelings of degradation, defilement, and dirtiness, sometimes for years after leaving prostitution.

In a study of prostitution survivors the following crimes were documented: 78% were victims of rape, 84% were victims of aggravated assault, 49% were the victims of kidnapping, 53% were victims of sexual abuse through torture, 27% were mutilated as a result of the torture, and 10 women disappeared or were murdered over a 14 month period. Murder is a fact of life for all prostituted women. In a study of 136 prostitutes, 82% of the respondents reported having been physically assaulted since entering prostitution, 55% had been assaulted by customers, 88% had been physically threatened while in prostitution, 68% reported rape in prostitution, and 83% had been physically threatened with a weapon.

Pimps play a vital role in the sexual exploitation of children. There are two types of pimps. In the first version, the pimp is a villain who lives off the victim, beats them, and makes false promises to keep them. In the second version, the relationship between the pimp and the victim is seen more as a bargained for exchange, where he protects them from police and perverts. In reality, pimps typically treat their women as their personal possessions and beat them to a pulp of they think or behave otherwise.

A power relationship in which prostitutes are subject to domination, violence, and torture by their pimps, as well as theft of their earnings, would be a more apt description. The vast majority of juveniles used in prostitution are initially recruited by a pimp or subsequently fall under the control of a pimp. Some data may be misleading due to the fact that many individuals do not recognize their present partner as a pimp, in spite of clear evidence to the contrary. The number of adolescents working for a pimp ranges from 30% to 84%.

A common misperception is that all pimps are male. However, pimps are not the only or major factor affecting an adolescent's decision to enter prostitution. Many young people start working the streets on their own or with the help of a friend or street peers. Violence rules much of the relationship between a pimp and the individual involved in prostitution. Pimps usually impose quotas of earnings on their girls, give them little money, beat them if they fail to meet their quotas, and often have a 'stable' of girls who work for them. Pimps most frequently beat them for not making enough money, being disrespectful to the pimp, violating some rules, or leaving, or threatening to leave.

Anyone who promotes, perpetuates, or knowingly derives some form of benefit from the traffic in child sex can be considered an exploiter. These exploiters include pimps, pornographers, booking agents, hard-core molesters, sex ring participants or organizers, publisher and printers of child sex newsletters or magazines, and madams and brothel owners who employ juvenile prostitutes. Any adult willing to take sexual advantage of a child is an eligible candidate for the role of exploiter.

Sex Offenders

Physically, sex offenders come in all sizes, shapes, colors, and nationalities, and for the most part they fit the 'boy/girl next door' or 'good neighbor' profile. In terms of education, their profiles span the gamut: ranging from those who never completed grammar school to those with Ph.D's. In terms of employment, their profiles range from simple laborers to work supervisors, from professionals of every category individuals who known and successfully operate their own businesses. In terms of economic class, the range spans from indigent to very wealthy. As regards to social adjustment, they range from social misfits to social giants who are often perceived as the pillars of the community.

As regards religion, all denominations are represented, including clergy from most of the denominations. As to marital status, it appears to have no bearing on the problem. Both single and married females and males sexually abuse. Offenders who organized sex rings to exploit children sexually were most often middle class and middle aged. Their primary access routes to the children were occupation, living situation, and other children. While many offenders did not have previous offenses, a large number did have previous sexual offenses. Because victims of child pornography and sex rings usually have been carefully seduced and often do not realize that they are victims, they repeatedly and voluntarily return to the offender.

Once involved in prostitution it is almost impossible to leave it. Once an individual enter prostitution a process begins which leads to entrenchment in the life. Many career paths are closed or remain unexplored as a result of an adolescent's decision to work in prostitution. The status needs of the individual actually encourage them to continue in street soliciting. Also, the lifestyle of prostitution is fast-paces and psychologically addictive. Factors that increase the lengths of time spent in prostitution are : involvement with a pimp, the use of drugs, and the unavailability or unwillingness to find other types of work.

Skills that adolescents acquire while on the street are not attractive to employers in the straight job market. The stigma related to a prostitution related charge only makes it more difficult for an adolescent to find straight employment. Once adolescents get the street smarts necessary to work successfully in prostitution, they often become complacent. Young people working in prostitution acquire new habits, lifestyles, and value orientations that are in some ways different from the straight world around them.

Exiting from prostitution in early years is fraught with dangers from within the system and rejection and abandonment from without. Generally, adolescent prostitutes see their involvement in street soliciting as being temporary, though few are able to articulate a plan for leaving it. A consensus on why leaving prostitution is difficult: the life brings some luxury and status, losing family support limits career paths, drug usage increases for some adolescents, the addictive lifestyle makes it difficult to leave, prostitution is an option for adolescents with few skills, street lifestyle and new values entice and trap adolescents, pimps are not the major influence or always violent, peers are a strong influence, and acceptance by the street makes leaving difficult.

Child Sexual Abuse

A section on sexual abuse of children is vital to the discussion of commercial sexual exploitation for several reasons. Primarily, abuse of any form makes the child vulnerable to anyone interested in exploiting them. In addition, sexual abuse is often a precursor to commercial sexual exploitation. A common definition of sexual abuse is the forced, tricked, or coerced sexual behavior between a younger person and an older person. The element of force is the key dynamic.

The elements of sexual abuse include manipulation of the child, coercion, force, threats, and virtually every kind of sexual behavior. The basic term sexual abuse of children comprises three elements: 1) a significantly older individual who 2) engages in sexual activity with someone 3) who is legally a child.

Both sexual and physical abuse are reported by large percentages of youth on the streets. In a 1991 survey conducted by the Wilder Foundation of eighty-one homeless youths in Minnesota, 51% of the girls and 12% of the boys reported having been sexually abused by an adult. Physical abuse was more commonly reported, with 62% of girls and 34% of boys reporting such abuse at the hands of an adult. Thirty percent of the respondents reported both sexual and physical abuse.

In a report prepared for the US Senate on the youth served under the Runaway and Homeless Youth Act in 1989, 26% of homeless youth and 29% of runaways reported physical or sexual abuse. It is well documented that victims of abuse, whether sexual or not, suffer from low self-esteem and depression and are more likely to be violent or abusive towards others.

Abuse can affect boys and girls differently. Boys often focused on proving their manhood, sometimes become sexually assaultive persons, and are often referred for sexual dysfuctions (e.g. impotence and premature ejaculation). Many also repeat their abuse behavior on a same age child. Girls can develop problems in their adult sex life, see sex as dirty or disgusting, may become an abusive parent without knowing why. Girls may tend to prostitute, become promiscuous, tend to marry aggressive battering husbands, tends to lose all goal motivation.

Many of the circumstances surrounding the sexual abuse of these children are also identified risk factors for AIDS. These factors include: promiscuous sexual activity with multiple partners, sexual contact which is physically traumatic, intercourse without barrier protection, genital lesions, and the use of illicit drugs. Studies of sexually exploited children indicate a variety of long-term emotional, behavioral, social and sexual problems.

Symptoms include physical problems of headaches, stomachaches, and sleeping and eating disorders; psychological reactions of fear and anxiety, depression, mood changes, guilt, and shame; social problems of school truancy, declining grades, and fighting; and sexual problems, such as heightened sexual activity, compulsive masturbation, exhibitionism, and preoccupation with sex and nudity. Running away from home, adolescent prostitution, suicide attempts, substance abuse, gender identity confusion, sexual dysfunction, and socially deviant behaviors have also been identified as possible consequences of untreated childhood sexual abuse.

Myths of Prostitution

Prostitution is a natural expression of sexuality and a necessity for inadequate sexual relationships. Actually juvenile prostitutes are often appalled at and damaged by the acts demanded of them. Participation in prostitution is often an threat to their physical well being. Prostitution is a victimless crime. Prostitution creates a setting whereby crimes against men, women, and children become a commercial enterprise. When a customer uses a juvenile prostitute for his or her own sexual gratification, he or she is committing the crime of child sexual abuse.

Juveniles freely choose prostitution. The fragile self-esteem and limited resources lead some girls to believe that they have no other choice but to enter the world of prostitution. Prostitution can be an exciting and glamorous life. In reality, juvenile prostitutes suffer pain, humiliation, and degradation at the hands of their pimps and customers. They are susceptible to sexually transmitted diseases and unwanted pregnancies.

The system of prostitution offers wealth to the participant. In truth, part of the strategy for control over the prostitute is for pimps and madams to keep them economically dependent upon the system of prostitution itself. Any profit is often spent as rapidly as it is obtained, reinforcing the efforts that go into prostitution. Prostitutes have power and control within the system. In reality prostitutes are controlled both by their customers and by their pimp. The more involved one becomes, the more difficult it is to leave.

Prostitution is a deterrent to sexual crimes. There is no evidence that prostitution deters sex crimes. Prostitutes can be victims of violent acts including rape and murder. In addition, young prostitutes can be easy victims for perpetrators. Prostitutes are from specific socioeconomic groups. Teenage prostitutes come from all socioeconomic groups. Juveniles make an educated decision to become prostitutes. Many case histories support the fact that entry into prostitution may begin in the teens or earlier. These histories reveal that the majority have been sexually or physically abused. For most of these young women the only way to stop the violence was to run away from home, which led to prostitution. This does not make for an educated decision.

There are laws to control prostitution. Historically there has been a unequal application of laws prohibiting prostitution. There is a difference between being a high-class prostitute and a streetwalker. In either situation the only people prostitutes have contact with are pimps, tricks, and other prostitutes.

6

Street Children and Juvenile Justice

In many countries around the world, children and adolescents who live and work on the streets suffer from wide-ranging human rights violations in so-called 'justice' systems. Each individual child has a story to tell. Street children are highly likely to come into contact with the criminal justice system in the first place due to discrimination and the circumstances in which they are forced to survive, regardless of whether or not they have actually committed a crime.

Due to outdated legislation they are arrested and face harsh sentences for petty (often 'survival') theft, substance abuse, begging and 'vagrancy'. Furthermore, they are less able to defend themselves from abuse once within the system due to limited or no contact with responsible adults who can speak up on their behalf, lack of funds to bribe their way out of the system, and the fact that their voices are not heard or respected. In short, street children are discriminated against and have their rights violated because they are poor.

Street children are seen as outsiders by society, often with only an outside chance of surviving and developing to their fullest potential. It is aimed at anyone with an interest in these issues and in particular: policy-makers in relevant government departments; personnel working in the various branches of the justice system; NGO practitioners working with street children and/or on juvenile justice issues; academics; human rights lobbyists; public and private donors; and actors in the UN and regional human rights systems. It includes:

— Descriptions - in the children's own words - of the treatment they receive at different stages of the criminal justice system;

— A framework of overarching concepts and recommended approaches to reform;

— An introduction to international human rights standards and guidelines on how to use them;

— Practical examples of projects and approaches from around the world;

— Specific recommendations for improvement, including recommendations from children themselves, targeted at different actors in the system.

The scope of 'juvenile justice' can vary. Juvenile justice is understood to comprise not only the treatment of children in conflict with the law, but also the need to address the root causes of offending behaviour and implement measures to prevent such behaviour. There are two major strands of work under this broad definition:

— Prevention - in order to ensure that children do not come into conflict with the law in the first place and therefore do not come into contact with the formal criminal justice system, and

— Protection - of children who are already in conflict with the law from human rights violations, focusing on their development in order to deter them from re-offending and to promote their rehabilitation and smooth their reintegration back into society.

In theory a 'juvenile justice system' is made up of the legislation, processes, institutions and personnel involved in the treatment of children accused of committing a criminal offence. Due to the specific needs and circumstances of children, this needs to be distinct from the workings of the regular adult criminal justice system. However, in reality there are three problems with the term 'juvenile justice system':

1. There is no one single 'system' but a complex mixture and overlap between many different systems: children pass through processes, institutions and personnel from a variety of different government departments, agencies and organisations such as the police, social welfare and probation departments, judiciary, lawyers, detention centres and prisons. Although these systems are supposed to be interrelated, coordinated and interdependent, in reality each sector has its own mandate, budget authority, regulations, governing body and political agenda. "Each one may act with the best of intentions and totally within its guidelines, but the effect of so many agencies making individual (or at best bilateral) decisions is that a 'non-system' is formed. In other words, there is no 'complex whole formed by interactive, interrelated, interdependent parts.' Complex, yes, but system, no." Understanding and respecting this complexity is key to implementing reform.

2. In some countries, even if a separate 'system' for the treatment of children (as opposed to adults) exists in theory, in practice children are often still processed through the adult criminal justice system. The term 'juvenile justice system' may therefore be misleading and this report often refers more accurately to the 'criminal justice system' in certain situations.

3. The term 'juvenile' is increasingly being criticised in international human rights circles as it is seen as a stigmatising label which detracts from the fact that the individuals in question are children and adolescents, entitled to special treatment and understanding, according to standards outlined in the UN Convention on the Rights of the Child and other instruments. Organisations such as Save the Children UK now use the

term 'child justice' as opposed to 'juvenile justice' to reflect these policy concerns. However, this shift in terminology has been developing over the past few years and, whilst appreciating current trends, the term 'juvenile justice' is still used in the title and other places throughout this publication as it is more widely recognised.

Street Children in Criminal Justice System

It is essential to understand from the outset that not all street children in criminal justice systems are criminals, but rather fall into three very different groups:

1) Children in actual conflict with the law: Some street children do engage in criminal behaviour ranging from minor to serious offences. These street children are in conflict with the law.

2) Children in perceived conflict with the law: Others may be arrested for activities that are officially criminalised in legislation but which the international human rights community calls for to be decriminalised as a matter of urgency. For example, street children are arrested for being victims of commercial sexual exploitation, for begging, 'vagrancy' and for 'status offences' such as truancy, 'running away from home', and being 'beyond parental control'. In these cases, although technically in conflict with the law, children in this category are actually victims of legislation that needs urgently to be reformed.

3) Children in need of care and protection: Some street children do not engage in criminal behaviour. Nevertheless, they may still be arrested randomly and illegally, on prejudiced suspicion of being involved in criminal behaviour, or they may be detained 'for their own protection'. In some countries, in the absence of adequate social welfare responses, the criminal justice system is used to warehouse homeless children

regardless of whether or not they have committed a crime.

Stressing the use of child-sensitive terminology and unless quoting references and identifying the titles of previous researches, words and phrases such as 'minor', 'juvenile', 'youthful offender' and 'juvenile delinquent' have been avoided in this publication. This is due to their negative and prejudicial connotations or the fact that they detract from the reality that the individuals involved are first and foremost children and adolescents. These terms have been replaced with more accurate references to 'child', 'adolescent', 'young person', 'child in actual conflict with the law', 'child in perceived conflict with the law' and 'child in need of care and protection'.

Amongst street-living children, girls are in a minority. This massive over-representation of boys living on the streets is carried over into the criminal justice system. For example, in Albania there were 386 boys sentenced in 1998 but only one girl . This low percentage of girls may be accounted for by their relative minority presence on the streets in the first place as well as differences in some countries in the way girls are processed through the system - for example in Pakistan it is reported that girls are more likely to be diverted from the system at police stations and in general girls are less likely to be prosecuted or to be given a custodial sentence than boys. "However, it is not clear to what extent these differences derive from more lenient treatment, from a lack of facilities available for female offenders, or from the divergent patterns of offending behaviour displayed by boys and girls." Nevertheless, this gender imbalance in the criminal justice system has major implications for the treatment of both girls and boys.

As criminal justice systems are traditionally orientated towards boys, girls are particularly vulnerable to human rights abuses. For example, due to lack of space in many police and detention facilities girls are often held in detention with female adults. Furthermore, limited numbers of female staff in the criminal justice system makes girls vulnerable to inappropriate handling and sexual abuse, particularly by law enforcement personnel. Because of their 'non-normative' sexual activity on the streets (possibly involving multiple partners, 'survival' sex in exchange for food, shelter and protection, and the difficulty in drawing boundaries between this and sexual abuse and commercial sexual exploitation), street girls suffer a perceived loss of rights over their bodies. This is compounded by gender stereotypes in male-dominated cultures which define these girls as not 'nice girls'.

Combined with a general taboo around sexually active children, especially girls, and even a fear of them, this results in exceptionally high levels of sexual violence against street girls. Finally, in general, "prisons are ill equipped to deal with young women who are damaged and who display extremely challenging and difficult behaviour. The numbers of juvenile girls within the system are small and as a result they are simply tacked onto the rest of the system with little recognition that their needs are different and separate from older women. It also means that they attract fewer resources..."

Studies shows that gender in relation to juvenile justice often highlight the particular problems faced by girls. However, "overall, neither the human rights movement nor the CRC movement is treating imbalances in the well-being of males as a human rights issue, or even a 'gender issue'". Abramson points out that, despite evidence that "the penal system, adult and juvenile, is the most heavily gendered institution in society", little - if anything - is being done by governments and child rights advocates to address the reasons why boys are so at risk in this area. He goes on to add that the general unpopularity or apparent lack of interest in addressing issues that disproportionately affect boys, rather than girls, is one of the most important reasons for the marginalisation of juvenile justice issues in the human rights movement.

Any reform of the criminal justice system therefore needs to take into account this gender imbalance in order to ensure that interventions are appropriate and effective. For example:

— Prevention programmes need to address why boys are more at risk than girls of coming into conflict with the law and accordingly identify and mobilise protective factors which are gender-specific;

— The minority of girls in the system need to be protected through the provision of adequate gender-sensitive staffing, facilities and services (including gender-sensitive health services);

— Psychosocial and rehabilitation interventions with girls and boys need to take into account differences due to gender (e.g. research has shown that street migration for girls is more traumatic and the rupture more permanent than for boys; programmes in Kenya, Senegal, Bolivia, Brazil and Guatemala report that girls on the street display more psychological damage than boys - a combination of both sexual abuse and rupture in the family ; the internalisation by girls of the effects of domestic violence, sexual abuse and family break-up may find expression in violent behaviour, depression, withdrawal and self-mutilation ; girls appear to grow out of crime more successfully and at an earlier age than is the case with boys - all of which have significant implications for professional counselling, family reintegration and other programmes);

— Programmes sensitising detention centre staff on methods of discipline which are not abusive or humiliating need to take into account any differences in the ways in which girls and boys are treated;

— Facilities for a full range of community penalties should be available to girls as well as boys in the local area, including community punishment orders and attendance centre orders. This might involve:

— ensuring that provision is in place to avoid the necessity of placing single girls alone with a group of boys;

— developing attendance centres for girls where these do not exist;

— providing child-care facilities where these are needed.

In short, "a gendered problem needs a gendered solution - regardless of the subject, and irrespective of which sex is on the winner/loser side of things." Practitioners must address the socio-economic and cultural factors that result in the massive over-representation of boys in the system whilst at the same time ensuring that service delivery does not discriminate against the female minority and that the particular needs of girls are not overlooked.

Reforming Juvenile Justice Systems

Reform of juvenile justice systems (or multiple, overlapping systems / 'non-systems') can take many different approaches. As with a tangled knot, there are problems in many areas and yet pulling at the knot in some areas may actually make matters worse. For example, attention to conducting physical repairs of detention centres may divert attention and resources away from programmes to ensure that children don't end up in detention in the first place. Improving parts of the system without analysing the whole can result in making bad processes function even more efficiently! This problem has also been described as the 'balloon effect' in juvenile justice reform: "we grab a hold of one part of the problem, and it bulges out somewhere else". Difficult decisions need to be made in the context of scarcity of resources, conflicting interests, lack of political will and negative media influence. It is therefore useful to have a common framework to refer to in order to help simplify complex decision-making.

Many images and stories portray street children either as helpless victims, dangerous criminals or heroic survivors. The reality is usually somewhere in between. They show incredible resiliency and initiative in the face of desperate circumstances. They have to be resourceful and strong in order to survive, but some do not survive. Others can only do so by breaking the law. Despite our generalisations, only by respecting their individual stories and characteristics can we understand and effectively address the causes of the problems they face.

Each child is unique and "even those living or working in the streets, are complex human beings with hopes and dreams whose problems need to be examined holistically, in relation to the individual circumstances in which they find themselves." In terms of juvenile justice system reform, this entails developing a range of options for intervention such that the most appropriate is implemented in individual cases. It also entails combating the generalised negative public perception of street children as criminals and/or as inferior beings, less deserving of respect and rights than others - an attitude which results in bringing children - often unjustly - into contact with the criminal justice system in the first place, and which impacts very negatively on their treatment once within the system.

Stereotyping and Dehumanisation

Not only are street children (especially those who actually live on the streets) an embarrassing, visible reminder of a society's failure to provide for and protect its most vulnerable children, but they are also considered by many to be a criminal threat to that very society. It is therefore easy and more comfortable to either not see them at all, to fear them as dangerous outlaws (or well on their way to becoming dangerous outlaws) or to see them as less than human. This perception results in them being transposed from 'children' to 'street children' to 'criminals' deserving of ill-treatment in the public's mind, the most extreme manifestation of which are the death squads and vigilantes made famous in Latin America.

Criminalisation and, to a lesser extent, dehumanisation are dangerous threats posed to vulnerable children in that they absolve people, especially the authorities, of the obligation to accord them their human rights. Criminalisation, stereotyping and dehumanisation impact on street children at both a collective and individual level and constitute the most significant underlying factors influencing their treatment in the criminal justice system: such negative generalisation and stereotyping obscures the individuality of boys and girls who live and work on the street and thus leads to inappropriate and often abusive blanket responses from the criminal justice system.

Criminalisation and dehumanisation at both the collective and individual level are inseparably linked: public opinion is shaped by the actions and attitudes of individuals and vice versa. Misconceptions are often based on the lack of objective, systematic and accurate statistics on juvenile crime, and the failure to distinguish between the causes and seriousness of offences. In other words, there is often a failure by the authorities, the media and the public to take into account why children and adolescents commit some crimes in the first place. For example, they may be victims of exploitation by others, the crimes may be status offences or may be necessary for the children's survival on the street.

There is also a lack of detailed categorization of offences - for example the fact that stealing a piece of bread or fruit from a vendor, or sneaking into a building to sleep may be categorized alongside much more serious crimes of theft and breaking and entering. In short, there is a failure to assess incidents on an individual, case by case basis. Combined with the lack of reliable statistics in relation to juvenile crime (due to lack of infrastructure, poor training, lack of systematised data collection methods, inconsistent categorisation of crimes and political manipulation of statistics) "this leads to unwarranted exclusion, suspicion, exaggeration of risk, marginalisation, unnecessary fears and overconfidence in methods which fail to correct."

One of the main influences on public opinion is the media and inaccurate, unrepresentative and sensationalist reporting contributes to the criminalisation of children and young people: "Alarming messages on increasing juvenile delinquency and thus for some people, possible obstacles for a full recognition of children as bearers of human rights, are not always based on sound information but are often emotional expressions related to isolated but indeed shocking events, such as homicide or murder committed by young children." The media can therefore fuel public fear and condemnation of street children.

Street children are considered to be "a blemish on the urban landscape and a reminder that all is not well in the country. Unwanted and considered human waste, these ubiquitous tattered, mainly black children and adolescents evoke strong and contradictory emotions of fear, aversion, pity and anger in those who view their neighbourhood streets, boulevards and squares as 'private places' under siege". In addition to vigilante and police violence and death squads, this negative public opinion and fear of street children in Brazil has resulted in strong public resistance to the urgently needed reforms which are required to implement the country's progressive child rights-friendly legislation: the Statute of Children and Adolescents (ECA).

An example of this is the ongoing intense public and political pressure to lower the age of criminal responsibility in Brazil. This would enable the authorities to put children and adolescents straight into adult prisons rather than the current system of detention in 'Centres for Socio-Education' (even though in some states conditions in these centres are appalling, and are to all intents and purposes similar to prison). Reliance on detention, even in these so-called 'socio-educative' centres, flies in the face of extensive evidence exposing the appalling cycle of violence and human rights violations against children in detention.

Detention of children in adult prisons is even worse. The movement to lower the age of criminal responsibility is due in part to an inaccurate perception that violent youth crime is prevalent, although it is stated that only 10% of all illegal acts are committed by adolescents, and these acts are more often crimes against property than against people. NGOs throughout Brazil have been lobbying intensively against this move.

Criminalisation at the individual level

Failure to regard street children as individual children first and foremost, (each defined by their unique personality traits, life stories, hopes and aspirations) contributes to the blanket discrimination suffered by them in the criminal justice system. In the same way that the negative impact of public opinion contributes to a hostile political and legislative climate as seen above, criminal stereotyping and dehumanisation are also integral to the majority of negative relationships experienced by street children at an individual level in the justice system. For example, just as collective public opinion can fuel a policy that encourages police round-ups of street children in general, similar opinions held at an individual level can lead to treatment such as beatings and verbal abuse:

> "Police see [street children] as a threat to tranquillity of society; misjudge them as thieves and troublemakers"; "I had to go to sleep on an empty stomach and got beaten up by the 'dadas' (bullies) and policemen" (Nepal).

In Egypt, Human Rights Watch reports that the police routinely use obscene and degrading language to humiliate and intimidate children during arrests, especially using terms such as 'bastards', 'whores', children of 'whores' or dogs, or making references to children's mothers' sexual organs - all of which are pointed out as being extremely offensive attacks on family and personal honour in Egyptian society. According to one 17-year-old,

"The government curses us. They curse us badly-curses of religion, of mothers, of fathers" (Egypt).

Racial Discrimination

Criminalisation and discrimination at both collective and individual levels can be further fuelled by racism if street children are perceived as belonging to particular racial or ethnic minority groups as illustrated by the following the case study.

Roma street children in the criminal justice system in Bulgaria

According to a 1996 Human Rights Watch report, between twelve and fourteen thousand street children are estimated to live in cities throughout Bulgaria. "Most street children are Roma [estimated 85%, possibly higher], for whom the unemployment rate in Bulgaria is estimated to be as high as 90% in certain neighbourhoods, and 70% on average. The Bulgarian national unemployment rate is reported to be 12.5%. The depressed socio-economic status of Roma people coupled with inadequacies in the Bulgarian educational system were often cited among the reasons for children taking to the streets."

"Roma are often perceived by the Bulgarian public to be a criminal element of society. For these reasons, street children are often subject to extreme violence and abuse at the hands of both skinheads and police. Police often harass and abuse the children because they perceive them to be criminals, and skinhead gangs regularly attack and beat the children because of their Roma identity."

'A group of skinheads snuck up on us and surrounded us. They were cursing us and saying 'dirty Gypsies, we will kill you.' We all started to run, but my brother was caught.

He was stabbed in the back with a knife. Then the skinheads ran away' [17-year-old girl, Sofia].

'[T]he worst beating I got was in Pleven by the bus station. Six skinheads caught me and started beating me and kicking me in the face with their boots. They knocked my teeth out. I didn't do anything to them. They beat me because I'm Roma' [13-year-old boy, Pleven].

In the words of one policeman: "...most of those kids are not Bulgarians, they're Roma." "He went on to comment that street children steal, that their parents force them to go out and beg, and that the children earn twice as much money as he earns as a policeman. When questioned about physical abuse of the children, he responded, '[o]f course if I catch a kid stealing, I'm going to kick his ass.' The significance of the ethnic identity of street children should not be underestimated in police attitude toward, and treatment of, street children. Human Rights Watch believes that Roma identity of street children may be a significant factor in their treatment by police".

"Street children, and Roma children generally, are particularly susceptible to confinement in Bulgaria's eleven Labour Education Schools. The Deputy Director of Slavovitza Labour Education School observed that '80% of the children [at Slavovitza] are Gypsies, mainly from large families. Most of them roamed the streets before coming to us'. It is estimated that Roma make up between 4 and 10% of the general population, thus indicating massive over-representation in the system."

Minority identity also affects access to complaints mechanisms: "These are problems which anyone who has been a victim of crime might encounter, but it is more so for the Roma people, who are less prepared to protest the irresponsibility of the judiciary organs".

Abusive treatment by police leads to a failure to report frequent racist attacks (sometimes several times a week) by skinhead gangs to the police. "Almost all the children we interviewed had suffered from such attacks. Despite the regularity of such attacks, children reported receiving little or no assistance from police. Those who did complaint to police said that police responded to their complaints with indifference, disbelief, and even suspicion." This fosters a culture of impunity for attackers.

Criminalisation, stereotyping and dehumanisation result from a failure to understand and treat each child as unique. Challenging these generalised, stereotyped attitudes, at the levels of both public opinion and individuals, is therefore key to any interventions to reform justice systems in favour of the most marginalised. The challenges must be met through sensitisation, public education and - wherever possible - breaking down the barriers between the children themselves and the individual decision-makers in local contexts.

The juvenile justice reform is the concept of choice. Based on experiences from organizations around the world, something that emerges very clearly is that work at an individual level with street children needs to be centred around choices. This approach can be seen as a three-stage process of understanding, expanding and empowering:

1. *Understanding choices* : We need to understand, from their own perspective, why individual children have made the choices they have: very often they have been confronted by limited choices or 'non-choices', for example when a boy or girl is faced with the dilemma: 'Do I stay at home and continue to be abused by my step-father, or do I take my chances of being abused on the street?'. Only once we understand the background to a particular child's situation can we attempt to identify a suitable intervention that we can work with them to implement. In the context of street children's involvement in the criminal justice system, such choices or non-choices may include: 'Do I steal or go hungry?'; 'Do I agree to have sex with the policeman or let him arrest me?'; 'Do I help in the older boy's robbery or get beaten up by him?'

2. *Expanding choices* : The next logical step is to help expand the choices available to them, for example, offering the option of residential shelters as an alternative to sleeping in a dangerous alleyway; the option of family reunification or group living; the option of less hazardous employment; the option of self-protection against sexually transmitted infections and HIV/AIDS; the option of someone to call in times of trouble who can intervene at the police station. It may be that, due to socio-economic and cultural constraints, there are fewer choices available to girls than boys in a given situation and therefore particular efforts should be made to promote gender equality in programming.
3. *Empowering children to make choices* : Even when choices are expanded, it can be difficult for children make the transitions necessary to implement those choices. The final stage is therefore empowering girls and boys to actually make, and carry through, their choices. This can be especially difficult in the case of children who are not used to having this freedom through (e.g.) a history of repeated coercion / abuse which can be inherently dis-empowering. This is often particularly the case with girls who have been subjected to limited decision-making in cultural contexts that are inherently disempowering to women and girls.

Likewise, many NGOs experience particular challenges with children who are substance abusers as their powers of analysis and clarity of thought / ability to see their own situation are diminished. The importance of this stage, however, is that the children - to the greatest possible extent within given circumstances - make educated choices for themselves, rather than having 'choices' made for them by others, no matter how well-intentioned. Children who are empowered are better able to protect themselves, assess and strengthen their own support networks, and take part in sensitization and collaboration efforts and other programmes needed for reform of the criminal justice system.

Relationship-building

Each child is unique, equally valuable (non-discrimination), has the potential and right to develop (right to life, survival and development), and the ability and right to contribute to that process (participation) ensuring that the most appropriate solutions are developed (best interests) and adequately resourced (implementation) - reform becomes child-centred. In other words, the child is put at the center of decision-making processes.

However, a child obviously does not exist in isolation from others. It is a matter of common sense that, the importance of family, community and other stakeholders, so too must reform of justice systems take into account children's relationships with the many stakeholders who make up the 'five pillars' of the system :

— law enforcement

— prosecution

— courts

— correction

— community

The aim of reform is to capitalize on the supportive relationships and minimize the impact of (or preferably avoid altogether) the abusive relationships. The issue of relationship-building in order to strengthen safety nets is particularly important in the case of street children whose relationships - particularly with responsible adults - may well have been damaged or ruptured.

All justice reform programmes depend ultimately on the individuals involved. In the existing system policy decisions at macro level are originated and promoted by individuals who then influence other individuals; individual police officers either abuse or help; judges make decisions at their individual discretion; politicians push for either punitive or restorative policies; journalists write either stereotyped or sensitive stories etc. The individual interactions with street children multiplying into public opinion and then influencing in turn yet more individuals. If this can be considered as a 'ripple effect', then so too can relationship-building and transformation, 'turning the tide' of criminalisation, stereotyping and discrimination.

Reform must therefore work at the level of relationships: "Good justice is good relationships. Bad justice is bad relationships."

— Prevention (of street migration, of first-time offending or of re-offending) depends not only on strengthening family, peer and community support networks but also on building relationship bridges between this level and macro-level decision makers who influence broader socio-economic policies;

— Diversion programmes depend on transforming bi-lateral and multi-lateral relationships between street children, police, social workers, community members, family etc.;

— Alternatives to detention depend on a street child's relationships and support networks being strong enough to produce an enabling environment to respond to their multiple needs.

In short, "programmes should be based on the philosophy of social reparation and restoration of damaged relationships." Two strands therefore emerge:

a) Sensitisation (working at the level of individual relationships) and

b) Collaboration (the multiplier effect of relationship building).

Sensitisation

Sensitisation is urgently needed amongst all the actors

involved in the criminal justice system, for example, lawyers, magistrates, donors, government advisers, civil servants, social workers, probation officers, families, prison staff and so on. Well-targeted, persistent advocacy aimed at key decision-makers and those who help to influence public and institutional opinion is essential to combat 'structural factors' that weigh against even the most well-meaning of individuals trying to improve conditions for street children. However, whilst acknowledging the need for engagement with multiple actors simultaneously across all branches of the justice system, the following examples focus on sensitisation programmes specifically in relation to the police as this is an area that has been identified by overseas organisations in many countries as a priority area for intervention.

There are many examples of sensitisation work with the police, including:

— Monthly 'open forums' held by NGOs where street children can ask the police questions and the police get to find out more about the situation of the children. This has helped to break down barriers and misunderstandings on both sides.

— Police training posters have been produced in the Philippines in sets of two versions: one with simple stages for the police to take when dealing with a child who is in conflict with the law and one with the stages for dealing with a child who is 'in need of care and protection'. The posters should be clearly displayed in the police station to act as a reminder that the two categories of children should be treated separately and clearly reminding them of the correct procedure to follow in each case.

— 'Children's Desks' in police stations staffed by police officers specially trained in dealing with children (very often women). All children are supposed to be dealt with through these desks rather than through regular 'adult' processes which are not suitable for them. This approach is in place, or being developed in many countries such as India: according to the Juvenile Justice (Care and Protection of Children) Act 2000, it has been proposed to have a Child Welfare Officer (CWO) in each police station especially trained to handle cases involving children and child abuse. Further, a Special Juvenile Police Unit is to be formed, made up of CWOs. In addition to this, "At least one police personnel from each station in the city has attended a 'sensitisation programme' and has been given necessary instructions on handling juvenile offenders and children". Meanwhile, 'Childline' volunteers will be visiting all police stations to display messages and interact with police personnel. These volunteers are also organizing street plays in slum areas to create an awareness on 'Childline'".

— Police training - either as part of the formal police academy curriculum, as official and regular in-service courses, or on an ad hoc basis: for example, in Angola, training of police responsible for children, conducted by an NGO in association with the Ministry of the Interior "has been successful in raising awareness of street children's problems and rights, and the level of mutual respect between children and police has increased. Both boys and girls are more willing to go to the police and report crimes of violence since the awareness-raising course, and the level of police violence has reduced." A police officer has been nominated to take responsibility for co-ordinating work with street children.

The majority of the police in India perceive street children as being a nuisance. They themselves are over-worked and underpaid and little or no time to help street children who are in trouble. Instead, it is easier to assume that they are criminals and treat them badly, even if they have not done anything wrong. A further problem is that the police in India are frequently 'rotated' around the country. Therefore, just as an

NGO has begun to develop a good relationship with particular officers, they move out of the area and the work must begin again.

Relationship Building at the Individual Level

Collaboration is the next step in capitalising on relationships built at the individual level. It is also essential in a context of the overlap of multiple systems and actors that makes up the 'justice system': "Collaboration by multiple stakeholders may be the only way to address the barriers to change that juvenile justice's 'non-system' character poses." Collaboration can effectively address delays in processing cases as well as helping to improve conditions in detention. Collaboration is essentially the glue that holds together the web of relationships between the five pillars of the justice system.

The Indian government has recognised the problems highlighted by many NGOs in relation to the treatment of children in the criminal justice system and in August 2003 the Juvenile Welfare, Correctional Services & Welfare of Street Children Department in Andhra Pradesh put into practice a scheme of co-management of the state's children's institutions with selected NGOs with a view to improving conditions for children in line with the CRC.

Under this scheme each institution will have a key NGO co-managing the institution and other member NGOs on a Committee to monitor implementation. This is one of several states developing such procedures under encouragement from the central government.

The NGO 'New Hope' has been appointed as the 'Nodal Agency' for the Observation Home at Rajahmundry and the local YMCA has been appointed for the Observation Home in Anantapur. Both of these organizations are project partners of The Railway Children. In addition, New Hope regularly visits the Observation Home in Warangal where their input is welcomed by the management and boys. In Vijayawada, there is a Child Rights Forum chaired by the mayor, and involving the police and other state authorities in addition to all of the NGOs working with street children in the city.

Role of the Community

The community has already been highlighted as one of the 'five pillars' of the justice system. In this context, the scope of the 'community' is very broad ranging and includes many of the most important actors in the lives of boys and girls living and working on the street. As highlighted previously, these relationships can either be positive (supportive) or negative (abusive). The examples listed below obviously represent an ideal situation towards which programmes can be oriented. For example:

— the child's family, extended family and / or 'alternative family' of supportive peers and friends: these act as the 'front line' of a child's protective and supportive factors and are thus key to any programmes aimed at the essential areas of prevention, diversion and alternatives to detention;

— specific influential and/or professional community members / service providers such as teachers, doctors, social workers and religious leaders who may be able to provide particular services and support to individual children as well as playing a key role in influencing local opinion in terms of awareness-raising and sensitisation to the needs and rights of street children;

— the business community, ranging from local shop-keepers to large corporations: these can play an essential role in prevention, protection and rehabilitation (through the provision of employment, development of local economies, support for income generation and micro-credit schemes for families in poverty, improvement in labour conditions through the development of corporate social responsibility, ensuring that any private security guards they hire are trained in child rights and made aware of child protection issues etc.);

— other community members such as neighbours: these can act as mentors or role models for girls and boys who live and work on the streets or for those at risk of taking to street life, act as an 'early warning' system to draw attention to situations of abuse and act as prison visitors to monitor conditions in detention and other institutions;

— civil society organisations such as NGOs, women's groups, church groups, children's clubs, unions etc.: these can act as facilitators and implementers of specific prevention and protection programmes, putting pressure on local and national governments to implement reform as well as offering fora for mutual community support, especially to at-risk families etc. In many countries and communities it is these organisations who play the essential catalysing role in reform of the justice system;

— academics: these individuals and institutions can provide much needed research to assist civil society organisations and governments to develop appropriate policies and interventions.

Sensitisation and collaboration at the level of the community is essential to establishing or improving the networks of support available to street children and involvement of the community should be a priority for any intervention.

Child Rights-based, Child-centred Approach

A child rights-based, child-centred approach obviously needs to take into account the specific circumstances of the individual children involved: relationships centred on the child are dependent on the child's individual personality and ability to communicate. "Under the vulnerability paradigm, children are viewed as passive, weak, dependent and even problematic and this particular paradigm is evident in the issue of street children. However, what is also evident is that street children are also 'smart enough to beat the system and they will beat the system in order to survive.'"

There has been a recent shift in the field of child development away from focusing on environmental risk factors towards consideration of personal resiliency and environmental protective factors that allow a child to survive the adversities of his or her environment. "The central idea behind this new paradigm is resilience. Resilience has been defined as the capacity to withstand, recover, and even grow from negative experiences". The resiliency concept is useful in that it can help to highlight the complexity of psychosocial disorders and their causes, it can help us to identify previously undetected possibilities for preventive action and "the idea of resilience keeps hope alive in clinical practice; however much the odds against a good outcome, we know that many children escape their ill fate."

Studies have revealed the following critical factors associated with resiliency: external supports and resources available to a child (e.g. family, school and community institutions); personal strengths that a child develops (e.g. self-esteem, a capacity for self-monitoring, spirituality and altruism), and social interpersonal skills acquired (e.g. conflict resolution and communication skills). In-depth interviews with 25 street children in Manila, Philippines revealed the following personal resiliency traits and protective environmental factors:

— *Internal strengths'*: sense of direction or mission and self-efficacy ("a positive perception of one's competence to perform certain tasks") / belief in self; social problem-solving skills - which "reinforce one's sense of competence and self-esteem" ; street survival skills - which, unlike problem-solving skills, "often involve self-damaging behaviour that heightens the risk of failure in a street child that is not resilient" ; adaptive distancing (ability to separate themselves physically and/or psychologically from risk factors in their environment, a trait which requires the ability to realistically appraise situations and to self-monitor); having a hobby or creative talent; realistic view of their environment; self-monitoring; self-control; intellectual capacity; 'easy' temperaments and dispositions - which helps foster good interpersonal relationships thus allowing others to treat them in a more positive manner; capacity to recognize and learn from mistakes made in the past; sense of humour.

— *Externally directed traits*': leadership skills; altruism; empathy; 'going along with a group to avoid confrontations' which can either be positive or negative, depending on the type of group in question.

— *Something bigger than oneself*': sense of morality; religion or faith in God.

Resiliency involves a process of interaction between individual and environmental factors, not fixed attributes or traits within an individual." It is this unique interaction between individual child and specific environment that brings us back once again to the need for an individualized approach when working with street children which focuses on children's choices: understanding why they make particular choices, expanding the choices available to them and empowering them to make those choices. As emphasized throughout, any interventions in the field of street children in the criminal justice system need to focus on minimizing the risk factors and emphasizing the protective factors in their relationships. Such protective factors include:

— Family protective factors: having family responsibilities; family traditions and rituals; having a warm bond with a sibling; warm positive relationship with a parent or other adult; positive adult modeling; supportiveness of child's abilities; high parental expectations.

— Environmental protective factors: agency intervention; opportunity for involvement in the community; school experience.

Competent functioning

While in jail, Bernard (aged 17) experienced being beaten up and being forced to clean the toilets. Moreover, his mother never visited him throughout his incarceration. Fortunately, however, his classroom adviser took pity on him and administered tests and quizzes in jail which he passed with high scores. He managed to study despite living in a difficult situation, a time he described that he had been "living like a dog". Despite the seemingly insurmountable burdens and in the presence of major life problems, Bernard had shown competence in his subjects, pulling through his tests. During the Regional Workshop, he revealed plans of momentarily becoming a construction worker so that he could continue his studies.

Self-reliant and Self-governing

James (aged 17) was caught while trying to steal an item inside a truck. He experienced violence in prison, but apparently he managed to deal with his life's struggles. The drawings he made exhibit his capacity to be a self-reliant and self-governing person. James drew a trishaw, explaining that he wanted to become a trishaw driver so he could buy rice for his mother. "So that when it rains, people will flag me down. It is better when you earn money out of sweat." James, who had also drawn the picture of a letter, said that he also wanted to become a mailman, so that people would be happy when he delivers them letters.

Reginald (aged 18) had felt bad towards his mother, who had taken a lover and even brought him to their home. He soon learned to use illegal drugs. Jailed for stealing a pair of trousers, Reginald experienced being slapped and forced to clean the toilet. He was afterwards released. According to Reginald, his brief experience in jail gave him the chance to think about things. This clearly shows that he possesses a therapeutic outlook that helped him change. "If I had not been caught, I would have turned out worse." Reginald also greatly understood the events in his life. His drawing of a wheel showed his forbearance. Through his drawing, he gave his views about life: "Our lives are sometimes at the top, sometimes at the bottom, but we can still surmount problems" Reginald said he dreamed of helping his family and sharing his happiness with them.

Jayson (aged 17) experienced sadness and boredom while in jail. "You would always be thinking especially when you have no visitors." Despite having experienced deprivation and dismal conditions while in jail, Jayson remained good and wholesome at heart. This goodness and wholesomeness was shown in his drawing, a puppet. Jayson explained that he wanted to become a clown, to make other people happy. Despite difficulties while living in jail, Jayson managed to find happiness, a happiness that he wanted to share.

Donald (aged 17) was no stranger to incarceration and the experiences of torture. However, with the educational and social support of an NGO on release from detention, he is recovering from his experiences. He drew a pencil, saying that his previous life was in shambles, like a broken pencil He displayed the determination to move on with life, saying that he would like to continue what he is doing - "making the pencil whole again." His words showed that he has been recovering from past wounds and is moving on with life.

Arrested for robbery, Marissa (aged 12) was jailed for three months. She experienced being shamefully photographed. Although she did not go through much hardship in jail, she admitted that the time she spent in jail and her experiences behind bars, particularly with the cell boss, had disciplined her. Having a firm sense of what is right and wrong, Marissa said that she does not want to go back to jail - "I have had enough". David (aged 15) meanwhile, was released on condition that he would become an asset - an informer. "I don't like to be an asset." Knowing that it was wrong, he refused and gained support from an NGO. David ably resisted the temptation of becoming an asset, which could have been his passport for a way out of jail.

In the context of the child rights-based approach to reform and the five key concepts outlined above, the final element to complete the set of guiding principles for the way forward in juvenile justice reform for street children is the prioritisation of areas for reform. In the context of extremely limited resources and competing priorities, there are four areas in which reform would help to break the revolving door cycle of street children caught up in the criminal justice system:

— prevention

— separation of criminal justice and social welfare systems

— diversion

— alternatives to detention

International Human Rights Instruments

There are a series of international instruments in relation to children in the criminal justice system that can be grouped as follows. The shaded instruments are legally binding on states that have ratified them. However, all other guidelines and rules still carry the authority of the UN and can be used to support advocacy based on the legally binding instruments.

1. UN Convention on the Rights of the Child (CRC)

In many ways the CRC is the most important legal instrument in relation to juvenile justice because it is legally binding on all countries except Somalia and the USA. It is therefore more powerful and more widely applicable than some of the other instruments. The most specific articles in relation to juvenile justice are Articles 37 and 40 :

Article 37 prohibits torture, cruel, inhuman, degrading treatment or punishment, capital punishment and life imprisonment, arbitrary or illegal arrest, detention or imprisonment; stipulates that arrest and detention shall only be used as a last resort and for the shortest appropriate period of time; outlines the right of children deprived of their liberty to be treated with humanity, respect and dignity in a manner that takes into account their age, to be separated from adults, to maintain family contact, to have prompt access to legal and other assistance, to challenge the legality of their detention and to expect a prompt decision in relation to any resulting action.

Article 40 more specifically covers the rights of all children accused of infringing the penal law. Thus it covers treatment of the child from the moment an allegation is made, through investigation, arrest, charge, any pre-trial period, trial and sentence. The article requires States Parties to promote a distinctive system of juvenile justice with specific positive rather than punitive aims. It details a list of minimum guarantees for the child and it requires States Parties to set a minimum age of criminal responsibility, to provide measures for dealing with children who may have infringed the penal law without resorting to judicial proceedings and to provide a variety of alternative dispositions to institutional care.

Although the decriminalisation of 'status offences' is not specifically mentioned in the CRC, the Committee on the Rights of the Child is increasingly raising this issue during its country reviews. Furthermore, the CRC's requirement that arrest and detention only be used as a last resort and for the shortest possible time is generally understood to prohibit the routine arrest and detention of children for status offences - an interpretation which the Committee has adopted in some of its concluding observations.

However, bearing in mind the need for a holistic approach and the fact that Articles 37 and 40 do not deal with broader - yet essential - issues of prevention, it is very important to set Articles 37 and 40 in the context of the overall framework of the CRC and its umbrella rights. These include:

— Art. 6 (the right to life, survival and development)

— Art. 3.1 (the best interests of the child as a primary consideration)

— Art. 2 (non-discrimination on any grounds)

— Art. 12 (the right to 'participation')

— Art. 4 (implementation - including of economic, social and cultural rights to the maximum extent of available resources)

This more holistic approach allows a broader scope for lobbying for reform from a child rights-based approach. Other CRC articles pertinent to street children and juvenile justice, including aspects of prevention, are:

— Art. 3.3 (standards of care in institutions and services)

— Art. 9 (separation from parents)

— Art. 13, 14 & 15 (freedom of expression, thought, conscience, religion, association and assembly)

— Art. 16 (right to privacy)

— Art. 17 (access to information / role of the media)

— Art. 20 (special protection and assistance for children deprived of a family environment)

— Art. 23 (children with mental and physical disabilities)

— Art. 24 (health)

— Art. 25 (periodic review of placements)

— Art. 27 (adequate standard of living)

— Art. 28 & 29 (right to, and aims of, education)

— Art. 30 (minority rights)

— Art. 31 (right to rest, leisure and play)

- Art. 32, 33, 34 & 36 (protection from economic exploitation / child labour, substance abuse, sexual exploitation and abuse and other forms of exploitation)
- Art. 39 (recovery and reintegration of victims of all forms of neglect, exploitation or abuse).

UN Riyadh Guidelines for the Prevention of Juvenile Delinquency

The Riyadh Guidelines represent a comprehensive and proactive approach to prevention and social reintegration, detailing social and economic strategies that involve almost every social area: family, school and community, the media, social policy, legislation and juvenile justice administration. Prevention is seen not merely as a matter of tackling negative situations, but rather a means of positively promoting general welfare and well-being. It requires a more proactive approach that should involve "efforts by the entire society to ensure the harmonious development of adolescents".

More particularly, countries are recommended to develop community-based interventions to assist in the prevention of children coming into conflict with the law, and to recognise that 'formal agencies of social control' should be utilised only as a means of last resort. General prevention consists of "comprehensive prevention plans at every governmental level" and should include:

- Mechanisms for the co-ordination of efforts between governmental and non-governmental agencies;
- Continuous monitoring and evaluation;
- Community involvement through a wide range of services and programmes;
- Interdisciplinary co-operation;
- Youth participation in prevention policies and processes.

The Riyadh Guidelines also call for the decriminalization of status offences and recommend that prevention programmes should give priority to children who are at risk of being abandoned, neglected, exploited and abused.

UN Minimum Rules for the Administration of Juvenile Justice: the 'Beijing Rules'

The Beijing Rules provide guidance to states on protecting children's rights and respecting their needs when developing separate and specialised systems of juvenile justice. They were the first international legal instrument to comprehensively detail norms for the administration of juvenile justice with a child rights and child development approach. They pre-date the CRC, are specifically mentioned in the CRC Preamble, and have several of their principles incorporated into the body of the CRC (explaining why Article 40 is by far the longest and most detailed article of the whole Convention).

The Rules encourage:

— The use of diversion from formal hearings to appropriate community programmes;

— Proceedings before any authority to be conducted in the best interests of the child;

— Careful consideration before depriving a juvenile of liberty;

— Specialised training for all personnel dealing with juvenile cases;

— The consideration of release both on apprehension and at the earliest possible occasion thereafter;

— The organisation and promotion of research as a basis for effective planning and policy formation.

According to these Rules, a juvenile justice system should be fair and humane, emphasize the well being of the child and ensure that the reaction of the authorities is proportionate to the circumstances of the offender as well as the offence. The importance of rehabilitation is also stressed, requiring necessary assistance in the form of education, employment or accommodation to be given to the child and calling upon volunteers, voluntary organisations, local institutions and other community resources to assist in that process.

UN Rules for the Protection of Juveniles Deprived of their Liberty: the JDLs

This very detailed instrument sets out standards applicable when a child (any person under the age of 18) is confined to any institution or facility (whether this be penal, correctional, educational or protective and whether the detention be on the grounds of conviction of, or suspicion of, having committed an offence, or simply because the child is deemed 'at risk') by order of any judicial, administrative or other public authority.

In addition, the JDLs include principles that universally define the specific circumstances under which children can be deprived of their liberty, emphasising that deprivation of liberty must be a last resort, for the shortest possible period of time, and limited to exceptional cases. In the context where deprivation of liberty is unavoidable, the following conditions should be fulfilled:

— Priority should be given to a speedy trial to avoid unnecessarily lengthy detention periods;

— Children should not be detained without a valid commitment order;

— Small, open facilities should be established with minimal security measures;

— Deprivation of liberty should only be in facilities which guarantee meaningful activities and programmes promoting the health, self-respect and responsibility of juveniles. Food should be suitably prepared, clean drinking water must be available, bedding should be clean and sanitary installations sufficient, clothing should be suitable for the climate, and preventive and remedial medical care should be adequate;

— Detention facilities should be decentralised to facilitate contact with family members and children should be permitted to leave the facilities for visits to their family homes;

— Education should take place in the community and children should have the opportunity to work within the community;

— Juvenile justice personnel should receive appropriate training. They should respect the child's right to privacy and protect children from any form of abuse or exploitation;

— Qualified independent inspectors should conduct regular inspections.

The JDLs serve as an internationally accepted framework intended to counteract the detrimental effects of deprivation of liberty by ensuring respect for the human rights of children.

UN Resolution 1997/30 - Administration of Juvenile Justice: the 'Vienna Guidelines' (1997)

This UN Resolution (also known as the Vienna Guidelines) provides an overview of information received from governments about how juvenile justice is administered in their countries and in particular about their involvement in drawing up national programmes of action to promote the effective application of international rules and standards in juvenile justice. The document contains as an annex Guidelines for Action on Children in the Criminal Justice System, as elaborated by a meeting of experts held in Vienna in February 1997. This draft programme of action provides a comprehensive set of measures that need to be implemented in order to establish a well-functioning system of juvenile justice administration according to the CRC, Riyadh Guidelines, Beijing Rules and JDLs.

African Charter on the Rights and Welfare of the Child (ACRWC)

When the CRC was written, it was important that it be applicable to countries and cultures across the globe. While this broad description of children s rights is relevant to all people, it became apparent that the situation of the African child was different from other regions. The Organisation for African Unity (now known as the African Union) responded by drafting the ACRWC, which guarantees children's basic rights within the context of African culture. For example, Article 21 of the ACRWC addresses harmful traditional practices common in many African countries that can violate the rights of children, such as corporal punishment, child labour, early marriage and female genital mutilation.

As with the CRC, the ACRWC contains a broad range of socio-economic provisions that can be referred to holistically, as well as the specific juvenile justice provisions of Article 17, 'The Administration of Juvenile Justice', which provides that:

— Every child accused or found guilty of having infringed penal law shall have the right to special treatment in a manner consistent with the child's sense of dignity and worth and which reinforces the child's respect for human rights and fundamental freedoms of others;

— No child who is detained or deprived of his/her liberty shall be subject to torture, inhuman or degrading treatment or punishment;

— Children are separated from adults in their place of detention;

— Every child shall be presumed innocent until proven guilty;

— Every child shall be afforded legal assistance in the preparation of his/her defence;

— The essential aim of treatment during the trial and if found guilty shall be his/her reformation, reintegration into his/her family, and social rehabilitation.

The Convention on the Rights of the Child and the other international guidelines include the following provisions:

— All children should be respected as fully-fledged members of society, with the right to participate in decisions about their own futures, including in official proceedings without discrimination of any kind.

— Children have the same rights to all aspects of due process as those accorded to adults as well as specific rights due to their special status as children.

— Children should be diverted from the formal system of justice wherever appropriate and specifically to avoid labelling as criminals.

— There is a set of minimum standards which should be provided to all juveniles in custody.

— Custodial sentences should be used as a last resort, for the shortest possible time and limited to exceptional cases.

— A variety of non-custodial sentences should be made available, including care, guidance and supervision orders, counselling, probation, foster care, education and vocational training programmes.

— Capital and corporal punishment should be abolished.

— There should be specialised training for personnel involved in the administration of juvenile justice.

— Children have the right to release unless there are specified reasons why this should not be granted.

— Children have the right to measures to promote recovery and reintegration for victims of neglect, exploitation, abuse including torture and ill-treatment, and armed conflict.

— States are obliged to establish a minimum age of criminal responsibility which is not set too low, but reflects children's capacity to reason and understand their own actions.

— States should invest in a comprehensive set of welfare provisions to contribute to preventing juvenile crime. This should include provision for very young children. Provision should involve the government, NGOs, churches, volunteers, etc.

Causes of Street Migration

The causes of street migration are inherently linked with the behaviours and strategies children subsequently use to survive whilst on the streets. These behaviours and strategies in turn impact on their vulnerability and treatment within the criminal justice system. In general, factors which cause girls and boys to leave home to live and work on the streets include:

— poverty

— ruptured family links (including neglect, violence and problems associated with 'reconstructed families')

— urbanisation

— HIV / AIDS

— conflict

— natural disasters

There is clearly an argument that any factor that causes children to come onto the streets automatically puts them at risk of contact with the justice system, but the discussion here will be limited to those factors which are more directly relevant to street children's involvement in the criminal justice system, namely poverty, ruptured family links, urbanisation and HIV / AIDS.

Poverty

The links between poverty and crime are well known , not only in terms of income poverty, but also in the way that poverty can restrict access to services such as education, access to justice, and how it can limit life choices and opportunities. However, it is important to stress that not all poor children become street children: poverty as a push factor in relation to street migration and crime must be seen within the broader context of supportive or non-supportive relationships of an individual child. Likewise, not all street children engage in criminal activities as a means of economic survival.

However, the choices available to children living and working on the streets can be very limited. Even making a deliberate choice not to engage in criminal activities is no guarantee of protection against involvement in the criminal justice system: poverty renders street children powerless to avoid arrest on the grounds of simply being in the wrong place at the wrong time. For those children who do 'choose' to become involved in crime, however, the links between poverty and survival explain clearly why the majority of crimes committed by street children are property-related offences. For example:

— In Malawi, statistics from 1997 show that 68% of registered offences were theft, burglary and robbery; a further 8% were 'vagabond': "a term ... representing obvious cases of street children" ;

— According to the most recently published government statistics on children in conflict with the law in Romania, it would appear that the vast majority are arrested on charges of robbery or theft of private property (84%), and that a massive 95% of all children arrested are boys from urban areas;

— According to research in Nigeria by the NGO Human Development Initiatives as part of the HDI / CSC Street Children and Juvenile Justice Project, between March - April 2003, 70% of boys detained for criminal offences in the Boys' Approved School, Isheri, Lagos, were there on charges of theft ;

— In the Philippines, in 2001, 54% of all crimes committed by children were for theft, a further 21% for 'use of volatile substances', 6% for robbery and 3% for 'dangerous drugs' - far outweighing the remaining 16% made up of physical injuries and rape.

In addition to being a push factor in relation to street migration and involvement in crime, poverty can also affect children's experiences once inside the system. Levels of corruption amongst police and other officials in many countries are particularly damaging to those who are unable to pay the necessary bribes for police 'protection', to prevent arrest, for early release from detention, and for more humane treatment within detention.

Incidents have also been reported of members of the public - with more money than the children - bribing officials to bring heavier penalties against street children, or even to proceed on false charges. Poor families are less likely to have the resources to intervene on behalf of their children, even in terms of maintaining contact through phone calls and travel expenses to visit or attend trials etc., let alone payment of bail and bribes. Furthermore, as with the children themselves - families may be disempowered through illiteracy and lack of status/social connections when dealing with police and judicial officers. Poverty is therefore one of the key links between street migration, survival strategies and treatment in the system.

Violence and Reconstructed Families

As borne out by testimonies from street children in the workshops organised as part of the Street Children and Juvenile Justice Project, ruptured relationships within the family - through neglect, physical, psychological and sexual violence, death, separation, abandonment, imprisonment of parents, divorce, re-marriage and the pressures on female-headed households etc. - play a key role in pushing children to leave home.

When discussing street children and family relationships, as well as appreciating that each child has their own story to tell, it is important to note that there are often significant differences between street-living and street-working children, the latter being more likely to maintain more stable and supportive relationships than those who have chosen - or been forced - to leave home.

There is strong evidence from around the world that violence often constitutes the critical differentiating factor between children who work on the streets, and the relative minority who actually live on the streets.

— According to research conducted in Peru, family violence and child mistreatment was the precipitating factor in 73% of cases of children migrating to the streets.

— 53 % of Guatemalan street children interviewed reported having been abused by a family member.

— Brazil - 1992 research: street-living children reported higher levels of corporal punishment at home (62%), compared to street-working children (23%). The same trend was evident in Ethiopia (1996).

In addition to violence, problems associated with 'reconstructed' families are a significant push factor. Large families resulting from poor family planning, multiple-partner relationships and - in some countries - polygamy, combined with the stresses associated with female-headed households (and increasingly child-headed households in the context of HIV/AIDS) mean that many children are not receiving the economic or emotional support they need for healthy development.

Combined with the weakening of traditional extended family support systems, some of these children are falling through the net. In 're-constructed' families children from previous relationships can end up bearing the brunt of any resulting power shifts within a changing household. This can manifest itself in the following ways: being treated differently in the house to other children, being shouted at and beaten more often, being asked to do a larger share of the work, not being given food or other goods or being made to feel like an intruder. This may be linked to either real pressure on resources or perceived pressure on resources. This resentment can be exacerbated if the child's 'direct' relation is out of the house for long periods of time leaving primary care of the child to the new partner.

Likewise if there is conflict between the child's direct relation and their new partner this can be taken out on the scape-goated child. Once on the streets, an individual child's experience of family relationships will either act as a protective factor, or as a risk factor. Positive family relationships can factor into choices not to get involved in criminal activities whereas ruptured or negative family relationships can predispose them to the opposite.

Ruptured relationships not only render street children more vulnerable to contact with, and abuse within, the criminal justice system due to lack of protection from responsible adults, but absence of parents or guardians to take responsibility for their custody and supervision means that street children are less likely to benefit from diversion programmes and alternatives to detention. It is essential that relationships are placed at the centre of efforts to reform justice systems at every stage, especially in the priority areas of prevention, diversion and alternatives to detention.

Rapid Urbanisation

Rapid and uncontrolled urbanisation is associated with an increase in crime rates while urban migration is often accompanied by disruption of social support networks, fragmentation of communities and increased strain on limited physical and financial resources. Children end up on city streets either having left home directly from rural areas, or via urban or peri-urban slum settlements following family break-up (possibly linked to the stresses of urban life mentioned above) or the need to earn money to take home to such areas.

Particular challenges arise in implementing justice reform in urban areas. It has been questioned whether fragmented and fluctuating urban communities provide a stable enough framework within which to implement the types of community-based traditional and non-formal restorative justice initiatives which have proved successful in rural areas. On the other hand, the 'popular' justice which has flourished in urban areas, such as vigilante violence, is subject to very limited checks or balances. Initiatives on prevention, diversion and alternatives to detention may also be affected in urban areas where street children may not only lack family ties, but also ties to their wider community.

However, the relationship between street children, urbanisation and crime is not simple. It also illustrates how very different situations can be from country to country, city to city and between neighbourhoods. The case study describes the mutually supportive relationship that certain groups of street children have developed with local community residents. The children have devised their own codes of conduct which strictly prohibit stealing from the local community on whom they rely for shelter, protection and the successful running of their small businesses.

In return, the local residents support the children's businesses, protect them from outside threats, and in some cases develop a more 'parental' role with them. Whilst there are also other, less stable groups of street children in the city who are more likely to engage in criminal activity.

HIV / AIDS can act as a push factor for street migration and consequently involvement in the criminal justice system in a number of ways :

— Children may be sent out to work or steal on the streets in order to supplement family income if economically productive adults become unable to work as a consequence of contracting AIDS-related illnesses;

— Children who have been orphaned by AIDS and who are not capable of being supported by extended family and/ or community members (who are themselves put under strain by the pandemic) may end up migrating directly to the streets;

— Children orphaned by AIDS or whose parents are ill with the disease may run away from abusive substitute carers;

— Children orphaned by AIDS might also move to the streets after finding themselves unable to cope with the pressures of looking after younger siblings in a child-headed household;

— Community alienation and stigma following the death of a family member, or as a result of suspected of being HIV positive, may also encourage children to move away from communities;

— "Girls and women in households touched by AIDS and by poverty frequently find their choices and possibilities so diminished that they have to turn for survival to the sex trade or to situations of lodging or work that expose them to sexual abuse and violence, increasing the risk that they themselves will die of AIDS." Human Rights Watch goes on to highlight that in Zambia, for example, police conduct round-ups of sex workers and charge them with loitering or indecent exposure. Usually, the women pay 10,000 kwacha (U.S. $2.30) and are freed in the morning; at other times, the police take the women's money or demand sexual services as payment.

HIV infection - or suspicion of infection - may render street girls and boys vulnerable to even greater discriminatory treatment once within the system. Furthermore, in the case of children orphaned by AIDS who are living and working on the street, the same issues relating to ruptured family links will apply.

Behaviour and Survival Strategies

Having examined some of the key factors that bring children onto the streets and into conflict with the law in the first place, this section will examine four examples of behaviours or survival strategies that girls and boys may engage in whilst on the streets that may further compound their vulnerability to contact with the criminal justice system and negative treatment once within the system.

One of the most common legal provisions discriminating against street children is the legacy of outdated 'vagrancy' legislation left over from colonial times. As an illustration, a study in Bombay reported that an astounding 74.6% of children sent to remand homes were on charges of 'vagrancy' or 'suspicion'. Huge numbers of children are being arrested and locked up simply for being poor and in the wrong place at the wrong time. 'Vagrancy' provisions criminalize poverty and demonstrate the confusion between social welfare and criminal justice systems as detention orders are often framed as 'safe custody' or 'protective custody orders'.

The international human rights community calls for an immediate decriminalisation of 'vagrancy' as well as status offences such as truancy and running away from home. Street children may be arrested on the grounds of 'vagrancy' either individually, in small groups, or in larger numbers as part of more systematic 'round-ups' or 'street sweeps' which are considered separately, below.

Progress has been made in some countries such as Uganda where being a 'rogue' or 'vagabond' have now been decriminalised under the Children's Statute (although this doesn't seem to have had much of an impacted on the ground as demonstrated by the current government policy of routinely rounding up street children). Likeiwse, in the case of Nigeria, although the government declared an amendment to the relevant sections of the Criminal Code in 1989, deeming it unconstitutional for the police to arrest anyone for "wandering" , the police still conduct raids and street children are still being arrested simply for being poor.

On the understanding that substance abuse is linked to individual choice, street children in many countries nevertheless abuse substances for a number of reasons, for example:

— to quell hunger;

— for escapism / to anaesthetise physical or emotional pain;

— as part of peer bonding activities linked to friendship and street gang culture;

— to keep street-living children awake for work and / or alert to possible violence;

— to facilitate sleep during the cold nights.

In many countries street children sniff glue due to its low cost and easy availability and this may be mixed with other substances such as petrol, as is the case in Kenya. Other substances used by street children include alcohol, tobacco, marijuana and, in some places, crack, amphetamines, cough syrups containing alchohol and/or codine, black market prescription pain medications and opium. Cocaine and heroine are generally less common due to prohibitively high prices.

The types of substances used by street children vary greatly, influenced by local circumstances, availability, cultural practices and geography (some countries / areas that lie in processing regions and/or along trafficking routes are particularly badly affected by high levels of drug abuse) and this list is in no way exhaustive or attributable to all countries. However, substance abuse is yet another risk factor that is likely to bring street children into contact with the criminal justice system for the following reasons:

— The practice of using drugs is, in itself, usually criminalized: As reported in 2001, offences in Brazil involving adolescents with drugs make up about 70% of all offences. Whereas middle class young people who consume drugs are considered in the context of a medical approach, young people from the lower classes who sell drugs are seen purely as criminals. This has led to a huge process of criminalisation of poor young people who overpopulate institutions for adolescent offenders.

— Committing crimes such as theft in order to satisfy addiction: "Addiction to glue sniffing is making street children more dependent on substances. This dependency is resulting in an increase in street children carrying out petty thefts. This trend, in the course of time, will lead children to ever more violent and unsocial activities." (Nepal) ; "Crack puts you crazy, like you're flying, and then when you come down, it'll make you do anything to get another fix, even rob your neighbours, your friends, your own family even... it's not like marijuana, which just makes you feel at ease with everybody..."

In terms of treatment in detention, drug addiction and/or withdrawal makes young people more vulnerable to exploitation (sexual abuse, recruitment for criminal activities, recruitment as informers, giving coerced testimony, etc.) by guards or other detainees who may have access to drugs. Also, for street children who engage in substance abuse, this can provide yet another weapon in the police arsenal with which to inflict abuse and humiliation.

Even if particular street children are not actually involved in substance abuse, they are often assumed to be. Populist perceptions that all street children are drug addicts have further restricted their access to basic services, while rendering them more susceptible to verbal abuse and humiliation at the hands of the public and police, regardless of whether not they are actually abusing substances. In addition to substance abuse being yet another a risk factor in relation to street children's contact with, and treatment within, the criminal justice system, it is also worth mentioning that valuable opportunities for counselling and therapy are being wasted throughout the system.

Medical and counselling services in detention are generally poor or non-existent. For example, in India: "Drug abuse and smoking in boys' homes is another major problem. Instead of sensitizing and educating these boys regarding the harmful effects of drugs, and motivating them to go in for de-addiction, the staff penalizes and ridicules them". There is a general failure to provide the necessary educational and rehabilitative programmes required to break the drug-crime cycle at any of the key stages of the system: prevention, diversion or alternatives to detention. This helps to perpetuate the 'revolving door' experiences of many street children on the streets and in detention.

For example, in Guatemala, "there is no detection of psychological issues, no treatment for drug withdrawal, and no programmes for drug addiction. When the children are released in six or twelve months, they haven't been helped. They go out, and they get back on drugs." Furthermore, lack of treatment for withdrawal can be particularly agonizing for children facing short term detention. Without specific services targeted at substance abusers, it is likely that reform efforts will be severely hampered. This is especially true given the immense challenges of working with street children who suffer from addictions: substance abuse interferes with their ability to engage in the 'choice' process that is key to interventions with street children (identifying the choices the child has already made, expanding the choices available to them and empowering the child to make those choices).

Street children are particularly useful to adult criminals for the following reasons:

— They are small enough to climb through windows and small spaces to assist in burglaries, and they are nimble enough to pick-pocket successfully: "I go inside a house first by opening the window in order for the other gang members to go inside and cart away all the things from the house."

— There is a plentiful supply of street children desperate enough (especially if they need money or drugs to support drug habits) to undertake unpleasant or dangerous tasks that adult criminals may be unwilling to perform, - e.g. as 'ants' in cross-border trafficking.

— They are easily threatened and controlled by using a combination 'of 'carrot and stick' approaches -i.e. through violence and intimidation offset with 'protection' and/or small gifts of food or drugs e.g..

— They are expendable and can be easily sacrificed (even killed) or used as scapegoats when an operation goes wrong: e.g. reportedly, street children who are being used as drug couriers and as accomplices to car-theft rings are killed when they learn too much or otherwise become a liability.

— They may be deliberately chosen for being under the age of criminal responsibility and are thus (theoretically) exempt from prosecution if caught.

— They are ideally placed to sell drugs amongst their peers.

The activities they commonly perform include theft (burglary, petty theft and pick-pocketing), commercial sexual exploitation, organised begging and drug vending / trafficking / general 'gopher' jobs for drug gangs. If a street child is arrested along with an adult, they run the risk of being detained and tried alongside them as adults, rather than being processed as a child. Involvement or coercion in adult criminal gangs may take place on an individual level, or in small groups, or as part of a more structured, organised criminal gang, syndicate or trafficking ring, as illustrated by the following examples.

Street Gangs

Street children's involvement in 'gangs' is often associated with criminal behaviour. However, it is extremely important to understand that the nature of gang activity varies greatly on a case by case basis. Just as it can be one of the main risk factors in an individual child's experience of crime, it can also be one of the main protective factors, depending on the nature of the gang, the character of the leader, the local environment, the extent and type of substance abuse engaged in and so on.

Street children join gangs in response to social exclusion, loneliness and the need for protection, in a society that has failed to provide them with their basic physical and emotional needs. In many countries it is a key coping strategy for survival in a hostile environment and the negative aspects of gang involvement must therefore be balanced against the positive ones. Negative aspects include violence (to maintain discipline and assert authority within the hierarchy of the gang as well as taking the form of inter-gang violence), introduction to substance abuse and potential for increased criminal behaviour.

On the other hand, positive aspects of gang involvement include mutual protection from outside threats, a sense of belonging, security and pride (often gained through undergoing harsh initiation rites), friendship and emotional and financial support (gang members may often share resources). Similarly, in the Philippines, the associations that street children form with their peers are often described by the term 'barkada' - a colloquial Filipino word with both positive and negative connotations which can be translated as "friend/s, gang, gangmates, peers, peer group, buddy/buddies, colleagues, and companion/s." Just as this term has both positive and negative connotations, the link between gang membership and crime is inconclusive in the Philippines: results of studies vary, suggesting that the commission of crimes does not necessarily mean that the children in question are part of a gang.

Different studies in the Philippines indicate that statistics for gang membership amongst children in conflict with the law range from 18.2% to 40.9%. Therefore in the Philippines, at least, whether gang membership is a contributory factor to the commission of an offence or not, may depend on the individual experience of the child. This brings us back once again to the importance of an individualized approach to street children.

The importance of gangs or peer groups as support structures for street children should not be underestimated: in the context of the criminal justice system, the potential to capitalize on the positive aspects of gangs, and minimize the negative aspects as much as possible, is key to the relationship-building that needs to underpin prevention as well as diversion efforts. "For the social worker attempting to establish contact with street children, the leader is [...] the key-element for approaching the group, and will often control the extent to which group members access or take advantage of external interventions."

An important feature of street life in Nicaragua and other countries in Central America is the increasing emergence of street gangs. According to one newspaper article from May 2003, "The influence of US gang culture is evident in poor neighbourhoods or barrios across Central America", with over 100 different gangs estimated to operate in Managua, the capital of Nicaragua. Membership in these groups has offered many from the poorer communities a way to fit into the new realities of post-conflict Nicaragua. As one Red Cross worker put it, "If home life is tough, children will look outside the home to get the love and support they need. Look around, you will see all these young kids hanging around the older gang members. They are the role models."

Many gang members agree: "Fundamentally we are friends who hang out together..." explains the leader of one, "We started this gang about five years ago to protect ourselves from other gangs." Most gangs are male only, and often act as the informal leaders of marginalized communities, while others develop into criminal groups and commit a range of offences from kidnapping to violent armed robberies to pay for deep-rooted drug addictions. Gangs will often cross each other in the fight for territory, sometimes for a few city blocks or a football field. Their weapons range from primitive sticks and knives, to home-made 'zip' guns, to AK-47 assault rifles and fragmentation grenades. There is an unofficial curfew restricting many parts of Managua at night and 40,000 gang members were arrested in 2001 alone.

The official response to street gangs in Nicaragua has been a mix of repression and attempts to open a dialogue with gangs and young people, and in Managua police have set up 'prevention committees' to visit gang members and their families. The organisation Ceprev has also worked with more than 3,000 pandilleros (gang members) over the past six years in one district of Managua with the aim of improving their relations with their families. Its director, Monica Zalaquette, says: "The problem is not economic poverty, it is the poverty of our family culture - that's what we have to change."

7

Children in Armed Conflict

The United Nations defines a child soldier as "any person under 18 years of age who is part of any kind of regular or irregular armed force or armed group [acting] in any capacity, including but not limited to cooks, porters, messengers and anyone accompanying such groups."The most widely accepted estimate is that there are currently 300,000 child soldiers worldwide.The recruitment of child soldiers occurs all around the world, yet their use is publicly sanctioned at varying degrees of acceptability.

For instance, more developed countries allow persons under 18 with parental consent to voluntarily join government forces, but only as trainees or cadets performing in limited capacities. Small numbers of youths (under 18) are active in forces associated with the United States, France, Germany, Japan, Australia, New Zealand, and Canada.Youth forces in these developed countries are often characterized as career development programs, and the utilization of youth forces for combat purposes are limited.

The use of child soldiers becomes especially problematic when children are abducted or coerced into joining government, paramilitary or rebel forces, as happens in many third world and developing countries. Children are easy to recruit because of their vulnerability and naïveté, but are often neglected once the conflict is over or when they leave the group. International groups have advocated for the rehabilitation of child soldiers, but children are often overlooked during official implementation.

DDR Programmes

Disarmament, demobilization, and reintegration (DDR) intervention programs are intended to bring security and stability to a region after a conflict. The three phases of DDR programs are sequentially imperative. First, Disarmament requires that combatants are stripped of their weapons, and DDR programs often utilize a trade-in system, such as weapons for cash. Demobilization constitutes the assembly and registration of ex-combatants, orienting former soldiers on the value of the DDR program, and transporting ex-combatants to desired locations at a time that is in-sync with civilian life, such as crop and school cycles. Finally, reintegration ensures social and economic assimilation through the personal empowerment of and financial incentives to excombatants.

Although child soldiers have much to benefit from appropriate DDR programs, they are frequently disregarded in the planning stages of DDR programs and excluded from DDR implementation. These programs predominantly focus on adult male soldiers, rarely include women, and often exclude children.The United Nation's Security Council recognizes the importance of DDR programs for child soldiers and war-affected children, but even with the help of international aid the responsibility and actual implementation of DDR programs ultimately lies with the government of the afflicted country.

The U.N. has taken many steps to protect the rights of children affected by armed conflict. To date, 72 nations have ratified the Optional Protocolto the Convention on the Rights of the Child on children involved in armed conflict, a document that establishes 18 as the minimum age of conscription into the military (Article 2) and requires that members of the military under age 18 be kept out of hostilities by "all feasible measures" (Article 1). This Protocol also requires governments to provide programs for the "psychological recovery and social reintegration" of former child soldiers, where necessary (Article 6).

Unfortunately, ensuring the successful reintegration of former child combatants is rife with complexities. Children who have known only violence are likely to resort to violence when solving personal problems. Those who have been forced to commit atrocities sometimes return to their homes only to be shunned and stigmatized by their own communities. Wars often uproot families, driving entire populations to seek shelter in refugee camps. These camps strain local resources, putting education and jobs out of reach for many refugee children and adults. In these conditions, with a shortage of food and no meaningful activities for children, armed groups find children in refugee camps to be easy recruits.

Some programs, therefore, target the situation of children in refugee camps to prevent children from recruitment, and to advance the process of rejoining society. For example, the International Rescue Committee has developed structures in Indonesia to supplement the local school system in order to provide for the influx of the displaced population.The following is a brief survey of several countries dealing with the problems of conflict, child soldiers, and DDR programs. It is clear that DDR is a long and complicated process, but one that brings about peace and hope for the future, especially for child soldiers.

Since 1980, Liberia has seen cycles of civil war and unstable governments, creating poverty and refugees. As a result, many children have been recruited to fight for government and opposition forces. In 2004, the UN warned that Liberian DDR programs were in funding jeopardy and that camps were "overstretched", potentially preventing 21,000 former child soldiers from receiving treatment.

Since 1983, the Southern People's Liberation Army has used child soldiers in a civil conflict with the Sudanese government. In March 2001, over 2,500 child soldiers were released. They spent four months in U.N. camps receiving education, and medical and psychological care. UNICEF estimates that another 9,000 child soldiers remain in Sudan.

Since 1986, 15,000 children have been abducted by the Lord's Resistance Army, an opposition group to the Ugandan government. Operation Iron Fist was launched by the Ugandan government in an effort to abolish the LRA; however, the policy merely pushed the LRA underground and in doing so, misplaced thousands of Ugandans. In 2003, the International Rescue Committee was able to successfully reunite over 1,500 former child soldiers with their families.

10,000 children have been known to have fought in Sierra Leonean armed forces. In the 1990's the "child armies" established a notorious reputation for brutality. In the summer of 2001, the Revolutionary United Front rebels released 600 child soldiers. The International Rescue Committee provided education, skills training, and psychosocial care to 100 of them. In 2002, a Sierra Leonean entrepreneur began a program to teach former child soldiers computer and programming skills.

Over 6,000 children fight in government and opposition forces around the Congo. In 2001, the U.S. Department of Labor funded $310,000 of an International Labor Organization program to collect vital information on child soldiers in Congo, Democratic Republic of Congo, Burundi, and Rwanda.

Over 7,000 children, including those from neighboring Namibia, were active soldiers in Angolan armed forces until the fighting ended in 2002. In 2003, the Angolan government, UNICEF, and community partners established a framework to provide former child soldiers with physical rehabilitation, psychological recovery, and social reintegration. The government has made plans to build thousands of new classrooms and has enacted goals to increase school attendance by 2015.

In early 2001, the Rwandan Patriotic Army (RPA) clashed with fighters from the neighboring Democratic Republic of Congo. After two weeks of combat, the RPA captured close to 700 child soldiers. Since August 2001, a UNICEF program has provided basic care and rehabilitation services for over 300 children, some as young as 10 years old.

Since 1986, 15,000 children have been abducted by the Lord's Resistance Army, an opposition group to the Ugandan government. Operation Iron Fist was launched by the Ugandan government in an effort to abolish the LRA; however, the policy merely pushed the LRA underground and in doing so, misplaced thousands of Ugandans. In 2003, the International Rescue Committee was able to successfully reunite over 1,500 former child soldiers with their families.

In Palestine's occupied territories, generations of children have been raised in areas of intense conflict. SOS Children, a charity organization for orphan and abandoned children, launched programs in the West Bank to help children affected by the conflict. They have made psychological support available to children in the region, treating about 2,500 children a year, as well as providing homes and primary schooling.

For decades, Afghani children have been known to fight with all forms of armed militias, but exact numbers remain unknown. UNICEF helped refurbish 200 schools, and in March 2002, over 1.5 million children enrolled for school. In early February 2004, UNICEF implemented a new reintegration program for 2,000 former child soldiers, and has plans for 3,000 more by the year's end. The program will create a comprehensive care plan and information database, including psychological and medical treatment, for each soldier.

UNICEF estimates a total of 8,000 child soldiers currently in Afghanistan. Under the tyrannical rule of Saddam Hussein, children aged 10-15 underwent mandatory three-week military training camps. USAID and other partners have undertaken the renovation of Iraq's education facilities while forming an

Iraqi government that will be more protective of children's rights.

In October 2003, UNICEF opened the first of three transit centers, where child soldiers released from the notorious rebel group, Liberation Tigers of Tamil Eelam, can stay for up to three months and receive educational and vocational training before they are to be reunited with their families.

In 1999, it was reported that 3,374 recruits in the government's armed forces had not yet reached 18 years of age. It is difficult to obtain accurate and current information on the use of children in either government armed forces or armed opposition groups. It may be that because the government denies its use of child soldiers, it has neglected to implement any DDR programs for those children that are affected by armed conflict.

As many as 70,000 children are involved in government and opposition armed forces despite national laws protecting children's rights and banning forcible conscription. More than 700 soldiers have been released since 2002 thanks to a program that verified soldiers' and prevented forced recruitment. The government has disbanded training camps used to hold street children and orphans until reaching recruitment age. These children were offered the opportunity to attend non-military training schools when the recruitment program was discontinued in 2000.

Though laws are in place to protect children from forcible recruitment by the government, reports indicate that children as young as 12 have been conscripted to serve in the armed forces. Military recruiters have been accused of aiding underage recruits in seeking false identification documents. In 2000, 10,400 children were estimated to be involved in government forces. There has been an alarming rate of injury and death among young conscripts. In 2002 Paraguay ratified the UN Optional Protocol on child soldiers.

In Rio de Janeiro, children are surrounded by violent drug-related gangs. The death rate due to firearms is comparable to that of a nation at war. Although there are many programs in the area that treat "at risk" children, to terminate the cycle of what has been called "Organized Armed Violence," Brazilian children may benefit from a DDR program that emphasized enhanced education and access to profitable job markets.

Human Rights Watch conservatively estimates that over 11,000 children are fighting with guerilla armies like the Revolutionary Armed Forces of Colombia-People's Army, the Camilist Union-National Liberation Army, and United Self-Defense Forces of Colombia. While in 1999, the Colombian government outlawed and prosecuted the recruitment of children in the military, in 2002, the government sought to expand the military by almost 20,000 troops. The plan called for the recruitment of "peasant soldiers", or in other words, poor children who were lured by economic incentives to join the violent conflict.

Separated Children

As in all situations of armed conflict, it is generally known that the armed conflict in Nepal has left children orphaned or separated from their parents and families. According to CWIN Children and Armed Conflict, January-June 2004, over 2,000 children have been orphaned due to armed conflict. In a 2003 assessment (based on a sample), Save the Children-UK extrapolated that at least 25,000 to 30,000 children may be separated from their families, explaining that it is difficult to determine what portion of these children have been separated due to the armed conflict or due to other reasons. This number is frequently cited as the most reliable estimate available about separated children. It is unclear whether these children have lost one parent or both parents.

Even when just one parent is killed or severely injured, children are left in vulnerable circumstances. They may have to drop out of school to work; or they are threatened by traffickers or face other vulnerable situations. As a result, families may send their children out of villages to district headquarters or to India and Kathmandu as a coping measure. Many such anecdotal stories have been communicated to Watchlist. Separated from their families, children find few alternatives to support their survival once they arrive in urban areas, and become even more vulnerable to exploitation and abuse, according to various news reports, such as "Selling Sex to Survive," published by the Nepali Times in April 2004.

According to one INGO operating in Nepal, a growing number of children are being separated from their families due to the armed conflict and an increasing number of "orphanages" or group homes for conflict-affected children are being set up. One example is the Sahara Children's Home in Nepalgunj, which houses approximately 60 boys and girls. Children who have lost one parent due to the conflict are generally accepted into the institutions, although in some cases the other parent and siblings may remain at home. No regulations currently exist for the operation of these institutions. UNICEF and ILO-IPEC are supporting the Ministry of Women, Children and Social Welfare and the Central Child Welfare Board in developing Comprehensive Minimum Standards for Care of Children in Need of Special Protection, with a special reference to residential care of children.

At least 5,000 children are living and working on the streets in Nepal, primarily in Kathmandu, Pokhara, Dharan, Narayanghat, Butwal and Biratnagar, according to CWIN. CWIN cites many causes for children ending up on the streets, including poverty, intensification of armed conflict and forced displacement due to armed conflict. Once on the streets, these children may take up a variety of odd jobs, such as begging, rag picking, portering and shoe shining. They are faced with hunger, lack of shelter, lack of clothing, vulnerability to trafficking and various forms of exploitation. The use and abuse of alcohol, glue sniffing and drugs are also problems for street children, according to CWIN.

On August 30, 2004, the Kathmandu Post reported that the Defense and Home Ministries have proposed a three-year security and development plan, prepared by the RNA, the Armed Police Force (APF) and Nepal police, which includes a proposal to "manage" the estimated 3,500 street children living in the Kathmandu valley, "Security Agencies Demand Additional Rs 11 Billion." According to the news article, management of street children is necessary because intelligence reports indicate that the Maoists are using street children to trace daily movements of high-level politicians and to transport explosives. No details were provided as to what "management" of street children would entail.

An estimated 2.6 million children are engaged in various forms of child labor in Nepal, according to "Different Forms of Child Labour: The Burning Issue of Child Exploitation in Nepal," which appeared in the October 2003 edition of the Concern, a publication of the Kathmandu-based NGO Concern Nepal. Children work in brick, cigarette and other factories; mines and quarries; agriculture; domestic service; restaurants; shoe cleaning; transportation; construction work; portering; commercial sex work; and other areas. Many organizations, such as Concern Nepal, have documented the often-dangerous labor conditions these young people face.

Years of armed conflict and political unrest have increased this problem, such that children who leave their villages for fear of abduction or recruitment, or in search of a functioning school, may end up in situations where they must work in dangerous conditions in order to survive, including commercial sex work.

For example, in 2001, the ILO-IPEC estimated that over 46,000 children were working as porters in Nepal, with the vast majority carrying loads over long distances and a small number carrying loads over small distances, Nepal: Situation of Child Porters: A Rapid Assessment. The armed conflict has likely increased the number of child porters working in Nepal and made their working conditions increasingly more dangerous. Child porters are particularly vulnerable to injury and death from landmines and UXO, as well as recruitment by Maoists, loss of educational opportunities and other threats directly related to the armed conflict.

The Coalition to Stop the Use of Child Soldiers reports in Child Soldiers Global Report 2004 that Maoist forces use adolescents as porters. Young people between 12 and 18 years old are working as porters for the Maoists in Hangyang, Phulbari, Nidhuradin, Change, Dhungesanghu, Phakumba, Sanku, Sinam and Thumdin VDCs, in Taplejung district, according to the Himalayan Times, "Maoists Using Children as Porters," November 6, 2004. The majority of these child porters are poor boys from the Rai, Limbu or Sherpa communities.

The increase in the number of girls fleeing armed conflict, together with a lack of jobs and poverty, has contributed to a new surge of prostitution in the Kathmandu Valley, according to the Nepali Times article, "Selling Sex to Survive." Much of this activity has shifted to massage parlors, cabin restaurants and cheap lodges, as police have increased vigilance on the streets. Women and girls in cabin restaurants interviewed by the journalist said they had fled their villages for fear of the Maoists who were trying to force them to join military training. The girls also said that some clients force them not to use condoms, or offer to pay higher prices for unprotected sex.

This combination of displacement, prostitution and unprotected sex increases the threat of HIV/AIDS. A reliable source in Nepal described to Watchlist the case of a young girl from Kanchanpur district who fled from her home due to the armed conflict. She eventually found temporary shelter in a hotel, where she was also forced into commercial sex work. After some time, she tested positive for HIV, but was forced to continue the commercial sex work.

Since the outset of the armed conflict, there has been a widespread pattern of "disappearances" by security forces, including children under age 18, as part of the government's counterinsurgency operations, according to AI. Between 1998 and mid-2001, AI recorded 130 "disappearances," including those of six children. Arbitrary detention of children in relation to the armed conflict is also reported.

According to AI, the most common pattern is for individuals suspected of involvement with the Maoists to be arrested by unidentified security personnel, often dressed in civilian clothes, and to be taken to army barracks or police stations, where they are held incommunicado in unacknowledged detention, Nepal: Escalating "Disappearances" Amid a Culture of Impunity, August 2003.

On February 17, 2004, at approximately 6 a.m., an estimated group of 15 security personnel in civilian dress arrested and detained Maina Sunuwar, a 15-year-old schoolgirl of Kharelthok VDC-6, Kavre district, according to Advocacy Forum, Illegal Arrest, Detention and Disappearance of a 15 Year Old Girl, of Kharelthok VDC-6, Kavre by Security Forces, February 19, 2004. The girl was arrested in place of her mother, who was an eyewitness to the rape and killing of her niece and two other children in Pokhari Chauri Village of Kavre district on February 12. When the police arrived at the home of Maina Sunuwar and found her mother to be out of the house, they arrested Maina instead.

In the days and months following Maina's arrest, her family and others made several attempts to locate her. On May 22, 2004, Advocacy Forum received a call from a diplomatic agency that had received a letter from the RNA stating that Maina had been killed after she attempted to escape from army custody. According to Advocacy Forum, the International Committee of the Red Cross (ICRC) also received a similar letter. However, the family members have never received a body or directly received any information about the case. They continue to search for their daughter. During an investigation into a related case, a reliable source reported to Advocacy Forum that Maina had been detained in an army barrack prison and during this detention she had been beaten and tortured.

The following three cases were documented by a reliable local source in Nepal: Nepali Tharu, a 15-year-old boy, permanent resident of Bhimapur-7, Bardiya district, was arrested from his own house by a group of approximately 70 security forces who came from Manpur Barrack on January 7, 2003. At around 1 a.m., while he was sleeping, they surrounded the house on all sides, entered, and arrested him for an unknown reason. His whereabouts remain unknown.

Gopal B.K., a 16-year-old male, permanent resident of Kohalpur-3, Banke district, was arrested at his house by an armed group of approximately 10 to 12 security forces in civilian dress who entered his house after having it cordoned off on April 26, 2002, at around 11 p.m., while he was sleeping. He was allegedly arrested for being a Maoist supporter. Before taking him away, the security forces tortured him. His whereabouts remain unknown.

Rajani Chaudhary, a 16-year-old girl of Suryapatuwa-2, Bardiya district, was arrested by security forces on April 16, 2002, at around midnight, while she was sleeping. A group of approximately five armed security personnel entered and searched the entire house and took her to Thakurdhaur Army Camp. Villagers estimated that 50 to 60 security personnel were present when she was arrested. She has not been seen by anybody since her arrest and her whereabouts remain unknown.

Following release from detention, young people may suffer from severe stress and anxiety. On January 11, 2004, Naresh Maharajan, a 17-year-old boy, committed suicide after learning that the police were planning to arrest him, according to Radjahni "Student Suicide," January 11, 2004. The boy had been detained for three months in 2002 under suspicion of being a Maoist. According to his family, the police had blindfolded him during his entire detention and tortured him in order to solicit names of suspected Maoists.

According to AI, torture, rape and death in police and military custody are reported almost daily.

Bonded Labor

As a remnant of the past feudal economic system, approximately 35,000-100,000 bonded laborers from the impoverished Tharu caste, called Kamaiyas, existed in five districts of Nepal until the government announced their freedom on July 17, 2000. This announcement was made after years of intense activism and lobbying by NGOs such as Backward Society Education (BASE) and others. After the announcement of their freedom, many of the laborers, including children, were evicted by landlords and were forced to live as squatters in temporary transit camps, in government supported camps or in self-erected thatch structures. They have lived with minimal, often insufficient assistance, and suffer from starvation, illness and lack of shelter, clothing and access to education.

In these vulnerable conditions, the camps of former bonded laborers have come under particularly intense pressure by both the Maoists and government forces in relation to the armed conflict. In 2001, local government officials burned down at least three camps in Kailali district, according to the Global IDP Project database. The same year, a delegation by Global Youth Connect reported that a visit to a camp was co-opted by a group of armed Maoists who gave a three-hour lecture on their ideology and solicited for recruits.

Role of International Federation of Red Cross and Red Crescent Societies

Day after day children continue to suffer from the many armed conflicts around the world, be it children recruited as soldiers, children killed, mutilated by land mines and children separated from their families or psychologically affected by these experiences. These children have a shattered childhood. They are of deep concern to the International Federation of Red Cross and Red Crescent Societies.

War affects the socialisation of coming generations, because it introduces new elements in the process of the individuals' social development. In periods of armed conflict, not only do children witness and participate in hostilities; they also suffer physical and mental wounds. These children have to learn to live with experiences such as separation from, or death of parents, interruption of education, the loss of confidence in people, the disintegration of the basic structures of society, loss of moral values, violence and destruction. These experiences affect the child's vision of the future.

As a result of forced displacements and desperate flight from the conflict zones, children find themselves alone, at the mercy of circumstances. Such children may be recruited by the armed forces or rebel groups, become victims of exploitation, violence and sexual abuse. The effects of land mines on children can stunt not only their bodies, but also their psychological, social and educational development. Many are abandoned because of their disabilities and the high costs of rehabilitation, or are discriminated against in their access to education. Others, who may be fortunate enough to receive medical attention, must learn to live with limitations that affect all aspects of their lives.

The International Federation works to improve the situation of the most vulnerable. Child victims of war are the most vulnerable of the vulnerable. Childhood has been stolen from them. Their future is affected by the consequences of their exposure to violent behaviour. Children living in a culture of violence or who are themselves perpetrators of violence are also likely to pose a social problem in civilian society even into future generations. Programmes of the International

Federation provide relief assistance and psychological and social support to facilitate reintegration into normal life to these children.

Programmes give priority to the special needs of unaccompanied children, since in addition to the problems normally faced by other children, they need to be reunited with their families as this constitutes the best environment to help them to overcome their traumatic experiences. Alternative solutions are sought when reunification is not possible. While focusing here on children affected by armed conflict we are also deeply concerned by other issues under item 13, related to the Rights of the Child.

Although the scale is different, nowadays almost all countries are affected by the phenomenon of children living on the street. The concept of street children has entered our vocabulary without being given a precise meaning and covering numerous situations: being orphaned, abandoned by their families, those who have run away for different causes, in many occasions linked with an environment of violence or poverty. To this can be added, more sporadically, specific circumstances such as natural disasters or armed conflicts.

In many countries, guerilla or government military groups force children into military service and used for purposes such as:

— cooks
— messengers
— sex slaves
— spies
— front-line combatants
— suicide bombers
— minefield sweepers

Girls comprise about one-third of the children forced into conflict, making them vulnerable to rape, sexual servitude,

HIV/AIDS, beatings, and unwanted pregnancies. Over the past 10 years, it is estimated that

— two million children have been killed in armed conflicts,

— more than six million children have been disabled

— 20 million have been left homeless

— 300,000 children below the age of 18 currently participate in armed conflicts in more than thirty different countries

Children as young as seven years old have been found participating in armed conflict. The problem is found on nearly every continent, but is most prevalent in Africa and Asia. Many countries in Europe and the Americas still accept children into their armed forces. A UNICEF survey of the genocide in Rwanda revealed that over 95% of the children witnessed massacres, over one-third had seen the murders of family members, and nearly two-thirds were threatened with death. Traumatic experiences of this magnitude will lead to:

— Extreme psychological and emotional trauma

— severe battle wounds

— loss of hearing

— loss of limbs

— blindness

— rejection by family and community

— disease (including HIV/AIDS)

— violence/abuse drug addiction

— rape and unwanted pregnancy

— malnutrition

— death

Throughout history, war has taken a heavy toll on children, but modern conflict affects them like never before. Children frequently are targeted for death, systematic rape, terrorization and ethnic cleansing in many countries. During the 1990s, more than two million children were killed as a result of conflict in more than 30 countries. Of those escaping death:

— more than six million suffered lasting injuries

— approximately 20 million were removed from their homes

— an estimated 100 million had their development interrupted by malnutrition or loss of education

Landmines deployed during these conflicts remain active in the ground and leave behind a legacy of terror that continues to kill innocent civilians and destroy communities. In many conflict ridden countries, children are kidnapped or forcefully conscripted into active military service. This practice occurs in both legitimate government military and nongovernment guerilla groups. In the absence of other work or education, some youth voluntarily join warring factions for survival reasons; others join to seek revenge. More than 300,000 boys and girls under the age of 18 are active soldiers in 34 conflicts around the world. Many have been forced to kill members of their own communities and families.

For example, since 1985 more than 12,000 children have been abducted and forced into combat by a group calling itself the "Lord's Resistance Army" (LRA) in northern Uganda. Moving from village to village, the LRA's soldiers kill other children who try to escape and systematically rape girls and use them as sex slaves. Similarly, guerrillas and paramilitary groups in Colombia abduct children for combat, accounting for up to 30% of some guerrilla units.

In addition to government complicity, kidnappings by guerilla groups and exploitation of poor children, the problem is worsened by the abundance of small arms and light weapons that make it easier for children to be exploited as soldiers. More than artillery, tanks and missiles, light weapons have terrorized people during and after conflicts. One half billion of these light weapons are circulating throughout the world resulting in larger and longer conflicts.

The international community responds to the plight of these children in a number of ways:

— diplomatic intervention

— demobilization efforts

— humanitarian assistance

— U.N. Security Counsel resolutions

— international treaties.

In many cases, there are few methods that effectively protect children in conflict either because governments are unable to do so, or they use child soldiers themselves. Rebel military groups are not obligated by treaties and are not held accountable.

The release of a number of children by government forces in Uganda and rebel troops in Sudan during 2000 and 2001 are very positive developments. On January 21, 2000, over 50 governments met in Geneva to establish an international agreement to prohibit the use of children in armed conflict. The gathering resulted in an approved Optional Protocol to the Convention on the Rights of the Child (CRC). This Protocol establishes 18 as the minimum age for:

— direct participation in hostilities

— compulsory recruitment

— any recruitment or use in hostilities by non-state armed groups

The protocol was adopted unanimously by the United Nations General Assembly on May 25, 2000 and opened for signature in early June.

Current U.S. policy allows for the recruitment of children 17 years of age into the U.S. military as long as parental consent is obtained. According to the U.S. Department of

Defense, 17-year-olds make up less than one half of one percent of active U.S. troops. In July 2002, the U.S. ratified of the Optional Protocol on the Involvement of Children in Armed Conflict. While ratification of this protocol will require little substantive change in U.S. policy, ratification will help create momentum toward universalization of the protocol's standards and enhance the U.S. Government's leadership in the global fight to end these assaults against children.

World Vision's commitment to this issue is rooted in the agency's extensive experience in directly assisting child victims of armed conflict. World Vision provides ongoing emergency relief, post-conflict reconstruction and peace building involvement through all stages of long-term conflicts. In northern Uganda, World Vision operates a center for former child soldiers where they are provided with care and rehabilitation services, and are then reintegrated with their families. This center has rehabilitated more than 5,000 children.

In Colombia, World Vision supports youth that are part of the Children's Peace Movement, which works for an end to the conflict within their own communities. In Cambodia, World Vision supports youth in demining programs, rehabilitation training and business skills training. After a conflict ends, child combatants require special treatment to re-enter society. Former child soldiers need medical attention, psycho-social counseling, education, family reunification assistance and job training.

During prolonged conflicts, World Vision advocates for informal education of noncombatants to help prevent children from stunted development and to help bring a measure of normalcy to those situations. On average, more children die from preventable causes, such as malnutrition and disease, as a result of conflict than children directly participating in conflict. Resources must be set aside to support children affected by conflict, in addition to demobilization and reintegration of child soldiers. World Vision believes that the protection of all children from armed conflict is essential, and addresses this concern through:

— humanitarian assistance to children during and after conflict

— child-focused community work to help address some causes of war

— peace building activities

— advocacy to improve opportunities for children

World Vision emphasizes these recommendations to national governments and international organizations, and focuses on practical steps within a comprehensive approach. World Vision believes that the Convention on the Rights of the Child and the Optional Protocols to the CRC provide a positive framework for action. As a Christian organization, World Vision is called to serve and protect children.

8

Refugee and Asylum-seeking

Some 13 million children are internally displaced within the boundaries of their own countries, others have been forced to flee - often to ill-prepared neighbouring countries with little capacity to support them, where they become refugees. Some refugee children and their families travel further afield to escape the horrors of conflict and constant displacement. Leaving their homes and communities - often in violent and frightening circumstances - has a major impact on children. Not only are their rights to be protected from the effects of conflict abused, but their rights - to education and decent healthcare for example - are also violated.

Children can be physically hurt in the panic and chaos of flight and, as a result of their experiences may be emotionally harmed as well. The health of refugee and displaced children can also be at great risk from malnutrition and diseases, especially measles, malaria, respiratory infections and diarrhoeal disease. In addition, refugee children often live in a situation of constant fear and insecurity - fear which is exacerbated if they have been separated from their families.

UNICEF has been supporting refugee children since its inception in the aftermath of the Second World War. While working to ensure that refugee children's immediate needs are met, A key aspect of UNICEF's approach is to try and create a sense of routine and normality for children who have witnessed traumatic events and fled their homes. Setting up lessons and opportunities to learn and play, even in the most difficult circumstances, is one of the ways UNICEF does this.

In Albania for example, during the exodus from Kosovo in 1999, 'child friendly spaces' were established in some of the refugee camps. These special tented areas are places where children can play, learn and receive health care and support in an area dedicated to them. Child friendly spaces are now routinely used in emergency situations. UNICEF also firmly believes that the best place for children to grow and learn is with their family. Therefore, when children have been separated from their families, UNICEF and its partners have implemented large-scale family tracing programmes.

Following the Rwandan genocide in 1994 and the resulting refugee emergency in the Great Lakes region UNICEF and its partners successfully traced the families of 100,000 children - caring for them before they were reunited. UNICEF UK is extremely concerned about the way child refugees and children seeking asylum are treated in the UK. When the UK Government ratified the UN Convention on the Rights of the Child (CRC) in 1991 it did so with certain reservations. One of these reservations suggests that children involved in asylum proceedings are not guaranteed the same rights as UK children. This runs contrary to one of the key principles of the Convention - that all children, regardless of their background or status are equal. Unequal treatment for this group of children is reflected in many areas of policy and practice.

This includes:

— The provision of vouchers to asylum-seeking parents in need rather than income support. The value of vouchers is less than income support and shops are not allowed to give change for them. Vouchers indicate that asylum-seeking families are 'different', making children a target for abuse when shopping with them, as well as having to travel long distances in search of shops accepting vouchers.

— Children arriving in the UK alone - either because their parents have been killed or because they have been separated from other family members - are not automatically 'looked after' by social services. Many of the 3,350 children who arrived in the UK alone last year were not fostered or accommodated in residential care, and many were thrown out of bed and breakfast accommodation as soon as they reached the age of eighteen. In some cases, children were even detained in adult prisons on arrival. A number of these children have disappeared since arriving in the UK - it is believed that 71 child asylum seekers, the majority girls, disappeared from the care of one local authority between 1995 and 2000. It is feared that they may have been abducted to work as prostitutes overseas.

At the beginning of the 21st Century the children of the world are facing an undeclared assault upon their childhood as they suffer as a result of poverty, sexual exploitation, abuse as well as becoming the innocent victims of wars and the HIV/AIDS epidemics.Ten years ago the UN Convention on the Rights of the Child was adopted and the UN Secretary General has stated "we have no higher priority, no prouder achievement, than our work for the rights of children!"

Millions of children are being orphaned as their parents die of AIDS related illnesses.The figures are unimaginable – already 11 million children in sub-Saharan Africa alone have been orphaned by the AIDS epidemic and reliable sources estimate that by 2010 there will be more than 30 million children orphaned by AIDS decimating parents.

Millions more are being orphaned by poverty and war. The most defenceless victims of the savagery of war are children who are terrorized, often sexually abused, mutilated, forced to participate in killing or enrolled as child soldiers.Ethnic wars target children as they represent the future and in the last 10 years alone 1.5 million children have died in wars. Long after war is over children continue to be traumatized by their brutal experience and to be at risk as the hundreds of thousands of landmines left as a deadly legacy of war continue to maim or kill 800 children each month. Millions of children live their entire childhood in refugee camps.

In many countries orphans are considered as outcasts.Throughout the world millions of children are kept in grossly sub-standard orphanages and other institutions, suffering from inadequate food, clothing, medical care, lack of stimulation and neglect.Medical care for orphans is limited and basic medical supplies are scarce.

Every week 250,000 children die - victims of avoidable disease and malnutrition - and millions more are condemned to suffer poor health and stunted growth.Education is vital to the development of children and is recognized as a universal human right.Yet the unpalatable truthis millions of children inherit a lifelong handicap as they do not receive even a basic education.

WomenAid International regards the current state of affairs as an unacceptable tragedy.Children alone cannot argue for their rights - they need advocates to help them understand their rights, to work actively on their behalf and to build global, regional and national coalitions to ensure the world community is made fully aware of the abuses perpetrated on children.As the second UN Special Session on the Rights of the Child (2001) approaches, "we the people" should demand less rhetoric from our governments and more real action to put rights into practice.All governments should end impunity for those who violate child rights.

A constructive, pro-active partnership between children, adults, all sectors of civil society, child rights and well-being non-governmental and inter-governmental organisations, and all governments is vital if the full rights and well-being of the children of the world are to be secured.

WomenAid International supports projects offering solutions to the problems of the most vulnerable children and families, through prevention, information, out-reach and training activities.Of special focus are children in especially difficult circumstances: - refugee or IDP children, street children, children in conflict with the law or at risk of being in conflict with the law, drug and alcohol addicts and children in institutions.

WomenAid Children of the World Initiative (WCWI) includes:-

— Child Rights and Well-being Advocacy Programme

— Children of the Silk Road Programme: practical assistance projects

— Orphan Kidz OK!: support for orphan focused projects and NGOs working with orphans.

WomenAid Children of the World Initiative (WCWI) aims to allievate suffering of children by:

— Providing urgent relief aid and support for children in distress;

— Promoting child rights advocacy and development and training 'Rights Educators';

— Supporting youth friendly clinics, safe spaces, crisis centres and shelters providing respite to children in crisis, including the provision of crisis telephone help lines;

— Providing street children with access to 'life skills' - resisting peer pressure, problem solving, decision making and negotiation skills; as well as resources available to meet their immediate needs;

— Establishing multi-disciplinary services for children traumatised by war and low-intensity conflicts;

— Increasing awareness of the impact of the HIV/AIDS epidemics upon children;

- — Formulating concrete orphan support policies and empowering orphaned children, fostering the spirit of self-reliance;
- — Mobilising effective community responses and strengthening childcare provision services, promoting the development of new models of care service delivery;
- — Encouraging organisational and institutional capacity building and providing financial and material assistance, as well as training;
- — Implementing rehabilitation and construction programmes;
- — Developing media advocacy programmes to increase public support for the rights of children.

Protection of Separted Children

Separated children are granted special protection under article 22 of the Convention on the Rights of the Child, which guarantees the protection and assistance of all refugee children, "whether unaccompanied or accompanied by his or her parents or by any other person," and calls on states to cooperate with the United Nations and NGOs in this regard. Article 22 also emphasizes the need for family tracing to reunify unaccompanied children with their families. In addition, separated children are entitled to "special protection and assistance" under Article 20. Children separated from their parents are entitled to the same rights as all other children.

Child abuse and exploitation are serious human rights issues that must be addressed. Under the Convention on the Rights of the Child, states are obligated to:

> Take all appropriate legislative, administrative, social and educational measures to protect the child from all forms of physical or mental violence, injury or abuse .

. . while in the care of parent(s), legal guardian(s), or any other person who has the care of the child.

Likewise, under the African Charter on the Rights and Welfare of the Child:

> Every child shall be protected from all forms of economic exploitation and from performing any work that is likely to be hazardous or to interfere with the child's . . . development,
>
> States . . . shall take specific legislative, administrative, social and educational measures to protect the child from all forms of torture, inhuman or degrading treatment and especially physical or mental injury or abuse, neglect or maltreatment including sexual abuse, while in the care of a parent, legal guardian or school authority or any other person who has the care of the child.

UNHCR guidelines on refugee children define unaccompanied minors as, "those who are separated from both parents and are not being cared for by an adult who, by law or custom, is responsible to do so." As stated above, this definition of "unaccompanied minor" is narrower than "separated children," because it does not include the many separated children living with extended family members in the camps. UNHCR policy calls for monitoring of care and protection of all separated children. The rationale for this is twofold: all separated children are entitled to special protection under international law and all separated children might be at risk of neglect, abuse, or exploitation. Nevertheless, UNHCR field staff have provided special protection only to those identified as unaccompanied minors, some 480 in the Guinean camps, excluding the vast majority of separated children. In addition, "unaccompanied" is actually somewhat of a misnomer, as most of these children are not completely on their own but rather are being cared for by other refugee families.

Thousands of refugee children in Guinea became separated from their families during the war, primarily during attacks on their villages or settlements in Sierra Leone. In some cases, children saw the RUF rebels abduct, mutilate, or murder family members. In other cases, families simply scattered during the panic of attacks. Family members, if still alive, may be dispersed across three countries: some may be found in refugee camps in Guinea or in Liberia, while others remain inside Sierra Leone.

Many children told Human Rights Watch that after they were separated from their parents a family or an individual among the thousands fleeing the conflict took them in and brought them to Guinea. Most of the children have become attached to these refugee families, akin to foster families, and refer to their foster mothers and other caregivers as "caretakers." One separated child explained:

I was in Koidu with my father and mother. We went to the bush to hide from the rebels, but they captured my mother and father. I was by a coffee tree when they killed my younger brother. I had no one left, so I ran away and I followed people here [to Guinea]. As I was crying, crying, a woman saw me and I explained my story . . . so the woman took me along with her. I now stay with this forced caretaker.

Adama H., a woman in Massakundou camp who cares for two separated children in addition to six of her own children, told Human Rights Watch:

I found the first child at a village in Kono district of Sierra Leone. I saw a group of people gathered around a sick child with a swollen stomach. I asked the child his name and where his parents were. He replied that his parents were lost in the attack. My youngest child begged me to take the child, carry him home, and maybe he would get better. I gave him some food and medicine. . . . From that time the boy has stayed with me. When I try to ask the boy about his family, he just says they got lost. We fled from village to village to the bush, moving a lot, fleeing the rebels. We didn't find the boy's parents, so we said he could stay with us.

Still other children are staying with a grandparent, aunt or uncle, or extended family member in Guinea. Even though they are with relatives, these children have sometimes been subjected to neglect, abuse, or exploitation, as those with unrelated caregivers have. Community leaders told Human Rights Watch that children cared for by an elderly grandparent can be especially vulnerable, as the elderly are frequently not strong enough to work or provide for them.

Families who care for separated children usually receive limited amounts of additional assistance to meet a child's needs, including a mat for the child to sleep on, medicine if the child is sick, and used clothes for the child to wear. They should also receive a food ration for every separated child living in the household, as they do for all family members. They do not, however, receive compensation for caring for separated children.

While many refugee families who have taken children in have done so with the child's best interest at heart, other families neglect, mistreat, or exploit these children for labor. Given the spontaneous nature with which these care arrangements were formed during the 1998 emergency influx, neither UNHCR nor any other organization had the opportunity to screen caregivers to determine whether they would act in the child's best interests. Better monitoring of existing arrangements, however, as well as screening prior to agency placement of a child with a caregiver should be urgent priorities.

Several children interviewed by Human Rights Watch stay in adolescent-headed households in which children, usually adolescents, provide care for other children. Particular problems may arise for the children being cared for as well as for the adolescents struggling to take on such responsibilities. The lack of special assistance to these households can result in everyone in the household, including young children, having to work to survive. Fatimata S., for example, is a seventeen-year-old girl in the Fangamadou camp who cares for six younger children: four siblings and two separated children she found who are not related to her. Fatimata S. had been pregnant when she fled from her village in Sierra Leone, but she miscarried during the trip to Guinea.

> I get no assistance, I can't go to school. I went to school in Sierra Leone, up to Form III. . . . The older children who stay with me don't go to school. The ten and fourteen year olds, my sisters, take care of domestic work in the house. They make sugar drink to sell in the market so we can buy soap and kerosene. They also work for Guinean citizens sometimes. The younger ones sometimes go to school, but they have to work, too. . . . Sometimes the neighbors give us food, they take pity on us. . . . I want to do something-any job. I'm just sitting idle but have no chance. I would like to be a nurse.

Despite the potential for neglect, abuse, or exploitation of separated children by their caregivers, it is generally in the best interests of the children to remain in family care settings. The solution is not for children to be placed in "children's homes" or "orphanages." As previously noted, there are many caregivers who have provided children with the necessary care and protection; and many who would like to do so were it not for the economic hardship they face. However, because neglect, abuse, and exploitation do exist, UNHCR must continually monitor these cases to ensure that these children receive the assistance they need, with host families that are willing to meet their needs, and that these families do not neglect, abuse, or exploit the children in their care.

Refugee community leaders, many of whom have taken separated children into their homes, repeatedly told Human Rights Watch, "It is part of our tradition for Sierra Leonean families to take in children who are in need; but it is not realistic to expect that they will treat them as well as they treat their own children." Community leaders, social workers, teachers, and separated children interviewed by Human Rights Watch stated that some caregivers use separated children as forced labor, deny them the chance to go to school, and physically and verbally abuse them. Others, who may have the best of intentions, find that they do not receive enough assistance to meet the needs of the separated children in their care. It is probable that many refugee children living with their parents are subjected to similar types of abuse or neglect to varying degrees. However, UNHCR and the Guinean government have a special responsibility to care for separated children under the Convention on the Rights of the Child and pursuant to UNHCR guidelines.

The most common form of labor exploitation separated children are subjected to is domestic labor. Other forms of labor commonly performed by separated children include gathering firewood in the bush and selling goods in the market. Many children also told Human Rights Watch that they sometimes work for Guinean citizens pounding rice or doing other agricultural work, for 300-600 GF or for a little bit of food per day. As noted above, those living in camps near the border with Sierra Leone have also been sent across the border in search of food.

Children described to Human Rights Watch having had the responsibility to provide for others in addition to caring for themselves, and sharing the hardships and work of a household in which everyone struggled for survival. Many, however, described having been exploited by their caregivers and others for whom they were obliged to work. The labor described in most of these cases went far beyond a share of a family's chores or participation in the work undertaken by all in the same household.

Bondu L. is a twelve-year-old girl from Kailahun district who lives with a caregiver named Margaret F. in Massakundou camp. On a typical morning, Bondu L. gets up, sweeps, goes to fetch water, goes to the stream to wash Margaret F.'s children's clothes, then washes dishes from the family's breakfast. Bondu L. said she does not get any breakfast. Afterwards, she gets bulgur wheat, which she pounds and cooks. Bondu L. tries to go to school two or three times a week, but she is not able to go when there is too much domestic work to do. She told Human Rights Watch that she needs books, pens, and a school bag. She does not know how to read. In the evening, the caregiver serves the bulgur Bondu L. prepared to her family, and leaves a little in the pot for Bondu L. to eat alone. Finally, Bondu L. washes up and goes to sleep.

Brama K. is a thirteen-year-old boy from Koidu town. He lives with his aunt and uncle and two cousins who are around his age in Massakundou. Brama K. described a typical day to Human Rights Watch.

I wash my face and go get water. Then I help my aunt with domestic work (sweeping washing dishes, fetching wood, etc.). Sometimes, if there is no money for food, I go to Kissidugou [a nearby town] to sell wood. . . . I make 500-600 GF a day for selling in the market and my aunt tells me what to buy with the money. . . . I go especially on Fridays and Saturdays, but even on school days if we need food. . . . If I am sick, my aunt still forces me to go and sell. If I refuse, then she refuses to feed me. . . . Sometimes she beats me if I say I am sick, she says I am just pretending. . . . My cousins don't come with me, they stay home with their parents.68

Abby T. is a fourteen-year-old girl who lives with her grandmother in Mangay camp. Before she came to Guinea, Abby T. was captured by RUF rebels, who held her for three weeks and raped her. She managed to escape from the rebels, traveled through the bush, and made her way to Fangamadou where she has an uncle. She then went to nearby Mangay camp, to stay with-and take care of-her grandmother and younger siblings who were already there. Abby T. told Human Rights Watch:

In the morning, I fetch water, sweep, and pray. Then I go to find a job for the day working for Guineans. I go towards Ouende-Kenema [a town approximately 15 km away]. Usually I pound rice. I work all day, until evening. I get no food, only 400-500 GF. Sometimes they don't even pay me until the next day, so I have to go back. I will be in the sun until evening. I feel pain all over my body. . . . I don't go to school . . . I want to work. I live with my grandmother and she is very old. I need to take care of her.

Kumba C. is a fifteen-year-old girl in Mangay camp who has crossed the border, at the request of her caregiver, to search for food in Sierra Leone. She told Human Rights Watch:

My problem is that, since I came to Mangay, I don't have anybody. My father was killed and my mother was captured by the rebels. I am living here with a woman. We met in Fangamadou, in Guinea. I went up to her and explained myself and said, "let me stay with you." She accepted, but she treats me bad. She discourages me. I work for her a lot. She never appreciates me. . . .

One time, the caretaker's husband told me to cross the border and if I did he would buy me clothes. I did, but he didn't buy me clothes. I crossed the border twice, went to get food and bring it back. I met the rebels at one village, but they didn't see me. The road is not safe. The rebels are sometimes there in the bush.

A refugee social worker in Mangay camp admitted to Human Rights Watch that he does not have the means to prevent this dangerous practice.

When there is no food, they go across the border. The caretakers ask us for help, but we don't get help from the head office, so there is nothing we can do. . . . Caretakers expect food to support the separated children. But they find that UNHCR does not come with food. The child then becomes a burden. Then they don't get to go to school, they have to go work to get money. Their health conditions are very poor.

Another social worker told Human Rights Watch "Some [separated children] go to school, but when the going gets rough, [the caregivers] prefer to send them across the border."

Psychological Abuse

In addition to the hardships faced by all children in refugee households, and the pattern of labor exploitation and the denial of education particular to separated children, these children are often also subjected to physical and verbal abuse and, in some cases, denied food and medical attention. Many separated children told Human Rights Watch they are beaten by their caregivers on a regular basis; almost all of them said they had been beaten within the week prior to the interview. Children told Human Rights Watch that they are usually beaten because they "waste time" or "make a mistake in their work."

Bondu L., the twelve-year-old girl who lives with a caregiver named Margaret F. in Massakundou, was both forced to work and regularly beaten. She said that Margaret F. beat her with a stick on her back two days before she spoke with Human Rights Watch because she "took too long" gathering firewood. Bondu L. explained to Human Rights Watch, "Margaret F. sometimes gets mad. If I don't work, she starves me. She also flogs me with a stick, over all parts of the body."

Human Rights Watch also found that some caregivers frequently verbally abuse separated children in their care. Most commonly, children said that their caregivers taunted them with the fact that they have been separated from their parents. Thamba M., a fifteen-year-old boy from Kangama in Kono District, lives with a woman named Finda A. in Massakundou camp. When the RUF rebels came to his village in Sierra Leone, he and his parents fled to the bush to hide. But the rebels found them and killed his parents. Only he managed to escape. Thamba M. told Human Rights Watch:

> My caretaker is sometimes nice, but sometimes she is cruel. One nice thing is that sometimes she will clean or do my laundry. But she makes me work. . . . And she beats me. For example, if I refuse to go fetch wood or if I come home late. . . . The last time she beat me was yesterday. She used a

cane and hit my hands and arms. She doesn't beat her own kids . . . Also, she shouts at me sometimes. She yells, "you don't have a mother."

Mameh G. is a nine-year-old girl in Massakundou camp, originally from Makeni. She lost her parents when the RUF rebels attacked her family's hiding place outside of Makeni-her parents fled in a panic and she was left alone. Mameh G. told Human Rights Watch:

> My caretaker gets mad at me sometimes. . . . If I stay at the water pump for too long, my caretaker will get mad and beat me. . . . The last time she beat me was yesterday. She was mad because I went out to the bush to fetch wood and I stayed out too late. ... . She rarely beats her own children. She beats me more. Also, when she gets mad at me she shouts, "you aren't my daughter."

Human Rights Watch also documented several cases of sexual abuse of separated children by members of their host families, as well as economic exploitation of girls-whereby girls feel coerced to work as child prostitutes in order to support themselves and sometimes their families. The issue of sexual abuse and exploitation of girls is discussed separately below.

Several children-including Kumba C., Bondu L., and Brama K., whose stories are described above-told Human Rights Watch that they are only permitted to eat once per day while members of the caregivers' families, like most refugees in Guinea, eat twice. Some separated children also said that they are only given bulgur wheat to eat, whereas the caregivers' families eat rice, Sierra Leoneans' customary staple. In the case of ten-year-old Ami in Fangamadou, her host family made her feel bad about eating at all. She told Human Rights Watch, "When the caretaker's kids eat, they shout at me. When I take food they get mad, so I can only take a little bit. They say, 'I don't know why you were mixed with me to shorten our food.'"

Several social workers told Human Rights Watch that some caregivers will take assistance earmarked for the separated children-including food, medicine, and clothing- and use it for their own families. A nun in Gueckedou town has taken in more than twenty separated children whose needs were not being met by their caregivers, and raises money from private sources to finance her operations. She described what happened to six children before she took them to live with her. Their mother was killed in Sierra Leone and their father was killed in an attack on a refugee settlement near Toumandou in Guinea:

> Their uncle took them from Toumandou. Only he didn't care for them-he took their belongings and abandoned them. I saw them and found a family to take care of them. I gave the family some food and medicine for the children each week. I returned each week to check up on them and it was clear to me that the family was not giving the children any aid or care. Two of them were very sick, on the verge of death. One of them [a seventh sibling] died, and another remained seriously ill. The family didn't give them the medicine I brought and they were not being fed enough. Finally, I had to take the children to live with me.

Denial of Education

Education programs have been available in the refugee camps since 1991 and currently primary education is available in every camp. Approximately 40 percent of refugee children attend school, which-although low by international standards-is similar to the rate among Guinean nationals and is relatively impressive in a refugee crisis of this magnitude. Adolescents, generally from ages twelve to eighteen, and girls of all ages, however, have relatively less access to educational programs. Even when children do enroll in school in the camps, however, they face many obstacles to effective learning. Many of the children Human Rights Watch interviewed who claimed to go to school-even those in advanced grades-were unable to read or write their own names.

The protracted nature of the conflict in Sierra Leone has had a profound impact on the education of Sierra Leonean children, with few receiving uninterrupted schooling due to insecurity, unrest, and displacement. A teacher in Massakundou camp explained to Human Rights Watch:

Lots of children are not going to school. It is even worse because many people in this camp were internally displaced within Sierra Leone during the first years of the war [which has been going on since. So there is more illiteracy as many did not go to school even in Sierra Leone. In addition, many children have been traumatized by the war and that also interferes with their learning.

Many separated children told Human Rights Watch that, although they try to go to school in the camps, they are unable to go on a regular basis because they have work to do. Sahr D. is a fourteen-year-old boy in Massakundou camp. He told Human Rights Watch that he attends school regularly and is in Class III, but he cannot read his own name. He explained:

Some days, there is work to do: fetching wood, washing clothes. Sometimes, after that, it is too late to go to school. . . . The caretaker's children work, too. But they don't have to work every day, like I do. . . . When I grow up, I want to be a carpenter. But I can't go for training to be a carpenter. . . . My caretaker says that, if I went for training, there would be no one left to do the domestic work in the house.

Christiana J., a twelve-year-old girl who spends her days doing domestic labor for her host family, told Human Rights Watch a similar story. "I want to go to school," she said, "but the caretaker doesn't allow me." Another problem is the very limited funding available for programs targeting adolescents. Many camps do not have secondary schools. Children in these camps wishing to attend secondary school must travel to a nearby village, often significant distances away, and pay school fees. Because of language barriers, English speaking Sierra Leonean refugees would have difficulty attending Guinean schools, which are taught in French. In addition, due to budgetary constraints in 1999, UNHCR was forced to eliminate almost all vocational training programs for the refugees. Another problem is that it can be difficult for adolescents lacking primary education to sit in class together with much younger children.

Teachers and other community leaders have remarked that separated girls, in particular, are pulled out of school at age ten to do domestic work. In Kundou-Lengo-Bengo, for example, out of 803 students, approximately 59 percent (472) are boys and approximately 41 percent (331) are girls. However, these percentages do not accurately depict the severity of gender discrepancies as few girls stay in school long enough to reach higher grades. Teachers in the camp explained to Human Rights Watch, "[there are less girls in school] because parents know that girls are more useful in the homes, more careful with small children. They work in the home, sometimes go out for food, or do child care when the mother goes out for food."

This is a common phenomenon in many countries, including Guinea and Sierra Leone. UNICEF has reported that, as of April 1998, 48 percent of all children were enrolled in primary school in Guinea (63 percent boys, 34 percent girls), and 50 percent in Sierra Leone (59 percent boys, 41 percent girls). However, 18 percent of boys, compared to only 6 percent of girls, were enrolled in secondary school in Guinea; and 22 percent of boys, compared to 13 percent of girls, were enrolled in secondary school in Sierra Leone.

Inability to Leave

Many separated children feel bound to remain with their caregivers out of a sense of loyalty for their having taken them in or out of guilt or fear. Community leaders have described labor exploitation of separated children by their caregivers as "a kind of slavery. . . . The child thinks she has to obey, that she can't go anywhere."

Abu B., a twelve-year-old boy from Koidu town, stays with a family he followed to Guinea from Sierra Leone. He, like other many separated children in Guinea, told Human Rights Watch that he feels he has no choice but to remain with an abusive caregiver who does not meet his needs.

> My caretaker is not nice. She doesn't let her daughter work, she makes me do everything . . . She beats me if I refuse to work. Sometimes she beats me for no reason. . . . I want to go to school because I want to be a doctor when I grow up. . . . Sometimes, I don't go to school, though, because the caretaker tells me to sell wood. I can't refuse because I am staying with her.

Mamusu P., a ten-year-old girl, small for her age, lives in Massakundou camp and comes from Koidu town. She stays with a caregiver who forces her to toil all day, only allows her to attend school one day a week, and beats her. Mamusu P. told Human Rights Watch that the caregiver's husband sexually molested her. Mamusu P. has an aunt and a sister who also live in Mangay camp, but told Human Rights Watch she would be afraid to try to leave to go stay with one of them because the caregiver threatened her.

> I won't try to go live with my aunt, because the caretaker said if I try to leave, she will beat me. She doesn't want me to leave because I do the domestic work. . . . What I really want is to stay with my sister. I'm afraid that man will try to touch me again if I stay with the caretaker.

During the interview, the social worker who was translating for Human Rights Watch invited Mamusu P. to come live with her family, but Mamusu P. said she couldn't leave her caregiver.

Role of UNHCR

It is essential to know which children are unaccompanied as children who are not being cared for by their families face a high risk of not receiving proper protection and care. While unaccompanied minors are usually taken care of by other refugees, experience shows that physical and developmental needs are not always met. It is essential that unaccompanied minors be identified as soon as possible because 1) these children require monitoring to make sure that their needs are being met, and 2) tracing for parents and other relatives must begin immediately.

According to its mandate, UNHCR is responsible for identifying separated children, monitoring their care, intervening if they are being abused or their needs are not being met, and tracing their families for eventual reunification. The guidelines on refugee children make clear that UNHCR protection officers, as well as community services officers, should be alert to the plight of separated children:

It may be very difficult to obtain reliable information about what goes on within families or communities. Often, such information reaches field staff as a result of other activities-for example, needs assessments for income generating projects or family reunification processing. Close cooperation between protection and community services staff is necessary, both in the identification of abuse and in deciding on the most appropriate intervention.

Human Rights Watch is concerned that UNHCR has not accorded protection of separated children in Guinea the priority it merits. Human Rights Watch met with many people, ranging from social workers who monitor separated children on a regular basis to senior protection and management staff in UNHCR, who seemed genuinely shocked to learn of abuses against separated children. In addition, social workers told Human Rights Watch that they had had little or no training in monitoring the care and protection of separated children and were surprised to learn that guidelines on refugee children, which they had never seen, existed.

In Guinea, UNHCR has largely delegated its child protection functions to its NGO implementing partners. Two local NGOs in Guinea, Service Chretien d'Animation pour le Developpement des OEuvres Sociales et du Secours (Secados) and CREA, maintain a network of paid refugee social workers in every camp, some of whom have been assigned to work with separated children. Some social workers whom Human Rights Watch met claimed they had not received complete instructions from their supervisors. Many had received little or no training and, as noted above, many were not even aware that UNHCR had guidelines on separated children or refugee children. In addition, social workers in Boudou camp told Human Rights Watch that they had not been paid for over two months and had not received funds or materials necessary to build an office for their work. In an effort to alleviate some of these shortcomings, UNHCR provided funding for an international NGO, IRC, to start a new program for separated children in 1999.

Under UNHCR guidelines as well as the Convention on the Rights of the Child, however, responsibility for protection of separated children falls squarely on UNHCR and on the Guinean government. The following sections discuss shortcomings in the identification of separated children, monitoring of their care, and response to cases of abuse. According to UNHCR's guidelines on refugee children, separated children typically make up 2 to 5 percent of a refugee population. Using this percentage and UNHCR's estimate of 305,000 Sierra Leonean refugees in Guinea, one would expect to find between 6,100 and 15,250 separated children among the refugee population.

As of March 1999, however, UNHCR had only registered 480 separated children. UNHCR staff in the field claimed that there are less genuine unaccompanied minors among Sierra Leonean refugees than typical because, in accordance with Sierra Leonean culture, many children have been taken in by relatives or extended family members and, consequently, do not fall within the technical definition of unaccompanied minors. However, this distinction should be irrelevant because, as has been noted above, UNHCR is responsible for identification and monitoring of all separated children, including those living with extended family members. Human Rights Watch is concerned that, due to the decision not to identify children with extended family members, thousands of children-many of whom are technically unaccompanied minors-are falling through the cracks.

Community services officers at UNHCR told Human Rights Watch that they, together with Secados and CREA, continually seek to identify separated children. However, despite the wide discrepancy between registered and projected figures, this does not appear to be the case in practice. In fact, several social workers interviewed by Human Rights Watch said that identification of additional separated children did not constitute part of their job description. Social workers in five camps introduced Human Rights Watch to children they knew to be separated children, although many of these children were not on their registration lists. UNHCR decided not to use the February 1999 census as a means of identifying separated children but had not made other plans to address the large discrepancy in numbers.

Although there were valid reasons for not using the census, UNHCR failed to take other necessary steps. Furthermore, as noted above, many separated children and other refugees categorized as vulnerable who had originally been registered were actually removed from registration lists as a result of the census and, consequently, have not received any assistance for months. UNHCR community service officers and social workers told Human Rights Watch that they are reluctant to register more separated children because they are concerned that families might lie, claiming that their own children are separated children in an effort to gain more assistance, for example extra clothing. However, it appears that this attitude has led to many children falling through the cracks.

Adama H. cares for two separated children in Massakundou camp as well as six of her own children. Her separated children call her "auntie" although they are not related. Adama H. told Human Rights Watch:

> When we arrived in Guinea, I registered one of the children with CREA. I couldn't register the other one, because she had been admitted to the hospital in nearby Kissidugou town. A social worker came once and gave me a mat, two pieces of clothes, and one soap for the boy whom I registered. One other time, a supply came for vulnerables: four kg of rice, two kg of beans, and ½ liter of oil. By the time the other child came from the hospital, the social workers told me that all the registration slips had been sent to Geneva already. They said I would have to wait for the next registration, but they did not say when that would be. I have never received any assistance for this girl.

Social workers in Massakundou camp told Human Rights Watch that, as far as they knew, there would not be another round of registration. The consequences of failure to register are serious for the children. It means that no one will monitor their care or intervene on their behalf in case of abuse, and that it will be nearly impossible for them to be reunited with their families. In the case of Adama H.'s separated children, the unregistered girl, a thirteen-year-old, told Human Rights Watch she works as a child prostitute with three different men a day because she does not have enough food to eat.

Even when separated children have been identified, UNHCR has not made sufficient efforts to monitor their care and protection. In this regard, UNHCR's guidelines on refugee children provide insufficient instructions for field workers on how to determine whether a child's needs are being met. The guidelines state:

> The quality of their care arrangements should be assessed and monitored . . . Intervention: if children are suspected of being abused, neglected or exploited, the situation must be investigated. . . . For example, when children are used as domestic servants, their developmental needs and needs for affection may be at risk. The guidelines explicitly direct

UNHCR staff to "protect [all] refugee children from employment that is likely to be hazardous to their health or to interfere with their education and development." However, aside from warning that domestic labor exploitation can be hazardous, the guidelines fail to discuss how to monitor for abuse, what indicators of abuse are, or how to respond. The Action for the Rights of the Child training program, discussed above, is in the process of developing a training module on exploitation of refugee children. When the training program is implemented, this should be an important supplement to the guidelines on refugee children, although it focuses primarily on labor and sexual *exploitation rather than other forms of abuse.*

When any abuse of children, including separated children, is discovered, the guidelines on refugee children instruct UNHCR staff to:

Make every effort to protect refugee children from abuse . . . Evidence of torture, physical and sexual assault, abduction and similar violations of the safety and liberty of refugee children call for extraordinary measures. Spare no effort to collect all the relevant facts, including corroborative evidence and identification of the culprits with a view to their apprehension. Retain legal counselors and ensure that offenders are prosecuted. Take measures which may prevent further incidence of such abuse.

The guidelines also note that "an alternative placement may have to be arranged" for separated children if abuse, neglect, or exploitation is suspected. However, in practice, even when social workers do detect mistreatment of separated children, their response is generally insufficient. Refugee social workers have few resources at their disposal and have seldom been able to do more than provide occasional assistance to the child or the family. In some instances, social workers requested assistance for the child from their head office, but never received a response.

Concerned social workers have even been known to offer abused or neglected children food from their own families' rations. Most frequently, social workers told Human Rights Watch that, if maltreatment is suspected, they would approach the caregiver and try to "encourage" him or her to take better care of the child-essentially by attempting to convince them to sympathize with the child's plight.

In some instances, severe cases of abuse of separated children have been reported to the refugee camp chairman. However, in most cases, little has been done in response, even when camp chairmen have attempted to intervene. Abu B., a twelve year old boy in Massakundou camp, stated that he once reported to a CREA social worker about his caregiver who beat him regularly, and the social worker promised to report it to the camp chairman. However, Abu B. had not been informed if his complaint was reported or if any action had been taken in response.

Human Rights Watch field research did not reveal any cases of abuse of a separated child by a caregiver in which the Guinean authorities had intervened. Alternative placement has rarely been arranged for separated children in Guinea. In one case, UNHCR conducted a search for the parents of a fifteen-year-old separated child who had been raped by her uncle in February 1999. As a result, they were able to remove her from her uncle's care and reunify her with her parents in another refugee camp. According to a UNHCR officer, however, social workers, camp leadership, and UNHCR had failed to heed repeated warnings that the uncle was a "risk" and "had his eye" on the girl. No intervention was made to remove her from the abusive household until after the rape was reported.

Family Tracing

According to UNHCR's guidelines on refugee children, family tracing and reunification are a primary goal in dealing with separated children. Tracing for parents or other relatives is essential. Begin tracing as early as possible. In addition to the possibility of family reunion, it can be very important for a child to know that someone is looking for his or her parents. Tracing will depend upon thorough documentation of the child's history, and often upon close cooperation across borders. Coordinate tracing efforts with the International Committee of the Red Cross (ICRC), for example by transmitting a copy of any registration / tracing request. This may increase the chances of locating relatives and avoid duplication of efforts.

Human Rights Watch is concerned that if, as discussed above, many separated children have not been identified or registered as separated children, then no efforts can be made to trace their families. Children who are living with extended family members have a right to tracing and reunification with their parents just as those with unrelated caregivers do.

Various organizations have been involved in tracing the families of Sierra Leonean separated children-including UNHCR, Secados, CREA, and IRC in Guinea and UNICEF and the ICRC in Sierra Leone. IRC, with funding from UNHCR, was planning to begin an aggressive tracing program in Guinea in March 1999, focusing on children under the age of five. Tracing efforts in Guinea, however, have not been systematically coordinated with efforts in Sierra Leone and Liberia, although parents are spread out in all three countries and, according to UNICEF, most of the parents are still in Sierra Leone.

UNICEF, for example, was working to trace the families of separated children inside Sierra Leone but was not doing so in Guinea. The ICRC, likewise, did not play an active role in tracing in Guinea, although its Red Cross Message Network (RCM) in Sierra Leone could be an important source of locating lost family members. It should be noted that, since December 1998, the security situation in Sierra Leone has made it extremely difficult for aid workers to conduct family tracing activities in the country.

UNHCR, UNICEF, members of the International Save the Children Alliance, IRC, and other international agencies are in the process of establishing a regional database to facilitate family reunification in West Africa. However, it has proven difficult to integrate different existing systems that are not compatible with one another. The project, for which planning began in July 1997, has been slow to get off the ground and is not yet operational.

To complicate matters, UNHCR staff in Guinea refer only to children living with extended family members as "separated children." However, this distinction in terminology is not entirely correct, nor is it useful. All children not with their parents, whether they are living with a grandparent or with a total stranger, are considered separated children and all of these are entitled to special protection. Unaccompanied minors are a subset of separated children: the groups are not mutually exclusive.

Domestic labor can be particularly hazardous for children. Human Rights Watch research in Guinea as well as other countries has revealed that child domestic labor is often performed under abusive conditions. Children are frequently required to toil from early morning to late night, and to be on call twenty-four hours a day. While they perform chores that might not normally be hazardous, the long hours exacerbate the negative impact the labor has on the child's well-being. Child domestic servants, particularly girls, are at a high risk of physical abuse and sexual exploitation from their employers. Separated children in Guinea, like child domestic servants in other countries, are rarely compensated for their labor. In addition, child domestic servitude can hamper the child's long-term development. The subservient attitudes required by employers or, in the case of separated children in Guinea, caregivers, can lead to low self-esteem-particularly when other children in the household are treated differently, for example being permitted to go to school.

Pounding rice entails using a heavy wooden pole, often much taller than the child, and pounding rice in a wooden bowl repeatedly. Other social workers are assigned to work with the elderly or victims of sexual abuse. Furthermore, it is likely that there could be even more separated children in Sierra Leonean camps in Guinea than in other refugee situations for two reasons. First, an estimated 65 percent of the refugees are children, as compared to 52 percent worldwide in refugee populations. Second, due to the horrific nature of the conflict in Sierra Leone, more children than usual were separated from their parents.

As has been noted above, separated children is a broad term which applies to all children who have been separated from their parents. Unaccompanied minors, who generally live with unrelated families, are a subset of separated children. For example, many separated children begin to call their caregever's "auntie" out of respect so social workers assume that they are related when they are not. Furthermore, as has been noted above, children with extended family members are often neglected or mistreated just as those with unrelated caregivers are.

Refugee social workers and international aid workers noted that in Guinea, as well as in other refugee situations, refugees have been known to claim their children are separated children or even give their children up so that the children could receive additional assistance.

9

Street Children's Experiences in the Injustice System

Police and Security Guards in Streets

The police may also be guilty of using their power to extort sexual favours, money or free child labour from street children. Harassment, threats, insults, exploitation and physical and sexual abuse may be carried out directly by the police, or by other members of the public with either active or tacit encouragement of the police. The police are therefore doubly responsible for human rights violations - as perpetrators themselves, and for failing to protect children from abuse by others. The children were also encouraged to relate their positive experiences with the police. By far the most common experiences of street children with the police are overwhelmingly negative, characterized by psychological, physical and sexual violence and arbitrary abuse of power, whether on the streets in the context of harassment, or in police stations.

Death Squads

We can see how criminalisation, stereotyping and dehumanisation at collective and individual levels can result in an array of human rights violations. Death squads are at the extreme end of that spectrum. It is important to point out that the state bears responsibility for these actions whether or not they are committed by representatives of the state. Where the perpetrators are state representatives (i.e. uniformed police) –the government's responsibility is direct. Where the perpetrators are non-state actors (i.e. vigilantes, private security firms, offduty police or street gangs), the government is still responsible on the grounds that it has 'failed to protect' its citizens.

Sexual Abuse

Sexual abuse affects both boys and girls. This features strongly in the repertoire of abuse of police power, ranging from use of derogatory language to rape. Sexual activities are often forced through violence or coerced through threats and exploitation.For example in exchange for freedom from arrest or detention, or for police 'protection' from others. Most' of the girls who took part in the project in the Philippines complained of being sexually abused by policemen and the boys also reported being sodomized or forced to perform sexual acts with other children.However, despite the much larger number of boys in the criminal justice system, the plight of girls tends to attract more attention due to their minority status and perceived additional vulnerability.

In Egypt, Human Rights Watch reports that "both girls and boys are at risk for sexual abuse and violence in police custody, but girls and women living on the street face additional pressures to enter into sexual relationships with police even when not in custody. Several girls and women reported that they had entered into relationships with police guarding parks and other public places, because they depended on the police to protect them from sexual violence by other men and boys."

Harassment

Harassment interferes with children's survival strategies,

resulting in loss of earnings and peace of mind. It may also result in other indirect effects such as causing them to be chased from areas of safety, making them more vulnerable to abuse at the hands of others. For example, in Bulgaria:

Bribery, Extortion and Corruption

In addition to extortion of sexual favours, low levels of pay for the police, combined with lack of accountability mechanisms, foster an environment where financial extortion, bribery and corruption are widespread. Powerless street children are especially vulnerable to this kind of abuse, either on the streets or in police cells. For Example, In Pakistan reported that policemen regularly harass the childrens for 'protection' money. That is a bribe that would allow the child in question to continue their survival strategies without interference. Some demand a share of the profits made by child vendors or extort an illegal 'fee' before allowing them to tout for business in their areas of patrol; others simply wait until the child has made a sale, and then snatch the money on the grounds that the child is 'a drug addict' and 'involved in crime'.

Many children are arrested on false charges and then offered release on payment of a fine. Street children also report that police use false arrests to get children to do odd jobs for them. This usually involves the child being detained for a few hours at the police station, during which time they are forced to clean cells and toilets before being thrown back onto the streets without charge.

In Egypt, both girls and boys told Human Rights Watch that police frequently extorted money in exchange for avoiding arrest, securing early release from detention, or gaining access to food during detention. Police officers told Human Rights Watch that they believed street children earned significant sums of money through begging or selling small items, a factor that may have contributed to police targeting such children for extortion during arrest and detention.

Arrest

Arrest may be with a warrant.As part of the project in the Philippines, some of the children indicated that good practice guidelines had been followed and that, their parents were called during interview, they were given food and advice by the police, they were referred to social workers and centres and they were allowed to go home while their cases were in progress. Likewise in Nigeria, children reported that some police helped to settle disputes and care for children.However, examples of negative experiences of the police during arrest unfortunately far outweigh the positive ones, as seen in the following examples.

In Nicaragua, over 20% of the children interviewed for the Street Children and Juvenile Justice Project country report testified that their arresting officers had failed to produce a warrant, court order or give any reason for their action at the time. Of the 44 files reviewed for this project, only 11 were found to have legal orders (warrants), suggesting the remaining 33 were all crimes where the child exhibited 'flagrant guilt'. Most appear to be picked up on charges of 'habitual vagrancy', 'disrespect to authorities' and 'alteration of public order' such as incidents involving drugs and fighting.Contrary to international human rights standards, legislation criminalizing 'truancy', 'running away' and 'vagrancy' may also be in place – to which street children are especially vulnerable.

Preventive arrest is subject to misuse which particularly discriminates against street children. A report from Bangladesh likewise reveals the injustice and abuse of socalled 'protective' or 'safe custody' provisions which have the effect of criminalizing children in need of care and protection: "Hungry children were picked up by the police with the temptation of food. There has been at least one case where the rape victim herself was detained while the assailant was left untouched." According to street children workshop participants in Kenya, reasons why street children are arrested by the police include loitering, carrying illegal weapons e.g. a knife, being caught smoking bhang, refusing to give in to the sexual demands of officers, being rude to or disrespecting police officers on duty, and to promote tourism, "since street children are seen as a nuisance to visitors."

The following statements from street children at the national workshop in Kenya reveal the potential consequences of arbitrary arrest not only for the children involved but also for society as a whole – i.e. the likelihood of encouraging criminality among street children if there is high chance of them being arrested whether innocent or not.

The manner of arrest may also violate human rights standards, for example use of force, unnecessary use of handcuffs or restraints, degrading treatment etc. In Nicaragua, just under half of those being detained reported being beaten by police at the moment of being captured, usually with a combination of fists, truncheons and being threatened with guns.According to the findings of a 1996 research conducted on the rights of the child in Nigeria, 40% of children in criminal custody said that their arrest involved the use or threat of physical force, 34% of a relevant sample size of 147 respondents stated that they had done nothing to warrant the use of force by the police, and 35.4% felt that they had been assaulted because they questioned their arrest or refused to make a statement. One-quarter of the respondents, however, admitted to resisting arrest. In further violation of legislative provisions, 35.8% of the respondents were handcuffed or otherwise restrained at the time of arrest.The use of handcuffs was also highlighted by children themselves who took part in the Street Children and Juvenile Justice Project in Lagos.

In Kenya, the children described being falsely accused and being transported to the police cell either in a lorry or car-boot. Also, "once they have arrested the children, police officers have a tendency of walking around with the children for long hours before reaching [the] police station". In Egypt, children arrested for being "vulnerable to delinquency" are commonly bound with ropes and forced to walk as a group to the station.

Once arrested, family members or guardians are rarely contacted by the police. For example in Nicaragua, 47% of children interviewed suggested that their families had found out about their arrest from sources other than the police (e.g. friends, onlookers) and 18% had no idea whether their family knew about their arrest or not. The children also said that the police never contacted NGOs for assistance in detaining children, despite this being a potentially valuable diversionary measure to reduce the child's contact with the more advanced stages of the justice system.

Humiliation

In Nicaragua, one boy described how he was stripped naked by police, taunted and left in a cell. This humiliation continued when his girlfriend came to the station to visit him, whereupon four officers ridiculed and made fun of him. Amongst the list of practices that street children in Nigeria complained of in relation to the police was the "enforced stripping of clothes even for female children."Street children in Kenya complained of the use of abusive language by the police – for example calling the children prostitutes or children of prostitutes.Likewise, in Egypt, Human Rights Watch reports that the police routinely use obscene and degrading language to humiliate and intimidate children during arrests, especially using terms such as "bastards," "whores," children of "whores" or dogs, or making references to children's mothers' sexual organs – all of which are pointed out as being extremely offensive attacks on family and personal honour in Egyptian society.

The 'regular' arrest and detention of street children on an ad hoc basis, police departments often conduct more extensive and systematic roundups. Common reasons behind the timing of such operations include:

— Cleaning' the streets prior to the arrival of visiting dignitaries to the city, international conferences or similar events;

— To coincide with the tourist season or the promotion of campaigns to encourage tourism;

— Preceding, or immediately following, local or general elections so that politicians are 'seen to be doing something' about the street children 'problem', revealing once again the influence of public opinion.

— As periodic 'new' initiatives, often prompted by the arrival of new personnel trying to 'make their mark' in relevant government departments;

— In order to use the children as scapegoats following high profile crimes in relation to which the public – and media – demand action;

— In response to residents' complaints of an increase in crime in a particular area. Street Children and Juvenile Justice Project pointed to the city askaris as the group that most frequently harass them, but they were also able to recall numerous incidences where personnel from the other forces had worked together on 'street sweeps'.

These apparently arbitrary and often spontaneous operations are reported to take place under cover of darkness, when there is less risk of public censure from passers-by or onlookers. Other sweeps are more carefully timed to coincide with the visit of a dignitary, an international conference or a holiday season in an effort to conceal the problem. From the testimonies of children at the national workshops, street sweeps usually involve beatings, requests for bribes and frequent detentions at police stations for those who refuse. Despite public and media protestations that round-ups are for the benefit of the children involved, especially in the case of systematic, as opposed to random, campaigns, roundups are usually undertaken in the context of the criminal justice system, rather than the social welfare system: the children are picked up by the police and held either in police cells or remand homes, or in separate facilities designated for particular 'street cleaning' campaigns.

Interrogation

Treatment by the police following arrest is often characterised by the same lack of respect for human rights shown on the streets and during arrest. For example, as part of the Street Children and Juvenile Justice project, children in Kenya highlighted the following injustices: rampant beating and torture by police officers; being forced or tortured to admit a crime or offence that they have not committed; changes being made to statements recorded by the police from the time the statement is taken to the time it is presented in court; and police officers not taking time and interest to investigate cases.

The human rights violations and experienced by street children on a daily basis in many countries around the world - are compounded by the general lack of monitoring, accountability and complaints mechanisms in place for the police and private security guards. Reasons are given below.

— Children are unlikely to complain directly to police about police abuse, due to the threat of repercussions and the knowledge that their word will not be taken seriously against that of a police officer;

— Abuses committed by police or security guards whilst in plain clothes can lead to problems in identifying and holding individuals responsible;

— There is often no special disciplinary unit within the police for the registering of complaints against officers, with no guarantee that complaints will be followed up or answered even if they are made;

— Children may not have physical access to the officials responsible for taking complaints, for example when the building has guards who refuse to allow street children to enter, or who require all visitors to show identity documents;

- The police themselves are the ones who make the determination whether or not to level a criminal charge against an officer who is accused of violating the law;
- It is extremely expensive and time consuming for an individual to bring a private criminal action against the police or another individual – often well beyond the means of street children and the NGOs that assist them– a process further hampered by corruption and inefficiency within many domestic court systems;
- Some countries, like Egypt, have no mechanism for private criminal action;
- NGOs are wary of antagonizing the police and jeopardizing their ability to work with street children – there have been cases where NGO involvement in cases has led to them being denied registration to work in the country.

All of these obstacles conspire to make it very difficult to successfully lodge and follow through a complaint against the police force.

Positive Experiences with the Police

The following 'positive' experiences of the police cited by street children in some countries.

- Some of these experiences identified by the children tend to represent the 'least bad' option available in difficult circumstances rather than a proactively 'positive' experience. This reinforces once again the concept of street children's restricted decision making in the face of 'limited choices' and 'nonchoices.

— These comments also demonstrate street children's resilience by showing how they are able to 'look on the bright side' of situations and turn negatives into positives as a coping strategy.

— The police currently represent one of the children's main points of contact for services such as medical attention, food and legal services, and a possible gateway to 'training' of some sort. The implication here is that there is a great lack of such services available by other means: it is unlikely that, given the evidence of a much greater likelihood of encountering negative rather than positive experiences, street children would choose contact with the police for social welfare support.

Some NGOs believe in the value of making use of street children's 'unavoidable' contact with the police by developing the role of the police as referral agents to transfer the children to more suitable services, other NGOs strongly believe that street children's contact with the police should be minimised and avoided altogether to the greatest extent possible. This lack of NGO consensus is the result of different experiences of the police in specific local contexts which can vary not only from country to country, but also from city to city and even from neighbourhood to neighbourhood within the same city.

Regardless of the variations in local contexts in the way in which police sensitization and training projects are delivered, based on the evidence of widespread human rights violations by the police and security guards outlined in this section, it is nevertheless important to highlight how essential such projects are in the reform of justice for street children.

Detention

Detention is most often used and only resort, often for the longest rather than the shortest possible time. Detention starts at the police cell and continues into remand and then usually as a preferred sentencing option. During this time, the child can be subject to multiple forms of abuse. Many street children involved in the juvenile justice system are locked up due to a lack of alternative facilities, their inability to post bail – even if it is offered, and lack of contact with responsible adults to whom they may be released. In the children's recollections, experiences in detention often merged into each other, regardless of the location or stage at which they were detained.

This is indicative that all detention is perceived by children as punitive and that the system fails to distinguish between the innocent and the guilty, between those already convicted and those unfortunate enough to have been picked up regardless of involvement in a crime. For this reason, the experiences related throughout this section from the children's perspectives are considered under the heading of 'detention' in general and are not separated by location or stage of the system unless specifically stated.

Remand Pre-Under-Trial Detention

According to international law, detention before trial "shall be avoided to the extent possible and limited to exceptional circumstances. However, in Pakistan, as of March 2003, out of a total of 2339 children detained in prisons alone in just four regions of Pakistan, 1942 (83%) were under trial, or waiting for their trial to start. In Kenya, the period of detention, although supposedly 24 hours or less, can actually extend to weeks and even months. Delays in processing and constant postponements are common due to lack of transport between the institutions and the court, delays in contacting parents or guardians, unavailability of judicial personnel at weekends, lack of coordination between departments responsible for investigating and writing reports, excessive workloads of probation and social services staff, bureaucracy and general inertia. In some cases, the combination of poor conditions and insecurity as to how long they will remain in the remand home pushes many children into pleading guilty for their crime whether or not this is actually true, simply because to do so usually resolves their case more quickly:

Detention in general can have severe negative impacts on the young person's own perception of themselves, their confidence and self-esteem. In the case of pre-trial detention, many children and young people feel as if they have already been labelled as an offender. This is particularly unfair in the case of street children who, are subject to arbitrary and illegal arrest regardless of whether or not they have committed any crime. Whilst considering the experiences of street children in detention outlined below, it should therefore be remembered that by far the greatest majority of them have not been convicted of a crime, and in many cases, due to the use of the criminal justice system to process social welfare cases, they have not even been detained for being in conflict with the law in the first place.

The right of every child to be separated from adults (unless it is considered in the best interests of the child not to be) is one of the key principles of juvenile justice administration . However, contrary to all of these international standards, it remains a common problem at both pre-/ undertrial and post-trial stages. For example, in Nicaragua, although arrested girls are usually separated by gender, they still often find themselves co-habiting with adult women prisoners due to space restrictions. Similarly, boys are frequently detained in the same cells as adult offenders, particularly in the Department of Managua, which suffers from considerable overcrowding. On average, it was found that just under 25% of the children visited in detention as part of the Street Children and Juvenile Justice Project were confined in the same cells as adults.

Similarly, in Nigeria and the Philippines boys reported that they were detained in the same cell with adult criminals, complaining in the case of the Philippines that they were sexually abused by other inmates and treated as slaves – e.g. they were forced to wash clothes and give massages.In

Pakistan the practice of detaining children with adults is so well entrenched that an attempt by some of the jail authorities at Sukkur Jail to separate boys from the adult prisoners reportedly led to riots inside the prison in the mid-1990s. It was painfully obvious that the rioting adult prisoners had a stake in keeping the children with them. In 1994, a medical examination was conducted of juvenile inmates of the Lahore Camp Jail revealing that 80% of the children had been sexually abused, most of them repeatedly. The jail authorities defended themselves by saying that the police had abused the boys while they were in custody at police stations before being sent to jails.

Physical conditions in Detention

The following case study from India illustrate common complaints about conditions in detention regarding food, healthcare, sanitation, sleeping arrangements, overcrowding and clothing as experienced by street children in detention facilities: Further examples of such problems include Kenya where, as part of this project, children complained of poorly ventilated and overcrowded police cells and overcrowded remand homes. In addition to complaints regarding lack / poor quality of food, lack of medical treatment and clothes, and "having to shave your head as if you had already been sentenced as guilty," the children also highlighted the corruption within Kenyan remand homes.

For example, they spoke of "staff diverting to their own pockets donations brought for the children by well-wishers;" staff colluding with outsiders to illegally engage girls as househelps; staff portraying a positive image of the institutions whenever there are visitors coming to the home; and teachers at the remand homes taking away valuables thatbelong to the children.

In many countries places of detention are little more than warehouses 'completely inadequate for any sort of child rehabilitation or development to take place,'with limited or no education or training facilities. At the worse end of the scale, the boredom of being locked up for most of the day is interspersed with "heavy and punitive labour"labour, beatings and humiliation; at the better end, dedicated staff struggle to provide basic education or vocational skills in difficult conditions with limited equipment and materials.

Sexual abuse, experiences on the street at the hands of the police and private security guards and when held in detention with adults, is also rampant in detention. As part of the Street Children and Juvenile Justice Project, children in Kenya, Pakistan and the Philippines highlighted this as a key complaint. One child at the workshop in Pakistan described being abused by a group of 8 policemen whilst in detention, while another suggested that abuse had become almost a standard practice among some officials. Examples of "severe police brutality" in Bulgaria are given by Human Rights Watch in a 1996 report and include children being beaten with electric shock batons, clubs, chains, rubber hosing, boxing gloves, and a metal rod with a ball at the end of it: "One boy was stripped of his clothing, doused with water, and beaten on the soles of his feet with an electric shock baton."Contrary to international guidelines, corporal punishment is frequently used as a form of discipline in remand homes and approved schools where staff lack understanding and training with regard to non-violent alternatives.

In addition to physical violence, the children also complained of degrading treatment and humiliation. For example, in Kenyan remand homes a degrading search usually conducted on children on arrival at remand homes without due respect gender e.g. a male teacher searching female children, and they have their heads shaved by broken sharp objects such as broken bulbs.Complaints regarding use abusive language are also common, such as police and other staff calling children prostitutes or children of prostitutes, and indicate yet again the extent to which children are degraded within the system. For example:

In Pakistan, degrading and humiliating experiences in juvenile cells in prison include brutal beatings, orders to sweep the floors with cloth strung in sewerage water, sitting crouched with bowed head and gaze locked downwards, use of fetters and solitary confinement.

In Kenya, although on the positive side street children participating in the workshop suggested that in remand homes they were at least assured of food, shelter and limited education, they nevertheless felt that such benefits were often outweighed by the negative aspects.'Positive experiences' in other countries appear to range from merely guaranteeing children basic rights to which they should be entitled anyway, to much more proactive and imaginative efforts by caring staff and authorities to improve services for children even in spite of resource constraints.

In Nigeria the children spoke positively of Social Welfare Officers in some of the homes, explaining that "they are caring; they take us to hospital; they help by going to our homes and talking to our parents; they stay with us and ensure that we are not alone; they take us to their houses." They also pointed out that, although conditions varied, in some schools, the children are "free to go to work for money, go to school, and feed themselves. Girls are spoken to nicely, advised, and treated as it they are the officers' own children."

Trial Hearing and Sentencing

Child's rights researchers in the Philippines as part of this project note that this trial period is often "a blur to the children, with the experiences not as vividly remembered compared to those during arrest or detention." In terms of the worst case scenario, testimonies from children in the Philippines include the following: the progress of cases was very slow due to frequent postponement; those who filed the case against the children do not often appear in court; children were persuaded by judges, lawyers and social workers to admit the charges "in order to speed up trial and enjoy suspended sentence"; they have difficulty in understanding court processes/hearings since the judge usually uses English - a language which these children could not understand.

Many children said that they were handcuffed on the way to and during the hearing, with the restraints removed only when the judge called on them and asked them to stand. Some of them even said that they were afraid of the judge who looked like a vampire to them in his black cape. During the hearings, they were fearful and nervous because they already believe that they have already been convicted. Many of them also felt ashamed for having to wear prisoners' uniforms. In Nicaragua, although there are slow improvements being made to ensure that children are remitted to a judge by the police within 24 hours, in places far away from the headquarters of the Criminal District Court for Adolescents in Managua, it is still not possible to comply with the term established by law.

In Kenya the children complained of: lack of legal representation; no witnesses or evidence presented during trial; use of false accusations and false evidence; children are often given 14 days in remand homes between hearings; they are not given sufficient time to explain their cases; no one seems to understand their problems; children are often forced to admit to an offence they have not committed; they are called bad names e.g. prostitutes.

Recollection of Reintegration

As with the experience of trial, in general the children's recollections of reintegration following detention were remembered less clearly than their experiences on the street and in detention. This may be explained by the fact that relatively few of them feel that they have undergone any 'reintegration' at all as in most cases the revolving door of the justice system has simply chewed them up and spat them back out onto the streets again without any preparation and with even more resentment and alienation from society than before. Detention – used so excessively throughout the system, and often so unjustly as a knee-jerk reaction to 'deal with' street children, regardless of whether or not they have committed a crime – only serves to reinforce separation of the child from protective societal networks and in many cases increases rather than decreases rates of recidivism. It is therefore not surprising that, given the general lack of 'restorative justice' options available at earlier stages of the system, and the lack of resources allocated to reintegration, that interventions at this 'final' stage have so much ground to make up.

Unfortunately, in many instances, children are simply not given the opportunity for reintegration. For example, in Davao City in the Philippines, there have been serious allegations that vigilante groups and informers (closely working with policemen and reportedly with the local government) have actually murdered former children in conflict with the law and that for this reason many children consulted as part of this project in that area preferred to stay in jail. At the less extreme end of the scale, children reported that they are the first to be apprehended if found near a crime scene, even if they are innocent.

Children in Lagos, Nigeria indicated how detention had failed to prepare them for mainstream society, indicating that: the vocational and educational preparation in the institutions are inadequate; government and private sponsors should do more for detained street children; foster parents should be provided for children who cannot trace their parents, rather than detaining them in homes; many children prefer reintegration into their own families where possible and that financial support should be provided to parents. Consultations with children throughout the country revealed a wide range of individual experiences, both positive and negative, but the positive experiences include: a social worker visited them in their homes to know their situation; the police implemented community programmes for children like sports festivals; their families received assistance from local officials; they were accepted by family, friends and neighbours. Civil society organisations play a huge role in reintegration.

10

Police Abuse and Arbitrary Detention

Street children throughout the world are subjected to physical abuse by police or have been murdered outright, as governments treat them as a blight to be eradicated-rather than as children to be nurtured and protected. Attention to street children focused largely on their pressing economic and social plight poverty, lack of shelter, denial of education, AIDS, prostitution, and substance abuse. With the exception of mass killings of street children in Brazil and Colombia, little attention was paid to the police violence and abuse inflicted on these children, or their treatment within the justice system through which they regularly passed.

Civil and political rights violations against street children were largely overlooked, symptomatic of the larger failure to take seriously the full scope of children's rights enshrined in the Convention on the Rights of the Child. The public view of street children in many countries is overwhelmingly negative. The public has often supported efforts to get these children off the street, even though they may result in police round ups, or even murder. There is an alarming tendency by some law enforcement personnel and civilians, business proprietors and their private security firms, to view street children as almost sub-human.

In Bulgaria, Guatemala, India, and Kenya, police violence against street children is pervasive, and impunity is the norm. The failure of law enforcement bodies to promptly and effectively investigate and prosecute cases of abuse against street children allows the violence to continue. Establishing police accountability is further hampered by the fact that street children often have no recourse but to complain directly to police about police abuses. The threat of police reprisals against them serves as a serious deterrent to any child coming forward to testify or make a complaint against an officer.

In Kenya, Human Rights Watch has worked with NGOs and street workers to encourage the establishment of a network for documenting and reporting police abuses against street children, and to improve children's treatment by police. Yet even in Guatemala, where the organization Casa Alianza has been particularly active in this regard and has filed approximately 300 criminal complaints on behalf of street children, only a handful have resulted in prosecutions. Clearly, even where there are advocates willing and able to assist street children in seeking justice, police accountability and an end to the abuses will not be achieved without the commitment of governments. With the exception of killings of street children in Brazil and Colombia, little attention has been paid to the constant police violence and abuse inflicted on these children, or their treatment within the justice system through which they regularly pass. Civil and political rights violations against street children have been largely overlooked, symptomatic of the larger failure to take seriously the full scope of children's rights enshrined in the Convention on the Rights of the Child.

Street children are charged with vague "offenses" such as vagrancy or loitering, or status offenses such as being "in need of protection or discipline," which effectively make children's poverty and homelessness, or status as children, a crime. They are often arbitrarily rounded up and detained simply because they are on the streets and appear to be homeless. Some street children are arrested and jailed because of their involvement in small businesses deemed to be illegal, such as unlicensed hawking, or are accused of petty theft, drug related crimes, or prostitution. Some are arrested as scapegoats, or in order to finger or catch others. Many police believe street children have information about crimes committed on their beat, or attribute crimes in the area to street children directly, imputing criminal associations and criminal activities to street children generally.

For whatever the alleged crime, from vagrancy to theft, street children face frequent roundups, being chased down by police and hauled off to jails. They are often held for excessive periods of time, for days and even weeks, under horrendous conditions, and usually mixed with adults. In jails they may be further beaten by police, or forced to pay bribes in order to be released.From jails, street children may be transferred eventually to long-term penal institutions, sometimes euphemistically called "homes" or "schools" where they may languish, out of sight, for years. Street children rarely have family members or other concerned adults able to intervene on their behalf. Family members are often not informed of their children's arrest and detention in the first place. Contrary to popular belief, many street children actually have family members and homes to which they might return periodically, and are not orphans.

Human Rights Watch has attempted to highlight the serious nature of the human rights abuses committed against street children by law enforcement personnel in Brazil, Bulgaria, Colombia, Guatemala, India, Kenya, and Sudan, and on the gross lack of police accountability for abusive actions. Widespread impunity and the slowness of law enforcement bodies to investigate and prosecute cases of abuses against street children has allowed violence against street children to continue unchecked. Establishing police accountability is further hampered by the fact that street children often have no alternative but to complain directly to police about police abuses. The threat of police reprisals acts as a serious deterrent to any child coming forward to testify or make a complaint against an officer. After witnessing and experiencing acts of brutality inflicted by law enforcement, it is no surprise that street children place little faith in the system to bring their tormentors to justice.

Even in Guatemala, where the NGO Casa Alianza has been singularly active in seeking police accountability for the rape, torture, and killing of street children, only a handful of prosecutions have resulted out of hundreds of criminal complaints filed. Frustrated with the failure of the national judicial system to address these cases, Casa Alianza and the Center for Justice and International Law brought a landmark case, involving the police killings of five street youth in 1990, to the Inter-American Commission on Human Rights, and subsequently to the Inter American Court of Human Rights, where the case is now pending. Still, violence against street children in Guatemala continues and the government is as slow as ever in responding to the abuse. The example of Guatemala demonstrates that even where there are strong advocates willing and able to assist street children in seeking justice, without the commitment of governments, the judiciary, and most importantly law enforcement itself, the abuses will continue.

Children's Rights

In 1999, the convention stood as the single most widely ratified treaty in existence. Adopted by the United Nations General Assembly on November 20, 1989, the promises of this historic document included children's rights to life; to be free from discrimination; to be free from military recruitment and to be protected in armed conflicts; to be protected from torture or cruel, inhuman, or degrading treatment or punishment; to be free from arbitrary deprivation of liberty; to special treatment within the justice system; and the rights to education, health care, an adequate standard of living, and freedom from economic exploitation and other abuse. The decade since the adoption of the Convention on the Rights of the Child was marked by some significant advances on behalf of children. Many countries used the convention as the basis on which to revise domestic legislation and improve protections for children, or have appointed pecial ombudspersons or envoys for children.

A 1996 United Nations report on the impact of armed conflict on children raised international concern about the plight of children in war, prompting varied initiatives to end the use of child soldiers and other wartime abuses. The number of children killed every year by antipersonnel landmines dropped in the wake of massive efforts to end the use of the weapon and the adoption of the1997 Mine Ban Treaty. The adoption of the statute for the International Criminal Court held out the hope of ending the impunity of those responsible for the recruitment of children under the age of fifteen in armed conflicts, as well as those who commit other war crimes, crimes against humanity, and genocide. The armed conflicts that raged in all quarters of the world produced appalling abuses of children's rights. Hundreds of thousands of children were pressed into service as soldiers. Millions became refugees displaced from their homes, often separated from their families, their future and safety uncertain.

Street children on every continent endured harassment and physical abuse by police. Even schools, intended to promote the healthy development of children, were the site of abuse. In some countries, the use of corporal punishment by teachers resulted in injury and even death. In others, gay and lesbian students endured harassment and violence by their peers while school authorities failed to intervene. Millions of children had no access to education, worked long hours under hazardous conditions, or languished in orphanages or detention centers where they endured inhumane conditions and daily assaults on their dignity, in violation of the rights guaranteed to them under the convention.

The tenth anniversary of the Convention on the Rights of the Child marked an important milestone. The rights of children were recognized as never before. But it also posed a challenge for governments and civil society to take stronger action to implement its provisions, strengthen protections, and fulfill the promises made to the children of the world.

Use of Children as Soldiers

In dozens of countries around the world, children were direct participants in war. Denied a childhood and often subjected to horrific violence, some 300,000 children served as soldiers in current armed conflicts. These young combatants participated in all aspects of contemporary warfare. They wielded AK-47s and M-16s on the front lines of combat, served as human mine detectors, participated in suicide missions, carried supplies, and acted as spies, messengers, or lookouts.

Physically vulnerable and easily intimidated, children typically made obedient soldiers. Many were abducted or recruited by force and often compelled to follow orders under threat of death. Others joined armed groups out of desperation. As society broke down during conflict, leaving children with no access to school, driving them from their homes, or separating them from family members, many children perceived armed groups as their best chance for survival. Others sought escape from poverty or joined military forces to avenge family members who had been killed.

Child soldiers were used in more than thirty countries around the world. In Sierra Leone, thousands of children abducted by rebel forces witnessed and participated in horrible atrocities against civilians, including beheadings, amputations, rape, and burning people alive. Children forced to take part in atrocities were often given drugs to overcome their fear or reluctance to do so. In Colombia, tens of thousands of children were used as soldiers by all sides to the country's ongoing bloody conflict. In southern Lebanon, when boys fled to desert or avoid conscription by the South Lebanon Army, an Israeli auxiliary militia, their entire families were subject to expulsion from the occupied zone.

Girls were also used as soldiers in many parts of the world. In addition to combat duties, Human Rights Watch found that girls were subject to sexual abuse and taken as "wives" by armed groups in Angola, Sierra Leone, and Uganda. Girls who were impregnated by rebel commanders were sometimes forced to strap their babies on their backs shortly after giving birth and take up arms against opposing forces. Some governments took positive steps. Colombia significantly reduced the number of under-eighteens in its national security forces after pledging to uphold a minimum recruitment age of eighteen.The U.K. government made a military aid agreement to the Sierra Leonean government contingent on non recruitment of children and the demobilization and rehabilitation of former child soldiers, although it continued to use sixteen-and seventeen-year-olds in its own military force.

Under the Convention on the Rights of the Child, the general definition of a child is any person under the age of eighteen. However, Article 38, governing children and armed conflict, uses fifteen as the minimum age for recruitment and participation in hostilities. This low standard of protection remained a glaring and troubling anomaly among the convention's other strong provisions. Several years after the convention's adoption, a U.N. working group was created to draft an optional protocol to the convention that would raise the minimum age for recruitment and participation in hostilities to eighteen.

In 1998, the recruitment of children under the age of fifteen and their use in hostilities was identified as a war crime in the statute of the International Criminal Court. Once established, the court will have jurisdiction to prosecute those responsible for the use of child soldiers. The use of children as soldiers was also recognized as a child labor issue. A labor treaty banning the worst forms of child labor, adopted in June 1999, prohibited the forced recruitment of children for use in armed conflicts. Established by six international NGOs, the coalition worked with national campaigns in more than thirty countries around the world, mobilizing political will and public pressure to end the use of children as soldiers. Despite this growing momentum, efforts to stop the use of child soldier did not reach fruition. Recruitment of child soldiers continued around the world, those responsible for their recruitment escaped justice, and key governments continued to resist efforts to establish and enforce the prohibitions necessary to end the use of children as soldiers.

The International Criminal Court (ICC)

In Rome, On July 17, 1998, delegates representing 160 countries voted by an overwhelming majority to establish a permanent International Criminal Court (ICC) to try persons charged with committing war crimes, crimes against humanity, and genocide. Upon its establishment, the court will provide a powerful deterrent to the conscription, enlistment, or use in hostilities of children under the age of fifteen years conduct defined as a war crime in the ICC statute. The statute also included other important measures to protect children in armed conflict: it recognized intentional attacks on educational institutions as a war crime, provided special arrangements for children as victims and witnesses, and exempted children below the age of eighteen from prosecution by the court.

Delegates reconvened at the United Nations headquarters for three weeks in July and August of 1999 to draft the rules of procedure and evidence for the court and the elements of the crimes covered by the statute. Two proposals introduced by the United States and by Costa Rica, Switzerland, and Hungary would have restricted the scope of the statute's provisions on the war crime of conscripting, enlisting, or using children in hostilities. The U.S. proposal would have required the prosecutor to prove that the accused knew the child in question was below the age of fifteen. The proposal by Costa Rica, Switzerland, and Hungary would have required a showing that the accused knew of or was "willfully blind" to the child's minority. In addition, both proposals would have required proof that the accused caused the child's conscription, enlistment, or use in hostilities.

Human Rights Watch said that the court should have jurisdiction over cases in which the accused recklessly failed to take steps to ascertain the child's age. Human Rights Watch also pointed out that encouragement, acceptance, or authorization of a child's enlistment or participation in hostilities should be sufficient conduct for the court to exercise jurisdiction.

Conflict with the Law

In some countries, reforms were under consideration but had not yet been enacted into law. Efforts to reform Guatemala's juvenile justice system stalled in early 1998, when the government delayed for the second time the implementation of a new Minors' Code that would represent a vast improvement over current legislation. Among other protections, the code would guarantee the right to a lawyer at government expense to children accused of crimes, would forbid placing children in protective custody in juvenile detention centers, and would end the practice of imprisoning children for "status offenses" such as running away or being homeless. A similar proposal was pending in Venezuela.

Brazil, one of the first to reform its national laws comprehensively in response to the Convention on the Rights of the Child, adopted its Children's and Adolescent's Statute in 1990. Ecuador and Peru passed Juveniles Acts in 1992, Mexico adopted its Law on the Treatment of Juvenile Offenders in 1991, El Salvador enacted a new juvenile justice law in 1995, and Nicaragua adopted a Children's Legal Code in 1998 after a two-year delay Grounded in the principle that all children possessed rights which must be respected by the state, these reform efforts represented a significant departure from earlier legislation directed exclusively at "minors" in "irregular situations" and in need of protection. Nevertheless, a large number of countries in the region and elsewhere in the world had not taken action to bring their legislation into compliance with the convention. In the Americas, Argentina and Paraguay, among others, retained outdated juvenile laws that did not adequately protect children's rights; in Colombia, the 1989 Juveniles Act was little more than a repackaging of earlier legislation.

Where legislative reforms had taken place, the practices in many countries fell far short of their new legal standards. In Mexico, as the U.N. Committee on the Rights of the Child observed in 1994, a large number of children complained of ill-treatment at the hands of police and military personnel. In Nicaragua, although the law provided that children should be housed separately from adults, children continued to be commingled with adults because of the lack of appropriate juvenile facilities. In the Dominican Republic, the government's near-complete failure to enforce the country's 1994 minor's code led to the confinement of hundreds of adolescents in adult prisons, where youth were not afforded sufficient protection, education, or rehabilitation.

Trial and Sentencing Practices

Human Rights Watch documented systemic failures to guarantee children legal rpresentation and otherwise provide them with fair hearings in Brazil, Bulgaria, Guatemala, India, Jamaica, Kenya, Pakistan, and Russia. Of particular concern were sentences that violated the International principle that deprivation of liberty should be a measure of last resort and for the shortest appropriate period of time and prohibiting measures that constituted torture or cruel, inhuman, or degrading treatment.

In many cases, children were detained arbitrarily or indefinitely on the basis of vague legalprovisions. In Kenya, Human Rights Watch's investigation found that street children were committed for years to juvenile correctional institutions after they were found to be "in need of protection or discipline" in summary proceedings without legal representation. Similarly, in Paraguay and other countries in the Americas that had not brought their laws into conformity with the Convention on the Rights of the Child, children were detained on the ill-defined basis that they were in a "state of danger."

In some cases, state authorities simply flouted laws intended to protect the due process rights of juveniles. Investigation in 1996, Bulgaria found that children were often detained in police lockups far longer than the legally permissible periods, without being formally charged, and without any judicial review. In India, police regularly detained street children without giving them any grounds for arrest and failed to bring them before magistrates in the time period required under India's Juvenile Justice Act.

In Jamaica, Trinidad and Tobago, and elsewhere in the English-speaking Caribbean, juvenile court judges were authorized to impose sentences of flogging for certain crimes. In addition, children in detention in these countries were subjected to corporal punishment as a method of discipline. Similarly, Pakistan's Hudood Ordinances permitted judges to include whipping, usually between fifteen and thirty lashes, as part of children's sentences; in practice, however, that portion of the sentence appeared to be routinely overturned on appeal.

In Kenya too, corporal punishment by cane or rod is authorized by law in sentencing children and as a disciplinary measure in correctional institutions for children. The imposition of corporal punishment is prohibited by international standards. Moreover, the U.N. bodies charged with monitoring states parties' compliance with the

International Covenant on Civil and Political Rights, the Convention against Torture and Other Cruel, Inhuman or Degrading Treatment or Punishment, and the Convention on the Rights of the Child have all indicated that corporal punishment is incompatible with those human rights treaties.

Conditions of Confinement

The practice of holding children in adult facilities, common in many parts of the world, exposed children to abusive conditions including physical and sexual abuse far worse than those they would have experienced in juvenile facilities. In Cambodia, for example, children were housed indiscriminately with adult detainees and reportedly sexually abused and subjected to other forms of physical and psychological violence at the hands of adults. In Guatemala, Human Rights Watch interviewed children commingled with adults who reported beatings and rapes by adults, and being forced to give up their clothing to adults, or to pay money to adults in order to get a place to sleep.

Children were subjected to appalling conditions of confinement that violated international standards. Often held with adults and subjected to beatings at the hands of guards and other detainees, children in confinement were frequently denied adequate food, medical and mental health care, education, and access to basic sanitary facilities. All of these children would eventually return to society, meaning that the failure to prepare them for their return was shortsighted as well as cruel, carrying enormous social costs.

Many youth in the United States were charged in the adult criminal system under state laws that made it easier for children to be tried as adults. Between 1992 and 1998, at least forty U.S. states adopted such legislation. A similar measure was pending at the federal level in 1999. Forty-two U.S. states detained youth in adult jails while they awaited trial. As a result, whether or not they would ultimately be found innocent, many children faced the prospect of spending six months to one year or more of their formative adolescent years behind bars pending trial.

In the U.S. state of Maryland, Human Rights Watch found that youth held in adult jails were subjected to the risk of violence at the hands of other juveniles and, in some facilities, from adult detainees. These risks were particularly high in the Baltimore City Detention Center, where some 150 adolescents faced daily risks to their personal safety, at times from fights condoned or even organized by corrections officers. Disciplinary measures there often appeared to be arbitrary and excessive, with many youth, and sometimes the entire juvenile section, receiving the maximum sanction of ninety days confinement to their cells. With few exceptions, the Maryland jails visited by Human Rights Watch suffered from serious deficiencies in the amount of education provided, a dearth of age-appropriate recreational activities, and an apparent lack of specialized training programs for staff in adolescent development and behavior management. In addition, children in all facilities reported that they did not receive enough to eat.

The South African government initiated a program in November 1997 to keep children out of the country's prisons, although delays in implementing the program threatened its effectiveness. Another deficiency in the program was that children between the ages of fifteen and eighteen who were accused of the most serious crimes would remain in adult prisons. In Bangladesh, the government accepted the need for improvements in conditions of confinement for children in conflict with the law, in particular noting in its 1997 supplementary report to the Committee on the Rights of the Child that "Too many minors are held in jails and police stations alongside adult offenders." In Jamaica, following the July 1999 release of the findings of a Human Rights Watch investigation of the practice of detaining children in filthy and overcrowded police lockups, the government announced that it would move all detained children to juvenile facilities.

Death Penalty and Juvenile Offenders

The ten executions of juvenile offenders in the United States represented more than half the known worldwide total, making it the worldwide leader in executing juvenile offenders. Five executions took place in the U.S. state of Texas; the states of Georgia, Louisiana, Missouri, Oklahoma, and Virginia each executed one juvenile offender in the same period. Sean Sellers, executed in Oklahoma in February 1999, was the first sixteen-year-old offender to be put to death in the United States in forty years. Seventy juvenile offenders were on death row in the United States as of July 1, 1999.

In positive developments, the highest court of the U.S. state of Florida ruled that the imposition of the death penalty on sixteen-year-old offenders was cruel and unusual punishment in violation of the state constitution; and effective October 1, 1999, the state of Montana abolished the death penalty for those under eighteen at the time of their crimes. As a result, nineteen of the forty U.S. states that permit capital punishment now prohibit the execution of offenders who were sixteen years old and younger at the time of their crimes; fifteen of the remaining twenty-one states restrict that punishment to adult offenders.

Kinds of Orphans

Throughout the world an unknown number of children, most likely in the hundreds of thousands, if not millions, were kept in orphanages and non-penal custodial institutions. Many were condemned to live a grim existence, and subjected to shocking and at times deadly levels of abuse and neglect.

Many children who ended up in orphanages had at least one living parent but had been abandoned because their families were poor, jobless, ill, or in trouble with the law. In countries that had restrictive population control policies, or where cultural traditions valued boys more highly than girls, babies and girls in particular were abandoned. In other cases, medical personnel pressured parents at birth to give up children born with disabilities, claiming that parents would be ostracized for raising a disabled child. For this reason, healthy children who were given up for financial or domestic reasons were often assumed to be "defective."

In Russia, children were abandoned to the state at a rate of more than 100,000 per year. In a 1998 report, Abandoned by the State: Cruelty and Neglect in Russian Orphanages , Human Rights Watch found that children in Russian orphanages were exposed to appalling levels of cruelty and neglect. They were beaten, locked in freezing rooms for days at a time, or sexually abused, and often subjected to degrading treatment by staff. Russian babies classified as "disabled" were segregated into separate rooms where they were changed and fed, but were bereft of stimulation and without medical care. At age four, these and other children faced another grave violation of their rights: those labeled retarded or "oligophrenic" were sent to locked and isolated "psycho-neurological internats," which were little better than prisons.Considered "ineducable," children in these facilities were restrained in cloth sacks, tethered to furniture, denied stimulation, and sometimes left to lie half-naked in their own filth. Orphans who survived to the age of eighteen moved on to an adult internat, removed from public view.

In the orphanages, children were physically punished not only by school staff, but by older children who were encouraged to beat up, bully, and intimidate younger ones. The use of cruel, inhuman and degrading treatment and punishment, including corporal punishment, public shaming, and isolation in freezing rooms was not uncommon. Children had no means of redress or complaint to protest ill-treatment and abuse at the hands of staff and older children. The practice of holding children in adult facilities, common in many parts of the world, exposed children to abusive conditions including physical and sexual abuse far worse than those they would have experienced in juvenile facilities.

Shocking abuses were also documented in Chinese orphanages, where infants suffered staggering mortality rates. Deprived of adequate food and basic medical care, orphans admitted into welfare institutions in 1989 faced less than a 50 percent chance of surviving for more than one year. Many institutions appeared to operate as little more than assembly lines for the elimination of unwanted orphans (especially girls), with an annual turnover of admissions and deaths far exceeding the number of beds available. At some facilities, the rate of death reached 90 percent.

Human Rights Watch found in Romania, that doctors who were forbidden to acquire medical information from outside the country carried out blood transfusions in a misguided attempt to improve the health of institutionalized orphans. Large numbers of children contracted HIV as a result. Children also suffered from inadequate food, housing, clothing, medical care, lack of stimulation or education, and neglect. As these conditions came to light, the international community responded. In the past decade, the European Union provided more than (U.S.) $75 million to improve the plight of abandoned Romanian children. Funds were directed not only towards emergency food, clothing, and medical care but also toward creating and implementing policies to prevent child abandonment.

In 1999, the United States Agency for International Development developed a program to channel (U.S.) $6 million to Russian organizations working to keep families together and further develop foster care and alternatives to institutional care for orphans and abandoned children. In China, staffing and medical care in orphanages improved, and the government worked to encourage adoption of abandoned children. Despite these encouraging developments, orphans and abandoned children continued to be institutionalized at alarming rates and too often failed to receive adequate care and protection.

While numerous international standards exist which protected the rights of children confined in penal or correctional institutions and settings, no comparable international standards exist to protect the rights of abandoned or orphaned children. Human Rights Watch advocated the use of alternatives to institutionalization of children wherever possible, including support for families or extended families, and foster care, with placement in small residential care facilities as a measure of last resort.

Child Labour

The International Labor Organization (ILO) estimated that 250 million children between the ages of five and fourteen were working in developing countries at least 120 million full time. Sixty-one percent of these were in Asia, 32 percent in Africa, and 7 percent in Latin America. Most working children in rural areas were found in agriculture; urban children worked in trade and services, with fewer in manufacturing, construction and domestic service. Only an estimated 5 percent of child laborers worked in export industries.

Despite the attention devoted to child labor in recent years, those addressing the issue were divided on how to proceed and considered a range of different approaches. Some urged that child labor be eliminated quickly and aggressively, including through the use of trade sanctions when countries or industries failed to act decisively. Others called for reforming the conditions in which children worked with a view toward gradual elimination. The issue of child labor, consideration of the immediate and direct consequences for children and their families could not be under estimated. The removal of children from the workforce had devastating results for some children when not accompanied with nuanced adjustment programs for their rehabilitation and education, and direct assistance. Children discharged from work found themselves on the street in prostitution or crime, or working in even worse conditions and for less pay.

The trade sanction approach seeking boycotts of employers or governments who permitted the use of child labor, or banning the importation of goods made with child labor was extremely difficult to monitor. Employers' assurances that they did not use child labor in manufacturing workplaces around the world were meaningless without effective and independent monitoring mechanisms in place. Child labor included a range of situations from the clearly hazardous and exploitative, as in the case of four-year-old children tied to rug looms to keep them from running away, to the benign or positive, seventeen-year-olds helping out on the family farm or working after school to earn some pocket money.

The ILO Convention Concerning the Prohibition and Immediate Action for the Elimination of the Worst Forms of Child Labor, adopted unanimously by the 174 member states of the ILO in June 1999, committed states party to take immediate steps to prevent, prohibit, and eliminate "the worst forms of child labor." The term child referred to anyone under the age of eighteen. Under the convention, the worst forms of child labor included the sale and trafficking of children, debt bondage, forced or compulsory labor, using children for prostitution or production of pornography, using children for illegal activities, particularly drug trafficking, and other work likely to "harm the health, safety or morals of children."

Cognizant of the dangers of banning child labor without also providing children with alternatives to labor, the convention obligates states parties to ensure that children removed from the worst forms of child labor be given direct assistance to ensure their removal, rehabilitation,and social reintegration. Most importantly, the convention mandated that children removed from labor e ensured access to free basic education, and wherever possible and appropriate, vocational training. Human Rights Watch worked on the issue of child labor in areas where the rights abuses were clear and acute, and which fell within the new ILO Convention's definition of "worst forms of child labor." We worked on bonded child laborers in India; the use of children as soldiers in armed conflicts around the world; and the employment of live-in domestic child servants in Sri Lanka. Throughout, Human Rights Watch emphasized the importance of providing education and rehabilitation in assisting children removed from these worst forms of child labor to truly end the practice.

In some countries, school officials routinely used corporal punishment to maintain classroom discipline and to punish children for poor academic performance. In other countries, authorities failed to intervene to protect minority children from harassment and attacks by other students. The failure of school officials to protect children from violence in school denied them their right to be free from all forms of physical or mental violence and the full enjoyment of their right to education.

In the United States and in other countries around the world, gay, lesbian, bisexual, and transgendered students too often experienced school as a place that accepted intolerance, ostracization, and violence against those perceived to be different. For the most part, school officials refused to intervene to protect these students, allowing what began as harassment to escalate to physical violence. Studies by the U.S. Department of Health and Human Services, the states of Massachusetts and Vermont, and the Seattle, Washington school district found that students who were subjected to harassment and violence at the hands of their peers frequently suffered from depression, low self-esteem, and an inability to focus on schoolwork; most alarmingly, the studies concluded that gay, lesbian, bisexual, and transgendered students were two to three times more likely to attempt suicide than their heterosexual counterparts.

School Corporal Punishment

School corporal punishment remained widespread and an accepted part of the class room experience for millions of children around the world, where the human rights violations inherent in its use went unrecognized. In many countries, the use of corporal punishment by teachers against children was explicitly authorized by law, making it a legalized form of violence against children.

The U.N. Committee on the Rights of the Child, the U.N. Committee against Torture, the U.N. Human Rights Committee, and the European Court and Commission of Human Rights took a strong stand against corporal punishment in schools on the grounds that it may rise to the level of torture or cruel, inhuman or degrading treatment or punishment. The Committee on the Rights of the Child was particularly outspoken, stating that the use of corporal punishment against children was incompatible with the Convention on the Rights of the Child, and it frequently proposed the revision of existing legislation and the development of education campaigns to prevent the physical punishment of children. The use of corporal punishment violated the right of children to be free from violence, debased their dignity and physical integrity, interfered with the development of their physical and mental health, and infringed on their basic right to education.

Kenya's School Discipline Regulations authorized the use of corporal punishment in schools but failed effectively to regulate its use. Nominal restraints were routinely ignored by teachers and the regulations rarely enforced. Teachers caned children for "offenses" such as tardiness, talking in class, wearing torn or dirty uniforms, being unable to answer a question, or failing to achieve target marks set on exams. These measures often resulted in bruising, swelling, and small cuts; at times, however, children suffered more serious injuries such as sprained or broken fingers or wrists, knocked-out teeth, internal injuries, and even death.

Research in Kenya found that the use of corporal punishment instilled a fear of the classroom for some children that impaired learning and at times led children to drop out of school altogether. Other research showed that corporal punishment could be a significant factor in the development of violent attitudes and actions in childhood and later life.

Police Abuse

Police abuse of street children is symptomatic of three problems:

— the increasing population of street children,

— the perception of street children as criminals,

— the lawlessness of police.

The rising number of street children is linked to India's burgeoning population growth: eighteen million children are added to the population every year, a rate that will result in India's mid-1993 population of approximately 902 million people doubling to 1.8 billion by about 2043. Rapid urbanization has also contributed to the problem. The Indian government's five-year plan for 1992-1997 reported: There has been a marked acceleration in urbanisation over the past two decades. If the present trends continue, urbanpopulation may account for about one-third of the total population by the turn of the century.

According to the United Nations Development Programme (UNDP), in 1960, 18 percent of India's population lived in cities. In 1992, this number had risen to 26 percent of the population. The UNDP estimates that by 2000, 29 percent of India's population will be urban-more than 261 million people. A major factor that contributes to rapid urbanization is the increased migration from rural areas to India's urban areas. Many of these migrants are landless agricultural laborers whose traditional occupations no longer exist or do not provide sufficient income, and who have come to the cities in search of employment.

In general, rural-to-urban migration can be explained by India's policy of development, which has favored urban, industrial development over rural development. While this policy did create greater industrialization and less reliance on agriculture as the engine of economic development, it did not alleviate rural poverty. According to the UNDP, 49 percent of India's rural population live at or below the poverty line. Some of these unemployed or underemployed people are forced to go to cities in search of economic opportunities. Cities provide a slightly better opportunity for these people. However, since the UNDP estimates that 38 percent of India's urban population is at or below the poverty line, this accounts for morethan eighty-nine million people.

A 1992 UNICEF study of street children in Bombay observed that the large-scale migration of families from rural to urban areas... has resulted in severe overcrowding, degrading work conditions, homelessness, deprivation of basic services and appalling living conditions in the city. Yet, to return to the village means starvation: to remain in the city means possible survival at least physically. Within this population are children, who may become street children when they arrive in the cities.

In Calcutta, to a great extent the issue of street children is closely associated with the process of fast urbanization that has been taking place in the major cities of India since the sixties. The children come to the city with high expectations and full of hopes that they would easily get jobs there and be able to live comfortably with their families. But except for the fortunate ones the dream is shattered in the case of many. Finding it very hard to make both ends meet they are driven to a life of precarious survival. No place to live, no job to support their family with, they are forced to take to streets as their homes and live on the meagre earnings that they somehow manage by doing various odd jobs. The railway stations and their surroundings, under flyovers and overbridges, and in unoccupied spaces they live in large clusters constructing tiny littie shanties with bamboo poles and plastic sheets or torn cloths.

Some of the children have been displaced as a result of development projects, like the Subarnarekha Irrigation Project which began in 1982 with aWorld Bank loan of $127 million. The goal of the project was to create irrigation for agriculture, industry, and cities, and hydroelectric power for the states of West Bengal, Orissa, and Bihar through the construction of two dams, two barrages, and seven canals. The World Bank estimated that 60,000 people would be displaced by the project, while NGOs estimated that the number of people displaced would be closer to 120,000.

Co-mingled with the migrant population and contributing to the phenomenon of street children is the local population of urban poor who were born in the cities, the temporary migrant families, children who travel to cities daily for work, and abandoned or orphaned children. All are subjected to the same economic and social problems that the poor throughout India face, including coping with significant increases in the cost of living. According to the World Bank, consumer prices increased 9 percent in 1990, 11.8 percent in 1992, 6.4 percent in 1993, and 10.5 percent in 1994, resulting in a 37.7 percent increase in consumer prices from 1990-1994.20 There has not been a corresponding increase in per capita income; in fact, per capita income has declined, from $340 in 1991 to $300 in 1996, according to UNDP figures.

According to NGOs, lawyers, and human rights activists working with street children, juvenile crime has been increasing, largely due to an increasing population of children and worsening economic conditions. The Swedish childrens' aid agency, Rädda Barnen, a member of a coalition of agencies affiliated with Save the Children, wrote in October 1995 that: Limited data reveals that, in 1991, 29,591 juveniles were apprehended for various crimes. Most of them were charged with theft, burglary and riot. Of those, 20% were children aged between 7 and 12 and 64% were between 12 to 16. Over 60% were from families earning less than Rs.500 a month. Girls formed 27% of juvenile offenders. Very little information is available on what happens to these children. Legal representation is rare and there are few facilities existing for the detention of children separately from adults. Little is known about the effectivéness of anyrehabilitation centres that may exist. Again, in India, juvenile crime rates are exploding.

Very little information is available because very little information formally recorded and what information is available is not reliable. For example, the National Crime Records Bureau (NCRB) reported that in 1992 there were 1,102 juvenile arrests in India's five largest cities (Bangalore, Bombay, Calcutta, Delhi, Madras). The same year, the United Nations estimated that the population of children in these five cities was 8,919,474, which would mean there was one arrest for every 10,746 children. The figures show that juvenile crime was extremely low in these cities, but the figures are questionable. In Calcutta, The National Crime Records Bureau (NCRB)reported thirteen arrests of juveniles in 1992. In a city that has over ten million inhabitants and over 1.2 million children, including an estimated 100,000 street children, thirteen arrests is a remarkably low number. It is about one arrest for every 94,000 children and even if all of the arrested were street children, it would be one out of every 7,692 street children.

An NGO representative in Bangalore told Human Rights Watch: Police use street children as a scapegoat for all sorts of things. They are corrupt and cannot arrest the real criminals. Street children are always there, and they are viewed by the police and public as criminals or criminals-in-waiting. The view of children as criminals, a culture of policing that includes brutal treatment and other abuses, and an increasing population of street children have led to consistent abuses against children by the police, leading most observers to believe that the police pose the greatest threat to the welfare of street children.

An NGO representative in Madras commented: The most common and pervasive form of abuse street children experience is by the police. They force them to clean the stations, they beat them, they take money from them, and they torture them into confessing to crimes or to name who committed them. The combination of an increasing population of urban children driven to the streets in order to survive with a brutal police force that views street children as criminals has led to a situation in which detention, torture, and extortion have become the norm, practiced in an environment of almost complete impunity.

Illegal Detention

Although prohibited under Indian and international law, the illegal detention of street children is common in every part of India. Arbitrary detention is illegal under Articles 21 and 22 of India's constitution. Sections 50, 56, and 57 of the Code of Criminal Procedure mandate that no person can be detained in custody without knowing the grounds for arrest, and that a detainee must be presented before a magistrate within twenty-four hours of arrest. Section 160 of the code prohibits the detention of males under the age of fifteen or females of any age for the purposes of investigation or questioning by the police. Article 9 of the International Covenant on Civil and Political Rights, and Article 37 of the U.N. Convention on the Rights of the Child prohibit arbitrary detention. India has ratified both.

The United Nations Minimum Rules for the Administration of Juvenile Justice, called the "Beijing Rules" because they were drafted in Beijing, state that all juveniles arrested have the right to counsel, notification of charges and the right to have a parent or guardian present at the time of arrest. Both the "Beijing Rules" and the U.N. Rules for Juveniles Deprived of their Liberty state that the human rights of juveniles should be protected and respected while in custody. Moreover, India's Juvenile Justice Act prohibits the detention of juveniles in either police stations or jails.

A 1992 study sponsored by the Indian Ministry of Labour and UNICEF on the plight of street children in Bombay noted: The most common complaint of street children without families was that they are rounded up and locked up by the police for two or three days merely on suspicion. This, they explained, was done to fill the "quota" which police are expected to do. Younger children are generally not caught; it is the older children the police have their eye on.

An NGO representative and human rights activist in New Delhi had a similar comment: For their reports and to make money, the police lock up a few children and majors [adults] everyday, only to release them later after having taken their money and/or beaten them up. A few are also presented to the magistrate to show proof that the police are performing their "duties."

The case of Anand, a thirteen-year-old ragpicker whom we interviewed on March 14, 1995, was typical. He was a pavement dweller who told us he lived with his mother, two brothers, and a sister "near a tree" in Triplicane, Madras. Because of their poverty, Anand had to work and spent much of his time on the street. He usually slept with other street children on the rail platform of Triplicane, a stop for the Madras local train. He earned about twenty rupees a day. He said he was ragpicking in January 1995 around 2:00 p.m. when two police officers came up to him. They told him they wanted him to pick up some garbage, so he went with them to the Zambazaar Police Station.

Anand told Human Rights Watch: When we were inside the station, the police started to beat me with their lathis and fists, calling me athief and asking me to tell them where some stolen articles were. I said I had no idea what they were talking about. The beating continued for some twenty or thirty minutes. Then I was put in the cell in the station reserved for criminals and left there for about two hours. At around 4:00 p.m., the police let me go, one of the constables having first grabbed me by the shirt, slapped me, and told me to get out.

No charges were filed, and no case was registered. It was the second time I've been detained without justification or explanation by the police.

A thirteen-year-old child from Bangalore, Palini lives and works on the street selling tickets to popular films that he buys up and then sells at inflated prices, a practice known as selling "black" tickets. Sellers of black tickets give the police a cut, according to Palini, but at the end of the month, they do not have any money and so they cannot pay. He said that on September 30, 1995, when he was working near the Movieland Theater, the police came and took him to the Upparpet Police Station in Bangalore. There he was made to take off all his clothes except his underwear. An inspector and two uniformed police officers held his legs while the inspector hit Palini's legs and feet with a lathi.

Palini told : He kept on asking me if I was selling tickets. There were about eleven other police in uniform and in plainclothes watching while they did this. They were yelling, "So you think you are a rowdy, your mother is a prostitute, you are the child of a prostitute!" They beat me for about half an hour. After this, they put me in the lock-up. There were around ten boys and three adults in there with me. They kept me in the cell until Monday. I think they kept me an extra day because my legs were so swollen. Before they presented me to the magistrate, they beat me again, the same way as before. Then they made me walk around and stretch my legs so that they would not look swollen. Then they presented me to the magistrate who fined me 300 rupees.I also had to pay two police officers forty rupees each because they allowed me to go to a shop owner to borrow money to pay the fine.

Palini said new policemen beat ticket sellers and take all of their money. Police who have been around longer take their money and only beat the children if they do not pay up. The going rate is five rupees for every twenty-five rupee ticket. If the tickets cost more or if the film is popular, the police take more. Palini said he pays anywhere from fifty to 400 rupees a day in bribes to the police.

Even though these acts are illegal, in reality, most children do not know that their rights have been violated and are intimidated by police, so they do not complain. NGO representatives and lawyers whom Human Rights Watch spoke to in Bangalore, Bombay, Delhi, and Madras said that even if children wanted to complain, magistrates, specifically in the remand and bail phases of dealing with an accused, do not spend enough time on any one case to provide the accused with a forum for complaint. The magistrate also relies on the First Information Report (FIR) to decide the status of the accused. The FIR is the first description of the alleged crime. Because is written at the discretion of police and has no input from the accused, the police can easily use it to frame false charges.

This is illustrated in a 1993 study of Bombay's criminal justice courts: the usual processing of the remand or first appearance of the accused was that an interpreter rapidly yelled the names of the accused and the police constable on duty seldom allowed the accused to remain before the magistrate for more than a few seconds. Often, they were pulled back even before they heard the next date of appearance. Consequently, they were forced to depend upon the policemen for this vital information. The magistrates, on their part, either briefly looked at the accused or continued with the court files. Most of the accused reported that "they did not get attention from the magistrate. Without making any enquiry or looking at them, remands were extended; the understanding of the accused was that the clerk calls names and accordingly they have to respond. The submission of the police officer was relied upon and as a matter of routine remands were granted mechanically." However, if the accused were produced in the court accompanied by an advocate, remand would not be extended in such a manner.

Magistrates fail to inform children of their rights or to check on the legality of police action. Moreover, magistrates routinely neglect to inform the accused of the charges against them. The Bombay study noted: After the accused are produced before the magistrate, the magistrate by statute, must inform the accused that they have a right to remain silent, that their testimony can be held against them, and they can have a reasonable amount of time to engage an advocate. Finally, if an accused person cannot afford private counsel, he has a right to court appointed counsel. In the magisterial courts of Bombay, it was observed that in all cases, the magistrates did not apprise the accused of his/her rights. In a majority of cases (95 percent) the accused were not even informed of the charges under which the police had produced them before the court. What is more, in nearly three-fourths of the cases no time was given to hear accused person's point of view.

The lack of adequate judicial oversight and the magistrate's reliance on the FIR and police accounts have contributed to an environment that allows police to illegally detain, beat, and extort money from street children without fear of scrutiny by the judiciary.

The Juvenile Justice Act

The Juvenile Justice Act, 1986, was enacted in an attempt to address the plight of children within the justice system. It was based on the United Nations Standard Minimum Rules for the Administration of Juvenile Justice (the Beijing Rules). Generally, this law, like constitutional rights and other legislation intended to protect children's rights, is ignored. The Juvenile Justice Act prohibits the detention of juveniles in police station or jails for periods longer than twenty-four hours. It also requires the registration of "neglected" and "delinquent juveniles" and requires that juveniles be sent back to their parents or guardians or to a remand home immediately following either their identification as a "neglected juvenile" or their arrest as a "delinquent juvenile." But, the act also makes the police responsible for identifying neglected juveniles and arresting delinquent juveniles.

The police actively abuse this authority, resulting in a pattern of arbitrary arrest, detention, extortion, and beatings of street children, and a practice known as the "round-up," in which children are detained in large groups and either sent to remand homes or disciplined in the police station. There are several reasons for the round-up. The act views children working in railway stations as "delinquent juveniles;" such children are frequently victims of the round-up.

In other cases, juvenile boards, the authority designated by the act to handle cases of neglected children and send them to the remand homes, pressure the police to fill vacant remand homes. NGO representatives and lawyers that Human Rights Watch spoke to said that becausethe shelters were ostensibly designed to care for both neglected and delinquent juveniles, officials fear that an empty home might invite criticism that the juvenile boards, the courts, and the police were not doing their duty. The round-up is also used as an expedient method of detaining possible suspects. Because police generally view street children as criminals, a round-up is an easy way to catch and interrogate them.

The 1992 UNICEF study in Bombay described the practice: When some property belonging to the public is lost/ stolen at the station, these children are rounded up and some even framed. To prove that they are not guilty, the children have to do their best to find the culprit and save their skin. Social workers, NGOs, human rights activists, and lawyers throughout India have documented such arbitrary arrests of street children.

The following series of incidents that occurred at the Bangalore Railway Station during 1995-96 is illustrative of the pattern:

— On June 29, 1995, forty boys aged between eight and fifteen were taken to the police lock-up by the RPF because government officials had complained about the security risks passengers at the train station faced from street children asking to carry their luggage. They also complained about the station being dirty. Consequently, the boys were beaten with lathis, verbally abused, and then warned not to be seen around the railway station's premises ever again. The police also demanded a payment of twenty-five rupees each as a bribe.

— On October 8, 1995, thirty-two boys aged eight to fifteen were apprehended by the RPF for being a nuisance around the station and begging passengers to carry their luggage. The RPF forced them to clean the ten railway platforms, the toilets, and the playground. Then the boys were stripped of all their clothes except underwear and put in the lock-up for three days. After three days, they were sent to remand homes because the juvenile board notified police that the homes were vacant and needed to be occupied.

— On February 1, 1996, two foreign tourists were robbed of a camera and $ 2,000 in the bus stand and railway station area. Thirty to forty boys, aged twelveto seventeen, were apprehended, beaten, and kept in the lock-up for four days. They were released after being photographed holding a slate on which their names, crime numbers, and the alleged offenses were recorded. The NGO working with street children filed a complaint with the police because the children were unlawfully arrested and offenses were recorded against them without any proof.

The Juvenile Justice Act, 1986, introduces itself as one meant "to provide for the care, protection, treatment, development and rehabilitation of neglected or delinquent juveniles and for the adjudication of certain matters relating to, and disposition of, delinquent juveniles." This well-meaning statement, in reality, reads, "Letting a child know in no uncertain terms that he is a criminal, therefore cannot live with his parents but with other little criminals, must work while other children play, is `asking for it' if sexually-molested or raped, is liable to be rounded up fiercely by the police on the slightest murmur of a crime taking place in any locality where he may be, is watched over by people who hate their jobs and couldn't be bothered about probing the child's mind to ensure that he never has to come back there again."

From police custody, the children may be sent before a juvenile board, or a juvenile court, headed by a magistrate with jurisdiction over juveniles who have been arrested on a criminal charge. Both the court and the juvenile board have the authority to send children to institutions known variously as observation, remand, special, or juvenile homes. Thus, regardless of their status as juvenile offenders, abandoned or orphaned children, or children awaiting trial, all children are remanded to the same institutions.

This situation was described by the additional commissioner of the Delhi police, Amod Kanth, who also runs a shelter for street children in Delhi: Rather than providing custodial care like parents provide, juvenile homes have degenerated into jail-like custodial centres. The Juvenile Justice Board, despite its authority, has remained a mute spectator to the pitiable conditions of the homes. The Juvenile Justice Act strongly advocates that children should not be kept in lock-ups as juvenile justice is distinguished from criminal justice. Most children arrested are non-offenders but the two categories-neglected children and juvenile delinquents are wrongly clubbed together.

The arbitrary nature of detention in observation homes has been documented in studies on street children. The joint reports on street children by the government of India's Ministry of Labour and UNICEF list some of the reasons children had been sent to remand homes: In Bangalore, the bulk of children were sent to remand homes on charges of theft, the second largest group were sent on "doubt". This means that 11.3 percent ofchildren were sent to remand homes without having been informed of the reasons.

The Bombay study reported that the majority of children were sent to remand homes on charges of vagrancy or suspicion. In other words, they were arrested because the police considered them vagrants or suspected they might commit crimes or may have committed a crime. But these children were never formally charged with any offense.

The Madras study found that 87.2 percent of children were sent to remand homes on "petty cases" or other charges not including drug peddling, loitering, theft, or robbery. The study commented: This analysis would not be complete without a reference to delinquency. The cross tabulation reveals that 109 boys and only one girl of the total sample of 2,000 had been remanded to a juvenile house of correction, a very small percentage indeed. But out of this small number, the cross tabulation reveals that seven of these children are between the ages of six and ten years. A shocking revelation about our penal system that such small children should be remanded at all.

The homes function as virtual prisons. Nationally, the capacity of the homes is estimated at 350,000. According to lawyers and NGO representatives working with children, the homes are poorly maintained, inadequately staffed, and are not rehabilitative. In addition to the appalling conditions, NGO representatives, lawyers, and children themselves consistently alleged physical abuse and sexual abuse.

A lawyer working with children in the remand homes told Human Rights Watch: The situation in remand homes is just as bad as what happens in the police station. The masters and older boys beat and molest the younger boys, there is rampant bribe taking. The conditions are bad. Children in remand homes have died as a result of severe beatings and other forms of torture. On March 6, 1996, fourteen officials, including six caretakers, two welfare officers, three cooks, and a security guard, of the Kasturba Niketan remand home in the Lajpat Nagar area of New Delhi were suspended in connection with the death of an eleven-year old boy, Rohit, who was allegedly beaten to death by an eighteen-year old boy, Dabloo. Rohit had been sentto the remand home after having been arrested for loitering. Apparently he had tried to escape from the home on March 2, 1996 and as punishment, a caretaker had ordered Dabloo to beat him. The Times of India reported that the caretaker, Subash, had been arrested on March 4, 1996 because he had told Dabloo to "teach Rohit a lesson."

The Statesman, a Calcutta-based national daily, reported that Dabloo had forcibly taken Rohit, rubbed oil on his body, forced him to bathe, and then hung him upside down from a wooden beam on the ceiling. Then Dabloo beat Rohit on his heels, back, and stomach. Later that evening, Dabloo beat Rohit again. On the morning of March 4, Rohit did not respond to calls of other children in the home and when the caretakers found him, he was dead. Children in the home said that despite Rohit's repeated cries for help none of the three caretakers on duty tried to investigate the source of the screams. This allegation was corroborated by the officer-in-charge of the Lajpat Nagar police station, Vijay Singh Chauhan, who said, "Despite being on duty, not one of them informed a senior official about the thrashing."

According to the post-mortem report, the body revealed several injury marks which could only have been inflicted over a prolonged period of time. The report also revealed cigarette burns on Rohit's genitals and observed signs of sexual abuse "which casts a shadow on the condition of other children in the Home." The Statesman also reported that: Residents of the area had also alleged that they would hear frequent screaming from the children's home and were convinced that the children were subjected to torture on more than one occasion.

On July 30, 1996, fourteen-year-old Hira reported to the Times of India that after he had been found on the streets by police, he had been detained in the Lajpat Nagar Remand Home for five years. Originally from Madhya Pradesh, the boy left home at the age of nine on an "impulse" which led him to Delhi. The police rounded him up on the street and he was sent to the Lajpat Nagar Remand Home. His parents were never notified of his detention and said, "We searched for our first-born for many months after he was missing. We thought he was dead."

Hira alleged that while in the home, he had been subjected to constant torture by Dabloo, who was arrested for killing Rohit. Hira recounted one incident of being beaten because he forgot to clean a teacher's room: I was asked to strip down to the waist, made to lie on the floor and my body was oiled. Then I was beaten with a stick until I fell unconscious.

On May 8, 1996, one hundred juveniles detained in the Rajkiya Kishore Graha juvenile home escaped, claiming that "...food shortage and atrocities had forced them to flee." The district magistrate, Ashok Kumar, concurred with these claims:

The inmates were indeed living in sub-human conditions at the juvenile home. Severe beatings and denial of food by the home officials had driven the boys to desperation and forced them to flee. The conditions in the home led one boy to say that, "It is better to live a life on the streets than lead a hellish life here."

There is some statistical evidence of conditions in the remand homes nationally. A number of the joint UNICEF and Ministry of Labour studies which interviewed street children who had been in the homes found that the majority of children reported that their treatment by staff at the homes and the provision of basic necessities in the homes was "bad"

Torture

Torture, usually in the form of severe beatings with fists, lathis, or other instruments, and kicking is a common feature of police treatment of street children. Beatings themselves are used extensively as a means of investigation, punishment, and retribution.

As an NGO representative in Madras told us: Regardless of the situation the police beat the children. I have seen broken bones, broken teeth, bruises, etc. The older a child is, the more horrible the treatment. They will tie boys down ina spread-eagled position and beat them, use knives or needles, they will hang them up by the arms and beat them brutally. The brutality of police in the course of investigating crime, especially in investigations of crimes against property, and as a form of retribution or punishment are acknowledged characteristics of police behavior.

A senior state police officer, Inspector-General I. Ravi Arumugam, described: An excerpt of his extraordinary statement, including the two charts which he used to describe illegal detention, torture and punishment, follows: The police short-cut is brutality and it has become a way of life. In a house breaking case, the process of making enquiries from various people, from the Modus Operandi Bureau and from the various fences of stolen property takes time: for the normal police officer it is faster to catch the servant in the house, hammer him and if it works and, at his instance, some stolen property is recovered well and good, otherwise tough luck for the complainant; the case goes undetected.

Of course, in India, the most superior short-cut is not to register the burglary at all; harass any one who comes to the police station so that an ordinary citizen would think several times before coming to report an offense. Brutality works even better in handling a law and order situation. And, sadly enough, under pressure it seems to be the natural response of police, regardless of country. Yet the desired change in police behaviour is not an impossible undertaking. The general awakening of society against police brutality is a good sign.

Investigation of Crime

During the course of crime investigations, expedience is not the only reason police resort to brutality. Section 25 of the Indian Evidence Act states that confessions made to a police officer while in custody are inadmissible. The provision is intended to prevent police from torturing suspects to gain confessions. But Section 27 of the Indian Evidence Act allows evidence obtained through confessions into court through a back door. For example, if a suspected thief is tortured into telling the police the whereabouts of stolen property or other facts not amounting to a confession, the police can then seize the stolen property or investigate the other facts and use this evidence against the accused.

In Indian Evidence Act, section 25 says that, "No confession made to a police officer shall be proved as against a person accused of any offence." This clearly shows. how a policeman is regarded in our country. Until this suspicious concept is removed from the law book, the police may harp on getting some evidence for the "hard-nut to crack criminals" under section 27 IEA, they are forced to use violence to extract information in a case.

However, instead of arguing that torture should be eliminated from investigations or that Section 27 should be amended or removed from the Indian Evidence Act because it leads to torture, Inspector-General Arumugam argues that Section 25 should be eliminated, thereby removing a suspect's only legal protection from torture when evidence is being gathered by police. The police routinely torture children in order to obtain both evidence and confessions.

Following are the Recommendations of Human Rights Watch, to improve the conditions of street children and abolish police abuse.

To India government:

— Implement the recommendations made by the National Police Commission in 1980, specifically those that call for a mandatory judicial inquiry in cases of alleged rape, death, or grievous injury of people in police custody and the establishment of investigative bodies whose members would include civilians as well as police and judicial authorities.

— Implement the Juvenile Justice Act in all states and Union Territories and amend the Juvenile Justice Act to provide for a complaints and prosecution mechanisms for cases of custodial abuse of children. These mechanisms should be constituted along the lines described in the National Police Commission's recommendations for the creation of civilian, judicial, and police complaints bodies for cases of police abuse.

— Implement the recommended amendments to the Code of Criminal Procedure made by the Parliamentary Committee on Home on March 4, 1996. These recommendations include a mandatory judicial inquiry in cases of custodial death or rape and compensation to families of people who have died in custody.

— Amend Sections 53 and 54 of the Code of Criminal Procedure so that medical examination (including age verification) is mandatory at the time of detention, in order to provide a medical record of the condition of the detainee. Subsequent examinations should be carried out at regularly scheduled intervals. This procedure would circumvent attempts by police officers to intimidate detainees not to complain of torture, and would also protect police from frivolous claims of torture because a complete medical record would exist for the duration of the detention. The order for a medical examination would be independent of the detainee and the police. The initial and final examinations should be done by different people to further ensure their validity.

— Amend Section 197, specifically Sections 3, 3A, and 3B of the Code of Criminal Procedure to delete the provision that requires government approval for prosecution of law enforcement officials when complaints of custodial abuse or illegal detention are alleged.

— Amend Section 43 of the Police Act, so that police cannot claim immunity for actions while executing a warrant in cases of illegal detention or custodial abuse.

— Amend the Trade Union Act to allow children to form and participate in trade unions. The Convention on the

Rights of the Child, which India has ratified, guarantees children the right of freedom of association.

— Review all laws relating to child labor and the Juvenile Justice Act to ensure that the implementation of these laws does not result in criminalizing children who are forced to work.

— Establish a civilian review board comprised of NGO representatives, judges, and lawyers to monitor police stations. Members of the review boards should be adequately trained and provided access to lock-ups and detention registers.

— Establish a high-level commission to investigate allegations of custodial abuse and killings of children.

— Complaints against law enforcement personnel should be promptly and thoroughly investigated by an independent agency with subpoena power and an adequately trained investigatory staff. This agency should be directly accessible to street children.

— Investigate all complaints of illegal detention, physical abuse, and killings of children by law enforcement officers, and prosecute to the full extent of the law those found responsible.

— Investigate all complaints of extortion and bribes from children, their families, or NGO representatives working with street children and prosecute to the full extent of the law those found responsible.

— Require the registration of each child taken to a police station, including the time, date, and reason for detention. The registers should be subject to frequent mandatory review by a judicial magistrate.

— Enforce payment of compensation for people who have been victims of custodial abuse, as per the Supreme Court decision in Nilabati Behara v.State of Orissa (1993) which ordered compensation in case of custodial death under Article 32 of the Constitution of India.

— Conduct a census of street children through city-wide surveys with the assistance of nongovernmental organizations (NGOs). Without an accurate estimate of the population of street children, it is difficult to plan and implement programs for their benefit.

— Promptly submit the report on India's compliance with the United Nations Convention on the Rights of the Child to the Committee on the Rights of the Child.

— Ratify the United Nations 1984 Convention Against Torture and Other Forms of Cruel, Inhuman, or Degrading Treatment or Punishment.

— Invite the United Nations Special Rapporteur on Torture and Other Forms of Cruel, Inhuman or Degrading Treatment or Punishment and the Working Group on Arbitrary Detention to India to investigate allegations of illegal detention, abuse and deaths of children in police custody.

To the United Nations:

—The United Nations Special Rapporteur on Torture and Other Forms of Cruel, Inhuman or Degrading Treatment or Punishment and the Working Group on Arbitrary Detention should visit India and investigate police abuse of street children.

— The United Nations Committee on the Rights of the Child should investigate the abuse and killings of street children by police in India.

— The United Nations Committee on the Rights of the Child should devote one of its theme days to police violence against street children.

To Nongovernmental Organizations Working With Street Children:

— Maintain detailed records of incidents of violence between police and children in order to monitor and document abuses by police. Submit these records to the National Human Rights Commission on a regular basis.

Bibliography

Abramson, B., 'Juvenile Justice: The 'Unwanted Child' - Why the potential of the Convention on the Rights of the Child is not being realized, and what we can do about it', August 2003

Abramson, B., 'Two Stumbling Blocks to CRC Monitoring: the Four 'General Principles' and 'the Definition of the Child'', September 2003

Assis Calundungo, S. de, 'Street Children in Angola', CEIS (Centro di Informazione e Educazione allo Sviluppo) in Petty, C. and Brown, M. (eds), Justice for Children: Challenges for Policy and Practice in Sub-Saharan Africa, Save the Children, June 1998

Cappelaere, G., 'Juvenile Justice 10 years after the Convention on the Rights of the Child (CRC): Some Reflections for Hopeful Perspectives', in Butterflies, My Name is Today, Vol. X., No. 2, Special Issue: 'Children in Conflict with the Law', 2003

Feely, F., 'Collaboration and Leadership in Juvenile Detention Reform', publication No. 2 in the series Pathways to Juvenile Detention Reform, Annie E. Casey Foundation

Gannon, K., 'Few Look out for Street Children', Associated Press, 20 April 2000

Inciardi, J.A. and Surratt, H.L., 'Children in the Streets of Brazil: Drug Use, Crime, Violence, and HIV Risks', Substance Use and Misuse, 1997

Kokic, M. 'Help for Nicaragua's Violent Slums', International Federation of Red Cross and Red Crescent Societies News, 18 September 2003

Moberly, C., 'The 'Voluntary Separation' of Children in Angola: Recommendations for Preventive Strategies', in Consortium for Street Children and University College Cork, Prevention of Street Migration: Resource Pack, 1999

Muigai, S., 'National Youth Service (NYS) will recruit Street Children at District Level', The East African Standard, 20 October 2003

Okagbue, I.E., 'The Treatment of Juvenile Offenders and the Rights of the Child' in Ayua, I.A. and Okagbue, I.E., The Rights of the Child in Nigeria, NIALS, Lagos 1996

Ordoñez Bustamante, Dr D., 'Family Structure Problems, Child Mistreatment, Street Children and Drug Use: A Community-Based Approach', in Consortium for Street Children and University College Cork, Prevention of Street Migration: Resource Pack, 1999

Rodgers, D., 'We live in a State of Siege' - Violence, Crime and Gangs in Post-Conflict Urban Nicaragua', Development Studies Institute, London School of Economics and Political Science, September 2002

Sinagra, L., 'Beneath Bucharest', City Pages.Com, 7 July 2001

Skelton, A., 'International Trends in the Re-emergence of Traditional Systems', in Stevens, J., Access to Justice in Sub-Saharan Africa, 2000

Stumpf González, R., (), 'Why Perpetuate an Old and Sad History? The Case of FEBEM, São Paulo', National Movement of Street Boys and Girls, Brazil, November 2000

Tandon, S.L., 'Fettered Young: Children in Conflict with the Law and Children in Prisons' in Butterflies, My Name is Today, Vol. X., No. 2, Special Issue: 'Children in Conflict with the Law', 2003

Uchena, T.P., 'Community Service in Zimbabwe' in Petty, C. and Brown, M. (eds), Justice for Children, Challenges for Policy and Practice in Sub-Saharan Africa, Save the Children, June 1998

Widdicombe, R. & D. Campbell (2003) 'Poor Neighbours Fall Prey to US Gang Culture', The Guardian, 27 May 2003

Index

STREET CHILDREN AND THE ASPHALT LIFE

STREET CHILDREN AND THE ASPHALT LIFE

(In 3 Volumes)

Volume 3

(Street Children and the Future Direction)

Editor

P.C. Shukla

ISHA

ISHA BOOKS

Delhi-110033

Street Children and the Asphalt Life

(Street Children and the Future Direction)

Rs. 2500 (Set)
Rs. 835 (Each Volume)

ISBN : 81-8205-212-2 (Set)
ISBN : 81-8205-308-0 (Vol. 3)

Published in 2005 in India by
Isha Books
D-43, Prithviraj Road,
Adarsh Nagar, Delhi - 110033
e-mail : ishabooks@hotmail.com

Laser Typesetting at : Global Printers, New Delhi
Printed at : Chawla Offset Press, Delhi

Contents

Preface

Street children are the casualties of economic growth, war, poverty, loss of traditional values, domestic violence, physical and mental abuse. Every street child has a reason for being on the streets. While some children are lured by the promise of excitement and freedom, the majority are pushed onto the street by desperation and a realisation that they have nowhere else to go. In many countries, street children are named after their main survival activities. What is obvious is that street children are poverty-stricken and their needs and problems are a result of wanting to meet basic needs for survival. They go through the struggle of providing themselves with basic things such as food, shelter, health and clothing. Providing targeted interventions that meet the needs of street children requires an understanding of who they are, what they need, what they do and how they can be identified.

It is estimated that there are between 10 and 100 million street children in the world today. These children live a transitory life style and are vulnerable to inadequate nutrition, physical injuries, substance use, and health problems including sexual and reproductive health problems. Some street children are part of entire families who live on the street. Others are born to older street girls. Some street children are 'on the street', which means that they still see their families regularly and may even return every night to sleep in their family homes. Children 'of the streets', on the other hand, have no home but the streets. Even if they occasionally spend time in institutions for

children or youths, they consider the streets to be their home. Although street children support themselves in many different ways, they need the assistance of caring adults and charitable services provided by governmental or non-governmental organisations. Despite peer solidarity and support through charitable services, street children have extremely high rates of morbidity, disability and mortality.

Improving the quality of life of street children is a difficult and challenging task. Street education is a very effective way to support street children as it occurs at locations where they live. Street education can involve many types of activities, for example, counselling about harmful effects of substances or about prevention of STDs, improving literacy and educating street children on the importance of seeking assistance on health issues or other social problems that could be addressed. It can be of vital importance in meeting the needs of street children in the areas of substance use, sex education, life skills, health education and literacy.

The present work in three volumes provides a comprehensive analysis of the problems of street children. The first volume *Selection and Enumeration of Street Children* narrates the status and burning issues of street children around the world. The second volume *Delinquent Street Children* discusses the crime trends among street children, the reasons that makes them criminals and the measures to reduce the delinquent activities. The third volume *Street Children and the Future Directions* discusses about the precarious future of street children. It explains the effective interventions to be taken to protect them from physical and mental vulnerabilities. This work will prove to be a useful reference material for sociologists, researchers, policy-makers, child welfare agencies and all who working for the empowerment of street children.

Editor

1

Defining Street Children

A street child is, of course, a minor, below the age of majority in the society in question. The age of majority invariably brings rights, responsibilities and expectations different from those of a child. In addition, the institutions and agencies of social assistance and control with which one comes into contact also tend to change. A street child spends at least a part of his/her days in the streets. S/he uses them as a place of congregation rather than simply as a channel for moving from one place to another. Street children reside on the streets full or part time and tend to generate their income there.

The United Nations defines street children as "boys and girls for whom 'the street' has become their home and/or source of livelihood, and who are inadequately protected or supervised by responsible adults." The definition suggests that a child in the street may be a working child, a school dropout, or a homeless boy or girl. Some agencies argue that the term "street children" is inappropriate because it creates an artificial category and diverts attention from the interconnected dimensions of child vulnerability.

Only a small minority of street children, however, are unattached or uninvolved with a family of their own. Throughout Brazil, about 90 per cent of street children either lived at home or maintained regular or at least occasional contact with their family. Tacon of UNICEF contends that throughout Latin America only 10 per cent are completely cut off from their family.

In a study in Juarez, Mexico, 44 per cent of the children were found to live with two-parent families, 20 per cent lived with their mother, and the remaining 39 per cent lived with relatives, other children or on the streets. Only 5 per cent of the children lived on the streets on a full-time basis and had severed contact with their family. Of those who retained family links, 15 per cent spent the majority of their nights sleeping on the streets. In Kumasi, Ghana, Korboe found that almost half of the street children live alone. A further 30 per cent live in a foster home where they are looked after by relatives or friends of the family under Ghana's traditional fostering arrangements.

The family of origin of street children tends to be atypical. Brown, for example, has found that in Kingston, Jamaica, over 90 per cent of street children came from female-headed households. In San Jose, Costa Rica, 78 per cent of a sample of street children came from families with a single parent or no parent. In Kumasi, Ghana, 60 per cent came from a single-parent or foster household. Kariuki reckons that, in Nairobi, female-headed households fare particularly badly because of women's inferior access to property rights and appear to generate many of the street children in the city. For many children, families are instruments of exploitation rather than protection. They so overburden their children with work that they grow up knowing little else. Perhaps it is so common that it is accepted as normal practice by many families to exploit their children and expose them to danger. In the worst cases, families intentionally injure their own children, for example maiming them as this improves the opportunities from begging.

UNICEF has estimated that there were some 100 million street children worldwide in 1992. Ennew and Milne reckons that some 71 million of these worked on the streets, about 23 million mostly work and live on the streets, and some 7 million were abandoned children. Glasser reports that there are significant numbers of abandoned children who live in institutions. In Brazil, for example, there are over 500,000 minors in government-related institutions. The large numbers of orphans in institutions around the world has been highlighted through media attention. Major catastrophes tend to generate orphan populations. Glasser recalls the devastating famines in the Soviet Union after World War I when as many as 5 million children were begging on city streets or were in institutions.

Most estimates for the number of street children in Latin America vary between eight and 50 million. The large range illustrates how difficult it is to count street children accurately. This is further exemplified at the national level. In Brazil for example, estimates have ranged from 7 to 30 million. Rizzini and Sanders and Lusk have observed that much of the variation in numbers is due to the lack of a standard definition of street children. Some have inflated their estimates by including all of those poor or 'marginalized' children who at times are found unsupervised around the streets. Others have also confused the issue by referring to street children as 'abandoned'. This leads to the erroneous impression that Latin American cities are filled with millions of children who have no family support.

Boyden has estimated that there are 500,000 street children in Sao Paulo and 200,000 children who work regularly on the streets of Lima, Peru. Probably only 6,000 (3 per cent) of the latter actually live in the streets. At least 1.5 million street children live and work in Mexico. In Mexico City, for example, there are estimated to be about 200,000 children who work on the streets. Bogota, Colombia, is said to have 130,000 street children; Quito, Equador, may have 6,000, and Asuncion, Paraguay, may have 15,000. The problem is not confined to Latin America. The National Coalition for the Homeless in the United States of America estimates that there are about 600,000 homeless children there at any given time, about one-fifth of the homeless population. Epstein estimates the figure at between 750,000 and 1 million.

India is estimated to have 44 million children working on the streets. In Africa, Ochola and others estimate that there will be about 32 million street children by 2000. By 1996, there were 50,000 in Nairobi alone. Worryingly, a rising proportion is abandoned, with no family ties at all, through the depredations of civil wars and HIV/AIDS. Even in quite small cities where there is a strong sense of communal care, there may be street children. In Kumasi, Ghana, for example, Korboe found between 1,000 and 1,500.

Different Types of Classifications

There have been many efforts to classify street children into some sort of typology, especially in order to identify the best ways to provide assistance to each portion of the whole. The following sections discribe the two different sets of such classifications. The first of these looks at the characteristics or behaviour patterns of the street children themselves, while the second looks at how behaviour corresponds to accepted community norms and family involvement.

Characteristics or Behaviour Patterns

UNICEF has developed a useful typology separating street children who live at home from those who do not. The experience of working children who live at home is evidently considerably different from the abandoned child who must rely on other children for protection, sustenance and nurture. It also takes account of the process whereby unsupervised children and child-workers can become fully-fledged street children. The typology differentiates between three categories, namely children at high risk, children in (or on) the streets and children of the streets. The children at high risk are boys and girls who live in absolute poverty in households that do not satisfy their basic human needs. They may spend time in the streets to work or 'hang out'. Through this, they are exposed to street culture, adult street workers, gangs, vagrants, prostitutes and homeless families.

In Latin America, these children can be found in poor neighbourhoods, living at well below the minimum wage. In Brazil, for example, more than half the children live below the United Nations poverty level. It is this marginal group that is at most risk of becoming street children. According to Lusk, about 50 per cent of all street children in Rio de Janeiro belonged to this group (which he calls 'family-based street workers'). They live at home full time and work on the streets full or part time. This group is less likely than other street children to be 'marginalized' or delinquent. They are predominantly from stable two-parent households and are the most likely of all street children to be attending school (73 per cent). These children are unlikely to be involved in crimes such as theft, assault or other illegal means of support.

They are not likely to be members of a gang or to be involved with the police and child welfare institutions. They tend to help to buy food or clothing, pay for school supplies or otherwise contribute to the household. They mostly work part-time in such jobs as shoeshine boys, candy vendors, beggars or car 'watchmen'. However, these children are exposed to the dangers of 'street society', an environment of gangs, drug dealers, police, beggars, criminals and other adults who would exploit them. There, where there is little privacy, comfort or safety, even the most occasional street worker is exposed to the drugs, violence and worker exploitation that characterise street culture. We can say that, the streets are a very effective 'school' of the wrong kind.

The second category in UNICEF's typology are children in (or on) the streets. These are youngsters who spend a substantial portion of their time in the streets, usually as child workers, often with parental encouragement. They tend to maintain a strong family link, but may sleep out occasionally,often owing to the distance from their household to the work-place, or to enable them to work at night when there may be less competition and better business. Others may find it impossible to travel home or to work by bus late or early enough for their work. Some of these children work all night whilst others get a few hours sleep wherever they can. Some may return home in the morning to get some sleep; others only go home every two or three days, spending the other nights together with children who do not go home on any regular basis at all.

Few among these children attend school regularly, but de Oliveira and others were impressed by the number in their study who were enrolled in school (37 per cent). Many will give some or all of their income to their family; some may not be permitted access to their home until some income quota has been met. Children in the streets are immersed in street culture and are exposed to its dangers - violence, police harassment and illegal drugs. According to Lusk some of these children (the 'independent street workers') suffer from a pattern of child abuse or lack of food and support, and tend to stay on the streets on a twenty-four hour basis at least periodically.

They begin to adopt the street culture and may eventually become children of the streets. These children tend to come from somewhat larger families than the 'family-based street workers', many of which have migrated to the city. In Lusk's sample, only 31 per cent of these children attend school. They are four times as likely to admit to involvement in illegal work, supplementing their earnings with shoplifting and petty theft. Well over half use illegal drugs and over a third belong to a gang. The most commonly used drugs are industrial glue, marijuana and cocaine. About two-thirds have been committed to a juvenile institution.

The third category in UNICEF's and Lusk's typology is children of the streets. These are those for whom the street has become a home, their primary environment for daily life. This group tends to be small compared with the multitude seen in many cities working as street vendors, performers, couriers, guides, beggars and prostitutes.

In Rio de Janeiro, some 15 per cent of Lusk's sample fell into this category. Called gamines in Colombia, huelepegas in El Salvador, tigueres in Brazil, these children of the streets have had their family ties severed through running away, abandonment, family disintegration or death of their parent(s). Many are abandoned or orphaned. The children of the streets tend to be older than the working children and tend to have run away and broken off contact with the family.

Compared with home-based street children, children of the street are less likely to come from a home headed by their father and less likely to have had access to running water or toilet facilities in their former home. Their parents are more likely to be unemployed, illiterate, uncooperative, less mutually caring and have higher levels of violence. Some of these children have no idea where their family is and others among them have been abandoned or orphaned. Over two-thirds have been physically or sexually abused - twice the norm for street children in general. Only a small fraction attend school and these do so only infrequently. The children of the streets in Rio "fulfil the popular pixote image of the hard core urchin".

Children of the street are socialised outside of the schools and the family with few conventional contacts with adults. Kariuki avers from experience Kenya that their parents could not afford to keep them in school. Despite this, Felsman and Lusk have described them as being positively adapted and entrepreneurial. On the other hand, their relationship to the larger society is predatory and exploitative, many supplement their income with illegal activity and in turn suffer harassment and violence. In Lusk's Rio de Janeiro study, fully 60 per cent of this group admit to making their living illegally and 80 per cent are open about their regular use of illegal drugs. They are at the very fringes of conventional social organisation. Social workers and street educators who work with this population state that these figures underestimate the nature of their behaviour in terms of crime and drug use.

The distinction between children in and of the streets can be very arbitrary as the children move between the streets and their homes depending on the weather, family dynamics, police harassment, or ecônomic conditions at home and in the street. Some of these children are so dislocated from mainstream society as to be identified by a street child advocacy agency as a fourth category: "the truly abandoned or orphanec child whose life revolves entirely around the street and whose only reference group is made up of other street children. CHILDHOPE estimates that 75 percent of the world's street children are those 'on' the street, 20 percent are those 'of' the street, and 5 percent are truly abandoned street children with no family ties".

Patel's Indian typology

In the Indian context, Pateli dentifies four groups of homeless or vulnerable children: children who live by themselves on the street (street children), children who work in hotels and restaurants (hotel boys), children of pavement dwellers, and children of construction workers. She also recognises that there are other groups of vulnerable children not included. In the city of Mumbai, the Missing Persons Bureau suggests that on average 200,000 people leave home annually. Of the 50,000 who are listed, 45 per cent are below the age of 16. Street children are distinctly different from pavement dwellers in that they have chosen to leave their families.

The children refer to themselves as 'Sadak Chap' (carrying 'the stamp of the street'). They are, by their own admission, roofless and rootless. While street children share occupations and some characteristics with these other children of the poor, they are unique in that they have broken all contact with their homes. They are children of the street. Without even rudimentary dwellings, these children live under bridges, on platforms of railway stations, working during the day, eating out of the wage they earn, and owning no more than what they wear on their backs. Their lack of permanent address, their wandering lifestyles, and their changing workplaces, make them a difficult group to locate.

However, Patel feels that the collection of information about this group, and the provision of state services for them, is an urgent need. Many inexpensive eating places, both registered and unregistered, illegally employ children known as 'hotel boys'; often from outside the city, as they are less likely to know their legal rights and are amenable to taking orders. It is estimated that some 50,000 are employed in 11,750 hotels, restaurants, canteens and teashops in Mumbai. Many children are pavement dwellers, living with their parents on the streets.

A study in Mumbai by the Society for the Promotion of Area Resource Centres (SPARC) in 1985 located around 6,000 households (27,000 people) living in one municipal ward, along three arterial roads. The children of construction workers are discussed separately. Most construction workers are unskilled, landless agricultural labourers who have left their village to earn a better living in the city. They are often recruited by subcontractors who come from the same area. Often these are persons to whom they are indebted, or who bring them to cities with the promise of a job. Workers live in makeshift homes on the site and, despite being in the city, are isolated from the mainstream of urban life.

Working conditions are hard, and their living environment even harsher. Their homes are usually bricks stacked without mortar, with tin or thatched roofs, and mud wall and flooring. The availability of water differs from site to site, and sanitation and drainage are practically non-existent. Schools, ration shops, health centres and other amenities are absent or the people are not eligible, or it is impossible for them to use the services because of the conditions attached, for example, opening hours. Many children live with their parents on construction sites in dwellings that are usually just bricks stacked without mortar, with tin or thatched roofs, and mud wall and flooring. Living on the construction site, amidst rubble, cement, stones and scaffolding, involves many dangers compounded by the lack of day care, education, health facilities and other social services. Some of the children are also expected to work.

Some people make distinctions among street children as "runaways (those who leave home without their parent's consent); throwaways (those forced to leave); system kids (those leaving social service system placements, such as foster care or group homes); and street youths (those who sleep on the street)".

In a study in Wales, for example, young people under 16 years are classed as runaways, since legally they cannot leave home without parental consent, but those 16 and over are called homeless. However, distinctions tend to blur and categories overlap. Other authors have differentiated categories of street children according to how long they have been on the streets and their age. However, it is usually secondary in importance to lack of family involvement and deviance.

Cosgrove's matrix of street children

Cosgrove suggests an approach that looks at how behaviour corresponds to accepted community norms and family involvement rather than at selected characteristics or behaviour patterns. Both the relationship of overall behaviour to accepted norms and family involvement are seen as continuums. However, he begins with a description of the extremes (the most negative and most positive) and a middle point.

The continuum of relatedness of behaviour ranges from essentially normative, through inconsistent, to pervasively non-normative behaviour. Each of the nine numbered cells in the matrix represents a category of children who are, who could become, or who resemble street children. Obviously, there will be some overlap among the categories. Cells 6, 8 and 9 make up the group generally considered to be street children. These are the children whose situations are fairly intractable to traditionally structured social services which have had little success engaging these youngsters, keeping them involved and producing positive outcomes.

Those in the two less severe categories (6 and 8) are usually more amenable to change than those in 9, because their ability to adapt to social norms and/or to relate to other people are strengths upon which new lives can be built. Those children who fall into cell 5 (in which family involvement is not strong and behavioural conformity vacillates) are prime candidates to join the ranks of street children. The children in cells 1, 2 and 4 are youngsters who may at first appear to be street children. Yet, they do only peripherally or accidentally associate with that lifestyle.

The groups include children who live, attend school, work, or are located, close to street children. Also included are adventurers or thrill seekers expressing their rebelliousness, testing their daring or seeking vicarious stimulation on the fringes of the 'street scene'. These youngsters are the least likely to become street children although proximity to the environment in which street children exist places them in danger. They are potential victims of kidnapping, confinement and being forced into prostitution.

Factors Affecting Street Children

Several related economic, social, and political factors have been linked with the appearance of street children. "Land reform, population growth, drought, rural to urban migration, economic recession, unemployment, poverty, and violence have all been implicated". Kariuki discusses several hypotheses for the origins of street children in Kenya. These are based on poverty, dysfunctional families and modernisation.

— The first hypothesis points out that poverty seems to cause some breakdown of families and moral valuespushing children in this situation into the streets in search of opportunities to earn some money to support themselves and their families. They may, however, also be responding to needs of their own, for open space where they can have some peace, supportive new relationships, or full responsibility for their own lives.

— The second hypothesis claims that street children are caused by dysfunctional families who abandon, abuse or neglect their children. This may result in teenage pregnancies, many arising from rape. Young women and girl victims become single parents and many set off for the urban centres in search of a livelihood. There, they and/or their children may end up on the streets.

— The third hypothesis blames modernisation, which leads to the breakdown of extended family values. The traditional ethos of the African family provided social security for victims of dysfunctional branches, absorbing children who needed care and preventing the phenomenon of street children. The presence of street children can be seen as an indicator that such traditions are being eroded by the modern culture of individualism. This trend has particularly affected the urban areas where the breakdown of these traditional support systems for poorer family members has led to greater disparities between the rich and the poor. Children living in the least favoured households suffer severe deprivation and tend to drift into the streets.

In high-income industrial countries like the United States of America, most street children have run away from home to escape physical or sexual abuse. Many homeless young people have received implicit messages from the family to leave (through physical abuse or neglect) until they finally run away. The main cause of children's being on the streets in developing countries, however, is poverty. While street children in the

United States of America come from all social classes and are overwhelmingly from neglectful or abusive homes, their Latin American, African and Asian counterparts should be seen primarily as workers.

Physical and sexual abuse are also major causative factors. A large number of the children fled from their homes because their real or step-parents had beaten or even burnt them severely. Although there are laws that protect children from the physical abuse of parents, they are not respected by any of the parties concerned. Work in Egypt also showed that, though poverty led families to break up, it was often associated with domestic violence. This domestic violence, and especially physical and sexual abuse of children, were among the main reasons why children ran away from their homes and took to the streets.

According to a study of girl street children in Nairobi, about 90 per cent come from households where physical and verbal abuse, alcoholism, and the like are problems. However, as more people are pushed to the economic periphery, children take to the streets to work and earn money because there is not enough at home either to keep them or to pay school fees. In Korboe's study in Ghana, many of the northern girls had migrated to Kumasi to raise money for cloth, storage bins, cooking pots and other paraphernalia to increase their chances of marriage.

In many lower income households the rational economic response has been to set children to work. Valladares found that 13 per cent of Brazilian children between 10 and 14 years of age are working full or part time. Among children aged 15-17, 40 per cent are employed. The optimal strategy for poor households seems to favour high fertility and limited education. This in turn provides an incentive for child street labour, which can lead to children-at-risk becoming street workers and, in some cases, 'children of the streets'.

Scanlon and others found that most street based children do not gradually move from home to street but establish themselves on the street early on. Most do intermittent, casual work such as hawking, cleaning and guarding cars, market work, begging, stealing, and prostitution. Some form quite structured gangs loosely based on the family but mostly they form less stable groups, adapted to the problems of street life, with diffusely defined roles and territories. Few street children in Latin America can be said to be on the streets in search of a 'Tom Sawyer-like' adventure or in pursuit of freedom from responsibility. They are 'pushed' into the environment by family poverty, neglect and violence, are 'pulled' into the street by the availability of work and income.

In a study of Bogota gamines, Pineda and others found that only one in ten claimed to have left home for 'adventure'. One in three of the children had left home owing to extreme poverty, one in four because of family disintegration, and one in five owing to physical abuse. A study of a broader group that included working children who lived at home found that children consistently referred to economic incentives as their reason for being in the street. In Ghana, Korboe found that, although poverty is the root cause for being on the street, it is not always the only one. The decision to venture into the urban street was prompted in part by children's frustration at their parents' seeming indifference to their emotional, financial and other needs. Parental neglect, multiple marriages, divorce or death are quite common reasons for leaving home but domestic violence is very rarely causal in Ghana.

Violence plays a seemingly increasing role in street children's everyday lives. At the extreme, street children are slaughtered by death squads. In Latin society in general believe that street children represent a moral threat to a civilised society that must be exorcised. The most frightening vigilantes, many of whom are involved with security firms and the police. Children living and working on the streets of Cairo are regularly rounded up by the police, often beaten, and then held in crowded detention centres where their heads are shaved. Some are transferred to corrective centres or other institutions where conditions are very poor. Such custodial institutions do not discriminate between criminals and those who have lost their way or those who have run away from their families. There is also a growth of violence among street children and between street children and adults.

The 7 per cent who belonged to gangs in Lusk and others' study of Juarez, Mexico, stated that their primary reason for being involved in a gang was for protection. Street children easily fall prey to temptations offered by their peers or adults. They are often robbed or have to pay 'protection money'. In addition and, perhaps more damaging for their personal development, street children are generally disparaged by the rest of society and consequently suffer from very low self-esteem despite their often considerable achievements in surviving.

Criminal Skills

All the children Bibars spoke to in Egypt were street children before they committed any kind of crime. However, the prevailing public and official view of homeless people and delinquent children in many countries is that of "trouble-makers and/or criminals by nature" - rather than victims of circumstances. The cycle for many street children begins with an abusive home which pushes them onto the streets. This leads to an arrest and finally to a corrective institution. From interviews carried out with institutionalised children, it became clear that they learn many more criminal skills during their stay in these institutions and they graduate as professional crooks. Leite and Esteves use the term 'creative' for the various ways that street children defy death, break institutional rules, transgress the laws of private property and local moral codes.

Many of these involve violence. Basic rights have been denied them, so their survival depends on artful, quick-witted actions. They know how to take advantage of a given situation to achieve results that may bring them an immediate advantage. Demonstrations of pity are not accepted unless these might prove useful. They are clearly aware that to receive requires a passive, submissive attitude and act whereas to take is something active, participative. This may be the reason why they steal in the streets - "it is so much more fun than begging".

According to Wright and others, about one half of the street children in Honduras have been arrested, while some 40 per cent have been imprisoned. São Paulo court figures show that the number of arrests of street children is increasing. However, there are few concrete data on crimes committed by street children to support the popular assumption that they are all thieves.

According to Leite and Esteves, the aggressive attitudes of street children stem from the impotence they feel in the presence of rules they cannot follow and are unlikely to succeed in. Their explosive bursts of anger, sometimes violent and aggressive, fighting and swearing, cannot be summarised simply as being quarrelsome or the products of bad education and vicious surroundings. Instead, it represents a different culture. The street children are trapped between their life circumstances and the dominant, ever-present values of the wider society around them that tell them how they should act.

Use of Drugs

Drug abuse is part of the reality of street life. A highly prevalent behaviour among street children in developing countries is glue sniffing. Several studies have shown that around 80 per cent of street children use drugs regularly. Glue is cheap and easily (and, often, legally) bought. It provides temporary but sure oblivion to cold, heat, hunger pangs fear, loneliness, and despondency. Unfortunately, children are quickly and easily addicted, and tend to spend whatever petty cash they have on glue, rather than on other necessities. Epstein reports significant drug involvement among street youths in the United States of America through injecting, smoking and inhaling substances from glue to heroin. She avers that this is part of behaviour traits expressing low self-esteem, withdrawal and listlessness, hostility and aggressiveness, and emotional neediness.

Physical Health

Little information exists on the general physical health of street children. Trauma and certain infections are more common among children of the street than among those based at home. However, street children's nutrition is no worse than other children from similar backgrounds. Indeed their begging and stealing activity might actually enhance the nutrition of street children as it allows access to relative expensive foodstuffs like meat. A study of Toronto street children showed that, though street children were basically healthy, many suffered from malnutrition and 50 per cent had the sexually transmitted disease chlamydia (tranchoma). They rarely seek medical advice but, when they are forced to do so, they are reluctant to be candid about their lifestyle.

The high level of intravenous drug use and involvement in prostitution, and the greater likelihood of gay or bisexual lifestyle, mean that street children are in the highest risk categories for contracting and transmitting HIV/AIDS and other sexually transmitted diseases. Street children are also more likely to be victims of rape. As their focus is on the present, street children find it difficult to bother about a disease that may not kill them for years to come. Effective HIV/AIDS education is vitally important but most pamphlets and books about HIV/AIDS are aimed at middle-class people with at least a high school education.

Most of it is not culturally relevant to street children who are often functionally illiterate. Such material provokes anxiety and children do not feel comfortable struggling through it. In Patel's study in Mumbai, street children were asked about their strategy for coping with illness. In her interviews with hotel boys, only a few had received help from their employers, the hotel owners. It is in the owners' interests to ensure that the boys are treated soon so that they may continue to work and do not infect other workers. Understandably, the boys do not see this as 'help'. Most rely on friends in their own networks. One-third of boys had no help when they were ill and a quarter was not taken for treatment. More than 70 per cent of the hotel boys sought treatment from private clinics; perhaps a comment on the failure of the public health system or that hotel owners who help them want quick solutions. Another factor is that a hotel boy is probably less willing than a street child to wait for long periods in a municipal dispensary due to the demands of his occupation.

Self-esteem

Many street children have negative feelings about being identified thus. De Oliveira and others found that many value street life as a learning process, and see themselves as resilient survivors in an environment that is hostile and potentially morally destructive. They recognise their own abilities in overcoming adversity and regret their derogatory label. They value themselves for what they are and many plan to become integrated into society in the future while keeping part of their street-acquired identity and values. De Oliveira and others found that the low self-esteem in which street children are said to hold themselves is less straightforward than it seems. Their research questions the validity of such statements and warned about the likely negative impacts of holding to them.

For example, labels such as criminals or thieves undermine their self-esteem and become believed by the children about themselves. Rejecting the labels (e.g., by claiming that they do not have to and do not want to be street children forever) may be an important defence mechanism for them. Objective testing of self-esteem is difficult, however. When street children make derogatory remarks about themselves, they may be doing so to satisfy researchers or to improve their chance of gaining some money from the sympathetic researcher.Through their harsh experiences, street children obtain valuable practical skills and survival instincts.

They are condemned to a life of meaningless existence by the general public, with negative stereotypes such as 'chokora pipas' (eaters from garbage bins). However, they see themselves differently. They have developed a 'subculture' with a clear social structure, leadership, recreation and work patterns, revolving around their day to day experiences. They use nicknames to reinforce a sense of belonging, identity and self-worth.

2

Human Rights Issues of Street Children

The turn of the twenty-first century has seen a change in most of the writing concerning street youth. The term street children itself has almost disappeared from the welfare and analytical literature, which now uses different appellations to refer to street children and other underprivileged groups. Children themselves, of course, are still on the streets, easily visible in the great majority of urban centers. What has been called the global or "worldwide phenomenon of street children" has neither vanished from sight nor effectively been solved. However, current perspectives tend not to demarcate street children so radically from other poor children in urban centers or to conceptualize the homeless in isolation from other groups of children facing adversity.

Welfare agencies nowtalk of "urban children at risk", which conceptualizes street children as one of a number of groups most at risk and requiring urgent attention. There is accumulated evidence that children move fluidly on and off the streets and that the street does not represent the sum total of their social networks or experiences. A dialogue between academics and welfare practitioners has also been instigated to broaden the insights gained by people working with different categories of unaccompanied, institutionalized, abused, refugee, street, or working children. In essence, the change in perspective reflects a shift of attention from the street as the primary focus of concern to the children themselves.

Identifying Street Children

Deceptively simple, the term street child has proved problematic. Abasic definition of the term is a homeless or neglected child who lives chiefly in the streets. The statement emphasizes two peculiarities about street children: the place they occupy (the streets) and the absence of proper contacts or links with adults in the family home and in society. This encapsulates much of the thinking behind studies of street children in the 1980s. Such work was concerned with establishing the hallmarks of a street lifestyle and the characteristics of street children in terms of their use of public spaces and their links with family and public institutions.

Street children is problematic for several reasons. First, it is a generic term that obscures the heterogeneity in children's actual circumstances. Second, it does not correspond to the ways many children relate their own experiences or to the reality of their movements on and off the street. Third, it is imbued with pejorative or pitying connotations. Fourth, it deflects attention from the broader population of children affected by poverty and social exclusion. Indeed, "street children" is a construct that reflects various social and political agendas. These are strong criticisms, which go some way toward explaining why "street children" is a difficult working concept and why other terms of reference or appellations have emerged in recent analytical literature.

Generic Term

The first difficulty, the need to recognize that street children are not a homogeneous group but experience very different circumstances and lifestyles, was already obvious more than 20 years ago. Welfare agencies, in particular UNICEF and Save the Children, have reworked their definition of street children many times, finding it difficult to devise meaningful statements about these children as people, to define various categories of street life, and more recently, to identify appropriate categories of "at risk" children. The term street youth, or street children conceals enormous variation in the experiences of youngsters who share the common condition of being 'out of place' in street environments, spending their lives largely outside the spheres typically considered appropriate for children, such as home, school, and recreational settings. The individuals concerned are all minors under 18 years of age, but from a broad age spectrum including teenage and near-teen youth as well as children as young as 5.

An early consensual definition of street children, formulated in 1983 by the Inter-NGO Programme for Street Children and Street Youth, stated: "Street children are those for whom the street more than their family has become their real home, a situation in which there is no protection, supervision or direction from responsible adults". The United Nations adopted the phrasing: "any boy or girl... for whom the street in the widest sense of the word... has become his or her habitual abode and/or source of livelihood, and who is inadequately protected, supervised, or directed by responsible adults. " For Save the Children Fund, "a street child is any minor who is without a permanent home or adequate protection" (UNESCO). There are three important elements in these definitions: the time children spend on the street, the street as a source of livelihood, and the lack of protection and care from adults.

Several terms in these definitions, however, have led to confusion. What is meant by home, family, protection, and a "responsible" adult? Such terms are conceptualized differently across cultures. Indeed adult-child relationships may be premised upon a radically different understanding of "normal" childhood. There are communities facing significant poverty where children are the prime caretakers of incapacitated adults and the prime income earners in the household, such that relationships of care, protection, and provision flow from the child to the adult rather than from the adult to the child. Being homeless is also variously rendered across cultures, as desamparado (defenceless, unprotected) in Latin America, furosha (floating) in Japan, and khate (rag-picker) in Nepal.

These terms evoke disaffiliation, transience, and marginal economic work, rather than notions of lack of home or abode. It has also been difficult to uphold the typology of children "of the street" and "on the street," established by UNICEF to differentiate street-based or home-based street children. The distinction here is between children of the street-who have a family accessible to them but make the streets their home-and child workers on the street-who return at night to their families. This terminology was promoted world-wide, but in practice it was found unsatisfactory as children themselves defied these generalizations.

Many children sleep both at home and on the streets, and they also spend significant periods of time in residential institutions like orphanages, refuges, or correctional establishments. Other distinctions have been made between abandoned and abandoning street children in the Third World, or between runaway and throwaway homeless adolescents in the West, according to the degree of family involvement, the amount of deviant behavior, or a range of sociological characteristics. These and other labels, such as children "without family contact" or "abandoned," lack precision and have been used ad hoc rather than analytically.

Today, the focus on discrete categories of street lifestyles has fallen into disuse. Efforts to devise a suitable definition and an appropriate typology of street children represented the first steps toward a useful conceptual framework to think about the children in question. A classification of children is still useful, as long as it is understood that categories are neither discrete nor necessarily homogeneous, and that they may not always coincide with children's own views about their lives. It is with these important provisos that current research makes distinctions between street and working children, between street-living and street-working children, between family-based street workers and independent street workers, or between homeless and working youth, distinctions that essentially uphold the original UNICEF typology. The category of street children may be "impossibly constructed", but there are few practical alternatives available-beyond local terms-to refer to these particular groups of children.

Inadequate Representations

A second criticism leveled at earlier studies of street children is that a simple focus on the street tends to promote a unidimensional account of children's lives, which does not do justice to children's actual behaviors and wider social networks.

Stigmatizing Label

The term "street children" has powerful emotional overtones. Common public responses are pity and hostility, with street children perceived as victims or villains. Ironically, the term "street children" itself was widely adopted by international agencies in an attempt to avoid negative connotations for children who had been known as street urchins, vagrants, gamines, rag-pickers, gluesniffers, street Arabs, or vagrants. It has been argued that the label street children, now so emotionally charged, does little to serve the interests of the children in question.

The term has a stigmatising effect, since the child is, as it were, allocated to the street and to delinquent behaviour. The term neither gives consideration to the experience or testimony of the children in question nor to other facets of their identity, which do not necessarily have any relevance to the street. Thus it becomes a cause of discrimination of the children and triggers or strengthens negative social reactions. The label "contributes to a social reaction towards them. Even programs of intervention for street children can result in their discrimination and stigmatization. This social reaction leads to stereotypes related to gender, ethnicity, and age; for instance, that all street girls are prostitutes and street boys junkies, and that younger children should be pitied but teenagers, especially dark-skinned ones, should be feared.

It also lumps together the homeless, a highly visible but minority group, with home-based streetworkers. Thus authors writing on street children (meninos de rua in Portuguese, ni˜nos de la calle in Spanish, enfants de la rue in French) will declare that they find the use of this generic term questionable-but retain it for lack of useful alternatives. Street children themselves may reject it as a pejorative label or conversely endorse it in order to define their shared identity.

A focus on street children-easily represented as the symbol of child poverty and social exclusion-concentrates attention toward only the most visible tip of a huge iceberg. As a target group for policy makers, street children have hijacked the urban agenda... to the detriment of other groups of disadvantaged urban children. Rizzini et al. also argued: "a focus on street children-however well-intentioned-deflects attention from the broader population of low income children and youth in poverty.... Most children's programs [in Brazil] have directed their attention to a relatively small number of children and youth in the most dire situations. " These authors find compelling reasons for changing policy and program attention in Brazil from street children to all children, with interventions giving social and developmental support "to all children and not just those who face specific risks, such as the risk of being abandoned or abused".

Focusing attention on street children can thus lead agencies to overlook or ignore the much larger problem of urban-and rural-poverty. For Lane, however, the distinction between "those that are at greatest risk of taking to street life and those who live in poverty is central to effective prevention strategies": not all disadvantaged children take to the streets, and those who do are most likely to slip though the nets of broad-based community interventions.

The public discourse on street children as victims of violence-particularly in Colombia, Guatemala, Brazil, and Honduras-has also distracted attention from the issue of widespread poverty and violence affecting children who live at home, and the quiet, private death that is hunger and disease. Indeed there are radically different understandings of violence linked to distinct social groups, reflecting distinct constructions of childhood. Such arguments highlight that international, national, and local action on behalf of specific groups of children in adversity (street youth, abandoned children, child laborers, sex workers) closely reflects the construction and management of a social and political issue.

Issues Related to Street Children

It has been argued that both the street children issue and the "homelessness problem" are constructs deftly manipulated to reflect the various agendas and interests of stakeholders such as the welfare agencies. For instance, very large estimates of the number of children in the street are produced to draw attention to the need for the agency's work. At best, these estimates rest upon largely elastic and nebulous definitions of homeless and working children. At worst, they are made up. The "arithmetic is as symbolic as the children involved". Many publications on street children impress upon their readership the sheer magnitude of the problem. The talk is of numbers, and the numbers cited are huge. Thus 100 million youth are said to be growing up in the streets of urban centers world-wide. Other estimates have 170 million living on the street, or give a range for street children of 30 to 170 million.

In Brazil alone, UNICEF estimated in the late 1980s that 7 million youth spent most of their time and/or slept on the street, and this figure readily came to designate homeless children. Hecht suggests the true number of homeless children in Brazil is less than 1% of that figure. The estimate of 7 million in Brazil is certainly an overstatement. Estimates will vary, of course, in relation to howa mobile population of children is counted and, most importantly, exactly who is considered for inclusion, because the term street children has different meanings in different regions. For example, in the Philippines, it denotes those who "spend most of their time on the streets yet who maintain some regular contact with a family". In contrast, it may denote more strictly those children who at night have no parental home to go to. Thus the estimates of welfare agencies are not always concerned with the same children.

Ennew states categorically: "Neither UNICEF nor the ILO (International Labour Organization) can give reliable or verifiable figures for the number of working children worldwide, including street children. A basic reason for the lack of accurate figures is that no one can agree on definitions. Numbers are often cited at the beginning of reports and descriptions of street and working children, but they have no validity or basis in fact".

The definition of homeless youth in industrialized countries is also elastic and can include those who sleep rough, live in shelters, squat, or double up with other families, encompassing the "literally homeless" and the "precariously housed". In Great Britain, Hutson & Liddiard have argued that estimates of homeless youth tend to be not only inflated by welfare agencies to legitimate their role, but also minimized by bureaucratic institutions to sidestep legal or financial responsibilities. In brief, the statistics are problematic: They reflect the particular agendas of organizations that collect them, and they are part of the construction and the management of homelessness as a social issue.

Human Rights

The United Nations Convention on the Rights of the Child,

which came into force in September 1990, has had a huge impact in defining conceptual frameworks and humanitarian concerns regarding children in adversity. The Convention asserted a number of rights for children worldwide, formulated basic principles to be applied, and created a legal obligation to put these rights and principles into practice. Concern for children in difficult circumstances was no longer a matter of humanitarian and charitable concern, but now is a legal responsibility falling on a state as party to the Convention. The Convention listed the areas where the rights and interests of children must be taken into account-for example, separation from parents, freedom of expression, health, education and employment-and enunciated that in all actions concerning children, "the best interest of the child shall be a prime consideration". This universal mandate was carefully worded to formulate a clear principle to empower intervention while leaving room for some flexibility and cultural interpretation.

Recent publications concerning street children have explicitly referred to children's rights and their best interests as advocated in the Convention. For instance, The Consortium for Street Children produced The Human Rights of Street and Working Children, devised as a practical manual for implementing the Convention. UNICEF's Implementation Handbook for the Convention, which adopted a wider brief, considered those who live and work on the street under the heading of "children deprived of their family environment". To these rights enshrined in international law, Ennew added some important yet unwritten rights for children outside society and "normal" childhood. These include the right for street children not be labeled, to be correctly researched and counted, to work and have their own support systems respected, the rights to privacy and respect for their individuality (including sexuality), and the right to be protected from exploitation by the media, activists, or fundraisers.

The Convention heralded a change in the prevailing discourse regarding street children and, more generally, children facing adversity. The emphasis moved significantly from highlighting the needs of vulnerable children to defending their rights as citizens. Earls & Carlson expressed this change of approach forcefully: "In recent years, the entire concept of childhood has been reconstructed... Children are citizens... The idea that they are simply immature creatures whose needs must be met by parents or other charitably inclined adults is becoming obsolete.

As citizens, children have rights that entitle them to the resources required to protect and promote their development. " Street children, however, are socially excluded, an exclusion that begins with lack of access to birth certificates and registration documents, lack of stability of residence, proper education, and health care: This group of children is deprived of citizenship rights. Advocacy on their behalf has therefore featured lobbying for inclusion of children's rights at the national level.

Yet the concept of "the child in need" still permeates "the everyday vocabulary" of social work. This construct draws a credible veil over any uncertainty or possible disagreement regarding which action might work in the "best interests" of children. It is easily taken for granted and applied indiscriminately to all children facing difficult circumstances. There are several reasons why this approach is unsatisfactory. First, the problem to be addressed is defined "as essentially individual and psychological, not social and structural". Second, the child is "classified as coming from an abnormal family and is constructed, through the language used, as deficient (having a need), weak (being needy), and a subject of charity".

The discourse about children's rights is revolutionary, yet one must tread carefully. The notion that children as individuals have inalienable human rights must be negotiated with the notion of group and family rights (giving children duties and responsibilities toward their elders) prevailing in many non-Western cultures. The notion that minors have rights usually raises questions regarding their developmental and social maturity: To respect or condone a child's choice to live on the streets, to grow up with peers rather than with a family, to work for an income, and to have sex is for many a morally unsatisfactory position.

Should the rights discourse be tempered with a measured consideration of children's capabilities-an appreciation of children as individuals with specific competences and maturity, able to discern and adopt those behaviors that, realistically, will improve their quality of life? To make rights contingent upon capacity is, however, problematic-especially where children are concerned, when adults remain the all-powerful adjudicators of their competences.

Another significant shift of emphasis, grounded in the UN Convention, was to recognize that promoting the best interests of children is not just a matter of protecting and providing for them, but of listening to them and fostering child participation. There is a careful balance to be struck between the three broad categories of rights in the Convention: rights to protection, provision, and participation. Adults are wont to emphasize the first two, being reluctant to let street children grasp participatory rights-other than by accident. The third set of rights recognizes that children are "agents of change in their own lives", which demands that adults recognize that children have agency and manifest social competency (shaping their lives for themselves). This drives the ethics of a program for research or intervention toward necessary consultation and child participation.

It has been forcefully argued that a portrayal of children as "vulnerable, incompetent and relatively powerless in society" is deeply problematic. To present street children as helpless victims of social discrimination does little to recognize their remarkable initiative and ingenuity in coping with difficult circumstances. For this reason, research has shifted emphasis from portrayals of vulnerability and dependency to a discussion of children's coping strategies in the face of adversity:

It may be more helpful to identify the factors that help children cope with adversity than to emphasize the problems in their circumstances. Thus, several discourses about street children compete for attention. One is journalistic, descriptive, and atheoretical, targeted to mass audiences; another is research-focused and aims to promote critical understanding and to influence effective policy development. Stark images of children's vulnerabilities (Portrait 1) coexist with a more dignified portrayal of their lives (Portrait 2).

Portrayals of street children (as victims, villains, dependents, or deviants) also have an impact on types of intervention. Interventions focused on "rescuing" children from the streets by placing them back at school or with the family have generally not provided lasting solutions because they tend to ignore children's own views and all that they have already accomplished for themselves. As stressed in a Save The Children publication, street and working children are not "objects of concern but people. They are vulnerable but not incapable. They need respect, not pity". The key to research and project design has changed to working with children rather than for them, thus giving prime importance to child participation.

The development of interactive and participatory research methods has hinged upon the realization that children have social agency and competency and are capable of making informed decisions about their lives and of expressing views and aspirations that may differ from the views held by adults. The call has been for novel ways of conducting research with children, ways that would prioritize their own perspectives and allow for their participation in the design and implementation of research objectives. These have included participation of the children themselves in the research process, not just as informants but as researchers, conducting interviews, taking photographs, or shooting videos of their world and of one another.

It has also led to new approaches for advocacy-a social mobilization of street andworking children at grassroots levels culminating in their participation, even ownership, of national and international forums in which children's rights issues were debated. These child-centered approaches do not, however, evade the issue of ethical concerns: involving children as participants rather than subjects raises its own set of ethical problems. The ethics of social research with children are not limited to securing informed consent and respecting children's views: They extend to appropriate ways of collecting, interpreting, and disseminating-without distortion-findings. They are complicated by the disparities in power and status between adults and children and by a consideration of age-related competence. And as Hecht noted for research in Northeast Brazil, there are considerable ethical challenges when working with street youth who lead very violent and vulnerable lives; many of these challenges are wholly unanticipated.

Children and Public Health

In current welfare literature, street children are a category of "children at risk. " This phrase has replaced the one "children in need" and even taken over UNICEF's appellations "children in especially difficult circumstances" abbreviated as CEDC, and "children in need of special protection" abbreviated as CNSP. Indeed in recent literature the generic category "urban children at risk" tends to replace the terms street and working children. But this term of reference may also be ambiguous, analytically unhelpful, stigmatizing for children, and manipulated to serve socio-political agendas. Is "risk" another one of these catch-all phrases that proves under close examination to be an unsatisfactory construct? It does raise the question: "at risk of what?"

Given the difficulties that beset earlier categorizations of children on and of the streets, Hutz & Koller suggested that "perhaps a more appropriate way of classifying street children would be in terms of the risks to which they were exposed" "and the protective factors available to them" (school, supportive social networks, caring adults). These authors noted, however, that risk assessment in research with street children is a particularly complex issue. In public health, risk factors are variables that predispose an individual to illhealth; the assessment of risk proceeds from a statistical measurement of those factors shown to affect health and well-being. In the case of street children, such risk factors include poverty, family dysfunction, ethnicity, gender, age, education, disability, work experience, and stability of residence.

However, it is tempting to generalize from a statistical (and largely empirical) statement regarding specific risk factors to a qualitative (and collective) categorization of the children in question. The quantitative approach to risk-a matter of ordering reality (rendering it into calculable form)-leads to a qualitative assessment of individuals as falling within at risk categories. Thus a statistical statement translates into a normative statement-a global narrative regarding groups of children-regardless of context. This leads to unhelpful assumptions of generalized vulnerability and represents a further instance of categorical thinking about children.

Moreover, although risk factors are based on the calculable, at risk discourses evoke the incalculable-a perception of fear or danger. Particularly when it comes to children, risk anxiety is focused on those who come under public scrutiny, fall outside accepted social boundaries, and are perceived as an endangered or a dangerous group. Risk management in relation to such children is fueled by risk anxiety, honed by "a climate of heightened risk awareness" and the construct of childhood as a protected state in which children should lead safe and carefree lives. In discourses about children, there is not only "a growing consciousness of children at risk" but also "a growing sense of children themselves as the risk... as people out of place and excess populations to be eliminated" or controlled.

Views about risk thus present an ambivalence in referring to groups who are especially vulnerable but also to groups who explicitly disturb or violate established social norms. It is precisely because street children are so visibly "out of place," many of them living a life of "inchoate rebellion" and selfdestruction characterized by violence, sexual exploitation, illiteracy, and haphazard nutrition, that they are the focus of intense concern-whereas their peers in urban centers, living at home in great poverty in slum and squatter settlements, are not.

Categorical statements about street children being the most at risk of negative physical, mental, and developmental outcomes abound in the literature. One striking example of the often polemical stance adopted regarding the health outcomes of a street existence is provided by de la Barra who claimed: "Being poor is itself a health hazard; worse, however, is being urban and poor. Much worse is being poor, urban, and a child. But worst of all is being a street child in an urban environment". As for homelessness, Wright maintained: "it is hard to conceive of a socially defined 'risk factor' that is of greater consequence for a person's physical wellbeing. " Over and above poverty, a homeless existence would expose "persons of all genders and ages" to a characteristic package of disorders identifiable "everywhere" across cultural contexts.

Indeed, by emphasizing the debilitating aspects of street life, most studies have brought street children to prominence as "a category of children whose life circumstances place them at physical and psychosocial risk". However, the assessment of risk is problematic because the statistics collected from street children are often suspect in their validity and reliability. Many studies feature samples that are small, ill-defined, or unrepresentative of the homeless or street child population. They also lack in rigor for want of appropriate comparison groups: Homeless street children tend to be compared with Western middle class children, the gold standard of childhood, rather than with local groups of poor, home-based children who arguably represent a more realistic lifestyle alternative for children in the streets.

Moreover, there are few comprehensive overviews of the literature, which includes unpublished academic theses, government reports, and advocacy materials, despite some attempts to produce a compilation of studies by topics or geographical areas. This makes it particularly difficult to distinguish the risks attributed to homelessness or street life from those associated with socioeconomic disadvantage. Indeed, one review of the health problems of U. S. homeless children asked whether "it is appropriate to focus exclusively on homelessness as a marker of risk" given that homelessness is "one event along the continuum of a child's experience of poverty". And if homelessness is "simply the most visible and exaggerated manifestation of chronic poverty, then broader policy questions must be raised".

In terms of physical health, some studies-explicitly designed to compare homeless with home-based children-have challenged the assumption that "all street children are pitiful, pale and thin, malnourished". They have highlighted the fact that street children had higher, albeit irregular, income than home-based children and relied on networks of solidarity and care within their peer group to buffer themselves against shortfalls.

In terms of mental health, criticisms have also been made of the view that street children necessarily suffer from negative developmental outcomes. Felsman and Aptekar are two authors who argue quite strongly that the majority of street children they have studied were "clearly without pathology", displayed better mental health than poor counterparts, and showed a high level of self-management. Rather than being the most victimized, the most destitute, the most psychologically vulnerable group of children, street children may be resilient and display creative coping strategies for growing up in difficult environments. Attention is here paid to streetwise behaviors and remarkable survival skills, which cannot however be equated with invulnerability or mature emotional development. There is also evidence of an habituation to stressful events, which extends to a downregulation of the physiological responses associated with stress.

In two studies using the hormone cortisol as a sensitive marker of anxiety and psychosocial arousal, average cortisol levels for homeless street children were similar to those of middle class children in Nepal and to those of home-based street workers in Ethiopia. In terms of engaging in drug-taking, survival sex, and HIV-risk behavior, studies overwhelmingly ascribe street youth, and street girls particularly, to an at risk category. But as with the measurement of mental health through psychiatric and psychological morbidity, the assessment of drug-taking and sexual health is fraught with significant methodological problems. Mere use of questionnaire data, without triangulation with other methods, is suspect and provides limited cross-sectional information.

Fewsurveys include the screening of home-based and street-based youth for markers of sexually transmitted infections, nor do they corroborate self-reports for common infections. Nonetheless, Raffaelli's review concluded that the weight of studies leaves little doubt that homeless youth are at higher risk of abusive sexual relationships and of sexually transmitted infections than are their peers. HIV in particular poses a dramatic challenge in Africa due to the magnitude of the AIDS epidemic and war-related instability, although to date very little research has been conducted on war, HIV-risks, and street children. Finally, because many street youth live harsh and violent lives, risks to health include death from violent trauma, suicide, accidents, and murder; however, fewsurvival statistics have ever been published. Those deaths represent a brutal end to pervasive social marginalization.

Social exclusion is also reflected in the risk of educational failure and poor cognitive performance-although street life can offer opportunities for nonstandard education.

Substantial evidence thus supports the view that street children are a category at risk, but there is also disagreement with a discourse that sets the characteristics of street life in global terms, associating the worst health outcomes with street children by ascription. Specific risks to health need to be rigorously investigated, and not overgeneralized to cover all aspects of health-physical health, mental health, sexual health-which constitute different benchmarks for risk assessment. Otherwise research and public health concerns are in danger of being led by a normative view of at risk categories and marred by a lack of conceptual clarity, rather than focused on the critical appraisal of what constitutes risk. This is true to the extent that the literature on street children is guilty of "systematically ignoring its own findings in favour of predetermined conclusions grounded in Northern, middle class mores".

As Sibert wisely indicated, what public health professionalswould really like to know is whether homeless street children are "uniquely disadvantaged or whether they form one end of the spectrum of poor children" with respect to risks to health. To achieve this, research on children in adversity needs to be quite extensively overhauled. As emphasized by Holden et al. for the United States, "research on children in poverty has already shifted from comparisons between children in low-income and middle-income families to in-depth analyses of processes mediating poverty's influences on developmental and health outcomes... To understand why some homeless children display a host of mental health problems and why others survive and succeed, attention should be focused on variations within homeless populations. " What is important to future research are the factors of risk and resilience that shape the long-term coping strategies of individual children, by developing their competence for negotiating high risk situations.

Resilience of Children

Influential research has argued that a helpful counterpart to the risk discourse is to focus attention on the resilience of children who manage to negotiate extremely difficult circumstances. As Rutter explained, resilience is the term used to describe the positive pole of individual differences in responses to stress and adversity. Rutter further emphasized that in the field of psychiatric risk research, there has been a shift of focus not only "from vulnerability to resilience, but also from risk variables to the process of negotiating risk situations". This represents a useful approach-one that is not constrained by categorical thinking but centers on identifying the protective factors that help individuals cope with adversity.

Research on resilience is by no means simple. In 1990, Rutter made a critically important argument: Research will gain very little if it confines itself to a mechanistic search for protective factors as those sets of variables that will predict resiliency with fair consistency (namely, personality features, family cohesion, and external support systems). Instead, it must appraise the developmental and contextual processes by which some individuals manage to negotiate adversity (why and how they maintain selfesteem and self-efficacy; how they managed to have effective social networks). It is wrong to assume that vulnerability or protection lies in the variable (e. g., social support) per se, rather than in the active role taken by individuals under adversity:

Resilience is a reflection of an individual's agency. It is also crucial, but obviously difficult, to appraise how protective factors may work in interaction with each other, to investigate their relative importance over a lifetime, and finally to confirm their relevance across different cultures. The majority of risk research remains based on comparison groups within a cross-sectional design. The overwhelming body of work on resilience concerns itself with industrialized countries, such that little information exists on children and adversity in other contexts.

Significantly, cross-cultural studies on street youth may not support unilateral conclusions regarding gender differences in coping with a long-term existence on the street, despite the argument that girls are at higher risk of negative outcomes than their male peers.

Current work with street children sees further studies on developmental vulnerability and resilience to be fundamental to both research and practical intervention. For street children present us with a "central and pervasive" paradox-"with evidence of developmental risk and vulnerability on the one hand and of resourcefulness, adaptability, and coping on the other". Indeed, researchers have been fascinated by both positive and negative aspects of their lives and personalities: Barker & Knaul describe them as "both needy and bold, exploited but street-smart entrepeneurs. " For Felsman, the paradox is that gamines in Colombia stand "at the intersection of human strength and vulnerability". These and other authors agree that the best approach is not to generalize over what common factors in street lifestyles lead to at risk situations, but to ask a different order of questions.

A pertinent issue relates to how key developmental stressors "combine to produce actual, not just putative, developmental vulnerability"; in many cases, it is the combination of multiple stressors rather than the experience of any single factor that defines an individual's vulnerability. Arguably, the concept of a street or homeless career-or the notion of street children having fluid careers-is another fruitful analytic device for moving the literature beyond its habitual snap shot descriptions of children, because it calls for data giving both time-depth and contextual information. The concept of career, used by Goffman and Becker in their studies of social deviance, can help appraise for street children the long-term outcomes of social experiences and negotiated identities.

For the homeless, self-perceptions and social experiences are the bedrock of career outcomes, as shown in the United

Kingdom by Hutson & Liddiard and in Nepal by Baker & Panter-Brick. It should not surprise anyone to find that the outcomes of homeless careers will differ by cultural context. In Northeast Brazil, Hecht reported that prison, insanity, or death were the common expectations of life for street children, while also in Brazil, Vasconcelos thus summarized the stark prospects for street girls: They "disappear. They are arrested or they die. They die from venereal diseases, they are sent to mental institutions, they die from abortion, or in childbirth, or they kill themselves. "

By contrast, in Nepal, Baker documented that homeless children could achieve stable employment, marriage and families of their own. It is not even well established why there are street children in certain cultures and not in others, given the paucity of comparative research linking global to local analyses. And while poverty and family dysfunction are ubiquitous causes for homelessness, poverty or abuse cannot be held as sole explanations for street children leaving home-when their siblings (and the majority of children) do not. An ethnographic focus on the careers of street children in comparison with their peers might help to achieve a more fine-grained understanding of such issues.

Careers are also profoundly influenced by ethnicity, gender, and disability, as well as age. Moreover, street life is often able to offer payoffs in the short-term, while compromising individuals in the long run. As Gregori noted, how Brazilian street children circulate in social spaces and negotiate with a range of institutions is marked by their status as legal minors; when they reach the age of majority, they face a difficult transformation of identity as the institutional support for minors falls away. A career perspective may be a way of articulating more cogently how rights articulate with risks for specific individuals, and how individuals themselves interpret the risks they face, the behavioral choices they make, and the social marginalization they experience.

3

Refugee Children

The term 'asylum-seeker' and 'refugee' have a specific legal meaning. An asylum-seeker is someone who has crossed an international border in search of safety, and refugee status, in another country. There are over 18 million refugees in today's world and the migration of refugees is a growing challenge to governments and non-governmental organisations alike. Although most refugee children live in poor countries there are probably over 120, 000 asylum-seeking and refugee children in the UK.

Status of Refugees

To be recognised as having refugee status, a person must have left his or her own country or be unable to return to it 'owing to a well-founded fear of being persecuted for reasons of race, religion, nationality, membership of a particular social group or political opinion. ' The 1951 UN Convention Relating to the Status of Refugees and its 1967 Protocol are the two international legal instruments that determine the rights of asylumseekers and refugees. Other human rights instruments have bearings on asylumseeking and refugee children. The 1989 UN Convention on the Rights of the Child enshrines children's rights, including:

— the right to judgements by the judiciary, welfare agencies and government that are taken in the best interests of the child (Article 3)

— the right to family unity and reunion (Article 10)

— protection of children without families (Article 20)

— ensuring that asylum-seeking and refugee children receive protection and assistance (Article 22)

— the right to liberty (Article 37).

It is frequently argued that aspects of the UK's treatment of asylum-seeking children contravene the spirit of the Convention on the Rights of the Child. Indeed, NGOs often highlight this in lobbying the UN. However, the UK has acceded to the Convention on the Rights of the Child with reservations, namely that children subject to immigration control, including asylum-seeking children, are excluded from rights that the Convention enshrines.

Asylum Applications

Asylum applications can be lodged at the port of entry or 'in-country' after arrival. Many of those who lodge asylum applications in-country have arrived as clandestine entrants to the UK. The closing of legal routes of entry to the European Union has meant that in the last decade greater proportions of asylum-seekers have been forced to use the services of traffickers to enter the EU. Families may take great risks to enter the EU, and there have been continued reports of deaths enroute, including of young children. In order to make an asylum application, the primary asylum applicant has to recount details of past persecution to the Immigration and Nationality Directorate (IND), part of the Home Office. On the basis of information given to the IND, a decision is made on the asylum-seeker's case. After full consideration of a case, there may be one of four outcomes:

— *Refugee Status:* Refugee status protects a person from being returned to his or her country of origin and confers other rights, such as the right to bring immediate family into the UK, the right to work and the right to most of the benefits of a British subject.

— *Humanitarian Protection:* This is a new immigration status introduced in April 2003. It is granted to asylum-seekers refused refugee status, who, if returned to their country of origin would face a serious risk to life from one or more of the following reasons the death penalty, unlawful killing, torture, inhuman or degrading treatment or punishment. Those who receive Humanitarian Protection usually receive it for a period of three years.

— *Discretionary Leave:* This is granted by the Home Secretary outside the provisions of the Immigration Rules. It is granted to people refused asylum who cannot be returned to their home country, or a safe third country. It is also granted to some unaccompanied children who cannot be legally returned home until they are 18. In April 2003, Humanitarian Protection and Discretionary Leave replaced the status of Exceptional Leave to Remain (ELR). Throughout the 1980s and 1990s most asylum-seekers who were allowed to stay in the UK, received ELR.

— *Refusal:* Asylum-seekers may be rejected without a full consideration of their case, at the port of entry after an application has been judged to be 'manifestly unfounded'. Asylum-seekers can also be rejected for 'non-compliance. ' Some 18 per cent of all decisions made in 2001 were rejections for non-compliance. Asylum-seekers may be rejected after full consideration of their cases. Once an asylum application has been refused, the applicant can appeal, leave the UK voluntarily, be removed or choose to 'disappear'. Some 20-30 per cent of appeals are usually successful.

Asylum-seekers may also have their cases rejected without being processed through the above 'full' asylum procedures; their cases being rejected as 'clearly unfounded'. Usually, those rejected in such a law have very limited rights of appeal in the UK; the Nationality, Immigration and Asylum Act 2002 will further restrict the right of appeal in the UK of this group. In addition to those who apply for asylum, the UK also hosts other population of forced migrants. They include those who have arrived on 'programmes' - Government-sponsored evacuations such as the Vietnamese, Bosnian and Kosovan Programme.

Here an immigration status is granted overseas and there is usually an organised reception programme. The Vietnamese were granted refugee status while Bosnians and Kosovars were only afforded temporary protection in the UK. Other endangered people including Afghans, Iraqis and Zimbabweans, have secured entry to the UK on new Home Office migration programmes. Other groups of forced migrants include those who fear persecution but never apply for asylum, relying on other immigration status or perhaps none at all. There are also migrations of refugees around Europe; movement into the UK made most significantly by Somalis who were originally granted refugee status in The Netherlands or Sweden. An estimated 9, 000 Somalis have arrived from the EU.

Demography

In 2002 some 85, 865 asylum applications were received in the UK. Including dependants, this amounted to 110, 700 asylum-seekers who arrived in the UK in 2001. Most asylum applicants are single and male; less than 25 per cent of applicants have had dependent children in recent years, although the proportions of dependent children do vary among national groups. During 2002, the four main countries of origin of asylum-seekers arriving in the UK were Iraq, Afghanistan, Zimbabwe and Somalia; countries beset by armed conflict, severe violations of human rights or both.

The Home Office publishes basic statistical data about asylum application and decisions, quarterly. The National Asylum Support Service, too, is meant to inform receiving health authorities and education authorities of asylum applicants dispersed to their area, but this system regularly breaks down. There is, therefore, little demographic data about the composition of asylum-seeking households or settlement patterns in the UK that would be of use to service providers, and Census data does not include information on immigration status.

An attempt to remedy this lack of data on refugee children has been made at the London Metropolitan University. By collecting local education authority (LEA) language and refugee surveys, Rutter concluded that there were about 80, 000 asylum-seeking and refugee children in UK schools in January 2002. In Greater London schools and LEA nurseries there were an estimated 62, 666 asylum-seeking and refugee children - their numbers comprised 6. 04 per cent of the total pupil roll in Greater London. In seven London LEAs, refugee children comprise more than 10 per cent of the total school roll. Outside London, only Manchester and Glasgow LEAs have numbers of asylumseeking and refugee children that approach that of London LEAs.

The largest groups of asylum-seeking and refugee children in schools are Somalis and Somali minority groups such as the Bravanese, comprising about 21 per cent of all asylum-seeking and refugee children in the UK. Sri Lankan Tamils are the next largest group and other large population include Afghans, Turkish Kurds, Iranians and Congolese. In many LEAs, there is great national diversity among refugee communities - in one London LEA the refugee survey showed children coming from 58 national groups. Asylum-seeking and refugee children are a very mobile population within the UK, owing to the temporary nature of housing allocated to asylum-seekers, and the fact that most refugees, once granted status, are then placed on a local authority waiting list for housing.

The analysis of data on asylum-seeking and refugee children, as well as of statistics produced by NASS (the National Asylum Support Service), indicate that secondary migration to Greater London is occurring. This is not a new phenomenon as there has been considerable secondary migration of other recent refugee groups to the capital. Push and pull factors in this secondary migration include existing community, family and friends, work and safety. Language surveys and refugee data show two other important trends. First, asylumseeking and refugee children are under-represented in LEA nursery schools and most classes of LEAs, and secondly, within an LEA, asylum-seeking and refugee children attend some schools and not others.

There have been major changes in asylum legislation and policy since the late 1980s, with new laws passed in 1993, 1996, 1999 and 2002. Legislative changes have been accompanied by negative media coverage, particularly in tabloid and local newspapers. Arguably, the impact of such coverage makes it less likely that central and local government will invest in good support services for asylum-seekers and refugees. Public hostility to refugees is also increased by negative media coverage. The legislative and policy changes have:

— built 'barriers', making the legal entry of asylum-seekers much more difficult. Such barriers include the requirement of a visa to enter the UK and placing immigration officers at overseas airports

— restricted asylum-seekers' social and legal rights, including rights to work, benefits, housing and higher education

— tightened the substantive by which asylum cases are judged, so that proportionally more asylum-seekers are refused refugee status or ELR than in the late 1980s.

These legislative changes target the legal protection of asylum-seekers as well as welfare and social support systems for them. All legislation that affects asylumseeking households will affect children's welfare. For example, proposals to remove some asylum-seekers' right to appeal in the UK against a negative asylum decision will obviously affect an adult asylum-seeker and his/her child dependants. The legislative changes comprise the:

— Asylum and Immigration (Appeals) Act 1993

— Asylum and Immigration Act 1996

— Immigration and Asylum Act 1999

— Nationality, Immigration and Asylum Act 2002.

Asylum and Immigration (Appeals) Act 1993

Among its many sections, this Act restricted rights to social housing for asylumseekers. From its implementation, asylum-seekers lost the right to be accepted as homeless if they had any other housing, 'however temporary', in which they could live. Moreover, while an asylum case is being determined, no asylum-seeking household could be offered a secure social housing tenancy. Schools, LEAs and organisations working with refugees noted increases in asylumseeking children's mobility from the implementation of the Asylum and Immigration (Appeals) Act 1993. Greater London OFSTED reports during the period 1993-1996 cited pupil mobility in some schools that had large numbers of asylum-seeking pupils as being 10 per cent in a year, and among the asylum-seeking pupils themselves as being 60-100 per cent.

High pupil mobility among asylum-seeking and refugee pupils remains a major challenge today, particularly in Greater London. Pupil mobility and poor housing affect children's welfare and educational achievement. Ill-health, cramped play and study space, difficulties in securing school places, stigmatisation of homeless pupils and difficulties in building social relationships within the school are effects described by practitioners. Continuity of care for refugee children with healthcare or special educational needs is adversely affected.

Other pupils, too, are affected by high pupil mobility: teacher time is spent settling in new students and it is difficult to deliver a curriculum with continuity in situations where there is high pupil mobility. There are therefore, social costs associated with high housing mobility.

Asylum and Immigration Act 1996

Further asylum legislation was passed in 1996, after the removal, in 1995, of Income Support from some asylum-seekers and then a reversal of this policy following legal challenges. The Asylum and Immigration Act 1996 had major effects on children's welfare. It barred asylum-seekers from being placed on a waiting list for social housing. It also removed the right to Income Support from asylum-seekers who lodged their claims 'in-country' as opposed to the port of entry. Families with children were instead supported by social services departments under the provisions of the Children Act 1989 and given a cash allowance and some form of temporary accommodation.

Many such families were moved to temporary accommodation outside Greater London, often in seaside towns in locations such as Southend, Great Yarmouth, Bognor Regis and Hastings. Some of the accommodation used was of very poor quality. There were problems securing legal advice and service providers usually had little experience in working with asylum-seekers and little access to interpreters. Securing funding to work with new population also proved a problem, as statutory funding sources such as the Ethnic Minority Achievement Grant rely on stable population in the allocation of funding through formulae. The duties placed on social services by the Asylum and Immigration Act 1996 may also have had long-term consequences on social services support to asylum-seeking and refugee families.

Immigration and Asylum Act 1999

By 31 March 1999, Greater London social services departments were responsible for 20, 421 asylum-seeking households without access to benefits and supported under the provisions of the Children Act 1989 and the National Assistance Act 1948. These local authorities were not being fully compensated by central government for support given to such asylum-seekers. After extensive lobbying from south-eastern local authorities, the Immigration and Asylum Act 1999 was passed and introduced far-reaching changes to the way that asylumseekers were to be supported and housed in the UK. The Act set up the National Asylum Support Service (NASS) as part of the Immigration and Nationality Directorate of the Home Office. To prepare for dispersal, the UK was divided into regional groupings, termed 'asylum consortia'. Each consortium appointed officers to plan for services for asylum-seekers.

During Spring and Summer 2000, NASS introduced a new voucher and dispersal system for all new asylum-seekers in the UK, apart from unaccompanied asylumseeking children. On arrival, any destitute asylum-seeker and dependants had the option of applying to NASS for a 'support only' package, or for support and accommodation. Until April 2002, support entailed a cash allowance of £10 per person per week, plus vouchers exchangeable at designated retail outlets. NASS also allocates housing to those that apply for it. A mixture of public and private sector accommodation is used in regions of dispersal. The NASS system has had a major effect on children's education and well-being, namely:

— Asylum-seekers may have a long wait in emergency accommodation in London prior to dispersal - far longer than the seven days planned by NASS. Most of the accommodation is in hotels previously or also used by homeless families. Some children living in emergency accommodation have stayed there so long that their parents have successfully got school places in London. Concerns about the quality of food in emergency accommodation for pregnant and nursing mothers has also been raised by healthcare practitioners and refugees themselves.

— Inefficiencies in the processing of NASS vouchers. Those applying for support from NASS may wait many weeks before support is granted. A proportion of NASS vouchers are also lost in delivery. This places stress on already destitute families.

— Housing quality for those opting for NASS 'support only' and remaining with a host family and/or friends is an issue of concern; it is inevitably overcrowded and this will affect children's well-being and ability to study.There is also an impact on the hosting household, whose living space and scarce household income is shared among more people.

— Housing mobility in London - anecdotal evidence from refugee support teachers is that many families who opt for 'support only' move between different types of accommodation, as hospitality is exhausted.

— Poverty: although voucher support was replaced by cash support on 8 April 2002, asylum-seekers are still supported at levels below income support. This is again of particular concern in Greater London, where those opting for 'support only' may be hosted by others on benefits. An account of the poverty faced by many asylum-seekers is provided in Poverty and Asylum in the UK where 85 per cent of a sample of refugee organisations reported that their clients experienced hunger on a regular basis.

— School uniform, a requirement by most primary and secondary schools, is outside the budget of families supported by NASS. Yet school uniform grants are discretionary and some LEAs do not award them at all.

— Secondary migration to London, once the asylum applicant and dependants have been granted refugee status or ELR, is high.

Nationality, Immigration and Asylum Act 2002

This will have far-reaching implications for young asylum-seeking children's welfare. The parts of the Act that deal with asylum will again change the support arrangements for some asylum-seekers. From 2002, many newly arrived asylumseekers will be held in non-secure 'Induction Centres' in London and the South East. Here they will lodge an asylum application, and, if needed, an application for support by NASS. After a period of time in the Induction Centre, the asylum-seeker may:

— go to a removal centre (detention centre) prior to removal from the UK. Two removal centres presently have facilities to detain children with their parents, prior to removal. Continued concerns have been expressed by children's charities about this detention of children, especially as accounts emerge of children being detained for substantial periods.

— move into the community, to live with family or friends, but be required to sign on at a reporting centre. Most asylum-seekers choosing this option are likely to be living in the Greater London area, with its large refugee population. At present, asylum-seekers who choose this option will continue to receive NASS support, but there is scope within the Bill for this to be removed at the Home Secretary's discretion. Refugee organisations believe that the eventual removal of this 'support only' option is likely.

— move to dispersal accommodation provided for NASS as before. At the time of writing, no extra money has been earmarked in order to make dispersal work and reduce secondary migration back to Greater London.

— move into an accommodation centre, where the asylum-seeker and his or her dependants will be expected to stay while their case is determined. The Home Office plans for the centres to be large, housing up to 750 residents.

Food, other necessities, healthcare and education will be provided in these accommodation centres and the asylum-seeker will only receive a small amount of pocket money. All of the accommodation centres will be located outside the South East and there are plans to set up four pilots to be operational by 2004.

The above changes are likely to affect children's welfare. Secondary migration to Greater London may remain at a high level if no extra funding is allocated to support arrangements in areas of dispersal. Housing in accommodation centres will increase isolation from the host community and prevent an asylum-seeker making local links outside Greater London. This, too, will encourage secondary migration to Greater London. The proposal to provide separate education in accommodation centres for children has attracted particular criticism.

Numerous studies have shown that, for refugee children, inclusion within mainstream education has special significance. Attending school may be a therapeutic and normalising experience for a child whose recent life experiences have been far from normal. Separate education has linguistic disadvantages - children have little or no social and academic interaction with native speakers of English - and asylum-seeking children are often successful ambassadors for their communities, therefore separate education will remove this aspect of community cohesion.

Separate education may prove difficult to deliver in accommodation centres. Unless the DfES sanctions disapplication, the accommodation centre contractors will be obliged to follow the National Curriculum. That there will be small numbers of schoolaged children of very different ages in accommodation centres gives an indication of how difficult it will be to provide education. The Nationality, Immigration and Asylum Act provides for other legislative changes that affect children. These are:

— A government resettlement programme for refugees admitted from abroad for resettlement in the UK, likely to be similar to the Vietnamese, Bosnian or Kosovan programmes. It is likely that such programmes will comprise a greater proportion of children than among 'spontaneous' arrivals.

— Sections that provide for the removal of the NASS 'support only' option if requested by the Home Secretary, or the removal of any NASS support. At present, significant numbers of asylum-seekers choose the existing 'support only' option, including many families with children. Most of this group remain within Greater London, near to existing communities. It seems likely that their removal of the support only option would not discourage many asylum-seekers from remaining in the capital. Instead it would only reduce their income, to the detriment of children's welfare.

NASS support was withdrawn from in-country asylum applicants without dependent children in January 2003 (this move is presently being challenged in the courts). Although not directly targeting asylumseeking children, it should be noted that many families from refugee communities - often with very few financial resources themselves - will feed and house destitute relatives and friends. There will be an indirect affect on children of families hosting destitute asylum-seekers as there was in 1996 after benefits were withdrawn from in-country applicants.

Changes to the detention procedures, including removing the right to bail. Concurrently, the Home Office is commissioning increased places in removal centres, including places for families, and has publicly stated that the detention of children may be 'an unusual but necessary step'. Children are a vulnerable category and detention has a harsher impact on them than on adults.

In addition to changes in the present legislation, the Government is likely to change support systems for unaccompanied asylum-seeking and refugee children, most of whom are presently the responsibility of a small number of local authorities in Greater London and the South East, with Kent County Council alone being responsible for over 1, 000 unaccompanied children, many of whom are moved to other parts of the UK. Options being debated are threefold. First, some four local authorities - Kent, West Sussex, Hillingdon and Croydon - would be responsible for assessing all unaccompanied children. Those children who needed homes would be dispersed around the UK. Finally, some of the case responsibility for these children would shift to the receiving local authority, an option that may require an amendment to the Children Act 1989.

Asylum-seekers lost the right to work in July 2002. This policy change may have indirect effects on asylum-seeking and refugee children. For example, asylumseekers may choose to remain in London and other big metropolitan areas where their chances of finding undocumented work are higher. Other non-asylum legislation and policy has affected asylum-seeking and refugee children.

The next decade is likely to bring further legislative and policy changes affecting asylum-seeking children. At a European level, too, there is also likely to be greater harmonisation of the reception conditions of asylum-seekers with a draft directive on reception conditions, as well as their rights to welfare, housing, education and healthcare. Although it is uncertain whether the draft directive will be passed, the trend is for greater harmonisation across Europe, and such changes will have a major impact on asylum-seeking children.

Needs of Refugee Children

Profiling of several researchers is useful for service providers. It is important to remember that within a given refugee community there is a great deal of heterogeneity, but needs and problems that manifest themselves with significant numbers of refugee children include:

— having an interrupted education in the country of origin

— having horrific experiences in their home countries and during their flight to the UK (for a small number, this affects their ability to settle and rebuild their lives)

— living with families who experience a drop in their standard of living and status in society

— changing care arrangements: losing parents or usual carers

— having parents who are emotionally absent

— living with families who do not know their legal and social rights in the UK, including their rights to basic services such as education and healthcare, and who encounter problems securing education, healthcare or benefits

— speaking little or no English on arrival.

The need for legal protection and a secure immigration status in the UK is a universal need. To be treated as a child, first and foremost, rather than an asylumseeker or refugee is a right that should underpin responses to these children. Asylum-seeking and refugee children are users of statutory services such as early years services, education, healthcare and social services. Such services, for example schooling, may be universal. Refugee children may also be users of targeted services, for refugees, for minority ethnic communities or for other identified vulnerable groups. Non-governmental organisations also run targeted support for refugee children.

Entitlements to Early Years Provision

Race relations legislation would indicate that asylum-seeking and refugee children have full entitlements to early years provision throughout the UK, although no government has issued any guidance on this. Refugee communities have a great need for quality early years provision. The age profile of refugee communities in the UK is younger than the non-refugee population - in 1996 some 77 per cent of asylum applicants were under 35 years - and it is likely that there are proportionally more refugee children under five than in the population as a whole. All research on employment among asylum-seekers and refugees indicates that the majority of these households are workless. Many refugee children grow up in poverty. Government commitments to abolish child poverty and to increase early years provision will, therefore, be of particular importance for refugee households. Access to good quality early years provision is also likely to be a cost effective intervention.

Children with positive early experiences of education are less likely to fail in school. Refugee Council research conducted in 1998 indicated that over 70 per cent of asylum-seeking and refugee children grew up in households where little or no English was spoken. Enabling a child from a non-English speaking household to attend a nursery before school starts will decrease the need for funded support in primary school. Access to early years provision may also enable refugee parents to attend English classes or obtain new qualifications. And for the most stressed refugee parents, a break from the demands of childcare may enable them to rebuild their lives, saving later interventions by health and social care agencies.

Initiatives of Potential Relevance

There has been an expansion of early years provision during the last five years, a policy central to government targets to reduce child poverty. In England, initiatives of potential relevance to refugee families include:

— *The Neighbourhood Childcare Initiative:* This is an area-based initiative that aims to create 45, 000 new daycare places in up to 900 neighbourhood nurseries (mostly voluntary sector), together with 25, 000 new places at child minders. The aim of this initiative is to improve access to childcare for working parents living in the most deprived areas

— *Sure Start:* This is an area-based initiative that aims to ensure that every child arrives in school healthy and ready to learn. It funds a range of projects including parent and toddler groups, advice sessions and provision in family centres. In Greater London a small number of Sure Start programmes have worked with refugee families, with some, such as Sure Start Edmonton, targeting these families. By March 2004 it is intended that 500 Sure Start projects will be working with 400, 000 of the most deprived children.

— *The Four-Year-Old Grant and the Three-Year-Old Grant:* All four year olds whose parents want to use nursery care are now guaranteed such provision - up to five two-and-a-half hour sessions during term time, achieved by payment of a grant to nurseries.

— *Early Excellence Centres:* These provide a range of early years education and family support services on one site, building on the pioneering work of the Dorothy Gardner centre in Westminster and others. Such centres provide nursery education, and services such as health visitor clinics, family literacy and English language classes, toy libraries, and surgeries offering welfare rights and other advice and services. It is intended that the funding for the 29 pilot Early Excellence Centres be expanded to fund some 100 such centres by 2004. Given the multiple social needs of many refugee families, Early Excellence Centres may usefully meet their needs and many are doing so already.

In 1999, the new English Early Years Development Plans were required to account for services provided for refugee children; an addition welcomed by refugee charities. Local authority social service departments are also required by the Department of Health to draw up Children's Services Plans - a product of collaboration between local authorities, health authorities, the voluntary sector and other appropriate groups. This creates another opportunity for planning for the needs of young refugee children.

Despite these and other central government initiatives, such as a commitment to better training for early years workers, it is likely that many refugee families are not reaping the full benefits of expanded early years provision. There is also no evidence to indicate that refugee communities groups are being helped to develop their own nurseries, parent and toddler groups or other provision. The reasons are complex, but mostly relate to a lack of bridge-building between early years partnerships and refugee community groups.

Regional, Local authorities and individual institutions

— Having a person with designated responsibility for refugees located within an early years team/partnership at LEA level.

— Effective multi-agency work, in particular ensuring that there are good links between health visitors and early years educators. Focus group discussion and visits indicated that such linking was weak in many areas.

— Conducting detailed ethnic monitoring of uptake of early years services.

— Child minding, which offers employment opportunities to refugee women. Local authorities can organise training courses targeted at refugee women, perhaps with English language support. Training should be coupled with a small grants scheme to enable the women to purchase toys and safety equipment.

— Ensuring availability of good quality outreach and consultation to gather information on needs and to inform refugee parents of the range of early years provision.

— Helping refugee community organisations to develop their own early years services, for example parent and toddler groups. Within Greater London, only five refugee community organisations presently run such services.

— Training early years workers to enable them to better meet the needs of refugee children. Refugee children need nurseries and playgroups that can:

  — meet their psychological needs by, for example, using play to help a child settle

  — respond to their language needs

  — challenge racism and promote cultural diversity

  — involve parents who may not be confident in speaking English

  — support families who may be experiencing stress and economic deprivation.

Growing Consensus

Despite growing consensus about good practice there are concerns about early years provision for refugee children. Refugee children presently have unequal access to early years provision. However, the analysis of language and refugee surveys conducted in 2002 does indicate an improvement in refugee children's access to LEA nurseries in some London LEAs since 1998, including three that had attempted to conduct outreach work among refugee communities. However, despite an expansion of early years provision, inequality persists. In one London local authority, where refugee children comprise 6. 5 per cent of all children, there were only nine refugee children within the area's nursery provision in 1997. Reasons for underrepresentation include:

Housing mobility: many LEA nurseries have waiting lists for places, and families move before a nursery place is available.

Lack of knowledge of local services: many refugee-producing countries in Africa and Asia have little or no early years provision. Asylum-seeking families arriving in the UK seldom know about the range of early years provision available. And since over 70 per cent of asylum-seekers speak little or no English, it is difficult for parents to find out about provision. In particular, they may not know about projects such as parent and toddler groups, one o'clock clubs, play buses and toy libraries.

Poverty: even parent and toddler groups that only make a small charge might be unaffordable for an asylum-seeking family that is forced to live on NASS support.

Cultural factors: in some refugee communities infants are always cared for by the mother and her extended family, so putting them in the care of strangers could attract disapproval. Other mothers, particularly those who speak little English, feel uneasy about young children being cared for by people who do not know their language, dietary arrangements, religion or customs.

Inaccessibility: some early years provision may not be accessible for large families without private transport.

Unwelcoming services: some types of early years provision, such as playgroups and one o'clock clubs, may be used by a regular group of children and carers who may make 'outsiders' feel unwelcome.

Most early years providers did not undertake good quality ethnic monitoring that would highlight differences in the uptake of early years services among refugee communities. Additionally refugee community groups felt that Early Years Development Partnerships and LEAs did not have accurate demographic information about the local population and this was a barrier to extending services for refugees and targeting resources.

There is little evaluation of service provision that takes into account refugee children's particular needs. Given that in some London local authorities, refugee children account for more than 10 per cent of all children, and a greater proportion of those living in low-income households, it would be reasonable to expect Sure Start evaluations to analyse its applicability to refugee children. Sure Start and the Neighbourhood Childcare Initiative are targeted at deprived families living in particular areas. Refugee children (and others) living in temporary accommodation in the more prosperous areas can be missed by area-based programmes.

Education

Asylum-seeking children, as well as those with ELR and Refugee Status have full entitlement to compulsory education throughout the UK. In England, the entitlement of asylum-seekers and refugees to compulsory education between 5 and 16 years is outlined in the DfES Code of Practice on School Admissions, Annex B, giving them the same rights to education as other children. Section 14 of the Education Act 1996 also obliges English LEAs to provide a full-time education to all children resident within the LEA. In Wales, the Code of Practice on Admissions 1999 secures the right to education for asylum-seeking and refugee children, and in Scotland their entitlement to education is premised on the Education (Scotland) Act 1980. Other legislation and guidance of particular relevance for asylum-seeking and refugee children in education includes:

— A legal right for free school meals if that family is in receipt of a means tested benefit or being supported by NASS or a local authority under the interim support scheme.

— English LEAs have a duty to provide certain educational support to children who are 'looked after' under Section 20 of the Children Act 1989, as are many unaccompanied refugee children under the age of 16 years. This duty requires the LEA to provide an officer who has responsibility for the education of 'looked after' children and an individual education plan and ensures that a child who has newly come into care is not out of education for more than 20 days.

— English and Welsh LEAs and schools must comply with the Race Relations Act 1976 and the Race Relations (Amendment) Act 2000. The latter obliges LEAs and other public bodies to positively promote good race relations. Additionally, the Commission for Racial Equality is tasked under the 2000 Act to prepare a statutory Code of Practice for LEAs and schools on how to fulfil their race equality duties. The new Education Code of Practice came into force in 2002.

— In England, OFSTED can inspect schools for social inclusion, including support for refugee children.

Government Responsibility

The DfES maintains a small team whose brief includes traveller education, refugee education and intercultural education. The team is located in the School Inclusion Division and has recently published guidance on the education of asylum-seeking and refugee children. OFSTED also employs three inspectors whose brief includes refugees. The Scottish Executive and the Welsh Assembly have members of staff whose brief includes refugee children's education, but neither has issued guidance about the education of refugee children. Central government's role includes the planning and implementation of targeted funding initiatives.

In England, three particular interventions are of particular relevance to young refugee children: the Ethnic Minority Achievement Grant (EMAG), the Vulnerable Children Fund and the Children's Fund. EMAG is part of the School Standards Fund and replaced the Home Office Section 11 Fund. The DfES provides 57 per cent of the grant, with local government being responsible for the remainder. EMAG is used mostly to fund English as an additional language support, although it also funds many refugee support teachers. The operation of the EMAG fund has attracted criticism and it is widely felt not to meet the needs of refugee children because:

— Funding is insufficient to meet refugee children's real needs. In reality, teachers' time is solely targeted at beginners in English. Few children who have achieved some competence in English receive additional help and EMAG does not meet the needs of children whose needs are more complex.

— Funding has decreased at a time when the number of children needing support has increased. A Section 11 fund of £130. 8 million in 1993/94 was cut to an EMAG fund of £83 million in 1998/99.

— There is no contingency in the EMAG grant. Local authorities have to make an annual bid for EMAG funds, yet the arrival of asylum-seeking children in a local authority is usually unpredictable, with many LEAs unable to claim monies for children who arrive mid-way through a financial year. As asylum-seekers began to be dispersed outside London, many coastal and northern local authorities complained that they were not receiving additional monies to meet the students' needs.

— EMAG is reluctant to allocate grants for funding dedicated educational psychologists and educational social workers to support refugee children. But good practice indicates that the complex needs of refugee children are best met by multi-disciplinary teams.

— EMAG does not fund home language teaching, even though this has educational and psychosocial benefits for refugee children. The DfES policy is that home language teaching is the responsibility of communities.

In response to the above criticisms of EMAG, the DfES introduced the new Vulnerable Children Fund in late 2002.

This new fund can be used to support travellers, asylum-seeking children and other children out of school. In 2003 its total budget will comprise £84 million. Spending on specific groups is not laid down by the DfES, although in bidding for its monies the LEA has to show how the bid is linked to the Education Development Plan. Unlike EMAG, its monies do not have to be devolved to schools. It could be used to fund items such as dedicated educational psychologists to work with refugee children.

It is a welcome development. However, the allocation of the Vulnerable Children Fund is based on an annual bid. There is no contingency. In 2002, the DfES rejected a contingency fund for large groups of asylum-seekers who arrive in an LEA or school outside deadlines for bidding for funds. The DfES-administered Children's Fund has the potential to fund non-governmental organisations working with refugee communities, as well as welfare support. It is also meant to encourage inter-agency partnership. One London LEA has successfully channelled £330, 000 of its Children's Fund to refugee projects. However, in other local authorities, refugee agencies as well as statutory service providers have complained that the Children's Fund has not been targeted at refugee communities.

In Wales, the Welsh Assembly makes grants available to local authorities for the support of children from ethnic minority communities. In Scotland there is no dedicated fund for such children's educational support, but funding is met directly by local authorities. There is no EMAG-like grant, as local authorities and the Scottish Executive argue that the needs of ethnic minority communities in Scotland can best be met by the appropriate delivery of mainstream local authority services.

The regional asylum consortia employ officers whose responsibility includes planning for the arrival of asylum-seeking children. In some, although not all consortia, there are coordinating meetings of education officers held under the auspices of the consortia. However, to date there has been little impact on actual educational practice (and also other services for children) and no consortia have facilitated cross-LEA services.

Regional and inter-LEA cooperation is more complicated in London - where at least 70 per cent of asylum-seeking children are resident. Here LEAs are small and many organisations, including OFSTED and the Audit Commission, have argued for greater cooperation. The London Asylum Seekers' Consortium (LASC) has not engaged in strategic planning. The Greater London Authority has produced a strategy report on asylum-seekers and refugees (as well as other relevant areas such as a children's strategy) but its remit does not extend to education or social services. The Government Office for London and the Association of London Government have had minimal involvement in refugee children's education in recent years.

During the last ten years there has been a growing consensus about good practice for refugee children at both LEA and school level. This consensus has developed with little intervention from central government; indeed, many aspects of present DfES policy are inimical to the successful educational integration of refugee children. At LEA level, good practice for refugee children is likely to include:

— multi-agency planning at a local authority level, involving education, housing, other statutory services such as FE colleges, the police and the health service, as well as non-governmental organisations
— ensuring that the Education Development Plan (EDP) and its Welsh and Scottish equivalents targets refugee children and involves schools, as well as community stakeholders in drafting
— access to good quality interpreting and translation services

— ethnic monitoring, including monitoring of the uptake of non-compulsory educational services such as early years and youth work provision, as well as educational achievement and school exclusions

— LEA admissions practices that facilitate the early admission of refugee children to school

— the active involvement of educational psychology teams in assessment of refugee children, therapeutic work with them, advice for teachers and other professionals as well as in-service training for teachers

— the employment of refugee support teachers/teams.

— programmes to support refugee community schools. About 40 per cent of all refugee children in the UK attend refugee community schools that may teach the home language, as well as supplementing the mainstream curriculum. A number of London LEAs fund and support such schools

— work by the youth service to ensure that refugee children have full access to youth clubs, leisure, mentoring, after-school and holiday projects and that refugee community organisations are supported in their development of youth services

— the active involvement of early years providers for services for refugee children

— work by libraries and leisure services to meet the particular needs of refuge communities, for example ensuring that refugees have access to books in their home languages.

In January 2002 some 34 local education authorities (LEAs) in England, Scotland and Wales employed specialist refugee support teachers or teams. A further two London LEAs have specialist refugee support teachers working with under fives. Job descriptions and working practices differ between LEAs, but refugee support teachers may; admit and settle asylum-seeking and refugee children into school before handing over responsibility for their education to mainstream and LEA teachers, provide a total package of support, including English language support for refugee children, support refugee children whose needs go beyond that of learning English, for example a child who is not coping as a result of an overwhelmingly traumatic past, act as a contact point within the local authority and represent education on multiagency working parties, act in an advisory capacity - organising in-service training and helping schools develop practices.

A small number of LEAs have multi-disciplinary teams located in education whereby teachers work alongside social workers and/or psychologists. One London LEA employed such a team from 1993-1998 comprising a coordinator, six refugee support teachers, a family support worker and a part-time educational psychologist. It appeared to be an effective way of working with refugee children and their carers. However the team was disbanded in 1998 after changes in educational funding. The employment of refugee support teachers appears to be particularly important in achieving good multi-agency coordination at LEA level.

Without specialist refugee support teachers, there is often less planning and support for refugee children. Other LEA staff may have designated responsibility for refugee children. These include bilingual classroom assistants working with specific refugee communities or linguistic groups, traveller educators, 'looked after children' educators and educational psychologists. Bilingual classroom assistants can offer real support to schools working with refugee children. As well as their linguistic skills, a good bilingual classroom assistant can promote liaison between home and school. For refugees, employment as a bilingual classroom assistant can also be the first step to achieving qualified teacher status in the UK.

Here there is also growing consensus about good practice for refugee children at school level, comprising much of the following:

— policies that draw on past experiences of working with bilingual children, promoting anti-racist and multi-cultural education and working with children in temporary accommodation

— an identified member of staff in the school who has responsibility for refugee children and access to information about refugee children

— in-service training on meeting the needs of refugee children

— an examination of school admission and induction practices, to ensure that refugee children are made to feel welcome

— specialist help and strategies for refugee children who are not coping as a result of their past and present experiences

— adequate support for children with English as an additional language

— encouragement to maintain and develop the home language(s)

— action to counter hostility and the racist bullying of refugees. This may comprise links with other organisations such as Race Equality Councils and community groups. School also need effective sanctions against racist bullying and to use the curriculum to promote ethnic diversity as positive

— good home-school liaison

Despite a growing consensus on what constitutes good education and quality provision for refugee children, there are continuing concerns about refugee children's education. These concerns, described below, have been articulated by refugees themselves, teachers and other educationalists. Some asylum-seeking and refugee children face major barriers in securing school places. In July 2001, the Refugee Council estimated that there were at least 2, 100 asylum-seeking and refugee children out of school in Greater London alone. There is anecdotal evidence that the situation has worsened since then, with the Children's Society estimating in October 2001 that there were at least 700 asylum-seeking and refugee children out of school in the London Borough of Newham alone.

An acute shortage of school places in some LEAs and these LEAs being unwilling or unable to fulfil their statutory duty to provide a school place 2 an unwillingness by some schools to admit refugee pupils. Although pupils with English language needs who arrive in English schools in Years 5, 6, 10 or 11 of their schooling no longer have to be included in English school or LEA league tables, the unwillingness to admit some refugee pupils has persisted.

This is most acute for those children who arrive in the UK aged 14-16, during an examination course, as many schools feel that they have little to offer such pupils 3 high housing mobility among asylum-seeking and refugee pupils, making for frequent moves of school 4 asylum-seeking and refugee parents being unaware of their rights to a school place and having no access to legal representation and/or advocacy to help them secure compulsory education 5 confusing school admissions procedures which differ greatly between LEAs and schools.

Underachievement

There is growing evidence to show that some groups of asylum-seeking and refugee children are underachieving in schools. These groups include Somalis, Turkish Kurdish boys and eastern European Roma. However, LEA data about refugee pupil achievement are variable in quality as, in many LEAs, ethnic categories used in data analysis are too broad to highlight underachievement among particular refugee groups.

Special Education

This is another concern articulated by refugee children. For example, of 32 children, many of primary school age, interviewed in Hackney in 1996, 19 report being the victim of racial harassment and seven had moved school as a result. Children reported verbal abuse, theft of personal items, spitting and physical attack. There is no research that analyses refugee children's experiences of the special needs system - a clear gap in knowledge. In 2003, research was conducted in one London local authority about Congolese children.

However, in four case study schools (secondary) examined by the author, it was found that refugee children were under-represented among those children on the stages of the SEN Code of Practice. No comparable studies have been done in primary schools. That the education funding system in both England and Wales does not meet the needs of refugee children is of growing concern and may contribute to school and LEA unwillingness to accept refugee children. Mainstream funding relies on an annual pupil census and geographically mobile children who arrive and leave between census dates attract no funding. There is a time-lag between a child arriving and funding being granted, as well as lack of contingency funds, either in mainstream funding or project funds such as the EMAG, available to local authorities and schools to support significant numbers of unexpected arrivals.

Out of Exile surveyed present youth work provision for young refugees. Almost all of this was offered by the voluntary sector and very little by local authorities. Refugee children also did not appear to be using much Education non-targeted local authority youth work provision. Although youth work is an issue pertinent to older refugee children to a much greater extent, there does need to be increased partnership between local authority youth work teams and refugee organisations. Another gap in provision is found in holiday projects that include English language support. An all too common scenario is of a refugee child who arrives in the UK in May or June, enrols at school and begins to learn until the summer holidays intervene. During this long vacation, many newly arrived

English language learners lose their existing English language skills.

Healthcare

Asylum-seekers, as well as those with ELR and refugee status, have full entitlements to most health services throughout the UK. Asylum-seeking children supported by NASS, however, have no right to supplies of formula milk granted to other families receiving means tested benefits. While many of the healthcare needs of refugee children are similar to non-refugees, asylum-seeking and refugee children do have specific healthcare needs.

- — securing access to healthcare
- — issues around language and communication
- — health issues relating to refugees' cultural or ethnic origin, for example, female genital mutilation, sickle-cell disease/trait and beta thallasaemia
- — health issues relating to refugees' arrival from poorer countries that have weaker primary healthcare systems and where certain communicable diseases may be endemic, or where immunisation may not take place
- — health issues caused by refugees' exposure to violence and persecution
- — health issues relating to welfare in the UK, in particular nutrition.

Asylum-seekers and refugees have the same basic entitlement to healthcare as other UK residents, with this entitlement being outlined in Health Circular (82) 15. However, many asylum-seeking families, as well as unaccompanied children, experience extreme difficulty in securing access to healthcare. The reasons for this are complex. Newly arrived asylum-seekers may not know how the British healthcare system works and that GP registration provides the route to accessing healthcare. Refugees may also not know the range of services available to them, for example the work of health visitors. Lack of fluency in English may prevent a refugee accessing services.

Asylum-seekers and refugees may be refused registration with a GP; research conducted in east London in 2002 indicated that 34 per cent of a sample of 116 children were not registered with a GP (Refugee Council, 2002). Even if registered, many asylum-seekers face bureaucratic hurdles in securing healthcare. In order for asylum-seekers supported by NASS or local authorities to secure free prescriptions and dental care, they have to complete Dept of Health Form HC1, return it to a Healthcare central NHS administration unit in order to be issued with HC2, a certificate of entitlement. The latter provides access to free prescriptions for six months, then the process has to be repeated. The fact that asylum-seekers and refugees are a very mobile population, particularly in Greater London, can also affect continuity of care.

Communication difficulties may prevent refugees from securing healthcare and also delay diagnosis. Face-to-face interpreters can be booked for planned appointments in most parts of London and other big cities, although they are often not available for appropriate languages outside big cities. There are telephone interpreting services that can be used, however using interpreters effectively is a task that requires skill and experience. Not all medical professionals possess this skill, particularly when examining children; this is an issue that could be remedied by more effective training.

Despite being illegal in the UK since the passage of the Prohibition of Female Circumcision Act 1985, this is still a major health concern facing some refugee communities in the UK. Girls generally undergo this practice at a young age: between six and eight years is common. It is a controversial issue, generating strong feelings among refugees and healthcare professionals. Female genital mutilation is practised in many African countries, as well as in Yemen and Oman, and in their refugee and migrant diaspora. It is carried out by

Muslims, Christians, Jews and animists. Many people believe it is justified by religious teaching, although it has no basis in any religious creed. In some countries, female genital mutilation is part of a girl's rites of passage into adulthood. In some societies, too, an uncircumcised woman is viewed as shameful and unclean. The practice is also used by families as a means of controlling girls' sexuality, and to deter them from marrying outside their ethnic group.

Female genital mutilation takes three forms circumcision, excision and infibulation. Circumcision involves cutting the hood of the clitoris, whilst excision involves the removal of the clitoris and all or part of the labia minora. The most severe form of genital mutilation is infibulation, which involves the removal of the clitoris, labia minora and part or all of the labia majora. The two sides of the vulva are then stitched together and eventually scar tissue forms. A small opening is left for the passage of urine and blood. In the UK, female genital mutilation is an issue which mostly affects the Somali, Sudanese and Yemeni communities. Although illegal, the operation still takes place in the UK, amid great secrecy. Other parents take their daughters to Africa or the Middle East during the summer vacation.

There are immediate risks to a girl's health, as well as long-term complications. An infibulated woman may suffer from chronic bladder and uterine infections. Sexual intercourse is likely to be painful for an infibulated woman. Complications during childbirth are unavoidable: in Somalia, a pregnant woman has her scar cut open and is then re-infibulated at every delivery. Labour is longer, and there is an increased risk of infection, maternal and child death and perinatal brain damage. Those working with young refugee girls need to be aware of the practice and its consequences. Girls who have been infibulated are extremely unwilling to take part in physical education. They may frequently be absent, as menstruation can be very painful. It will also take an infibulated girl a very long time to pass urine: in schools where children have little privacy this can lead to questions, teasing and desperate embarrassment.

In both African and European countries there are promising initiatives among women's groups and from governments, aimed at ending the practice of female genital mutilation. Legislation in the UK prohibiting female genital mutilation came into force in 1985, with the Prohibition of Female Circumcision Act. Female genital mutilation has been incorporated into child protection legislation by local authorities, and there have been nearly 40 cases where there has been action to protect girls at risk. But intervention is often difficult, and many social workers face the dilemma of whether intervention will permanently divide a girl from her family.

There are a number of useful summaries of communicable diseases common among refugee populations. These infections vary according to the countries from which Healthcare refugees have fled. Particular conditions to be aware of include gastrointestinal infections, parasites, tuberculosis and malaria. However, diagnosis of these conditions is often delayed in the UK. That primary healthcare breaks down in conditions of conflict also means that refugee children may not have received routine immunisations. Responding to HIV/AIDS among refugee children requires national planning. In much of sub-Saharan Africa the rate of HIV infection is high. In the Democratic Republic of Congo and Zimbabwe, both major refugee-producing countries, the ante-natal prevalence of HIV is so high that between 10-20 per cent of all children born have been vertically infected with HIV.

Great stigma is attached to HIV infection and among many asylum-seekers there is the fear that HIV/AIDS will prevent an award of refugee status or ELR, and therefore treatment is often delayed. A recent court case granted formula milk to an HIV positive mother who was being supported by NASS, but the judgement only related to this woman. There have been other cases where HIV positive mothers have not been able to access formula milk. While excellent treatment, advice and support is available from the NHS and community groups, these services are mostly located in London and Manchester. There has been little research conducted in the UK about the psychological profiles and responses of refugee children. There is undoubtedly a significant number of refugee children whose life experiences manifest themselves in psychological distress.

There is a growing body of research about nutritional status of refugee children -malnutrition among refugee children is not as uncommon as might be expected in a wealthy country. Those asylum-seekers who have spent time in refugee camps may suffer from malnutrition, as might those asylum-seekers who have had lengthy land journeys through many countries. Asylum-seekers and refugee children living in bed and breakfast hostels or in NASS emergency accommodation are also vulnerable. Hotels may lack cooking and hygienic food storage facilities; cooked food that is provided in emergency accommodation is not always acceptable to children.

In emergency accommodation and NASS full board accommodation, formula milk is not provided - even where a mother is HIV positive. Neither is appropriate weaning and infant food usually provided. NASS-supported women are also not provided with formula milk tokens, although this is being legally challenged by the Child Poverty Action Group, acting on behalf of an HIV positive woman. It is debatable whether asylum-seekers, supported by NASS at levels below Income Support, can achieve a balanced diet. Concerns have also been raised about the nutritional contribution of free school meals. This was attributed to children wasting free school meals because the foodstuffs were largely unfamiliar or did not conform to religious requirements.

While schools in urban areas have addressed this issue and now provide halal meals, it is likely that some refugee children are still nutritionally vulnerable. More optimistically, research undertaken in 2000 on refugees' nutritional status showed that some groups of refugees may have better nutrition than other low income families. Refugee women's family feeding strategies were examined. These women provided a balanced diet for their families, despite being supported by local authority vouchers under the provisions of the Children Act. They achieved this by sharing shopping and cooking. The maintenance of breastfeeding was also high, as a result of support systems among the women.

As in education, a number of projects have been set up to improve refugees' access to and experiences of healthcare. The Department of Health has policy staff with responsibility for refugee healthcare and is in the process of developing national guidance on healthcare. Awareness of healthcare issues is improving and a new internet-based healthcare information exchange - harpweb - is serviced by the University of East London. Some of the asylum consortia have health working groups, mirroring provision in education. A number of health authorities have funded direct work with refugees. Such responses include salaried GPs working with asylum-seekers living in hostels.

The Healthcare South East London Health Authority employs a team whose responsibility includes the homeless and refugees. It was responsible for planning a Health Action Zonesfunded project working in Lambeth, Southwark and Lewisham with refugee children. Some six staff are employed working with unaccompanied children, providing training for healthcare, educational and social care staff and improving planning and coordination in south London. A number of primary care trusts employ health visitors with responsibility for homeless and refugee families. Additionally, some primary care trusts have salaried bilingual health advocates working with particular groups of refugees. Education providers commission the school medical service.

Non-governmental organisations also provide health advice and support. There are a growing number of healthcare projects working with refugee children - for example the Medical Foundation, described below. Barnardo's Positive Options provides support for children and families affected by HIV/AIDS, as do a number of Londonbased community groups such as the Ugandan Community Relief Association. However, outside Greater London there is very little support for asylum-seeking and refugee children affected by HIV/AIDS.

Social Service

Asylum-seeking and refugee children have the same entitlements to protection and social care as other children in the UK. Recent case law has established that Social Services are responsible for funding community care for asylum-seekers supported by NASS, while NASS is responsible for basic levels of support. Refugee children who are cared for by parents present themselves to social services departments, for assessment and support under the provisions of the Children Act and other relevant legislation. However, no national statistics exist that monitor refugee children's assessment outcomes, uptake and support by social services departments. It is not known whether refugee children are under-represented or over-represented in the cases assessed and supported by social services departments.

Child Protection

There is very little data or research on child protection issues among refugee communities. Showed the overrepresentation of Congolese children on the Child Protection Register in one London LEA. Neglect caused by parental hours of work was an issue in this local authority. Physical punishment and severe inter-generational conflict were also indicated.

— Hostel accommodation may put children at risk.

— High mobility may prevent continuity of support from social services, or in the worse case children being put at risk as they move across local authority boundaries.

— Social workers' levels of awareness about refugee children's backgrounds and specific needs were often felt to be poor.

— There are some child protection issues specific to certain communities, including female genital mutilation among refugees from Africa and the Yemen, and child marriage among some eastern European Roma. Much more work needs to be carried out with community groups and community leaders in order to ensure the protection of children who may be at risk.

While Victoria Climbie was not a refugee, many of the issues raised by her tragic death are of relevance to social services departments, the police, healthcare providers and others concerned with the protection of refugee children. It is hoped that the recommendations of the inquiry into her death may also improve child protection systems for refugee children.

In 2000 some 2, 733 asylum-seeking children arrived by themselves in the UK and were identified as unaccompanied asylum-seeking children by the Immigration and Nationality Directorate of the Home Office. Casework statistics from the Refugee Council's Panel of Advisers for Unaccompanied Refugee Children indicate that most of those referred to the Panel were between 13 years and 18 years old, with less than 3 per cent of referrals being for children under 8 years old. Both statistics, however, underestimate the numbers of unaccompanied refugee children under 8 years old. This is because many refugee children cared for by older siblings, relatives or friends do not always come to the attention of the Home Office, social services or the Refugee Council.

Unaccompanied refugee children come from a variety of countries. In 2000, the main countries of origin were Afghanistan, Iraq, the Federal Republic of Yugoslavia, Somalia,

Sri Lanka and Turkey. Their numbers include many more boys than girls. The majority of the UK's unaccompanied asylum-seeking and refugee children are the responsibility of social services departments in Greater London and the South East. Kent, West Sussex, Hillingdon and Croydon support the greatest numbers of them.

Unaccompanied children have many of the same needs as other groups of refugee children, for example the need to learn English. In addition, some refugee advocates argue that unaccompanied children are the most vulnerable of refugee children, because they lack the support of a family. It should be noted that family separation or loss, however, never occur in isolation - an unaccompanied refugee child will have experienced other traumatic events, such as war.

British asylum law currently makes little distinction between adult and unaccompanied child asylum-seekers, although there are some concessions. At present, an unaccompanied child who does not qualify for refugee status (almost all) will be granted Discretionary Leave until their 18th birthday. No unaccompanied child has been removed from the UK since the early 1990s. At present the Home Office is leading a review of support for unaccompanied asylum-seeking children, as a result of lobbying by local authorities in London and the South East. Some of the review process is being undertaken by the Social services provision Unaccompanied Asylum-Seeking Children Forum.

The Home Office also administers the Special Grant for Unaccompanied Asylum Seeking Children, which is payable for support offered under Section 17 and Section 20 of the Children Act 1989, although not all local authorities who support such children receive it. In England, the Department of Health coordinates the Children and Families from Overseas Network - a forum on refugee children whose membership comprises social services departments and non-governmental organisations. Its agenda has been dominated by issues about unaccompanied children. Central government has also encouraged some good practice initiatives. In 1995, the Department of Health published practice guidelines and a training pack on unaccompanied refugee children.

Non-statutory Organisations

A number of non-statutory organisations provide support services for refugee parents and/or refugee children. These comprise: larger refugee agencies such as the Refugee Council or Refugee Action, refugee-led community groups, organisations that work with a range of vulnerable groups, for example the Children's Society.

The approach of most of the larger refugee agencies has been that of providing support for adult refugees as carers of young children. As a consequence, only a small amount of the work of the larger refugee agencies is directly targeted at young children.

The Refugee Council has employed an education adviser since 1988, with a brief of improving educational provision for children aged 0-18 years. Her work has included lobbying central and local government, supporting practice initiatives, initial and inservice training and producing publications for those working with refugee children, as well as children themselves. The education adviser has also serviced an information-sharing forum called the Steering Group on Refugee Education comprising the DfES, LEAs and non-statutory organisations involved in refugee education in London and the South East.

The Refugee Council also employs an unaccompanied children's policy adviser, located with the education adviser in its policy team. Her role has been to lobby and assist in the development of better services for unaccompanied asylum-seeking and refugee children. Since the majority of such children are above 13 years of age, the unaccompanied children's adviser has been less involved with work targeted at younger refugee children. Another key member of staff is the women's adviser, whose job it is to assist community groups, including those working solely with women, to develop services. The Refugee Council has not employed a social services adviser since 1994.

The Refugee Council undertakes some direct work with unaccompanied refugee children, running the Panel of Advisers for Unaccompanied Children - advocates who help present children's needs to the Immigration and Nationality Directorate of the Home Office, social services and other service providers. Most of its clients are aged 13 and over, although a small number are under eight years. Additionally, the Refugee Council, as well as Refugee Action, Migrant Helpline, The Refugee Arrivals Project and the Scottish Refugee Council are involved in commissioning and supporting refugee families in NASS emergency accommodation prior to dispersal. The quality of some of the emergency accommodation has attracted criticism, as has the diet offered to families and children.

Refugee Action is another large refugee organisation working in England, offering advice for newly arrived refugees and supporting community development. It does not work directly with refugee children, although it carries out community development work with refugee women. The Refugee Arrivals Project, with bases at Heathrow and Gatwick, provides advice for new arrivals (including many families) as well as other forms of support. It has recently employed a member of staff to work with unaccompanied children, a small proportion of whom will be under eight years.

Other large refugee agencies such as the Scottish Refugee Council, the Welsh Refugee Council, Refugee Education and Training Advisory Service (RETAS) and Migrant Helpline have concentrated on supporting adult refugees as carers. Of the larger refugee agencies, the Medical Foundation for the Care of Victims of Torture undertakes the greatest proportion of direct work with refugee children. Its remit is to support those who have survived torture or other forms of organised violence. Most of its work is carried out in London. The support offered is multidimensional: assessments for asylum applications, basic advice, small grants, individual, family or group psychotherapy, physiotherapy, other medical interventions, art therapy, a befriending scheme for unaccompanied children and so on.

The Refugee Council estimated that there are over 650 active refugee community organisations in the UK, with the majority being located in Greater London. Such organisations vary in size, function, and access to funding and stability. All offer basic advice on issues such as immigration status, housing and benefits. A number also offer English language classes and careers advice. Cultural events are another common activity. Most refugee community organisations serve a specific community or ethno-linguistic groups. A small number attempt to serve all communities in the locality, acting as a forum, for example Lewisham Refugee Network. Most refugee community organisations are located in Greater London, although some of the larger urban areas such as Manchester and Birmingham also host many such groups.

However the small towns and cities, in which much dispersal accommodation is located, may only have one local refugee support group to serve all communities. Approximately 35 groups in London are refugee women's groups - for example the Somali Refugee Women's Association. A small number of other refugee community organisations run women's activities as part of their work. Young children are frequent visitors to community organisations, but very few groups run activities specifically for them. At the time of writing only six refugee community organisations in Greater London run playgroups or parent and toddler groups. Many community organisations run 'Saturday' schools; the Resource Centre for Mother Tongue and Supplementary Schools list 257 refugee schools in Greater London alone.

Secondly, the agenda of some community organisations is male-dominated. Children's welfare is thus considered the prime responsibility of women and a private task, centred on the home. This again may prevent some organisations from developing projects for refugee children. There will always be some refugees who have no contact with community groups, including many with parental responsibilities. There may be no group in their locality - an issue for many asylum-seekers dispersed by NASS. Some refugees may be unwilling to have contact with a particular group, for personal or political reasons. Those planning and delivering services for young children should, therefore, not over-rely on community groups.

4

Education for Street Children

Inability of finance to education lead the children to steet. Children have to work to help their parents. Children help with looking after their younger siblings so that their parents can work. Parents/patrons do not know about the procedures of enrolment. Parents do not realise the importance/benefit of long-term education. Parents do not know that their children have the right to study in a formal school. Children do not have legal papers. Children cannot follow the learning speed of the class without support from school or teachers.

How does one ensure quality, appropriateness, accessibility and flexibility of non-formal/appropriate education policies for children at risk of taking to the street?

To improve quality: equip schools to improve quality of the learning environment; continue to hire better qualified teachers and social workers.

Improve appropriateness and flexibility: Support for students: Provide additional support . Teachers should help prepare and promote a timetable with students outlining what subjects need to be studied each evening and for how long. Raise awareness of parents regarding the importance of quality education. Support for teachers and social workers: Support and train school and community social workers, or interested teachers and school officials to address the needs of disadvantaged children. Train teachers to better instruct children with special learning and emotional needs . Provide training for teachers in basic behavioural psychology, child psychology, social work, and child rights. In teacher meetings, try to organise discussions among teachers regarding difficulties and possible solutions to classroom management issues.

Improve accessibility: Raise awareness about possible solutions to payment issues. Inform guardians of disadvantaged students that they may pay school-related fees in instalments instead of in one lump sum. Schools, government, and INGOs should identify organisations and companies willing to help improve poor schools and alleviate costs for poor students. Utilise MOET directives that allow children without birth certificates and/or resident permits to enrol. Use directives that provide fee reduction and waivers for orphans and low-income children. Identify pre-school aged children and organise meetings with their guardians to raise awareness of enrolment criteria. Provide clear information on the importance of securing a birth certificate and how to get one. In addition to existing meetings, organise additional parent / community meetings and activities to further improve the relationship between parents and the school. Improve and revise the quality and content of all parent meetings to improve parent involvement.

Discrimination in Quality of Education

Some still view allowing street children to study as a favour rather than a right to education (formal or non-formal). Discrimination in quality of education: Street children are usually provided with low quality education because it is free.

Recommendations

— Ensure quality, appropriateness, accessibility and flexibility of non-formal/appropriate education policies for children at risk of taking to the street.

— Professionalise social workers/street educators by providing focused training in street work.

— Diversify training methods including training sessions, newsletters, information sharing sessions among street educators.

— Increase public awareness about children's rights, especially right to education.

— Improve quality of education for street children.

Basic Education Programme

UNESCO in perspective - 'Education for All': The Dakar Framework of Action in the World Education Forum (April 2000) called for international commitment to respond to the rapid increase of children and youth at risk in the areas of early childhood care; access for all children (especially girls, children with special needs and marginalised youth) to primary education; learning needs and skills development; prevention of gender disparities in primary and secondary education; quality and measurable education. In support of this commitment, UNESCO provided assistance to five countries in the region:

— *China*: basic education programme for migrant youth

— *Indonesia*: street literacy and non-formal training for children in need of special protection

— *Philippines*: non-formal training programme for street children and out of school youth

— *Thailand*: non-formal education for children in the railroad communities

— *Mongolia*: non-formal training and livelihood education for children and youth and families in therural areas

The overall challenges / critical issues and corresponding recommendations to provide / integrate life skills, literacy, basic education, vocational skills and interventions to prevent the increase of street children are presented in the table below:

Challenges/Critical Issues	Recommendation
Dysfunctional family set-up	1. Capacity building / training programme for parents, service providers and community leaders on responsible parenting.
	2. Parent-Child training programme.
School drop-out	1. Short skills and development training programme.
	2. Strengthen and advocate government support through active coordination with related government agencies.
Risk and vulnerability to	1. Community development activities
criminal behaviour	such as sports activities, youth camps and seminars where the youth are not only participants but co-organisers.
	2. Self-assessment workshops to help view their strengths and weaknesses.
Child labour	1. Skills development training for children at risk.
	2. Orientation / seminar for children to inform their rights and protection.
	3. Continuous coordination with NGOs, GOs and People's Organisation.
Gender disparities	1. Advocate at the national / local government level on rights and protection against gender disparities.

	2. Training and capacity building on gender sensitivity.
	3. Skills development training open to young men and women.
Urban migration	1. Outreach programme to improve opportunities for education, livelihood and other social services that are reinforced in rural areas.
	2. Development of life skills programme in rural areas.
Weak implementation of programme due to lack of capacity of service providers (e.g. teachers, street educators)	1. Training needs assessment for facilitators and service providers.
	2. Training and capacity-building programme for facilitators and service providers.
Insufficient funding for educational programmes	1. Advocacy for government to support social development programmes and to allocate budget at local level.
	2. Develop available resources into income-generating projects.

Enhancing through Street Educators

The roles and responsibilities can be many and various. Some of them are:

— *Assessment*: obtaining correct and relevant information about the situation of street children and the available resources. This helps in prioritizing the needs and problems of street children.

— *Responding to needs and problems*: responding to the immediate needs and problems of street children within the boundaries of available resources.

— *Teaching/educating*: imparting knowledge, skills and appropriate attitudes to street children to help them in preventing or minimizing their problems and in seeking help when necessary.

— *Community mobilization and advocacy*: stimulating both the street children and the community to take action and adopt workable means as solutions by creating awareness about existing needs, problems of street children and about potential resources. Advocating and supporting the street children's cause can strengthen the political will of the government to provide protection and welfare of street children and family units.

— *Management*: planning, implementing, evaluating activities, identifying and linking different resources within the community and ensuring collaboration with relevant government bodies and other organizations.

To be able to carry out these responsibilities it is important to have or acquire certain characteristics, knowledge, skills and attitudes. Experience of working with street children, basic skills of communication and the ability to share information with street children and information on them with other key people and organizations, e.g. government officials, business people, police etc. and basic skills for documenting their work, will be useful.

It is not always easy to work with street children. Street children often become hardened victims of a society that feels threatened by them. Peer pressure, cultural and working conditions of the street are other difficult issues that you will have to deal with. A major task for effective street education therefore is to establish a working relationship with the street children. For this, you will have to spend time on the street to know the world of street children, so that a trusting relationship can be established. The challenge is how to cope with the limitations that you come across.

Characteristics of Street Educator

To be an effective street educator you need to possess or acquire certain characteristics. You should:

— Have knowledge, skills and appropriate attitudes.

— Have the desire to learn continually. This would involve being aware of your limitations and seeking help when necessary.

— Have integrity, maturity, and a sense of responsibility, patience and sympathy.

— Have determination, enthusiasm and motivation.

— Be creative and resourceful.

— Be able to work in a participatory style and encourage everyone to contribute ideas and make decisions.

— Believe in empowering street children by setting up opportunities for them to recognize and develop their own skills by building self-confidence.

Street educators must possess appropriate knowledge, skills and attitudes to be able to work with street children effectively.

— *Knowledge*: Knowledge relates to information and understanding of facts and principles. Knowledge can be acquired by reading reports about street children, talking to street children and other key leaders in the community, conducting assessments on street children and learning from experience.

— *Skills*: A skill is the ability to do something well. You will need to learn certain skills in order to transfer them to street children. Skills can be learnt through practice and demonstrations.

— *Attitudes*: Attitudes are tendencies to think or behave in a certain way. Attitudes include values and beliefs. They can be expressed in what you say, what you do or do not do, e.g. if you do not recognise the plight of street children and do not believe that they need help, your non-caring attitude can be reflected in the way you interact with them. Attitudes develop over a long period of time and are the hardest to change.

To work with street children you will have to understand the culture of the street and the ambitions and resources available to the child. To be effective, be flexible enough to accept the realities of working with street children. You will need to develop the capacity to reflect and relearn over and over again as you work with street children. For example, if you wish to use peer influence for the betterment of street children, you need to understand how peer groups are organized. Influential peers will have to be identified. Look for individuals who can communicate and express the group feelings, needs and aspirations.

— Mobilize the group for action.

— Organize the group and initiate team spirit.

— Produce workable ideas and encourage group members to adopt and maintain skills and strategies.

Communication Skills

Communication is the process by which a message is passed from one individual to another. It is one of the most important tools that you have to influence the life of the street child. It is a key to understanding the street children, their world and a means to establishing a trusting and working relationship with them and the community. A street educator communicates all the time, for example when taking on the responsibility of imparting knowledge, influencing attitudes and teaching street children skills. Communication skills are also important for advocacy and community mobilization. Working with street children requires you to have effective communication skills.

Communication is a two-way flow of information. It involves both sending (sender to audience/receiver) and receiving (audience/receiver to sender feedback) information. The second part of the process (audience to sender) is also referred to as 'feedback'. Communication can be through the use of words (written or spoken) or without words (gestures and appearance).

Verbal Communication

Verbal communication involves three main processes:

(a) listening,

(b) speaking and

(c) feedback.

One needs to develop certain skills in each of these areas to be able to communicate effectively.

Skillsful listening

Listening carefully to street children can assist you in understanding their interests, ideas and needs. Few adults in the life of street children have bothered to listen to their worries and difficulties. Attentive listening conveys to them that you believe they are important and have the right to be heard. Listening to them when they talk about their problems also makes them feel better. Experience suggests that listening may be more important than talking for eliciting co-operation and building relationship. Skillful listening involves:

— *Making eye contact with the child*: This shows that you are interested and do not disapprove of what the child is saying, and that you are not embarrassed by their situation. Avoid eye contact with the child if it is considered impolite or threatening in the local culture.

— *Paying attention to the street child*: Do not appear distracted or in a hurry when the child is speaking. Allow the child to finish sentences before making comments. Communicating is more than spoken words. The tone of the child's voice, the rate of speech, the expression on his or her face can tell you what he/she might be thinking. _ Treating the street child as an individual. Try not to make assumptions about the street child based on the behaviour of the group. Avoid being judgmental and show acceptance of the child.

— *Speaking skills*: Good communication between two people requires using a common language. Street educators and street children sometimes have difficulty in fully understanding each other because of differences in language. If you have not spent time on the streets, you may not know the special words and expressions that street children use. The following can assist you to speak effectively:

a. Speak clearly, coherently and audibly.

b. Use clear expressions and words.

c. Complete the message and stay on the subject of discussion. Encourage the child to speak by nodding your head or using short phrases like "hmm," "really?" "What happened next?" or "What else happened?"

d. You could also use key words as prompts, e.g. a street child may say, "He is good to me, but... " you could just respond by saying "but?"

e. Avoid pushing the child to say more than he or she wants to say. Remember, talking only helps when a person is ready to talk. Respect a young person's right to be silent.

Providing feedback can be a two way process. Repeating to an individual what they have said can provide helpful clarification to them. It also provides them with an opportunity to tell you if you have misunderstood what they have said. Give feedback to the street child, but also encourage the child to give you a feedback about what he or she feels about the communication. Feedback is effective when it is:

— Constructive and not judgmental.

— Clear, specific and essentially correct.

— Given immediately after the message or action.

Show acceptance of the children. Do not ignore the children.

Non-verbal Communication

Communication without words can help in understanding the street child and to be understood by him or her. Facial expression, body movement, gesture, posture, type of clothing and distance between the street child and street educator are important determinants of the communication process. Non-verbal communication says a lot about your attitudes or those of the street child. To be effective, ensure that both non-verbal and verbal communication are conveying the same message. When communicating with a child or another individual, avoid letting eyes wander while listening as you might miss some information. Pay attention to any disparity between verbal and non-verbal communication. Suggest the need to shift strategy, e.g. if the street child's eyes become tearful even though he is speaking smoothly, you may have to stop your exploration on a particular subject.

When you work on the street wear simple clothes. If you do not want to be perceived as distant, accept food if a street child offers you food, or join in a game but wear simple dignified clothes for advocacy work. Maintain an encouraging posture: In some cultures, leaning forward may encourage communication, whereas slouching and crossing the arms can indicate lack of interest and create a barrier to free communication. Smiling and showing approval, e.g. by nodding, if this is appropriate, can encourage a street child to continue speaking.

— *Communication strategy*: The audience for a message may be street children or members of the community. It is important to pick a communication strategy that will reach your intended audience. A personal unstructured approach works best for most of the communication with individual street children. For this approach the street educator is guided by street children's needs, and the opportunities that come up, so that no fixed schedule for imparting messages is followed. This approach may not be the best approach for advocacy. A more focussed strategy in which the intended message is put across in a precise manner would be preferable.

— *Methods of communication*: You may want to consider the following methods of communication when planning activities on the education of street children and advocacy:

— *Communication using speech*: this can be by formal face-to-face meetings or informal conversations (either directly or through telephone calls) or by a public address system.
_ Communication using written words: this can be through articles, letters, books, leaflets, poems or songs.

— *Through visual means*: this can be through films, videos or illustrations.

— *Environment*: For effective communication to take place, the environment should not be too noisy. There should be as little distraction as possible. If the topic is of a sensitive nature, privacy may need to be ensured (issue of confidentiality will be discussed in Module 5). Try going to the corner of a room or taking a walk together.

Trusting Work Relationship

The fundamental work of street education is to build relationships with street children that are based on mutual trust, respect and a commitment to personal growth. The process of establishing trust with street children is often difficult because many street children have learned not to trust people. The street educator must come across as a person who is genuinely committed and who practices what he or she stands for. Communication plays an important role in establishing such a trusting working relationship with street children.

Engaging is the process of encouraging a street child in having a relationship with you. One good way to start the process of building a trusting relationship is to join in when they play games such as football, pinball, hide-and-seek or in something that they normally like to do. You can also join in when street children are working. Help them wash cars, search for food, or carry things. Avoid imposing activities as it would make you appear as an authority figure rather than a facilitator and a friend.

World of a Street Child

Street children are more likely to trust you and spend time with you if you already know something about their world.

— *Language*: many groups of street children have their own special language, which is not known to outsiders. This special language helps to unite them. Learn some aspects of their language in order to understand them and communicate effectively with them. Using the terms they use can help build their trust in you.

— *Community*: knowing the physical and social characteristics of the area or locality where street children spend their time can assist you in your work. The physical characteristics are structures such as streets, sidewalks, markets, theatres, recreational areas, public buildings, and empty spaces. The social characteristics of the neighbourhood include sources of food, danger zones, sleeping locations, work places, and areas for using substances. Once you have made a map of the neighbourhood, you will have some idea of where to go in order to engage the street children. The social characteristics can be marked with a code that is explained at the side of the map.

Documenting and Reporting

Documentation helps in monitoring the progress of the individual street child. Recording and reporting can also help in monitoring progress and in identifying problems in a street children's project. Documents are necessary for communicating with other agencies and are a source of information for other people who want to become involved in street education.

Some programmes have a provision for keeping records on individual street children and for recording daily, weekly or monthly activities. Each team will have to decide what would work best.

— *Intake forms*: Street educators usually like to keep a record of how many and what type of children they are working with. They use an intake form for this purpose. The form is usually completed after a street educator has met the street child a few times on the street or at a centre. This information helps in the case assessment and development of action plans. Some programmes include assessment information and initial action plan as closing sections on the intake form, while others ask street educators to document the case assessment process separately. Find out about the type of forms used in your locality to document information about street children. You can then develop your own form. Key areas on which information should be obtained are:

a. Identification e.g. name, age, gender, date of birth, usual address, family background.

b. Description of the child, physical appearance, physical and emotional problems.

c. Other information e.g. reasons for leaving home, any arrests, special needs.

— *Log books*: A log book is a record of daily encounters between street educators and street children. Log books are often used by street educators who move frequently from one location to another. Each day, the street educator records the names of the street children met, the locations visited and the work done.

— *Case progress notes*: Some street educators, especially those who work in centres or institutions, prefer to keep information about each street child separately. These records are called case progress notes. If the workers see a street child daily they may make only one entry each week, but if they see the child only occasionally, they may write a progress note after each meeting.

The way records and reports are kept can contribute to their effectiveness. Whatever methods of recording and reporting are used, they should be of value.

They must:

— be clear and readily understood (they should have no complicated terms)

— be presented in logical sections

— stress important points

— be precise (avoid unnecessary details and repetitions)

— be kept confidential such as not using names on sensitive documents that might be incriminating

— be kept is a secure place

— be accessed by a limited number of people and not by the general public

Helping Refugee Children in School

Education, in particular language support, is often the route to self-sufficiency and a new life. It is based on material from the British Refugee Council's publication "Helping refugees in schools", but also takes additional material from a seminar held in Minsk, Belarus on March 29th and 30th 2001 entitled "Working with refugee children and building tolerance in the classroom", which brought together around 40 teachers, local and national government officials and NGO representatives from Belarus, Ukraine, Russia and Moldova with staff and speakers from UNHCR, the UK and Poland. Education is vital for refugees, whatever their age. Forced by persecution to leave their own countries, refugees often arrive in a new country traumatised and disorientated.

In Russia, children are not able to apply for asylum individually before the age of 18, especially if they have been provided institutional care as this is considered to be a form of State protection. In Ukraine an individual can ask for asylum, but children below 16 are automatically included in their parents' application. In Belarus, children are able to apply for refugee status individually but in 2000 only two such applications were made, as unaccompanied children are usually resettled by UNHCR. In Moldova, pending the creation of Government structures, UNHCR extends international protection to the persons of its concern, registers asylum seekers and conducts refugee status determination procedure under its UNHCR mandate. The asylum application is made by the principal applicant, which includes his/her family members as well.

In Russia, regional Migration Services are responsible the refugee status determination procedure, under the auspices of the Ministry of Federal Affairs, National and Migration Policy of the Russian Federation. The Ministry also runs the Appeals Commission. Decisions of the Migration Services and the Appeals Commission can be appealed in the courts. Applicants are denied access to the determination procedure for violation of time limits for those crossing the border illegally, or for transit through 'safe third countries', which included the countries of Central Asia. Russia has also recently introduced a regulation on temporary asylum, although the mechanism for implementing it is yet to be developed. Russia also has a separate law for 'forced migrants', former citizens of the former Soviet Union who came to Russia from other ex-Soviet republics.

In Ukraine, regional Migration Services consider asylum applications. There are 27 of these as well as the Kyiv City Migration Service. The activities of the Migration Services are supervised by the State Department for Nationalities and Migration within the Ministry of Justice, which also runs an Appeals Commission which considers rejected applications together with the district court in the region where the application was made. The decision of the Appeals Commission can in turn be appealed in the courts. At the border applicants should be referred to the nearest Migration Service and, while time limits exist for applicants crossing the border illegally, these limits are rarely enforced. The procedure takes varying amounts of time depending on the region, with applications lodged in Kyiv taking the longest to be considered. In general, though, a first instance decision is normally given within two months of the application being lodged.

In Belarus, applications are lodged with the Migration Service, overseen by the Committee on Migration within the Ministry of Labour. Advice to new asylum-seekers is given by the Refugee Counselling Service, a project of the Belarusian Movement of Medical Workers, in Minsk and Vitebsk. The asylum-seeker then makes their application to the Migration Service and, if rejected, may return to the RCS for further advice. Many applicants do not have their claims registered because the applicant failed to apply within three days of entering the country illegally, or because they transited through a 'safe third country'. Nonetheless, there has been a sharp decrease in the number of oral rejections at the admissibility stage, which has led to an increased recognition rate. It should also be noted that Chechens are not admitted into the refugee status determination procedure because, under the Union Treaty with Russia, citizens of Russia should have the same residence rights as Belarusian citizens.

In Moldova, asylum seekers are required to address their asylum request to UNHCR's implementing partner NGO "Society for Refugees of the Republic of Moldova" (SR), which registers asylum seekers and conducts initial interviews. Upon registration, asylum seekers are advised and assisted to petition the Presidential Commission invoking the Constitutional provision on asylum. During the refugee status determination procedure, a protection letter is issued for a 3-month term, which can be extended while the case is being analysed. The protection letter is a basis for registering with the authorities and to receive various forms of UNHCR assistance. After close scrutiny of all available facts adduced by asylum seekers to support their claim, the file together with the interview results are transferred to UNHCR which reviews the facts and formulates a final decision or requests additional information.

The asylum seekers are informed in writing about the final decision. There is no government authority with responsibility for awarding refugee status, so once the asylum-seeker has received the protection certificate their rights are regulated by Moldovan legislation on foreigners and stateless persons. Refugee status protects a person from being returned to his or her country of origin. It gives other rights, such as the right to family reunification. In Russia, some asylum-seeker and refugee children attend regular schools through the intervention of NGOs, UNHCR or individual parents. Most, however, attend special 'stop-gap' classes because they have limited knowledge of Russian or are denied access to the regular education system. In Ukraine, children of concern to UNHCR have the right to primary education regardless of the legal status of their parents under the UN Convention on the Rights of the Child. In Belarus, the law "On Education" decrees that primary education is compulsory.

The Belarusian legislation also proclaims the principle of non-discrimination and equality for all children, including asylum-seekers and refugees. In Moldova, UNHCR and Save the Children intervene to try to ensure access for refugee children to schools. In late 1999 the Ministry of Education issued two orders regarding access to the primary education for the children of non-Moldovan citizens in order to comply with the obligation as a party to the Convention on the Rights of the Child. In fact, all four countries have ratified the UN Convention on the Rights of the Child, which should provide for education for children regardless of the legal status of their parents.

Refugees are people who have survived persecution in their home countries. For those who flee, their recent experiences may have been horrific. Aspects of their life after arriving in Eastern Europe can also cause stress for families. Here are some examples of problems for refugee children in Eastern Europe which can induce stress:

— Children are often exposed to violence, for example in temporary accommodation centres

— Harassment by law enforcement officials of parents or guardians

— Children are unable to deal with psychological aspects of flight due to temporary lack of permanent housing

— Uncertain length of stay in Eastern Europe

— Need for young people to help with family income generation which can prevent them from attending school

— Children often live with people other than their own parents in overcrowded accommodation

Educational and Social Needs

Young refugees are a diverse group who have a wide range

of educational and social needs. But significant proportions of refugee children

— Have an interrupted education in their countries of origin
— Have had horrific experiences in their home countries and flight, and for a small number this may affect their ability to learn and rebuild their lives
— Have suffered a drop in their standard of living and other major changes in their lives
— Are not cared for by their parents or usual careers
— Have parents who are emotionally absent
— Are living with families who do not know their educational and social rights
— Speak little or no Russia, Ukrainian, Belarusian or Romanian when they arrive in Eastern Europe
— Suffer bullying or isolation in school
— Find it difficult to study in the further or higher education sector because of their immigration status or lack of access to benefits.

Unaccompanied Children

Many refugee children arrive are unaccompanied when they arrive in Eastern Europe. Several live with relatives, making it difficult to produce precise statistics on the number of unaccompanied minors. Many are also resettled soon after arriving as they are considered to be a particularly vulnerable group. For example, in Russia there are no unaccompanied minors at present officially registered with UNHCR, as those children with no relatives in the country have been resettled, while in Belarus, of the 11 unaccompanied minors reported to the Refugee Counselling Service in 2000 only two applied for refugee status as the rest were resettled. Some unaccompanied children have seen members of their family arrested or killed.

Other unaccompanied children are sent abroad when life becomes too dangerous at home or they are faced with conscription. The families of unaccompanied children are alive, but contact with them is usually limited and the pain of separation is great. Other children arrive in the care of an elder brother or sister, or other relatives. This group of children may never become known to social services departments and may not receive the support that they require.

During the Minsk seminar participants from Russia, Ukraine, Belarus and Moldova listed the factors which had the greatest effect on refugee children in the classroom in their countries.

In Ukraine,

— There is no special problem of access to schools or of obtaining leaving certificates, although there are very few asylum seekers who attend school.

— The NGO ADRA runs a social centre, offering preparatory classes for asylum seekers children before they enrol in schools. They help them catch up on missed years of education, and learn the language. They have voluntary student teachers as well as teachers from the asylum seeker community.

— The social centre has had to intervene in local schools to prevent tension between the Ukrainian and Afghan children. This tolerance building initiative has on the whole been successful. The lack of information about different cultures leads to many problems with tolerance and understanding.

— The social centre is planning an international festival soon which will involve the participation of the local schools which asylum seekers attend.

— Parents: there is a need to work with Ukrainian parents to increase tolerance and combat xenophobia. Teachers and psychologists also do not always have an understanding of refugee issues.

In Moldovak,

— Absence of refugee law/ Govt. refugee status determination procedure

— There are three main NGOs working with refugees: Save the Children on social issues, Charity Centre for Refugees on cultural issues and the Society for Refugees on legal issues.

— Children can learn Romanian at the Charity Centre for Refugees

— Children of refugees/asylum seekers have free access to primary education, however, the parents have difficulty to contribute extra cost to school for repair etc.

— The children are insecure, and the absence of documentation exacerbates.

In Russian Federation,

— Lack of normative legislation allowing asylum seeker children access to schools

— Asylum seekers do not have the right to go to school. In some regions compromises are made and the situation is easier. But the situation in Moscow is difficult - some children attend school but local legislation forbids.

— Many asylum seekers do not have the documents (propiska) necessary to allow them to travel to and from school and therefore the children are afraid

— Asylum seekers are not always able to obtain the necessary medical documents to allow them to attend school. There are some NGOs helping with this but it is not enough

— Conflicts between Russian and asylum seeker children are common.

— There is a lack of knowledge of Russian among asylum seekers

— Economic problems prevent school attendance; for example, some parents cannot afford travel costs of the price of a school uniform

In Belarus,

— There is a generally humane attitude towards refugee children regardless of race

— Asylum seeker children are given help to catch up with the other children

— There can be a lack of tolerance on the part of Belarusian parents,

— Medical certificates are needed for each child, which cost money

— School leaving certificates depend on the local authority, and are not issued to all asylum seekers

— Temporary foreign citizens do not have the right to education but, without refugee status, it is impossible for refugees to be permanently registered as resident in Belarus

— Lack of knowledge of legislation by asylum seekers

— Adaptation to culture and language difficult

— Cultural traditions and language of the asylum seeker are not always preserved. Need for education in mother tongue as well

— Racism

All students who arrive after the start of the year need special induction procedures. Induction aims to help students settle into a new school and become effective learners, in as short a time as possible. Good induction practices are particularly important for refugee children, as almost all new refugee students will arrive in a school mid-term. Refugee children also come from countries where the education system is very different schools may be organised in a different manner, and the style of teaching is usually more formal.

Investing time in developing good induction practices is cost effective, as this may prevent problems arising at a later date. A refugee child may have experienced a multiplicity of different stressful events, both in their home country and abroad. Most refugee children are able to cope with these stresses, but some children remain unsettled or psychologically vulnerable. A small number of refugee children manifest disturbed behaviour and require specialist support from the school psychological service, child guidance clinics or NGOs. The various events which refugee children undergo can be described as a combination of loss, trauma and change

Refugee children may have lost parents and other key carers, brothers and sisters, extended family and friends. They may have lost physical items such as their home, material possessions and favourite toys. Exile also results in the loss of familiar surroundings, familiar ways of doing things, and perhaps their parents' attention and support in a new country.

Trauma

A trauma is an overwhelming experience that a person is not able to cope with. Refugee children may experience multiple traumas such as:

— High intensity war

— The destruction of their homes

— The violent death of family or friends

— Getting separated from family

— Injury

— Arrest of members of their family

— Being arrested, detained or tortured themselves

— Being forced to join the army or militias

— Rape
— Grave shortages of food, water or other necessities
— Fear of discovery or arrest
— Hostility in their new homeland
— Material deprivation

Refugee children may experience major cultural changes, including learning a new language and a new set of cultural norms. Refugee families may also experience a drop in their standard of living and status in society. As a result of exile, there may be changes in a child's relationship with his or her parents refugee children may see their parents as being vulnerable or dependent. Parents may also become more protective or authoritarian or sometimes emotionally absent. After traumatic experiences it is normal to manifest strong emotional reactions, but with time these usually lessen. Refugee children's reactions to traumatic events are very variable and many factors influence a refugee child's psychological well-being.

The duration and intensity of traumatic events, the child's age, the child's personality and character, the quality of child care and the refugee child's experience in a new country all affect how a child will come to terms with being a refugee. Some factors - adverse factors - make it more likely that problems will arise. Protective factors help safeguard a child against psychological distress. Protective and adverse factors were listed in relation to two fictional refugee children. Adverse factors included changes in child care such as having new carers, or experiencing difficulties with parents. Other adverse factors may include material deprivation, isolation from members of one's own community, bullying at school and seeing exile as being inexplicable.

Protective factors included having parents/carers who are able to give good quality child care, having access to other people who can give friendship and support, particularly other refugees from the country of origin. Having some understanding of the reasons for exile is also a protective factor, as is being happy in a new school. The school can play a very important part in helping to minimise adverse factors and maximise protective factors. Providing emotional support for refugee children is an integral part of any school's refugee policy. Schools can consider the practices set out below:

Understand about education

One of the most important things that a teacher can do is to talk to refugee children, listen to what they say and take their communication seriously. To be effective in doing this a teacher has to make a regular time to be free and have some degree of privacy. A room or office can be used for this purpose at break time or after Strategies for individual children Where a particular child gives cause for concern it is important to observe that child's behaviour in a variety of situations. The school should avoid jumping to immediate conclusions or labelling the child. The teacher should try and find out about the child's background and reasons why he or she is behaving in that way. Children can be asked why they are feeling angry or sad. After this, the school can think about a strategy for the individual child.

Working with parents/carers

If a child experiences difficulties at school it is essential to develop good communications with parents or carers at the earliest opportunity. A school must use an interpreter for this, if one is needed. Sometimes parents' or carers' and children's problems may be interlinked.

Knowing when to refer

Sometimes a refugee child manifests disturbed behaviour for a protracted period of time and does not respond to support strategies. In such instances a school should consider referring a child with expertise in working with traumatised refugee children. It is worth finding out as much as possible about relevant agencies in the local area. Is there anyone at school who is experiences in working with refugee children, or children from different cultural and linguistic backgrounds. There may be staff in local child guidance clinics, or in voluntary sector organisations who may also be able to help.

The presence of some of the following behaviour may indicate that a refugee child is not coping:

— Losing interest and energy or being very withdrawn

— Being aggressive or feeling very angry. Some refugee children copy the violence they have seen around them

— Other children may be unable to put their feelings into words and use violence as an outlet

— Lack of concentration and feeling very restless

— Repetitive or intrusive thoughts about traumatic events, or repetitive play and drawings

— Physical symptoms such as poor appetite, eating too much, breathing difficulties, pains and dizziness

— Not thriving

— Self-injury or self-abusing behaviour

— Losing recently-acquired skills and faculties, for example keeping dry at night

— Nightmares and disturbed sleep

— Crying and overwhelming sadness

— Being very nervous and fearful of things such as loud noises

— Difficulties in forming relationships with other children

Aautobiographical techniques

Children can be encouraged to write about themselves, their home country or their present circumstances and feelings. Such autobiographical techniques are frequently used with refugee children as a way of helping them develop understanding of complex events and feelings. Younger children can make a scrapbook or picture book about themselves. They can also use paints and crayons and work with an adult to write captions for their drawings.

Play and drama

Schools can use play, games and drama with small groups of children, to explore such issues as fear and trust, to help newly-arrived children settle in. It may be helpful to schedule in some time to play to help young refugee children settle in school.

Pastoral curriculum

Bereavement will affect everyone at some time in their lives, and learning about death and loss is important to all students. Some schools have developed excellent resources about bereavement for use in religious education or personal and social education. But not all schools tackle these issues. Where there are refugee children in a school, the pastoral curriculum can be used to examine bereavement and loss. In that way refugee children will not feel so different, and will realise that other children sometimes suffer similar experiences.

Homework clubs

Some schools set up homework or after school clubs for refugee children, or other groups such as those living in temporary accommodation. These can be a way that refugee children can gain the support of peers. Adult volunteers from refugee communities can be approached to help in homework clubs. There are also sources of funding that can be utilised to pay volunteer and other expenses.

Counselling

A small number of refugee children will need more interventions. Some schools offer individual or group counselling to children who have suffered abuse or stressful experiences. Such counselling may be facilitated by teachers who have obtained professional qualifications, or by outside agencies.

Learning the host language

When teaching children who are starting to learn the host language, it is important to find out the extent of their former education, in particular if they are literate in their mother tongue, if they have had educational difficulties in their home country, or if they have previously studied the subject offered in the school timetable. Some refugee children may not have attended school in their home country and may not be literate. This group of children will need considerable support when they first arrive, to enable them to learn to write and develop other skills.

The following suggestions may help a beginner participate more fully in lessons:

— The student can sit next to a sympathetic friend who could help with translation when necessary. At the same time, it is reasonable to expect the beginner to learn some phrases and greetings in The host language

— Use as much visual support as possible by having diagrams, flash cards and illustrated dictionaries and glossaries for reference

— Schools should have bilingual dictionaries for all those children who need them

— Teachers should talk to beginners individually. Both teacher and student should know each other's name and be able to say it clearly

— Beginners should be encouraged to join in with practical activities such as distributing equipment, when they will have to make verbal contact with other pupils

— Collaborative group activities are helpful when learning the host language, as is planned student talk during a lesson. But the beginner should be placed in a group with those who are best able to involve him or her in the learning task.

— Students should be encouraged to ask for help when they do not understand work

— Reading material can be made easier by oral discussion, relating it to a student's own experience. If reading material is recorded onto a cassette, a student can listen and read simultaneously.

— Bilingual books and other interactive teaching aids can be obtained if available and if resources allow.

— Short vocabulary lists should be provided in each lesson.

— Instructions on work sheets should be clear and follow the same format.

Joe Flynn from Manchester Local Education Authority's Ethnic Minorities Achievement Service spoke on the need to keep developing the academic achievement of the asylum seeker children, even if they did not have a good grasp of the language. In particular, he referred to the Cummins framework for language learning.

Development in Home Languages

Refugee children need to be able to develop their home language(s) as well as learn the host language. Many refugee families aspire to return to their home country, so will need to be fluent in its language. The maintenance and development of the home language is also important in a child's cognitive development and promotion of positive identity. Schools should include community language and dual language books in class and school libraries. It is important that schools give value to students who speak two or more languages. Schools could, for example, run language awareness courses for all students and bilingual children can contribute to them.

Many refugee children in Eastern Europe attend supplementary schools. These are usually organised by refugee community organisations or by NGOs. Here refugees study the languages of their home country, as well as receiving religious education and participating in leisure activities. Some such schools also help children with subjects such as host language tuition or Maths. In Eastern Europe such schools are sometimes seen as a replacement for regular schooling. However, as was clearly expressed at the Minsk seminar, supplementary schooling should be seen as just that - a useful addition to the education which should be offered within the regular school system.

Countering racism and xenophobia

Many refugee children report isolation and racist bullying when they first arrive in a new school. Given popular misconceptions and increased public hostility to refugees, this is hardly surprising. It is important that schools have consistent policies to deal with bullying and racial harassment and that the school curriculum is used to explore issues such as migration and human rights. Refugee children should know who they can speak to if they are being bullied. The school should have clear guidelines to deal with bullying, and these should be understood by all pupils and staff. The pastoral curriculum can be used to challenge bullying and racial harassment.

Some schools have introduced peer mediation to deal with bullying. It should be noted that children can be bullied between school and home. The school curriculum can be used in many imaginative ways to help children understand contemporary issues such as conflict, refugee movements, migration and human rights. Programmes of civic education can encourage all students to see refugees as human beings, to help them develop empathy towards those forced to flee and a commitment to justice. Some resources aimed at encouraging understanding of human rights were offered to participants. Here are some ideas:

— The Language and Literature curriculum can focus on texts involving refugees and migration, or look, for example, at how the media examines the issue of miration.

— History projects can look at the history of migration, the human effects of the Second World War, international humanitarian law, the Arab-Israeli conflict, oral history or a local historical study

— Religious education can be used to examine accounts of migration in different religious works, as well as contemporary moral issues such as the arms trade, war, poverty, social justice and responsibility to others

— Geography can be used to study migration and the impact of refugee movements on a host country

— Art classes can be used to produce campaign material

— In primary schools, cross-curricular projects can be carried out

Irina Korenyak from UNHCR's regional training office in Ankara stressed that Article 22 of the 1951 Geneva convention states that all refugee children have the right to primary education, while Article 22 of the Convention of the Rights of the Child states that governments should ensure that all asylumseeker children as well as refugee children should have free access to education in the country in which they are applying for asylum. This reflects the fact that early years provision is very important for refugee children who come from homes where little of the host language is spoken.

Nonetheless, refugee children are very underrepresented in early years provision such as nurseries and playgroups, and user-use facilities such as toy libraries and clubs. This may be because refugee parents may not know the range of early years provision that exits. It may also be due to the fact that many refugee parents are unhappy about leaving very young children with strangers from outside their own community. Here are some questions to consider when examining early years provision for refugee children:

— Are there any waiting lists or are needy children prioritised?

— Has anyone from the school or playgroup visited refugee communities to make them aware of the services on offer? Is any material produced in a language the refugees will understand?

— Does the local authority monitor the provision of early years education?

— Are refugees involved in the running of the nursery or playgroup?

— Can refugee parents contribute things such as food ideas, stories and information about festivals to the nursery? Are there plenty of toys, pictures and books that represent the diversity of local cultures?

— Is there plenty of opportunity for young children to play freely and express themselves with material such as paint, clay, sand, toys and figures that represent a child's family? Children may need support in expressing and reconciling difficult feelings.

Vulnerable Adolescents Group

Asylum-seekers who arrive during adolescence may be a particularly vulnerable group. They will have arrived in the middle of examination courses. They may be unable to progress to further or higher education because of their immigration status. It is important that young refugees have their educational needs fully assessed when they arrive in school or college. Young refugees need specialist advice on employment which takes into account issues such as their legal status or lack of familiarity with the local job market. For those young asylum-seekers who wish to go onto higher education, they need extensive support with securing a place and the financial resources to accept it.

5

Policymaking for Street Children

Homelessness

Early home leaving can lead to homelessness if insufficient protective factors exist for a young person. The implication is that both prevention and early intervention strategies are important. Early home leaving occurs in a climate of family conflict, a felt lack of emotional support, grief and loss, or environmental characteristics which remove the protective factors around young people to the point where the young person is kicked out, or is effectively compelled or feels compelled to leave. This is not to suggest that young people were not at times active contributors to the difficulties experienced in families. However, in almost all cases there were other significant and preceding issues in the family. Early home leaving also occurs because of state intervention, where the safety of the child or young person and their continued residence in the family are seen as mutually exclusive. Protective factors are:

— access to a parent who they felt can understand and listen to them;

— relatives or friends who provided alternative sources of support to parents;

— access to community youth services where a young person can gain information and personal support;

— a supportive teacher or school counsellor who could provide information or support; and

— a supportive and responsive rather than punitive school environment.

Most young people will return to the family home on one or more occasions, they will leave again if they believe nothing has changed. The implications of this for early intervention are numerous. They include helping parents think through their response to find the one which is most helpful, when their young person returns home or subsequently makes contact. Given that in many cases support external to the family is not sought until a crisis within the family or home leaving has occurred, the immediacy of service response is a critical indicator of the effectiveness of early intervention services.

While an interest in the prevention of youth homelessness dates back to the 1970s, the language and concepts of early intervention are far more recent, with the HREOC setting out the overall agenda in a way that has remained substantially unchanged since 1989. An examination of the policies and programs reveals government responses since this time have been mixed, with outstanding features being the failure of the States to deliver adequate welfare services to young people, and the emergence - through tied Commonwealth-State programs such as the Adolescent /Family Mediation and Therapy Program and SAAP - of specific models of service which have an early intervention capacity.

Other Commonwealth programs such as STAR have included as possible targets young people who are homeless and at risk of homelessness. This has allowed some localised, sporadic and generally timelimited developments relevant to early intervention to occur. Some States such as Victoria, have introduced specific programs relevant to early intervention, while most have done little beyond that required under joint contribution to Commonwealth programs. The current dominant programmatic strategies by Australian governments involve:

— an increased commitment to adolescent/family mediation and support services;

— school-based at risk strategies that are largely focused on school retention and which largely develop responses within an individualised construction of at risk;

— a range of other programs aimed at prevention of homelessness which involve pilot, short-term initiatives at the local level, generally conceptualised within a vocational training, education or employment framework; and

— coordination and articulation of services strategies primarily focused on introducing individualised case management, and clear case management location.

Perspectives of Young People

Young people see their relationship with parents, or step-parents (where there are changed family structures) as central to their capacity to stay at home. Many would remain living longer at the family home if there was a level of change in critical areas.

When young people seek assistance they have mixed experience, with communication-based support being described as helpful or unhelpful to a similar extent. It is clear that young people often find that a counsellor, teacher or other service provider breaches what they consider to be the trust and implicit confidentiality of their conversations. There are also reports of service providers dismissing the young person principally on the basis of parental deference. There is a clear implication for a wide range of services and practitioners to explicitly examine from an ethical perspective the nature of their service relationship with young people and to develop practices which are respectful of them.

Perspectives of Parent

The parents interviewed indicated a high level of concern, distress, embarrassment and sometimes anger for what had happened, and yet consistently indicated they had a high level of concern for their children. From the perspective of the parent, it is the young person who is most often seen as "the problem", or as having problems which need addressing. This was further confirmed in the case studies, where service providers frequently indicated that the most common parental request for response from service providers often amounted to a request to "control" or "fix up" the young person.

The reasons for home leaving also cited by parents include negative peer influence and the availability of income support arrangements. This stands in some degree of contrast to the significant levels of difficulty, instability, mobility and problematic behaviour such as alcohol misuse, aggressiveness, or abuse reported by parents as usually occurring in the home in the period preceding the home leaving. The parents interviewed did not include the feelings and perspectives of their children as issues contributing to home leaving.

Although there was a degree of similarity in parents' and young people's definitions of home at one level (where people feel loved, safe, supported) parents did not, as young people did, include in their definitions specific behaviours which indicate how such feelings are developed and maintained (through listening, getting problems sorted out, talking to each other). This, together with a tendency to blame, and exclude their own role in the process of early home leaving from discussion, supports the view that parents have a substantial blind spot in respect of the antecedents of early home leaving.

The implications for parent support and education strategies include the need to examine the notion of home from a child's perspective, for parents to develop the capacity to self-reflect on the behaviours that are consistent with their own notions of home, and to develop skills in discussing these matters with children. The survey findings reveal that 58% of the sample of agencies reported working with parents or guardians "virtually always" or "often"; and only 6% "virtually never". These results stand in sharp contrast with parents who repeatedly stated during interviews that they were unable to access support, and were frequently not consulted about their young person's situation.

In many interviews parents maintained that they felt perpetually "judged" by service providers as inadequate parents or guardians. Seventy per cent of the parents related extreme difficulties in accessing support for their son or daughter. Interview and survey data suggest that many parents cannot find services to respond to their needs despite significant attempts, or that they are not aware of how to access those services which are available. There is a serious need for an increase in parent support services and an increase in community awareness about the kinds of support and services available to parents and guardians confronting an issue associated with youth homelessness or early home leaving.

Across the stories told by young people and parents, there is a high level of consistency at several levels. Both groups speak of the need for communicationbased support, and of gaps or breakdown in communication within their families. Both groups speak about significant levels of conflict, physical violence (whether presented as discipline or not), and grief and loss. In the experiences of both groups, changes in family structure appear to be significant factors in the process leading to early home leaving and homelessness. There are striking similarities in terms of unmet need, cited in terms of lack of access to or support from service providers; inadequate provision of suitable short-term respite accommodation for the young person, especially where there is alcohol or substance abuse or an issue of intellectual disability; and inadequate counselling to deal with the grief and loss experienced by parents and young people.

For both groups, schooling and contact with school staff tends to be more negative than positive, and there are disturbing similarities in the stories of parents and young people who speak of schools providing inadequate support when the young person demonstrated disruptive behaviour, a decline in academic performance, learning difficulties, or truancy. The experiences of young people and parents with regard to schools strongly suggests that school systems need to engage in critical self-reflection about the impact of school policies and practices on young people who are vulnerable. In both groups, physical violence: hitting, striking, slapping, occur as a part of family life. In more than half of the young people's interviews, episodes of physical violence are related.

In the parents' group, serious physical violence is related in one-third of cases and one in six parents indicated sexual abuse of a female child in the family. Physical violence was often mentioned in these and other cases in the context of being necessary discipline. This calls into question not only the issue of young people's right to be protected from physical violence, but what constitutes appropriate discipline for children and young people. In many cases, the resort to physical means of discipline appears to be used as a means of authoritarian control or a lashing out rather than reasonable "discipline". A number of parents in the sample spoke with alarm about young people's "rights", as if information to young people about their right not to be the subject of physically violent discipline presents a threat to family life.

It is not only important to value parents and their role but to do so in a way which does not reduce young people to objects for coercion and manipulation. The issue of children's rights is important and should include the child's "right to relationships" with people they need to provide the safety and security necessary to emotional and physical well-being. This incorporates, but goes beyond, a purely legalistic notion of rights to one which requires a set of behaviours and attitudes to children and young people which reflect a view of them as people with views and feelings which cannot be routinely ignored. Parent and institutional behaviours consistent with this right to relationship include listening to young people, developing two-way communication, demonstrating commitment to children and young people over time, and ensuring that a young person's perspective is gained when matters concerning them are determined.

Perspectives of Service Provider

The research proceeded on the basis that early intervention into and prevention of homelessness among young people required a variety of intervention sites and goals, and would be substantially affected by various contextual matters. This proved to be the case. Given this, it becomes difficult to suggest specific models of practice that are likely to be transportable unless this occurs in institutional environments where there is a degree of consistency across services. While state secondary schools and child protection and alternative care systems, along with Commonwealth funded welfare, education and employment programs, have the capacity to endorse and resource particular service models across states and sometimes across Australia, a significant degree of variability in the specific models developed can be assumed as necessary to account for these contextual factors.

In order to analyse models of early intervention practice it is necessary to consider whether the diverse practices and goals of different models can be classified into broad practice approaches. A number of these approaches are usually in combination in a specific service model. There are six broad approaches to young people and service responses to them are discernable. It is of interest that these same approaches can be discerned in relation to parent strategies. We have called these approaches as:

— a treatment and control approach;

— an individual therapy approach;

— a developmental approach;

— a rights-based approach;

— a relational approach; and

— a transitional/independent living approach.

The treatment and control approach involves a view of young people in a period of adolescence where they are essentially unstable, in a period of "storm and stress", or in effect, a period of abnormality. From such a perspective, young people need controlling or treatment by either parents, or if not parents, then services and other agencies such as school and police. Issues of home leaving are seen essentially as the fault of willful young people who are "bad" or "mad", who are led astray by peers, government inducements, youth workers or their own pathology. Parent-child relations are painted as static and as threatened by calls by the young person for greater autonomy. This approach when applied to parents, is one where parents are universally blamed and viewed as inherently uncaring and/or unstable.

In research literature the "storm and stress" analysis has been rejected as an empirically supportable basis for understanding adolescence. This approach provides legitimacy for excluding young people who experience difficulty from sources of social and family support. The individualised therapeutic approach is aimed at bringing about change in, or treating, the individual from a position of empathy, often stated as a client centered perspective. It is essentially a deficit approach and includes a range of mental health, drug rehabilitation and individual counselling strategies.

A third approach operates from a developmental perspective, where young people are seen as being in need of personal development, socialisation, guidance and stability of lifestyle in order to successfully make various necessary transitions, including from living at home to independent living. Where these conditions do not exist, a young person risks not making the transition successfully. Such an approach generates strategies focused on individual young people, often seen as being at risk. Two variations of this approach seem reflected in the data. In the first an active process of diagnosis occurs, where young people are identified as at risk through the application of particular risk factors.

The second approach involves creating an environment where young people will self-identify as requiring support. This is an important distinction as young people themselves do not use the notion of at risk as a way of understanding themselves. Both approaches often involve strategies for the development of skills or competencies by the individual, sometimes through specifically developed programs. When all young people are considered "at risk" these strategies are applied universally, for example, through the inclusion of conflict resolution or parenting curriculum in school. When applied to parents, a developmental approach focuses on education regarding parenting styles and skills.

A fourth perspective sees young people essentially as individuals with legitimate perspectives, feelings, and rights in the same way as other people. From this perspective, embodied in the United Nations Convention on the Rights of the Child (CROC), young people have a right to protection, to education, to relationship with their families, and a right to be heard in decisions made which affect them. Implicit in this perspective is the view that parents and other social institutions such as schools only partially acknowledge the personhood of children and young people. Strategies with this orientation reflect an acknowledgement that young people do have rights and that they have a right to know what these are. In CROC, these rights include the acknowledgement of parents as the primary caregivers for children and so should not be assumed to be anti-parent.

Practices which seek to include rather than exclude parents, to improve relationships, can be pursued, though this can be in tension when at the expense of other rights of the young person, such as the right to safety. The relational approach sees young people as being in interdependent relationships with parents, other family members, and even communities, where ongoing implicit or explicit negotiation of the nature of the relationship and associated norms is required. Responses which heighten communication and mutual understanding between young people and their parent/s are prioritised. Such an approach views the notion that young people are in transition to independence as simplistic and failing to understand the importance of family relationships to the social and emotional well-being of people throughout the lifespan. This relational orientation is reflected in young person-family counselling, strategies to link young people and parent/s, and mediation and systemic family therapy approaches.

The highest priority of such strategies is improved relationships and support within the family. While individual work may occur with different family members, these are seen as necessary accompaniments to the whole of family work. A final approach is oriented to the provision of and/or support of young people in accommodation or housing that is independent or transitional. This approach could be termed a transitional/independent living approach. It is most often cited as relevant when the family situation has been broken down for a considerable period of time, usually as a result of abuse or when a young person is needing or wishing to live independently and is of an age where there are no requirements for the involvement of the state welfare authorities.

Such intervention usually falls outside the arena of early intervention with young people under 16, given the long-term process homelessness that young people of this age usually have as antecedents. It is a common approach used with young people 16 and older. These approaches are not mutually exclusive. Indeed, in respect of best practice it is usual to see a number of approaches combined in a particular service model.

Family-Focused Services

Family-focused services were broadly divided into general family support services, family mediation and therapy services and alternative care services. General family support services are more oriented towards work with parents and together with alternative care services seem to have comparatively less involvement with young people and families once home leaving has occurred, than family mediation/therapy, and young people-family mediation. Family-focused services generally receive a significant proportion of referrals from statutory welfare authorities with referrals from young people and parents themselves often limited because of a lack of sufficient resources or a restricted mandate.

The overall impression from the data is that familyfocused strategies regarding early home leaving and homelessness among young people are best coordinated by those services which have clear and articulate pro parent and pro young person frameworks and practices. The adolescent-parent mediation and therapy services are outstanding examples of this, demonstrating a deep appreciation both of the experiences and perspectives of young people and the value which young people themselves place on family relationships, a respect and empathy for parents, and a commitment to continue to seek family restoration or at least a level of reconciliation well after home leaving has occurred.

Generic family support services are sufficiently focused on or understanding of the issues and interests of young people within families to coordinate this work effectively, though this could well be the case in particular services. This new type of young person-family service has emerged only recently, largely through the Commonwealth funding of adolescent-family mediation services. It provides an obvious site for the coordination of specialist adolescent-family-focused work which arises from the involvement of schools, general youth services and other service providers. Such services have an important role to play in providing specialist support to a range of agencies in professional development and training and in community education.

Vital to best practice is a framework for practice which contextualises the difficulties families experience, rather than simply viewing difficulties as signals of a dysfunctional family. It is notable that best practice agencies do not pathologise families (parents or young people), but see them as operating in stressful circumstances from a social justice perspective. The emphasis is on validating parents while at the same time being clear about the basic rights of young people to a safe and supportive home. This combination of relational, rights, developmental and therapeutic approaches requires substantial insight regarding macro and micro perspectives on practice with families and with young people, and can only be undertaken with a strong commitment by the service to professional support, training and ongoing reflective practice.

These young people-family services are clearly focused on early intervention in direct practice, yet can play an important role in developing greater protective factors particularly at the situational level, through involvement in community awareness raising activities, policy development, and preventive education in schools. Protective and alternative care services have a clear role to play where there are long-standing or serious family issues, given the link between these issues and subsequent homelessness. State intervention is reported by a wide range of respondents as a substantial source of systems abuse and an active ingredient in the creation of homelessness. A variety of respondents indicated the need for greater emphasis on providing support to families where there are protective concerns, and the need for specific services for adolescents and their families.

The level of notifications of abuse of young people is not seen to be matched by services to those adolescents and their families. While in part this may be attributable to the difficulty in gaining sufficient alternative care placements in the community; the insufficiency of services and tendency to target services to younger children were cited as ongoing barriers to effective intervention. The case studies indicate that best practice involves using practices which deal with protective concerns while maximising the extent to which unproblematic family processes can continue. Best practice also involves service providers regarding the young person as a person with basic rights, which includes the right to be actively involved and heard in all aspects of the case planning process.

There is clear evidence that SAAP-funded services are engaging in family-focused work, and in particular with parents of young clients. Best practice in a SAAP service involves having a readiness and a capacity to engage with the families of young people, as well as to support young people in other areas of need. Services which are accessed by a significant number of young people under 16 are clearly moving in this direction.

Linkage with a specialist young person-family worker or service appears vital if SAAP services are to effectively explore the family options young people have. The dilemma remains as to how in policy and practice SAAP will deal with young people under 15 years given the resilience of this group as users of SAAP, and the lack in many cases of alternative options for these young people. The extent to which Youth and Parent Services in Adelaide involve parents in the alternative accommodation aspect of their work deeply challenges the long-held assumption that location in another family is a relatively benign strategy. Indeed it could well be that such placements, which may have some parent involvement aspects, actually contribute to the process of young people becoming detached from families more than is necessary. If family reunification is genuinely sought the YPS model of practice and some of the principles it is based on are well worth further application. This said, a view was raised a number of times in the research that the removal of, or location of the young people away from their home was in many cases detrimental.

At a time when it is becoming increasingly recognised that the perpetrator rather than a victim of domestic violence should leave the family home while the matter is dealt with, it is of concern that young people should be the ones to leave when there are protective concerns or when substantial family issues exist. Given that such relocation often actively contributes to early home leaving and homelessness, it is time these practices are examined more fully with a view to young people remaining in the home when, for example, physical or sexual abuse indicates another family member or resident should be held accountable, and change their behaviour. The needs of families from non-English cultural backgrounds receive some level of response by a number of services. However, as the research of Prince indicates, models are required which can respond to the needs of families where English is not the preferred family language.

Schooling System

The results from the survey and the parent interviews indicate that schools represent a significant source of referrals, and that they are an important site for both prevention and early intervention. Interview data arising from young people and parents revealed that schools were the institution most frequently identified as the first to be aware that the young person was having difficulties, though these factors did not present as related to early home leaving or homelessness. This potential for schools to be "first to know" cannot be overlooked when framing responses aimed at early intervention into youth homelessness. The interviews with young people (and parents) revealed a pattern of declining school performance as a consequence of pressures at home.

In a significant number of cases, leaving home was given as a reason for dropping out of school, and at times school expulsion or difficulty was a contributing reason for early home leaving. At the same time, interviews with more than one-third of parents identified the transition from primary to high school as a significant and detrimental turning point in the lives of their sons and daughters, with the same number of parents citing truancy and suspension/exclusion as a part of their young person's school experience. Half of the parents identified problems with their young person's school academic performance. In any discussion of best practices as they exist in school settings, it is essential to consider what dilemmas or constraint s exist for school s trying to implement best practice.

Given the credentialling demands generally placed on Australian secondary schooling systems, there are limitations on their capacity to adopt early intervention and prevention strategies. While secondary schools do respond to the social, emotional and welfare needs of students in a variety of ways in, general they do so in ways which often fall short of responding to the needs of those students who are homeless or most vulnerable to homelessness. Such students are often seen as difficult and in need of significant additional support or attention within a disciplinary or behaviour management framework.

The challenge for schooling systems and individual schools is to address academic and vocational goals and yet be responsive to the social and emotional wellbeing of young people from the widest range of circumstances. Clearly schools cannot do this alone. By networking more efficiently, by breaking down barriers between teachers, welfare workers, youth workers and other professionals, schools can better achieve the multiple goals demanded of them by an increasingly complex society. This ability to network in the community, to draw upon the resources of specialised personnel in meeting all the life needs of young people, seems an essential ingredient of schools which strive for successful practice.

Three strategies seem to typify current best practice. These are the involvement of youth and community services inside the school, in roles of contributors to the curriculum, sources of information in the playground, providers of specific support services in rooms located at the school, in active support of guidance officers and teachers regarding particular students, and in teacher in-service training. Second, it involves the schools' use of these agencies in the community through referral, participation in interagency networks, and school support of systems for external case management where significant welfare or family issues exist for the student. Finally, best practice in schools involves schools recognising that the institutional structures and processes of the school must be consistent with prevention and early intervention agendas.

Best practice does not involve simply adding on early intervention and prevention features to the school without considering in very explicit ways the level of supportiveness experienced by students in the school generally, and the impact of policies related to exclusion, suspension, behaviour management and truancy. At the same time, barriers between home and school need to be consistently tackled, with parents and young people encouraged to build partnerships of learning with teachers and school personnel. School authorities need to develop more flexible timetabling, including evening and weekend classes, so that young people and parents can better access school services.

The unmet need by parents for support and educative input can clearly be partially met at schools due to the image they have as community rather than welfare services. There are issues here for teaching as a profession, and for teacher-training authorities. The past decade has witnessed increasing levels of criticism directed at teachers, and teachers have learnt to move quickly into "siege" positions when attacked. There is some parallel here with parents, who need first to be validated rather than attacked for their perceived failings. It is essential therefore to "sell" any changes in schooling to the teaching profession, to validate the enormous difficulties inherent in their work, and to help them see the benefits in changing.

While schools are hypothetically ideal sites for early intervention given the almost universal attendance of children, in practice there are a number of cautions. There are some things it appears schools can do well, for example, brief intervention that provides perspectives and information to parents and young people at critical times; curriculum which develops life skills and information about the existence of social supports, and ways to deal with difficulties. Schools can also respond well to young people once they have become homeless particularly in respect of ensuring (in concert with youth and community services) that there are additional supports to allow students to continue schooling while they live out of home, as evidenced by the Ardoch Foundation approach. In this respect schools can become a site for the delivery of welfare services integrated into the school and delivered in a non-stigmatising way.

Schools can be an excellent site for some aspects of prevention work, and can play an important role in early intervention, though this latter capacity is heavily dependent on their frameworks for viewing and responding to young people issues and their capacity to operate in the genuinely collegial and open manner with other community and specifically youth services. Schools do not often engage in young personfamily work that is substantial. This is the arena of specialist young people-family mediation and counselling services who are best placed to do this work.

The critical issue with schools is how to liaise and connect into such services. The critical issue of family relations involves having a practice framework that regards young people as people with views and feelings that must be heard, and strategies which enable an increase in positive regard towards the young person within the family. In general there is little evidence of empathetic institutionallysupported practice frameworks in schools, as perceived by the young people who are homeless or likely to become homeless.

While some schools exhibit strong values in this regard there is wide variation in school philosophy and management approach. It appears that identifying students who are at risk and targeting specific strategies at these students is problematic. A narrow "at risk" approach will run the danger of labelling and stereotyping students. It reflects too closely an approach to students at the institutional level of the school that is essentially "doing to" rather than listening to and engaging with students. Further, there is evidence that the current general trend in Australia is to promote supportive school environment policies while the actual practices of secondary schooling are operating from a more behaviour management perspective, and at risk strategies involving active identification could very easily be subsumed subtly and despite the best intentions into this pervasive orientation.

Young people are particularly concerned about confidentiality, and this raises the thorny question for schools of who is the primary client? Schools, it could be argued, do not perceive or reflect in their processes the view that students are their primary client but rather operate on the basis that the primary client is the community, parents, and society generally. The question of the practice frameworks used for best practice in schools is vitally important. Young people who are homeless or who are close to homeless will generally not respond or access a "treatment and control approach" or a response that does not include important protections for them, which are in turn embodied in a rights approach.

While there can never be total confidentiality, there is a need for response frameworks that encourage access by students and build trusting relationships. At risk strategies, if employed, should focus on self-identification strategies rather than enter the ethical and dubious quagmire of diagnostic techniques to identify the at risk young people. Schools can certainly use skills in the community and youth sectors, and work in partnership with agencies who do essential coordination.

Youth Services

There has been a certain public perception that youth services are in some way antagonistic to or do not engage with parents. Young people most commonly self-refer to youth services, the youth services in the survey indicated that parents were the referral source at 50% of that level. More than half of the youth service respondents indicated that they worked with parents virtually always or often. It is also relevant that youth services did not cite the provision of accommodation as a critical early intervention strategy, although little work was directed specifically at the support of parents.

A number of early intervention and prevention service models are located in youth services. In addition, some of those discussed under the familyfocused services, such as the SAAP youth accommodation service with a specialist individual and family worker, identify as youth services. The approaches used by youth services vary considerably, however it is reasonable to suggest that there is a strong recognition that a relational approach is important in respect of young people and early home leaving. This is accompanied by a view that young people have the right to be safe, to be heard, for the privacy of discussions to be respected unless permission for disclosure is given, and to seek and be given information and support as a person.

A developmental approach is also present in most youth service approaches with parenting, life skills, conflict resolution, or some educative component for young people and parents (separately) viewed as important components of most models. Services in the mental health area indicate an emphasis on an individual therapy approach. The transitional/ independent living approach is most clearly evident in youth accommodation services which cater primarily for young people 16 and over, and in those services where few resources are available to undertake the time consuming work associated with parent and family liaison. Both generalist and specialist youth services can play a vital role in early intervention. A number of service models are worthy of specific mention.

The Drum Youth Resource Centre is a model clearly replicable to other urban areas. It has a preventive orientation in building up protective factors regarding young people's access to information and easy access to support, where young women in particular are catered for, as well as a capacity to undertake basic early intervention work which links into schools as a matter of routine and family counselling as needed. Such a basic yet integrated youth service facility with health, legal, family relations and accommodation components colocated could be seen as an essential community resource in all suburban and satellite areas with a significant population of young people, and as a fundamental ingredient in the town plans of growing regional and satellite communities.

In small rural towns youth services of any description struggle to exist on short-term and low levels of funding. They respond to a very broad range of needs and the only way they can effectively undertake early intervention or prevention work is by developing strong links with other key people, particularly specialist workers in the area, such as in community health services, in schools, and in the police. Given the diversity of issues these agencies work on and the fact that early home leaving issues do not constitute a great deal of this, such a strategy would need to be developed in the context of responding to a variety of needs of young people and families in rural areas. The importance of a national telephone counselling service for young people and parents cannot be underest imated.

Universal access to immediate and confidential support is likely to have significant application particularly in regard to early intervention. It is clear SAAP youth services are orientating to include relations between young people and parents/caregivers. There is however a distinct difference between the degree of insight, and the practices developed in those SAAP agencies with a concentration of clients in the 12 to 15 age range. These services have obviously developed an orientation to include family relations work to some degree in their role.

The link between child protection intervention and homelessness is evident. While the rationale for intervention (abuse to a child) is not questioned, the removal from abuse appears to come in some instances at the cost of systems-induced homelessness. The continued lack of sufficient service supports to adolescent young people with protective concerns is clearly problematic given the emergence of effective practice models for these young people and their families.

The removal of abused young people is seen as unfair by some young people and service providers. While it is important not to generalise to all family contexts, these respondents indicated that, in their experience, adolescents were often inappropriately seen as the ones who should be relocated when they were the subject of abuse. Although some parents made very positive comments about their experience with police, the data from surveys and interviews supports the view that intervention from police, although in many instances positive, often does not involve effective referral of the young person or parent to an appropriate service provider.

These results strongly suggest the need for better communication channels to be developed between police and service providers working in the area of young people. This might entail educational and professional development programs which inform police of the factors associated with youth homelessness, and of appropriate avenues for referral and support for those young people and parents who present with difficulties associated with early home leaving. Infrastructures which build links between "first to know" agencies and other support services have the potential to result in better mechanisms for early intervention.

Equally there is a need for health professionals, including psychiatrists, to reconsider their response frameworks when dealing with issues surrounding early home leaving. This may mean careful consideration of "pathology" models which focus on the young person as the source of problems in families. Best practice in the area of early intervention requires services to incorporate as a minimum, aspects of relational and rights-based approaches. These models recognise that early intervention responding to early home leaving must recognise and respect the personal perspectives of both young people and parents where each has a right to be safe and heard. They are relational in that they work with both parents and young people specifically around home leaving and returning issues. Individual therapy and developmental approaches are used to supplement these core approaches as needed.

Protective Factors

Successful prevention and early intervention means recognising the need for protective factors, and providing support networks which assist in this regard. Throughout the course of the case studies, and during interviews with parents and young people, reference is made to the families lacking support networks. These networks might be other family members, friends, or community-based. There is also a recognition in the field that some localities, by virtue of their isolation, lack of social infrastructure, low socioeconomic profile, and high levels of unemployment, represent localities where there is likely to be a lack of community resources to sustain and encourage such support networks.

Early Intervention and Prevention

There is a need to acknowledge that many families are undergoing stress, particularly in the current climate where structural and external factors such as unemployment interact with factors such as family conflict. Massive changes to the labour market involvement of young people in Australia and many other nations have resulted in changes to home leaving patterns. These changes require a fundamental reconsideration of what protective factors families, and specifically young people and parents require if the level of interdependency emerging between them is to be sustainable. This is particularly true in families where financial resources are already minimal.

There is a need to recognise and publicly acknowledge that some young people in families where there are substantial long-term relationship issues, cannot or may not wish to live at the parent/s home. In this case, policies and programs have to address the needs of young people living independently. The models of service which met the requirements of best practice most clearly identified by parents, young people and service providers are those which offer non-stigmatised openly available services to all, and from this point were able to link people to other tiers of more specialist or specific support. In short, there is a need for sensitive systems of service delivery which encourage self-identification of support needs.

Prevention approaches are best conceptualised as universal, and as building protective supports. Such supports can occur at a number of service systemlevels, and include the provision of community education and life skills education. Services conceptualised as responding to young people at risk of homelessness should emphasise placing support service close to and accessible to young people and parents. These should be articulated to more specific service supports to deal with various levels and types of need. It is possible that an approach which emphasises identification of at risk young people could not only have a stigmatising effect but could also have a netwidening effect.

Early intervention strategies cannot deal with or ameliorate the social and structural dynamics which produce and sustain homelessness. Early intervention strategies can have preventive impact at the level of the individual and the level of the family and so reduce the numbers of young people who become homeless as a result of early home leaving. This said, there is the broad issue of young people's place in contemporary Australia, where even if many or most young people remain at home, significant numbers will need to live in independent households for one or a number of reasons. Study, employment, unsatisfactory circumstances at home or simply the desire to live independently mean that the prevention of homelessness ultimately returns to the core issues of poverty and housing affordability.

Conversely the long-term processes that lead to early home leaving in many circumstances cannot be addressed by early intervention strategies. Issues of abuse prevention and domestic violence, a re-examination of the place children and young people have when parents separate or repartner, whole family homelessness, the poverty and general lack of adequate housing for many Aboriginal people, and the broader socioeconomic stresses facing families are of vital importance in the prevention of homelessness among young people.

It is critical that there develops a positive and supportive view of young people generally, rather than there be a continuing view that young people, particularly those from low income circumstances and indigenous young people, are inherently problems and threats to social order. Images of the troublesome adolescent as a stereotype, reinforced through negative media portrayal, can themselves create additional distance between young people, their parents and the rest of the community. Such images provide legitimacy for a "doing to" approach to young people instead of an approach of engaging and listening. As young people gain information from a wider range of sources and remain for longer periods at home, the imperative is that our picture of who young people are and the nature of our relationship with them needs to alter. There is a need for substantial community and parent education, in order that these dominant perspectives are challenged.

Status Implementing Street Children

Implementation of a street children project should be systematic and must follow a series of steps. The main steps in the implementation process are

— *Situation assessment* : this leads you to decide on the problems that need to be addressed.

— *Strategic plan* : this states the objectives and outlines the strategies, activities, and resources (human and financial) that are needed and a plan for implementation of the activities.

— *Project implementation* : this is the process of conducting all the activities.

— *Monitoring and evaluation* : monitoring is a process of continuous assessment of the project, while evaluation measures the impact of the project at defined time points.

— *Revising the strategic plan* : lessons learnt through monitoring and evaluation could be used to rewrite the plan, and improve it in terms of relevance and feasibility.

— *Sharing information* : information obtained from the project should be disseminated so that others may benefit from it.

Conduct a situation Analysis

Assessing the situation to determine priorities for intervention is the essence of the strategic approach to planning. Situation analysis helps you to understand street children as individuals and the social environment in which they live. This would enable you to identify their problems, set objectives for interventions and to plan services and support. The Modified Social Stress Model could be used as a framework for carrying out the analysis. Methods for conducting a situation assessment are presented in Module 5 (Determining the needs and problems of street children). Information should be gathered on a continuous basis as the initial situation may change.

Develop a Strategic Plan

The strategic plan is a document that serves as the framework for implementation of the street children project. It represents an agreement among the team members of the project about the target group that the project is supposed to benefit, the problems that are going to be addressed, and the approach to intervention. CAC members may be consulted during the process of developing the strategic plan as they have experience in providing various services and in long-term planning. Inputs from street children ensure that the programme actually addresses their needs, and it enhances the credibility of the project in the target group. The main components of a strategic plan are;

Aim of the Project

The aim should be based on the situation analysis. It should fit in with the basic mission of your agency and should complement the activities of other programmes that involve street children. A clear aim helps in setting the priority of activities to be undertaken.

Objectives of the Project

This is an expansion of the aim of the project. The objectives will set the direction of the project. Each objective should be Specific, Measurable, Achievable, Realistic and must give a Time-frame to accomplish the activities (SMART).

Outline of the Strategies

Outline of appropriate strategies and the components of each strategy should be drawn for each objective, e. g. if education is an objective, components of the strategy could be training in life skills, health education, peer education or vocational training.

List of Activities, Time Frame and Assignment of Responsibilities

For each strategy, list the activities that need to be implemented and determine a realistic time frame for each activity. Activities should be placed in a chronological order. Responsibility for each activity should then be assigned.

Budget

Make a budget estimate of the cost of each activity. Indicate against each activity the resources that already exist, as it will help in decisions regarding the final allocation.

Develop a Plan for Monitoring and Evaluation

The plan for monitoring and evaluation of a programme should be made at the time when the goals and activities of the programme are being planned. Developing a monitoring and evaluation plan later may become difficult if the objectives were not stated in an objective and measurable manner. Monitoring involves a day to day follow up of activities. It is an ongoing activity that helps in the identification of problems that need to be corrected. A set of indicators is usually required for appropriate monitoring. Evaluation requires comparing the information collected at the start of the project to information obtained after the implementation of the project.

Other Considerations for a Strategic Plan

Project sustainability : A project is said to be sustainable if it has the potential to stay operational as long as the need for it exists. Projects become more sustainable if they have community support and are integrated within or are associated with the local sectoral structures. Support for your work may grow as the community learns more about street children and their needs.

Future directions : In a strategic plan, there is a place for ideas about long-term goals and potential projects that can be implemented in the future.

Implement the Project

This is the stage where you actually start or expand projects and services for street children.

Recruit a team of interested people : People have different skills and they have access to different types of resources. People from different institutions (e. g. health), organizations and ordinary community members can be recruited as team members.

Hold an organizational meeting for team members : Provide information on the project in order to gain support. All issues should be discussed and clarified. Unless the team goes through the process of reaching a consensus before real work begins, members of the team may constantly be pulling the project in different directions. Plan meetings in advance to ensure that all the invitees attend. Everyone on the team should have a copy of documents concerning the situation of street children in your community.

Train team members : Depending on the background of the team members, you may have to provide training on specific topics e. g. development of educational materials, community development, referral procedures, and specific interventions such as counselling or group therapy techniques. Training activities could be repeated for volunteers or staff who join the project later. If there are few training resources in the beginning, limit the team to those who already have some skills and experience of working with street children.

Involve the community : Community support is crucial for any project or intervention to be successful. The Community

Advisory Committee can be instrumental in changing the community's attitudes towards and knowledge about substance use and other problems among street children. Involving street children representatives at all stages of project implementation could be quite useful.

Budget : Make a budget estimate of the cost for each activity. Indicate against each activity the resources that already exist, as it will help in making decisions about the final allocation.

Develop a plan for monitoring and evaluation : The plan for monitoring and evaluation of a programme should be made at the time when goals and activities of the programme are being planned. Developing a monitoring and evaluation plan later may become difficult if the objectives were not stated in an objective and measurable manner. Monitoring involves a day to day follow up of activities. It is an ongoing activity that helps in the identification of problems that need to be corrected. A set of indicators is usually required for appropriate monitoring. Evaluation requires comparing the information collected at the start of the project to the information obtained after implementation of the project.

Monitor and Evaluate

Monitoring : Monitoring enables you to check the quality of activities and whether the project is on course. Corrective measures can therefore be taken in time. The ongoing nature of monitoring helps in taking care of problems that had not been visualized at the beginning of the project, and new problems that may have arisen after the completion of the initial situation analysis.

Evaluation : Evaluation is a process by which you find out whether your project is having an impact on the target group. External assistance (external experts) may be required for unbiased evaluation. Street children, street educators and community members can provide unique perspectives and should be involved in the evaluation process. The impact of the project can be determined by comparing information obtained recently with the baseline information. Every project should be evaluated from time to time.

Revise the strategic plan

Once you have received information about the progress of your project or projects, it may be necessary to revise (and rewrite) the strategic plan. This should be an on-going process. An outreach project on prevention of substance use may fail if the area is infested with drug dealers who use and sell substances to street children. The project should then be modified and the activities should be carried out at a centre for street children.

Share What You Have Learned

Giving feedback should be a part of the project's structure. Clear and direct feedback reduces uncertainty, solves problems, builds trust, strengthens relationships and improves the quality of work. Sharing information is essential for networking with key persons and organizations and for enhancing support. Share the information with,

Street children : They need to know what they have achieved and how they have failed. This could act as a motivating factor for them to work harder to improve their situation.

Street educators : They need to direct their efforts at what is feasible and effective.

NGOs : They may be able to extend their assistance and resources to your project.

WHO : Mental Health and Substance Dependence (MSD) - They may be able to provide technical support and other resources.

6

Future Health Care for Street Children

Substance in Health care must be an important part of healthier life management of street children. This approach may help in reduction of risk behaviours without the need for specific interventions, such as detoxification.

Substance in Health care

These complications can result in behaviours such as anxiety, panic, agitation, anger, hallucinations, confusion and disorientation. At times, street children can be managed by placement in any safe and supervised setting, e. g. a child who is intoxicated with alcohol. Medical assistance may be needed under other circumstances, e. g. detoxification from heavy use of barbiturates, as it is associated with the risk of convulsions and delirium (confusion, hallucinations). You may have to respond to intoxication, overdose or withdrawal by providing adequate immediate care and appropriate referral. Specific conditions of street children:

— Anxiety, agitation or panic.

  — Approach the street child in a calm and confident manner.

- Move and speak slowly and reassure the child. Do not leave him or her unattended.
- Minimise the number of people attending to the street child.

— Anger, aggression.

- Do not touch the street child unless absolutely necessary.
- Speak in a calm, reassuring way. Keep your own emotions in check.
- Address the street child by name when talking to him or her.
- Do not challenge or threaten by the tone of your voice, eyes or posture.
- Allow the street child to talk about his or her feelings and acknowledge them.

— Altered perception, hallucinations.

- Explain perceptual errors, for example, "the pink elephant you see is not real, it is just the substance you have taken, you are safe".
- Create a simple and uncluttered environment.
- Place child in well lit surroundings to avoid the possibility of perceiving things wrongly.
- Protect the street child from harm.

— Confusion, disorientation.

- Provide frequent reality orientation by asking simple questions.
- Remove unnecessary equipment to avoid injuries.
- Provide explanations as to what is going on around the child.

  — Do not leave the child alone.
  — Place child in well lit surroundings to avoid the possibility of perceiving things wrongly.

— Unconsciousness:

  — Shake the child and call his or her name. If there is no reaction, check breathing.
  — If the child can be revived, get him or her up and moving.
  — If the child is not breathing, start mouth-to-mouth resuscitation.

When faced with a street child experiencing any of the above mentioned conditions (intoxication, withdrawal, overdose), be alert to other physical problems or illnesses that may co-exist with substance use. Street children may also get intoxicated with or may have withdrawal symptoms of many substances (polysubstance use). Seek further assistance from a health service. If possible, try to obtain a sample of the substance that has been taken. Health care personnel may want to examine it or may run a test on the sample.

Goal of Detoxification

The goal of detoxification is to provide safe and humane withdrawal from substance(s) dependence. The procedure for detoxification will depend upon the type, combinations and pattern of use of substances in question. Detoxification for hypnosedatives should occur in a medically supervised setting because withdrawal from these substances can result in death from convulsions and heart failure. If the withdrawal symptoms are not expected to be severe and if there is a person to supervise the detoxification, there may be no need for hospitalization or constant clinical care. Selfdetoxification is possible for solvents, cannabis, stimulants and cocaine. Medical assistance may however be needed to ease the withdrawal process.

Your main role will be supporting the street child before, during and after the detoxification process. Support, motivating and structure are more necessary for street children than adults because of their developmental stage, and their impaired nutritional and general health status. Supporting a street child through withdrawal can be a good opportunity to engage the street child and motivate him/her to participate in further treatment. Support can include:

— Dispelling myths and fears about detoxification.

— Helping the street child toaccess and use the health system (for example, taking the street child to a detoxification clinic or experienced health care worker).

— Monitoring the general health of the street child.

— Supporting and involving the street child's family when possible.

— Identifying and supporting other people who can support the street child during and after detoxification.

Referral and Goal Setting

After providing the necessary immediate care, refer the street child to another service. When deciding on the service, assess whether the street child requires:

— Intensive treatment in a health facility or treatment centre or a residential environment.

— Sessions of a particular intervention, such as counselling.

— A casual drop-in centre.

— Linkage to a supportive adult or a more functional peer in the local community.

A well-developed network of appropriate services can help you in getting in touch with services or resource persons who can tell you what you want to know. The services required might not exist in the area or might not be child-friendly.

Where such a network does not exist and if you have the necessary skill, train community members to provide the interventions and support that street children need.

It is also important to prepare yourself and the street child for the possibility of setbacks in the process. Street children need to be aware that if one referral does not work out, it does not mean that the problems cannot be solved. Other options can be tried. Street children might have to use a number of services before they achieve their goals.

Goal setting (case planning/action planning) is an important component of assessment and case management. Goals should be negotiated with the street child. The goal should be specific and observable, and broken up into short-term, achievable targets. Plans should be reviewed regularly, and updated to take into account the changing nature of street life, the current availability of resources and services, developmental issues, and the fluctuating motivation that street children typically display.

Motivating the Street Child

The street educator responding to the needs of street children may sometimes feel frustrated when he/ she is trying to help street children control or stop risky behaviour because they may not change at the desired pace. It is essential to realise that the change process can take a long time and proceeds through stages that are described below on the next page. It would also be helpful to consider these stages in relation to life skills. It is necessary to know how to encourage a street child to respond positively to the action plan. Motivational Interviewing (MI) is a technique that can help you to achieve this.

Stages change and appropriate response

The pre-contemplation stage: During this stage, the street child engaged in risky behaviour is not considering giving up his or her behaviour. Try to form a relationship with the child and raise his or her awareness of the consequences of risk behaviour. Avoid pushing him or her too hard! Get them involved in thinking about changing their lives.

The contemplation stage: At this stage the street child begins to think about doing something regarding his or her behaviour. Help the child by discussing the advantages and disadvantages of risky behaviour, and those of stopping.

The action stage: At this point, the street child attempts to stop or minimise his or her risk taking behaviour. Help him or her develop the needed skills and strategies (life skills). The child will need to figure out the situations (associated with people, places, feelings or things) under which he or she is more likely to adopt risky behaviour. Once identified, these situations can be eliminated, e. g. throwing away equipment like syringes, using condoms during sexual activity, avoiding friends who use substances or finding a job to avoid boredom.

The lapse stage: After trying to take action as described above, the child can resume their risk taking behaviour. This should not be seen as failure, but simply as a part of the process of change. Prepare the child in advance for this stage and then help him or her get through it. When the child is ready to try to stop the behaviour again, help him or her make a more effective plan of action.

The maintenance stage: Now the individual wants to consistently practice the desired new behaviour. Help the street child develop a healthy lifestyle, which might include moving into a safe environment such as home, finding activities that keep him or her off the streets, and spending free time with children or adults who do not encourage or participate in risk behaviour. Encourage the child to make a self-assessment on how well he or she is able to maintain the selected acceptable behaviour by monitoring himself/ herself and by recognizing when he/ she is entering risky situations.

MI enables the street child to convince himself/ herself about the need to change risk behaviours. It can be used at the time of the initial assessment to increase a street child's readiness to change, and at later stages for reinforcing and maintaining the positive behavioural change. MI does not involve coercion or confrontation.

There are five broad principles underlying MI:

— *Express empathy:* You should be able to express acceptance and respect for the street child. This is often done through skillful reflective listening (listening carefully to the child and letting him or her know that you understand him or her).

— *Develop discrepancy:* A discrepancy between present behaviour and important goals will motivate change. The child should present the reasons why he or she should change.

— *Avoid arguments:* Arguments should be avoided because they are counter-productive, as the child becomes guarded and does not let you know his or her problems.

— *Roll with resistance:* Resistance on the part of the child is a signal to change strategies. Statements that a street child makes can be reframed slightly to create a new momentum towards change.

— *Support the child's sense of ability to change:* Belief in the possibility of change is an important motivator, so support the child's hope in the range of alternative approaches available. Acknowledging that the child is responsible for choosing and carrying out personal change can foster his/her self-belief.

Reproductive Health Problem

Street children who have sexual and reproductive health problems including HIV/AIDS and STDs. You should be able to recognize these problems, provide immediate care and refer the street child for professional care. The street child should also be taught to look for these signs and taught how to seek support and supervision from a health care worker. Four conditions are specifically described abortion, emergency childbearing, STDs and HIV/AIDS.

Abortion

A child who has undergone an abortion or an unsafe abortion may complain of:

— Fever.

— Abdominal pain.

— Abnormal discharge or bleeding from the birth canal.

— A street girl may tell you that her menses have not been regular or have stopped.

— The child may be confused.

A street girl needs expert support as she could develop serious health complications. Refer the child to a health facility immediately.

Emergency Problems in Pregnancy

Emergency problems or danger signs in a pregnant street child include:

— Bleeding from the birth canal.

— Abnormal discharge.

— Fever.

— Fits or swelling of feet.

Pregnant street children are at high risk for these conditions. If a street child has these signs, refer the child to a health facility immediately. Sometimes the need to deliver the baby may be urgent. This could be due to a variety of reasons, some of them being that the street girl may not be aware that she has been experiencing labour pains and realises too late. Or perhaps she may not even know what labour signs are. If you happen to be confronted with an emergency child delivery situation, stay calm and do the following:

Preparation

— Reassure the street girl that you will try and provide the best support you can given the situation.

— Find a comfortable and private place for the delivery to take place.

— Help her to assume the most desired comfortable position.

— If water and soap are available wash hands with soap under running water.

— Put clean cloths under the mother where the baby will be born.

— Do not examine the street girl's birth canal.

The birth of the baby and immediate care of the baby

— Let the baby be born on its own.

— Do not pull out the baby.

— Do not push on the abdomen.

— With a clean cloth in your hands, receive the baby.

— Listen for the baby's first cry.

— If the baby cries and looks healthy, place the baby, covered in a cloth, on the mother's body. Explain that this is important as the mother's body helps to keep the baby warm.

— Make sure that the weight of the baby does not pull on the cord and that you place the baby on the mother's body without causing a pull on the cord.

— Quickly wipe away any water (mucous) from the baby's mouth and nose.

— Keep the baby warm at all times.

— Continue to reassure the mother and inform her what you are doing.

If there is heavy bleeding before the afterbirth comes out

— Ask the mother to try and pass urine to make room for the afterbirth.

— Ask her to breastfeed the baby without interfering with the birth of the afterbirth.

— Gently rub the mothers womb until you feel the womb become hard like a ball.

— Continue to do this from time to time if the bleeding continues until help arrives or until you reach a health facility.

— Putting the baby on the breast soon after delivery will also help contract the womb and consequently control the bleeding from the birth canal.

Delivery of the afterbirth and care of the mother

— Reassure the girl that she has done well so far and that you have requested for transport or help but will stay with her until then.

— Do not pull on the cord to force the delivery of the afterbirth.

— Allow the afterbirth to come out on its own. Some times it may take as long as 20 minutes. Stay calm and wait patiently.

— Once the afterbirth is delivered, wrap it in a cloth and place it with the baby.

— Make the mother comfortable.

— Ask her to breastfeed the baby, making sure that the baby's nostrils are not being blocked.

— Record all what you have observed and done during the process and give this information to the health worker.

— If possible, accompany the street girl to a health facility especially if no health worker can be found in the area.

Sexually Transmitted Diseases (STDs)

If a street child has complaints such as:

— Sores on the genitalia.

— Discharge from the penis or vagina.

— Pain on urinating.

Provide advice on the need for treatment and refer them for appropriate care at a health facility.

HIV/AIDS

Street children affected by AIDS may suffer from frequent infections. In this situation, you may have to advise them on many issues such as nutrition, hygiene, dental care, psychological support and medications. Seek advice from health workers on how you can provide support and care to a street child affected by AIDS. To give you some idea on the extent of the care and support required when a street child has HIV/AIDS, a few issues are addressed below.

Anxiety and depression

When a street child is made aware of his condition he will experience mental problems such as shock, confusion and constant fears about the condition. A child who is anxious will :

— Have no appetite to eat food.

— May feel short of breath.

— Will be shaking and feeling very worried and may be jumpy.

— Experience sensation of the heart pounding.

— Sweat and could feel like fainting.

— Experience difficulty in sleeping and concentration.

A child experiencing depression can express this in the following ways:

— A feeling of hopelessness.

— Feeling tired and lack of energy.

— Finds no pleasure in the surroundings.

— May be irritable.

— Unable to concentrate and has poor memory.

— May be waking up in the morning or have difficulty getting to sleep at night.

Mental health problems such as anxiety and depression could make the child have difficulty dealing with everyday life situations. In the case of depression, it could lead to the child wanting to harm him or herself even to the point of considering suicide. Encourage the street child to express his or her thoughts and feelings. Give them an opportunity to go through the grief by simply talking and listening to them. Although you may not be in a position to provide support beyond this, it is important to find someone who can find the necessary support for the child such as the social worker. Since the event of HIV there are a number of support groups that have been established in most communities.

Role of Voluntary Counselling and Testing (VCT)

At the beginning of the HIV epidemic, HIV testing was used

mostly for clinical confirmation of suspected HIV disease. At the present moment, people are encouraged to attend voluntary counselling and testing services to find out their HIV status. If the test is negative, one can be encouraged to adopt preventive measures to prevent future infections. In the case that the result is positive, individuals and families can be helped to learn to leave positively, access appropriate care and support early, learn how to prevent transmission of the infection to sexual partners and plan their own future and that of their family.

You may come across a situation when a street child wants to know if he or she is infected with HIV and may wish to have an HIV test done. Good counselling will assist the street child to make informed decisions and cope better with the outcome of the test, help him or her lead more positive lives and prevents further transmission of HIV. Although HIV/AIDS counselling is usually provided by trained counsellors, street educators if trained in counselling, are better placed to provide effective counselling, advice and support to street children. Counselling requires good communications skills. Testing for HIV requires two types of counselling. These are: a) Pre test counselling. b) Post test counselling.

Pre test counselling

The aim of pretest counselling is to provide information to the street child about the technical aspects of testing and the various implications of being found to be HIV positive or negative. Testing should be discussed as a positive act that is linked to changes in risk behaviour, coping and increasing the quality of life. The main issues to be considered in pre testing counselling are:

— The street child's personal history of risk behaviour or exposure to HIV.

— The street child's understanding of HIV/AIDS including methods of transmission and experience in crisis situations.

Assessment of risk

Example of issues to consider:

— Frequency and type of sexual practices especially unprotected vaginal and anal intercourse or unprotected sex with prostitutes or other street children.

— Being part of a group with high prevalence for HIV infection (injecting drug users, prostitutes etc).

— Having received a blood transfusion or other blood or body products.

— Exposure to non-sterile invasive procedures such as tattooing. The Modified Social Stress Model is a useful tool in assessing the risk for HIV infection.

Assessment of understanding

Assess the need for HIV testing by asking the street child these questions:

— Why the test is being requested?

— What are the behaviour patterns?

— What does the street child know about the test and its uses?

— What are the street child's beliefs and knowledge about HIV transmission and its relationship with at risk behaviour?

— Has the street child sought Voluntary Counselling and Testing (when, from whom, for what reason and what was the result)?

— Has the street child considered what to do or how to react if the result is positive or negative?

Preparing the street child for pre test counselling

A decision by the street child to be tested should be an informed one. Try and get an informed consent from the street child. An informed consent implies being aware of the possible implications of a test result. Prepare the street child by discussing :

— confidentiality and informed consent for HIV testing

— implications of the test result whether negative or positive

— ways to cope with knowing the HIV status

— sexuality and sexual practices and

— exploring emotional coping mechanisms and the availability of social support

— explaining how to prevent transmission of HIV

— correcting myths, misinformation and misunderstandings related to HIV/AIDS

Post test counselling

Post test counselling helps to put the street child at ease. Find a quiet place to discuss the results, whether negative or positive. It is important to have the street child repeat the information presented. Give the street child time to reflect on the results and understand the next course of action. Counselling and other support activities should address the feelings of shock, fear, loss, grief, guilt, depression, anxiety, denial, anger, suicidal thinking, reduced selfesteem and spiritual concerns. Therefore, continued counselling and support should also take place to help improve the street child's quality of life as well as to enhance his or her ability to cope and make informed decisions about life choices and ongoing care. The result of the test must be kept confidential only when the need to share it with others arises (shared confidentiality). These others may include family members, loved ones, care giver or trusted street children or friends.

Care for HIV infected street children

Care for infected street children must be comprehensive across a continuum. Comprehensive care involves a network of resources and services which provide holistic, comprehensive, wide ranging support. A continuum of care includes care between hospital, home or other institutions of care over the course of the illness. It is important to recognize that one single approach to the care of HIV infected street children can not be effective.

Nutritional problems

Street children most of the time have inadequate nutrition. This situation becomes even worse when they have AIDS due to some of the other factors related to the condition such as:

— Infections in the mouth that could cause difficulty in swallowing (fungal infections in the mouth, mouth sores, infections of the gums and teeth).

— Nausea and vomiting.

— Prolonged diarrhoea.

— Depression and anxiety.

— Fever from any source.

What the child would require

The child should be encouraged to eat all the food that is familiar in the location in a balanced form. A balanced meal will comprise of these groupings:

— *Body building foods*: These are rich in protein, iron and calcium. Examples of these are eggs meat, fish, milk, groundnuts, peas, beans and soya.

— *Energy-giving foods*: Energy giving foods include, potatoes, yams, cassava, sugar, vegetable oils.

— *Vitamin rich foods*: Included in this group are dark green leafy vegetables, orange coloured vegetables and fruits. These types of food protect the body from infections. Cooking for too long destroys the vitamins in these foods.

Emergency Assistance in Bleeding

Apart from problems directly related to substance use, street children may experience other conditions needing emergency assistance. The most commonly seen conditions among street children based on the findings of the WHO street children project included:

- Unconsciousness (due to trauma, or overdose from a substance).
- Severe bleeding.
- Shock, dizziness.
- Intoxication.
- Burns (from fire, electrical, or chemical).
- Cuts and wounds.
- Broken bones.
- Emergency childbearing.

In this section, elaboration on two techniques is made, which are related to unconsciousness and severe bleeding. To be able to perform first aid on the conditions mentioned above you need to be trained. Many organizations such as hospitals, medical clinics, and the Red Cross or Red Crescent Societies in your community may be offering training courses in first aid. If you are already trained, it is important to go for refresher courses from time to time. As street educators you need to develop the ability to know what type of problems you can handle on your own and those to refer to health care professionals. The environment of street children is violent and they may be far from places where they can get support. To get you started on some first aid techniques only two situations are elaborated here.

There is a potential for acquiring infections from the victim or transmitting infections to the victim during provision of first aid. It is advisable to have a first aid kit at all times when you work on the street if you have been trained in first aid skills. Protective devices should be used whilst giving first aid during resuscitation and control of bleeding or in any situation when contact with body fluids may occur. These protective devices can include gloves, if available, or simply a clean cloth. Prior to performing first aid, ensure protection to yourself, people around the incident and the victim. For example:

— Remove pieces of glass on the floor.

— Control traffic to ensure the safety of all involved. For example, a car accident in the middle of the road.

— If in a violent environment, find appropriate support to protect yourself and others.

Mouth to Mouth Resuscitation

Mouth to mouth resuscitation is given to someone whose breathing has stopped. The objective is to blow air into the victim's respiratory tract. In general, mouth to mouth respiration has not been implicated in the transmission of infections such as HIV. However, there is a significant risk of the infection if a street child is bleeding from the mouth or has an open sore around the mouth. If you are bleeding from the mouth or have sores around the mouth you may also pass infections to the street child.

Bleeding can be external (as a result of a cut on the skin). In this situation blood is visible and obvious. Internal bleeding occurs inside the body and blood may leak through a natural opening such as the ear. Sometimes, blood cannot be seen if the bleeding occurs in an internal cavity like the abdomen. When controlling bleeding avoid contact with body fluids when possible and do not touch anything that may be soiled with blood or other body fluids. Use any protective barriers that are available, gloves or a clean dry cloth. The following is what you can do to control bleeding:

External bleeding

- Small cut.
  - Wash your hands under running water (Hands should also be washed after you complete the procedure).
  - Gently wash away the dirt with clean water.
  - Apply a small dressing if necessary, otherwise keep it open.
- Bleeding heavily from a cut.
  - Apply pressure using your hand to stop the bleeding.
  - Elevate the limb if it is an arm or leg which has been cut.
  - Cover the cut with a pad and apply a bandage.
  - If the bleeding does not stop, add another pad and bandage or cloth without removing the previous dressing.
  - If the bandage is on a limb, frequently check the fingers and toes to ensure that they remain warm. If they are getting cold, loosen the bandage to let the blood circulate.
  - Refer to a health facility for stitches and immunization that can protect the street child from getting tetanus.
  - Apply a small dressing if necessary, otherwise keep it open.
- A cut where a broken bone is protruding
  - Ask someone to assist you to support the broken arm or leg.
  - Place a clean cloth over the cut and bone.
  - Build up padding around the bone and gently bandage this in place keeping the limb still.

  - — Frequently check the fingers and toes for blood circulation. They should remain warm.
  - — Transport the child to a health facility making sure that the injured part is kept still.

— A cut with an object sticking out.

— Do not press on the cut. Pinch the cut around the object.

— Place a clean cloth loosely over the cut and object.

— Keep the injured part raised. If there is a broken bone, keep the injured part still.

— Frequently check for blood flow in fingers and toes. Ensure they remain warm at all times.

— Transport the street child to a health facility.

Internal bleeding

If a street child is loosing blood inside the body, it may be seen coming from the nose, ear, faeces, urine or in the vomit or the birth canal. This will depend on the location of the injury. Sometimes it may not be visible at all as blood may be collecting in a cavity of the body. Here is an example of bleeding from the nose and ear.

Nose bleeding: Ask the child to sit down with head tilted slightly forward. Ask him or her to pinch the soft part of the nose and breathe through the mouth, avoiding blowing or sniffing. The pressure is applied just in front of the bridge of the nose, not only at the tip of the nose. If bleeding does not stop, refer for expert care.

Bleeding from the ear: Bleeding from the ear may indicate a head injury or damage to the ear drum. If there is only a scratch on the outside of the ear, treat it as a small open wound. If bleeding comes from inside the ear it is much more serious and requires expert attention. Place the child in a sitting or lying position, head tilted with bleeding ear down. Cover ear with a clean cloth and refer to a health facility.

Children with Reproductive Health

The WHO defines reproductive health as a state of complete physical, mental and social wellbeing and not merely the absence of disease or infirmity in all matters relating to the reproductive system and to its functions and processes. This definition suggests that people with adequate reproductive health have a satisfying and safe sexual life, can have children, and can make a choice as to whether they would like to have children and if so, when and how to have them. Street children who have sexual and reproductive health problems including HIV/AIDS and STDs. Although the typical age of a street child varies from place to place, the age range includes children in the adolescent period. Sexual behaviour begins before adolescence; during adolescence, major physical and psychological changes occur.

These include rapid physical growth and development, social and psychological maturity which bring about enormous social and psychological pressure. Young people, especially boys are exposed to continued pressure from peer groups as sexual experiences may be viewed as achieving or demonstrating competence. Street children are exposed to situations that make them vulnerable to sexual and reproductive health problems on a day to day basis. Their vulnerability to these situations is increased by their lack of understanding of the changes associated with adolescence, the lack of knowledge and skills which could help them to make healthy choices and their inability to access the appropriate services.

The Modified Social Stress Model is then presented as a framework for understanding the factors that may contribute to these health problems. The six components of the model (stress, normalization of behaviour and situations, effect of behaviour and situations, attachments, skills and resources) influence the likelihood of risk behaviours. An understanding of these factors may be helpful in developing intervention strategies related to sexual and reproductive health including HIV/AIDS/STDs.

Sexual Health

In broad terms, sexual health is a personal sense of sexual well being as well as the absence of disease, infections or illness associated with sexual behaviour. As such, it includes issues of self-esteem, selfexpression, caring for others and cultural values. Sexual health can be described as the positive integration of physical, emotional, intellectual and social aspects of sexuality. Sexuality influences thoughts, feelings, interactions and actions among human beings, and motivates people to find love, contact, warmth and intimacy. It can be expressed in many different ways and is closely linked to the environment one finds oneself in. The environment can hinder or enhance sexual expressions.

Development of Adolescent

Adolescence is the transitional period between childhood and adulthood. It begins with the biological changes associated with puberty and proceeds through a process of psychosocial changes. Each aspect of maturation does not develop at the same rate. Development in adolescence can be uneven and deviations from the norm can cause alarm in the adolescents and those around them. The general information below will give you an understanding of the importance of sexual reproductive health among street children, most of whom are in this phase of development.

Puberty refers to the sequence of physical events by which a child is transformed into a young adult. The characteristic physical changes include those in the reproductive organs and the external genitalia in both sexes, breast development and hip enlargement in the female, facial hair growth and change in voice-pitch in the male. Puberty leads to menarche (onset of menstrual flow) in females and to the onset of ejaculation (of seminal fluid) in males.

Adolescents select characteristics from many people, - peers, parents, teachers, relatives, religious leaders and famous people. They blend certain of these people's features with their own characteristics to become a unique new person. The new person or identity is not one's final self, but it forms the basis of what one will become. If adolescents manage to work through the contradictions of this process they will develop positive and healthy feelings towards themselves.

The advent of sexuality and the need to manage it in some way are major features of the adolescent experience. Uncertainty, conflict and a struggle often accompany the awakening of sexual feelings over appropriate avenues of expression. Cultural factors also play an important role in the psychosocial aspects of adolescent development and in the sexual conduct and meaning adolescents generate concerning sex.

Adolescence serves as the intermediate stage between the shaping experiences of the gender in childhood and the development of the full-blown male or female adult identity. Sexual activity may signify different things to different people. Such meanings are derived from collective, individual and interpersonal experiences and expectations. Below are some of the important meanings attached to sexual experiences by street children:

Comfort sex: Street children have a great need to fill the void of normal relations because many have left their families or do not have a family. Street boys sometimes describe sex as "play between friends". Comfort sex is often exploitative in nature, even though such a relationship provides the child with shelter, basic needs and protection.

Sex for power: Sometimes, street children use sex as a way of expressing physical power. The younger street children comply for fear of being beaten. Some street boys have said that they have sex with prostitutes because it is a symbol of strength and being a 'real man', and to show friends that they are in control. Sex is used to control other street children and make them obey demands and respect 'hierarchies' on the street. A street child in Mwanza, United Republic of Tanzania said, "he rapes me because he wants me to know who is in power".

Initiation sex: This type of sex occurs to initiate newcomers to the group. It is thought to be a way of making the new street children feel they 'belong'. It is a passage to identity formation. Usually the victims are threatened with violence if they do not agree. Most street children see this type of sexual experience as something inevitable.

Sex for punishment: When a street child is found not to be 'going along' with the group (norms), they may be punished for not abiding by the 'rules'. Sexual assault is used as a way of punishing a street child.

Consequences of Child Sex

Risky Sexual Behaviour

A risky sexual behaviour is one that increases the likelihood of adverse sexual and reproductive health consequences. These health consequences may include unwanted pregnancy, unsafe abortion, HIV/AIDS and STDs. Examples of such behaviours are: sexual activity under the influence of substances, sexual intercourse with drug users, unprotected sexual intercourse, commercial sex/survival sex/prostitution, and unprotected sex with a same sex (particularly between males) partner. Risky sexual behaviours in some countries in which the WHO street children project on substance use implemented assessment are given below:

— *Sexual activity under the influence of substance*: Substance use may influence sexual behaviour in ways that increase the risk of acquisition of HIV and other STDs. The street child's decision on sexual behaviours such as whether to use a condom during sexual activity, whether to negotiate for sex or to use force (rape) depend on the level of intoxication. In general alcohol and other substance use often accompany the early sexual experiences, especially among boys.

— *Sexual intercourse with substance users*: Having unprotected sex with substance users can lead to sexual and reproductive health problems because such persons are more to likely engage in risky sexual behaviour. The risk of acquiring HIV infection through unprotected sex from a sex partner who injects substances is particularly high.

— *Unprotected sexual intercourse*:Unprotected sex is common among street children. This could result in a variety of sexual and reproductive health problems. Street children spend a lot of time in settings where casual sexual encounters occur. Their risk of acquiring blood borne diseases and STDs such as HIV, syphilis and hepatitis is increased by the fact that they often have sex with persons at high risk for these diseases.

— *Commercial sex/survival sex/prostitution*: Sometimes street children engage in this type of sexual activity due to the immediate need to secure food and shelter, or as a means to obtain substances or to support their families.

— *Same sex sexual activity*: Street children sometimes have sex with other street children of the same sex. This is much more common among boys. In addition, street boys are often sexually exploited by older men. Engaging in unprotected sexual intercourse can lead to acquisition of STDs.

— *Sexual violence*: Sexual violence including rape is very common on the streets. Both street girls and boys are at risk. The perpetrators may be strangers or people known to them. Sexual abuse may also occur within the family e. g. forced sex with a stepfather. Because of the unprotected nature of the sexual intercourse, there is a high risk of STDs and other reproductive health problems.

Consequences

Early and unwanted pregnancy: Street girls may become pregnant because of unprotected sex. Because the reproductive system is not fully developed, they are prone to complications related to childbirth such as premature delivery and obstructed labour. These can cause injuries or death to the baby and the mother. The baby born to such mothers may have a low birth weight and may be prone to infections and illness. Coping with the needs of the child may be difficult for a street girl.

Unsafe abortions: Pregnant street girls may feel pressured into terminating their pregnancy. They often have no one to turn to for support and advice and they may not have access to reproductive health services for safe termination of pregnancy. They may seek the services of unqualified persons or induce the termination themselves. Unsafe abortions could lead to infections, bleeding, or even death. Damage to the reproductive organs can cause infertility (inability to have children). The stress of the experience could also lead to psychological problems such as depression.

Sexually transmitted diseases, HIV/AIDS: STDs and HIV infection are consequences of unprotected sexual intercourse with an infected individual. The risk of STDs increases if a person has more than one sexual partner, or a partner (including prostitutes) who has other sexual partners.

HIV Infection

Sexually transmitted diseases and HIV infection are among the commonest health problems in the area of sexual and reproductive health in the world today. These conditions are a major cause of morbidity and mortality among the young. It is estimated that one in every 20 adolescents worldwide contract sexually transmitted diseases each year. 34. 3 million people are now living with HIV the virus that causes AIDS. Already, 18. 8 million people around the world have died of AIDS. 3. 8 million of them children. Half of the people who acquire HIV become infected before they turn 25 and die from AIDS before their 35th birthday. By the end of 1999 the epidemic had left an accumulative total of 11. 2 million AIDS orphans. Orphans are defined as those having lost their mother before reaching the age of 15. Street children are particularly vulnerable to HIV/AIDS/STDs because of their circumstances.

Sexually Transmitted Diseases

STDs are diseases that are passed from one person to another mainly through sexual intercourse. The most common STDs are: chlamydia, syphilis, trichomonas, genital warts, chancroid, genital herpes, hepatitis B and HIV infection. Some STDs, such as syphilis and HIV can also be transmitted through exposure to contaminated blood and from a pregnant woman to the unborn child. During your work with street children, you may encounter children needing help or treatment for STDs. Awareness of some of the common complaints will help you recognize or suspect the presence of these conditions. You could then refer the child for expert care. A street child complaining of any of the following may have a sexually transmitted disease:

— Abnormal discharge from the penis, anus or vagina.

— Burning or pain on passing urine.

— Pain in the abdominal or groin area with fever.

— Pain during sex.

— Blisters, rash or sores on the genital organs.

HIV destroys certain white blood cells that form an important component of the immune system. As the power or ability to resist infections depends on the immune system, such individuals become vulnerable to many types of infections, even those that heal quickly in people with normal immunity. The destruction of the protective white blood cells takes place gradually and therefore a person may be infected with the virus for many years without feeling unwell. As the virus is present in the body, the potential for spreading the disease exists even during this period. After this initial dormant period, the person develops swelling of lymph glands, fever, loose motions, loss of appetite, loss of weight, and fatigue.

After a period varying from six months to as long as 10 years, the illness becomes more active and serious infections and related conditions occur. This stage of the illness is known as AIDS (Acquired Immunodeficiency Syndrome). Almost all HIV-infected people will ultimately develop HIV-related disease and AIDS. Remember that the complaints attributed to HIV/AIDS (fever, loose motions, loss of appetite, loss of weight, fatigue, skin lesions etc.) are common and are also seen in many other diseases. There is no way that anyone could diagnose that the street child has HIV or AIDS by simply looking at him/her. The presence of HIV infection can only be confirmed by a blood test.

Since the discovery of the virus in 1983 by scientists in France, the routes of transmission were confirmed. HIV infection can pass from one person to the other through the following ways:

— Through unprotected sexual intercourse: a person infected with the HIV virus can pass it on to another when his or her body fluids (e. g. semen, vaginal fluids or blood) enters the other person's blood stream through unprotected sexual (vaginal, anal and oral) intercourse. The virus can enter the bloodstream through cuts, abrasions etc. on the body surface or mucosa. A street child's (street girl) immature vaginal mucosa can easily be broken during sexual intercourse, facilitating the entry of the virus into the body. Sexually transmitted diseases increase the risk of transmission of HIV because some of them cause genital ulcerations or sores which can facilitate the entry or transfer of the HIV infection. ??Through contaminated blood or blood products: such as receiving infected blood, using contaminated needles and syringes when injecting drugs, or through skin-piercing equipment contaminated with HIV. The pattern of substance use among street children can have an influence on HIV transmission in two ways:

— Due to practices connected with the administration of the substance e. g. sharing needles and syringes or mixing the substances in the syringes contaminated with blood. ??Substance can affect perception, judgement and behaviour, making it more likely that they would engage in unprotected sexual intercourse especially with other substance users using injectable substances.

— From an HIV infected mother to the child: this could occur during pregnancy, childbirth and in infancy through breast-milk.

Even with the current level of knowledge, HIV/AIDS generates fear and misunderstanding in many people. HIV/AIDS is surrounded by many myths among people in many countries. It is important to understand how HIV/AIDS is perceived in the local community in order to develop appropriate educational messages. Illustrated below are some examples of common misunderstandings about HIV/AIDS.

Modified Social Stress Model

The Modified Social Stress Model can be used as a guide to understanding factors that may contribute to the vulnerability of individual street children to engage in sexual behaviour at a young age, or to have unprotected sex. Understanding the combined effect of the six factors listed in the model will assist you in planning interventions that will reduce the risks associated with sexual and reproductive health behaviours.

Most examples given were compiled during field activities by the WHO street children project on substance use.

Stress

A number of stressors can have a profound influence on the reproductive and sexual behaviour of the street child. These include lack of companionship and acceptance, sexual abuse and unwanted sex, economic pressure from family and adolescent development. ??Lack of companionship and acceptance: a street child may get involved in a sexual relationship to decrease the stress of feeling lonely or to fit in with the norms of their street groups. ??Sexual abuse and unwanted sex: forced sex is common among street children. It may take the form of initiation into the group, or exploitation of the weak by the stronger ones. Street children experience significant stress related to lack of control over such encounters. ??Economic stress and pressures from families: street children may engage in commercial sex, for economic reasons. This may be their own decision or their family members may force them into this. Children who engage in prostitution may not be able to refuse unprotected sex for fear of losing customers.

A street child is more likely to engage in early, unprotected sex if this behaviour is accepted as normal in their environment. Problems related to pregnancy and childbirth are more likely if they are accepted as normal and unavoidable. At times, society accepts or promotes patterns of sexual behaviours and situations which contribute to reproductive health problems among street children. This includes

Media advertising: Street children often get their information about sexual and reproductive health issues from the media. Sex and substance use are often presented in the following way in the media:

— Sexual themes are used to sell many products in the media in ways that make sex seem very exciting and desirable or as something very normal. Such images influence sexual behaviour among street children.

— Sex is rarely presented as having any negative consequences. Sexual relationships presented rarely incorporate ideas and images that promote or support responsible sexual behaviour (e. g., delaying sex until older, using condoms and other contraceptives to prevent sexually transmissible infections and unwanted pregnancy). Such presentations increase the possibility that the street child will indulge in risky sexual behaviours.

— Advertising shows stereotyped images of men and women, showing men in dominant, unfeeling roles and women as submissive. This encourages the role of force in sexual encounters.

Pornography: Pornography exists in a variety of forms (videos and films, magazines, photos, sculpture and drawings) within all cultures. Pornography is presented in a much more attractive manner than many of the materials used to promote responsible sexual behaviour and consequently significantly influences the norms that shape sexual behaviour and attitudes towards relationships.

Culture: Attitudes towards sex and sexuality are a basic part of every culture. Such attitudes are influenced by religious, social and economic factors. The expectations and norms (accepted practices) of the society greatly influence how the street child perceives sexual practice and activities. Such practices affect the sexual and reproductive health of an individual. For example, if sex may be accepted only within marriage in a culture where early marriage is the norm, it would protect against infections, but it would be associated with problems related to early pregnancy and childbirth. The attitude towards the role of men and women is interrelated within each culture to sexual behaviours and practices. The low status or value placed on girls or women increases the likelihood of sexual reproductive health problems in them, e. g. men may demand sex as their right and may refuse to accept the responsibility for contraception.

Sexual Experience

If the street child's earlier sexual experiences were positive, he or she is more likely to seek these experiences. If sexual activity brings feelings of power or control to someone who otherwise feels powerless, such feelings may be sought through aggressive sexual demands or violence against others. Street children may enter a sexual relationship to avoid the feeling of loneliness or rejection or to feel desired and accepted. Sex is often used like substances, to help street children forget worries and anxiety or for relaxation, pleasure or comfort. Negative sexual experiences decrease the chance that a child will indulge in sexual activity. Early and unwanted sex may also lead to distorted perceptions of sexuality.

The people who are supposed to be protecting them may sexually assault street girls and boys in some situations. One of the lasting effects of child sexual assault can be a difficulty in forming and maintaining intimate, trusting relationships. Some of these children keep forming relationships with potential abusers and others become frightened of developing closeness with anyone. Being raped or raping others is a common experience among street children. Street children report use of substances to enable them to tolerate physically and emotionally painful sexual encounters.

Attachments

Street children are more likely to have positive sexual and reproductive health if their strongest attachments are with people who support and practice responsible sexual behaviours. Attachments to people who take advantage of them, or allow or encourage risky behaviours increase the vulnerability of street children. Trading sex for friendship and protection is common.

Skills

There are many skills which can enhance street children's ability to plan and carry out responsible, healthy choices related to sexual behaviour and substance use. These can directly and indirectly decrease their vulnerability to sexual and reproductive health problems. The skills can be grouped into life skills, practical skills, and performance, vocational and livelihood skills. Life skills can help street children resist sex or have safer sex. Similarly, life skills such as problem solving and critical thinking help in healthy decision making. Practical skills like knowing how to use a condom are essential for the practice of safer sex. Livelihood skills would decrease dependence on survival sex.

Resources

There are many resources that have a positive influence on sexual and reproductive health among street children. The resources can be internal (within the child) or external (in the community).

— *Essential information*: information that covers key points about growth and development, contraception, STDs, the relationship between treatment of STDs and HIV prevention, and counselling for HIV/AIDS testing are critical for street children. External resources include:

— *Reproductive health services:* if services are to make a difference to the reproductive health of street children, it would be necessary to have health care providers who can work with street children in a supportive, non-judgemental way.

— *Drug treatment programmes:* treatment for substance use may contribute to a decrease in STDs/HIV infection.

— *Key commodities:* condoms and other contraceptives need to be easily available to street children. In some places, condoms /contraceptives are not generally available to the population at large because of logistical, religious or cultural reasons. In other places condoms or contraceptives may be available to adults but not for street children because service providers or shopkeepers may feel that street children should not have sex.

7

Children's Participation

The right and the ability to advocate on one's own behalf, to be in control and a part of decision making processes and interventions. This form of participation of children and youth enhances the concept of civil society participation and strengthens democratic processes. Children's participation should enhance children's personhood. Often their individual growth is side lined, especially when they are a part of an organisation. Children's participation should also be in keeping with their capacity and ability (milestones of development) and contribute positively to the process of children's growth and development. However, all this operates within the context of children's rights and their participation is the means by which children realise their rights.

The 'levels' of children's participation are a combination of the nature of children's participation and the structures in which they participate. Children may participate as individuals or through their organisations or as representatives of their organisations. Children's participation may take place formally or informally and with or without structures. Their participation may be initiated by the children themselves or by adults or as a result of a partnership between children and adults. Roger Hart's Ladder of Participation has actually been rather misleading as it more aptly describes the role of adults vis a vis children's participation, rather than the levels of participation of children.

The role that adults play in the arena of children's participation is a wide spectrum. On the one hand it ranges from resisting children's participation to being facilitators of children's participation and ultimately, partners. Adults play these roles consciously and unconsciously and their roles could vary depending on the situation and the children they are with. Children are political, economic, ecological, socio-cultural and spiritual (religious) beings. There are several arenas where children do and can participate that satisfy one or several aspects of their personhood. The arenas of participation are several and varied, the home, school, work, and community, going further to state and international levels.

All the above constitute the ecology of children's participation. To enable children's participation to happen constructively and effectively and in a way that is positive for children, they need to be empowered. The three essential elements of empowerment are: an organisation or forum, access to and use of relevant information and access to resources (structural, material, human and financial). We the adults can play a proactive role if we wish to enable children's participation. However in order to perform this part adequately, we need to prepare ourselves. This has to be done with utmost seriousness and honesty. And perhaps the first lesson is that we will have to unlearn many things before we can 'learn'.

The concept of 'the best interest of the child', an underlying framework for the realisation of the CRC implicitly guarantees the participation of children in all decisions concerning them and the CRC is the first international instrument that very strongly advocates for the participation of children and their right to form associations. The CRC may be divided into three areas of focus. They are the three P's. The articles concerning the protection of children, those related to the provision of services to children and those concerning participation or the recognition of children as political beings with both civil and political rights.

Children have asserted their right to intervene in their environment and change it for the better. As a result many of us have realised that the active and equal participation of children in all matters concerning them is both realistic and beneficial. However in order to enable this we adults and adult led organisations have to examine ourselves critically and redefine our roles, sometimes to the extent of unlearning what we thought to be 'right' and reconstructing ourselves closer to the children's paradigm. Unfortunately, though children's right to participation is a much discussed and heavily debated issue, very few have actually been able to translate this into action and make it a ground reality. There are perhaps some elements related to children's rights such as those related to the physical well-being of a child that could be universal and context neutral for example, children inhaling toxic substances, carrying heavy weights etc.

Participation of Civil Society

In several countries of the world, various factors, including the system of education has resulted in social stratification, the increased marginalisation of thousands of people and their political exclusion. This has drastically reduced the participation of civil society. The entire situation is aggravated by the fact that the state is no more accountable and has abdicated its duty and in some cases become the violator of people's rights. There are no safety nets, no protection for the weak and the entire social fabric is unravelling. In such a situation children find work a preferred option to schooling, as it gives them an illusion of participation, an identity - the feeling of belonging and meaning to life. However this does not encourage the individual's participation in democratic processes.

The key to rectify this situation is to enable meaningful, informed and active participation. This also means enabling participation of children and fulfilling article 12 of the CRC.

However for children to participate meaningfully they require an organisation or platform where they can come together and share experiences and evolve an identity.

Level of Participation

Children's participation is no different from that of adults. Children may represent themselves as individuals or be represented by their organisations or they may even represent their organisation. When they represent themselves, they tend to focus on issues that concern them personally. As members of an organisation they tend to voice larger/common concerns that in turn become the concerns of the organisation. Children's participation is no different from that of adults. Children may represent themselves as individuals or be represented by their organisations or they may even represent their organisation.

When they represent themselves, they tend to focus on issues that concern them personally. As members of an organisation they tend to voice larger/common concerns that in turn become the concerns of the organisation. When children participate as representatives of their organisations they bring with them the mandate of their entire organisation. Their responsibilities increase, as they have to ensure the optimum use of opportunities to raise the issues of the members. This also implies a very high level of accountability and we have seen children's organisations that have several checks and balances in place to ensure that this accountability is respected and maintained. It is important to point out that issues related to 'representation' should also be considered important for the participation of adults.

Children may participate in formal or informal consultations. In both these scenarios, they may or may not be listened to and their inputs may or may not be taken on board. It is possible that children are a part of formal consultative structures - such as advisory boards - in which case there is a better chance of their opinions and concerns forming a part of the decision. Children may also be a part of joint decision making structures where children are an integral part of the decision making process. In this set up children have optimum impact. Their contribution becomes most potent when they are using formal structures and spaces as representatives of their organisations and it is in this form and level of participation that they can most significantly contribute to policy level decision making processes.

Children's organisations and movements have multiple and unique histories. Their birth, evolution and maturity may take on different paths based on the context in which children function, on the issues they wish to address, on their ideological frame and vision. The mechanisms for empowerment and the structures for participation should be created at all levels of decision-making from home to local governance. Only then will education become relevant to the lives of marginalised children and enable them to use this newfound knowledge to transform their lives and their schools. Crucial to this process are the need for structures and forums where children can participate in an organised and meaningful way. These structure need to apply to all the arenas of a child.

Children belonging to organisations, unions and movements in several parts of the world have begun to quite definitively define their own paradigm of development and reshape the world closer to their vision. They have made significant contributions to policies and programmes resulting in interventions that are (probably for the first time) appropriate and sustainable.

The right of children to organise and participate in decisions regarding themselves does not mean that they have all the answers, nor does it mean that we, as adults, are absolved of our responsibilities towards our children. It is only giving them the first step towards being able to defend themselves and reshape their future. We must also be prepared for the fact that children will say things we do not necessarily agree with, they will ask embarrassing questions for which we do not have ready answers and they will disagree on the stands they take based on the differing realities they face. But we must be willing to accept this. The concerns of working children need to be put on the agenda and discussed. Their questions must be answered and only if we accept this challenge will we be any closer to finding solutions that work.

Child Development

Their engagement among themselves and with adults has to be seen within three important frameworks by those of us who wish to initiate or enhance children's participation. We need to recognise and respect the personhood of children, have knowledge about child development and understand and internalise children's rights as a key principle. Getting to know a child, as an individual in her/his own right is not easy to achieve. On first meeting a child, there are several factors, which influence the understanding of that child. More often than not, bias and social stereotyping influence this understanding.

Often children are categorised by the way policy and programmes are designed. Children categorised as one constituency may actually have diverse needs. For instance 'working children' or 'children in bondage'. While planning interventions, all children of one 'category' may be assumed to have common characteristics - such as 'all working children are voiceless' or 'all children in bondage are ignorant'. The assumption is that children within a category are homogeneous. As a result the individual characteristics of each child, their individual strengths, their specific concerns and interests get overlooked.

Often children end up conforming to these descriptions of themselves. For instance, a girl may see herself as more disempowered than her male counterparts and a Harijan boy may think of himself as down trodden. While this may be true within the existing socio-economic and cultural situation of that child, these perceptions cannot be allowed to undermine the 'inner character and qualities of the child'. It is this inner character of a child which defines her/his individuality and personality.

We need to find ways to reach the inner child and assist children to recognise their strengths and assist them to overcome their shortcomings. It is critical to build relationships with children that are based on mutual trust, affection and most of all respect. Only then will we be better equipped to constantly question, challenge and change the stereotypes and prejudices surrounding children. When children were drafting their definition of 'Work we can and cannot do ' they initially felt that many forms of that they were performing were actually acceptable; the reason being, that were able to do it. It is only when they examined the same work within the perspective of their rights and more importantly, their developmental milestones that they began to distinguish between work that was acceptable and unacceptable. There is a distinct difference between children's perceived needs and their rights and we adults often confuse our perceptions of children's needs with children's rights.

Reasons for Participation and Protagonism

— *Children's participation:* Participation is a natural instinct. From the moment they are born, children begin to participate. They participate in order to communicate and to establish links with their environment. They participate in order to gain an identity and a membership in the community. They find meaning in their lives through their participation. Gradually, through their participation, they intervene in their external environments.

— *Children's protagonism*: The spiral of Children's Protagonism illustrates the reasons for children's protagonism and was arrived at based on the history and evolution of the working children's movements from around the world.

— *For survival*: For children who are in difficult circumstances, marginalised and oppressed, their first and foremost need is that of survival, obtaining basic needs such as food, clothing and shelter and the livelihood to get these.

— *To end discrimination*: Once basic needs are met the need to end discrimination would become important. For example, working children would demand equal pay for equal work, etc.

— *For positive discrimination*: Once the above is accomplished the next step would be to demand and access rights that are due to them as children. For example, working children would demand that they work fewer hours than adults do and have access to quality education in their free time that is compatible to the formal system and appropriate to their needs.

— *To solve causes*: The solving of causes or the redefining of structures that oppress and marginalise children would be their next area of concern. For example, eradicating poverty, strengthening the services available to children and increasing the employment opportunities for the adults in their communities. This would also include the participation of children in governance.

— *To realise a vision of a new world*: And finally children would like to intervene in reshaping society closer to their vision of the world they would like to live in. This would demand that adults enter into a democratic partnership with them.

Forms of Participation

Children's participation can take numerous forms. Thousands of children are members of Bhima Sangha and Makkala Panchayats. They demonstrate participation in so many new and different ways. Ways that we adults sometimes fail to notice or recognise. The fact that a child has walked 7 kilometres to a meeting, the fact that she had to work harder and quicker to finish her household chores, the fact that he had to bring along his baby sister and mind her - these are all acts of participation - even if at the meeting the child may seem quiet or less vocal than other children. It is an act of solidarity, an act of belonging and commitment to the group and most of all a personal contribution to a larger cause. Participation therefore is not restricted to meetings or formal platforms.

Each child is a complex individual with a unique social, cultural, political, social, environmental and spiritual identity. This identity is critical to the child and yet a dynamic one, continuously transforming through interactions with the external world as well as through internal reflections. Children constantly interact with other children and adults in a wide range of arenas. Starting with their respective families and going up to the international forums, children can and sometimes do interact and influence processes.

Children who seek to participate encounter many obstacles, within their own homes and outside. They have to constantly negotiate in order to make time and space for themselves. We should also remember that when a child participates in a platform or forum that is visible to us adults, such as conferences, that child has probably negotiated at several levels, home, work, school, community, peers, etc. in order to be there. This would mean participation in all these arenas. Our responsibility as adult facilitators is to enable and equip children to handle this.

Then we need to create the structures for participation so that children may use this to reduce the pressures on them and release them from exploitation. It is only through such participation that the state can be made accountable. This participation in political space by children will also enable other marginalised groups such as women; tribal communities etc. to change their immediate situations, and to strengthen and redefine our democracy.

Thousands of children are now participating in the governance of their villages. Adults that were traditionally feudal, patriarchal and gender insensitive have become the advocates for Children's Rights. Many of them do not even know about the Convention on the Rights of the Child. They see a value in the active and equal participation of children as they have seen this translated into overall benefit for the whole community.

Adults' Role

The Ladder of Participation by Roger Hart is often used to represent levels of children's participation. However what it depicts are not levels of children's participation but the varying roles adults play in relation to children's participation. It denotes the control and influence adults have over the process of children's participation. It also indicates adult responses to children's participation. The term 'Ladder' is a misnomer as it implies a sequence, where as in reality one level may not necessarily lead to the next level; for instance, manipulation of children may not lead to children being used as decoration as a natural next step. If we take it that Roger Hart depicts a wide spectrum of scenarios of adult roles viz a viz children's participation that range from the negative to the positive, we suggest a modified version of the same as follows:

1. *Active resistance*: There are adults who actively resist children's participation. These adults belong to several categories. Some of them feel that children should not be burdened with participation. Some believe that children do not have the capacity to participate and hence cannot make informed choices. Some hold the view that children are very easy to manipulate and hence their participation may be used only to further adult agendas. Some adults in this category take very strong positions against children's participation and actually mobilise support and lobby against it. They do so because they are very aware of the power of children's participation and hence do not want to forfeit their power.

2. *Hindrance:* There are adults who hinder children's participation. Some of them may be against children's participation and they may come in the way of children's participation either overtly or covertly. They block opportunities for children and discourage children from participating. There are others in this category that may voice their support to children's participation, but the manner in which they interact with children may actually hinder children's participation. They may intentionally or unintentionally undermine the ability of children and may end up making children feel inadequate and reluctant to participate.

3. *Manipulation:* There are adults who manipulate children. Some adults may coach children to voice what they want or cleverly interpret what children say/do to suit their own interests. Sometimes this manipulation is very obvious, yet often it may be quite subtle - and may be carried out in ways children find very ifficult to notice, let alone counter. There are other adults who may manipulate children in order to 'get the best performance' out of them - and according to the adults, this may be done in the best interest of the child. Sometimes manipulation takes on emotional overtones as children often have emotional ties with the adults they interact with closely. Manipulation is a very subtle and sensitive area. This critique has been often used to discredit children's participation. Even the best child facilitators could end up manipulating children unintentionally and unconsciously. The only way to guard against this is to be constantly vigilant.

4. *Decoration*: There are adults who treat children more or less like decorative objects, where they are expected to basically add colour to the proceedings. Children are called to present bouquets or sing songs - and not much is made of their presence.

5. *Tokenism*: There are adults who bring in children to take mileage from their presence and pretend that children have been given opportunities to participate. The adults may not manipulate children to speak on their behalf, yet they do 'use' the presence of children to be counted as 'advocates of children's rights' and to be politically correct.
6. *Tolerance*: There are adults who bear with the notion of children's participation as some one higher up (such as a donor agency) thinks it is important. In some cases, children themselves may have demanded to be listened to. Adults then go through some consultative exercises with children but do not give any value or credit to the process or the outcome.
7. *Indulgence*: There are adults who find children's participation 'cute' and 'interesting' and are willing to provide limited spaces for children to voice their opinions. They keep prompting children to speak up and try to keep the environment friendly. They may listen to the opinions expressed by children with interest, but may not follow them up with seriousness. These are mostly one time events and very little comes out of such 'participation'.
8. *Children assigned but informed*: There are adults who work with children with some seriousness. The adults in this category decide on what needs to be done, but keep children well informed. They encourage children to be actively involved in the activities. They will guide children to implement the task, but do not expect children to input into the larger design of the process.
9. *Children consulted and informed:* Some adults believe in consulting children and keeping them involved. The adults take the lead role but inform the children about the situation and seek their opinion. They try to give children a sense of ownership over some aspects of the

process, but under their supervision. The adults are still in control over the process, but they keep it flexible to incorporate the suggestions and concerns of the children.

10. *Adult initiated, shared decisions with children*: There are adults who initiate a process or a programme, but are clearly willing to share the decision making space with the children. They see it as a collaborative interaction. Even though initiated by them, they make it a joint effort. Here too children and adults may take on different roles, yet those roles are defined by mutual consent.

11. *Children - initiated, shared decisions with adults*: There are children and their organisations that call the first shot, and invite adults to collaborate with them. Children ensure that adults are jointly involved in deciding what needs to be done and share the ownership of the process and the outcome. Within the collaboration, children and adults may take on different roles, yet those roles are defined by mutual consent.

12. *Children initiated and directed*: There are children and their organisations that are in total control and they may or may not involve the adults. If they do decide to involve the adults, they will work out the framework in which the adults are to participate. Children will continue to keep the process under their control and will have the total ownership of the process and the outcome.

13. *Jointly initiated and directed by children and adults*: There are adults and children who have developed a partnership and they jointly initiate and direct the processes. They have joint ownership of the idea, the process and the outcome. They may play different roles, based on mutual consent. This relationship is possible only when both the adults and children are empowered and are able to pool their respective strengths to achieve a common objective, in partnership with each other.

These roles neither are watertight compartments nor are they purely black or white scenarios. Thirteen of them have been spelt out, yet there is a wide range of shades between them. We have seen adults play all these roles sometimes intentionally or unintentionally. It is possible that the same group of adults play one or several of these roles with the same group of children or different groups of children at different times.

But in situations where children have control over their own spaces and participation, they are in a position to negotiate with adults from a point of strength. They can then actively determine the roles each of them take on in a given situation. It is this, which actually determines the level of children's participation. There are some who argue that the responsibility or duties of adults decrease with children's participation. This however is not true. There is actually a relationship of direct proportion between children's participation and adult responsibility.

Right to Participation

Children's right to participation is a new concept to both adults and children. This is a difficult concept to understand and more difficult to practice, as both adults and children are not normally used to this. The existing relationship we (adults) have with children normally does not allow for their active and equal participation. At present, adults are in total control. We reserve the right to advocate, intervene and decide on behalf of children. We also have socialised children to 'listen to' adults. This absolute control also gives us the possibility to abuse children. Children should have the right and the ability to resist this. It is only then that adults will be accountable for their actions.

If we recognise children's right to participation the nature of our relationship with children will have to dramatically change. It will have to change in many ways. First it will have to change from one of either independence or dependence to one of interdependence. Secondly it will have to be a participatory relationship that is bottom up and not hierarchical or top down. We also need to ensure that we do not perpetuate existing hegemonic structures and practices. This relationship will have to be based on democratic principles and processes. This new partnership built on a foundation of participation will have to be based on democratic principles. Some of the elements that determine the true nature of this partnership are given below:

Nature Partnership

This partnership will have to be based on negotiations between the adult and the child. The adult may set the frame for this relationship based on two criteria, one the development needs of the child and the rights of the child. This will be based on approximations. This frame has to be honestly negotiated with the child and mutually agreed upon. We should be careful not to manufacture consent. However, we must be prepared for the fact that as the child develops s/he will question, challenge and dismantle this frame. The role we have to play, as adults, is to prepare for this eventuality and gently put a larger, more challenging frame in place. Again the process of negotiation and challenging will be repeated.

In the initial stages the frames are set with the concerns of the child as primary and central. This will determine that all our actions are child focused and child centred. The negotiation therefore between the child and us is based on our perception of what is good for the child and their perception of what is good for them. It is only gradually that our concerns can be brought into this equation. As the child grows and develops it is healthy for the child to recognise and respect our concerns and our needs as well.

We have to recognise the importance of the frame. We all need frameworks within which to function even if these frames are to be broken down and replaced. In fact that is one of the functions of the frame. A challenge to work towards and surmount. But frames are necessary as they give us a sense of safety while we need it. The total lack of a frame would lead to anarchy and loss of direction.

For those of us who work with children it is easy to 'feel sorry for them', 'care for them', 'even love them' but to make the leap to 'respecting them' seems difficult. The word 'respect' means so much more. It means respecting the child's situation, perceptions, attitudes, ambitions, reasoning and needs. It means listening to the child and really hearing what the child is saying even when the child's means of communication may not be only words. Though this requires a mindset or major shift in paradigm it also requires a knowledge base and a set of skills and tools that make one proficient at this.

Empowering Children

Our role would be to enable children to occupy and use decision-making spaces effectively to change structures and programmes to those that improve the quality of their lives and that of their communities. To do this, the children need to gain strength through collective action, own and use information and be able to access and utilise human and material resources.

We need to prepare ourselves for this new role. We need to provide children with the knowledge and skills to organise themselves, access information and resources and understand structures, be they political, socio-cultural or economic.

Capacity Building for Adult Facilitators

For adults, the most important starting point is to view children as holders of rights. This requires a paradigm shift and it challenges us to redefine our relationship with children. It is also important for us to equip ourselves with a sound body of knowledge regarding personhood of children and their developmental milestones. These form the basis on which facilitation skills may be acquired to enable children to attain their full potential as protagonists. We need to develop indicators that will give us an honest understanding of the processes we are facilitating so that we are able to create spaces where both adults and children can become empowered.

Rights and Responsibilities

The determining of rights and responsibilities of children and adults within a partnership is an issue that requires inquiry and debate. Not much work has been done in this area and this gap has led to simplistic arguments about balancing children's rights with equal responsibilities. Children's participation does not mean the abdication of adult responsibility. When children's participation is low or nil, adult responsibility is also low or nil. There is no accountability by adults or children. However, as children's participation increases, adult responsibility also increases in twice that proportion.

It is a partnership that adults have to enter into with children, it involves adults sharing power with children, it means listening to and understanding really what children are saying and acting on the basis of a consensus. We need to prepare ourselves for this new role and we also need to provide children with the knowledge and skills to organise themselves, to access information and resources and to understand structures, be they political, socio-cultural or economic. It is also important for adults to protect their arenas of participation, so that we do not usurp children's spaces or manipulate them.

The rights and responsibilities of adults and children are not always equally balanced. At no point in ones life are rights and responsibilities equal. Adding a right does not necessarily mean adding on a corresponding responsibility. A baby has all her rights, but practically no responsibilities. Similarly, senior citizens or mentally challenged individuals. Rights and responsibilities are determined by age and ability of the individual.

8

Empowering Street Children

The street children phenomenon cannot be analyzed in isolation. Street life has specific kinds of problems (drug addiction, sexual promiscuity and abuse, work exploitation, involvement in criminal activities, and violence by police, other adults, and rival gangs) and attractions (freedom, adventure, peer solidarity) that call for ad hoc interventions. No term has yet been coined to capture both the peculiar nature of street life and its interconnection with other aspects of vulnerability.

Street Children at Risk

Children and youth may be categorized according to the level of risk they face in being disconnected from family and society. The lower the level of risk, the larger the scope for preventive and untargeted programs. Street children are at the so-called tertiary level, which is where risk has turned into concrete reality and targeted special protection programs are required. Obviously, action is also essential at the primary and secondary level to prevent more children from choosing the street in the future. The emphasis here is on tertiary level interventions, however, to promote the positive development of children who are already in that situation.

Although street children are a well-known reality in many countries, it is difficult to provide a clear picture of them. These children spend intermittent periods with their families, or move from one city to another, depending on the time of year and their circumstances. Since many do not have identity papers or birth certificates, there are no official statistics on their number. For any given country, figures on street children may oscillate with the source of information (the government, NGOs, research institutions) and whether the issue is a development priority.

The United Nations International Children's Emergency Relief Fund (UNICEF) has estimated there are about 100 million street children worldwide, half of them in Latin America. Experts consider this a guess estimate used for advocacy purposes, however, and recently the agency itself abandoned it. Needless to say, figures depend on definitions. If one distinguishes between children in the street and those of the street, the second group is actually fairly small worldwide, but the figures increase when the first is included.

In Eastern Europe, for instance, where street children represent an alarming recent phenomenon, most of them maintain a relation with their family and sometimes with school.While the number of children of the street is considered very low in Western Europe and the United States, if children in Roma communities and youth 'hanging around" in street gangs are included, the picture changes dramatically.Because "counting" street children is so complex and the results often uncertain, all figures should be treated with caution. Additional research would be needed to quantify the actual levels in different countries. "Flows" rather than "stocks" should be considered, given the everchanging nature of the phenomenon. These problems should not hinder countries from devoting time and resources to urgent interventions. Even where street children are few in number, there is no excuse for lack of action: on the contrary, early interventions are more likely to prevent the problem from escalating in the future.

Reasons for Selecting Street Life

Child disconnection is closely associated with the vulnerability of segments of society, often in a context of economic liberalization and growing inequality. Reduced land security contributes to the swelling of urban slums where many street children work to support their family. In some countries, inadequate public expenditures undermine the education system's capacity to cater the needs of vulnerable children. The transition from state to market-dominated society temporarily weakens communities' capacity to protect their young members. In both poor and rich countries, family isolation and the weakening of social capital may aggravate parent's abusive behaviors.

Nevertheless, some general observations can be made about the immediate factors that lead children to choose a street life, as these should inform the content and modalities of ad hoc interventions. Children end up on the streets for one or more of the following reasons:

— *Low family income*: Many work in the street to contribute to family survival.

— *Homelessness*: In both rich and poor countries, the lack of proper housing pushes entire families into the street.

— *Neglect and abuse*: This problem may be associated with parents' drug addiction and alcoholism, or the lack of time spent in significant interaction.

— *School failure.*

— *Loss of parents*: Loss of parents due to armed conflicts, natural disasters, HIV/AIDS and other epidemics, and refugee problems.

Each street child's history is a unique blend of several of those elements. While material hardship is a major factor in putting children at high risk, not all materially deprived children become disconnected from the family. Evidence suggests that the quality of family relationships plays a fundamental role.

In Brazil, for example, children of the street reported higher incidents of corporal punishment (63 percent) compared with children working in the street but still in contact with family (23 percent). In Ethiopia, children of the street reported significantly higher levels of abuse at home than family-based street children.

Lack of communication in the family and other emotional problems are crucial factors of child disconnection in industrialized countries. In addition, peer pressure can be an important trigger. Many young children have been encouraged or even forced into the street by older siblings and friends who have already set foot on that path.

Resources of Street Children

The majority of street children in the world are aged 10 or older. Street children reached by existing programs tend to be somewhere between the ages of 8 and 18. However, there is evidence that the average age of street initiation may be decreasing in some regions.Most countries appear to have more street boys than girls. Street girls may be less visible, but they are clearly an understudied reality. They are also exposed to violence and sexual abuse by peers and adults, and more likely to be engaged in prostitution.

In Europe and Latin America, street children frequently belong to ethnic minorities, such as Roma in Southeastern Europe, Afro-Caribbean peoples in the United Kingdom, and descendants of Africans in Brazil. Street work includes odd jobs, petty trading, and services. Because of the lack of protection in these jobs, there is a greater risk of exploitation and of encountering health hazards. Many children make a living through illegal activities such as begging, selling drugs, petty theft, and prostitution. Street work is less common in poor communities in the United States and Europe.

Instead, children there just "hang around" in gangs and often become involved in deviant behavior. Many street children do not go to school; others perform poorly in class and are at high risk of dropping out. Because of the peculiar nature of their life and problems, the skills required to survive on the street, and the lack of parental support, these children find it difficult to adjust to standard school curricula and school discipline. Also, as mentioned earlier, many street children have never had, or have lost, their birth certificates, a document vital to legal and civic existence.

Although underlying and immediate causes of the street children phenomenon may differ, the range of problems that children suffer once in the street present some similarities across regions: poor education status, low self-esteem, and emotional disorders, violence and exploitation by peers and adults, early and unwanted pregnancies, sexually transmitted diseases and HIV/AIDS, and drug abuse. In Latin and Central America, a very high number of street children are victims of brutality by police and other adults. The specific nature of these problems calls for specialized, ad hoc programs. The fact that these problems get worse the longer children have been in the street provides a strong rationale for early interventions.

Street children are not merely a problem that needs to be addressed. They are resourceful human beings, many of whom have decided to seek a better life. In a number of countries, some have even become community leaders and activists in social movements, not to mention valuable peer facilitators in NGO programs. The idea of focusing on street children as resources-not just as victims or threats to society-is in line with the U.N. Convention of the Right of the Child, which underlines the need for the empowerment and participation of children. In sum, street children fall into a variety of categories, and their number is difficult to determine. The phenomenon has long existed in many regions, but in others it is just emerging.

Underlying and immediate causes include deteriorating social capital and poverty, low family income, lack of housing, school failure, neglect and abuse, armed conflicts, and epidemics. Life in the street is associated with child-specific physical and emotional problems that call for specialized and early programs. Various interventions are available to address street children's problems.

Education is a key component of all, usually combined with health, job training, basic assistance, or income generation. A simple classification can be drawn up on the basis of their main features. The first distinction is between programs providing services directed primarily at the child and those that involve schools, families, and communities as well, or that include advocacy, lobbying, and social mobilization. Another difference is that some provide residential services for a small number of children for a certain amount of time, while others focus on nonresidential or outreach services to a larger number of children on a less continuous base.

However, most residential programs carry out some outreach work in the street to establish the first contact with their beneficiaries. Interventions also vary with the age of the target group. Those geared to young children concentrate on basic assistance and school and family reintegration, while activities aimed at adolescents also include job training, legal defense, housing, and sexual health.

Most of the 18 programs are carried out by NGOs, although some are components of multiagency development programs at the municipal level. Some of these interventions are still in an initial stage, and information on their impact is not available. Nevertheless, they represent interesting models of partnership between NGOs and local government in this area.

NGO Programs for the Child

Ciudad Don Bosco

The program consists of four stages. First, children are

contacted in the street and encouraged to spend a night at the program shelter. Second, activities begin for children who decide to stay in the center, focusing on behavioral changes, basic schooling, socialization, and developing self-esteem skills. Third, children attend formal primary and secondary school provided by the program. And fourth, technical training for the labor market is provided for adolescents. Throughout the four stages, the program evaluates and takes care of participants' basic health, nutrition, psychological, social, dental, and occupational needs.

A period of time is spent observing, conducting medical tests on, and holding discussions with each child, after which an interdisciplinary group of professionals prepares a strategic plan for each. These plans recommend how best to respond to psychological, educational, nutritional, and health needs, and they are regularly revised. Children also provide input by expressing their feelings in open groups and therapy sessions. The collective work of professionals ensures that recommendations follow an integrated approach and are tailored to stimulate self-awareness and self-confidence in each child.

Work with Street Children: Growing within the Family

This program is an "innovative initiative" of Portugal's Third Program of Fight against Poverty. The target group consists of children in downtown Lisbon who have broken away from their families in a more or less radical way, often depend on illegal activities for their livelihood, stay overnight in places frequented by vagabonds, and have begun to exhibit antisocial behavior. The aim is to reestablish connections between street children and their families and communities, through street work, the transmission of positive values, family counseling, and the creation of a network of community resources and services in support of street children.

The project team is composed of professional educators. A number of youth who were once street children themselves now assist the team in reaching their peers in the street. The implementing agency collaborates with the Ministry of Education and public schools to reintegrate children into the schools or to prevent them from dropping out. A key activity has been to train public school teachers to facilitate communication between children at risk, community services, and the family. This approach makes it possible to closely monitor difficult cases and help them do better at school.

An "Alternative School" for street children has also been established that draws on the skills of educators and teachers after regular school hours to help children do their homework and to increase their knowledge of school curricula; they organize field trips and visits to city museums, parks, libraries, and other educational centers. The program coordinates with school cafeterias to provide extra meals to needy children and organizes awareness-raising sessions concerning children at risk and how to prevent them from dropping out of school.

Axê Program, Salvador

Number of children reached: 3,000 (about 20 street children in Salvador) Description: Project Axê has received international recognition for its imaginative educational work with marginalized children in Salvador. Practicing what Axê calls the pedagogy of desire, project facilitators stimulate the child to develop interest in school through artistic and recreational activities, as well as other non formal methods of education. Axê´s approach is designed to reach children on the streets and strengthen their desire to stay in school and learn. Through a strong partnership with the State Secretariat of Education, Project Axê has been able to integrate its pedagogy into the public school system. Following are some specific program activities:

—*Outreach services*: A bus parked in the city center is used to reach out to children spending time in the streets and to raise their curiosity. A street educator informs children about the fun-filled activities taking place on the bus and invites them on board, where they can watch a video, draw, and sing or read books. If the children show an interest, they are also invited to become students at any of Axê's educational or training centers. The project also provides food, medical care, legal protection, assistance with identity documents, and some financial aid to replace what was being earned in the street.

—*Early childhood education project*: Using theater, dance, and song, the program engages children from marginal neighborhoods in learning activities relevant to their reality and cultural heritage. Currently, educators are using African theater to teach children about their rights and responsibilities as Brazilian citizens. Artistic techniques of this kind allow children to actively participate in their own learning. The project also provides literacy classes and attempts to reintegrate children in regular schools.

—*School monitoring*: Through a partnership with the Secretariat of Education and more than sixty public schools in the state of Bahia, Axê is able to enroll street children into the public school system and monitor their performance. A condition of enrollment is that a family member sponsor the child. Once enrolled, the child spends the morning in instructional classes, while afternoons are devoted to the arts (dancing, theater, singing, or drawing). The School Monitoring Program also trains teachers in alternative methods of education. Production workshops. Children participate in productive activities such as paper-recycling, printing, and a fashion workshop. The emphasis is on quality, and the goods produced are sold at competitive, non subsidized prices in two shops in the tourist area of downtown Salvador. Workshops are also meant to prepare participants to enter the world of work by increasing their ability to concentrate, reinforcing their motor skills and emotional equilibrium, and helping them form new habits and behaviors.

—*Vocational training for those aged 16 and older*: Agreements are signed with public and private companies able to give children job training and eventually hire them. The program works closely with the local municipality to avoid duplicating services already offered to street children. It also tries to coordinate its activities with programs geared to children at primary and secondary risk, which can refer their difficult cases to Axê. Given the importance of learning in its philosophy, the program relies on highly skilled educators rather than volunteer staff.

Cultural Support for the Social Integration of Street Children

The ASIS program has three main components:

1. outreach services, such as medical assistance and help in obtaining identity papers;
2. incentives to join the program residential center, when feasible; and
3. activities at the center designed promote the social and professional integration of teenagers and youth.

ASIS's approach is to design an individualized educational plan that draws on a young person's cultural background, capacities, and aspirations. Integration in the labor market is seen as a process that requires not only professional skills, but also the capacity to obtain information, formulate realistic plans and expectations, find jobs, and constantly update knowledge. The ASIS project team working toward these ends includes teachers, social workers, medical staff, and psychologists.

An important part of this process is to provide information on short- and long-term job opportunities and the advantages/disadvantages of each. In addition, ASIS provides training in skills that are in demand in the labor market, support and advice during the job search process, continuous follow-up with employers once the youth has been hired, and training in additional/alternative occupations to enable the youth to obtain extra revenues or a fuller social reintegration. It also encourages young people to do volunteer and community work, to cultivate skills needed to increase their marketability, to reestablish contact with their families and, when this is not feasible, to search for independent housing. ASIS teaches youth how to communicate better and tries to convey the practical and psychological skills that are needed to live independently, such as how to manage one's money and time. To assess the program's impact, the staff keeps track of all beneficiaries who have left the residential center.

The Bridge over Troubled Waters

Bridge over Troubled Waters, Inc. was founded in Boston in 1970 to serve runaways, homeless youth, and other youth in the street through a multiservice approach. One of its services, called street outreach, consists of having street workers meet daily with runaways, homeless youth, and other young people at risk in areas where they gather, to explain Bridge services and refer them to appropriate community services. Recognizing that street youth are usually wary of social service agencies and mistrustful of adults in general, educators try to establish trust through non threatening dialogue and a consistently caring attitude. As part of its health services, Bridge places a mobile medical van on the street every weekday, offering free health care and teaching youth how to seek assistance at hospitals and clinics.

Bridge's dental clinic offers a full range of oral treatments. The in-house medical clinic provides physical exams when clients begin substance abuse counseling or enter the residential program. Runaway services consist of a 24-hour/ 7-day-a-week response, which offers emergency housing and counseling. Educators attempt to reconcile families of runaway or high-risk youth, and to facilitate contact and communication between them and those in Bridge's care. When family reunification is not an option, they also provide stable alternative living arrangements. Bridge also provides the following services:

—Transitional day program. It has an open day center where youth can take part in recreational and confidence-building activities. Breakfast and lunch are provided. o Counseling services. These include long-term substance abuse counseling, personal counseling, basic survival services, family counseling, and referrals. Because the youth are not forced to attend sessions, they feel comfortable talking freely, and are able to begin addressing the root of their problems.

— Education/preemployment program. Bridge provides educational, preemployment, guidance, and job development services necessary for youth to enter and advance in jobs, training programs, or higher education. It offers adult education classes to help young people meet the literacy standards required for the high school equivalency degree. Courses combine academic instruction with training in professional, computer, job search, and life skills. o Residential components. Bridge's Transitional Living Program, single-parent house, and cooperative apartments offer youth an opportunity to acquire life, social, and educational skills in a safe, drug-free, and nurturing environment, while enjoying the full range of other Bridge services. The objective is to help young residents develop the self-esteem and capacities that will enable them to return to their communities as responsible adults. o Referral services. Bridge maintains a wide network of affiliations with agencies that provide specialized services, including hospitals, mental health centers, educational programs, homeless shelters, and multicultural services.

Casa Alianza Program

Casa Alianza is an NGO dedicated to the rehabilitation and defense of street children in Central America. Its ultimate purpose is to provide children with an opportunity to leave the street, rather than improve street life. For this reason, educators do not offer food or clothes to street children but encourage them to join a crisis center, followed by transition homes and group homes only in cases where family reintegration is impossible. One of Casa Alianza's primary goals is to reintegrate the child in the family. To this end, it offers phased-in support for children and families to reunite and find solutions to their difficulties. Each phase lasts about one month.

The first phase consists of meeting the basic needs of children in a crisis center and building trust. In the second phase, educators hold preliminary interviews with families and explore the feasibility of reunification. Each child has his/her own plan, tailored to the specific situation and individual's needs. Phase three includes counseling to families and children, self-help groups and therapy, financial assistance to parents, job training, and identification of a support network in the community. In the fourth phase, children gradually reunite with their families, under the supervision of educators. The program provides for a minimum two-year follow-up, which in some cases includes material support to enable families to take care of the child.

Services in Guatemala City and Mexico include a mums-and-babies program to address the problems of street girls who have become pregnant against their will, most of them as a consequence of sexual abuse or prostitution. This program offers individual and group therapy, child-care training, vocational training, and pediatric and gynecological treatment. Drug rehabilitation residential centers have been established in Guatemala, Honduras, and Mexico. Here, children receive intensive occupational, individual, and group therapy and some vocational training. After about three months, they are accepted in the program's transitional homes or are reintegrated into their families.

The program has also set up a legal aid office in each participating country. The first center was opened in response to the brutal murder of a street child by the police in Guatemala. These four offices provide legal defense to hundreds of children who are victims of violence at the hands of the authorities and bring cases of the violation of children's rights before specialized regional and international commissions. They also assist children with matters of civil law, such as the acquisition of birth certificates and identity cards. The HIV/AIDS program, another important endeavor, provides sex education and information on the prevention of sexually transmitted diseases. Casa Alianza in Mexico has a residential program for children at the terminal stage of AIDS.

"Vivere" (Living) Program

C.A.T. is an Italian NGO with a long history of working with drug addicts, prostitutes, juvenile offenders, and youth who spend much of their time roaming in the streets. It works in close cooperation with Florence's municipal and social services. The "Vivere" program consists of a mobile unit (van) that travels in neighborhoods where adolescents spend much of their time in the street. At each stop, educators organize parties and concerts and offer friendship and counseling, and information on drug abuse, contraceptives, and AIDS. They distribute free condoms and provide instructions on their use. The van provides a space for young people to meet and talk. Children with specific problems are referred to local public services.

The program is sponsored by the local municipality, in collaboration with a local radio station, which advertises its street activities and events. In its first phase, the program focused on observing street activities and mapping streets, to compile information on the daily itinerary and gathering places of adolescents in the city. Educators then established the first contact with youth by spending time in the places identified (bars, discos, public gardens) and initiating casual conversations and recreational activities. This led to daily interaction, with educators and adolescents discussing, planning, and organizing activities and projects together, including video production, dances and musical events, focus groups and surveys, and artistic expression.

The program invited youth to design a questionnaire on HIV-related behaviors, which was to be distributed among their peers. Educators also help youth obtain access to community services. The van is equipped with a bulletin board posting information on job opportunities, municipal sports and recreation activities, available public services. Educators meet public service providers regularly to make them aware of the specific needs of young people in the street. Evidence of impact: Focus groups indicated that the program gave youth a forum in which to express themselves without fear of being judged, even when discussing their sex-related, illegal, or deviant behaviors.

Young people who have participated have developed self-confidence, a better knowledge and use of existing community services, and a more proactive approach to the search for jobs. About 2,000 adolescents have been informed about the prevention of HIV/AIDS and instructed on how to use condoms. A number in this group have become actively involved in disseminating information on HIV/AIDS prevention among their peers. The municipality of Florence recently adopted the program model, by supporting street work projects in other deprived city neighborhoods.

Health Peer Counseling

YPIC is a youth-serving NGO with an integrated approach that includes health services, population and environment education, job creation, life skills, and rural and community development. The activities most focused on youth in the street are its health services. The program selects young people between the ages of 10 and 24 and trains them in different aspects of HIV/AIDS control and prevention, so they can reach out to their peers in the street. Individuals are selected for this task on the basis of their commitment and leadership skills. These "peer promoters" are trained by Ministry of Health representatives in seven-day workshops on the necessary skills in health education, counseling, and service delivery. Youth are taught communication skills and how to use information, education, and communication material such as flash cards, posters, and brochures.

Trained peer promoters are then put in charge of HIV/AIDS education in villages and schools, and one-to-one counseling in the street. Peer promoters listen to other youth to learn their needs, spread information, and refer difficult cases to program staff when requested. They use photos, video, and drama to communicate messages and maintain interest among participants. The same youth-to-youth approach is used to provide condoms and other contraceptives at subsidized rates, or free, and to teach other youth how to use condoms. In addition, the program provides continuous training to staff members as well as to peer counselors in leadership, youth work, management, and planning.

Family-Level Programs

JUCONI's services are designed to help children leave the street and to prevent their siblings from taking to street life. Their target includes three specific groups:

1. children who live in the street,
2. those who work in the street and live with the family, and
3. those who work in street markets but do not always live with the family.

The primary objective of this program is reintegration, which is to be achieved via three phases. In the first or "operation friendship" phase (1-6 months), educators have intensive contact with children in the street, providing them with recreation and counseling. Street children are offered emergency medical services and prepared for life away from the street. Activities with working children also involve the family and include complementary schooling and help with identifying new sources of livelihood.

The second step toward family and social integration consists of "intensive change" service. Depending on their individual circumstances and needs, children are involved in informal education, complementary schooling, recreation and life skills, and visits to the child's school and workplace. Children working in the market readily participate in a group environment and are therefore attended in day centers located near the market. Working street children receive help at home, as part of their family unit. Street-living children need particular attention, especially if they are to return to their family, and thus are hosted in a transitional half-way house. At the same time, the program provides counseling and other services to their families, to prepare them to reintegrate the child.

The third phase is the "sustaining change" phase, also called the follow-on. For two to three years after the child has left the intensive change service, program educators continue to visit the child and his or her family and provide counseling and therapy. Follow-on can take place either in the family or in any other structure where a child has found a place. The second objective of the program is prevention (among siblings and families). Once streetliving children are back home, the program begins to work with the entire family, including brothers and sisters. The siblings of street-working children participate in program activities almost from the beginning of the "operation friendship" phase.

Younger brothers and sisters of market-working children are introduced to a Montessori-type kindergarten, while their older siblings take part in day centers in the "intensive change" phase. Evidence of impact: More than 80 percent of children improve their opportunities in education, work, and personal development after participating in the program for one year. In 1994, UNESCO called it the most innovative and promising program of its kind.

American Family Inns

Since 1991 American Family Inns has provided transitional housing to homeless families and has integrated educational, vocational, and family support services into the residential setting. This stable, structured environment provides parents and children with access to a wide variety of programs, one of which is offered through the child development center. The center follows a variation of the High/Scope curriculum, developed at the University of Michigan and aimed at developing a child's sense of control and initiative. Teachers organize weekly conferences with parents to discuss the child's needs and progress and to involve the family in all aspects of early childhood education.

Another aspect of the program is the Brownstone School, which provides after-school education to children aged 5 to 13, to compensate for their limited access to education opportunities. The theory behind this endeavor is that children who are behind should not be placed in a "slow lane" or a remedial program to catch up, but in a program similar to those for "gifted" children. The model developed by Henry Levin emphasizes a low student-to-teacher ratio, active teaching of concepts, analysis and problems solving, interactive learning tools, and fieldwork. High expectations, clear deadlines, and stimulating didactic material are also key components of the process.

The program motivates parents to work with teachers and children. "Learning contracts" based on subject areas chosen by the children are drawn up to involve parents in monitoring school performance. The organization also offers family literacy workshops, family trips, and family projects such as community gardens. Still other services are provided through the Healthy Living Center for recreational and cultural activities. Children are encouraged to express themselves in drama, dance, and poetry. By participating in sports teams and boy scout groups, children learn cooperation and social skills. The center also organizes workshops on substance abuse, AIDS, pregnancy, and crime. Parents are encouraged to meet staff members regularly and discuss the capacities and needs of their child.

Crucero Program

EDNICA is a Mexican NGO dedicated since 1989 to the development of community initiatives in favor of street and at-risk children and youth. EDNICA offers special education, medical attention, and drug treatment; youth leadership training and involvement in community affairs; and opportunities to work off the street, in existing local economic activities. The organization believes that the problems of street children need to be addressed through family and community efforts rather than short-term assistance. The NGO's activities are guided by two main principles. The first is that community institutions should be involved. Therefore EDNICA implements its programs in partnership with existing local organizations.

After an initial period of capacity-raising, it gradually transfers the implementation and planning responsibilities to community hands and moves to other city neighborhoods. The second is that existing community resources should be mobilized in support of program activities. To this end, EDNICA has established a pool of locally available resources (through private business, local government, and civil society initiatives) to devote to addressing the problems of street children. This involves community mapping and the establishment of formal agreements among community members and services.

The EDNICA Crucero Program works through the local parish San Pedro Apostol. This parish is active in awareness-raising activities that can help to modify attitudes toward street children among local merchants, taxi and bus drivers, and small business owners. These members of the community tend to discriminate against and sometimes harass children in the street. The program gradually involves them in finding solutions to the problem. Shop owners, for instance, are asked to monitor the number of new children joining the street so as to facilitate early intervention.

The parish also helps reestablish positive relations between street children and their families through counseling and referral to community services. By working with families, the program also reaches street children's siblings and helps prevent them from getting into the street. A similar program has been implemented by the San Felipe de Jesus Parish west of Mexico City. Evidence of impact: Community members now have a more positive attitude toward street children; family ties with community services have been strengthened, making child rearing easier; and after four years of collaboration with EDNICA, the San Felipe de Jesus Parish is now implementing the program independently from the NGO's funding and supervision.

Community Mobilization for the Protection and Rehabilitation of Street Girls' Prostitution

CHILDHOPE initiated this program in late 1995 in Pasay City, an area known for widespread child prostitution. Its objectives were to

1. raise community awareness of the problem;
2. develop a local capacity for advocacy and service provision among NGOs, government workers, and volunteers;
3. reach out to children in streets and bars and provide shelter, care, and rehabilitation services to prostitutes and abused girls under 18 years of age;
4. involve families in the rehabilitation process; and
5. improve girls' self-esteem and awareness of their rights.

The program has established a municipal task force that works with churches, schools, NGOs, police, and local government. Its function is to train local officers and community stakeholders to promote support for young prostitutes; train volunteers in family counseling and group therapy; lobby for the passage of a law protecting sexually exploited children;

conduct outreach work in the street; operate a drop-in center for girls; and help rehabilitate and reintegrate prostitutes in the community.

Task force members oversee various program activities. For example, a local religious group that runs a day-care center and shelter is in charge of the girls' rehabilitation, and NGO street educators help reach girls in the streets. Twenty-two local schools have formulated a plan of action to fight prostitution, which includes incorporating child rights in school education, identifying abused and prostituted school children, counseling them, referring them to appropriate services, and conducting orientation sessions on child prostitution with parents. In addition, 195 community volunteers have been trained in advocating support for these girls in their neighborhoods and places of work.

The Undugu Society

The program was established to address the needs of young street workers in Nairobi, the so-called parking boys and girls. Initially focused on child rehabilitation, it gradually turned its attention to the communities where children originated, recognizing that it needed to address not only the symptoms but also the root of the problem. The Undugu Society carries out a variety of urban community development projects as well as providing direct services to street and working children. Activities are identified and designed in consultation with the community. These include

1. an alternative primary education program for children in low-income neighborhoods;
2. primary and secondary school scholarship programs to assist low-income children and youth who want to remain in formal schools;
3. an urban agriculture project that serves to generate income for youth who live in the street;

4. a community health program that includes primary health care, family planning, and AIDS prevention;
5. a housing assistance program that upgrades slum dwellings;
6. production units that provide training in practical skills of trade and technical assistance in marketing goods and services; and
7. job placement.

In this last area, the Undugu Society's strategy is to link street youth with informal sector artisans. When youth enter the program, Undugu asks them to identify an artisan in their own neighborhood with whom they would like to work. If the situation is suitable, Undugu negotiates an agreement with the youth and the artisan under which the NGO will provide training in marketing and basic practical skills while he or she works with the artisan. After the apprenticeship, the youth returns to Undugu for training in small business management skills. A business Advisory Unit and Industrial Design Department offer loans and help participants improve their marketing and product design.

Programs Geared toward Policies and Laws

The street children (Meninos de Rua) movement in brazil

This movement was initiated in the early 1980s, when a number of government agencies and UNICEF signed an agreement to study street and working children in Brazil. Known as the Alternative Street Children Project, this endeavor focused on supporting national seminars and other dissemination activities that would allow educators and NGOs from different regions to organize a common platform. By 1985 a directorate was elected for the new organization taking shape, now called the National Movement of Street Boys and Street Girls. The movement captured the attention of the media when the first national meeting was held in Brasilia in May 1986. At that time, Brazil was beginning a transition to civilian democracy. The meeting was attended by about 500 children delegates who reported on their experiences with police violence, which eventually led the Brazilian Parliament to hold special hearings on the issue.

The movement upheld the principles of the International Child Right Convention (ICRC) promulgated by the United Nations and struggled to incorporate them into the new legal system that was being formed in Brazil. In the late 1980s, various government ministries, NGOs, and other organizations (including UNICEF) joined in the process that led to the formation of the National Commission on the Child and the Constitution, in order to coordinate various advocacy efforts and to help draft a constitutional clause on children's rights. On November 20, 1988, the government approved Article 227 of the new Brazilian Constitution, which incorporates and extends the basic content of the ICRC. On July 13, 1990, legislation was passed implementing the Child and Adolescent Statute. The statute calls for radical changes in the rights accorded to children, the way children in trouble should be helped, and in decision making about these issues.

Street children program and legal changes in bulgaria

In the past two years, the Bulgarian government has been preparing a national Child Welfare Reform, with the assistance of UNICEF, the United Nations Development Program (UNDP), and, lately, the World Bank. Under this reform, Bulgaria's child care system will be reorganized to better address the needs of institutionalized children and of children from disadvantaged families and economically depressed areas.

Bulgaria is one of the 10 countries supported by the King Baudouin Foundation and Soros Foundations program for street children, which operates in partnership with the World Bank. Bulgaria's program has provided grants to nine NGO projects and has financed training and networking activities and public awareness campaigns. With the training and funding obtained under this program, the selected NGOs were able to upgrade the quality of their interventions and to gain funding and recognition by public authorities. Systematic cooperation was established with key government agencies at the local and central level. The program's support of public awareness campaigns also brought media and public attention to street children issues.

Funded NGOs increased their cooperation and new incentive was given to lobbying activities. Street children organizations supported by the program, in cooperation with other NGOs dealing with children, and put pressure on legislators to incorporate a component on street children in the new legislation. Thus the Child Welfare Reform includes provisions to ensure financial support for street children programs.

Multiagency Programs

UNICEF: Urban Basic Services Program

The Urban Basic Services Program originated in an initiative spearheaded in the late 1970s by a local university. The aim was to address Olongapo's acute social problems. As part of this venture, social researchers at the university helped create neighborhood and municipal committees and trained community volunteers to identify local needs and propose interventions. In 1985 the initiative gained UNICEF support and was incorporated into the agency's Urban Basic Service Program. Cooperation was established with the City Health Office, which consulted volunteers and researchers on how to design its primary health care system.

Research conducted under the program revealed the magnitude of the street children problem and the lack of government interventions in this area. It was concluded that to be effective a program for street children had to have an integrated approach. Furthermore, community action had to aim at reducing the pressures that led children to leave home in the first place, as well as provide rehabilitation services.

In 1987 Olongapo municipality took charge of the Urban Basic Services Program and established an Inter-Agency Council (IAC) to coordinate services for urban poor women and children. The IAC was composed of representatives of 13 government departments and 13 NGOs organized into steering committees on health and nutrition, education, water and sanitation, livelihood, community organizing, and services for street and working children. An education program for street children was launched with the objective of reintegrating children into the formal school system. The local government agreed to reduce the costs of books and uniforms, to waive school fees to poor families, and, through the Philippines Educational Placement Test, to allow children to reenter school at their level of competence, often skipping several grades. The program is an important example of what can be achieved through the collaboration of community, government, and NGOs.

Inter-American Development Bank Support to Social Reforms for the Development of Children and Youth

The aim of the program is to support the development of children through their better integration in the family, school, and community. It is divided into two components: municipal participatory plans and institutional strengthening. The municipal participatory plans are prepared in 20 municipalities by a commission comprising members of local government, NGOs, and community organizations. Plans are based on a diagnosis of local problems affecting children and must emphasize cooperation among different sectors.

Activities eligible for program funding include early childhood development, preventive health, education and dropout prevention, recreation and culture, violence prevention, rehabilitation and protection of street and working children, reproductive health, and family and community strengthening. New components may be added if shown to be a cost-effective way to tackle community problems. By the end of the program, local governments are expected to assume full financial responsibility for the execution of the plans. The objective of institutional strengthening is to raise the public sector's capacity to design, support, and supervise decentralized and multisectoral interventions for the development of children through the efforts of community organizations and NGOs. This component includes training, special studies, strategic planning, education campaigns, and monitoring and evaluation of state and municipal activities.

NOVIB Social Co-investment Program

This program was launched by Mexico City Municipality, with the support of the Dutch NGO Novib, as an experimental approach to meeting the needs of vulnerable groups in the city. The basic purpose was to support better coordination among public sector and civic organizations in order to maximize resources and increase the impact and sustainability of interventions. The initiative provided grants to eight NGO projects dealing with the sexual and reproductive health of women, cultural activities for youth, support to indigenous immigrants, participatory rehabilitation of city historical center, social center, community child development center, and a street children project.

A program general committee was established that included the selected NGOs, other civic organizations, the municipality, and donors. The committee was in charge of defining the program development strategy, planning activities, and monitoring and evaluation, to ensure that the overall aim of meeting the needs of vulnerable social groups would be achieved. Participants consider the program to be a first important step toward complementing the efforts, resources, and methodologies of public and civic sectors of society. Participation in the program also helped NGOs mobilize additional resources.

Long-term Development of Child

The chances for positive, long-term child development will depend in part on the lessons learned from past experience. The lessons of the programs just discussed revolve around the use of trained professionals, a development-related focus, reaching children where they are, individualized attention and tailor-made services, children's participation, inclusion of physical and mental care, involving family and community, lobbying and advocacy, integration of services, networking and institutional cooperation, and links with programs at first and second level of risk.

Trained Professionals: Goodwill is not enough to ensure a positive, long-term impact on children. As the programs described earlier demonstrate, little can be accomplished without the help of experts. The Axê program, for instance, relies on highly trained professionals for its education activities, and the Casa Don Bosco makes use of interdisciplinary teams of experts to assess children's needs and build life plans. Some programs, such as the Health Peer Counseling in Ghana, include continuous training activities for their volunteers and staff.

Development-Related Focus: Good programs are not limited to basic assistance to children in the street. Rather, they incorporate development-oriented activities through integration into the family, school, and labor market. In the long term, mere assistance does not in fact motivate children to strengthen connections with the family and society. The ongoing provision of food, clothes, medicines, and shelter may even help to perpetuate the problem by making street life bearable and intensifying a child's dependence on programs.

In some cases, children have learned "to make use of street educators as a survival strategy," taking advantage of the most attractive outreach or residential services offered by the educators, "who often, quite literally, competed for the child's attention."By contrast, development-oriented practices actively promote links between children and social institutions. They teach their participants a wide array of practical and emotional skills that will enable them to function in different social contexts. Integration is a long-term process, and good programs follow up their cases sometimes for several years.

Family Reintegration: In principle, reuniting the child with the family is the most desirable outcome of a program. This general objective must, however, take into account the family's capabilities and will to receive and protect its child, and the child's wish to go back. In some cases, families are ready to have their child back if programs can help them get a job or a house. In others, parents have died, moved to other marriages or cities, have lost interest, or are not psychologically fit to raise a child. Whatever the circumstances, reintegration is a gradual and delicate process that requires counseling for children and parents, confidence building, conflict resolution, and, sometimes, financial help.

In cases when it is not advisable for the child to rejoin the natural family, programs need to identify alternative solutions such as foster families, adoption, or community homes. Flexible and individualized approaches are those most likely to succeed. Follow-up activities are also necessary to make sure that reintegration is a long-term success. The Casa Alianza Program in Central America provides a possible model in this sector.

School Reintegration: Helping children return to school-or remain in it-presents many challenges. For one thing, children may have developed health, psychological, and behavioral problems that affect concentration, discipline, and school social relations. For another, many street children have more skills and life experience than their peers, but these are not taken into account in normal school curricula. Furthermore, teachers and pupils may not be ready to accept the street child. For these reasons, education programs should emphasize learning and critical abilities and general life skills, rather than traditional pedagogy. At the same time, they should teach the standard curricula to enable children to enter the mainstream of the education system and labor market. It is also essential to train and sensitize school staff to overcome stereotypes, accept and integrate street children, and pay attention to their specific skills and needs. The Axe' program provides a good example of how this can be done.

Integration in the Labor Market: Traditional job-training programs based on the simple transmission of technical skills have failed in the past because the imparted skills do not meet labor market needs, children are unable to adjust to the working environment, employers are reluctant to accept them, and the labor market imposes structural constraints. The experience of Axê in Brazil, however, shows that even these efforts will have a limited chance of success in contexts of high unemployment.

Integration into the labor market should be based on the young person's specific capacities and desires. As demonstrated by the ASIS program, particularly promising interventions seem to be those that follow participants step by step through the various professional and emotional challenges involved in entering the world of work, from spelling out professional aspirations to holding down a job.

Reaching Children Where They Are: Children cannot be forced to leave the street, and programs need to respect their right to stay there if they wish. The correct approach is for educators to socialize and initiate dialogue right in the street, hoping that at some point the young person will become aware of other possibilities and be ready to change his or her life. Building trust is fundamental, as many young street people have had traumatic experiences with adults and do not trust them. Educators are nonjudgmental, and the modalities of interaction are based on children's schedule and rhythm of daily life. Several of the programs establish a phased-in transition to allow the child to gradually leave his or her street habits: after a period of befriending in the street, children are encouraged to join center-based activities and residential structures. The Axê project in Salvador, JUCONI project in Mexico City, and Ciudad Don Bosco all take this approach.

Individualized Attention and Tailor-Made Services: Every street child has its own needs, medical and family history, skills, and aspirations. The complex combination of reasons that have taken him or her into the street is also unique, as is the situation that he or she would face once back in the family. Promising programs thus invest time and multidisciplinary expertise in assessing the individual situation of each participant and in designing tailor-made life plans and services. In Ciudad Don Bosco, for instance, participants are divided into groups, and activities are designed according to the stage of a child's life transition. Programs must also build on the positive resources-skills, cultural background-of the children involved, to enhance their self-confidence and chances for a successfully independent life.

Children's Participation

Much of the literature on children's programs emphasizes that children should participate in their design in order to ensure positive and long-lasting outcomes. The special life experience of street children makes them potential leaders and advocates for the development of their communities. Thus it is also important to recognize them as one of the powerless groups in society. In the 1980s, street children involved in NGO programs in Brazil became part of a national struggle for political, economic, and legal changes in their favor. Their participation contributed to the movement's positive achievements at the end of that decade.

Health Care

Programs need to pay special attention to physical and mental health, either through their own specialists or by referring children to community services. Because of the special nature of their physical condition, street children tend to require immediate treatment, most often for injuries from accidents or abuse, malnutrition, respiratory and intestinal infections, skin diseases, sexually transmitted diseases, HIV/AIDS, and drug addiction. They are usually the survivors of traumatic experiences in the family and in the street itself, and they need to reconcile themselves with their life history to find meaning and healing. Many children will need individual or group therapy and counseling to turn their lives around.

Public health workers should become familiar with the specific needs of street children, and children need to know where services are and how to ask for help. The program Bridge over Troubled Waters is one that puts such effort into mediating between its young participants and community health services. Medical issues can also be addressed by having peer volunteers obtain information in a nonjudgmental way on subjects such as sexual health and drug addiction, or to convey educational messages and information. Substance abuse or HIV/AIDS infection cannot be prevented or controlled without an understanding of the specific needs and behavioral patterns of those affected.

Involvement of Family and Community

The circumstances in which street children find themselves are a reflection of the vulnerability of their social environment. The street gives them a new sense of belonging and of emotional and material function that the community and family failed to provide. That is why many go back to street life after periods in shelters and foster homes, or after being reunited with their parents. Therefore it is important to strengthen the capacity of the family and community (including the school) to receive and take care of their young members.

As the Family Inns Program shows, parent involvement can increase the chances of school reintegration. In particular, a family's recognition of the importance of education and its active participation in learning activities have been found to help children succeed in their studies. Poor families may also need help to cover education expenses. In response to this need, some programs provide scholarships for a certain length of time. Family-level programs can also have a preventive function. The Juconi Program works with street children's siblings who are still with the family to prevent them from following the same path. Note, too, that it is also essential prevent and treat violence and sexual abuse at the hands of the family. This kind of abuse is among the first reasons that children leave home.

Community-level programs in the sample focus on job creation, education, advocacy among relevant stakeholders, the improvement of school and other basic services, and the strengthening of social capital. To help overcome negative stereotypes, they also call for greater awareness of the problems and risks faced by street children, and of the reasons why they are in this situation. Promising programs are ones that identify and strengthen the network of community resources available for street children and that train community members who play a significant role in a child's life, such as the police, shop owners, health staff, and teachers. Recall that the Pasay City Program fought girl prostitution by having all significant community members involved in the advocacy and rehabilitation efforts.

"It is not the lack of knowledge or means that is at the root of our most serious social problems. We basically know what to do and how to do it. What is lacking is the power to effect change." No matter how technically sound, stand-alone programs provide only partial solutions to the problems of street children. Their opportunities in life are directly affected by national laws and policies on education, social protection, health, child labor, juvenile crime, social work, adoption, and many other factors. NGO involvement in lobbying and advocacy at this level can spur changes in the environment affecting children and strengthen the impact of more typical services. The massive social mobilization of street children and educators resulted in the introduction of the Brazilian Child and Adolescent Statute, and with the contribution of NGOs' lobbying, a street children component has been included in the Child Welfare Reform in Bulgaria.

A lesson learned from these experiences is that strong NGO networks make the public aware of the street children's cause. The involvement of the mass media and the quality of information that they provide are also key factors. In all the cases mentioned, support by international agencies and donors provided further legitimacy to NGO efforts in the eyes of their governments. In Bulgaria, donor support has increased the capacity for local lobbying and campaigning, which contributed to NGOs' positive achievements. Finally, the Casa Alianza Program shows that advocacy and legal defense are essential to protect the rights of street children from police violence and the abuse of other adults and to raise public awareness of this issue.

The health, educational, survival, and emotional needs of street children are often impossible to address separately. A drug-addicted, ill, or malnourished child will not be able to benefit from education; children require psychological support before being ready to reunite with their families; job training works better if it is provided in conjunction with counseling on health and life skills; recreation, sport, and culture are essential to gain children's trust, and to motivate them to participate in other program activities.

Up to now, NGOs have played a central role in street children programs, in most cases providing those services that local and national government could not afford. Compared to public service staff, their educators are more experienced in street work and outreach services, flexible methodologies, and the capacity to involve and mobilize poor communities. However, with their limited reach and duration, NGO programs alone are not enough to significantly reduce the number of children in the street, nor are meant to be. Many of them are in fact more effective when they remain small scale.

A better division of roles and models of institutional cooperation between NGOs and public sector seems necessary to adequately promote the positive development of street vulnerable children. The experience of some programs suggests that, thorough networking with other governmental and nongovernmental service providers at the local level, NGOs can overcome their isolation and increase their impact. Several programs for instance contemplate training schoolteachers, health staff, social workers, and police to enable them to meet the specific needs of street children. Axe' works in network with service providers in the city, so that information on children at risk is shared, and an effective case management can take place.

In some cases, NGOs innovative experiences, rather than being a substitute for government action, have been used as a model to be replicated and mainstreamed by public services. The HIV/AIDS services and transitional living structures experimented by the "Bridge Over Troubled Waters" program have been replicated by national health and social services. It must be noted that the role of street children NGOs vis a vis public services differs from poor to rich countries in our sample.

In the first, nongovernmental organizations tend to provide separate services in areas where the public network is absent or low quality. In rich countries the network exists and quality is higher, but children at risk may not have access to it. The purpose of NGOs here is to be a link between young people and available services. The involvement of local governments, schools, health services, and other public institutions is also necessary to create a favorable environment for children who decide to leave the street.

Street Children and Community Advocacy

When a community is involved in street children projects, it comes to realize that the problem of street children is a problem for the whole community. It also comes to understand that problems of street children have multiple causes and need multiple responses. Community involvement gives the people a feeling that they 'own' responsibility for the problems of street children, the project, and the future of their children. Resource persons emerge and the community permits its resources to be utilized for the betterment of the street children. A system or structure for collective action is developed or activated within the community which leads to the improvement in the lives of street children. Some examples of ways in which community involvement benefits street children are given below:

— The stigma, discrimination, and human rights abuse that street children face are lessened.

— Street children get greater access to services as people become more sensitive to their needs.

— Introduction of services, which may otherwise have been rejected, is facilitated, e.g. drug treatment facilities.

— The issue of street children becomes politically sensitive. This provides an opportunity to influence government policy.

— Prospects for better funding, resources, and services improve when the people who control funding see that street children have community support.

Community involvement strengthens the ability of people to solve their problems using their own resources and it generates in them a feeling of ownership of the project and the project becomes sustainable.

Since most of the issues in substance use, sexual and reproductive health and rights and laws affecting children are sensitive issues, it is important that community leaders are in agreement on their approach otherwise they may undermine the initiative. To be able to engage the community in activities you need to understand the community well, especially how it responds to street children and how it affects their lives. To do this you must:

— Identify opinion leaders and have informal discussions with them and with street children.

— Get to know the profile of the community to identify any special features which will influence their involvement.

— Find out how they feel about the activities you want to introduce.

— Find out if they agree with the proposals.

— Determine any conflicting interests.

Rights and Laws

United Nations Convention on the Rights of the Child outlines the basic rights of children and the responsibilities of the governments to protect children. Street children have the same rights as other children and the same laws should apply to them. A summary of the convention is given below:

Importance of Understanding about Rights and Laws

Street educators should familiarize themselves with rights and laws for the following reasons:

— Street children often get into conflict with legal authorities. Street educators at times need to act as unofficial advocates for them. To carry out this function, street educators need to develop working relationships with the local police, military, court authorities, centres for juvenile offenders and lawyers.

— Sometimes street educators are regarded with suspicion by the authorities because of their close association with street children. At times the authorities might mistake street educators as people who exploit street children. For your own protection, you need to know about your own rights and about laws regarding street education.

— While working on the streets, street educators may find contradiction between local and national/ international rules, or a discrepancy between the written rules and actual practice. On behalf of street children, the street educator might feel the need to bring about changes in laws or in law enforcement.

You should learn about the following:

1. Police powers.

   — The circumstances under which the police can stop, search and question a street child or enter the home of an individual or a youth centre; whether they need a warrant.

   — Reasons why a police officer can detain or arrest a street child and the length of time a child can be legally held without being charged with a crime.

   — Whether the police have the right to interrupt or interfere with a gathering of street children in a private place or in a public place.

   — Under what circumstances can the police stop and question a street educator.

2. Child protection.

   — The age at which children are regarded as adults by the legal system.

   — Whether it is permissible for street children to be held in the same detention facilities as adults.

   — Existence of sentencing options for children and adults (e.g. group homes or camps).

   — Whether juvenile records are destroyed when a child becomes an adult.

— What the street educator can do to obtain the release of a street child in custody.

3. Legal aid.

— Existence of free legal aid for children who are arrested or sent before a court, and how you can obtain legal aid for a street child.

— Availability of attorneys who might work on the behalf of street children without a fee, if legal aid is not available.

4. Laws regarding street educators.

— Existence of legal protection for street educators.

— Whether there are restrictions against street educators contacting street children or providing support to a street child who goes before a court.

5. Confidentiality issues.

— Legal requirements about reporting assault or abuse to authorities e.g. physical or sexual assault by an adult on street children.

— The street educator's legal responsibilities if he or she witnesses a street child committing a petty or serious crime.

— The street educator's legal responsibilities if a street child discloses that he/ she had committed a crime.

— How to respond when a street child is in possession of illegal substances and/ or is using and selling substances.

— Legal requirement about reporting HIV status to a street child's family members.

Information on rights and laws affecting street children can be obtained from law professionals, governmental bodies and from members of the Community Advisory Committees.

HIV and Children's Rights

Street children are at a high risk of acquiring HIV infection and less capable of coping with the consequences of HIV. An adaptation of relevant human rights for HIV/AIDS patients is given below.

— The right to education and information: street children should have access to education and information on HIV prevention.

— The right to non-discrimination: a child's HIV status should not lead to discriminatory treatment.

— The right to health: street children should not be denied access to health care and prevention services because they are HIV positive, e.g. services for STDs or clean injection equipment.

— The right to privacy: street children should be protected against mandatory HIV testing and their HIV status should be kept confidential.

— The right to liberty: street children must be protected against imprisonment, segregation or isolation for being HIV positive.

— The right to education and work: street children should be given the right to education and work even when they are HIV positive.

— The right to marry and have a family: a street child should not to be denied marriage, and a street girl should not be forced to undergo sterilization or abortion if she is pregnant.

— The right to social security, assistance and welfare: HIV positive street children should have access to social security, assistance and welfare.

— The right to freedom of movement: HIV positive street children need not be subjected to travel restrictions.

—The right to seek and enjoy asylum: street children should be permitted to seek asylum even when they are HIV positive.

Community Advisory Committee (CAC)

You will need the help of a core group of community representatives to be effective as a community mobilizer and to act as an advocate for street children. This core group of community representatives is referred to as the Community Advisory Committee. A Community Advisory Committee is an essential component of community oriented projects. The main objectives of establishing a CAC are to:

— Share knowledge, responsibilities and resources.

— Support those who are working directly with street children.

— Link street children projects to the community as a whole and to influence the way in which the community acknowledges and responds to street children.

Coordination with appropriate local and national government and examining other projects is a vital part of developing plans for your project. By including a wide range of influential and well-respected members on the committee, the CAC is in a position to significantly change the attitudes of the community, e.g. members with political experience can help in building support for street children projects. By allowing people from different segments of the community to serve as advocates for the project, the CAC promotes a sense of selfhelp, self-reliance, and community ownership of the strategies developed to support street children. In this way, the CAC advocates for street children and helps them gain access to resources and services.

The effectiveness of the advisory committee depends at least partly on the people who are selected as its members. The advice of the children should be taken when candidates are being short-listed. Focus group discussions with street children could help you in identifying people and organizations that they are in contact with (e.g. religious groups, legal authorities, health services), and in ascertaining their perceptions towards these people and organizations (e.g. police, school). Do not include anyone whom street children do not trust or respect.

CAC may need to be modified to suit the local situation, e.g. for practical reasons, one may split the CAC into two groups, one dealing more with local issues (a group comprising street children, parents of street children, those providing direct services to street children) and another dealing with the responsibility of improving access to services and advocacy. Coordination between the two groups is essential. Apart from this, there is a need to increase the participation of street girls on CAC and 'councils'.

— One or two individuals assume the responsibility for organizing the advisory committee. They arrange the initial focus groups with street children and select individuals or organizations from the community as potential members and invite them to join the CAC.

— The committee elects a chairperson to run committee meetings. One of the organizers usually takes the role of secretary during meetings. The secretary takes down the notes and circulates it among the participants, and keeps a record of all the activities of the committee.

— At the first meeting, the organizers explain that the committee has an advisory role, and members get to know each other (skills and resourcefulness).

— Soon after the first meeting, a workshop may be held for the committee. This is an occasion to present new information to members who may not be informed, and to collect information from members who may already know quite a lot about various issues relevant to the life and health of street children.

— The committee decides on the location and the frequency of meetings. Monthly meetings are recommended, but more may be necessary at the beginning of the project.

— During regular meetings, the committee is informed about any new developments. The committee then interprets this information and recommends appropriate responses. It takes an active role in the development and on-going review of the strategic plan.

— The committee may also decide to monitor all local projects concerning street children. This helps the committee in identifying gaps in services, preventing duplication of services, facilitating the sharing of resources, and in starting collection of information on the effectiveness of various projects.

Street Children Network

An important lesson that WHO has learned through its work on substance use with street children is that a network of local people who care about street children is needed, as it may not be feasible to keep the whole community motivated and active. A street children network is a group of people who agree to communicate among themselves about issues relevant to street children. Members can share ideas, information and resources. Such a network responds swiftly to the needs and problems of these children. Once the network gets large enough, someone in the network can answer almost any question about street children. The advantages of a street children network include:

— It has a positive influence on the community perception of street children.

— It helps street children to move from the edge of society and become full members of the community.

— It brings different groups of people and organizations together to collectively advocate for specific policies, attitudes and practices in support of the health and well being of street children.

— It influences policies and attitudes to a greater extent as compared to isolated efforts by individual organizations and people.

Sometimes, it is advantageous to link specific problems with specific organizations, e.g. street girls with women's organizations; HIV infection with Health Care; delinquent children with lawyers.

Mobilization of Community

Mobilizing the community begins with providing information on substance use, sexual and reproductive health among street children and children's rights and laws. Once aware of or sensitized about these issues, the community is likely to support proposed activities and to become activelly involved.

To mobilize and motivate the community you should:

— Encourage participation through the Community Advisory Committee.

— Avoid prejudice. Make it clear that anybody can play a role in alleviating the situation of street children.

— Approach the community with great respect and humility. There is always something to learn from the community and its culture about the way the work can be done.

— Establish good relationships. Work hard at establishing good relationships. This may be difficult in the beginning but once you know how the community functions, you may find it easy and fulfilling.

Street children project staff and volunteers, members of the Community Advisory Committee and street children have used many strategies successfully to promote awareness and support for the needs of street children and related project activities. Such strategies have included newspaper and radio interviews, talks with community leaders and community groups, presentations at schools, workplaces, at sports events, in the street and market places and in religious settings. Many street children projects have found that it is very beneficial to join a network of organizations concerned with promoting the rights and well being of street children. Projects have found that the collective actions of as many groups as possible are needed to advocate successfully for particular issues related to the rights and entitlement of street children.

Communicating with other members of the community on behalf of street children may also be an important part of your work as a street educator. This type of work is called advocacy. The goal of advocacy is to eliminate some of the causes of the problems of street children by persuading individuals, organizations, and governments to change policies and practices. An example of advocacy would be encouraging health officials to change policies that prevent children and youths from receiving health care without the presence of their parents or guardians. Advocacy for street children usually works best when it is conducted within the framework of the community's own cultural norms and governing system. Like all parts of street education work, advocacy should always emphasize the strengths and rights of street children.

9

Ensuring Positive Future for Children

Education has always been important to Americans. In every community, teachers, principals, superintendents, and school board members work to ensure that students have the knowledge and skills they need to be productive members of society. Public schools have a mission to serve all children, to provide quality teaching, and to ensure academic success. In recent years, new challenges have taken education to the top of the national agenda. The new economy has greatly increased the demand for literate, highly skilled workers. Public education systems are expected to level the playing field for young people so that all will benefit from-and contribute to-expanding opportunities.

Materials prepared for a 1999 Education Summit of governors, business and education leaders declare, "The real challenge for public education will be to lift the academic proficiency of the more than 12 million impoverished and disadvantaged young people who struggle with reading, mathematics, and science. These children have the most to gain from a system that expects more of them."Everyone, from the President to state legislators to letter-writers in local papers seems to agree: more must be done to help more students achieve higher levels of academic success -especially in under-performing urban schools and school systems. There are many ways to measure student learning, but the current political climate attaches paramount importance to standards based reform and testing.

The responsibility to improve student scores to meet state-established standards is felt most intensely by the professionals -teachers and administrators - who work inside the schools. Education leaders must improve curriculum and instruction, prepare new teachers, and develop the skills of those who are already in classrooms.

Community Building

The community building field in urban centers is typically neighborhood focused. In cities across the nation, local citizens are coming together to improve the lives of children, their families, and the communities where they live. Organizations of many kinds, including community development corporations, neighborhood-based organizations, faith-based groups, settlement houses and others see themselves as part of a growing movement to identify and capitalize on the strengths and assets of neighborhoods in order to solve local problems. Frequently, these groups form coalitions to address local issues and change the way public and private organizations do business.

Community building encompasses a variety of approaches, including community organizing and community economic development. Organizing initiatives build social and political capital by empowering residents to mobilize themselves and their assets. Community economic development initiatives build physical and economic capital by increasing economic and physical infrastructure and opportunity through housing, job creation, transportation and related initiatives. A Rockefeller Foundation publication describes community-building as "self-renewing efforts by residents and professionals to engage in collective action, aimed at problem-solving and enrichment, that creates new or strengthened social networks, new capacities for group action and support, and new standards and expectations for life in the community."Through all of these approaches, community builders emphasize building personal and institutional relationships as a prerequisite to change. By developing local leadership and creating coalitions, community builders ensure that buildings and streets are well maintained, affordable quality housing is available, and residents have access to jobs, training and good schools. They employ a range of strategies to achieve these goals. Increasingly, education is on their agenda.

Some educators and community builders are discovering how much they have in common. In cities, suburbs and rural areas, schools are looking for ways to improve the performance of their students. Community builders, especially in urban areas, are looking for opportunities to do the same - along with organizations focused on youth development, family support and improved delivery of human services. The result is a national movement toward community schools - partnerships in which organizations join forces with schools to develop activities, supports and opportunities that enhance student learning, and build stronger families and communities.

These partnerships seek to create schools as vital centers of community life, with families, youth, principals, teachers and neighborhood residents working together to promote high educational achievement and positive youth development. Community schools serve community residents by providing child and youth development, employment, immigration, housing, and related human services. They open the school building and its resources for extended hours, expanding assets available to members of the community, and making effective use of community resources.

As community schools grow and mature over time, they establish deep relationships in the community-with school staff, parents, community organizations, and children and youth. Many engage youth in service learning projects that improve the community and help students understand the connection between school and life. A preliminary review of evaluation resultsdocuments the accumulating evidence that these partnerships have a positive impact on the lives of children and families. Many community schools have been able to demonstrate results in improving students' attendance at school, and reducing disciplinary problems and risk taking behavior. They document increased parent involvement with schools and improved family functioning. Families also report improved access to health services for their children.

Some initiatives were able to document an impact on the whole community, with lower violence rates, safer streets, and reductions in family mobility. Deep community-school relationships combine inside expertise with outside resources and support. They have a dual benefit: by expanding the services, supports and opportunities available to young people, they increase their opportunities for learning and development; by strengthening the school as the universally available public institution in the community, they increase assets available to community residents.

These insider/outsider relationships are not easy to craft and sustain over time. School staff can be so immersed in, and sometimes overwhelmed by, the growing demands of accountability that they don't always recognize the help community members have to offer. Community builders often do not fully understand the education system they are trying to change. Community builders and citizens often find themselves outside, while education professionals work toward reform, by themselves, inside the school.

Sticking Points

IEL's conversations with leaders in education and community building shed considerable light on the reasons why they struggle so often with insider/outsider issues. As institutions, schools and community organizations have contrasting structures, organizational cultures, and approaches to leadership. Their perspectives on schooling, citizen involvement, accountability, and partnership styles differ significantly. This section describes some of these differences and the "sticking points" that frequently arise.

Issues of institutional power and resources often underlie tensions between schools and community building organizations.

Schools: Public schools are governed by single-purpose Boards of Education, endowed with substantial power-to construct buildings, employ staff, and decide how education dollars are spent. This governance design was intended to protect schools from the politics of local general-purpose governments. Whether or not they have been successfully shielded from political pressures can be debated, but it is clear that public school systems control large amounts of funding from local, state and federal sources.

School systems are complex, hierarchical organizations. Specific roles and functions are attached to a wide array of staff positions, and individuals must possess specific degrees and qualifications to meet state level credentialing and union contracting requirements. Individuals acquire status and attain promotions through formal selection processes. As large employers, schools are often key institutional players in the community - whether or not they form and sustain relationships with community residents. While many school districts have a separate Office of Community Relations, staff in these units usually does not have authority over site principals. As a result, "community affairs" and matters of curriculum, instruction and school management are typically not well connected.

Community builders: Community building organizations are typically much smaller, more fluid, less hierarchical entities, with structures that are more horizontal than vertical. Funding typically relies on short-term grants rather than stable funding streams so organizational energy is continually expended in seeking out new income sources. Staff is hired and advanced by demonstrating skills and their ability to work effectively with members of the community. Credentials are valued but not always required. Because funding levels for community-building entities often fluctuate, individuals may work in a variety of roles over a comparatively short period of time and exercise considerable autonomy and decision-making discretion.

Sticking points: Differences in organizational size, structure, and staffing can easily lead to communication problems between schools and community organizations. Community builders may find it difficult to sort out messages from within the school hierarchy. School staff may find it hard to communicate with people whose communication style and values reflect the community rather than a specific discipline or profession. Community builders may find "working through channels" arduous and exasperating while their lack of knowledge about "how things are done" can frustrate school personnel. School staff may also mistakenly assume that community builders with flexible schedules are not putting in a full day's work.

Criteria for Leadership

Schools: Organizational culture and leadership are closely connected. In schools and school districts, leadership is based primarily on the authority inherent in specific positions. Public education is organized so that leaders at various levels operate within a defined range of responsibility - for example, conducting a specific program, managing large amounts of public funds, or operating a school that serves hundreds of students. School organizations typically provide few opportunities or incentives for leadership that crosses boundaries to bring new people or new ideas to the table.

Community builders: In community-building organizations, opportunities for leadership are more fluid. Leadership is exercised beyond the organization, as well as within it. Individuals with the ability to build relationships become leaders - within the organization, with community residents of all ages, and with individuals at all levels of various organizations and institutions. The relationship-building process is valued as a way of showing respect for individuals and as a tool for creating consensus and uniting the community.

Sticking points: Differences in the roles and expectations of leaders may lead to friction when partners fail to recognize the legitimacy of both kinds of leadership - the one based on credentials and training, and the other on relationships. Misunderstandings are most likely to occur when partners fail to take the time to build relationships, trust, and appreciation for one another; when school personnel misjudge the abilities of people who may not have advanced degrees; or when community-builders underestimate the challenges, responsibilities and obligations that high-level school leaders face.

Role of Schools and Schooling

In communities where school reform efforts and community-builders attempt to work together, there is often a clear contrast in the way that community-builders and education leaders define the role of schools and schooling.

Schools: The current strong push for improved student performance as measured by test scores has led many educators to emphasize classroom-based, academic learning. Some education reform experts argue that if schools are to succeed they must not attempt to do too many things at once, or operate too many separate programs that don't relate to their primary mission of teaching and learning. This focus means that schools may curtail time spent on the arts, on leadership development, even on recess and physical education, in order to spend more time on academics.

Community builders: Community organizations recognize the importance of academics, but they see a broader role for schools in supporting human development. They expect public schools to help develop young people's personal and social skills, and stress connections between skills learned in school and "real life" outside the school. Along with James Comer, a nationally known psychiatrist and school reform leader, they believe that schools must build positive, trusting relationships with students, parents and community members as a prerequisite to children's academic achievement.

Sticking points: As education reform focuses more exclusively on academic achievement, these differences in views about the role of schools and schooling can create considerable distance between school personnel and community builders. Educators sometimes feel that community members do not understand the magnitude and complexity of the challenge to improve student achievement. Community builders worry that a " laser-like" focus on academics ignores opportunities essential to enabling achievement in life situations as well as the classroom.

Accountability

Schools: Educators' accountability for student and school performance has high visibility in most communities. Education reform today is standards-driven. Many states have adopted universal expectations for what students should know and be able to do in subject areas including reading, writing, and mathematics. States and local districts are establishing systems of "high stakes" testing in which all students must demonstrate specified achievement levels in order to move to the next grade - or to graduate. Schools are expected to improve teaching and learning so that every student can achieve the standards. Accountability for results, as measured by test scores and comparisons among schools, is publicized in local newspapers and on the Internet. The careers of school leaders and the placement and/or retention of teachers can depend on their students' success in meeting education standards.

Community builders: Community organizations are not subject to the high expectations for results that schools experience. They are often supported by short-term grants and gifts from public and private organizations. While they are accountable to funders for meeting the goals of their funding, their efforts are not routinely subject to public scrutiny nor are they expected to produce large-scale change. Funders recognize the difficulty of holding individual providers accountable for outcomes that require a comprehensive approach. It is also extremely difficult to measure community builders' most important work: building relationships and leveraging joint efforts within and across organizations.

Sticking points: School personnel who see their jobs-and their student's futures-on the line are sometimes unwilling to share power and resources with partners who appear to have less to lose. As long as test scores are the only measure of accountability, partnerships between schools and community builders may experience imbalance and tension.

Power, Race And Class

Community builders and school personnel also differ on how they view power - its sources and purpose.

Schools: Educators tend to focus on institutional power, based on size, authority and resources. For example, when we asked a group of high level school administrators who had participated in an IEL leadership programfor aspiring urban superintendents about their community building involvement, they pointed to efforts to connect with other organizations - businesses, government agencies and community organizations with the potential to expand school resources. These positive relationships reflect an orientation to traditional sources of power. Relationships tend to be valued when partners bring resources.

Community builders: Community builders are more likely to see people as their primary source of power -and their ability to mobilize support for a specific agenda as the primary use of this power. Most community building organizations work in urban low-income communities where the residents may be predominantly African American, Hispanic, and/or Asian. The major resource in these communities is the hard work and motivation of the people who live there and want to improve their lives.

Community residents may be uncomfortable or suspicious about becoming involved with large public institutions. In part, this distance may reflect differences in race and class between top-level school administrators and the communities they serve. Because decisions about substantial amounts of school funding are made inside school and district hierarchies, some parents feel that the school is an "island" - a different world set apart from the rest of the community.

As schools employ high stakes testing to determine students' academic future, community members in urban areas may perceive that students' low achievement reflects insufficient effort on the part of schools to provide resources in low income communities as well as the isolation of schools from the community.

Sticking points: Both institutional and people power are necessary to improve student learning and build communities. But connecting them is often difficult. School administrators are likely to look for partners with demonstrable "clout" and to disregard the potential power in organized groups of residents and family members. Because community building organizations in low-income communities do not bring sizeable resources or community influence to the table, their members often feel that they are not valued or courted by school administrators.

Collaboration and Conflict

Both educators and community builders use collaborative strategies to move forward. Community builders frequently refer to the "table" as a metaphor for the way the work gets done, as well as a place for meeting and discussion. But conflict also is a tool for community builders.

Schools: School site councils, or teams, have the potential to create collaborative "tables." A study of the changes in Chicago's schools under local control concludes that principals in productive elementary schools share leadership with teachers and parents and promote social trust as a key feature of the schools' culture. "These principals are accessible; teachers and parents feel that they 'really listen' and that there are opportunities to influence important affairs."Community builders. According to community leaders, collaborative tables must go beyond increasing communication. They should minimize inequalities in power based on resources, race and class. "No table should be built where someone has more power because of their title," says Nancy Aardema, director of the Logan Square Neighborhood Association in Chicago. Through collaboration, the community can broaden support for educators' efforts to improve results for local schools. "Strong community organizations can take some of the politics off the backs of the principals," said Aardema, who has firsthand experience in getting principals and teachers to talk about working in the community. Community builders sometimes confront what they see as recalcitrant school bureaucracies. The Marshall Heights Community Development Organization chose to confront the District of Columbia Public Schools over delays in rehabilitating its neighborhood high school, while continuing to work in partnership with that school and others.

Sticking points: Community builders and educators differ on the importance they attach to conflict-both within and outside of collaborative partnerships. For educators, conflict is a sign of something going wrong; for community builders, it is seen as a valuable tool for change. Many community builders see conflict and confrontation as essential tools for equalizing power relationships and creating positive change. School leaders with an inside strategy for decision-making may find it easier to suppress debate than to allow strong disagreement. Community builders can help school leaders understand why conflict occurs, and learn from it when it does.

Involvementp of Family

Both schools and community-building organizations work actively to involve parents in school matters, but in different ways.

Schools: Schools emphasize parent involvement, organized by school staff. In many schools, workshops and meetings teach parents about how to support their children's academic learning. Parent involvement activities often take place inside the school building, using "school" language and meeting formats. Schools believe that, for children to reach standards of academic achievement, parents must actively monitor their child's schoolwork, attendance, and homework.

Community builders: Community building organizations are more likely to emphasize parent participation and leadership in school reform and community improvement. They take a strength-based approach by building families' confidence in dealing with schools, helping families navigate school bureaucracies and develop their skills not only as their children's first teachers but also as their best advocates. Parents build relationships with other parents and work together to make schools more responsive and accountable to the entire school community.

Community builders also help school staff to engage parents. Joanna Brown, who worked to develop parent-led bilingual committees at elementary schools in Chicago's Logan Square neighborhood, sees her work as helping school staff learn to respect parents and their heritage.

Sticking points: All parents, regardless of their background, can benefit from an ongoing, school-sponsored parent involvement program. However, not all educators value the more advocacy-oriented approach supported by community building organizations. Parents who have had little formal education or negative experiences with schools may be reluctant to participate in school-organized activities, especially if they are cast in the role of students who must be taught, rather than as adults who have a great deal to teach.

Community Partnerships

Schools: Most urban schools are underfunded and chronically short on resources, from pencils and paper to skilled teachers. Staff is often more willing to work with outsiders when that involvement increases resources for the school and makes their difficult jobs easier. Community partners who can make a tangible contribution to the school by bringing services and supports to create a Family Resource Center in unused space, for example, or providing a continuous source of trained volunteers, are readily welcomed.

Community builders: Community builders seek to increase opportunities for education and self-determination for residents of all ages, and to better use all the assets in the community -including school buildings and equipment financed by local property taxes. Although public schools are underfunded in many urban areas, they often have assets that exist nowhere else in the community, including classroom, gymnasium, and auditorium space; office equipment and computers; purchasing power; and the energy and talents of young people. Community builders view partnerships as "two-way streets," with schools giving to the community, as well as receiving support from it.

Sticking points: Community builders and many educators believe that actions taken to benefit communities ultimately benefit schools. Tough issues frequently arise when community builders ask schools to share use of school facilities and equipment, respond to parent challenges to school policies, and deal with community concerns about school performance. The " two- way street" is difficult to establish and maintain.

Building Relationships

Despite the sticking points they encounter, many schools and community building organizations are working together to benefit children, families, and communities.

Develop the school's capacity to work with families and community residents. Most school staff has not been trained to work with parents and members of the community, especially those from different ethnic and socioeconomic groups. The Philadelphia Public School District has instituted an on-the-job leadership development program in which principals with successful community-engagement track records serve as mentors for aspiring administrators.

Increase community leadership and participation. Community-school partnerships can be designed to develop family members as leaders so they can be comfortable and effective - inside the school as well as outside in the community. An extensive parent-mentoring program designed by Chicago's Logan Square Community Association (LSNA) has built a cadre of informed, involved parents who have established relationships with teachers and are poised to play expanded leadership roles. LSNA also worked to ensure that its parent mentor program truly contributed to parents' personal development.

Build the assets of children and adults in the community. The Marshall Heights Community Development Organization in Washington, DC sponsors a series of family field trips to museums and other educational resources in the community. In addition to their educational value, these trips provide an opportunity for adults in the community to interact and build relationships in a stress-free setting.

Broadening Accountability Efforts

Develop shared responsibility. Accountability efforts are most effective when they clarify school and community commitments, require all parties to maintain appropriate and accurate records of their work, and make the results public.

Involve community members and represent community interests in school planning and problem solving. School leaders who have conducted intensive community engagement efforts attest to the value of involving stakeholders in finding solutions to tough issues. These school leaders understand the needs of the whole community, not just a few individuals. "Logan Square Neighborhood Association comes united," says Carlos Azcoitia, Deputy Chief Education Officer for the Chicago Public Schools. "We know where the community stands."

Develop education and community coalitions to ensure shared accountability. In Rochester, NY, for example, a cross sector community effort to coordinate efforts to support children and families includes the mayor, the superintendent of schools, and representatives of higher education and community based organizations. It works to set priority results and track progress toward achieving them, while reducing conflict and duplication among individual school and community improvement initiatives.

Rules of Engagement

Given the similarities and differences between the education and community building sectors, it is important to understand that working relationships between the two sectors' leaders must be mutually rewarding. They must consistently attend to building relationships, strengthening assets, and ensuring positive outcomes for young people. The following "rules of engagement"-with suggestions for both educators and community builders-come from our conversations with experienced practitioners on both sides.

We believe that the future of children, especially in our most disadvantaged communities, demands that all sectors of our society work together. The following actions can help to expand the dialogue among educators and community builders, and build a strong foundation for joint action. Form additional tables to engage more educators and community builders in the conversation. Educators and community builders should expand the opportunities for dialogue between the sectors at the local, regional and national levels. Part of the work for educators involves explaining the goals and process of school reform to community builders and enlisting their active involvement in improving local schools.

For community builders the task is to help educators appreciate the capacity they bring to schools for student support, support for educators and the development of a strong constituency for public education. Dialogues among educators and community builders in communities across the country can help to expand the assets available to strengthen students' learning and development. School leaders and community building organizations can use this essay as a catalyst for dialogue about ways to work together.

Help educators to learn more about community and community building, and community builders to learn more about education in their formal preparation and during professional development and conference opportunities. Most education leaders report that working with community members, especially residents of urban communities, was something they had to learn on their own, by trial and error. It was largely absent from their professional preparation.

New, highly visible initiatives to recruit new leaders for schools and strengthen the skills of current leaders are being developed across the country. Designers and funders of these initiatives should include experiences in working with community in general and with individuals and organizations that seek to build community capacity in particular. They should also consider implementing the principles of distributive leadership in schools so that no single individual is expected to conduct all leadership functions. Many community builders also need to know more about schools and education reform.

The efforts of the National Community Building Network in this arena can be a model for other community building initiatives at the local, state, and national levels. Local leadership programs also focus on schools and community building relationships. Promote the joint efforts work of community builders and educators in strengthening and supporting the attainment of their shared missions. As community builders and educators work together, they can concentrate on opportunities to contribute to the attainment of their shared missions. For example, community builders can help to strengthen parent involvement in schools and expand students' productive use of out-of-school time for extended learning.

Educators can find ways to expand access to school facilities and other resources, while schools and community members can work together in projects to improve schools' appearance and safety so they become assets in the community. And schools and community builders can work together to ensure that students are safe when they travel to and from school.

Provide resources to strengthen and sustain the work of community builders in supporting education reform. Community-building organizations can play a vital role in improving public education. But many community building organizations will require additional resources to be able to work effectively with schools. Public and private funders can support community building organizations' presence and participation in education reform efforts.

Strengthen the internal capacity of school districts to work with community. Few school districts are effectively organized to work with community builders and other community organizations. School districts need assistance in thinking through how they can most effectively interact with community builders and other community-based organizations so they can build strong sustaining partnerships. Research also is needed on existing organizational models that may have potential applicability to other districts.

Enhance capacity of intermediary organizations to connect school and community. Because of the "sticking points" outlined in this report, it is often difficult for schools and community builders to work effectively together in the absence of third party intermediaries. Such entities exist in a number of communities and are proving to be valuable resources.

Further examination of this role and development of intermediary capacity is needed. Support additional research and information gathering. This analysis emerges primarily from the experiences of four communities. It is important to gather additional information about the work of community builders and education reform in order to strengthen the focus of funders - local, regional and national - on the potential in this relationship. One outcome of this ongoing work might be the development of indicators of success for community building and education, including evidence of relationships, results, and influence on site-based governance.

Global Movement for Children

All the possible opportunities, benefits and pitfalls surrounding children and participation were at issue in the lead-up to the UN General Assembly Special Session on Children in May 2002. This was something of a test case of meaningful children's participation at the international level, which took UNICEF, governments and non-governmental organizations into genuinely new territory. Starting with the World Summit for Children in 1990, there was increasing recognition of the importance of children's participation, based in large part on the Convention on the Rights of the Child, and increasing readiness to try to make participation possible in international conferences. By 1997, when UNICEF conducted a systematic review of children's participation in its own work, a total of 302 UNICEF-supported programmes reported young people's involvement, with particularly high rates of involvement in Central and Eastern Europe and the Commonwealth of Independent States and in Eastern and Southern Africa.

The preparations for the Special Session on Children started early, involving extensive regional consultation: young people's organizations participated in high-level meetings in Beijing, Berlin, Cairo, Kathmandu, Kingston, Panama City and Rabat to review progress since the World Summit for Children and to guide action for the future. The formal preparatory gatherings in New York for the Special Session provided opportunities for experimentation and for learning from inevitable mistakes.

In the run-up to the Special Session, the Global Movement for Children brought together adults, adolescents and children; campaigners, counsellors and crusaders for child rights: those who cared about forging a world fit for children. While recognizing that children and adolescents cannot be expected to challenge the world's misplaced priorities on their own, this energetic alliance embraced the idea that the job could not be done by adults without the passion and perspectives of children.

The primary focus of the Global Movement for Children was a major worldwide campaign called 'Say Yes for Children', launched at events around the world beginning in March 2001. Adults and children alike were asked to say 'Yes' to a pledge - "I believe that all children should be free to grow in health, peace and dignity" - and to support the Global Movement's 10-point agenda for action. They were then asked to identify the three action priorities that they considered most important. The participation involved in a campaign of such a mass scale is bound to be limited. But this element of interactivity whether over the Internet or on widely distributed paper forms - undoubtedly helped draw both children and adults into the process.

By the time the 'Say Yes' pledges were presented to Nelson Mandela and Graça Machel at the Children's Forum in New York in May 2002, the total number - far exceeding expectations - stood at nearly 95 million, including 20 million from China and a remarkable 16 million (one in four of the population) from Turkey. With the overwhelming number of pledges coming from children, the three issues identified as most urgent were education, discrimination and poverty. More importantly, the drive to involve as many people as possible provided a focus for promoting discussion and raising awareness of child rights - as in Peru where 800,000 children 'said yes'.

In East Asia, 10 countries took the opportunity to hold a National Children's Forum as part of the 'Say Yes' campaign. They then sent representatives to a regional forum in the Lao People's Democratic Republic and selected a delegation of children to the UN Special Session on Children to represent the region. In the Syrian Arab Republic, a national seminar saw 150 children aged 6 to 12 discuss the Convention on the Rights of the Child with writers, artists, educational experts and television producers. The children presented a list of recommendations to the Prime Minister, which included their request for a children's parliament, and said they now dared to hope for change.

The 'Say Yes for Children' campaign allowed an arc of participation for millions of children and young people, who could trace a path from the pledge they made in their local communities to leaders such as Nelson Mandela and Graça Machel, and from them to the UN General Assembly Special Session on Children, and on into the outcome document and a declaration by world governments.

The 400 plus children who travelled to New York City in May to attend the Special Session came from more than 150 countries. Most were in their teens, though some were as young as age 10. Some had been selected rather than elected, either by governments or by NGOs, and thus could not be considered representative. On the other hand, many had been chosen not just for their confidence or eloquence but because they were already passionately engaged in advocacy for children's rights or had launched their own campaign.

The Children's Forum, which lasted for three days, was opened by the UN Secretary-General and closed with a ceremony presided over by Nelson Mandela, Graça Machel and Mrs. Nane Annan as guests of honour. Between these two events, the only adults present were interpreters and facilitators. Children started off in regional groups, establishing the ground rules of respect for each other and 'unity in diversity' that were to govern their time together. They then divided into groups to discuss eight key issues, which they had identified as exploitation and abuse, environment, protection from war, children's participation, health, HIV/AIDS, poverty and education. Rapporteurs were elected, as was a group delegated to draft a common statement.

The children's impact at the Special Session extended far beyond the Children's Forum itself. The presence and participation of children changed the style of the event, infusing proceedings with a directness, idealism and honesty that are too often absent from such international meetings. At press conferences and feedback meetings, child delegates explained their achievements and articulated their expectations with astonishing assurance - not to mention a freshness of approach that compared favourably with the often dry exchanges between adults elsewhere.

In 'Intergenerational Dialogue' workshops child delegates met face to face with prime ministers and princes, ministers and heads of international agencies. The children's passionate frankness was often remarkable. When 16-year-old Fatoumatta Nduré from the Gambia, for example, welcomed participants

- including the President of Mozambique and the King of Lesotho - to the Intergenerational Dialogue on Africa that she chaired, she said, "Welcome first to the children of Africa. And second to all child-friendly adults. " It is impossible to measure the positive overall impact of children's participation at the Special Session - though its empowering, transformative effect on each child's life is easy enough to imagine.

One cannot but feel that only good can come from this intense interaction between children and the men and women with power to make a difference in the world. The UN Security Council, for example, held a formal meeting on children and armed conflict during the Special Session, and three children - from Africa, Asia and Europe - whose lives had been affected by war addressed the Council.

We are the World's Children

After discussion and debate during the Children's Forum, an event preceding the United Nations Special Session on Children, some 400 young people agreed on a statement to be presented to world leaders. Gabriela Azurduy Arrieta, 13, from Bolivia and Audrey Cheynut, 17, from Monaco were chosen by their peers to represent them. As the Special Session commenced on 8 May 2002, these two young delegates to the Forum stood before the General Assembly and delivered their message. On this historic occasion, for the first time ever, children formally addressed the UN General Assembly on behalf of children, giving voice to their vision for a better world.

A World Fit for Us

— We are the world's children.

— We are the victims of exploitation and abuse.

— We are street children.

— We are the children of war.

— We are the victims and orphans of HIV/AIDS.

— We are denied good-quality education and health care.

— We are victims of political, economic, cultural, religious and environmental discrimination.

— We are children whose voices are not being heard: it is time we are taken into account.

— We want a world fit for children, because a world fit for us is a world fit for everyone.

In this world,

1. *We see respect for the rights of the child*:

   — governments and adults having a real and effective commitment to the principle of children's rights and applying the Convention on the Rights of the Child to all children,

   — safe, secure and healthy environments for children in families, communities and nations.

2. *We see an end to exploitation, abuse and violence*:

   — laws that protect children from exploitation and abuse being implemented and respected by all,

   — centres and programmes that help to rebuild the lives of victimized children.

3. *We see an end to war*:

   — world leaders resolving conflict through peaceful dialogue instead of by using force,

   — child refugees and child victims of war protected in every way and having the same opportunities as all other children,

   — disarmament, elimination of the arms trade and an end to the use of child soldiers.

4. *We see the provision of health care*:

— affordable and accessible life-saving drugs and treatment for all children,

— strong and accountable partnerships established among all to promote better health for children.

5. *We see the eradication of HIV/AIDS*:

— educational systems that include HIV prevention programmes,

— free testing and counselling centres,

— information about HIV/AIDS freely available to the public, orphans of AIDS and children living with HIV/AIDS cared for and enjoying the same opportunities as all other children.

6. *We see the protection of the environment*:

— conservation and rescue of natural resources, awareness of the need to live in environments that are healthy and favourable to our development,

— accessible surroundings for children with special needs.

7. *We see an end to the vicious cycle of poverty*:

— anti-poverty committees that bring about transparency in expenditure and give attention to the needs of all children,

— cancellation of the debt that impedes progress for children.

8. *We see the provision of education*:

— equal opportunities and access to quality education that is free and compulsory, " school environments in which children feel happy about learning, " education for life that goes beyond the academic and includes lessons in understanding, human rights, peace, acceptance and active citizenship.

9. *We see the active participation of children*:

— raised awareness and respect among people of all ages about every child's right to full and meaningful participation, in the spirit of the Convention on the Rights of the Child,

— children actively involved in decision-making at all levels and in planning, implementing, monitoring and evaluating all matters affecting the rights of the child.

10. *We pledge an equal partnership in this fight for children's rights*. And while we promise to support the actions you take on behalf of children, we also ask for your commitment and support in the actions we are taking - because the children of the world are misunderstood.

We are not the sources of problems; we are the resources that are needed to solve them. We are not expenses; we are investments. We are not just young people; we are people and citizens of this world. Until others accept their responsibility to us, we will fight for our rights. We have the will, the knowledge, the sensitivity and the dedication. We promise that as adults we will defend children's rights with the same passion that we have now as children. We promise to treat each other with dignity and respect. We promise to be open and sensitive to our differences. We are the children of the world, and despite our different backgrounds, we share a common reality. We are united by our struggle to make the world a better place for all.

Turning Back

There is no turning back to an era when children suffered in silence, when they waited on the world's protection and charity. The Convention on the Rights of the Child has transformed the landscape irreversibly. Its 54 articles contain not only a clarity of thought and care of phrasing unusual in instruments of international law but also a rare wisdom of which the world should be justly proud. That it has been nearly universally accepted is a tribute in itself. The effect of the Convention continues to be profound. From Malaysia to Mexico, Namibia to Norway, with every passing day more children understand more about their rights, and those living and working with them understand more about how to respect those rights. While work in child participation is still tentative, uneven and relatively unevaluated, there are lessons that cannot be unlearned.

One of the broadest, most profound lessons of all is that children are capable of much more than is normally thought: at virtually every age from birth onwards children's capacities are greater than previously imagined. Children will rise to meet the challenges in front of them. But for the millions of children caught up in armed conflict or condemned to a half-life of sexual slavery or hazardous labour, the challenges are far greater than any child should have to bear. The world must protect its children far better than it does at present, even as it opens the door to their participation. And open the door it must. Not only because the children who walk through it will be better able to protect themselves, but also because we cannot design a world fit for children without carefully listening to what they have to say.

Democracy is neither easy nor guaranteed. As UN Secretary-General Kofi Annan reminds us, "One of the greatest challenges to humankind in the new century will be the struggle to make the practice of democracy truly universal. "If we are to meet the goals of 'A World Fit for Children' and attain the Millennium Development Goals, if we are to change this divided, damaged, conflict-ridden world by advancing the practice of democracy, if we are to make the world truly fit for all people - we will only do so with the full participation of children and young people.

Bibliography

Burgess, C. (1990) "The street-wise children." In Southern Africa Today November 2.

Cemane, K.B. (1990) "The Street Child Phenomenon". In Social Work Practice. 1(90): 2-5

Cerrans, M. (1992) "A signal of alarm: 5 million street children in Africa". In South African Outlook. 122(1): 11-12

Chetty, V.R. "Street Children: Victims/Deviants? Paper presented at The Violence and Corruption: "The Crimes of Africa?" Conference. September 1993. Located at the Social Justice Resource Project. University of Cape Town.

Cockburn, A. (1990) *Street Children: Understanding the Problem.* Located at Child Welfare Resource Library. Cape Town.

Dantu, R. (1985) "A study of Juvenile Vagrancy in Cape Town". *School of Social Work,* University of Cape Town.

De kock, R. (1987) "The garbage scavengers". In Indicator Southern Africa. 4: 51-55

Giles, C. (1988a) Street Children - what makes them tick? *Paper delivered at the National Association of Child Care Workers Conference on Street Children.* July 1988. Cape Town.

Harvey, E., (1989) Draft Report of a Pilot Study on the Street Children Phenomena. Report from the Department of National Health and Population Development. Pretoria.

Hickson, J; graydon, V. (1989) "Twilight Children": The street children of Johannesburg. In Journal of Multicultural Counselling and Development 17: 85-94

Keen, J. (1988) "Street Children, Bush Children, Dump Children". In The Child Care Worker. 6(1): 12

Kramer, S; MC Lachlan, F; Osler, B. & swart, J. (1986) "Street Children - Four Perspectives". In Paper 40. Institute for the Study of Man in Africa. University of the Witwatersrand.

Le roux, J. (1992) "Street Children as Manifestation of an Anti-Child Culture in South Africa". In *The Journal of Pedagogics.* 13(2): 87-98

————, (1994) "Street Children in South Africa and Thailand: findings from a comparative study". *In The Journal of Pedagogics.* 15(2): 53-62

————, (1995) "Street Children": A man-made phenomenon. In The Journal of Pedagogics. 16(1): 31-39

Maphatane, M. "Understanding support systems for black street children and their families: an ecological perspective". In Social Work Practice. 2(94): 22-30 July 1994.

Maree, P.J. (1990) "Street children: The present situation in the RSA and possible reasons for this phenomenon". *Paper presented at Street Children: An Educational Perspective.* Symposium conducted at the University of Zululand, Umlazi.

Index